Smart Legal Contracts

Smart Legal Contracts

Computable Law in Theory and Practice

Edited by

JASON GRANT ALLEN & PETER HUNN

OXFORD
UNIVERSITY PRESS

OXFORD
UNIVERSITY PRESS

Great Clarendon Street, Oxford, OX2 6DP,
United Kingdom

Oxford University Press is a department of the University of Oxford.
It furthers the University's objective of excellence in research, scholarship,
and education by publishing worldwide. Oxford is a registered trade mark of
Oxford University Press in the UK and in certain other countries

© Jason Grant Allen & Peter Hunn 2022

The moral rights of the authors have been asserted

First Edition published in 2022

Impression: 1

All rights reserved. No part of this publication may be reproduced, stored in
a retrieval system, or transmitted, in any form or by any means, without the
prior permission in writing of Oxford University Press, or as expressly permitted
by law, by licence or under terms agreed with the appropriate reprographics
rights organization. Enquiries concerning reproduction outside the scope of the
above should be sent to the Rights Department, Oxford University Press, at the
address above

You must not circulate this work in any other form
and you must impose this same condition on any acquirer

Public sector information reproduced under Open Government Licence v3.0
(http://www.nationalarchives.gov.uk/doc/open-government-licence/open-government-licence.htm)

Published in the United States of America by Oxford University Press
198 Madison Avenue, New York, NY 10016, United States of America

British Library Cataloguing in Publication Data

Data available

Library of Congress Control Number: 2021946680

ISBN 978–0–19–285846–7

DOI: 10.1093/oso/9780192858467.001.0001

Printed and bound by
CPI Group (UK) Ltd, Croydon, CR0 4YY

Links to third party websites are provided by Oxford in good faith and
for information only. Oxford disclaims any responsibility for the materials
contained in any third party website referenced in this work.

Contents

List of Abbreviations	xi
List of Contributors	xiii

Editors' Introduction   1
Jason Grant Allen and Peter Hunn

1 Wrapped and Stacked: 'Smart Contracts' and the Interaction of Natural and Formal Language   23
Jason Grant Allen
   A. Introduction   23
   B. What is a 'Smart Contract'?   26
   C. Is a Smart Contract Really a 'Contract'?   33
   D. Smart Contracts and Conventional Contract Law   43
   E. Conclusion   52

2 End-to-End Smart Legal Contracts: Moving from Aspiration to Reality   54
Sir Geoffrey Vos, MR
   A. Introduction   54
   B. Where Are We Now?   56
   C. The Thesis   58
   D. A Preliminary Issue: Property in English Law   59
   E. Current Developments in English Law   62
   F. What Can be Done Once Any Legal Impediments to the Use of Smart Contracts Have Been Identified?   64
   G. Further Questions About Smart, Legally Enforceable Contracts   65
   H. An Inbuilt Dispute Resolution System for Smart Contracts   66
   I. Conclusions   68

3 Making Smart Contracts a Reality: Confronting Definitions, Enforceability, and Regulation   70
Justice Aedit Abdullah and Goh Yihan
   A. Introduction   70
   B. The Definitional Debate: What is a 'Smart Contract'?   71
   C. The Enforceability of Smart Contracts   73
   D. The Statutory Regulation of Smart Contracts   78
   E. Conclusion   78

vi CONTENTS

4 Smart Contracts and Dispute Resolution: Faster Horses or a
   New Car?   79
   Justice Stephen Estcourt AM
   A. Introduction   79
   B. Smart Legal Contracts and Dispute Resolution   80
   C. Conclusion   85

5 Why the Ricardian Contract Came About: A Retrospective Dialogue
   with Lawyers   88
   Ian Grigg
   A. Introduction   88
   B. The Origins of the 'Riccy'   89
   C. The War of the Wordsmiths   93
   D. Random Experiences on the Ricardian Journey   100
   E. Enter 'Smart Contracts'   102
   F. Conclusion   105

6 Smart Contracts: Taxonomy, Transaction Costs, and Design
   Trade-offs   107
   Alfonso Delgado De Molina Rius
   A. Introduction   107
   B. Contract Taxonomy   109
   C. Smart Contracts and Contract Law: A Transaction Costs Approach   119

7 A Model for the Integration of Machine Capabilities into Contracts   142
   Natasha Blycha and Ariane Garside
   A. Introduction   143
   B. Grounding the SLC Concept—The Space Ship Scenario   146
   C. The SLC Model—Foundational Components   146
   D. The SLC Model Drafting Principles   155
   E. Conjoined Method   157
   F. Smart Boilerplate   165
   G. Clause Classification   175
   H. The Legal Status of Automated Contract Performance   176
   I. The Legal Void of the Digital Economy   177
   J. Conclusion   179

8 Six Levels of Contract Automation: The Evolution of 'Smart
   Legal Contracts'   182
   Susannah Wilkinson and Jacques Giuffre
   A. Introduction   182
   B. Automation and Digital Transformation   184
   C. Smart Legal Contracts   186
   D. Analogy Between Automation of Contracts and
      Autonomous Vehicles   191
   E. Conclusion   203

9	Smart Contracts as Execution Instead of Expression *Eric Tjong Tjin Tai*	205
	A. Introduction	205
	B. Definition and Principal Characteristics of Smart Contracts	206
	C. Smart Contracts and the Role of Interpretation	211
	D. Extensions to Smart Contracts? Oracles and Libraries	217
	E. Implementing Contract Law in Smart Contracts	219
	F. Conclusion	223
10	Smart Contracts: The Limits of Autonomous Performance *Tian Xu*	225
	A. Introduction	225
	B. De-constructing Autonomous Performance: Three Core Functionalities	227
	C. Documentary Credit: Analogue Autonomous Performance	230
	D. Comparative Analysis of Smart Contracts and Documentary Credit	233
	E. Conclusion	244
11	Techno-Legal Supertoys: Smart Contracts and the Fetishization of Legal Certainty *Robert Herian*	246
	A. Introduction	246
	B. Prelude: The Persistence of 'Supertoys'	249
	C. Smart, but not Intelligent, Contracts	252
	D. Legally Weak?	257
	E. Conclusion	265
12	Languages for Smart and Computable Contracts *Christopher D Clack*	269
	A. Introduction	269
	B. The Language Stack	271
	C. Natural and Formal Expression	278
	D. Semantics	283
	E. Computable Contracts	292
	F. Conclusion	303
13	The Mathematization of Legal Writing: The Next Contract Language? *Megan Ma*	305
	A. Introduction	305
	B. A Primer on Translation	307
	C. Logical Ancestors and the Formalistic Return	310
	D. A Study of Code	315
	E. Observations and Implications	322
	F. Conclusion	325

14 Beyond Human: Smart-contracts, Smart-Machines, and
    Documentality   327
    David Koepsell
    A. Introduction   327
    B. Social Objects and Documents   328
    C. Conclusion   337

15 Smart Contract 'Drafting' and the Homogenization of Languages   339
    Siegfried Fina and Irene Ng (Huang Ying)
    A. Introduction   339
    B. Language, Contract Drafting, and Lawyers   340
    C. Smart Contracts and Language Homogenization   342
    D. Language Homogenization   344
    E. Impacts of Language Homogenization by Smart Contracts   347
    F. Conclusion   352

16 Practice Makes ... Pragmatic: Designing a Practical Smart Contract
    Legal Architecture   353
    Scott Farrell, Hannah Glass, and Henry Wells
    A. Introduction   353
    B. Interoperability   355
    C. Certainty   357
    D. Flexibility   358
    E. Accountability   362
    F. Safety   365
    G. Conclusion   367

17 Lawyer Meets Developer: How Interdisciplinary Collaboration
    Builds Smarter Legal Contracts   369
    Madeleine Maslin and Joshua Butler
    A. Introduction   369
    B. The Emerging Taxonomy of Interdisciplinary Collaboration   371
    C. The Relative Benefits of Different Ways of Working   374
    D. Lawyers, Standards, and Emerging Technologies   379
    E. Conclusion   382

18 Not Up to the Job: Why Smart Contracts are Unsuitable
    for Employment   383
    Gabrielle Golding and Mark Giancaspro
    A. Introduction   383
    B. Background to Smart Contracts in Employment   385
    C. Why Smart Contracts are Unsuitable for Employment   388
    D. Conclusion   395

19 The Legal Consequences of Automated Mistake   397
    Simon Gleeson
    A. Introduction   397
    B. *Quoine Pte Ltd v B2C2 Ltd*   398
    C. The Law of Mistake   403
    D. Integrating Cyber-contracts with the Law of Mistake   412
    E. Commercial Certainty   416
    F. Conclusion   419

20 Dispute Resolution for the Digital Economy: DLT as a Catalyst
    for Online Dispute Resolution?   420
    Charlie Morgan, Dorothy Livingston, and Andrew Moir
    A. Introduction   421
    B. Setting the Scene   422
    C. Drivers and Obstacles to Online Dispute Resolution   428
    D. Is DLT an Additional Catalyst for ODR?   435
    E. The Road Ahead: Multidisciplinary Collaboration   451
    F. Conclusion   452

Bibliography   455
Index   499

List of Abbreviations

ACE	Attempto Controlled English
ADR	Alternative Dispute Resolution
AI	Artificial Intelligence
AMIX	American Information Exchange
API	Application Programming Interface
ASCII	American Standard Code for Information Interchange
B2C	Business-to-Consumer
BCL	Business Contract Language
BSI	British Standards Institution
BTC	Bitcoin
C2C	Consumer-to-Consumer
CBDC	Central Bank Digital Currencies
CFG	Context Free Grammars
CLLS	City of London Law Society
CNL	Controlled Natural Language/Constrained Natural Language
CPU	Central Processing Unit
DAML	Digital Asset Modelling Language
DAO	Distributed Autonomous Organization
DeFi	Decentralized Finance
DLT	Distributed Ledger Technology
DSL	Domain-Specific Language
DSML	Domain-Specific Modelling Language
DSPL	Domain-Specific Programming Language
EDI	Electronic Data Interchange
EFT	Electronic Funds Transfer
ETH	Ether
ETRN	Equity and Trusts Research Network
EU	European Union
EUBOF	European Union Blockchain Observatory and Forum
EVM	Ethereum Virtual Machine
FIBO	Financial Industry Business Ontology
FIDE	International Chess Federation
GDPR	General Data Protection Regulation 2016/679
HMCTS	Her Majesty's Courts & Tribunals Service
HTML	HyperText Markup Language
ICANN	Internet Corporation for Assigned Names and Numbers
ICO	Initial Coin Offering
IDE	Integrated Development Environment
IMF	International Monetary Fund

IOSCO	International Organisation of Securities Commissions
IoT	Internet of Things
ISDA	International Swaps and Derivatives Association
IT	Information Technology
LAO	Legal Autonomous Organization
LIFT	Law, Information, Future, Technology
LPA	Law of Property Act 1925
LPS	Logic-Based Production System
LTDP	Lawtech Delivery Panel
MCOL	Online Money Claim Procedure
NFT	Non-Fungible Token
NLP	Natural Language Processing
OCR	Optical Character Recognition
ODR	Online Dispute Resolution
OWL	Web Ontology Language
PGP	Pretty Good Privacy
SCL	Simplified Contract Language
SHA-1	Secure Hash Algorithm 1
SLC	Smart Legal Contract
UDRP	Uniform Domain Name Dispute Resolution Policy
UKJT	UK Jurisdiction Taskforce
UNCITRAL	United Nations Commission on International Trade Law
VPL	Visual Programming Language
WJP	World Justice Project
XML	Extensible Markup Language

List of Contributors

Justice Aedit ABDULLAH

Jason Grant ALLEN

Natasha BLYCHA

Joshua BUTLER

Christopher D CLACK

Justice Stephen ESTCOURT AM

Scott FARRELL

Siegfried FINA

Ariane GARSIDE

Mark GIANCASPRO

Jacques GIUFFRE

Hannah GLASS

Simon GLEESON

Yihan GOH

Gabrielle GOLDING

Ian GRIGG

Robert HERIAN

Peter HUNN

David KOEPSELL

Dorothy LIVINGSTON

Megan MA

Madeleine MASLIN

Andrew MOIR

Charlie MORGAN

Irene NG (Huang Ying)

Alfonso Delgado De Molina RIUS

Eric TJONG TJIN TAI

Sir Geoffrey VOS, MR

Henry WELLS

Susannah WILKINSON

Tian XU

Editors' Introduction

Jason Grant Allen and Peter Hunn

Background

The idea behind this volume was first articulated in a Call for Papers circulated in August 2019. Blockchain-based 'smart contracts' were becoming the object of increasing (and increasingly mainstream) legal attention. A raft of questions had arisen going to their legal treatment and implications. However, our intuition was that these smart contracts—and Distributed Ledger Technology ('DLT') implementations generally—were only an instance of a much broader topic of interest. There were deeper questions, and higher stakes, than the immediate question whether any given 'smart contract' could fulfil the requirements of contract formation or confound the operation of doctrines like mistake or rectification (for example). They were, rather, the vanguard of a broader, even secular development towards the digitalization of law. The Call thus set out a number of themes surrounding the notion of 'smart legal contracts' in a technology-neutral fashion, ie, including but not limited to blockchain-based smart contracts. The idea was to gather investigations of technology-mediated contract formation, performance, and dispute resolution that would mark the field, establish some basic points regarding terminology and the deeper theoretical questions, and so provide a point of orientation for the growing literature on the topic.

The initial impulse was provided in an article by Allen first published in the *European Review of Contract Law* in 2018.[1] This article set out an argument that lawyers should look at technological developments without adopting any *a priori* position on the legality or alegality of any particular technological artefact; the relevant question is whether a given set of facts presents all the elements of a 'contract' or not. The focus was squarely on the role of language in human activities such as 'contracting'—whether 'smart' or conventional. While much of the literature at that time was focused on the legal implications of the *automation* of contractual performance, Allen argued that the implicit encoding of (some or all) contractual provisions in a *formal language* would be equally or more important for contract law in the long-term. Most importantly, the article set out the view

---

[1] See J.G. Allen, 'Wrapped and Stacked: "Smart Contracts" and the Interaction of Formal and Natural Language' (2018) 14(4) *European Contract Law Review* 307–43.

that technologically-mediated contracts were best seen as composite creatures, including conventional 'legal' elements (mostly on paper) as well as technological elements. Allen described this approach as a 'contract stack', in which a 'smart' layer rests within and interacts with other layers. A version of this article, which was circulated with the Call and an invitation to critical engagement by chapter authors, appears as Chapter 1 of the present volume.[2]

A speech by Sir Geoffrey Vos, then Chancellor of the High Court of England and Wales, entitled 'End-to-End Smart Legal Contracts: Moving from Aspiration to Reality' provided another important impulse.[3] An extended and updated version of Sir Geoffrey's speech forms Chapter 2 of this volume. It, too, was circulated with the Call to provide contributing authors with a common point of focus. At its core, it sets out a similar set of assumptions regarding the legal treatment of 'smart' contracts (whether blockchain-based or otherwise). The overriding mood is one of optimism that the law—and the common law systems in particular—are well-placed to accommodate novel contracting technologies.

The consultation process and publication of the landmark *Legal Statement on Cryptoassets and Smart Contracts* ('*Legal Statement*') by the UK Jurisdictional Taskforce ('UKJT') of the LawTech Delivery Panel[4] in November 2019 reinforced the impression that no impediment stood, in theory, to prevent encoded contracts being 'real' contracts—however they are encoded. However, it also confirmed that theoretical effort would be helpful to understand these new contractual forms and to answer the questions they would inevitably raise.[5] Alongside his work with the UKJT, during this time Hunn led both commercial and open-source initiatives, including the Accord Project, a non-profit, collaborative initiative under the Linux Foundation developing an ecosystem and open source tools specifically for smart legal contracts.[6] While the *Legal Statement* was not circulated with the Call, it was referred to and forms part of the backdrop of the present volume.

In addition to the open Call, solicitations were made to leading and emerging authors in academia and legal practice, as well as members of the judiciary working on the legal accommodation of emerging technologies. Submissions from disciplines other than law, particularly computer science and the humanities, were expressly invited, as were collaborations between authors from different backgrounds. Further, the Call invited submissions with a practical as well as a

---

[2] We thank the *European Review of Contract Law* and De Gruyter for the permission to reprint this article.
[3] https://www.judiciary.uk/announcements/speech-by-sir-geoffrey-vos-chancellor-of-the-high-court-cryptoassets-as-property.
[4] Now the LawTechUK Panel.
[5] See <https://technation.io/lawtech-uk-resources/#cryptoassets> accessed 13 August 2021. The UKJT was chaired by Sir Geoffrey. Hunn was, and remains, a member of the UKJT.
[6] See <https://accordproject.org/> accessed 19 July 2021. Among other things, Hunn chairs the working group of IEEE P2963, a standard which establishes common requirements for the development of computable contract templates: see <https://standards.ieee.org/project/2963.html#Standard> accessed 19 July 2021.

theoretical focus, namely to explore what it would take for 'smart legal contracts' to enter mainstream commercial practice within a coherent legal framework. Comparative analysis was expressly invited, but it was stipulated that doctrinally-focused chapters should include analysis of at least one common law jurisdiction to keep the collection tightly coherent.

The focus and framing of the Call reflected the fact that innovation in the design and application of code-based contractual provisions, particularly in the context of DLT, was leading development of the very legal theory that those innovations themselves presupposed. The Call thus invited submissions on a cluster of questions, including:

- *The concept of 'smart (legal) contracts'.* Are blockchain-based smart contracts 'smart' or 'contracts' at all? Should we be concerned with such 'smart contracts' only, or is the relevant concept broader? If so, what alternative terminology might we consider, such as 'computable contracts' or 'smart legal contracts'? What is a 'contract', and what do current developments teach us about that concept itself? Is the core of the concept the idea that a single body of symbolic data might be *both* executable code *and* human-readable text that validly expresses legal relationships? How do we account for the 'wrapping' of conventional legal prose around code? Is the metaphor of a 'contract stack' a valid way of conceptualising the interaction between 'encoded' and 'conventional' components of a contract?
- *Interactions between 'smart contracts' and prevailing legal doctrine.* Accepting that blockchain-based smart contracts are an important category for theory and practice, what relationship do smart contracts have with the concept of a 'legal contract' and with conventional legal doctrines? What doctrines are most challenged by code that purports to perform or express contractual obligations?
- *The legal basis of 'smart legal contracts'.* Assuming that 'smart legal contract' is a valid conceptual category, what is the legal basis of such a contract, and what issues would it raise for conventional legal doctrines? These might include issues in private international law or doctrines such as formation, the incorporation of terms, and equitable remedies. What impact do questions of anonymity, pseudonymity, and (the appearance of) non-human agency hold?
- *Design principles, elements, and emerging best practices.* How should lawyers and engineers approach the design of 'smart' contracts? Are any principles or best practices emerging? What conceptual, infrastructural (ie, technological), and institutional elements are clear at this stage? What role do dispute resolution mechanisms play in the concept of 'smart legal contracts' and in their commercial adoption?
- *Use cases for 'smart' contracts.* What are the present and future applications of and 'smart (legal) contracts'? Are the use cases limited to financial

transactions, or are there broader use cases? What role might smart (legal) contracts play in organisation or governance?

Authors were invited to engage critically with the adequacy of these questions: Were they (all) the right ones to be asking? At that time, no judicial precedents on the legal treatment of smart contracts yet existed, so many of the problems had to be framed in the abstract. In particular, the claim that blockchain-based 'smart contracts' were operating in a manner extraneous to the law, while in our view unconvincing, had a degree of plausibility that it definitively lacks today; work on smart *legal* contracts had barely begun.

Hunn joined Allen as co-editor in early 2020. His expertise was instrumental not only in selecting and organising chapters, but also in developing the substance of the volume and the collaborative process between the editors and authors to ensure a volume that, while not aiming for a handbook-type treatment of the subject, would make a targeted contribution to these fundamental questions. Despite the fast-moving pace of market developments in this space, we are confident that this book will represent a landmark point in the legal literature on 'smart contracts' for some time to come.

Choosing a Nomenclature in Default of an Accepted Conceptual Framework

As the foregoing list of questions makes clear, the first problem faced in formulating the Call was the correct *term* to use in the absence of consensus on what *concept* we were dealing with. Following the ground-breaking work of the *Legal Statement*, we opted for the nomenclature 'smart legal contracts' as a term to contrast with 'smart contracts'.[7] 'Smart contract' had already received acceptance in reference to DLT-based implementations of computer code that have the propensity to operate, or appear to operate, as a form of contract (or as a functional equivalent to a contract). Often, such a 'smart contract' does *not* operate as a contract at law at all, despite having a similar functional effect. The use of the term to address a broad spectrum of applications, encompassing both agreements with contractual effect and code without legal consequences, gives rise to a need to distinguish between the two, regardless of similarities in form.

'Smart legal contract' is a somewhat inelegant construction for two reasons. First, from the lawyer's perspective, the word 'contract' implicitly denotes something 'legal'. Secondly, the term mixes terminology, connoting popular and

---

[7] This nomenclature is generally attributed to Josh Stark, 'Making sense of Blockchain Smart Contracts' (Coindesk, 4 June 2016), <http://www.coindesk.com/making-sense-smart-contracts/> accessed 19 July 2021.

technical notions of (i) a specific technology implementation (ie, blockchain), and (ii) alegality, or agnosticism towards legal effect. These points notwithstanding, it expresses aptly, in our view, the idea of a contract 'encoded' in software and therefore a 'computable' contract that retains its contractual nature despite adopting particular technological characteristics.

Readers will notice that authors sometimes opt for different terms in their respective chapters. Several of them have advanced their own terminological (and conceptual) schemes in prior work, which in many cases have been influential. Despite these differences, all chapters were formulated against the background of the same Call, and all engage with the questions set out above. It would have been inappropriate, especially in 2019, to insist on any given term, but it is hoped that the volume, taken as a whole, contributes to the formation of a stable consensus around the concepts we are dealing with and the appropriate words to denote them. In our view, 'smart legal contract' is likely to become an accepted term in virtue of its use to date in instruments such as the *Legal Statement*, but other candidates such as 'computational contract' are equally, if not more, attractive.

Choosing a Point of Departure

Although work on the expression of legal, including contractual, terms in formalistic logic and computer code date back several decades, the idea of 'smart' contracts is generally associated with Nick Szabo's foundational work in the mid-1990s,[8] and this generally serves as the point of departure for the contemporary discussion. In fact, there is a danger of disconnect between the extensive literature and the current debate about smart contracts, which it is hoped this volume will help to bridge. Many of these early efforts were made from a computer science background and were focussed on expert systems. The current wave of engagement with computational contracts (including this volume) is being led by lawyers and has been catalysed by developments in DLT. In our view, the legal perspective is essential and we hope that this volume will help to show the true importance of this crucial technical work.

---

[8] See N. Szabo 'Smart Contracts' (1994), <https://www.fon.hum.uva.nl/rob/Courses/InformationInSpeech/CDROM/Literature/LOTwinterschool2006/szabo.best.vwh.net/smart.contracts.html> accessed 19 July 2021; N. Szabo, 'Smart Contracts: Building Blocks for Digital Markets' (1996), <https://www.fon.hum.uva.nl/rob/Courses/InformationInSpeech/CDROM/Literature/LOTwinterschool2006/szabo.best.vwh.net/smart_contracts_2.html> accessed 19 July 2021. Earlier work on computational law (broadly defined) includes L.E. Allen, 'Symbolic Logic: A Razor-edged Tool for Drafting and Interpreting Legal Documents' (1957) 66 *Yale Law Journal* 833; R.M. Lee, 'A Logic Model for Electronic Contracting' (1988) 4(1) *Decision Support Systems* 27; A.L. Tyree, 'The Logic Programming Debate' (1992) 3(1) *Journal of Law and Information Science* 111. See also M. Calejo *et al.*, 'Logic Programming and Smart Contracts' (2020), <https://www.remep.net/wp-content/uploads/2020/06/Miguel-Calejo_Logic-Programming-and-Smart-Contracts_ReMeP2020.pdf?x45466> accessed 23 December 2021.

We will take Szabo's 1997 article 'Formalising and Securing Relationships on Public Networks' as illustrative of the relevant concept.[9] Szabo starts by observing that a memorialized set of promises, reflecting a 'meeting of the minds', is the 'traditional way to formalise a relationship', and that it would be inefficient to reinvent the wheel entirely; however, new technologies can be harnessed to improve every phase of the contractual lifecycle to provide 'new ways to formalise and secure digital relationships which are far more functional than their inanimate paper-based ancestors.'[10]

The Szabo smart contract is a dynamic technological artefact[11] whose structure is informed by economic analysis (cost of breach), that can be used to automate and so guarantee 'performance' such that traditional 'legal enforcement' is made redundant:

> The basic idea of smart contracts is that many kinds of contractual clauses (such as liens, bonding, delineation of property rights, etc) can be embedded in the hardware and software we deal with, in such a way as to make breach of contract expensive (if desired, sometimes prohibitively so) for the breacher.[12]

Szabo's broadly techno-libertarian ethos is evident in the assumption that it is desirable to use economic incentives to circumvent conventional legal processes (rather than, for example, just rendering them more efficient or effective). However, at this stage at least, some degree of conventional legality was implicit—in our view, a greater degree than is sometimes recognized to be the case today.[13] It is fair to say that Szabo's view of the interrelation of law and technology is subtle.[14] The original Szaboian 'smart contract' is, in our view (and regardless of whatever else might have been said subsequently) clearly a 'contract, properly determined' that

---

[9] N. Szabo, 'Formalising and Securing Relationships on Public Networks' (1997) 2(9) *First Monday*, <https://doi.org/10.5210/fm.v2i9.548> accessed 19 July 2021. For background, see also P. Cuccuru, 'Beyond Bitcoin: An Early Overview on Smart Contracts' (2017) 25(3) *International Journal of Law and Information Technology* 179; V. Gatteschi et al., 'Technology of Smart Contracts' in DiMatteo et al., *The Cambridge Handbook of Smart Contracts, Blockchain Technology and Digital Platforms* (Cambridge University Press 2019); D.T. Stabile et al., *Digital Assets and Blockchain Technology: U.S. Law and Regulation* (Edward Elgar 2020), 215–65.

[10] Szabo (n. 9).

[11] For discussion of what a 'technological artefact' is, see C. Lawson, *Technology and Isolation* (Cambridge University Press 2017), 80 *et seq*.

[12] Szabo (n. 9).

[13] For example, Szabo sets out an outline of a formal language he intended to 'unambiguously and *completely* and succinctly as possible, specify common contracts or *contractual terms*': see Nick Szabo, 'A Formal Language for Analysing Contracts' (2002), <https://www.fon.hum.uva.nl/rob/Courses/InformationInSpeech/CDROM/Literature/LOTwinterschool2006/szabo.best.vwh.net/contractlanguage.html> accessed 19 July 2021. However, a synoptic/diachronic analysis of Szabio's various contributions, and the evolution of his thinking, is beyond our present scope.

[14] See also the discussion in F. Möslein, 'Smart Contracts and Civil Law Challenges' in I. Chiu and G. Deipenbrock (eds), *Routledge Handbook of Financial Technology and Law* (Routledge 2021) 27.

happens to be 'smarter' than its paper forbears through provision of an inherent means of operationalization.[15]

So much is implicit in Szabo's oft-cited vending machine example.[16] A machine that *vends* does not just deliver goods, it *sells* them—by accepting payment and delivering goods, it encodes a legal workflow, albeit without any of the conventional legal processes such as the creation of a written instrument. Things really get interesting, however, as vending machines go digital: 'Smart contracts go beyond the vending machine in proposing to embed contracts in all sorts of property that is valuable and controlled by digital means. Smart contracts reference that property in a dynamic, proactively enforced form, and provide much better observation and verification where proactive measures must fall short.'[17] For example, a car with a 'smart' lock can switch itself off on default of repayment to protect a secured creditor. The idea is not just that the car can be immobilized at will, but 'lawfully', pursuant to the contractual agreement made between the buyer/debtor and seller/creditor. Szabo's article concludes with the idea that 'the law of the Internet' will be provided by a 'grand merger of law and computer security': 'If so, smart contracts will be a major force behind this merger.'[18]

Presented more than a decade prior to Satoshi Nakamoto's Bitcoin Whitepaper of 2009;[19] the Szaboian smart contract was obviously not dependent on blockchain technology as we currently understand it.[20] While the Bitcoin protocol implements a purposefully constrained notion of a smart contract for the transference of the Bitcoin cryptoasset between network participants,[21] a generalized implementation of 'smart contracts' arose much later, with the development of Ethereum.[22] The creators of Ethereum adopted the term to refer to blockchain-based scripts[23]

---

[15] See P. Hunn, 'Smart Contracts as Techno-Legal Regulation' (2019) 7(3) *Journal of ICT Standardization* 269.

[16] See Szabo (n. 9). ('A canonical real-life example, which we might consider to be the primitive ancestor of smart contracts, is the humble vending machine. [...] The vending machine is a contract with bearer: anybody with coins can participate in an exchange with the vendor. The lockbox and other security mechanisms protect the stored coins and contents from attackers, sufficiently to allow profitable deployment of vending machines in a wide variety of areas.')

[17] Szabo (n. 9).

[18] *Ibid.*

[19] S. Nakamoto, 'Bitcoin: A Peer-to-Peer Electronic Cash System'. <https://bitcoin.org/bitcoin.pdf> accessed 19 July 2021.

[20] Szabo did, however, expressly envisage many of the technical characteristics of blockchain and other DLT protocols in their implementation, see Szabo (n. 9) and N. Szabo, 'Secure Property Titles with Owner Authority' (1998), <https://nakamotoinstitute.org/secure-property-titles/> accessed 19 July 2021.

[21] A Turing-incomplete scripting language consisting of a limited set of operation codes (or 'opcodes'): <https://developer.bitcoin.org/reference/transactions.html> accessed 19 July 2021.

[22] V. Buterin, 'A Next-Generation Smart Contract and Decentralized Application Platform' (2013). <https://ethereum.org/en/whitepaper>; G. Wood, Ethereum: A Secure Decentralised Generalised Transaction Ledger (2014). <https://ethereum.github.io/yellowpaper/paper.pdf> accessed 19 July 2021. See also <https://ethereum.org/en/developers/docs/smart-contracts> accessed 19 July 2021.

[23] An 'algorithm' is the series of steps to be performed in order to solve a problem (a solution). A 'script' is an instantiation of a particular solution. An algorithm may be implemented in different scripts and different scripts may use different algorithms to solve a particular problem.

of any arbitrary mathematical complexity, including the creation and transfer of cryptoassets and 'tokens' representing other assets such as legal rights against counterparties and in things. In the context of Ethereum, the implicitly *contractual* (that is, implicitly *legal*) aspect of 'smart contracts' has been somewhat obfuscated by a technology-centric recasting of the concept.[24] In this context, the notion that the label 'smart contracts' is a misnomer has received notable support,[25] especially among lawyers, prompting attempts at reframing away from legal, and towards more technical, terminology such as 'transactional scripts', 'stored procedures', or 'persistent scripts'.[26] At this stage, however, the horse has bolted and the nomenclature seems here to stay.

Stated in the abstract, the core area of inquiry is the complex relation between technological artefacts (be it a vending machine, a smart lock in an automobile, or a cryptoasset) and the 'world of law'. Can *any* artefact entail the redundancy of 'conventional law', or does it simply imply the creation of a contract, eg, through acts such as making a vending machine available to the public ('offer to all the world') or feeding it coins ('acceptance by performance')? In our view, the advent of code no more replaces the legal figure of the contract than the advent of writing and (later) printing. The roots of this question dig down into deeper questions about the existence and nature of 'cryptolaw'—the relationship between patterns of social and economic interaction mediated by emerging technologies such as DLT, and blockchain, in particular.[27] This enquiry in turn raises yet deeper questions about the ontology of legal objects (such as complex relational positions of invisible 'rights' and 'duties', aka 'contracts') and the artefacts (mainly documents of speech acts[28]) through which they are created and maintained.

The Focus of this Volume

As this discussion suggests, the definition and legal status of blockchain-based smart contracts is not the focus of this volume. In fact, our intention all along has

---

[24] Subsequently, Vitalik Buterin expressed regret at his choice to use the term, preferring instead 'persistent scripts': https://twitter.com/vitalikbuterin/status/1051160932699770882.
[25] See Allen (n. 1); E. Mik, 'Smart Contracts: Terminology, Technical Limitations and Real World Complexity' (2017) 9 *Law, Innovation and Technology* 269; J.M. Lipshaw, 'The Persistence of Dumb Contracts' (2019) 2 *Stanford Journal of Blockchain Law & Policy* 1; K.E.C. Levy, 'Book-Smart, Not Street-Smart: Blockchain-Based Smart Contracts and The Social Workings of Law' (2017) 3(1) *Engaging Science, Technology, and Society* 1.
[26] See S. Cohney and D. Hoffman, 'Transactional Scripts in Contract Stacks' (2020) 105 *Minnesota Law Review* 319.
[27] See, eg, C. Reyes, 'Conceptualising Cryptolaw' (2017) 96(2) *Nebraska Law Review* 384; D. Fox and S. Green (eds), *Cryptocurrencies in Public and Private Law* (Oxford University Press 2019); P. De Filippi and A. Wright, *Blockchain and the Law: The Rule of Code* (Harvard University Press 2018).
[28] See, eg, the discussion in M. Hildebrandt, 'Text-driven Jurisdiction in Cyberspace' (30 April 2021), <https://doi.org/10.31219/osf.io/jgs9n> accessed 19 July 2021.

been to curate the first concerted investigation of 'smart' contracts *not* limited to the blockchain context. However, it would be inappropriate to exclude blockchain-based 'transactional scripts' from scope, and this volume contains a number of blockchain-specific chapters, reflecting the importance of current developments in that technology space. In fact, most chapters discuss blockchain-related developments in some degree of detail.

In a meaningful sense, the submissions we received—which now comprise this volume—have vindicated a number of intuitions and hypotheses framing the Call. At the time, four things seemed tolerably clear to us. First, many blockchain-based smart contracts encoded things *relevant*, at least, to parties' legal relations. We could see no reason why *some* blockchain-based smart contracts should not embody or evidence a 'contract'—provided the elements of contract formation were, in all the circumstances, present. This was the approach taken by the UKJT *Legal Statement*, too, which put the point crisply:

> There is a contract in English law when two or more parties have reached an agreement, intend to create a legal relationship by doing so, and have each given something of benefit. A smart contract is capable of satisfying those requirements just as well as a more traditional or natural language contract, and a smart contract is therefore capable of having contractual force. Whether the requirements are in fact met in any given case will depend on the parties' words and conduct, just as it does with any other contract.[29]

Secondly, however, it seemed equally clear that many blockchain-based smart contracts were, at most, *parts* or *elements* of a contract, not the whole thing. It seemed to be unnecessary and unhelpful to exclude the 'off-chain' elements simply because *part* of the relevant documentary structure was recorded in a blockchain data structure. Thirdly, efforts were already underway to make conventional contractual forms 'smarter' by harnessing more expressive digital tools to record contractually relevant information and effectuate contractually relevant actions, including digital tools that had nothing to do with blockchain. Finally, taking all of those things together, there seemed to be value in exploring how the elements of a contract at law interact with novel technical elements—be that markup text, blockchain-based smart contracts, or other forms of encoded component.

Our approach treats the composition and execution (in the computer science sense) of code as any other human behaviour which the law falls to interpret and give legal effect to—or not. A contract, of course, requires mutual assent,[30] but following the dominant 'objective' theory of contracting, the relevant intention is to

---

[29] UKJT *Legal Statement*, [8].
[30] Lord Steyn, 'Contract Law: Fulfilling the Reasonable Expectations of Honest Men' (1997) 113 *Law Quarterly Review* 433; *Raffles v Wichelhaus* [1864] EWHC Exch J19.

sell you my car, not to *form a contract* to sell you my car.[31] By the same token, I might subjectively intend to sell you my car *without* creating a contract at all, but from the legal perspective the very concept of 'selling' has 'objective' contractual entailments. Much like "Monsieur" Jourdain in Molière's *Le Bourgeois Gentilhomme*, some of us might find that we have been speaking in 'contractual prose' all along without being aware of that fact.[32]

There is, perhaps, an implicit imperialist claim by the legal systems of the world here: state-based legal systems recognize each-other, and allow parties a great degree of latitude to choose the governing law of their contracts. But together, they insist on forming a jigsaw of contiguous jurisdictions. Gaps are not conceivable within this conceptual scheme. Freedom of contract does not allow parties to remove, by consent, their contracts from the world of law entirely, or to erect a wholly private, idiosyncratic legal system. Every human dealing must be subject to *some* law, jurisdiction established by some connecting factor—even in cyberspace.[33]

If we accept this legal point of view—which we think lawyers generally must—the question becomes whether apparently (and sometimes avowedly) alegal 'smart contracts' might be relevant in a mediate way, for example by providing evidence of a transaction such as a 'sale' or providing clues as to the terms of that contract of sale. As Allen asked of the vending machine in 'Wrapped and Stacked':

> [If a vending] machine's discriminator is defective and it does not dispense the right product (or the right change), what do I do in the absence of a written contract with the machine's owner? Where would I find the terms of the alleged contract of sale to argue (possibly before some tribunal) that the machine's owner owes me performance or damages in lieu?[34]

The answer, of course, is that the relationship between the vending machine operator and the consumer is still 'contractual', but its terms must be derived somehow from the available evidence. The one potential difference is that, while vending machines are not very expressive—their terms are 'encoded' in gears and levers—a 'smart contract' is itself a *text-based* instrument. Text is inherently more susceptible of interpretation by lawyers and courts than technological artefacts of the mechanical age.[35] This approach suggests that popular arguments that blockchain-based

---

[31] See, for example, J.M. Perillo, 'The Origins of the Objective Theory of Contract Formation and Interpretation' (2000) 69(2) *Fordham Law Review* 427.

[32] 'My faith! For more than forty years I have been speaking prose while knowing nothing of it, and I am the most obliged person in the world to you for telling me so.' See J.P.B. de Molière, *Le Bourgeois Gentilhomme* (Paris 1670).

[33] See J.G. Allen and R.M. Lastra, 'Border Problems: Mapping the Third Border' (2020) 83(3) *Modern Law Review* 505; D.J.B. Svantesson, *Solving the Internet Jurisdiction Puzzle* (Oxford University Press 2017).

[34] Allen (n. 1), 314.

[35] Granted, this distinction is not categorical, it merely raises questions about how far down the 'stack' we need to go to find legally-relevant answers. Text-based instruments may have physical world

smart contracts bring their users outside the realm of 'law' are a harmful distraction and an impediment to achieving the necessary legal certainty.

It further suggests that the legal treatment of machine-readable text can be seen, at least in part, as a *problem of translation* and as a problem akin to the *incorporation of terms*. In any event, it seemed to us clear that software-encoded agreements can no more be 'alegal' than any other human endeavour. Even when new technologies mediate new forms of human action, the law cannot, by its nature, remain passive. Further, and more fundamentally, things like driving, on the one hand, and effecting transfers of economic value, on the other hand, are not really the same. The latter category of action inherently presupposes *normative* structures— at the very least, the transitive passage of some kind of entitlement from one person to another. Although some might argue blockchain to provide a mechanism for the purely *de facto* 'holding' of certain assets or positions *vis-à-vis* other persons, we think that developments over the first decade of its technology much rather speak to an incorporation of blockchain within the world of law than the opposite.

In most important respects, then, the conceptual tradition of this volume owes far less to Szabo's 'smart contract' or Buterin's 'persistent script' than to Ian Grigg's 'Ricardian Contract'.[36] The Ricardian Contract was developed by Grigg, also in the 1990s, as an intentional engagement with law and its conventional structures. It is a method of implementing a document as a contract at law, and linking it to financial systems to record an issuance of value. Pre-empting later developments in DLT, the Ricardian Contract incorporates cryptographic security protocols. The Ricardian paradigm would later become a core design pattern for connecting *conventional legal prose* with *executable code*, which is the central concern of this book. We are very pleased to have a retrospective dialogue with lawyers from Grigg in the volume.

Smart Legal Contract Language and Technology-Mediated Social Artefacts

In light of all this, the most interesting site of development seems to be the *combination* of 'smart' and 'conventional' layers in contracts, seen as complex artefacts. As Allen argued in 'Wrapped and Stacked', contracts should be recognized as complex legal institutional entities whose parts interact. DLT is not the best starting point

---

implications. Source code, often written in a programming or scripting language, is translated to, or interpreted and executed as, machine code used to *directly* control the *physical* circuitry of a computer. Computers are used to control all manner of physical infrastructure from cars to power plants including, of course, vending machines.

[36] See I. Grigg, 'Why the Ricardian Contract Came About: A Retrospective Dialogue with Lawyers', Chapter 5 in this volume.

for an enquiry, nor indeed is the apparently 'agentive' nature of the digital artefacts concerned.[37] While automation of contractual performance is the obvious advantage of encoding contractual terms in machine-readable 'prose', just as important is the impact that inevitably has on the way that a contract is *written*, ie, composed of structured symbolic data comprising a set of operators expressing both actions and modes of obligation in the future in a legally-relevant way.

From this approach, the conclusion reached by the *Legal Statement* in fact follows inevitably: there is no barrier to a single instrument, written in formal language, embodying both the 'legal contract' *and* its automated mechanism of performance. However, this raises fascinating and perplexing questions of language. For example, what language might be intelligible both for a human reader and for a machine? Given the fundamentally different nature of natural (human) and formal (machine) languages, how the processes of 'translation' between one language and another will work. How are elements that are not accessible to a human 'incorporated' into the contract which, though recorded in some written medium, is a social artefact that ultimately rests on shared understandings, interpretations, and societal consensus between human beings? In addition to such conceptual questions, a host of practical questions have already begun to arise for this new, digital domain within contract law. What consequences follow from the fundamental differences between natural and formal languages' ability to express terms such as 'reasonableness' or 'fitness'? What workarounds might be available, such as sources of 'truth' outside the software platform? How are those going to be incorporated as a matter of 'legal design'—itself a burgeoning field of innovation and scholarship?

In our view, the 'contract stack' metaphor is a powerful way of framing these questions, and to a great extent subsequent developments bear that out. A blockchain-based smart contract, for example, might be incorporated into a 'legal' contract in a manner not categorically different to a formal appendix, such as a mathematical accounting formula. As nobody would argue that a technical appendix is not part of the contract, a technical appendix that comprises executable code should not be seen as categorically non-contractual, either. The core idea is the *interaction* of different elements with each other.[38] Allen advanced[39] the metaphor of a 'stack' as a pithy encapsulation of this approach:

> In computer science, a 'technology stack' refers to the underlying elements of an application, ie, the languages and software products that the application

---

[37] By 'agentivity', we mean the apparent ability of the artefact to perform actions like bidding, accepting, or transferring payment in an appropriate digital environment. See eg, D.A. Cruse, 'Some Thoughts on Agentivity' (1973) 9(1) *Journal of Linguistics* 11.
[38] Allen (n. 1), 311.
[39] Both Hunn and Allen arrived at a similar conceptual structure and terminology independently of one another in their work in 2017 and 2018 respectively. The Accord Project provides one of the first open source implementations of smart contracts built around this concept.

is built on. This, I think, provides a way of describing the various components of a contract as a complex entity... A paper contract comprises (i) the spoken words through which the contractual terms were negotiated and against which the text was drafted, (ii) the written text, and (iii) legal rules implying terms and governing construction. The written text (ii) is often highly complex, with cross-references incorporating various documents. Further, the legal rules (iii) are generally fairly strict in the way that they circumscribe (i) the words outside the text, especially pre-contractual negotiations. In a smart contract, (ii) is complemented (or supplanted) by code which is also, incidentally, wholly or partially executable by a machine. Depending on the design of the smart contract, the code component of the written layer of the contract stack may be comprehensive or cover only a small part of the contract as a whole. The type of formal language in which this code is written will also be relevant to the complexity of the contract stack, eg, whether it is a compiled or interpreted language; a compiled language, which translates ("compiles") machine-readable code from the human-readable source code, will add another sub-layer within this layer of the stack.[40]

Obviously, if we had to write 'Wrapped and Stacked' again today it would look different. Not least, the literature has grown in size and sophistication, and the process of editing this volume itself has provided us with valuable insights into the concepts discussed there. The structure of the argument in that article (as readers will see) perhaps could have teased out some of the issues of blockchain-based *versus* non-blockchain based 'smart' layers more clearly, or distinguished more clearly between different approaches to constructing the 'contract stack'—for example, merging human-readable and machine-readable language into a single text or somehow pairing specific code-based elements with a more conventional stack. The volume demonstrates a multidisciplinary crystallization of the core concepts supporting the notion of a contractual stack: a framework of interaction between code (which may take various architectural forms) and natural language positioned within a legal environment, which is well-established.

The contract stack approach is agnostic to the concrete shape that a 'smart legal contract' takes in practice. Nothing *per se* speaks against one body of structured symbolic data being a human-readable 'contract' (with all the legal consequences that entails) *and* a technological artefact that effectuates some degree of performance automation. However, this is not the only permissible design pattern, and many implementations of 'smart legal contracts' will continue to pair elements that are only human-readable *or* machine-readable (but not both) rather than attempting to merge them into one single text. Both approaches are discussed in this volume, many instantiations will be more hybrid than ideal-type, and time

---

[40] Allen (n. 1), 330.

will tell which approach establishes itself as the preferred one for which applications and contexts. By whatever approach, the interrelationship of text and code to form a contractual artefact capable of both recording and performing contractual agreements is fast becoming an established form for the co-ordination of commercial relationships. Their interaction is critically important and practically necessary.

The exact implementation of the constituent components will present important techno-legal considerations and trade-offs. When should code be run 'on-chain' or 'off-chain'? When, and how, should the code of a contract be initiated or stopped? Will the code be embedded within the text or implemented independently of it? As this new contractual paradigm develops, these and other interesting legal and practical questions will raise the opportunity to critically assess the application of the doctrines of interpretation, rectification and remedies, jurisdiction and conflict of laws, and technology standards, to smart legal contracts, amongst others.

Although it does not form part of the volume, the UKJT *Legal Statement* has already become established as a historically significant document in this emerging field and could usefully be read with it. The *Legal Statement* was intended to clarify the legal position of, and principles applicable to, cryptoassets and smart contracts under English law, and represents the most comprehensive legal exposition, both from a procedural and substantive perspective, of the subject matter under the law of any single jurisdiction to date.[41] Importantly, the *Legal Statement* supports the position that a smart legal contract is capable of satisfying the basic requirements of an English law contract and, as a corollary, that English law is capable of accommodating smart contracts and their associated technological machinery through established principles of contract law.[42]

At the time of writing, there are numerous forthcoming developments relating to smart legal contracts. Key amongst these is the Law Commission of England and Wales' project on smart contracts led by Professor Sarah Green as part of the 13th Programme of Law Reform.[43] The resultant report and proposals will present an assessment of the ability of the common law to accommodate smart contracts, including a 'hybrid' combination of code and natural language. It is our view that this concept will solidify as the foundation upon which future legal and practical developments will be built. As such, we anticipate that this volume will take a landmark position in the emerging literature on smart legal contracts.

---

[41] Whilst not binding law, the *Legal Statement* is an influential persuasive source. In *AA v Persons Unknown who demanded Bitcoin on 10th and 11th October 2019 and others* [2019] EWHC 3556 (Comm), its analysis of cryptoassets was adopted by Bryan J. at [57]–[59].

[42] Including the recordation and operationalization of a contract through use of source code and cryptographic primitives: UKJT *Legal Statement* (n. 29), [136], [150]–[152], [158].

[43] Law Commission, *Smart contracts: Call for evidence* (December 2020), [1.8]. See <https://www.lawcom.gov.uk/project/smart-contracts> accessed 19 July 2021.

EDITORS' INTRODUCTION 15

Overview of Chapters

The volume comprises twenty substantive chapters. Chapter 1, which appears immediately after this Introduction, reproduces 'Wrapped and Stacked' and provides the reader with an overview of the background issues which chapter authors were invited to consider and critically assess. This chapter has been summarized sufficiently above.

The volume then moves to a dialogue between leading judges in England and Wales, Singapore, and Australia. In Chapter 2, 'End-to-End Smart Legal Contracts: Moving from Aspiration to Reality', Sir Geoffrey Vos MR asks how 'smart contracts', broadly defined, might move from a technologically feasible aspiration to legal and commercial reality. Originally written during the UKJT's investigation into the legality of 'smart contracts' in English law—and expressly avoiding pre-emption of the *Legal Statement*—Sir Geoffrey's chapter (i) suggests that a firm *private law* foundation was needed, (ii) draws attention to the need to consider end-to-end digital contracts with a subject matter other than cryptoassets, and (iii) suggests that a built-in dispute resolution system would provide important commercial certainty. Stressing the need for lawyers and coders to work together, Sir Geoffrey's chapter moves from the basic question (are 'smart contracts' capable of giving rise to binding legal obligations?) to the application of conventional legal doctrines to legal contracts written wholly or partly in code. On the whole, Sir Geoffrey expresses a characteristically pragmatic and sanguine view, particularly regarding the ability of traditional contract doctrines of formation to accommodate new forms of agreement memoranda.

In Chapter 3, 'Making Smart Contracts a Reality: Confronting Definitions, Enforceability and Regulation' Justice Aedit Abdullah and Yihan Goh SC pick up on Sir Geoffrey's practical question. They work through a number of issues likely to arise as the courts are called upon to adjudicate matters concerning different degrees of contract automation. These include, for example, contract formation *via* algorithm and vitiating factors such as mistake or fraud.[44] Responding to Sir Geoffrey's preference for active judicial common law development, Justice Abdullah and Professor Goh weigh the merits of legislative intervention and call for the development of legal rules that balance the interests of party autonomy, legal certainty, business efficacy and the protection of the public interest, broadly defined.

In Chapter 4, Justice Stephen Estcourt AM addresses the crucial question of dispute resolution in our increasingly digital world. Justice Estcourt focusses on the competition between state courts and new, often private (and sometimes

---

[44] Mistake, of course, was an issue in the Singapore International Commercial Court decision in *Quoine Pte Ltd v B2C2* [2019] 4 SLR 17 and is the subject of Chapter 19 by Simon Gleeson.

blockchain-based) dispute resolution services that are emerging in 'cyberspace' to meet the needs of underserved markets. Using the example of Kleros,[45] Justice Estcourt engages critically with the reasons why consumers might turn to private justice alternatives and explores what the courts might do to maintain values, such as the rule of law, in the face of competition. He also examines recent developments including the UKJT's *Draft Dispute Resolution Rules*,[46] published in early 2021, which represent a world-first effort to incorporate private online dispute resolution ('ODR') into the conventional legal system through the gateways of arbitration and appellate review. In conclusion, Justice Estcourt makes some observations on the interaction of technology and law that frame the volume as a whole.

The volume then moves to 'theory' and includes chapters by legal scholars and computer scientists (and a few that are both) exploring definitions and taxonomy and taking a deep dive into the question of language. This part commences with Chapter 5 by pioneer financial cryptologist Ian Grigg, 'Why the Ricardian Contract Came About: A Retrospective Dialogue with Lawyers'. The Ricardian Contract, he explains, was designed to capture the semantic essence of a financial instrument and link it to legal prose. Its architecture presents a human-readable, contractually significant document, digitally signed and including markup tokens such that a computer program can extract important values. The Ricardian paradigm is conducive to thinking about the question at the heart of this volume, and we hope that this will encourage a more 'Ricardian' inflection to the subsequent literature.

Chapter 6 by Alfonso Delgado De Molina Rius, 'Smart Contracts: Taxonomy, Transaction Costs and Design Trade-offs' starts with a taxonomy of 'contracts' ('smart' or not) in order to define the subject matter more precisely: we must understand what a 'contract' is before asking about 'smart' contracts. Reflecting on the mismatch between lawyers and computer scientists, particularly in the context of DLT, Rius argues that computer scientists have been denied a chief benefit of the law—a recursive body of experience, developed over centuries, to streamline socially and commercially beneficial behaviour. Rius uses the framework of New Institutional Economics to assess the relative strengths and weaknesses of smart contracts and focusses, in particular, on some of the trade-offs inherent in using varying combinations of natural and formal language to structure a contractual relationship.

In Chapter 7, 'Smart Legal Contracts: A Model for the Integration of Machine Capabilities and Contracts', Natasha Blycha and Ariane Garside present a compelling approach to implementing the concept of 'smart legal contracts'. In so doing, their chapter provides a number of both conceptual and practical insights. In particular, it provides a complement to Allen's 'contract stack' and introduces a number of pertinent distinctions when it comes to looking at the different ways that legal and technical elements are combined to instantiate a 'smart legal contract'. On a

---

[45] <https://kleros.io> accessed 19 July 2021.
[46] <https://technation.io/lawtech-uk-resources> accessed 19 July 2021.

practical level (in our terms) it presents a way to 'wrap' computer code and natural language and to 'stack' a legal contract within a data source and an execution layer. In so doing, this chapter provides insight into the mode of interaction between components of a contract that are more conventional (ie, based in natural language prose) and more formal (ie, based in a more expressive and operational machine-executable code).

In Chapter 8, 'Six Levels of Contract Automation: Further Analysis of the Evolution to Smart Legal Contracts', Susannah Wilkinson and Jacques Giuffre expand on the Blycha and Garside model with an analysis of the different degrees or 'levels' of automation. Identifying and contrasting a 'unified' and 'paired' approach to the combination of natural and formal language components (and identifying the Blycha and Garside proposal as an instance of the 'paired' approach), Wilkinson and Giuffre work by analogy with international standards of vehicle automation to present a graduated scale of contract automation. By so doing, this chapter seeks to provide a starting point from which to develop a framework for discussion of legally enforceable automation of contractual performance.

In Chapter 9, 'Smart Contracts as Execution Instead of Expression', Eric Tjong Tjin Tai asks what blockchain-based 'smart contracts' are able to do by way of contrast to conventional ('legal') contracts. Smart contracts, he argues, upset the traditional functions of interpretation by providing an automated execution chain without requiring human-readable expressions. Smart contracts do not however, do away with the necessity of *translating party expectations*. Contracts derive from the mutual desire of parties to realize a project in the world as expressed in a document. Translation into the relevant language and interpretation over the contract's life-cycle is unavoidable—but will look different for a contract with 'smart' components. Because code does not, as such, express 'meaning', smart contracts are good at some things and poor at others; parties deploying them always accept a certain derogation of the *ex post* protection afforded by contract law. Though smart contracts may achieve a high degree of compliance with contract law, *lacunae* are an inevitable result.

In Chapter 10, 'Smart Contracts: The Limits of Autonomous Performance', Tian Xu points to the institution of documentary credit as an established mechanism for effecting autonomous contract performance in a commercial setting. Considering novel forms of contract automation in light of functionally similar, but paper-based, instruments sheds light on smart legal contracts and their potential deployment. Xu explores a number of concrete issues arising from this comparative exercise, including some potential limitations to applying smart contracts to scenarios beyond digital asset transfers, how dispute resolution mechanisms should be designed to complement automated contractual performance, and capital cost implications which might arise where parties seek to replace human intermediaries with smart contracts.

In Chapter 11, 'Techno-Legal Supertoys: Smart Contracts and the Fetishization of Legal Certainty', Robert Herian brings a valuable critical perspective. Underpinning the question of smart contracts' legal treatment are three overlapping legal and extra-legal factors: (i) apprehensions surrounding the definition and reliability in fact and law, (ii) uncertainties regarding remedies at law and in equity, and (iii) fetishization of the perfectibility and certainty of smart contracts (particularly by non-lawyers). Drawing on the idea of 'supertoys' in science fiction literature, Herian argues that the legal legitimacy and certainty of smart contracts rests on fundamental principles of contract law, not on imaginary or quasi-legal conditions determined by the limits of coding and design. As expectations of right and wrong are inherent in the idea of a 'contract', contract law remedies are crucial even for blockchain-based smart contracts to operate reasonably. Far from intelligent 'solutions' to longstanding 'problems', much smart contract design is legally simplistic and ignores critical aspects of contract law and theory.

The stage so set, the volume then takes a deep dive into the theory of computation, language, and law. In Chapter 11, 'Languages for Smart and Computable Contracts', Christopher Clack asks how we might increase confidence in the ability of computer code to express the intention of commercial parties. This question, he argues, requires an exploration of natural and computer languages, of the semantics of expression in those languages, and of the gap that exists between the disciplines of law and computer science—particularly when they come to concepts like 'meaning'. Clack explores some current research directions and explains the importance of language design in the development of reliable smart contracts, including the specific methodology of (in his terms) 'computable contracts'. Introducing the notion of a 'language stack', Clack sets out some thoughts on the 'translation' or 'conversion' of terms between languages and provides a detailed and practical overview of the essential layers in the language stack. This chapter promises to be not only an important point of reference for lawyers, but also a practical guide for developers encoding the terms of a legal agreement in a computer language. In particular, it provides a comprehensive overview of the different languages designed for computable contracts, including *inter alia* blockchain-based smart contracts and Ricardian contracts combined with a detailed examination of the semantic and syntactic features of those languages.

In Chapter 13, 'The Mathematisation of Legal Writing: The Next Contract Language?', Megan Ma explores the history of attempts to formalize legal language (and, thereby, the content of legal norms) from Aristotle to Descartes to Leibniz and uses this context critically to assess the current wave of innovation. Noting the implicit marginalization of 'interpretation' that language formalization entails, Ma addresses the conundrum of the significance of *medium* in contract drafting. By identifying the logic of the languages concerned, Ma's chapter tackles methods of legal writing, arguing that analysis of the components of legal and programming languages enables a richer dialogue on the sociological implications of translating law into algorithmic form and provides a context in which to consider what contextual understanding may need to exist to 'interpret' contractual language.

In Chapter 14, 'Beyond Human: Smart Contracts, Smart Machines, and Documentality', David Koepsell brings two crucial considerations to bear, again with a focus on blockchain-based smart contracts. First, he looks towards the future when increasingly intelligent machines perform (or mimic) functions of human agency such as negotiating the terms of a contract or forming a written contract. Secondly, he looks to the conceptual resources of social ontology and of the theory of 'documentality' in particular to shed light on that question and the other questions raised by computable, code-based expressions of legal language. Drawing on previous work on the nature of documents 'beyond paper' and their role in constituting social reality, Koepsell argues that legal rules and classifications will require adjustment to account for the types of social objects and agents that will arise.

In Chapter 15, 'Smart Contract "Drafting" and the Homogenization of Languages', Siegfried Fina and Irene (Huang Ying) Ng tackle an under-appreciated implication of the rise of 'encoded' contracts: homogenization of the languages involved, both natural and formal. This has various dimensions, ranging from the marginalization of languages other than English (languages with smaller speaking communities, in particular) to the loss of lawyers' traditional monopoly over contract drafting. Fina and Ng also discuss the standardization of programming languages used for encoding contractual agreements, and the potential impacts of artificial intelligence in the future.

Finally, the volume moves to 'Practice' and contains a number of incisive interventions, mostly by legal practitioners working at the coalface, on the design and application of 'smart legal contracts', their impact on conventional legal doctrine, and future directions in adjudication. In Chapter 16, 'Practice Makes … Pragmatic: Designing a Practical Smart Contract Legal Architecture', Scott Farrell, Hannah Glass, and Henry Wells identify and summarize five core considerations that have arisen in designing what they term the 'legal architecture' for smart contracts. The authors assess the importance of interoperability, certainty, flexibility, accountability, and safety in the design and development of a suitable legal architecture for smart contracts, and advance these as guiding techno-legal attributes for the design and development of implementations of the 'contract stack'.

In Chapter 17, 'Lawyer Meets Developer: How Interdisciplinary Collaboration Builds Smarter Legal Contracts', Josh Butler and Madeleine Maslin assess the growing need for, and approaches to, cross-functional collaboration in the development of smart legal contracts. In analysing common means of co-ordination between computer scientists and lawyers, the authors consider the importance of a tripartite framework of consortia, partnerships, and standards in order to bring together the necessary infrastructure for the practical development and adoption of smart legal contracts.

Chapter 18, 'Not Up to the Job: Why Smart Contracts are Unsuitable for Employment', by Gabrielle Golding and Mark Giancaspro highlights some of the potential drawbacks with the use of smart contracts *qua* legal contracts. The chapter discusses the oft-cited issues of subjectivity, discretion, and flexibility as they pertain to smart contracts and discuss how they have the propensity to operate as technological constraints in the operation of employment relationships.

Simon Gleeson moves in Chapter 19 to address the first major judicial decision on smart contracts and conventional contract law, *Quoine Pte Ltd v B2C2*[47] in 'The Legal Consequences of Automated Mistake'. The chapter compares the application of the law of mistake to human acts and those performed algorithmically by machines. In assessing the decision in *Quoine*, Gleeson advances an argument that algorithmically formed contracts are not susceptible to the same, traditional, analysis as contracts formed between human counterparties; concluding that recourse to equity is required to address automated mistakes that would otherwise result in a contract between humans being disregarded at law.

Chapter 20, 'Dispute Resolution Fit for the Digital Economy: DLT an Additional Catalyst for ODR?' by Charlie Morgan, Dorothy Livingston and Andrew Moir look at the role of smart legal contracts and their associated technologies as a catalyst for change in the institutional resolution of disputes generally. Their chapter asks what the most effective ODR process would look like for resolving the disputes relating to smart legal contracts. The chapter reviews the possibility of resolving DLT disputes through online mechanisms, and explores the promise and challenges of DLT-based dispute resolution within the digital economy.

Conclusion

In sum, these twenty chapters provide the most comprehensive overview to date of the core questions of 'smart legal contract' theory and practice. As the first major work dedicated to the topic, this volume has been curated to introduce the interdisciplinary foundations of smart legal contracts. The selected contributions demonstrate the variety and complexity of the issues pertaining to, arguably, the most important development in commercial co-ordination in a generation.

Substantively, this collection demonstrates the necessity of applying rigorous legal analysis to software-enhanced contracting. Technological design and implementation generates legal consequences, sometimes even against the subjective intentions of contracting parties. This calls for future work to define

---

[47] *Quoine Pte Ltd v B2C2* [2020] SGCA(I) 02.

blockchain-based 'smart contracts' that are not, all things considered, 'contracts' at all. Over time, the terminology of 'smart legal contract' might recede in favour of alternatives such as 'computational contracts'; for the time being, however, it remains an essential heuristic. In any case, the notion of 'smart legal contracts', as a composite of natural language and code, will continue to define future developments and is essential to understanding the current wave of applications 'in the wild' and in the pipeline. We expect that a 'unified' or 'merged' design pattern will emerge as the predominant form of 'contract stack' over time—not least as languages intelligible to machines *and* humans evolve and lawyers become more technically savvy. However, 'paired' contract stacks are likely to remain appropriate in many use cases and may prove to be a preferred option for important categories of user. In either case, the 'contract stack' will remain complex and will always contain elements extraneous to the technological artefact in which the relevant agreement is (mainly) recorded and instantiated.

From a disciplinary perspective, it is evident that the scope for future of scholarship in this area is rich and vast, catalysed by constant technological, legal, and regulatory developments. The coming years may well see the most concentrated activity of any area of law, including significant regulatory developments, law reform projects, technological advancements, and standards programs. It is hoped that this work will provide a core point of reference for scholars and practitioners to guide and inform the development of law, policy, and practice concerning 'smart legal contracts' in such initiatives.

Acknowledgements

Originally, this book was intended as a special issue of the *Journal of Law, Information and Science*.[48] As 2020 presented unique circumstances, factors compounded to make that impossible. We would like to extend our thanks to the Oxford University Press editors for helping our project take its final shape and all of our authors for their insightful engagement with the subject matter and for their dedication and patience over the time this book was in production.

We would like to thank our chapter authors, who were extremely cooperative with the peer review and the editorial review process, in many cases indulging us in multiple back and forth iterations to ensure a set of chapters that speak to a truly coherent set of concerns. Despite these delays and the break-neck pace of market developments, these excellent chapters remain an incisive and impactful contribution to the emerging literature.

---

[48] Back content of the journal is available at <http://www6.austlii.edu.au/cgi-bin/viewdb/au/journals/JlLawInfoSci/> accessed 18 July 2021.

A volume of this standard would not have been possible without a dedicated corps of peer reviewers around the world. We benefitted from the considerable expertise of our review pool. In particular, we would like to thank a number of leading women scholars who were unable to contribute chapters but volunteered their time as reviewers. Thanks also to Marco Mauer, Christoph König, Connie Beswick, Samuel Camp, and Emilia Buccella for their assistance, at various stages, with the editorial process.

During the early phases of this project, Jason Allen was a Senior Fellow at the Weizenbaum Institute for the Networked Society and would like to thank the Institute for its financial support and Professor Björn Scheuermann and Research Group 17: Trust in Distributed Environments for their collegiality as hosts. The Weizenbaum Institute kindly brought Peter Hunn to Berlin in late 2019. Clifford Chance LLP (UK) very generously sponsored a prize for early career scholars, judged by Sir Geoffrey Vos MR and the firm's partner Simon Gleeson. We would like to congratulate Megan Ma for her winning submission on the mathematization of legal language.

1
Wrapped and Stacked

'Smart Contracts' and the Interaction of Natural and Formal Language

Jason Grant Allen*

A. Introduction	23	2. The contract and the speech act(s) creating it	37
B. What is a 'Smart Contract'?	26	3. Smart contracts as 'legal contracts'	40
1. The evolution of 'contractware'	27	4. Smart contracts: 'wrapped' or 'stacked'?	42
2. Digital contractware	28	D. Smart Contracts and Conventional Contract Law	43
3. Distributed ledger technology	30	1. Smart contracts in the courts: illegality, jurisdiction, and procedure	43
4. A working definition	32	2. Towards a smart(er) contract law	45
C. Is a Smart Contract Really a 'Contract'?	33	E. Conclusion	52
1. Natural and formal languages	36		

A. Introduction

Since the launch of Ethereum in 2015, lawyers have become increasingly aware of the challenges and opportunities of so-called 'smart contracts'. The emerging literature on the topic ranges from stressing business as usual[1] to predicting the end of contract law as we know it.[2] Despite this literature, however, we are some way

---

* This chapter is an amended version of J.G. Allen, 'Wrapped and Stacked: "Smart Contracts" and the Interaction of Formal and Natural Language' (2018) 14(4) *European Review of Contract Law* 307 with the permission of the ERCL and De Gruyter.

[1] For example M. Raskin, 'The Law and Legality of Smart Contracts' (2017) 1(2) *Georgetown Law Technology Review* 305 argues that there is 'little difficulty situating smart contracts within existing contract law'; J. Cieplak and S. Leefatt, 'Smart Contracts: A Smart Way to Automate Performance' (2018) 1 *Georgetown Law and Technology Review* 418 stresses the continuity of automated contract *performance* and enforcement with the well-established practice of automated contract *formation* through electronic signature services; A. Cohn, T. West, and C. Parker, 'Smart After All: Blockchain, Smart Contracts, Parametric Insurance, and Smart Energy Grids' (2017) 1 *Georgetown Law and Technology Review* 273 argues that smart contracts are enforceable under existing US law, particularly federal statutes governing electronic signatures and transactions.

[2] See eg, A. Savelyev, 'Contract law 2.0: "Smart" Contracts as the Beginning of the End of Classic Contract Law' (2017) 26(2) *Information and Communications Technology Law* 116.

from a general consensus on (i) what 'smart' contracts actually are, (ii) whether a national legal system should recognize these phenomena as 'contracts' in the ordinary legal sense at all, and, (iii) in either case, what problems they might entail for the conventional doctrines of contract law.[3] There is little consensus on the definition of the term, either among computer scientists or lawyers.[4] The technologies on which many of these instruments rely are still new, and their use is evolving. Though it means tracking a moving target, it is necessary for lawyers and legal academics to define what exactly we are dealing with. In this chapter, I take these interrelated questions in turn and focus attention on what is, in my view, the most salient feature for lawyers: the formalization of contractual language into a system of operators expressing actions and modes of obligation in the future.

Section 2 provides the necessary background. Discussion of smart contracts often begins in the context of distributed ledger technology ('DLT'), particularly 'blockchain'[5] and 'cryptocurrencies'.[6] Because blockchain raises specific issues, it is preferable to start at a more basic level and to round back on blockchain-based 'smart contracts' in the second step. First, I explore the notion of a 'smart' contract—and how digital instruments differ from paper ones. The feature most often stressed is the automation of some or all contract performance through the fusion of contractual terms with the computer code that executes performance of those terms. I expand on a classic exposition that points to the vending machine as an 'industrial-age smart contract' based on analogue (ie, mechanical) technology. In the case of an old-fashioned vending machine, the vendor's terms of trade are 'encoded' into the gears of the machine as the passage of time is encoded into a mechanical clock. The key to remember is that to 'vend' is to *sell*, not just *dispense*; the machine (i) performs a sale but it also (ii) encodes the terms of that sale (in whole or part). If this idea is grasped, the more complex vending processes that have appeared recently make more sense once their information age technology is understood. In other words, although smart contracts' agentive function—performing coded actions autonomously—deserves examination, this chapter concentrates instead on the *formalization of contractual language*. Making contractual prose track computer code reliably and predictably, by whatever means, entails a formalisation of the natural language (such as English) that lawyers use. This not only informs the challenges smart contracts pose to contract law, but also the opportunities that smart contracts present for the development of contract law in the coming decades.

---

[3] See K. Werbach and N. Cornell, 'Contracts Ex Machina' (2017) 67 *Duke Law Journal* 313, 317.

[4] See C.D. Clack, A.V. Bakshi, and L. Braine, 'Smart Contract Templates: Foundations, Design Landscape, and Research Directions' (15 March 2017), arXiv:1608.00771v3, 2.

[5] Use of the definite article with the noun 'blockchain' is a fairly reliable indicator of 'buzz'.

[6] By using the term 'cryptocurrency' I do not want to assume the status of any particular token as 'currency' or 'money', I am merely using the term current in general parlance. See eg, J.P. Smit, F. Buekens, and S. du Plessis, 'Cigarettes, Dollars and Bitcoins—An Essay on the Ontology of Money' (2016) 12(2) *Journal of Institutional Economics* 327.

Section 3 turns to the question whether a 'smart contract' is a 'contract' at all, or whether the term itself is a misnomer, as has been argued in the context of blockchain-based 'smart contracts'. Taking a technology-neutral approach, I observe that, in a 'smart contract', automation of contractual performance is achieved through the structured coding of information in symbols that are machine-readable *and* (to a greater or lesser extent) human-intelligible, such that a human can predict what the machines will do. Such smart contracts thus implicitly claim to merge the legal object of the contract with its mechanism of performance in a single written instrument. Some proponents of smart contracts assume such a merger and stress the completeness and self-containment of smart contracts—even their isolation from the national legal system. Many empirical applications of 'smart contracts' are, however, only performance mechanisms 'wrapped' in a conventional contractual framework. In such cases, the term is certainly a misnomer and should be avoided. However, some commentators go so far as to suggest that a smart contract can, conceptually, never be anything more than the performance mechanism of a 'legal contract'. Against this view, I argue that there is no barrier to a single instrument, written in formal language, embodying both the contract as such and its automated mechanism of performance. A more sophisticated view of the ontology of contracts themselves—legal entities created and maintained by speech acts and documents—suggests that we should see contracts as a 'stack' composed of several 'layers'. This opens up exciting horizons for understanding the future directions contractual law and practice could take. *Contract stacks* will, increasingly, contain 'smart' components. Rather than delineating sharply the 'smart' contract from its 'legal' wrapper, we should regard both as parts of a complex legal institutional entity whose legal and technological parts—including also the mandatory and default rules of any relevant legal system(s)—interact. The smart contract layer is incorporated into the stack in a manner not categorically different from conventional contracts with formal appendices, such as mathematical accounting formulae. Nobody would argue that a technical appendix is not part of the contract, and so a technical appendix that comprises executable code should not be seen as categorically non-contractual, either.

The *dynamics of interaction* between a contract's layers could, in time, influence legal theory and practice profoundly. Understanding this potential impact requires us to engage with the nature of language, and in particular with the interaction of formal and natural languages, in a legal institutional context. Assuming that some smart contracts, at least, really are 'contracts', Section 4 turns to the challenges and opportunities that smart contracts present for conventional contract law. Many smart contracts purport to create a cyber business entity, a private currency, or private regulatory system, raising a raft of issues beyond contract law.[7] Again, these

---

[7] Including consumer and investor protection, capital markets law, corporate governance law, and international private law: See eg, D.G. Post, 'How the Internet is Making Jurisdiction Sexy (Again)' (2017) 25(4) *International Journal of Law and Information Technology* 249; J.A.T. Fairfield,

important questions deserve independent examination. The current discussion is limited to contract law proper. I argue that smart contracts are neither business as usual nor the end of contract law as we know it. While innovators and investors might wish to build a New Jerusalem outside national law, the more 'smart' contracts (of whatever kind) are treated as 'real' contracts, the more they will interact with national contract law. The courts will, therefore, need to consider their interpretation and enforcement. I set out the main issues that I think are likely to arise, which mostly concern the translation between formal and natural language. In conclusion, I argue (by reference to English law, primarily) that contract law is broad and supple enough to absorb smart contracts, though it is likely that they will exacerbate some existing problem areas in the law and create some new ones. Smart contracts will, above all, challenge the courts' approach to ambiguity in contractual language, and in particular the proper treatment of code-based clauses that have a result that is intuitively perverse to any common-sense agent. Lawyers and legal academics must carefully consider the role of equitable remedies in the context of contracts drafted in whole or part in executable code. At the same time, smart contracts present an opportunity for a fundamental rationalization of contract law doctrine to follow the formalization of contractual language. In order to ensure that the formalization of contractual language does not leave too much of conventional contract law behind, it is imperative for lawyers to get involved in the effort to create smart contracting languages.

B. What is a 'Smart Contract'?

The term 'smart contract' is generally attributed to a slew of papers by Nick Szabo from the mid-1990s. Szabo defined a 'smart contract' as 'a set of promises, specified in digital form, including protocols within which the parties perform on these promises.'[8] Another classical account that is generally taken to describe a 'smart contract' is the so-called 'Ricardian contract' presented in the early 2000s by Ian Grigg.[9] Grigg's concern was to create a document form that reconciles the

---

'Smart Contracts, Bitcoin Bots, and Consumer Protection' (2014) 71 *Washington & Lee Law Review Online* 35, 39.

[8] See N. Szabo, 'Smart Contracts: Building Blocks for Digital Markets' (1996) 16 *Extropy* <http://www.fon.hum.uva.nl/rob/Courses/InformationInSpeech/CDROM/Literature/LOTwinterschool2006/szabo.best.vwh.net/smart_contracts_2.html;> N. Szabo, 'Formalizing and Securing Relationships on Public Networks' (1997) 2(9) *First Monday* <http://firstmonday.org/ojs/index.php/fm/article/view/548/469> accessed 13 April 2018; see eg, Chamber of Digital Commerce, *Smart Contracts: 12 Use Cases for Business and Beyond* (December 2016), <http://digitalchamber.org/assets/smart-contracts-12-use-cases-for-business-and-beyond.pdf accessed 2 March 2022> accessed 13 April 2018.

[9] See I. Griggs, 'Financial Cryptography in 7 Layers' (*Financial Cryptography Fourth International Conference*, Anguilla, 21–24 February 2000) <http://iang.org/papers/fc7.html;> I. Griggs, 'The Ricardian Contract' (Proceedings of the First IEEE International Workshop on Electronic

inherently contractual (ie, legal) nature of a financial instrument with the requirements of being an integral part of a digital automated payment system. This which entailed defining parameters to connect legal prose to the sections of computer code that will perform the actions mandated in that prose.[10] More recently, C.D. Clack, A.V. Bakshi, and L. Braine have observed that a number of definitions are currently in use, and that a distinction is often made between definitions that focus on the fulfilment of contractual obligations by 'software agents' and those that focus on how 'legal contracts' can be expressed and implemented in software. On this approach, a 'smart contract' is an *automatable and enforceable agreement*: 'Automatable by computer, although some parts may require human input and control. Enforceable either by legal enforcement of rights and obligations or *via* tamper-proof execution of computer code.'[11]

Numerous questions and ambiguities remain in all of these approaches, particularly relating to the connection—often implicit rather than expressed—between the computer code and the (invisible) world of legal rights and obligations. As a starting point, however, we might say that a 'smart contract' is (i) a recording of a *legal agreement* between parties that is (ii) written in a *formal, ultimately machine-readable language* rather than a natural language such as English, and whose text incorporates (iii) an algorithm which *automates some or all performance* of the agreement. This means that the performance and enforcement of a smart contract does not rely to the same extent on the parties' own further actions or on the intermediation of a trusted authority (such as a court) to interpret and enforce the parties' mutual promises. But it also means that the parties will have had to reduce at least some operative part of their 'legal' agreement into writing in a language with a high level of formality, such that it can be interpreted and performed by a machine.

1. The evolution of 'contractware'

Discussions of smart contracts often begin in the context of cryptocurrencies and blockchain data structures, because current developments associated with these technology layers have cast smart contracts into the limelight. The most basic idea expressed in Szabo's early work, however, was that contractual terms have long been embedded in systems to ensure performance, usually by making breach

---

Contracting, San Diego 6 July 2004) <http://iang.org/papers/ricardian_contract.html> accessed 13 April 2018 (pp 25–31).

[10] See I. Grigg, 'On the Intersection of Ricardian and Smart Contracts' (July 2016), <http://iang.org/papers/intersection_ricardian_smart.html> accessed 13 April 2018; I. Griggs, 'The Sum of All Chains— Let's Converge!' (*Financial Cryptography*, 29 April 2015) <http://financialcryptography.com/mt/archives/001556.html> accessed 13 April 2018.

[11] Clack *et al.* (n. 4), 2.

impossible or prohibitively expensive. A review of the evolution of 'contractware', ie, technological artefacts designed to embody and perform contracts, helps to frame the issues raised by smart contracts.

Szabo points to vending machines as an illustration. All vending machines contain some process—whether analogue or digital—that responds to actions by agents in the world outside with a predetermined conditional output. These conditionals reflect and embody the contractual terms of the sale. The profound implications of this comparison are due to a deep parallel between algorithms and contracts as sets of if/then conditionals. A legal agreement consists of a set propositions of conditional logic; if A delivers late, then B has/has not a right to refuse delivery, etc.[12] A vending machine automates the process of operation (eg, performing delivery) by encoding a set of conditional logic that responds to a very restricted set of permissible inputs in its gears, rendering much human agency superfluous. *If and only if* the right coin is inserted, *then* the machine will dispense the goods. In so doing, it also renders (albeit at a high level of abstraction) the conditional logic of the contract of sale into its cogs, gears, and levers.

Of course, vending machines have come a long way since their early mechanical history. Modern vending machines contain sophisticated computers, and accept payment from credit cards, mobile wallets, etc, so we must leave this illustration behind. However, we will return in Section 3 to the question whether the set of conditional logic encoded in the vending machine's internal processes is really the 'contract' or merely a 'mechanism of performance'. Already we can anticipate some of the central questions that arise. For example, if the machine's discriminator is defective and it does not dispense the right product (or the right change), what do I do in the absence of a written contract with the machine's owner? Where would I find the terms of the alleged contract of sale to argue before some tribunal that the machine's owner owes me performance or damages in lieu thereof?

2. Digital contractware

Where early 'computers' were mechanical devices that performed a limited range of functions, such as a mechanical shop till with a direct mechanical process that encoded the desirable function, modern computers are universal machines that can be programmed with any number of functions. Digital 'contractware' thus renders the terms of a contract not into mechanical clockwork, but into symbols which a computer can read (ultimately in binary on/off code) and respond to. The

---

[12] Indeed, the law generally, as Max Raskin notes, is a set of conditionals; the general function of the courts is to take a series of inputs, run them through a series of legal conditionals, and then have an agent (such as a bailiff) enforce their output: M. Raskin, 'The Law and Legality of Smart Contracts' (2017) 1(2) *Georgetown Law Technology Review* 305, 312.

symbols that comprise a modern coding language (like C++, Python, or the smart contracting language Solidity) correspond ultimately to true *machine code*, which identifies physical locations in a micro-processor which perform functions desired by the programmer, with predictable outcomes. It is perhaps instructive to remind ourselves that modern coding languages are already the product of impressive developments to make symbols (which ultimately identify physical addresses in a hardware system) intelligible to human programmers. Making that symbol also encapsulate what humans take to be the substance of a complex social practice—the law of contracting—is the challenge behind digital contractware.[13]

In a modern vending machine, an internal processor is attached to digital sensors that identify coins and a computer-operated lever mechanism to deliver the goods. Their input and output is not encoded in gears but rather is governed by rules written in a *formal language*. This language is, hypothetically, readable by both humans and machines with predictable outcomes—ie, humans can programme in this language with a set of expected actions in mind, and the machine's output will conform to those expectations. That is, one could read the code and determine what was meant to happen. For something be constitute 'contractware', the rules so (en)coded must reflect both the legal terms of the agreement between the parties and the linguistic constraints of the formal language, ie, its formal logic of operators and conditionals. Essentially, therefore, digital contractware requires the formalization of at least some of the legal process of contract formation, performance, and enforcement into a machine-readable syntax, such that performance of the contract terms comes to approximate 'execution' of the 'code' in which the contract is written. For example, in Szabo's proposal for a formalized contract drafting language, the legal obligation to dispense candy is expressed in machine-readable terms that resemble something like JavaScript.[14] As I argue below, the language in which we make agreements *cannot but influence those agreements themselves*, and this is why smart contracts have the potential to influence contract law profoundly.

The penultimate development to date is the digitalization of both means of payment and of goods themselves. As the subject matter of contracts and the means of performance are moved into cyberspace, the scope for using smart contracts and the potential advantages for doing so increase. Consider the most straightforward case, electronic payment for an e-commerce transaction: information passes

---

[13] Thanks to James Scheibner for his advice on this point. An overview of the evolution of digital agreements is given in K. Werbach and N. Cornell, 'Contracts Ex Machina' (2017) 67 *Duke Law Journal* 313, 319 and following; see also H. Surden, 'Computable Contracts' (2012) 46 *UC Davis Law Review* 629. See also R. Turner and A.H. Eden, 'Towards a Programming Language Ontology' in G. Dodig-Crnkovic and S. Stuart (eds), *Computation, Information, Cognition—The Nexus and the Liminal* (Cambridge Scholars Press 2008).

[14] See N. Szabo, 'A Formal Language for Analyzing Contracts' (2002) <http://www.fon.hum.uva.nl/rob/Courses/InformationInSpeech/CDROM/Literature/LOTwinterschool2006/szabo.best.vwh.net/contractlanguage.html> accessed 13 April 2018.

between my computer, an online seller's server, and our respective banks' servers.[15] If this process satisfies the conditionals embedded in the online store's code, an instruction is sent to an agent which delivers the goods, as it were.[16]

This final stage may be automated two ways. First, the physical delivery of a physical good may be automated, as where a drone delivers my DVD.[17] Secondly, the product itself may subsist in digital form. For example, the content of a DVD is just information that instructs my machine to perform certain functions. In this case, I may get my feature film simply by being given access to digital information without any physical good (storage medium). In effect, the need for physical delivery is made redundant by the virtualization of performance.[18] Significantly, my counter-performance is digitalized and automated as well. Once I have entered my credit card details into Amazon.com, for example, my click sets off a cascade of instructions such that the balance of my account on my bank's digital ledger is depleted by *n* units and the balance of the seller's account with its bank is increased by *n* units (minus transaction fees along the way). Indeed, the accounting records which form the fabric of the financial system are now almost exclusively digital. This makes finance perhaps the most obvious use-case for smart contracts.

3. Distributed ledger technology

The final development of which we must take notice is the use of blockchain data structures to record and verify flows of information between nodes in a computer network. A blockchain is not stored on any one computer or server, but is replicated on each of the nodes running the relevant protocol—a virtual super-computer—and the integrity of the chain of transactions is protected by the protocol's cryptography and consensus features.[19]

---

[15] See J.H. Sommer, 'Where is a Bank Account?' (1998) 57(1) *Maryland Law Review* 1 for an overview of bank-based electronic payments at the dawn of the e-commerce era.

[16] This transformation often involves turning traditional goods into a type of service, or a hybrid, ie, granting licenses to access digital content rather than selling traditional goods such as storage media with that content in analogue or digital form. This is significant in its own right but peripheral to my substantive point.

[17] See F. Giones and A. Brem, 'From Toys to Tools: The Co-Evolution of Technological and Entrepreneurial Developments in the Drone Industry' (2017) 60(6) *Business Horizons* 875.

[18] The global entertainment and media market was estimated to be US$1.9 trillion in 2016 and to increase to US$2.2 trillion by 2021: see IQ Magazine, 'Value of the global entertainment and media market from 2011 to 2021 (in trillion U.S. dollars)' <https://www.statista.com/statistics/237749/value-of-the-global-entertainment-and-media-market/> (citing PriceWaterhouseCoopers data) accessed 13 April 2018.

[19] See N. Szabo, 'The dawn of trustworthy computing' ('Unenumerated' blog, 11 December 2014) <http://unenumerated.blogspot.de/2014/12/the-dawn-of-trustworthy-computing.html> accessed 2 March 2022. In short, transactions are protected by cryptographic puzzles, which other nodes in the network need to solve in order for a transaction to be recorded as a link in the chain. Each block incorporates an encrypted reference to the previous block, and so on, so that no block can be changed without changing the entire chain. Nodes check each other's work, ensuring the integrity of the record by means such as an anonymous and probabilistic 'Byzantine consensus'. The so-called Byzantine Generals

Blockchains have become familiar largely due to the success of the 'cryptocurrencies' Bitcoin[20] and Ethereum.[21] There has, in particular, been a flurry of innovation using Ethereum-based applications since its launch in 2015. These businesses often issue digital 'coins', which are intended to circulate as a private currency, but which often mirror an issue of securities to raise capital.[22] An Ethereum blockchain, however, can be used to record transaction data irrespective of the subject matter, and many applications extend beyond payments.[23] In an early empirical analysis, Massimo Bartoletti and Livio Pompianu propose a taxonomy of blockchain-based smart contracts according to their intended application in 'financial', 'notary', 'game', 'wallet', and 'library'[24] domains. In the 'financial', 'notary', and 'wallet' domains, applications range from certification of ownership, crowdfunding venture capital, and collective investment schemes, to the certification of documents, copyrighting digital art files, and identity services, to ancillary services that enable digital payments. We could therefore expect, and have indeed seen, smart contracts to crop up in a plethora of commercial and financial contexts.

Problem is an abstraction in computer science terms for how a distributed system deals with dysfunctional components: see L. Lamport, R. Shostak, and M. Pease, 'The Byzantine Generals Problem' (1982) 4(3) *ACM Transactions on Programming Languages and Systems* 382. Blockchain-based systems achieve communication between the network of potentially dysfunctional components using public and private key communication. This process is driven by an incentive mechanism, a reward for each node that dedicates processing power to solving the puzzle (and thus verifying the authenticity) of a transaction. This means that an agent can trust the outcome of a blockchain without trusting any other agent in particular. Only in the case that a malicious agent controlled 51 per cent of the network's nodes or more would this consensus mechanism break down.

[20] Bitcoin, the first cryptocurrency based on a distributed ledger, was launched in 2009. See <www.bitcoin.org> and in particular S. Nakamoto, 'Bitcoin: A Peer-to-Peer Electronic Cash System' <https://bitcoin.org/bitcoin.pdf>.

[21] Ethereum is currently the second most important cryptocurrency after Bitcoin. Its main innovation is that it is a so-called 'Turing complete' virtual machine. While the Bitcoin protocol is only capable of calculating the transaction of Bitcoins, the Ethereum software was designed to be able to compute anything (that is computable). This was to create a platform for a much richer suite of smart contracts. See <https://www.ethereum.org/> and V. Buterin, 'A Next-Generation Smart Contract and Decentralised Application Platform', <https://github.com/ethereum/wiki/wiki/White-Paper>. Turing-completeness has been controversial; more recently Vitalik Buterin, one of the creators of Ethereum, has expressed a preference for 'rich statefulness' instead of 'Turing completeness'. See for example Buterin's tweet of 18 April 2017 <https://twitter.com/VitalikButerin/status/854271590804140033?ref_src=twsrc%5Etfw&ref_url=https%3A%2F%2Fhackernoon.com%2Fmedia%2Ffab472fb800755fae284b5b118e4396d%3FpostId%3De650db7fc1fb> all accessed 13 April 2018.

[22] The volume of capital raised by early-stage companies via an 'Initial Coin Offering' or ICO surpassed the amount raised through traditional Venture Capital investment in July 2017, according to a widely-cited report by investment bank Goldman Sachs. See <https://www.cnbc.com/2017/08/09/initial-coin-offerings-surpass-early-stage-venture-capital-funding.html> accessed 13 April 2018.

[23] See Chamber of Digital Commerce, *Smart Contracts: 12 use Cases for Business and Beyond* (Washington DC, December 2016); M. Walport, *Distributed Ledger Technology: beyond block chain* (UK Government Office for Science 2016); see also the Outlier Ventures tracker of blockchain startups at <https://outlierventures.io/startups/browse/> (accessed 13 April 2018).

[24] M. Bartoletti and L. Pompianu, 'An Empirical Analysis of Smart Contracts: Platforms, Applications, and Design Patterns' in M. Brenner et al. (eds), *Financial Cryptography and Data Security Proceedings 2017* (Springer 2017).

The connection between smart contracts and cryptocurrency is not accidental, because smart contracts lend themselves particularly well to manipulating assets such as digital tokens that take the form of *immaterial objects*.[25] While they could be used to regulate access to physical assets (for example using remotely controlled solenoid locks or ignition switches),[26] the core use case of smart contracts would seem to be where the subject matter of the contract is an immaterial object which can be manipulated directly by the smart contract algorithm. It is important to remember that many traditional securities are immaterial objects, too, consisting in a digital computer entry kept by some financial intermediary.[27] Indeed, even 'real' property appears in the eyes of the legal system as land registry entries which exist in an informational domain (ie, the servers of a land registry),[28] which also lend themselves to the application of blockchain data structures and smart contracts.[29] This makes a large part of our financial economy *prima facie* open for the application of smart contract technology.

4. A working definition

To sum up, then, it seems possible to say that a 'smart contract' is a piece of text in a formal language that purports to contain both (i) a written instrument embodying and recording contracting parties' mutual promises and (ii) code that performs and/or enforces those promises on a digital computer.[30] For the time being, only human beings make contracts,[31] but we outsource tasks in negotiation, execution,

---

[25] See J.G. Allen, 'Property in Digital Coins' (2019) 8(1) *European Property Law Journal* 64; see also P. Cuccuru, 'Beyond Bitcoin: An Early Overview on Smart Contracts' (2017) 25(3) *International Journal of Law and Information Technology* 179.
[26] For example, slock.it (the team that brought us The DAO—see Section 4) aims to automate access to Airbnb properties, among other things, using smart contracts.
[27] See B. Smith, 'How to Do Things with Documents' (2012) 50 *Revisti di estetica* 179, 183.
[28] Christian von Bar calls land parcels—the legally constituted entity that delineates an area on the surface of the land or a stratum of air as an object of property rights—as 'normative things with a physical substrate': C. von Bar, *Gemeineuropäisches Sachenrecht* (CH Beck 2015), 249.
[29] The Government of the Republic of Georgia signed an initiative with the Bitfury Group Limited to register land titles on the Bitcoin blockchain in April 2016: see L. Shin, 'Republic Of Georgia To Pilot Land Titling On Blockchain With Economist Hernando De Soto, BitFury' (*Forbes*, 21 April 2016) <https://www.forbes.com/sites/laurashin/2016/04/21/republic-of-georgia-to-pilot-land-titling-on-blockchain-with-economist-hernando-de-soto-bitfury/#57d3903e44da> accessed 13 April 2018. See, eg, L.D. Griggs et al., 'Blockchains, Trust and Land Administration: The Return of Historical Provenance' (2017) 6 *Property Law Review* 179 for a discussion of the application of DLT to land title registration.
[30] See P. Cuccuru, 'Beyond Bitcoin: An Early Overview on Smart Contracts' (2017) 25 *International Journal of Law and Information Technology* 179, 185.
[31] Actually, this is a little more complicated: *personae fictae* such as corporations make contracts, too, albeit through human agents—the acts of the human being are legally the acts of the corporation, but the law only attributes the acts of human beings to corporations such that corporations cannot act without human organs. These lines are blurring as human beings increasingly act through algorithms, but the acts of a software agent are attributed the human being in question and thence to the corporation. We are not at the stage yet where a corporation may act directly through software agents, although innovations such as distributed autonomous organizations ('DAOs') are pushing the envelope.

and performance to algorithms because they are quicker, more efficient, or more reliable. Digital contractware combines the written contract and the algorithm which performs these tasks in one highly structured language-based digital instrument housed in the memory of a computer network. Although the automation of performance is often stressed, equally important is the *formalization of contractual language* that smart contracts entail, as 'contracts' (or parts thereof) are written by programmers in languages that include more formal systems of logical operators. But are these instruments really 'contracts', or is it misleading to think of them as such?

C. Is a Smart Contract Really a 'Contract'?

Lee Bacon and George Bazinas observe that the term 'smart contract' is used to refer both to 'software code that embodies a contract', and to 'contracts expressed in executable code'.[32] It is, however, not straightforward that any given instrument really can embody both the contract—a legal object created when certain conditions are satisfied—and the code that performs it. According to Cheng Lim, T.J. Saw, and Calum Sargeant, for example, the term is a misnomer: 'smart contracts' are merely computer programmes that parties use to *perform* their contracts, and are not properly called 'contracts' at all. A so-called 'smart contract', they argue, operates irrespective of the absence or presence of legal indicia (such as consideration), and indeed independently of the legal context itself. (This ambiguity was evident in the Clack *et al.* definition above, for example, which equiparates 'legal' with 'technical' enforcement.) Although code may cover some, or even all, of the functions of a contract (such as recording obligations, regulating the relationship between the parties, and providing a blueprint for execution) it is not self-standing and cannot be seen as if in a legal vacuum. In particular, legal doctrines such as mistake and misrepresentation form part of the legal contract and this, in some cases, must impinge on the operation of the 'smart contract' execution mechanism. Lim *et al.* therefore draw a bright distinction between the 'smart contract' and what they call the 'legal contract', and express doubt that a code-based instrument can ever merge with the legal contract.[33]

Such views have force, in my view, for two reasons. The first reason is that, empirically, many of the software processes currently hailed as 'smart contracts' are

---

[32] L. Bacon, ' "Smart Contracts"—The Next Big Battleground?' (June 2017) *Finance & Credit Law* 1.
[33] See C. Lim, T.J. Saw, and C. Sargeant, 'Smart Contracts: Bridging the Gap Between Expectation and Reality' (Oxford Business Law Blog, 11 July 2016) <https://www.law.ox.ac.uk/business-law-blog/blog/2016/07/smart-contracts-bridging-gap-between-expectation-and-reality>. The terminology of 'smart legal contract' was suggested by Josh Stark in 2016; see J. Stark, 'How Close are Smart Contracts to Impacting Real-World Law?' (*Coindesk*, 11 April 2016), <https://www.coindesk.com/blockchain-smarts-contracts-real-world-law> accessed 13 August 2021.

indeed more accurately described as performance mechanisms. Many financial institutions, for example, are using smart contracts more to determine their own financial position (with the advantages of granular detail and real-time reporting) than to replace conventional paper contracts with a counter-party. In other words, many of the use-cases of smart contracts bandied about in whitepapers, blogs, and forums are aspirational rather at this stage. The second reason is that *no* legal relationship can exist in a legal vacuum. In order to be enforced as a contract by a national court, it is right to point out that that court would have to be satisfied that the 'smart contract', and the relationship it purported to structure, possessed all the indicia of a contract according to the relevant national law(s). This type of argument should be seen against overblown claims that smart contracts can operate without any overarching legal framework, and that they represent a technological alternative to the legal system as a whole.

But problems lurk beneath both of these reasons, which take some effort to unpack. Taking the second point first, it is important to remember that significant economic activity takes place outside national legal systems. Although the global order of national jurisdictions and private international law fairly cover the globe in a seamless web of norms, there are interstitial spaces.[34] We do not need imagine two stateless castaways swapping fish for coconuts on the high seas to accept the basic proposition that, while economic activity nestles within the substrate of a legal system where one exists, it can also thrive outside national law.[35] Trying to understand smart contracts, and how they might change the contract law of the future, is therefore not an exercise best undertaken from a perspective that stipulates national law indicia in strong terms *ex hypothesi*. Given the fundamental challenges that Internet-based commerce poses for the system of territorial-based jurisdiction as a whole,[36] it seems disingenuous to deny at the outset that a trans-national body of norms might arise to regulate trans-national e-commerce and e-finance. We can see parallel developments, for example, in the law of intellectual property with the Creative Commons licensing protocols, which then reverse-engineer 'ports' to national legal orders.[37] Globally dispersed open-source communities

---

[34] The medieval *lex mercatoria*, for example, stands in counter-point, as do (to a lesser degree) international regimes such as the Convention on the International Sale of Goods.

[35] We do not need such examples because, empirically, a great many individuals live nominally under the law of a nation-state but operate, as economic agents, almost entirely within informal economies with informal normative orders; they never actually interact with the national contract law they live under. Hernando de Soto, for example, describes the formal legal economy of developed countries as the inside of a 'bell jar', while four fifths of human society exists outside it: see H. de Soto, *The Mystery of Capital* (Black Swan 2000).

[36] See D. Sventsson, 'The Holy Trinity of Legal Fictions Undermining the Application of Law to the Global Internet' (2015) 23(3) *International Journal of Law and Information Technology* 219.

[37] See eg, <https://wiki.creativecommons.org/wiki/Version_3#Further_Internationalization> accessed 13 April 2018. More recently, Creative Commons has shifted away from porting to simply creating uniform CC licenses irrespective of jurisdiction.

are a fascinating *situs* for development of normative order outside the nation state. As so many smart contract proponents are ideologically committed to an Internet beyond national jurisdiction, the denial of contractual status to formal language-based digital instruments seems oddly out of touch with the techno-libertarian[38] challenge that smart contracts are intended to mount to contract law as a sphere regulated by national law. Thus, while I agree that there is a gap between expectation and reality, and that strong aspirations for smart contracts are misguided, we should not dismiss the challenge they pose offhand.

As to the first point, which is the more important one, it is clear that at least *some* smart contracts purport to combine the document which creates the contract with the digital means by which the parties perform their obligations under it. Partially this is a question of definition, and in particular of whether one wishes to focus on (i) the code-based automation aspects of a 'smart contract' or (ii) on its ability to express the terms of a legal agreement. As I have argued above, (i) is relevant but (ii) is the more interesting for legal theory, as it entails the formalization of contractual language and the combination (or indeed merger) of contractual terms with machine-parsable code. When one adopts a broader definition, as I have done in this paper, it becomes necessary to examine the legal status of smart contracts and at least to ask whether they are legally cognisable as contracts in the conventional sense.

For example, we might ask whether a piece of code might not satisfy the writing requirements under a statute of frauds, and we might define a 'smart contract, properly so called' as a piece of code that does. Attempts to capture the terms of a legal contract in code should be taken seriously. In my view, it is at least conceivable that they will achieve some degree of success in the near future, if they are not doing so already.[39] The problem seems to rest on a conceptual dualism between the contract and its written embodiment.[40] To address this problem successfully, it is necessary to explore how we encode information for human and machine interpretation, what legal entities such as 'contracts' actually are, and how such entities arise through documentation. I will take these matters in turn.

---

[38] See eg, A.D. Thierer and C. Wayne Crews Jr, 'The Libertarian Vision for Telecom and High-Technology' (Cato Institute, 3 April 2001), <https://www.cato.org/publications/techknowledge/libertarian-vision-telecom-hightechnology> accessed 13 April 2018.
[39] See H. Diedrich, *Ethereum: Blockchains, Digital Assets, Smart Contracts, Decentralised Autonomous Organisations* (CreateSpace 2016), 94, cited in J.M. Sklaroff, 'Smart Contracts and the Cost of Inflexibility' (2017) 166 *University of Pennsylvania Law Review* 263, 279.
[40] Similar issues arise in the context of accounts—is an 'account' the ledger of debits and credits between two parties, or the 'actual', 'true', or 'objective' state of credit and debt? How do we determine that the account exists, let alone where it stands, apart from its embodiment in some medium of recording—whether a person's memory, tally-sticks, paper, or digital records? See eg, *WH Smith Travel Holdings Limited v Twentieth Century Fox Home Entertainment Limited* [2015] EWCA Civ 1188; See J.H. Sommer, 'Where is a Bank Account?' (1998) 57(1) *Maryland Law Review* 1.

1. Natural and formal languages

Szabo speaks of 'wet' and 'dry' code,[41] but it is perhaps better just to speak of 'natural' and 'formal' languages. Natural languages such as English have evolved from human prehistory to the present day within more or less organic linguistic communities. Formal computer languages such as C++ or Solidity are much more recent and have been intentionally constructed not only to allow communication between members of a human community, but to programme deterministic agents (ie, machines which ultimately follow a binary logic encoded in transistor states). Both natural and formal languages consist of structured, symbolic content, but they differ in several important respects.

Linguists study three main aspects of language. First, all languages have *syntax*—a logic inherent in devices such as pre-, in-, and suffixes, articles, and word order that express logical relations such as subject-object relations, action, transitivity, temporality, etc. Natural and formal languages have similar syntactic properties, when viewed at a certain level of abstraction, although the syntax of natural languages is more path-dependent and generally less rigorous than that of formal languages.[42]

Secondly, linguists study *semantics*, or the meaning that different words and combinations of words have.[43] The semantic content of natural and formal languages is very different—so much so that, even assuming the formality of legal language assumed by traditional legal studies,[44] the semantic content of a natural language is difficult to formalize and make machine-readable. There are more shades of meaning and ambiguity in natural language than would ever be possible in a formal language. This is partly because machines are not good at drawing inferences from the context in which words of natural human language are uttered as a tool for resolving ambiguity.

---

[41] This tracks the idiom of referring to the human brain as 'wetware' mirroring the 'hardware/software' dichotomy, but the colourful metaphor does not seem to add much. See N. Szabo, 'Wet code and dry' ('Unenumerated' blog, 24 August 2008), <http://unenumerated.blogspot.de/2006/11/wet-code-and-dry.html> accessed 13 April 2021.

[42] The habit of gendered nouns, for example, originally expressed something meaningful about the world to a hunter-gatherer or agricultural society, but has become essentially meaningless today in most gendered languages which assign it to inanimate objects like rocks and abstract objects like centimetres that are wholly alien to the idea of gender.

[43] We could study the syntax of a sentence like 'the dog chased the cat' without knowing what a 'dog' or a 'cat' is, or what it is 'to chase'. Assuming a knowledge of English syntax were possible without any knowledge of its semantics, we would know (i) that the dog was doing the chasing, (ii) that the cat was the one being chased, and (iii) we are reading of an event that happened in the past and is complete. (I do not assume such a neat division between syntax and semantics.) Equally we would know that a sentence like 'the dog chased the cat tomorrow' contains a logical error. A sentence like 'the dog weighed the Thursday', on the other hand, is syntactically correct but is nonsense.

[44] See P. Goodrich, 'Law and Language: An Historical and Critical Introduction' (1984) 11(2) *Journal of Law and Society* 173.

In other words, computers are not so good as human agents at the third element of language, *pragmatics*. Pragmatics, the newest branch of linguistics, studies what words mean in the context in which they are uttered—ie, not by reference only to the utterance as an isolated unit of meaning but as part of a discursive exchange against a background.[45] As in normal speech, the commercial and social context of a legal utterance informs our judgment of what the parties actually meant. However, the pragmatics of legal language is peculiarly institutionalized; the institutions of the legal system (such as courts) always claim the residual authority to interpret contractual utterances in light of the law's historical lexicon. Context is especially important to interpreting and constructing the meaning of utterances in legal language, even while legal language strives for a greater degree of formality than every day speech. Ambiguity always subsists, however, and the scope of permissible context, its role in interpretation, and the relationship between interpretation and construction is controversial.[46]

This background perhaps helps to clarify what lies at the core of the smart contract project: An effort to formalize the language in which contractual promises are expressed to the extent that the written instruments we now call 'legal contracts' are combined with, or merge into (ultimately) machine-readable code. It is, first and foremost, a project to change the way that parties express their promises; while the benefit of automation arises in virtue of this formalization of legal speech, it should not be the focus of attention for lawyers interested in smart contracts as a development. Our focus should be on the way that computer scientists are setting about 'hacking' the quasi-formal language in which contractual obligations are now expressed and recorded. This represents the primary challenge to contract law as a product of lawyers' lore, and the point to which we can make the most positive contribution to the development of the smart contract movement.

2. The contract and the speech act(s) creating it

A 'contract' is a kind of promise that meets the requirements of some legal system (not necessarily one's own) and generates, within that legal system's logical universe, special 'legal' consequences in a way that non-qualifying promises do not. To understand contracts, it is useful to draw on the conceptual resources of

---

[45] Two syntactically and semantically identical utterances can have completely different meanings depending on the context—I might say 'I'm going to kill you!' in the context of a game with my son, or in the course of a bar-fight, with very different implications. See S.C. Levinson, *Pragmatics* (Cambridge University Press 1983) for a classical overview.

[46] English lawyers and judges do not generally distinguish between interpretation and construction as discrete activities, but our counterparts across the Atlantic do: see G. Klass, 'Interpretation and Construction in Contract Law' (Georgetown Law Faculty Publications and Other Works 1947, 2018) <https://scholarship.law.georgetown.edu/cgi/viewcontent.cgi?article=2971&context=facpub> accessed 13 April 2018.

Oxford linguistic philosophy and the related field of social ontology. A contractual promise (like all other acts-in-the-law) is an *intentional speech act*. That is, when I offer to sell you my car, I am not making any truth claims, but doing an action; I am not *saying* something so much as *doing* something by uttering words.[47] The question is whether that speech act is cognisable by the relevant legal system.[48] Assuming the pre-conditions of our chosen legal system are met, my utterance has legal effects[49]—it changes our respective legal positions.[50] In this, a contractual undertaking is more like a ritual incantation (eg, the consecration of 'holy ground', the declaration that a person is 'unclean', or the naming of a ship) than it is like everyday speech. When we perform these acts, *the world itself changes*.[51] In particular, performative speech acts in conventional systems like law create new things. J.L. Austin called his speech act theory 'legal phenomenology', because it explains how things come into existence out of thin air—contracts, marriages, rights, debts, corporations, promises, etc.[52] These things are invisible and their existence fundamentally mind-dependent, but they are as 'real' as the legal system itself can purport to be.[53]

Consistent with their basis in speech acts, contracts can be formed by oral utterances as well as by written ones. Indeed, the proto-typical contract is an oral one evidenced by a handshake or other gesture, ideally in front of witnesses drawn from the normative community whose collective practices and beliefs sustain the existence of contractual promising as an institution (and whose collective force will be called upon to *enforce* the promise if the parties' relationship breaks down). Thus, as a basic premise, we can stipulate that speech acts create legal objects like contracts[54] whether the words are uttered in spoken or written

---

[47] I do make the implicit assertion that I own the car, etc, but the 'contracting' part is a declaration that I promise to sell it to you, not any of these assertions.

[48] For example, they may not be legally cognizable as a contractual promise because I use the wrong form, or because I am not recognized as an agent with contractual capacity.

[49] See J.L. Austin, *How To Do Things With Words* (Oxford University Press 1962), 19.

[50] On legal position generally, and how it can be modelled formally in a manner useful to understanding code as law', see L. Lindahl, *Position and Change* (Riedel 1977).

[51] See A. Reinach (J.F. Crosby trans), *The Apriori Foundations of Civil Law* (1983) 3 *Alatheia* 1, 9; B. Smith, 'How to Do Things with Documents' (2012) 50 *Revisti di estetica* 179, 181; A. Brinz, *Lehrbuch der Pandekten Band I* (2nd edn, Deichert 1873), 211 on 'invisible legal effects'. Reinach was a lawyer and part of the Munich phenomenological school—see A. Salice, 'The Phenomenology of the Munich and Göttingen Circles' in E.N. Zalta (ed), *The Stanford Encyclopedia of Philosophy* (Winter 2016 Edition) <https://plato.stanford.edu/archives/win2016/entries/phenomenology-mg/ > accessed 13 April 2018. See generally K. Mulligan (ed), *Speech Act and Sachverhalt: Reinach and the Foundations of Realist Phenomenology* (Springer 1987).

[52] See P. Amselek, 'Philosophy of Law and the Theory of Speech Acts' (1998) 1(3) *Ratio Juris* 187.

[53] The role of speech acts reveals deep parallels between law and computer science as disciplines built on some kind of modal logic: see eg, R.H. Thomason, 'Conditionals and Action Logics' (AAAI Spring Symposium 'Commonsense 2007', 26–28 March 2007, Stanford University) <www.ucl.ac.uk/commonsense07> accessed 13 April 2018.

[54] Whether they create 'institutional facts' or 'social objects' is a matter of debate between social ontologists—John Searle, for example, takes a 'reductionist' view that does not admit of the existence of social objects as such and explains institutional facts (effectively as emergent) in terms of collective intentional states within a community; Maurizio Ferraris, on the other hand, considers social objects

form.⁵⁵ As David Koepsell and Barry Smith explain, however, the spoken word is transient, and the increasing complexity of society has proceeded with (and through) the inscription of performative utterances in more enduring, written form.⁵⁶ As a result, documents have come to play an increasingly important role as category of performative act. As Maurizio Ferraris argues, documents are not just an 'accessorial' element of social reality, but are rather its 'condition of possibility' insofar they ensure the fixation of individual and collective memory.⁵⁷ Documents inscribed on media such as clay, stone, leather, and paper support the existence of both more complex social objects (consider the complexity of a joint stock company's financial records compared to those of a medieval partnership) and more enduring ones (consider the immortality of a modern corporation, as a separate legal person, compared to a partnership which is an aggregation of partners as natural persons).⁵⁸ Tampering and destruction are avoided by the best currently available institutional and technological means.

What, then, is the relationship between a contract and the documents recording the speech acts that created it? Before turning to the more complex case of smart contracts, let us consider the normal case. As a preliminary, not all documents that evidence the existence of a social object are necessarily involved in its creation. Imagine that we use our smartphones to make a video recording of an oral contract whereby I contract sell you an apple for $1.00. The video records the legally operative event, in the case of English law the coincidence of offer and acceptance, but it is not identical with the event; the recorded speech acts of declaration themselves change our legal position and cause the contract to come into existence, not the *recording* of the speech acts. So, an oral contract, according to Koepsell and Smith, is *ontologically non-dependent* on documentation. In other cases, documents play both a 'recording' and an 'object-generating' role. Under the law governing my marriage, for example, the celebrant's act of signing the marriage certificate was the operative act that created a 'marriage'. Accordingly, that document plays a dual role.⁵⁹ However, I would not cease to be married even if the original and only copy

---

as more ontologically real or material. This is not a question that we have to answer here; it is sufficient to accept the intuitively obvious fact that invisible, immaterial entities do exist in the legal domain and are treated by the legal system as 'real', and that we need to explain their existence carefully if we wish to avoid accepting the existence of faeries, too. Social ontologists attempt, in various ways, to square the circle and all of them have insights which can be usefully applied in law. I attempt to do so ecumenically without, however, adopting inconsistent premises.

⁵⁵ Like 'speech' in American constitutional jurisprudence, we can even recognize gesture—consider purchasing three apples for one dollar by communicating with hands and feet in a foreign market-place.
⁵⁶ D. Koepsell and B. Smith, 'Beyond Paper' (2014) 97(2) *The Monist* 222, 222.
⁵⁷ See M. Ferraris, 'Perspectives of Documentality' (2012) 2 *Phenomenology and Mind* 41, 41; M. Ferraris, *Documentality: Why it is Necessary to Leave Traces* (R. Davies tr, Fordham University Press 2012).
⁵⁸ See A.W. Crosby, *The Measure of Reality: Quantification and Western Society 1250–1600* (Cambridge University Press 1997), 204 and following.
⁵⁹ D. Koepsell and B. Smith, 'Beyond Paper' (2014) 97(2) *The Monist* 222, 224.

of our certificate were destroyed in a house fire. The law would provide ways and means for us to prove the existence of our marriage and some authority would issue a replacement certificate, not declare us married *do novo*. A 'marriage' *qua* social object is, then, *proto-typically dependent*. A bearer bond, on the other hand, is *specifically dependent* on the existence of the document. If such a negotiable instrument is lost or destroyed, the object itself lapses into non-existence.[60]

It seems fair to say that ordinary written contracts are *proto-typically dependent on documentation*. The written contract (for example under the parole evidence rule and 'entire contract' clauses) purports to embody all the relevant speech acts and determine the contract's content authoritatively. But of course, as Lim *et al.* rightly point out, content is added to the contract as a result of the result of speech acts by other entities—eg, speech acts ('Acts') of the legislature, rulings of regulatory bodies, judgments of the courts. These incorporate terms into the contract, sometimes retrospectively, to complement the terms defined in the parties' contractual speech acts.[61] Court judgments, particularly, have a special status because they may determine what the speech acts that created the contract actually meant at the time, in the eyes of the law, at a much later date.

3. Smart contracts as 'legal contracts'

What does this tell us about the distinction between the 'legal contract' and its 'code-based performance mechanism'? On the one hand, it partially confirms the idea that smart contracts are not 'contracts', insofar as it underscores a dualism between the 'legal contract' (an invisible legal object created by speech acts) and the instrument(s) that record(s) the relevant speech acts. However, on the other hand, it reveals a fundamental problem. As noted above, any contract *per se* exists independently of the writing that creates it. Additional content is provided to the contract by the legal system; the definitive content of the contract 'floats' in suspense until it is interpreted (by a court, in the last instance). To identify the contract with the writing that creates it directly—to view the contract in a legal vacuum—might even exclude some of its most important terms. If we deny that smart contracts can *ever* be 'legal contracts', we would have to deny that conventional ('paper') contracts are 'legal contracts', too: *A written document ('contract') is ontologically distinct from the legal object ('contract') it creates and purports to embody.*[62] By way of

---

[60] Ibid., 226.
[61] See also Clack *et al.* (n. 4), 5.
[62] See the discussion in S. Macaulay, 'The Real and the Paper Deal: Empirical Pictures of Relationships, Complexity, and the Urge for Transparent Simple Rules' (2003) 66(1) *Modern Law Review* 44; Z.X. Tan, 'Beyond the Real and the Paper Deal: The Quest for Contractual Coherence in Contractual Interpretation' (2016) 79(4) *Modern Law Review* 623.

illustration, consider the doctrine of rectification, by which the written terms of a contract itself are later changed to reflect the 'true' legal position formed by the parties' speech acts at the relevant time.

There is no conceptual reason why a formal language instrument—recorded on a blockchain or elsewhere—cannot be a 'legal contract' in the same sense that a natural language instrument stored on paper is a 'legal contract'. Even though a contract arises from the agreement of two contracting parties, a contract is not just a meeting of the minds, it is one that has been *expressed* through performative speech acts and *recorded* in some lasting format.[63] As Kevin Werbach and Nicolas Cornell rightly note, blockchain-based smart contracts erode the distinction between executory and executed contracts insofar as they set an unstoppable chain of actions and responses in motion, and this challenges the conventional remedial role of contract law.[64] But this does not mean that they are categorically not contracts. It is simply an empirical question of how far the smart contracting project has come along in terms of developing a formal contracting language—ie, how accurately that formal language captures the syntactic and semantic content of ordinary legal English and how it deals with the problems of pragmatics.[65] Distinguishing between the phenomenon of a written memorandum and the epiphenomenon of a contract *qua* legal object is important, but it is the start rather than the end of a fascinating enquiry into the ontology of acts-in-the-law and the legal objects they create in the context of new technologies.[66]

New technologies are not only regulated by the law—they are they leaven by which legal institutions themselves change and evolve. Take the advent of writing, the invention of paper, the creation of double-entry bookkeeping, or electronic data interchange ('EDI').[67] By filling forms, registering, conveying, validating, attaching, etc, we change the world.[68] From ancient Mesopotamia to the present, innovations in information and communications technology have enabled social and economic developments which the law has then structured and regulated using the same technologies. Smart contracts are an important part of the next chapter in this age-old story.

---

[63] See M. Ferraris and G. Terrengo, 'Documentality: A Theory of Social Reality' (2014) 57(3) *Revisti di estetica* 11.
[64] K. Werbach and N. Cornell, 'Contracts *Ex Machina*' (2017) 67 *Duke Law Review* 313, 335.
[65] In this respect, while languages such as Solidity are attracting much attention, future developments are likely to occur in the context of more advanced programming languages. See eg, Clack *et al.* (n. 4) for further discussion.
[66] See D.R. Koepsell, *The Ontology of Cyberspace* (Open Court 2000), Chapter 2; P. Brey, 'The Social Ontology of Virtual Objects' (2003) 62(1) *American Journal of Economics and Sociology* 269; N. MacCormick and O. Weinberger, *An Institutional Theory of Law* (Reidel 1986), 51.
[67] See H. Surden, 'Computable Contracts' (2012) 46 *UC Davis Law Review* 630, 639.
[68] See also A.W. Crosby, *The Measure of Reality: Quantification and Western Society 1250–1600* (Cambridge 1997), 204–5.

4. Smart contracts: 'wrapped' or 'stacked'?

How, then, do we characterize 'smart contracts'? Bearing the above qualifications in mind, it is neither inconceivable nor conceptually incoherent for a (single) writing to express a legal contract in formal language and thereby render it both intelligible to humans and executable by machines. What emerges is simply a new form of contract stack.[69] An oral contract stack contains (i) spoken words (recorded in the memories of the parties and their witnesses or on some other medium such as video) and (ii) the legal rules which a) imply terms and b) give words their legal meaning.[70] In a conventional ('paper') contract, we have (i) the spoken words through which the contractual terms were negotiated and against which the text was drafted, (ii) the written text, and (iii) legal rules implying terms and governing construction. The written text (ii) is often highly complex, with cross-references incorporating various documents. Further, the legal rules (iii) are generally fairly strict in the way that they circumscribe (i) the words outside the text, especially pre-contractual negotiations, which are allowed only exceptionally.

In a 'smart contract', (ii) is either complemented or supplanted by code which is also, incidentally, executable by a machine. Depending on the design of the smart contract, the code component of the written layer of the contract stack may be comprehensive or cover only a small part of the contract as a whole. The type of formal language in which this code is written will also be relevant to the complexity of the contract stack, eg, whether it is a compiled or interpreted language; a compiled language, which 'translates' machine-readable code from the human-readable source code, will add another sub-layer within this layer of the stack. Again, this reinforces the impression that the ultimate goal of the smart contract movement is (or should be) to develop a formal language which is intelligible to humans *and* executable by machines to use for the whole or part of the written layer of a contract stack in appropriate use-cases. Another, equally important, goal is to concretise the arrangements in place where the 'smart' component is only part of a stack composed of more conventional layers.

In light of this discussion, the stronger techno-libertarian claims that smart contracts herald the end of contract law as we know it reveal themselves as oversimplifications of the contract stack. Most smart contracts will remain wrapped in a more conventional legal framework, including paper instruments in a natural language, that govern aspects of the parties' relationship around the software

---

[69] I was inspired by a passing comment in a conversation with Björn Scheuermann to adopt this term from computer science to explain the complex structure and sources of contracts, which I think is generally underappreciated by lawyers who see the contract as a monolithic entity that is later subjected to remedial doctrines. 'Tech stack' refers to the underlying elements of an application, ie, the languages and software products that the application is built on. I have not developed the analogy into a mature one; if I have used it infelicitously, the source of the error is with me.

[70] An important category of these rules govern which words count as part of the contract, which aspects of the context are relevant to its interpretation, and how these are to be determined in evidence.

processes which render core performance, and most smart contracts (along with their paper wrappers) will remain, from any reasonable view-point, nested in a national contract law regime (not necessarily the law of the forum). The *dynamics* of this wrapping and stacking provides the focus for the balance of this paper, in which I explore the interaction between formal and natural languages in the context of English contract law. As both of these are embraced by the notion of stacking, and as stacking more accurately brings a stable structure to mind, I think it is better to speak of 'stacking layers' than 'wrapping' smart performance mechanisms in paper contracts.

D. Smart Contracts and Conventional Contract Law

In this section, I briefly mention some issues concerning the legality of smart contracts and the problems of jurisdiction and procedure they will raise for national courts. I cannot, however, explore these issues fully, and they warrant an independent examination at a later date. I focus instead on eight issues in contract law proper: (i) the syntax of legal operators; (ii) translation from natural to formal language and *vice versa*; (iii) the unintentional loss of semantic richness; (iv) the intentional loss of semantic richness; (v) the relational aspect of contracts in the real world; (vi) changing canons of contractual interpretation; (vii) textualism and contextualism; and (viii) the place for equity in the changing landscape.

1. Smart contracts in the courts: illegality, jurisdiction, and procedure

In his original contributions, Szabo stressed the continuity of smart contracting with conventional doctrine and practice, and assumed the continuity of the legal background to smart contracts (ie, property law, criminal law, etc) as well as those doctrines of contract law that remain relevant in his new paradigm. It would take too long to start from scratch, he argued; the aim is to extract principles and practices from the 'laws, procedures, and theories' that we have inherited in order to develop useful 'digital institutions' more quickly.[71] The idea is thus not one of a radical displacement of paper-era contracts, but an augmentation of long-established practices with new digital tools and the integration of paper-era practices into the new digital economy.[72] However, the future which many smart contract enthusiasts envisage—especially within the blockchain context—is one in which

---

[71] N. Szabo, 'Formalizing and Securing Relationships on Public Networks' (1997) 2(9) *First Monday*, <http://firstmonday.org/ojs/index.php/fm/article/view/548/469>, 1 accessed 13 April 2021.
[72] *Ibid.*, 4.

technology disrupts established processes and practices more radically, from the way contracts and negotiated and recorded to the way performance is audited to the way that business organizations themselves are formed and run.

The first and most obvious point in this context is the potential for conflict between the terms of a smart contract and the mandatory terms of the applicable law (or laws). Max Raskin distinguishes between 'strong' and 'weak' smart contracts. The former entail prohibitive costs of revocation and modification, where the latter may be revoked or modified after the contract has been executed. The 'stronger' or 'harder' a smart contract is, the further it will cast its own projection of the parties' legal position from that of objective (ie, state-projected) legal reality.[73] The most obvious example is the situation where the terms of a smart contract are illegal, either from the outset or in virtue of a supervening change in the law. This is not a conceptually challenging issue. In fact, this is no different to the case of an ordinary contract: we may agree to terms that are unenforceable or even illegal under the laws of a relevant national legal system.

The problem is, however, sharpened by the self-executing nature of the smart contract and by the potential for parties to transact in contravention of national law and its institutions. In effect, much of the innovation behind smart contracts is driven by the zeal to remove economic transactions from the purview of national law *in toto*. For innovators of this bent, the perceived failings of the legal system[74] outweigh its perceived benefits. The flight response is reflected in a reformist agenda within national legal orders, as well, for example the desire to reorganize the corpus of legal knowledge, make it machine-readable, and to oust legal professionals from their position as gatekeepers through market forces.[75] Jeremy Sklaroff points to a larger project associated with the so-called 'Californian ideology' to substitute human-controlled public institutions with automated digital processes within which individuals can order their private affairs.[76] Incidentally, it is perhaps no accident that many innovators are from former Soviet jurisdictions where confidence in public institutions is traditionally low, or that a particular American brand of libertarianism has succoured this movement.[77]

Many smart contracts may never come before a national court for practical, rather than legal reasons, as their parties seek anonymity and the ability to dispense with trusted intermediaries. The ideological commitment to non-contestability in

---

[73] See generally D.W.P. Ruiter, *Legal Institutions* (Kluwer 2001).
[74] Or rather, the global system of national legal systems, international law public and private, and para-statal alternative dispute resolution systems.
[75] Some of these processes are discussed in R. Susskind, *The End of Lawyers? Rethinking the Nature of Legal Services* (Oxford University Press 2010).
[76] J.M. Sklaroff, 'Smart Contracts and the Cost of Inflexibility' (2017) 166 *University of Pennsylvania Law Review* 263, 1; on the so-called Californian ideology, see R. Barbrook and A. Cameron, 'The Californian Ideology' (1996) 6 *Science as Culture* 44.
[77] This observation is rather conjectural, but see, eg, <https://themerkle.com/eastern-blockchain-financial-liberation-through-crowdsales/> accessed 13 April 2018. The paragon example is perhaps Ayn Rand herself.

traditional forums may undermine the rule of law, which thrives in a space typified by deliberative, normative disagreement by reference to shared higher-order norms.[78] The strength of the impetus behind this project is, in my view, at least partly a function of the quality of the response of the profession, the academy, and the bench to current developments. The law often responds *ex post* to innovations in the way that commerce is transacted. By remaining pro-active and receptive to the affordances of new technologies, legislatures and courts can perhaps even pre-empt some of the push and pull factors that might lead subjects to (attempt to) opt out of the order of national legal systems. The core challenge in this is to formalize contractual language without losing too much of the breadth, depth, and nuance of contract law itself—and to ensure that a legal language drafted for machine intelligibility continues to serve the needs of its human constituency.

2. Towards a smart(er) contract law

Leaving illegality, jurisdiction, and the rule of law, then, to one side, what issues will smart contracts raise for *contract law* in coming years? In my view, most problems will relate to the 'smart' layer of the contract stack interacting with its 'conventional' layers, ie, paper documents, the background of the parties' dealings, and the applicable rules of national contract law such as statutory implied terms. These problems will relate to the fact that natural languages have looser syntax and richer semantics than formal languages, and that machines are bad at pragmatics.

The following eight issues represent challenges and opportunities. They are areas in which contract law will have to adapt, and in which computer scientists and lawyers should work together closely. If addressed properly, they are all areas in which contract law could itself be improved through increased formalization of contractual language.

a.) Logical operators in contract drafting

The first and most obvious point relates to contractual syntax. At the moment, not only is contractual language ambiguous, but the contractual logic behind it is fuzzy. That is, not only do we struggle with the inherent ambiguity of natural language to express exact ideas, but we lack consensus on a rigorous logic of contractual operations. Two centuries after Bentham presented his 'logic of imperation' as a branch of logic 'untouched by Aristotle',[79] and a century after WN Hohfeld's attempt to

---

[78] See M. Hildebrandt, 'Law *as* Information in the Era of Data-Driven Agency' (2016) 79(1) *Modern Law Review* 1, 27.

[79] J. Bentham (J.H. Burns and H.L.A. Hart eds), *An Introduction to the Principles of Morals and Legislation* (Athlone 1970), 299. Bentham's logic used the operators 'obligation', 'prohibition', and 'permission'. The first attempt to organize relationships of legal obligation into a logical scheme was in fact made by Gottfried Wilhelm Leibniz in the late seventeenth century, but Leibniz' account remained unpublished until much later: See L. Lindahl, *Position and Change* (Reidel 1977), 11; G.W.

formalize the way we speak about legal relations with a structured, constrained vocabulary,[80] it is not uncommon to hear efforts to systematize deontic logic dismissed by lawyers as 'academic'. Practitioners and judges routinely use words like 'right' and 'privilege' in an unstructured, undisciplined manner. This kind of posture is, in my view, increasingly untenable. My point is not that we should all accept the Hohfeldian scheme (or any other particular scheme) but that we need, now more than ever, to reach a broad level consensus that *some* more formal logical scheme is necessary. We urgently need a logic of jural relations and operators, and we need an agreed, constrained syntax to talk about them.[81] This will not only involve a logic of obligation and prohibition, but also of actions and their consequences within the contract's legal and technological framework.

This is the area in which lawyers probably have to challenge their own preconceptions most radically, not only to understand smart contracts in the first place but to respond to them adequately and to harness their potential to influence contract law *praxis* positively as well as to disrupt it. Formal languages may lack some of the semantic richness and nuance of natural languages, but they are more logically rigorous. Embracing some of this rigour and developing a more standardized vocabulary to describe the states of a contract and the actions of its parties is a worthwhile and exciting project and ought to be welcomed by lawyers.

b.) Translation (there and back again)
Disputes concerning smart contracts will require the translation of an instrument's formal language into natural language. A basic characteristic of artificial languages is that they can be fully circumscribed and studied in their entirety, so they have to be understood by human users in a meta-language—ultimately a natural human language such as English.[82] Post-breach negotiation, for example, or disagreements about the intended function of the code, would take place in legal English with references to the formal language used to draft the smart contract.

In fact, a smart contract is already the product of translation from a natural language into a formal one. The language of a smart contract will start its life as an idea (in natural language, or something like it) in the mind of a developer, or a discussion between developers, in response to a design brief (more likely in natural

---

Leibniz, 'Elementa Juris Naturalis' in *Sämtliche Schriften und Briefe 1. Band* (Preussische Akademie der Wissenschaften 1930), 465.
[80] See W.N. Hohfeld, 'Fundamental Legal Conceptions as Applied in Judicial Reasoning' (1917) 26 *Yale Law Journal* 710; see P. Schlag, 'How to Do Things With Hohfeld' (2015) 78(1) *Law and Contemporary Problems* 185.
[81] See for example E. Tjong Tjin Tai, 'Formalising Contract Law for Smart Contracts' (Tilburg Private Law Working Paper Series 06/2017) <http://www.ssrn.com/link/Tilburg-Private_Law.html> accessed 13 April 2018.
[82] C.A. Gunter, *Semantics of Programming Languages: Structures and Techniques* (MIT Press 1992), 4.

language) given by a client, possibly mediated by a conventional lawyer.[83] It will then be rendered into a machine-parsable language, and back again in the case that the machine has done something undesirable and the parties have to argue about it. (As discussed above, depending on the structure of the formal language, this will also include translation from source code to machine code. I will assume that the language is sufficiently reliable that this element of the translation is unproblematic.)

Essentially, the challenge is to ensure that the terms written as down in the formal language by a programmer are isomorphic with the natural language on which it is based. This is difficult because of the way that natural and formal languages work. It is not possible at the present time, in my view, and may never be fully possible. Even should we design systems which generate a natural and a formal language version simultaneously, it is impossible to say that their semantic content will be *identical* in all possible future states of the contract. What is probably needed is a much more wide-spread and long-term project of creating smart contracting language which parties can then adopt as a comprehensive 'private dictionary' for drafting purposes with predictable interpretations under national law.[84] This is an involved, long-term project, that will require the involvement of conventional parties including lawyers.

c.) The unintentional loss of semantic richness

In consequence, there is a real risk that those now working on smart contract drafting languages (such as Solidity) will try, but fail, to capture the richness of existing contract law. The syntax will usually be the easiest part to translate, as operators can be explained in terms of their causal effects within the relevant universe.[85] As suggested above, this might even exercise a salutary influence on the law, or at least galvanize lawyers into bringing their own house in order. The semantics of legal concepts will prove more difficult. The semantics of most formal languages less complete than we would like, and the semantics of natural languages are inherently ambiguous. Some central concepts of English contract law are among the most ambiguous of all. Consider how contractual terms such as 'good faith', 'best endeavours', or 'reasonable delay' would be defined in a formal language. True, 'big data' may promise opportunities for mining opinion from large constituencies within the relevant community, or indeed to distil judicial precedent in new

---

[83] Human thoughts might be informed by the structure of a formal language but no-one really *thinks* in C++. Much as a lawyer's thoughts are informed the structure of contractual language; she will 'think' in categories of contract doctrine, in contrast to the layman client who will brief her in terms of relationships and commercial objectives. Of course, to some extent we all operate with our own private dictionary, and so it is difficult to say categorically that all my thoughts start their existence in 'English', as opposed to *my* English. But the general point, I think, is good.

[84] I thank Philipp Thurner for our discussion on this subject, which helped to clarify this point.

[85] See eg, Massimo Bartoletti and Roberto Zunino, 'A Calculus of Contracting Processes' (University of Trento Technical Report #DISI-09-056, October 2009).

ways. But the core of a concept such as 'reasonableness' is flexibility and sensitivity to context, which is inherently difficult for machines. This presents a greater risk of dimorphism and incorrect translation: The greater ability of human agents to construct meaning from context presents the danger that human parties will understand their agreed terms to mean one thing, and their machines will understand it to mean something entirely different.

d.) The intentional loss of semantic richness

The critical input of computer scientists into the eldritch world of law is something which I, personally, welcome as a healthy cross-pollination of disciplines concerned with 'doing things with words'. But if, instead of carefully developing a new and better language for expressing contractual obligations, we subject contract law to a casual weekend hackathon, we will surely discard some things of value. For example, many would hail the abolition of 'good faith' as a step in the right direction. But it would also raise serious problems from the perspective of consumer and investor protection, among other things, especially in the case of retail investors putting money into an initial coin offering.

More importantly, as Sklaroff argues, the ambiguity and flexibility of natural languages actually create efficiencies to which some appear blind. The straitjacket of immutable, unstoppable code requires parties to know (or attempt to know) everything relevant about every possible future state of the contract. This is costly in the due diligence phase and the drafting phase, as every contingency has to be imagined and negotiated. When affairs nevertheless take an unexpected turn, it raises the costs of responding to breach by making informal negotiation impossible. Once initialized, a smart contract creates a 'permanent and unalterable link between the terms of the contract and the information system it manipulates', which lasts until the transaction is complete.[86] Totally inflexible contractual performance might sound attractive, but will bring its own difficulties and inefficiencies when the universe conspires to 'alter the equilibrium of the contract'.[87]

A more promising line of development might be to think carefully about how the smart layer (which may be a blockchain-based 'smart contract') and the rest of the contract stack interact, and to factor a human element into the stack where this could create efficiencies. For example, one response to the difficulty of making 'good faith' comprehensible to a machine might be to include a mechanism whereby a smart contract stops and refers a matter to a human third-party (who holds the ability to reinitiate the process) to define a term. We might call this a 'semantic oracle', as it would mirror the use of so-called 'oracles' as external sources

---

[86] J. Sklaroff, 'Smart Contracts and the Cost of Inflexibility' (2017) 166 *University of Pennsylvania Law Review* 263, 18–19.
[87] S. Vogenauer and J. Kleinheisterkamp (eds), *Commentary on the UNIDROIT Principles of International Commercial Contracts* (Oxford University Press 2009), commentary to Article 6.2.2.

of data relating to the conditions of contract performance in blockchain systems.[88] Most oracles are algorithms that provide third party information such as weather data or stock prices scraped from some database, but there is no reason why a human institution could not perform a similar function in giving semantic content to difficult terms—especially when circumstances have changed in unpredictable ways.[89] The result of such an approach would not be a techno-libertarian post-law utopia, but it would be a much 'smarter' contract stack.

e.) Keeping contracts based in relationships between (human) agents
Likewise, Donald Robertson stresses the importance of flexibility in international contracts, and in particular the principle of 'good faith' as a basis on which to adjust the operation of a contractual relationship after the event.[90] Parties actually value relationships, which endure beyond transactions, far more than some innovators seem to recognize. Accordingly, it is important for lawyers (who do appreciate this fact) to consider how smart contracts might be used to structure long-term relational contracts, instead of just trying to obviate the need for a meaningful relationship between the parties.[91] Robertson argues that good faith and fair dealing are the essential features of international contract law, especially in the context of the adaptation of contractual obligations once a contract has become 'executive' and performance initiated. It is noteworthy that smart contracts occupy the same space between regimes of national law, but purport to deal with the problem of uncertainty and risk in exactly the opposite manner.

f.) Textualism and contextualism (in a new context)
The formal nature of smart contracts adds a new dimension of complexity to existing controversies about the 'formal' *versus* 'contextual' interpretation of contractual language.[92] Take, for example, Lord Hoffmann's fifth principle in the classical case of *Investors Compensation Scheme Ltd v West Bromwich Building Society*,[93] ie, that we should not assume that parties have made a linguistic mistake in complex, formal documents, but that, if we conclude from the background that something must have 'gone wrong with the language', we should not impute to the parties an intention which they plainly could not have had. *Investors Compensation Scheme* was an application of a principle laid down earlier by Lord Diplock that, 'if detailed syntactical and semantic analysis of words' 'flouted business common sense',

---

[88] I thank Miëtek Bak for suggesting this nomenclature.
[89] See V. Buterin, 'Ethereum and Oracles' (Ethereum Blog, 22 July 2014), <https://blog.ethereum.org/2014/07/22/ethereum-and-oracles/> accessed 22 November 2017.
[90] See D. Robertston, 'Contracts in Crises' [2014] *AMPLA Yearbook* 221.
[91] See generally A. Cunningham, 'Decentralisation, Distrust & Fear of the Body—The Worrying Rise of Crypto-Law' (2016) 13(3) *SCRIPTed: A Journal of Law, Technology and Society* 235.
[92] See eg, Z.X. Tan, 'Beyond the Real and the Paper Deal: The Quest for Contractual Coherence in Contractual Interpretation' (2016) 79(4) *Modern Law Review* 623.
[93] *Investors Compensation Scheme Ltd v West Bromwich Building Society* [1998] 1 All ER 98.

the words should be made to yield before the business common sense.[94] This, and related principles, have given rise to complex discussions about what context is relevant and about what evidence of context is admissible. The present status of this principle, and of the so-called 'contextual' approach to contractual interpretation generally, is currently being undermined in the jurisprudence of the UK Supreme Court, and is generally in a state of flux across the Commonwealth jurisdictions.[95]

The alternative to Lord Hoffmann's contextual approach, which is establishing itself in English law, looks at the 'natural' or 'ordinary' meaning of contractual language in the first instance, and only looks to context if there is ambiguity in the contractual language. (The *ICS* approach looks first at the context to determine what the words mean, and therefore whether there is any ambiguity in the first place.) The new approach, led by judges drawn from a commercial law background, may prove itself to be problematic where the content of a contract is determined in whole or in part by a code-based instrument. The problem, as I see it, is this: If code is capable of execution, it would appear to be (by definition) clear in meaning and not ambiguous; if ambiguity is prerequisite for context to play a role in interpretation and/or construction, the court might never get to the point of asking whether the algorithm's product is really what the human parties intended—even in perverse cases.[96]

However, things can go wrong with the drafting of smart contracts, too. A prominent example is the incident involving an entity called 'The DAO'.[97] A smart contract allowed investors to pool their money into an investment vehicle that would operate without human organs. Naturally the code allowed for investors to withdraw their funds. However, the code also allowed users to exercise the removal function recursively, that is to make repeated withdrawal requests, without checking whether the requests exceeded the investor's original contribution. Intuitively, this would appear as a bug, rather than a feature, of the software. A certain user (or users) discovered this function and used it to remove about US $50m (of a total fund of about US $150m) into a so-called 'child DAO' hived off from the parent fund. The DAO community responded to this action as a 'hack' rather than

---

[94] See *Antiaios Compania Naviera SA v Salen Rederierna AB* [1985] AC 191.
[95] See Sir G. Vos, 'Contractual Interpretation: Do Judges Sometimes Say One Thing and Do Another?' (2017) 23 *Canterbury Law Review* 1; see eg, P.S. Davies, 'Interpretation and Rectification in Australia' (2018) 76(3) *Cambridge Law Journal* 483.
[96] See *Arnold v Britton* [2015] UKSC 36, which upheld a clause (containing a simple mathematical formula) that would require lessees of some holiday shacks to pay £1,025,004 per year for garden maintenance in the 99th year of the lease while others, with a slightly different version of the contract, would pay only £1,900 for the same services.
[97] See D. Siegel, 'Understanding The DAO Hack' (Coindesk, 25 June 2016), <https://www.coindesk.com/understanding-dao-hack-journalists/> accessed 13 April 2018. The acronym stands for 'Decentralised Autonomous Organisation', essentially a body without human organs. The legal cognoscibility of entities of this kind is another question for an independent examination. See A. Cunningham, 'Decentralisation, Distrust and Fear of the Body: The Worrying Rise of Crypto-Law' (2016) 13 *SCRIPTed: A Journal of Law, Technology and Society* 235.

the legitimate use of a feature. The 'hacker(s)', however, quite claimed rightly that the terms of the smart contract explicitly excluded any extrinsic material as an aid to interpreting the code's functioning. The majority of The DAO community took a different view, and in the end a group of insiders short-circuited the consensus mechanism in the (supposedly immutable) code to perform what is called a 'hard fork' in the blockchain—effectively, they colluded to wind the clock back and start a new chain of transactions. There are now two competing records of the events, each claiming to be authoritative.

Because so many blockchain-based smart contracts are (still) being drafted with the intention of excluding context entirely, principles of contextual interpretation will be even more difficult to apply. The DAO incident again demonstrates that inferences drawn from the context (including the background intention of the parties, and the background intention of those who drafted the formal language) are crucial to the interpretation of the 'smart' (ie, coded) layers of the contract stack.

g.) An evolving canon of interpretation

By its very nature, a formal language may do unexpected things from the point of view of a human observer. For example, the problem with The DAO appears to have been one of language *design*, not just language *use*.[98] This opens a debate about the intended function of the whole language, not just that of a portion of code written in it. The semantic content of a formal language is informed by the question of what the language itself was intended to do. Unlike natural languages, formal languages are created rather than evolved. For example, the programming language Simplicity is presented as a 'new language that maintains or enhances the desirable properties that Bitcoin Script has while adding expressiveness', and its creators name five 'design goals'.[99] The legal meaning of a phrase in Simplicity could therefore plausibly be informed by the stated intention to improve on its predecessors. The law may have to develop its traditional canons of interpretation based on this feature of formal languages. It may be necessary, in due course, to use documents such as this as we would use a dictionary or grammar. Again, this will entail discussion (in a meta-language) about the developer's intended meaning at the time of drafting. But it will be difficult to determine the status of this or that statement in the canon of interpretation, especially in the context of open-source languages on which a large number of programmers have collaborated, over many versions and over a long period of time.

---

[98] See N. Atzei, M. Bartoletti, and T. Cimoli, 'A Survey of Attacks on Ethereum Smart Contracts (SoK)' in M. Maffei and M. Ryan (eds), *Principles of Security and Trust: POST 2017 Proceedings* (Springer 2017), 164.
[99] See R. O'Connor, 'Simplicity: A New Language for Blockchains' (Blockstream Blog, 30 October 2017) <https://blockstream.com/simplicity.pdf> accessed 13 April 2018.

h.) Whither equity?

Finally, smart contracts will raise issues surrounding the equitable doctrines that do so much work in contract law—from estoppel to rectification to specific performance. First, many of these doctrines intervene in the normal process actually set out in the words of the agreement. To the extent that an automated process is unstoppable, even in light of changes in the parties' legal relationship, smart contracts may come into direct conflict with equitable doctrines earlier and more frequently than any other part of contract law. This also relates to the points made above about complete contingency drafting and the unknowability of the future. Secondly, the techno-libertarian ideology driving smart contract innovation is inherently antagonistic to the tradition of Aristotelian equity in English law. As Lord Ellesmere said the *Earl of Oxford's Case*,[100] chancery exists because our actions are so diverse and infinite that it is impossible to make any general law that will cover every interaction and not fail in some circumstances. Equity specifically involves a departure from parties' legal rights, including their contractual rights, based on very human considerations. Equity is peculiarly vulnerable in the context of smart contracts—but, paradoxically, the latter's rigidity calls out for more, rather than less, equitable supervision. So far, the interaction between smart contracts and equity seems to be entirely neglected in the literature.

E. Conclusion

'Smart' contracts—up to and including blockchain-based 'smart contracts' are neither business as usual, nor end of contract law as we know it. The normal mode of the law's development is the refurbishment of existing concepts and doctrines in the wake of social and technological change. The disruptive potential of smart contracts equals that of innovations in corporate organization and finance in the eighteenth and nineteenth centuries, and the pace of change is more rapid. The potential for disruption is particularly acute in the context of automated contractual performance, especially using tamper-proof processes that are unstoppable once initiated and cannot respond to changes in the state of the world or the legal position of the parties. Rather than focussing on the potential for disruption, however, lawyers, judges, and legal academics should look at the positive influence that these developments might have for legal theory and practice more generally.

In particular, smart contracts could act as a catalyst for the increased formalization of contractual concepts and the language used to express them. In advance of any of issues coming before the courts, the legal academy has an important role to play in explaining the role of language in law and in computer science, and forging

---

[100] *Earl of Oxford's Case* (1615) 1 Ch Rep 1.

a common vocabulary with computer scientists. Much of the groundwork has already been laid in the philosophy of language, on which both disciplines already draw. The point at which linguistic philosophy and social ontology meet is, in my view, a particularly rich seam of conceptual resources waiting to be exploited. I have stressed the importance of speech acts contained in documents, or document acts, in the construction of our social, economic, and legal world. This is essential to understand a world in which algorithms can interact with the information systems which maintain these domains. As a result, we need to engage actively and constructively with the computer science community whose innovations (and ideology) are, at present, marking out the field.

At the moment, conversations are still in progress regarding the syntactic structure and semantic content of smart contracting languages themselves. We lawyers need to ensure we take up a place at the table while the conversation is still in terms we can understand and to which we can contribute. The challenge is to ensure that parsing contractual language to be machine readable does not exclude too much of contract law, on the one hand, and on the other to ensure that the strictures of received legal doctrine do not stifle worthwhile technical, business, and legal innovation. In particular, we need to reconsider current debates in the law of contract interpretation in light of smart contracts, and think carefully about how to preserve the operation of equitable doctrines that affect the parties' legal position pre-contract or mid-performance.

2
End-to-End Smart Legal Contracts
Moving from Aspiration to Reality

Sir Geoffrey Vos, MR[*]

A. Introduction	54	F. What Can be Done Once Any Legal Impediments to the Use of Smart Contracts Have Been Identified?	64
B. Where Are We Now?	56		
C. The Thesis	58		
D. A Preliminary Issue: Property in English Law	59	G. Further Questions About Smart, Legally Enforceable Contracts	65
E. Current Developments in English Law	62	H. An Inbuilt Dispute Resolution System for Smart Contracts	66
		I. Conclusions	68

A. Introduction

The legal treatment of 'smart contracts' is rapidly becoming one of the most important legal subjects of our generation.[1] Smart contracts may be taken to be enforceable legal agreements expressed to a greater or lesser extent in computer code. The classic definition derives from the various writings of Nick Szabo, who defined a smart contract as a set of promises, specified in digital form, including protocols within which the parties perform on these promises.[2]

---

[*] The Rt Hon Sir Geoffrey Vos is at the forefront of judicial engagement with emerging technologies globally, especially in his roles as Chancellor of the High Court of England and Wales (2016–2021) and now Master of the Rolls. Sir Geoffrey is a member of the LawTech UK Panel and chairs its UK Jurisdiction Taskforce.

[1] An earlier version of this chapter was published, under the same title, in (2019) 26(1) *Journal of Law, Information and Science* EAP 1 and is reproduced here with permission. Some updates have been made, but for the most part the discussion reflects the situation at the time of writing for historical purposes. It is based on a lecture entitled *Cryptoassets as property: how can English law boost the confidence of would-be parties to smart legal contracts?* delivered on 2 May 2019: <https://www.judiciary.uk/wp-content/uploads/2019/05/Sir-Geoffrey-Vos-Chancellor-of-the-High-Court-speech-on-cryptoassets.pdf> accessed 8 July 2021. I would like to acknowledge with gratitude the great assistance in the preparation of the lecture and this Chapter provided by Dr J.G. Allen and Ms Anca-Gabriela Bunda, both former judicial assistants.

[2] N. Szabo, 'Smart Contracts: Building Blocks for Digital Markets' (1996) 16 *Extropy* <http://www.fon.hum.uva.nl/rob/Courses/InformationInSpeech/CDROM/Literature/LOTwinterschool2006/szabo.best.vwh.net/smart_contracts_2.html> accessed 8 July 2021.

Sir Geoffrey Vos, MR, *End-to-End Smart Legal Contracts* In: *Smart Legal Contracts*. Edited by: Jason Grant Allen and Peter Hunn, Oxford University Press. © Jason Grant Allen & Peter Hunn 2022.
DOI: 10.1093/oso/9780192858467.003.0003

In a recent analysis of the notion of smart contracts as legal contracts, properly so called, Dr Jason Allen, my former judicial assistant, has suggested that a smart contract is a recording of a legal agreement between parties that is written in a language that is both human-intelligible and machine-readable, whose text incorporates an algorithm which automates some or all of the performance of the agreement.[3] These definitions suffice for present purposes. In practice, smart contracts have a close association with distributed ledger technology ('DLT'), particularly blockchain data structures, and with 'cryptoassets' such as Bitcoin and Ether.

In this chapter, I ask what is needed for the promise of smart contracts to move from technologically feasible aspiration to legal and commercial reality. In the speech I delivered at the University of Liverpool in early May 2019,[4] I examined how English law could respond to the technological developments behind smart contracts in a manner that encourages their responsible use and increases the confidence of market participants in their legal underpinnings. One of the major obstacles observed was the early association of smart contracts with specific cryptoassets, bringing with them security issues, poor commercial practice, and legal uncertainty. In this paper, I shall touch on these questions—which I think are unavoidable—but concentrate on (i) the legal basis, and (ii) the design principles, of what may be called 'end-to-end smart legal contracts'.

There a body of learning on the topic has emerged since the rise of Bitcoin, the blockchain technology on which it rests, and an explosion of other 'crypto-currencies'. Somewhat disconnected from an earlier literature on the formalization of legal logic, the first wave of literature on 'smart contracts' from the 1990s onwards generally staked stronger or weaker techno-libertarian claims and buttressed them with legal theory, or rejected them and sought to undermine their feasibility or desirability.[5] A meaningful and intentional dialogue between the two sides of the

---

[3] J.G. Allen, 'Wrapped and Stacked: "Smart Contracts" and the Interaction of Natural and Formal Language' (2018) 14(4) *European Review of Contract Law* 307, 313, following a review of some of the current definitions.

[4] At a joint event with the Northern Chancery Bar Association.

[5] One of the earliest sources on law and logic is L. Allen, 'Symbolic Logic: A Razor-Edged Tool for Drafting and Interpreting Legal Documents' (1957) 66 *Yale Law Journal* 833, and there is a significant literature in this vein produced by a number of projects around the world including those at Imperial College London—see eg, A.L. Tyree 'The Logic Programming Debate' (1992) 13(1) *Journal of Law and Information Science* 111. On the more recent blockchain-based discussion, see A. Cohn, T. West, and C. Parker, 'Smart After All: Blockchain, Smart Contracts, Parametric Insurance, and Smart Energy Grids' (2017) 1(2) *Georgetown Law and Technology Review* 273; M. Raskin, 'The Law and Legality of Smart Contracts' (2017) 1(2) *Georgetown Law Technology Review* 305; J. Cieplak and S. Leefatt, 'Smart Contracts: A Smart Way to Automate Performance' (2017) 1(2) *Georgetown Law and Technology Review* 418; A. Savelyev, 'Contract Law 2.0: "Smart" Contracts as the Beginning of the End of Classic Contract Law' (2017) 26(2) *Information and Communications Technology Law* 116; K. Werbach and N. Cornell, 'Contracts Ex Machina' (2017) 67 *Duke Law Journal* 313; P. Cuccuru, 'Beyond Bitcoin: An Early Overview on Smart Contracts' (2017) 25 *International Journal of Law and Information Technology* 179;

debate now seems to have emerged. There is not only evidence of deeper engagement by lawyers in the technical features of smart contracts, but also of deeper engagement by innovators with the questions of law and legal theory their innovations provoke, and a realization that if emerging technologies are to be widely adopted, their promotors must be pragmatic about the legal implications of what they are doing.

This paper takes English law as its subject, but it can be considered as part of a broader discussion, particularly given the borderless nature of the technology and the global structures of twenty-first century finance. Discussion across jurisdictional boundaries will enhance the collaboration between common law jurisdictions for which I have striven in other contexts.

B. Where Are We Now?

My starting point is to ask why smart contracts have taken so long to become ubiquitous. We have been discussing how and when they may take over the world of mainstream financial services, for example, for several years. Yet, smart contracts have thus far not made their breakthrough into reality. So far as I am aware, there has not yet been an end-to-end smart legal contract in financial services or in any other sector.[6]

It is possible also that many of the most useful applications of the algorithms touted as 'smart contracts' are not, in fact, as end-to-end 'legal' contracts at all. Instead, the most useful applications may be as components of more conventional legal relationships such that talk of 'contracts' is inaccurate.

But allowing for this, one of the premises of this paper is that end-to-end smart legal contracts will not become mainstream without a legal infrastructure. Rather, the notion of an end-to-end 'smart legal contract' entails the existence of multiple layers, some legal and some technical, which will interact. Those crafting them should perhaps begin with that kind of output in mind, and our terminology should reflect the complexity of contracts as legal phenomena themselves. In this context, Dr Jason Allen has suggested that we adopt the metaphor of a 'contract stack' comprising multiple layers, some technical and others conventionally legal.[7] That is one way of making a point that is certainly worth investigating.

M. Durovic and A. Janssen, 'The Formation of Blockchain-based Smart Contracts in Light of Contract Law' (2018) 6 *European Review of Contract Law* 753.

[6] By this I mean a legal relationship which is structured by and around an algorithmic expression of the parties' mutual undertakings which is machine-readable and, ultimately, executable.

[7] J.G. Allen, 'Wrapped and Stacked: "Smart Contracts" and the Interaction of Natural and Formal Language' (2018) 14(4) *European Review of Contract Law* 307, 331.

Another answer to the question of why end-to-end smart legal contracts have taken so long is, I think, that mainstream investors are unwilling to part with real money without the assurance that there is a legal foundation for their engagement.[8] Thus far, the legal uncertainty that pervades the use of cryptoassets for financial transactions has meant that the starting line has not been crossed: the early days of smart contracts were characterized by a close association with cryptoassets and, therefore, uncertainty by association.[9] We may soon see greater clarity on the legal nature and regulatory status of cryptoassets. So, it is to be hoped that, to the extent that there remains a close association between smart contracts and cryptoassets, some of this collateral uncertainty will begin to dissipate. Further, as I see it, despite the close association of smart contracts with blockchain technology, a smart contract (defined broadly) is possible without either a cryptoasset as its subject matter or using cryptoassets as a medium of payment. It is, therefore, worthwhile to explore the notion of 'smart' contracts beyond the context of cryptoassets.

Moreover, the use of smart contracts would be advanced by greater clarity in relation to (i) the legal enforceability of contractual provisions expressed in code, (ii) how such provisions will be interpreted, and (iii) what parties can do when things go wrong with the code. It is perhaps only when these matters are clarified under some applicable law that smart contracts will begin to be widely used for mainstream applications.

I should, in this context, say two things about the technologists and innovators. First, I do not want to suggest how those more intimately concerned with the development of FinTech, LawTech, and RegTech solutions might achieve their objectives. Innovation is best left to innovators and not pre-empted by judges. My intention here is to open up some lines of enquiry that I think may be important in the common law's unending task of keeping up with changes in technology and commercial practice.

The second is that there appears to be a considerable divide between coders and lawyers. Many of the coders involved in the development of smart contracts think they have no need for lawyers or law, because the answer is built into the code. As I see it, lawyers and judges need to be persuasive on this point. We need to explain *why* a legal foundation to smart contracts is not only desirable but essential. In two words, the answer is: investor confidence. If smart contracts are to become part of the mainstream, investors will need to be able to invoke legal remedies in appropriate circumstances so as to avoid fraud and ensure a dependable market. Some coders, however, still seem to be developing technology so they do not have to wait

---

[8] See eg, ISDA/King & Wood Mallesons, 'Smart Derivatives Contracts: From Concept to Construction' (Whitepaper, October 2018), <https://www.isda.org/a/cHvEE/Smart-Derivatives-Contracts-From-Concept-to-Construction-Oct-2018.pdf>, 12.

[9] See eg, Q. DuPont, 'A History and Ethnography of "The DAO", A Failed Decentralized Autonomous Organization' in M. Campbell-Verduyn, *Bitcoin and Beyond: Cryptocurrencies, Blockchains, and Global Governance* (Routledge 2017).

to see what the legal position turns out to be. Part of the persuasive exercise on which lawyers need to become engaged will be to address the misunderstanding that the law does not apply to these new technologies in an apparently borderless environment. The technological community will need to understand why they actually do need both (i) a legal foundation and (ii) built-in dispute resolution—something to which I shall return.

C. The Thesis

The thesis in this Chapter is that the common law, and in particular English law, is in a good position to provide the necessary legal infrastructure to facilitate smart legal contracts if, but only if, any necessary legislative reforms are kept simple. This brings the advantages of the common law sharply into focus. The common law is dependable and predictable and able to build on clear principles so as to apply them to new commercial situations. The objective should be to identify and, if necessary, remove any fundamental legal impediment to the use of smart contracts. We should try to avoid the creation of a new legal and regulatory regime that will discourage the use of new technologies rather than provide the foundation for them to flourish.

There are two important and substantive distinctions: the first is between law and regulation, and the second is between rights and remedies. One must understand the underlying legal position before one starts to regulate the use of smart contracts and cryptoassets. What will ultimately be of most significance to those using smart contracts will be the remedies that they can obtain when things go wrong. But, like regulation, one cannot reliably ascertain the appropriate remedies before one has properly analysed the legal rights with which one is dealing.

It is fashionable to characterize new technologies as disruptive, and indeed in many respects they are. But disruptive technologies which have lasting value are more aptly described as foundational. They may, to some extent, disrupt the *status quo* of commercial practice, but more significantly, they provide a new foundation for those practices.[10] This is something that we all should keep in view—the lawyers to temper their scepticism, and the coders to focus their innovations most constructively.

Removing the legal impediments to the use of smart contracts in the way I have suggested would provide commercial entities with the ability to contract as they wish, and ensure that new foundations are available for economic and financial activity. It may very well be easier said than done, but let me explore the possibilities.

---

[10] See M. Iansiti and K. Lakhani, 'The Truth About Blockchain' (2017) 1 *Harvard Business Review* 118.

D. A Preliminary Issue: Property in English Law

The first problem, as I have said, is the legal uncertainty surrounding the nature of cryptoassets. Although the focus of this chapter is on the legal status of smart contracts, I think it would be inappropriate to embark on such an investigation without due regard to the 'property question' surrounding cryptoassets, given their close connection in concept and practice. In other words, although the law relating to 'smart legal contracts' may need to be applicable to 'smart' contracts unrelated to cryptoassets, it seems likely that the two will remain connected.

In this regard, it is tempting to think that we are the first generation of judges and lawyers faced with innovative types of financial assets. But that is not so. Back in the eighteenth century, judges were in a similar position as new kinds of financial instruments were proliferating. In *Nightingale v Devisme*,[11] Lord Mansfield had to decide whether stock in the East India Company was money. He held that it was not. But he observed that '[t]his is a *new species* of property, arisen within the compass of a few years'. Lord Mansfield may have been wrong. Trade in stocks had, in fact, been common in London for seventy-five years before 1770. But it was not until the late nineteenth century that treatises on investment securities and stock exchange transactions appeared.[12]

It is now necessary to think for a moment about how property is regarded by the common law, and in particular English law. The single biggest question that has been raised in this area is whether cryptoassets can be regarded as property under the current law. It is increasingly common to see lawyers assuming that cryptoassets are capable of being property—or, perhaps more accurately, being the objects of property rights.[13] There has recently been more explicit engagement with the details of this assumption and the complexities of how established notions of property might or might not apply in this new context.[14]

The tendency to assume that cryptoassets are property is based on the intuitively sound premise that the law follows the economic reality it purports to govern. The market, nationally and internationally, is treating cryptoassets with various

---

[11] *Nightingale v Devisme* (1770) 98 ER 361.
[12] J.S. Rogers, 'Negotiability, Property, and Identity' (1990) 12 *Cardozo Law Review* 471, 476.
[13] For example, in *B2C2 Ltd v Quoine Pte Ltd* [2019] SGHC(I) 03 in the Singapore International Commercial Court, Simon Thorley QC considered specifically whether cryptocurrencies were property for the purpose of being held in trust. He said at para [142]: '[i]t is convenient to consider the second certainty, certainty of subject matter, first. Quoine was prepared to assume that cryptocurrencies may be treated as property that may be held on trust. I consider that it was right to do so. Cryptocurrencies are not legal tender in the sense of being a regulated currency issued by a government but do have the fundamental characteristic of intangible property as being an identifiable thing of value'. Cryptocurrencies, he said, meet the classical requirements of intangible property. 'Whilst there may be some academic debate as to the precise nature of the property right, in the light of the fact that Quoine does not seek to dispute that they may be treated as property in a generic sense, I need not consider the question further'.
[14] See in particular S. Gleeson, *The Legal Concept of Money* (Oxford University Press 2018), Ch 9; D. Fox and S. Green, *Cryptocurrencies in Public and Private Law* (Oxford University Press 2019), Ch 6 and Ch 7; J.G. Allen, 'Property in Digital Coins' (2019) 8(1) *European Journal of Property Law* 1.

characteristics as economic assets. In general, the law should try to serve the needs of society. That should include its economy and financial system. Divergences between the law and the market without a sound basis in policy or principal are probably best avoided. It seems to me that nothing about cryptoassets *per se* makes them more or less unattractive than, say, ordinary securities.[15] The latter can also have some potentially harmful effects, as the global financial crisis of 2008 demonstrated. There may be a good case for the prohibition of some types of cryptoassets, and for the encouragement of others. Such regulatory action might, for example, be based on the character of the issuer, the intended and actual use of the cryptoasset, or the risk to consumers and the financial or monetary system. But none of that is a good reason to treat fundamentally similar assets differently in terms of their legal status as objects of property rights. Whilst possible, treating similar assets differently at the level of legal principle, rather than regulation, is a somewhat heavy-handed technique that is perhaps better reserved for more marginal products.

I shall not, in this paper, be obsessing over the fine definitional distinctions that exist between, for example, different species of cryptoassets, such as utility tokens, exchange tokens and security tokens. These are important regulatory questions, but they comprise a second stage of analysis, and it is on the basic legal questions that I wish to focus here.[16] As I have said, there is a clear distinction between the legal issues that underpin the mainstream use of cryptoassets on the one hand, and the regulatory issues that will undoubtedly arise once those legal issues have been resolved, on the other hand. Before one starts to regulate economic activity, one needs to understand precisely the activity that is being regulated.

Continental legal systems often start such discussions with an axiomatic definition of the types of things in which property rights can exist, and some exclude intangible objects from the catalogue *ex hypothesi*. English law and other common law legal systems tend to start from the other direction by focussing attention on the scope and content of property rights themselves.[17] English lawyers have a clear, perhaps undue, focus on remedies. This can be seen from the leading English cases on the question of property rights in intangible, informational objects.[18]

It is worth observing first that, for the purposes of English law, section 205 (1) (xx) of the Law of Property Act 1925 defines property quite broadly as including 'any thing in action, and any interest in real or personal property'. This legislative

---

[15] If a broad definition of 'cryptoassets' is adopted, this is not a controversial claim; it does not exclude the possibility that *certain* types of cryptoassets (for example 'privacy coins') are *per se* problematic from a regulatory perspective.

[16] See A. Blandin *et al.*, *Global Cryptoasset Regulatory Landscape Study* (Cambridge Centre for Alternative Finance, 16 April 2019) <https://www.jbs.cam.ac.uk/faculty-research/centres/alternative-finance/publications/cryptoasset-regulation/#.XO5PXaRS-Uk> last accessed 28.02.2022.

[17] See F. Pollock, 'What is a Thing?' (1894) 10 *Law Quarterly Review* 318.

[18] See, in particular, *OBG Limited v Allan* [2007] UKHL 21, [2008] 1 AC 1, *Your Response Limited v Datateam Business Media Limited* [2014] EWCA Civ 281, and *Armstrong DLW GMBH v Winnington Networks Ltd* [2012] EWHC 10 (Ch).

provision leaves much unsaid about the English law of property. It does, however, allude to the principal division between real and personal property, as well as identifying things in action—conventionally called choses in action—as a special class of personal property.

There appear to be two main issues facing the recognition of cryptoassets as property in English law. First, whilst an intangible asset can undoubtedly be property in English law, a cryptoasset does not in all cases generate a right against another person like a chose in action or money held in a bank account; the latter is, of course, generally a right, evidenced in writing, against a counter-party. Some cryptoassets represent 'off-chain' value (whether tangible things or rights) and some do not. It would seem that cryptoassets representing external value are more easily assimilated to the category of choses in action than those that do not. The latter would seem to be a hybrid, a 'new species of property, arisen within the compass of a few years'.[19] The question then arises how they are to be accommodated in the taxonomy of English (or any other) law of property. Secondly, different cryptoassets are represented by different informational structures—most importantly, there is an 'account model' and an 'unspent transaction output' or 'UTXO' model. It may be necessary for the law to distinguish between these types of cryptoassets and to treat them differently for certain purposes—that is an open question at this stage. It is potentially very important; the precise nature of the cryptoasset may affect the ability to possess it and the remedies that can be employed in English law such as conversion or theft, for example.

But it is notable that the Law of Property Act 1925 only provides that property 'includes' choses in action and any interest in real or personal property. There is no statutory reason why a new form of personal property could not be recognized in English law, provided that it represents some form of value and falls within Lord Wilberforce's definition in *National Provincial Bank v Ainsworth*,[20] being 'definable, identifiable by third parties, capable in its nature of assumption by third parties, and [having] some degree of permanence or stability'.[21]

Put in the way suggested by Moore-Bick LJ in *Your Response Limited v Datateam Business Media Limited*,[22] the catalogue of intangible property could be identified first by reconsidering the dichotomy between choses in possession and choses in action, and secondly, recognizing a third category of intangible property, which could possibly be susceptible of possession and amenable to the tort of conversion. Overlooking the inherent difficulties associated with possession of digital objects, for the sake of argument at least,[23] that would have the benefit of accepting as

---

[19] *Nightingale v Devisme* (1770) 98 ER 361 per Lord Mansfield.
[20] *Bank v Ainsworth* [1965] 1 AC 1175.
[21] Ibid., 1248.
[22] *Your Response Limited v Datateam Business Media Limited* [2014] EWCA Civ 281.
[23] See J.G. Allen, 'Negotiability in Digital Environments' (2019) (July/August) *Butterworths Journal of International Banking and Financial Law* 459.

property anything which is owned by one person and can be sold and transferred to another person as property within, as Stringer J put it in New Zealand, 'both the popular and legal meanings of the term'.[24]

In this entire discussion, I think it is important to leave intellectual property out of the debate. It would make the whole exercise far less likely to succeed if there were an attempt to re-characterize the well-known species of nationally and internationally statutorily-recognized intellectual property rights.

Databases may also require separate statutory reconsideration. I do not, however, think that the *Datateam* case necessarily provides an insuperable obstacle to the recognition of cryptoassets as property under English law. Although both databases and cryptoassets consist of structured symbolic data, there are differences both in their technical composition and in their use that may justify different legal treatment.

E. Current Developments in English Law

Recently, the UK Government established both a FinTech Delivery Panel and a LawTech Delivery Panel. I am a member of the LawTech Delivery Panel and chair of its UK Jurisdiction Taskforce (the 'UKJT'), which was established with the objective of demonstrating that English law and UK jurisdiction can provide a state-of-the-art foundation for the development of DLT, smart contracts, artificial intelligence, and associated technologies.

The UKJT had conducted a public consultation at the time that this chapter was originally written.[25] This consultation sought views from lawyers and coders on the identification of the key issues of legal uncertainty as they affect the status of cryptoassets and the usage of smart legal contracts in the law of England and Wales. The UKJT has, since this chapter was written, published in November 2019 its *Legal Statement on the status of Cryptoassets and Smart Contracts*, prepared by

---

[24] In *Jonathan Dixon v The Queen* [2015] NZSC 147, the NZ Supreme Court held that digital files comprising video CCTV footage held on a computer system could be property for the purposes of the New Zealand Crime Act. They said at paragraph 38 that they considered 'that the fundamental characteristic of 'property' is that it is something capable of being owned and transferred. In *New Era Printers and Publishers Ltd v Commissioner of Stamp Duties*, Stringer J held that anything which is owned by one person and can be sold and transferred to another is property within both the popular and legal meanings of the term'. In *Jonathan Dixon v The Queen* [2015] NZSC 147, the NZ Supreme Court held that digital files comprising video CCTV footage held on a computer system could be property for the purposes of the New Zealand Crime Act. They said at paragraph 38 that they considered 'that the fundamental characteristic of 'property' is that it is something capable of being owned and transferred. In *New Era Printers and Publishers Ltd v Commissioner of Stamp Duties*, Stringer J held that anything which is owned by one person and can be sold and transferred to another is property within both the popular and legal meanings of the term'.

[25] See <www.lawsociety.org.uk/policy-campaigns/articles/lawtech-delivery-panel/> accessed 8 July 2021. A public consultation was held on 4 June 2019 in London.

leading experts in the field. The *Legal Statement* has received some favourable judicial consideration.[26]

I do not intend, in this Chapter, to pre-empt the answers that are to be provided by the UKJT's *Legal Statement* with the benefit of the public consultation. What I will say, however, is that even if the answers are obvious, I think it will be useful to state them definitively so that the industry can move forward with a more secure legal understanding.[27]

The principal question in relation to cryptoassets is under what circumstances, if any, either a cryptoasset or a private key would be recognized to be an object of property. Ancillary questions relate to how such objects of property are to be dealt with, which could potentially become problematic in the context of securitization, bailment, and remedies.[28]

Moving on to smart contracts, the principal question is whether a smart contract is capable of giving rise to binding legal obligations, enforceable in accordance with its terms. Ancillary questions include:

(i) How would an English court apply general principles of contractual interpretation to a smart legal contract written wholly or in part in computer code?
(ii) Under what circumstances would an English court look beyond the mere outcome of the running of any computer code that is part of a smart legal contract in determining the agreement between the parties?
(iii) Is a smart legal contract between anonymous or pseudo-anonymous parties capable of giving rise to binding legal obligations?
(iv) Could a statutory signature requirement[29] be met by affixing a private key?

---

[26] See *Ruscoe v Cryptopia Ltd (in Liquidation)* [2020] NZHC 728 (Gendall J); *A v Persons Unknown* [2019] EWHC 3556 (Comm) (Bryan J); and *Quoine Pte Ltd v B2C2 Ltd* [2020] SGCA(I) 02 (Menon CJ).
[27] See <https://technation.io/lawtech-uk-resources/#cryptoassets> accessed 8 July 2021.
[28] Ancillary questions relating to cryptoassets include:

(i) If a cryptoasset is capable of being recognized as property, is it a chose in possession, a chose in action or another form of personal property?
(ii) Is a cryptoasset capable of being the object of a bailment?
(iii) Under what circumstances would a specific unit, as opposed to a fungible cryptoasset, be considered identifiable, as distinct from other units of the same cryptoasset recorded to the same address?
(iv) Can security validly be granted over a cryptoasset?
(v) If so, what forms of security may validly be granted over a cryptoasset?
(vi) Can a cryptoasset be characterized as 'property' for purposes of the Insolvency Act 1986?
(vii) Under what circumstances, if any, would a cryptoasset be characterized as being (a) a documentary intangible or document of title; or (b) an 'instrument' under the Bills of Exchange Act 1882; or (c) negotiable?
(viii) Can cryptoassets be characterized as 'goods' under the Sale of Goods Act 1979?
(ix) Is a distributed ledger recording cryptoassets capable of amounting to a 'register' for the purposes of the Companies Act 2006 or the Uncertificated Securities Regulations 2001?

[29] For example, in the context of a disposition of an equitable interest (under s53(1)(c) Law of Property Act 1925 (LPA)) or of a legal assignment (under s136(1) LPA)?

(v) Could a statutory 'in writing' requirement be met in the case of a smart legal contract composed partly or wholly of computer code?

These questions will be capable of adaptation in most common law jurisdictions, and indeed more broadly. Whilst their answers will, in some respects, be jurisdiction-specific, there will be significant cross-jurisdictional comparisons to be drawn.

Again, without pre-empting the legal statement commissioned by the UKJT, the answer to some of these questions may seem pretty clear; I do not see the question of the legally binding nature of a smart contract as being so complicated as the property question. The juxtaposition of code and prose in a smart contract seems to me quite easily soluble: the parties will decide whether the code or the prose is to govern any given state of affairs within a contractual engagement. Many issues of jurisdiction and dispute resolution can and should be similarly treated. If agreement were to emerge amongst market participants, end-to-end smart legal contracts might become reality.

The question would then become what form legal clarification ought to take. It might give the market confidence if the legislature were to say expressly that a contract composed wholly or partly of computer code were capable of constituting a legally binding contract under English law, but I am far from certain that it is necessary to do so.

F. What Can be Done Once Any Legal Impediments to the Use of Smart Contracts Have Been Identified?

There are, as it seems to me, two possible approaches to achieving the objective of identifying and removing any fundamental legal impediment to the use of smart contracts. One could, as I have said, try to create an entirely fresh statutory regime for the use (and perhaps the regulation) of cryptoassets and smart contracts. Alternatively, one could seek to remove by legislation only the most fundamental legal impediment(s), leaving the common law to do the rest.

In suggesting that the second of these alternatives may be preferable, I am being both pragmatic and adventurous. Pragmatic, because I would not expect an entirely fresh statutory regime to be capable of completion within any reasonably limited timescale. There would need to be a full Law Commission report and consultation, followed by an extended Parliamentary process that would be lengthy in normal times, let alone in the UK's current political circumstances. I am being adventurous, I think, because not all commentators agree that the common law is up to the task that I am suggesting for it. Lord Hodge SCJ has delivered two excellent lectures on this subject. In the most recent one entitled 'The Potential and Perils of Financial Technology: Can the Law adapt to cope?' delivered in Edinburgh on

14 March 2019,[30] he said that it was clear that it was not practicable to develop the common law to create a suitable legal regime for FinTech. He continued by saying that '[t]he judiciary does not have the institutional competence to do so. The changes in the law which are required are not interstitial law the making of which is the long-recognized task of judges; they will require inter-disciplinary policy-making and consultation which a court cannot perform when resolving individual disputes and developing case law'.

How then could the most fundamental legal impediments be removed by legislation, leaving the common law to do the rest? First, let me say that I would no more wish to pre-empt any future work by the Law Commission than I would to anticipate the outcome of the UKJT's deliberations.

As it seems to me, however, if it were clear (a) that a right to value recorded on any kind of distributed ledger is indeed a species of property, and (b) that a smart legal contract composed wholly or partly of computer code is capable of constituting a legally binding contract under English law, I do not see why the other questions posed by the UKJT would not answer themselves.[31] Moreover, I think that many of the ones that remain unclear can be solved by the parties or coders of new smart legal contracts writing some appropriate provisions into their code.

G. Further Questions About Smart, Legally Enforceable Contracts

Questions as to the design and the layers of an end-to-end smart contract will depend on the relationship it is used to structure. In my view, it is difficult to conceptualize the design principles and elements of smart contracts independently of their use-case. There would be considerable value in achieving further clarity on how these protocols are currently being applied and how they are likely to be applied in the near, mid, and longer term.

Some generic questions about the design of smart legal contracts, however, can perhaps usefully be asked at this stage. For example:

(I) Where does an end-to-end smart contract start and finish? What elements or layers does it embrace or implicate?
(II) Are all these layers incorporated by the parties' intentions or are elements implied or imposed by law?
(III) How do the technical and non-technical 'layers' of a smart legal contract interact?

---

[30] See <https://www.supremecourt.uk/docs/speech-190314.pdf> accessed 8 July 2021.
[31] Which is essentially what the *Legal Statement* expressed as its opinion after this Chapter was written.

66   SMART LEGAL CONTRACTS

(IV) How could parties ground their smart contracts in the law of a jurisdiction?
(V) What will determine which jurisdiction they choose?
(VI) How would the principles of private international law operate in this context, especially where the smart contract concerns cryptoassets to which conventional notions like *lex situs* do not straightforwardly apply?
(VII) Will smart contracts always be closely associated with cryptoassets and blockchain data structures?
(VIII) If so, what will those cryptoassets and blockchains look like?[32]

The purpose of this Chapter is to raise, rather than to answer, such questions. However, I think, as I have said, that two points are clear. It is essential that there is a sound and well-understood legal foundation for smart contracts to be built upon. I would not wish to pre-empt what form this legal foundation might take. The most obvious, perhaps, would be a 'wrapper' for the smart contract that specified, in conventional terms, what the code-based parts of the smart contract were intended to do (including their intended legal effect, eg, effecting the transfer of rights).[33]

Secondly, there will need to be some dispute resolution mechanism to give parties confidence to commit funds under smart legal contracts. Parties can do much to make the legal basis of their relationship explicit, and to set out their intentions regarding the interaction between the law and its processes and the code and its processes.[34] The second of these observations is of critical importance and warrants some further elaboration.

H. An Inbuilt Dispute Resolution System for Smart Contracts

An in-built dispute resolution mechanism would, I think, be a desirable feature of any end-to-end smart contract.[35] Parties should obviously think about what will happen when things go wrong before they do. Coders, as I have said, often like

---

[32] Compare IBM's use of blockchain and smart contracts summarized at <https://cointelegraph.com/news/ibms-blockchain-patents-from-food-tracking-and-shipping-to-iot-and-security-solutions>, and the Dubai model at <https://2021.smartdubai.ae/> accessed 8 July 2021.

[33] See eg, Clifford Chance, 'Are Smart Contracts Contracts?' (August 2017), <http://globalmandatoolkit.cliffordchance.com/downloads/Smart_Contracts.pdf> accessed 8 July 2021.

[34] In this context, the steps taken by the International Swaps and Derivatives Association in the context of its Master Agreement are much to be welcomed. See ISDA, 'Legal Guidelines for Smart Derivatives Contracts: Introduction' (January 2019) <https://www.isda.org/a/MhgME/Legal-Guidelines-for-Smart-Derivatives-Contracts-Introduction.pdf>; ISDA, 'Legal Guidelines for Smart Derivatives Contracts: The ISDA Master Agreement' (February 2019), <https://www.isda.org/a/23iME/Legal-Guidelines-for-Smart-Derivatives-Contracts-ISDA-Master-Agreement.pdf> accessed 8 July 2021.

[35] See eg, J. Rogers, H. Jones-Fenleigh, and A. Sanitt, 'Arbitrating Smart Contract Disputes' (2017) 9 *Norton Rose Fulbright International Arbitration Report* 21.

to think that no dispute resolution will be required. But they are wrong, because human beings and corporate entities managed by human beings are likely to enter into smart legal contracts. Such entities are capable of making representations and, therefore, misrepresentations, about the effect of a particular piece of computer code. Coders also need to realize that they themselves may quite genuinely make mistakes. We all can.

There is, of course, much talk of the immutability of code. But it is nonetheless clear that things can and do go awry with computer language, just as they do with legal language. Sometimes we say things we do not mean, or fail to express in words the most important part of our intended meaning.[36] Moreover, the world changes around us in ways that can as much affect the language we have used as it can affect the agreed operation of computer code. The failure of code to capture all contingencies[37] and the danger that vulnerabilities in the code may be exploited by opportunists is evident from the notorious DAO incident.[38] This is a nub of disagreement within the cryptocurrency movement, too. Lawyers have been attuned to this for some time. As Lord Ellesmere said in the *Earl of Oxford's Case*:[39] 'Men's Actions are so divers[e] and infinite, that it is impossible to make any general Law which may aptly meet with every particular Act, and not fail in some Circumstances'.

The courts serve an invaluable role as the ultimate arbiter of disputes between parties where all efforts to reach a commercial solution have failed. But judicial or arbitral adjudication is, in reality, the last instance of dispute resolution. Alternative dispute resolution, including mediation, ODR, and early neutral evaluation, are now well-established online and in commercial and financial centres around the world. Commercial entities will wish to consider what kind of dispute resolution they wish ultimately to adjudicate their disagreements, should they occur. This holds as true for smart contracts, and end-to-end smart legal contracts in particular, as it does in more conventional legal relationships. In terms of smart contracts, one could envisage mechanisms that might halt a smart contract's automatic performance (a) at the behest of one party, (b) with the agreement of both parties, (c) at the discretion of a trusted third party, and/or (d) upon the occurrence of some specific event. There could perhaps be a trade-off between the rigours of immutability and ensuring the existence of satisfactory remedies for impropriety or the unexpected.[40]

---

[36] See *Investors Compensation Scheme Ltd v West Bromwich Building Society* [1998] 1 WLR 896, 913 (Lord Hoffmann).
[37] See J.M. Sklaroff, 'Smart Contracts and the Cost of Inflexibility' (2017) 166 *University of Pennsylvania Law Review* 263.
[38] See S. Falkon, 'The Story of the DAO—Its History and Consequences' (*Start It Up*, 25 December 2017), <https://medium.com/swlh/the-story-of-the-dao-its-history-and-consequences-71e6a8a551ee> accessed 8 July 2021.
[39] *Earl of Oxford's Case* (1615) 21 ER 485.
[40] Since this Chapter was written, the UKJT has published in April 2021 its Digital Dispute Resolution Rules intended as an arbitral or expert process for inclusion in digital transactions including smart contracts. The rules are available at <https://technation.io/lawtech-uk-resources/> accessed 8 July 2021.

My tentative conclusion, therefore, is that one of our first objectives should be to devise a built-in species of dispute resolution specifically designed for smart contracts, so as to ensure a legal infrastructure for future contracting parties. I am thinking of an expedited dispute resolution process entrenched in the code itself, which would allow ultimately for ADR, arbitration or judicial resolution. Such a newly devised approach should not frighten the coders. It would be proportionate and thought through, but it would provide the legal certainty and investor protection that I regard as essential.

This debate has also, in my opinion, some potentially serious implications for the rule of law. Our society has the right to demand that technology and technologists are not exempt from or above the law. That is probably obvious to a lawyer, but it is in this generation by no means a given. In order to win the argument, lawyers and legal systems will need to adapt so as to ensure their future relevance to new forms of transaction.

I. Conclusions

I conclude by returning to the question implied by the title to the lecture on which this Chapter is based: how can the common law (and English law in particular) boost the confidence of would-be parties to smart legal contracts?

First, there needs to be an identification of whether cryptoassets are, or are not, property under English law.[41] If they are not, a quick and simple legislative approach could be considered. Any such approach could, indeed should, recognize the realities of present day financial and economic markets.

Secondly, it is necessary to consider where smart contracts might be used outside the context of cryptoassets. Having done so, it may be hoped that the flexibility and ingenuity of the common law would do the rest. It could surely, with that starting point, solve the issues that have been raised as to the difficulty of taking security over cryptoassets and entering into valid and binding end-to-end smart legal contracts. It will, at that stage, be for the regulators to ensure that they have structures in place to protect against abuse.

As part of what I am suggesting, as I have said, lawyers and our legal system will need to put forward a persuasive case so that all market participants can see the economic benefits of their innovations being governed by a system of law. The main argument will be economics itself in the shape of investor confidence.

---

[41] See the UKJT's *Legal Statement*.

If all that is achieved as a matter of urgency, I would expect the common law, and English law and UK dispute resolution in particular, to prove a popular foundation for the trillions of smart legal contracts that we may then expect to be entered into annually.

I hope this Chapter provides a little food for thought, and I am pleased to see that the questions it has posed have provoked such a rich and varied set of answers in the chapters that follow.

3
Making Smart Contracts a Reality
Confronting Definitions, Enforceability, and Regulation

Justice Aedit Abdullah and Goh Yihan[*]

A. Introduction	70	2. The consideration and exchange problem	76
B. The Definitional Debate: What is a 'Smart Contract'?	71	3. Vitiating factors and smart contracts	76
1. What do we want out of smart contracts?	72	D. The Statutory Regulation of Smart Contracts	78
C. The Enforceability of Smart Contracts	73	E. Conclusion	78
1. Intention and automation	75		

A. Introduction

As Sir Geoffrey Vos rightly puts it in his chapter, the legal treatment of 'smart contracts' has become one of the most important legal subjects of our generation.[1] Even as smart contracts raise interesting possibilities for legal practice, however, there remain a number of important issues that must be dealt with before they can become ubiquitous. In this short chapter, we suggest that the use of smart contracts will require us to confront some basic questions concerning definitions, enforceability and regulation. Answering these basic questions will help to pave the way forward for making smart contracts a reality in legal practice.

---

[*] Justice Aedit Abdullah was appointed Judicial Commissioner in 2014 and High Court Judge of the Supreme Court of Singapore on 30 September 2017. Among other duties, Justice Abdullah is in charge of the transformation and innovation efforts within the Singapore judiciary.

Goh Yihan is Dean and Professor of the Singapore Management University Yong Pung How School of Law. He is Principal Investigator at the SMU's Centre for AI & Data Governance and a Co-Investigator at the Centre for Computational Law. He was appointed Senior Counsel in 2021.

[1] Sir G. Vos, 'End-to-End Smart Legal Contracts: Moving from Aspiration to Reality', Chapter 2 in this volume.

B. The Definitional Debate: What is a 'Smart Contract'?

The fundamental question that should be asked is what really is a 'smart contract'? This is not just an academic question. Indeed, the legal analysis of smart contracts have been rendered difficult (perhaps more difficult than it should be) by inconsistent understandings of this term. If we do not know what it is that we are seeking to promote or regulate, any subsequent discussions about such matters would be problematic.

The starting point would be Nick Szabo's influential, early exposition of the concept. On this analysis, a smart contract is an agreement whose performance is automated.[2] Thus defined, algorithmic contracts which are self-performing amount to smart contracts. This has been termed the *narrow definition* of smart contracts. Similarly, Philip Paech defines a smart contract as 'computer code that is designed automatically to execute contractual duties upon the occurrence of a trigger event'.[3] As he goes on to explain, unlike a traditional contract, the performance of a smart contract cannot be stopped, whether by the parties themselves or a third party. This emphasis on automated performance explains why smart contracts have been linked to blockchain, even though these two technologies were conceived independently of each other. Again, as Paech explains, the certainty of execution is ensured by a blockchain network, since the record of a blockchain network on which a smart contract is stored is supposed to be absolutely immutable and its execution automatic.[4] This ensures that there is no subsequent review of the contract after formation.

In contrast to this narrow conception of a smart contract, Allen has suggested that a 'smart legal contract' is simply a recording of a legal agreement between parties that is written in a language that is both human-intelligible and machine-readable, whose text incorporates an algorithm which automates some or all of the performance of the agreement.[5] This is clearly a *broad definition* that readily transposes 'smart contracts' to many commercial arrangements regardless of the specific technology used. Indeed, this broad understanding of what a smart contract is will often infuse elements of automation, speed and autonomous decision-making alone or together with the core feature of automatic execution.[6] This definition can

---

[2] A. Savelyev, 'Contract Law 2.0: "Smart" Contracts as the Beginning of the End of Classic Contract Law' (2017) 26 *Information & Communications Technology Law* 116, 120.

[3] P. Paech, 'Law and Autonomous Systems Series: What is a Smart Contract?' *Oxford Business Law Blog* (9 July 2018).

[4] *Ibid*.

[5] J.G. Allen, 'Wrapped and Stacked: "Smart Contracts" and the Interaction of Natural and Formal Language' (2018) 14(4) *European Review of Contract Law* 307, 313.

[6] Paech (n. 3).

include smart contracts which can learn from previous decisions and use that information to make future decisions.

What might be a workable definition from these various definitions of a smart contract? While it may be tempting to achieve academic precision, this may not be necessary for a legal analysis of smart contracts. Rather than having to agree *exactly* on what a smart contract is, it is possible to accept that there are different understandings of a smart contract, so long as we are clear what the *functions* of a smart contract can be. In this regard, we need to clearly identify the functional results of the relevant mechanisms.[7] For example, the process may be to perform repetitious actions a human could perform; or it may process unstructured data and perform actions following complex algorithms; or it may learn from previous decisions and their effects.[8] Thus, to take the last example, if the smart contract enables the automatic production of contractual arrangements,[9] legal questions may arise as to the degree of consent needed before the contract is enforceable. This is an example we will explore shortly.

1. What do we want out of smart contracts?

Yet, the application of legal principle to analyse smart contracts is only half the equation. We should also be clear of the clear policy considerations that drive smart contracts. The first is party autonomy. It is trite to say that contract law aims only to facilitate, rather than dictate, what parties can enter into. This is essence of the freedom of contract. The Singapore courts have variously referred to the freedom of contract as the 'norm',[10] and the courts are reluctant to interfere with the parties' choice as to the substance of their agreement. This may be even more so in relation to smart contracts. Paech suggests that the use of smart contracts may lead to the situation where court decisions do not exert the same authority as in the traditional contracting context.[11] This is because, should a party claim that a contract is unenforceable for, say, reasons of illegality, a court cannot, like for a traditional contract, order that the smart contract not be carried out. Similarly, if a party claims that the contract was entered into as a result of a mistake and seeks rectification, a court would likewise be powerless to do anything about the smart contract. This leaves the aggrieved party with only damages, which may sometimes not be the best remedy for that party.[12] Be that as it may, the courts may have to assume that parties enter

---

[7] Ibid.
[8] Ibid.
[9] Ibid.
[10] See, eg, *CKR Contract Services Pte Ltd v Asplenium Land Pte Ltd* [2015] 3 SLR 1041, [17].
[11] Paech (n. 3).
[12] Ibid.

into smart contracts with full knowledge of these consequences, such that the recognition of party autonomy may translate into the courts acknowledging that their powers can be further constrained than with traditional contracts.

Second is the need for certainty. It is again trite to say that contracts are meant to promote certainty for the parties. The contract law of Singapore, which is based on English law but has since developed independently, is able to provide such certainty for contracting parties by the articulation of clear principles. Thus, in order for the same to be said for smart contracts, the law governing them must be clear. In part this flows from understanding the functions we are trying to govern, but it also concerns the broader question of whether statutory intervention is needed to achieve this certainty. At the end, we must not lose sight of the simple fact that parties enter into contracts—smart or otherwise—so that their commercial affairs are governed with certainty.

Finally is the promotion of business efficacy. It should be recognized that there are clear commercial benefits that follow from making smart contracts, however narrowly or broadly they are defined, binding in law.[13] For example, treating smart contracts as enforceable contracts would make them assignable for value. If there is a secondary market in futures contracts for that particular commodity in question, the computer-generated agreements should be tradeable on the secondary market. This requires such contracts to have the same legal status as other agreements. Secondly, the use of smart contracts, especially in financial markets, is a fact regardless of the legal treatment of such agreements. This, by itself, is a sign that doing business through smart contracts is more efficient in some areas than doing it through other media. The law should follow commercial practice and uphold such agreements.[14]

C. The Enforceability of Smart Contracts

If we adopt a functional analysis of smart contracts as we have suggested above, then are they are enforceable by traditional principles of contract law? It is trite law that a contract is enforceable if the parties have shown a mutual intention to be bound and if the contract is supported by consideration. In so far as intention is concerned, both offer and acceptance constitute the traditional theoretical starting points in the formation of a contract under Singapore law.[15] The law in this area

---

[13] T. Allen and R. Widdison, 'Can Computers Make Contracts' (1996) 9 *Harvard Journal of Law & Technology* 25, 50.

[14] *Ibid.*, 51.

[15] This includes implied contracts as well: see the Court of Appeal decision of *Cooperatieve Centrale Raiffeisen-Boerenleenbank BA (Trading as Rabobank International), Singapore Branch v Motorola Electronics Pte Ltd* [2011] 2 SLR 63, [46] and [50].

follows English law and is relatively straightforward, although technical in nature. Indeed, there appears to have been little controversy in practice with regard to the rules in this area of contract law.

The Singapore courts have affirmed the objective principle. For example, in the Court of Appeal decision of *Bakery Mart Pte Ltd (in receivership) v Sincere Watch Ltd*,[16] Chao Hick Tin JA, who delivered the judgment of the court, reaffirmed the basic principle that:

> Where negotiations are protracted the court is entitled to look at all the circumstances and apply an objective test to determine whether the parties had reached an agreement as far as the essential terms are concerned, or whether the parties intended to reserve their rights pending a formal agreement.[17]

How then should these trite principles of formation apply to contracts made by computer systems operating via algorithms? The first point that may be made, as Eliza Mik has suggested, is that contract law does not dictate how agreements should be made.[18] Thus, the intention to contract can be expressed in any manner; this can be done through oral communication, in writing and most certainly, in code. Thus, a contract created through code is just as enforceable as one expressed in a foreign language.[19]

But what of smart contracts that are automatically entered into by algorithms that are programmed to do so automatically? Can we still find the requisite intention in such contracts? Algorithms execute these rules on the basis of data inputs. The decisional parameters and rules for weighting them can be set by the algorithm's designer.[20] Advanced algorithms employ machine learning, in which the algorithm self-adjusts based on its own analyses of data previously encountered, partially freeing the algorithm from predefined preferences. Algorithms have much to offer—indeed, they offer speed, lower transaction costs, and efficiency in decision-making, thereby enabling the user to enjoy lower cost and higher quality products.[21] Furthermore, artificial intelligence coupled with the analysis of big data enable algorithms to make more complex choices. Computer scientists predict that as more data about human actions and choices are accumulated and analysed, algorithms may know us better than ourselves.[22]

---

[16] *Bakery Mart Pte Ltd (in receivership) v Sincere Watch Ltd* [2003] 3 SLR(R) 462.
[17] [2003] 3 SLR(R) 462, [22].
[18] E. Mik, 'Smart Contracts: A Requiem' (2019) 36(1) *Journal of Contract Law* 70.
[19] Ibid.
[20] M.S. Gal, 'Algorithmic Challenges to Autonomous Choice' (2018) 25 *Michigan Telecommunications and Technology Law Review* 59, 65.
[21] Ibid., 61.
[22] Ibid., 61.

1. Intention and automation

This technological change goes to the heart of autonomous human choice.[23] The user, voluntarily and willingly, removes himself from the decision-making process. He still chooses which algorithm to employ and may set at least part of the decision parameters. But other choices then follow automatically. Further, due to developments in deep learning, a process by which the algorithm's decision parameters are continuously updated and refined based on data analysis, the user might have no information about which parameters underlie the algorithm's choice, or how much weight is given to each parameter. Alternatively, the user might not have the capacity or the permission to exercise effective control over the algorithm's choices.[24]

The crucial difference between an algorithm and a person determining terms is that a computer rather than a conscious human being is implementing the rules.[25] When a human makes a choice, ordinary principles of liability and agency clearly link the acts of the human to the company she works for. However, the same may not be possible when algorithms are involved. When we have more complicated algorithms, the ability of a human to anticipate the result of the algorithm is limited. Indeed, as Lauren Scholz points out, this is precisely the reason why we use algorithms: they can consider a breadth of data and number of conditions that no human could.[26] However, decision-making algorithms can have emergent properties, that is, actions in manners not predictable by their developers. How the law should react to algorithmic contracts would depend largely on what the algorithm is doing and the extent of human input.

In sum, there will need to be modifications made to existing contract law to accommodate the formation of contracts made by deterministic algorithms. Specifically there would be a need to decide that human intention need not underlie the making of an offer or an acceptance, at least as far as computer-generated agreements are concerned.[27] In other words, the law would hold that the human trader's generalized and indirect intention to be bound by computer-generated agreements is sufficient to render the agreements legally binding. This would extend the accepted principle that a person who signs a contract without reading it is nonetheless bound by its terms. It is difficult to construct any intention relating to the specific terms of the agreement and the fact that an agreement is made is sufficient.[28]

Thus, applied to computer-generated smart contracts, it might be said that if a person can be bound by signing an unread contract, it would seem reasonable to

---

[23] Ibid., 66.
[24] Ibid., 63.
[25] L.H. Scholz, 'Algorithmic Contracts' (2017) 20 *Stanford Technology Law Review* 128, 134–35.
[26] Ibid., 135.
[27] Allen and Widdison (n. 13), 44.
[28] Ibid., 44.

say that by making the algorithm available, the human operator would be bound by the agreements it generates. As Patrick Atiyah rightly argued, the truth is that a party is bound not so much because of what he intends but because of what he does. He is liable because of what he does for the good reason that other parties are likely to rely upon what he does in ways which are reasonable and even necessary by the standards of our society.[29] In both situations, there is a realization that the relevant acts are likely to result in an agreement on which there will be reliance, and hence there is a sound basis for treating the agreement as a legally binding contract.[30]

2. The consideration and exchange problem

If smart contracts are narrowly defined as computer programmes that enable the performance of obligations pertaining to the transfer of assets, including crypto-assets, then it is clear, as Mik points out, that there is no reciprocity required to constitute consideration under traditional contract doctrine.[31] In this narrow sense, smart contracts operate as a result and in performance of an agreement.[32] The question of enforceability would not even arise in this case because the smart contract is merely a tool to enforce the underlying agreement. However, it is equally clear that if we were to take a broader meaning of smart contracts, questions of reciprocity and consideration must be addressed. This is especially so if we take a functional analysis and regard that smart contracts can be vehicle of agreement itself, as opposed to a tool used to enforce an agreement.

3. Vitiating factors and smart contracts

With the above discussion on formation in mind, how then should the doctrine of mistake be applied to smart contracts that are automatically created pursuant to an algorithm? It is useful as a starting point to consider the possible mistakes that may be made in this situation. In a different context, Chopra and White identify three types of errors that may be relevant for our analysis:[33]

- Specification errors: the algorithm applies its pre-programmed rules, but the rules are not specified carefully enough.

---

[29] Patrick Atiyah, *Essays on Contract* (1990), p 22.
[30] Allen and Widdison (n. 13), 44.
[31] Mik (n. 18).
[32] *Ibid.*
[33] S. Chopra and L. White, 'Artificial Agents and the Contracting Problem: A Solution via an Agency Analysis' (2009) 2 *University of Illinois Journal of Law, Technology & Policy* 363, 371.

- Induction errors: a discretionary algorithm incorrectly inducts from contracts where the user has no objections to a contract the user does object to.
- Malfunction errors: software or hardware problems whereby the principal's rules or parameters for the agent do not result in the intended outcome.

Turning first to specification errors, these errors arise mainly where the algorithm is deterministic. Thus, where the algorithm's rules are not specifically or correctly programmed, an error results. Correspondingly, a mistake that may be operative in law can arise. Specification errors can also arise for non-deterministic algorithms, such as where the parameters of decision are not specified correctly. When the algorithm searches for an answer, an error arises because the specific parameters within which it is supposed to find the answer are not correctly specified. However, specification errors may not be relevant for truly autonomous algorithms since, by definition, such algorithms do not depend on specific programming to operate.

Turning then to induction errors, such errors arise mainly where the algorithm is non-deterministic. This is because the algorithm is here supposed to induce an answer based on the parameters ascribed to it. Correspondingly, where the algorithm makes an error in its determination, albeit within the correct parameters, an induction error arises. This may correspondingly result in an operative mistake in law. This may also apply for truly autonomous algorithms which may induce an answer based on available information, albeit not within a set of pre-programmed parameters. The present state of technology, however, is such that most algorithms are deterministic. Indeed, even so-called non-deterministic algorithms may, broadly speaking, be deterministic in so far as the decision-making parameters are all fixed beforehand.

Finally, turning to malfunction errors, it is quite clear that this can apply to all kinds of algorithms, since these errors are a result of a software or hardware issue that can arise regardless of the nature of the algorithm concerned.

It must again be said that these types of errors are not exhaustive. But they give a good starting point with which to understand how errors (and correspondingly, legally operative mistakes) can arise in the context of smart contracts entered into by algorithms.

Many of the issues surveyed above can probably be addressed by incremental developments in the common law. Some which are foundational may call for regulatory intervention to at least put these contracts on a firmer doctrinal footing. But an important area for possible legislative intervention which cannot be readily left to the common law is in the protection of consumers and others who may be at a disadvantage in navigating the demands of smart contracts. Similar concerns will also inform the statutory regulation of smart contracts to be discussed in the next section.

D. The Statutory Regulation of Smart Contracts

The common law is of course a reactionary creature, in that it reacts to disputes brought before it but does not generally prescribe for scenarios that have not arisen. Thus, the certainty needed for smart contracts to flourish cannot be provided by the common law on its own but will require a legislative framework that addresses the fundamental issues clearly and unambiguously. However, such a legislative framework also cannot be taken too far, as a code would likely stifle the future growth of the law in this area. Thus, alongside that legislative framework, sufficient room for flexibility and incremental development must come from case law that interprets the legislation.

There have been, as Mik suggests, multiple attempts to regulate smart contracts.[34] One example she raises is the statute passed by the Arizona state legislature in February 2017 which provides that 'smart contracts may exist in commerce. A contract relating to a transaction may not be denied legal effect, validity or enforceability solely because that contract contains a smart contract term'.[35] Such a statute is a good example of one which declares that smart contracts are enforceable, subject to conditions and definitions that it lays down. This is helpful because, until smart contracts come before the courts, the courts cannot declare on their own accord that smart contracts are enforceable and, if so, on what terms. In a fast moving space like smart contracts, it is helpful for the legislature to step in at an early stage and clarify basic questions surrounding smart contracts, such as their enforceability. Such clarificatory attempts should not too radically change the law. After all, as we have briefly canvassed, traditional contract law can be applied to smart contracts with little modification. It would cause too much uncertainty if statutes were designed to upend that stability.

E. Conclusion

Ultimately, the way forward requires the courts and legislature to grapple with the key foundation principles at play: party autonomy, respecting the need for certainty and business efficacy. Both the legislative framework and the case law must also respect the likely development that some, if not many, of those using smart contracts will probably want systems that are almost wholly self-contained (aside from necessary oracles), minimizing outside involvement or reference to external provisions or decision makers, such as judges. The law and the courts should respect such self-containment as a manifestation of party autonomy, save for areas where wider public interest, such as public order or morality, and the protection of the vulnerable, calls for intervention.

---

[34] Mik (n. 18).
[35] Ariz Rev Stat 44-7061 (2017).

4
Smart Contracts and Dispute Resolution
Faster Horses or a New Car?

*Justice Stephen Estcourt AM**

A. Introduction	79	2. Blockchain-based functional alternatives to legal processes	82
B. Smart Legal Contracts and Dispute Resolution	80	3. Recent developments in England and Wales	84
1. The challenge for conventional law	81	C. Conclusion	85

A. Introduction

In the opening chapter of this volume, Sir Geoffrey Vos makes the point that the emerging body of learning on 'smart contracts' has proceeded in waves, and that the current wave of literature is characterized by dialogue between lawyers and others (particularly technologists and entrepreneurs) that have traditionally taken a 'disruptive' approach to law. That kind of dialogue is typified by this volume itself. The major thesis of Sir Geoffrey's article is that the common law, and in particular English law, is in a good position to provide the necessary legal infrastructure to facilitate 'end-to-end smart legal contracts'—which he defines quite broadly as contracts with code-driven elements—provided any necessary legislative reforms are kept to a minimum. This, he says, is because the matter brings the advantages of the common law sharply into focus: 'It is dependable and predictable and able to build on clear principles so as to apply them to new commercial situations.'[1] I agree wholeheartedly with his observation that 'smart legal contracts' will only begin to

---

* Justice Stephen Estcourt AM is a Judge of the Supreme Court of Tasmania. Prior to his appointment in 2013, Justice Estcourt practiced as a Queen's Counsel, principally in commercial and administrative law practice in the appellate courts of Victoria. A former president of the Australian Bar Association and a Foundation Fellow of the Australian Academy of Law, Justice Estcourt has a special interest in the application of emerging technology to the judicial system.

[1] See chapter 2. Thanks to the editors Jason Grant Allen and Peter Hunn for their comments on the draft of this chapter.

be widely used for mainstream applications when they clearly provide for the legal enforceability of their contractual provisions.

He offers the tentative conclusion that one of the first objectives should be to devise a built-in species of dispute resolution, entrenched in the contract code itself, so as to ensure a legal infrastructure for future contracting parties. In this chapter, by way of reply, I will engage with the question of dispute resolution in the context of 'smart legal contracts'. Sir Geoffrey has in mind an expedited dispute resolution process, which would allow ultimately for alternate dispute resolution, arbitration, or judicial resolution. I agree with the thrust of that conclusion; however, my inclination is that what will emerge is a new species of dispute resolution existing, to a certain extent, in tension with the legal system as we know it. The question is the extent of that tension and how it is to be resolved. I would like respectfully to offer the view that, even if one assumes that the current literature demonstrates that the protagonists are engaging in a conciliatory understanding of each other's position, the emergence of autonomous, decentralized, third-party dispute resolution applications are likely to become attractive to consumers, at least in certain contexts. Such systems will enable the filling of the void in end-to-end 'smart' contracts constituted by the absence of a mechanism for, not just the recording of their terms and their performance in the ordinary course, but complete performance and enforcement in the event of an alleged breach.

B. Smart Legal Contracts and Dispute Resolution

Sir Geoffrey makes, with respect, the very valid point that, despite the close association of smart contracts with blockchain technology, a broad definition of 'smart contracts' is possible that is technology neutral. Writing in 2018, Jason Allen observed that the various distributed ledger technologies on which 'smart contracts' rely are still new, and their use is evolving.[2] He argued that '[t]hough it means tracking a moving target, it is necessary for lawyers and legal academics to define what exactly we are dealing with'.[3] I agree. Taking a firmly 'legal' perspective open to the role of emerging technologies in contracting, Allen argued that there is no barrier in principle even to a single contractual instrument, written in 'formal' (coded) language, embodying both the agreement between the parties and an automated mechanism for its performance. Although it deviates from some other approaches to 'smart contracts', this must also be true. Indeed, I would suggest that unless the automation of both contractual performance and/or enforcement are achieved through the execution of coded actions— autonomously, yet intelligible

---

[2] J.G. Allen, 'Wrapped and Stacked: "Smart Contracts" and the Interaction of Natural and Formal Language' (2018) 14(4) *European Review of Contract Law* 307, 310.
[3] Ibid.

to humans—then it cannot be said that the contract is anything more than a document recording an agreement coupled with an executable mechanism for consideration if the parties' obligations under their agreement are fulfilled uneventfully. Absent such dual, automated functions, smart 'contracts' (if they could be called that at all) would be constrained in their scope of their commercial application.

1. The challenge for conventional law

It is for these reasons that global, open-source, decentralized systems, such as Ethereum,[4] are likely to provide the technological foundation for new forms of contractual co-ordination and dispute resolution. Indeed, it is my own view that the march of artificial intelligence will inevitably see consumer demand for quicker and cheaper outcomes to commercial disagreements. So many facets of daily life and commerce will be amenable to faster outcomes that it is difficult to imagine that society will remain satisfied with the leisurely pace of the current judicial process. It is of note in this regard that Sir Geoffrey sets out the opinion of Lord Hodge, that it is clearly not practicable to develop the common law to create a suitable regime for fintech[5] because 'the judiciary does not have the institutional competence to do so' and because the changes in the law 'will require inter-disciplinary policy making and consultation.'[6] Moreover, as Allen points out,[7] 'the problem is sharpened by the self-executing nature of smart contracts and by the potential for parties to transact in contravention of national law and its institutions.'[8]

Courts may still be involved with questions as to how legal doctrine should be applied when contracts are drawn up and executed by computer systems with limited human involvement.[9] However, smart contracts formed and automatically enforced *via* the medium of these systems will not always require—or allow without some preliminary process—recourse to the law or the courts. 'Turing-complete' smart contracts are arbitrarily programmable, meaning developers can use them to build any kind of application. These decentralized applications known as 'dapps' may be said to be 'trustless' in the sense that they will run as programmed, without the need for (or, in many instances, the possibility of) intervention. They will almost certainly be the vehicles for some 'smart contracts' intended

---

[4] See <https://www.ethereum.org>. See also V. Buterin, 'A Next-Generation Smart Contract and Decentralised Application Platform' <https://github.com/ethereum/wiki/wiki/White-Paper> accessed 8 July 2021.
[5] The integration of technology into offerings by financial services companies in order to improve their use and delivery to consumers.
[6] Lord Hodge, 'The Potentials and Perils of Financial Technology: Can the Law Adapt to Cope?' (First Edinburgh Fintech Law Lecture, University of Edinburgh, 14 March 2019) <https://www.supremecourt.uk/docs/speech-190314.pdf>.
[7] Allen (n. 2), 332.
[8] Allen (n. 2), 332.
[9] *Quoine Pte Ltd v B2C2 Ltd* [2020] SGCA(I) 02.

by parties to be 'real' contracts. The apparent rise and rise of 'decentralized finance' or 'DeFi' in the last two years is an indication of the potential for blockchain protocols to enable financial innovation that does not always sit within established legal categories or regulatory perimeters, for example in the lack of a centralized intermediary. The details of the legal treatment of these new transaction flows is still being worked out.

Alongside the 'smart contract' phenomenon is the more familiar problem that the Internet (and associated technologies) facilitates transactions within and across jurisdictional borders, making conventional oversight, enforcement, and adjudication more complex. This is giving rise to a new category of cross-border disputes that may not be well-served, even by established alternative dispute resolution mechanisms such as arbitration.[10] Because globalisation and digitisation both, at once, *enable* and *require* contracts to be negotiated and formed over the Internet, it is difficult to see how contracting parties will not look to online solutions to disputes arising from their agreements. That is to say, that the age has been reached when consumers of dispute resolution will be able to opt for a system based on simplicity, efficiency and economy, and may well be prepared to do so, even at the cost of the loss of intimate involvement in a human managed process and the loss of the imprimatur of a state court. This is where conventional judicial processes will face competition from private sector providers, who are seizing the opportunity to provide parallel means of dispute resolution through technological innovations.

2. Blockchain-based functional alternatives to legal processes

Blockchain-based dispute resolution systems[11] represent one of these core innovations. The fundamental rationale underpinning blockchain-based dispute resolution systems is that online commercial co-ordination should be resolved through online means of dispute resolution. The juxtaposition of an online economy characterized by automation, pseudonymity, and decentralization with offline institutions and traditional methods of rendering justice is stark. Blockchain-based dispute resolution systems seek to provide a means of administering justice in a manner commensurate with the form and manner of the co-ordination between the parties.

---

[10] S. Nappert and F. Ast, 'Decentralized Justice: Reinventing Arbitration for the Digital Age?' (2020) *Global Arbitration Review*. Cf. B.E. Howell and P.H. Potgieter, 'Uncertainty and Dispute Resolution for Blockchain and Smart Contract Institutions' (2021) *Journal of Institutional Economics* 1.

[11] See eg, Kleros (C. Lesaege and F. Ast 'Kleros, Short Paper v1.0.7' (2018) <https://kleros.io/whitepaper.pdf>; Aragon (Aragon Network Whitepaper), <https://github.com/aragon/whitepaper>; Jur, White Paper v3.0.0 (March 2021), <https://jur.io/wp-content/uploads/2019/05/jur-whitepaper-v.2.0.2.pdf> all accessed 8 July 2021.

The archetypal system is designed to function as a decentralized, autonomous third party, to arbitrate disputes through blockchain-based 'smart contracts'.[12] This 'third party' is typically comprised of a number of pseudonymous 'jurors', often algorithmically selected, that vote to resolve a dispute in favour of given party. Each stage of the process is algorithmically defined in the 'on-chain' smart contract. Invariably, at the start of a transaction, an on-chain cryptoasset escrow is initiated using a smart contract. The escrow will encode the conditions—typically release by a counterparty or the arbitral third party—for the release of the cryptoasset. In the event that the counterparty does not release the escrowed asset, the transacting parties may resort to the dispute resolution mechanism incorporated into the smart contract. The arbitral procedure is defined by the specific system used. The parties may define the parameters, such as the number of 'jurors' that may vote on the outcome and the available remedies, prior to formation of the smart contract. Typically, the party escrowing the asset may elect to execute the arbitral process at any point after the formation and instantiation of the smart contract. The exact procedural details will depend upon the system being used and the parameters defined, *ex ante*, if any. Most systems require the parties to provide evidence, often without a defined discovery process or procedural rules, to support their argument. Jurors often have little to no latitude to compel further evidential discovery. Similarly, parties are often afforded no ability to counter or rebut arguments.[13] The dispute is resolved, subject to any appeal process, often by an (economically incentivized) simple majority vote.[14] Jurors that vote in the majority typically receive tokens (a form of cryptoasset native to the dispute resolution system) staked by jurors in the minority.

This arbitral form, whilst nascent, may indicate the future of online dispute resolution. As Federico Ast, founder of Ethereum-based dispute resolution platform 'Kleros', has quipped (by reference to an apocryphal attribution), if Henry Ford had asked his customers what they wanted they would have said 'faster horses', not cars.[15] It remains to be seen how such smart contract-based systems are used in practice. It is likely that such systems represent a component of the justice system as commercial arrangements become increasingly digital in form and function. This is increasingly true, in my assessment, unless there is jural engagement not only in the emergence of blockchain applications but also in the adaptation to

---

[12] See Y. Aouidef *et al.*, 'Decentralised Justice: A Comparative Analysis of Blockchain Online Dispute Resolution Projects' (2021) 4 *Frontiers in Blockchain* Article 564551.
[13] An appeal process may be incorporated, but often involves the addition of more jurors rather than a formal process for litigating the merits of a prior finding. See, eg, <https://blog.kleros.io/the-kleros-juror-starter-kit> accessed 2 March 2022.
[14] Often supported by Schelling point game theory: W. George, 'Kleros and Mob Justice: Can the Wisdom of the Crowd Go Wrong?' (2018) <https://medium.com/kleros/kleros-and-mob-justice-can-the-wisdom-of-the-crowd-go-wrong-ef311209ea36> accessed 8 July 2021.
[15] 'Cryptoeconomics: Can blockchain reinvent justice systems?' <https://blogs.thomsonreuters.com/answerson/cryptoeconomics-blockchain-reinvent-justice-sytems-kleros/> accessed 8 July 2021.

formal language of the traditional language of open textured contract law concepts such as, for example, 'good faith' and 'co-operation' or 'best endeavours' and 'reasonable delay'.

3. Recent developments in England and Wales

Despite the significant technological advances that make these systems possible, equally significant development remains necessary for their maturation into a genuinely parallel juridical system. There are valid concerns with the quality of private decentralized dispute resolution processes,[16] procedurally, substantively, and legally. The economic incentive mechanisms and absence of guidance for pseudonymous jurors may impact the integrity and quality of outcomes. Encoding procedures through smart contracts may constrain the ability to satisfactorily address disputes beyond a certain degree of complexity. This is certainly true in respect of the ability to adequately encode suitable evidence management processes into the systems in order to provide users with the appropriate mix of efficiency and rigour in the administration of disputes. These concerns, ultimately, have ramifications for the rule of law. The 'coherence' of a decision, for example, may not guarantee that it is 'legal' in any traditional sense—either that it will be accepted by a court in parallel or subsequent proceedings, or indeed that its substance or procedure reflects the demands of any 'legal system' properly so called. Sir Geoffrey concludes that the smart contract dispute resolution debate has potentially serious implications for the rule of law and that society has the right to demand that technology and technologists are not exempt from or above the law. Again, I respectfully agree, and I agree also that in this generation that is by no means a given. He suggests that 'in order to win the argument, lawyers and legal systems will need to adapt so as to ensure their future relevance to new forms of transaction'.[17]

In this regard, the recent work of the UK Jurisdiction Taskforce ('UKJT'), chaired by Sir Geoffrey, gives cause for optimism. Following its landmark—and so far well-accepted[18]—*Legal Statement on Cryptoassets and Smart Contracts* of 2019, the UKJT turned its attention to online dispute resolution and in early 2021 released the first version of its *Digital Dispute Resolution Rules* ('the Rules').[19] The Rules can be incorporated into a contract, digital asset (blockchain 'smart contract') or digital

---

[16] See Howell and Potgieter (n. 10).
[17] See Sir G. Vos MR, 'End-to-End Smart Legal Contracts: Moving from Aspiration to Reality', Chapter 2 in this volume.
[18] In *AA v Persons Unknown* [2019] EWHC 3556 (Comm), for example, the *Legal Statement* was cited with approval by Bryan J.
[19] UK Jurisdiction Taskforce, 'Digital Dispute Resolution Rules', <https://technation.io/lawtech-uk-resources/#rules> accessed 8 July 2021.

asset system. Their stated purpose is to facilitate the 'rapid and cost-effective resolution of commercial disputes', particularly those involving emerging technologies including cryptoassets, cryptocurrency, 'smart contracts', distributed ledger technology, and fintech applications.

The Rules allow parties to resolve disputes by arbitration rather than judicial determination. Unlike other arbitration rules, a key objective is maximise flexibility in the procedure to ensure suitability to the technologies concerned, and to ensure speedy determination by arbiters with the necessary technical expertise. They are short, provide for a speedy process, and encourage the use of technology in that process. They 'interoperate' with the Arbitration Act 1996, which sets out default alternatives for circumstances not expressly dealt with by the Rules themselves. The Rules further allow for expert determination of particular issues in a dispute subject by party agreement.

They are novel in allowing for arbitration on a very short turnaround with decisions implemented 'on-chain' and are tailored to provide optional anonymity for the parties to a dispute resolved under them. They avoid the potentially difficult choice of law problems that arise with geographically distributed parties through choice of law (and would appear designed to encourage the choice of English law). Of relevance in light of the foregoing discussion, the Rules accept peer-to-peer and other online processes as 'automatic dispute resolution processes' and makes their outcome legally binding. They seek to provide a default framework that 'wraps' such automatic dispute resolution processes, within which secondary disputes—such as whether the procedural integrity or proper functioning of the automatic process. Drafted with extensive consultation with the technical community, the Rules seem to have found initial favour with smart contract-based dispute resolution systems.[20] This is particularly notable as they provide a framework to address a number of the issues identified with current system design.

C. Conclusion

Initiatives like the Rules provide some deeper insight into the question whether the conventional law—with or without extensive legislative intervention—is capable of delivering something more than a 'faster horse' itself, and whether it is capable of accommodating private sector innovations. The reference to horses invites a few reflections on the broader themes in this volume. In an influential speech on 'Property in Cyberspace' Judge Frank Easterbrook warned against the proliferation of sub-disciplines within the law based on current technological developments.

---

[20] See *ibid.*, [8].

The best way to learn about the law applicable to niche endeavours, he argued, was to 'study general rules':

> Lots of cases deal with sales of horses; others deal with people kicked by horses; still more deal with the licensing and racing of horses, or with the care veterinarians give to horses, or with prizes at horse shows. Any effort to collect these strands into a course on "The Law of the Horse" is doomed to be shallow and to miss unifying principles.[21]

The 'Law of Cyberspace', was, he argued, susceptible to the law of the horse critique. The answer was to 'develop a sound law of intellectual property, and then *apply* it to computer networks.'[22] The current work on the application of property law principles to digital assets might inspire a different conclusion today,[23] but this is a salutary warning to focus on the legal substance of new developments rather than accepting their novelty at face value. The law's conventional categories and processes are *prima facie* capable of application to new technologies, and too much legal pre-emption of what those technologies are would unduly constrain their very development. The Fords of this world should be allowed to provide the market with automobiles, not just faster horses.

A little later, against this argument—which he observed to be an odd way to open a conference on 'The Law of Cyberspace' in 1996—Lawrence Lessig argued that legal perceptions and rules would need to evolve with the growth and evolution of cyberspace itself.[24] Pointing to the different modes of 'regulation' that might apply to any given action,[25] Lessig pointed to the law, extra-legal social norms, the market, and the 'architecture' of the relevant domain of interaction—then the Internet, now also DLT and 'Web 3.0'. According to this argument, the software that constitutes cyberspace *implies* a set of constraints on how one can behave within it. While the substance of the constraints vary, the protocols that determine them are selected by those writing the code and are 'regulative' in the same way that the architecture of 'real space' is regulative—think of geographical distance or a speed bump. The constraints encoded within any domain of cyberspace reflect, in turn, the values of those encoding them. These values might favour copyright consumers or copyright owners, for example.

Saliently to the question at hand, Lessig turned to the idea of 'code displacing contracts'. Because cyberspace has the appearance of being *prima facie* free of

---

[21] Judge F. Easterbrook, 'Cyberspace and the Law of the Horse' (1996) *University of Chicago Legal Forum* 207, 207.
[22] Ibid., 208.
[23] For example, the UNIDROIT Study LXXXII on Digital Assets and Private Law, <https://www.unidroit.org/work-in-progress/digital-assets-and-private-law>.
[24] L. Lessig, 'The Law of the Horse: What Cyberspace Might Teach' (1999) 113(2) *Harvard Law Review* 501.
[25] See also L. Lessig, 'The New Chicago School' (1998) 27 *Journal of Legal Studies* 661.

'legal' constraints, it was then (and is now) often said that contract, rather than 'law', governs online behaviour.[26] An architectural feature (such as the need to provide your name to access an Internet domain in which a service is provided) is, indeed, often understood as a contractual matter—a conditional offer of access, on the provider side, and acceptance of that condition, on the user side. But, although they might have a contractual 'wrapper' (such as in an end user license agreement), the bare fact of an architectural constraint is not, itself, a 'contract'. In particular, the kind of public values that underlie every 'enforced contract'—what the contemporary debate might call a 'legal contract'—are absent in the case of a bare architectural feature.[27] In 'real space', obligations are conditioned by norms of competition law, consumer protection, principles of equity, and remedies such as rectification, too:

> The cyberspace analogue has no equivalent toolbox. Its obligations are not conditioned by the public values that contract law embraces. Its obligations instead flow automatically from the structures imposed in the code. These structures serve the private ends of the code writer; they are a private version of contract law. But as the Legal Realists spent a generation teaching, and as we seem so keen to forget: contract law is public law. "Private public law" is oxymoronic.[28]

Whatever one's preference on the question of private legal ordering, Lessig's concerns go directly to the heart of the questions this volume sets out to explore, and indeed to the concept of 'smart *legal* contracts' itself. In my view, it underlines the importance of ensuring, as the Rules have sought to do, that code-based dispute resolution alternatives that would appear to challenge law's inherent regulative function should be integrated into the broader fabric of the legal system. The next few years will be crucial in the development of legal rules and procedures that are appropriate and adapted to the needs of delocalized and decentralized markets. As typified in the present volume, the collaborative effort of judges, legal practitioners and scholars, technical experts and entrepreneurs to shape that development will be crucial.

---

[26] Lessig (n. 30), 530.
[27] *Ibid.*
[28] *Ibid.*, 531.

5
Why the Ricardian Contract Came About
A Retrospective Dialogue with Lawyers

*Ian Grigg**

A. Introduction	88	5. The hash as identifier	99
B. The Origins of the 'Riccy'	89	6. The form of the contract	99
1. Research	90	D. Random Experiences on the	
2. Deep dive	91	Ricardian Journey	100
3. Resistance level	92	1. Contracting, not contracts	102
C. The War of the Wordsmiths	93	E. Enter 'Smart Contracts'	102
1. A practical computer-contract places		1. The Bitcoin unit	103
human first	94	2. The sum of all chains	104
2. A signed digital—readable—document	94	3. The governed blockchain	105
3. Markup	96	F. Conclusion	105
4. The identifier	98		

A. Introduction

How do you issue a financial instrument onto the Internet? How do you securely negotiate a financial agreement over the Internet, and not end up in court? How do you capture all of the legal significance of a deal in such a way as to reduce confusions and empower traders? The Ricardian Contract is a tool to meet these goals—a method to capture the essence of any deal for Internet trading.[1] This chapter will show how it came to be, and why it came to take the form it took. It will also show its relationship to the current topic of 'smart contracts'.

---

* Ian Grigg is a pioneer financial cryptographer who created the world's first cryptographically secured 'virtual exchange' in 1996 with digital cash and assets expressed as Ricardian Contracts. He co-invented triple entry accounting, a concept that does for events *between* firms what double entry accounting did to accounts *inside* the firm. Today, Ian dedicates his primary efforts to innovations in social savings and identity. An early version of this article was presented at R3's first Smart Contract Templates Summit, London/New York 2016.

[1] I. Grigg, 'The Ricardian Contract' (2004) IEEE 1st Workshop on Electronic Contracting <http://iang.org/papers/ricardian_contract.html> accessed 6 July 2021.

Ian Grigg, *Why the Ricardian Contract Came About* In: *Smart Legal Contracts*. Edited by: Jason Grant Allen and Peter Hunn, Oxford University Press. © Jason Grant Allen & Peter Hunn 2022. DOI: 10.1093/oso/9780192858467.003.0006

In early 1995 I was sitting in Finance 1 classes at London Business School learning about the marvels of the 'zero coupon bond'. The 'zero' is a promise to pay a sum on a date. An issuer will write a zero coupon bond to raise capital to finance good works, do those works, and pay back slightly more on the stated date; their peculiarity is that it is hard to get anything simpler as a financial instrument.

This very simplicity gives the zero a special role in finance: we can build a *mathematica financia* or financial language modelled on debt. A dollar due on a given date can be used to compose many advanced financial products. For example, take a zero and make it defaultable: it could pay out, or not pay out by a certain date. Add an event by which it does not pay out, and we now have an *option*. Apply mathematics to the option over the zero and we eventually get Black-Scholes, the formula that predicts a price for the option, and arguably did more than any other factor to drive the modern finance industry in the late twentieth century.[2] The takeaway here is that the zero is the *atomic unit of finance*. The relevance of this was to be found in Amsterdam, seat of the world's oldest stock exchange—and in the 1990s, the start of a new revolution in finance.

B. The Origins of the 'Riccy'

In Amsterdam, my cypherpunk friend Gary Howland was working with other cryptographers and programmers to make an entirely new and interesting form of the dollar: David Chaum's invention of 'digital cash' that could be transmitted across the Internet and arrive safely and *untraceably* at a recipient.[3] In the mid-1990s, this cryptographic money was terribly exciting; the web was only just seeping onto the public consciousness, and already e-commerce was squeaking its first post-natal cries—*where's the money?* Chaum's eCash was the answer. The money was everywhere, nowhere and in Amsterdam, all at the same time; his formula to preserve monetary privacy was a sensation in an already hyperbolic market inspired by the browser, the World Wide Web, and thousands of startups. While watching my professor turn one zero into many—into options, the Ho Lee binomial model, into Black-Scholes—my mind was swirling with the impact of this new Internet dollar.

Suddenly, in class, it clicked into place: eCash was more or less a zero coupon bond. There was no explicit payment date, but so what? If we could issue a dollar on the net, we could also issue a zero, and if we could do that, we could use the finance techniques unfolding on the board in front of me to issue practically everything else. This connection brought the excitement of the new Internet, the new

---

[2] On the Black-Scholes model, see M. Del Giudice, F. Evangelista, and M. Palmaccio, 'Defining the Black and Scholes Approach: A First Systematic Literature Review' (2015) 5 *Journal of Innovation and Entrepreneurship* 5.
[3] D. Chaum, 'Blind Signatures for Untraceable Payments' (1983) 82(3) *Advances in Cryptology Proceedings of Crypto* 199–203.

eCash to the boring old zero, to finance classes, and to me. If eCash was exciting to geeks and boring to the City, what was exciting in finance? Derivatives! Shares! Commodities! Especially, derivatives could be constructed as composites of the zero coupon bond and complicated formula followed. Efficient market hypothesis! Black-Scholes! Profits!

If I could reduce Chaum's eCash into the tokens of finance known as zeroes, I could also issue all of the financial instruments that humanity had dreamed of. Suddenly, eCash became exciting to financiers as well as geeks. In 1994, DigiCash did not appear to be thinking of finance, but Nick Szabo was:

> Another area that might be considered in smart contract terms is synthetic assets. These new securities are formed by combining securities (such as bonds) and derivatives (options and futures) in a wide variety of ways. Very complex term structures for payments (i.e., what payments get made when, the rate of interest, etc.) can now be built into standardized contracts and traded with low transaction costs, due to computerized analysis of these complex term structures. Synthetic assets allow us to arbitrage the different term structures desired by different customers, and they allow us to construct contracts that mimic other contracts, minus certain liabilities.[4]

1. Research

Gary Howland and I resolved to give it a go—to build a crypto system to issue any financial instrument on the net, and trade it. Like many computer scientists in the 1990s, we embarked on a journey to build an Internet of finance, a long journey that in time became known as 'Ricardo' after the British Economist who discovered that free trade is better for everyone. Gary Howland concentrated on the lower cryptosystem, called SOX, and I concentrated on the higher financial application.[5] My first step was to research all of the financial instruments out there and pick one as a minimum viable product. I chose bonds because I perceived them to be simple, because I had studied them in class, and because the market was easy to enter. Bonds were simpler than other financial instruments. Equity, for example, was harder to model; commodities required an underlying; derivatives included all their own complexity as well as reference to an underlying. The simplicity of the bond's certain payouts was attractive. Bonds were also lightly regulated in comparison to some other types of security, making for a market that seemed to have

---

[4] N. Szabo, 'Smart Contracts' 1994 originally: szabo.best.vwh.net/smart.contracts.html but can be found at <https://web.archive.org/web/20011102030833/http://szabo.best.vwh.net/smart.contracts.html> accessed 6 July 2021.

[5] G. Howland, 'The Development of an Open and Flexible Payment System', 1996 <http://systemics.com/docs/sox/overview.html>.

low barriers to entry—important for a small fintech startup. Either way, rightly or wrongly, at the time I perceived bonds to be a market that was easy to enter.

What complexity did exist in bonds was found in two parts:

- **a set of coupons** of fairly definable dates and payments, which from a programmatic perspective seemed quite tractable, and
- **a set of terms and conditions** which I felt also could be modelled, indeed which intuitively I felt was easy to model.

It may strike the reader at this point that choosing bonds was naïve and misinformed. In retrospect, it was naïve, as the ease of entry was only superficial. In practice, corporate bonds were a big boys' game—only the largest corporations issued bonds, and nations and supra-nations were the favourites. Banks and brokers were the intermediaries, and unlike today, the holders of last resort. All the players were quasi-regulated or directly-regulated in some fashion, so this was a market easily defended. I was to find that not only would a fintech upstart not be able to enter this market, I'd have to create an entirely new market—eg, small bonds to small companies. Inept indeed for a self-claimed student of strategy, but this mistake was critical to that which followed.

2. Deep dive

I then turned to investigate what complexity existed in a bond, because I reasoned that we had to capture all that complexity into our system. In those days, bonds on paper still existed, and it was possible to identify the basics more easily by looking at the old paper-issued debt instruments. A typical bond is a document with three major components:

- **A set of parameters:** an issuer, a face value, a date of payment, an amount for interest payments, a schedule. These were regular and easy to model in computable-name, value pairs.
- **'Coupons':** dated payments of interest. Finance classes had taught me that each coupon was just another zero coupon bond and therefore, if I could figure out the general case of how to issue a zero coupon bond problem, then I'll have solved the problem for coupons as well.
- **The fine print:** the terms and conditions that varied the basic or standardized form.

I declared the first and second parts easy, which left the fine print. As a computer scientist, I was convinced that the field of law was overdue for disruption, and that clearly we could model the content into some form of database layout or domain-specific language. Especially when the terms were clearly laid out, as on many older bonds. Most modern bonds, however, had been computerized, and had adopted much more complex prose for their terms. The model was the same, but it seemed that, as we left behind the discipline imposed by needing to fit it all on a single piece of paper, the quantity of clauses exploded.

At some point, I realized that a bond was nothing more and nothing less than a contract, which was serendipitous because—although all financial instruments are contracts at heart—only the bond so clearly presents itself in this way. Contracts were a new mystery, but they too were modelled by lawyers as a set of 'elements':

- A party and a counterparty,
- An offer and an acceptance,
- Consideration of goods or services in one direction balanced by considerations of cash in the other,
- Terms and conditions.

I felt that the complexity of finance was unravelling: there was a contract agreed at the beginning, and there was performance of that agreement to follow. This separation of the lifecycle of the bond into two separate spaces led to a glimmer of hope—if we could render that division into code, dividing agreement, and performance would make the job of each of the halves so much easier. Understanding the bond contract then appeared as a (complicated) task of reducing legal English into a database of fields. I charged into terms and conditions with gusto. I would reduce the whole lot into tag-values or SQL[6] tables or expressions or language or something. Then, the rest of the accounting system that Gary Howland was building could handle the performance from all this information. This I could do because I was a Computer Scientist!

3. Resistance level

Yet, the bond resisted. The clauses were not that clear, nor standardized, nor even settled. I discovered that each and every issuance of debt copied from its forebears, but each new bond was an opportunity to tweak, to fix, to turn the conditions for some kind of incremental benefit. Bond legal prose tended to grow over time, in ways that we could not predict; no two bonds were directly equivalent. This was an important challenge—why would anyone trust their valuations to a new cryptographic system that failed to capture all that was in a bond?

---

[6] SQL is a domain-specific language used in programming, typically for relational databases.

I also discovered a pattern of fighting the last war: every bond debacle would result in new clauses. The cynical amongst us would say the lawyers were turning opportunity into fees, but it is human nature to tinker, and indeed there are always improvements to make. Worse than continuous evolution, I got the sinking feeling that the use of language was combative—it could be used to hide asymmetries which favoured the issuer over the holder. My unfortunate conclusion, then, was that it was impossible to convert all of the English language as used in bonds into a data language or schema so long as it was under the Byzantine influence of legal wordsmiths.

C. The War of the Wordsmiths

That left some options. Could I get rid of the wordsmiths? No—not in my lifetime, nor the lifetime of our startup. Would a suitably good algebraic formulation render the English prose redundant? No—for better or worse, some of the concepts could only be explained in human language for reasons of vagueness, uncertainty, unpredictability or even low probability. Why spend pages over an event that only happens once in a blue moon? It is efficient for the clauses to be incomplete wherever the future is both unknown and a contingency is unlikely. Yet, for us programmers, incompleteness in English is a showstopper. Could I convert some of the contract? The most part of it? The important part? Even the answer to this question appeared to be 'No'!

I had a sinking feeling that rendering the contract into computer language would be a bad thing. If the English language were being used as a battleground between the parties, then the use of the languages and data structures of computing would simply add more power to their weapons. Unless the conversion was a perfect one between English and a computational language, I would simply be adding more room for more trouble. These were consequences I did not want to foresee; I did not want to be the expert witness called to court to explain why the computer language said the opposite of the legal prose. And this applied to even the simple elements of the contract—the face, and the issuer for example. If there was duplication of any form, there was even more room for trouble.

At that point, perhaps, a principle emerged: Simplify! Marketing classes taught me that consumers paid double for a simple product. Security thinking told me that more complex models result in more insecurity. At that time, I was becoming suspicious that systems of Internet security were failing because they thrust too complex a model onto the poor user. Simplicity not complexity was the key to security, something I later captured in the aphorism—*there is only one mode, and it is secure*—which I later found out to be embedded in the 6th principle of Auguste Kerckhoffs exposition of military cryptography:

> Finally, it is necessary, given the circumstances that command its application, that the system be easy to use, requiring neither mental strain nor the knowledge of a long series of rules to observe.[7]

1. A practical computer-contract places human first

At some point, the inspiration hit me to flip my logic upside down. Keep the document as is—in legal English in all its juridical glory—and let the computer do the work of extracting the information it needs *after the fact*. Instead of converting up front for ease of programming, convert lazily for ease of contract writing. We fight for the users, not the developers. Suddenly, it all made sense. The document had to be readable primarily by humans, and only secondarily by the computer. I had been wrong to want to place the computer first, in part because I'd been seduced by the financiers' drive to value the financial instrument, and by the developers' drive to 'automate all the things.' But my goal had never been that, it had always been to issue a financial instrument. Valuation was the task of users; let them do the hard lifting, let the marketplace find a way to reduce a contract to a database. Embedding ten or so fields into the text in computer-readable fashion was an easy problem, whereas getting humans to work with computer layout was intractable. The contract for digital issuance had to be in plain human language, and everything else followed.

My goal then became to tweak the document to capture the variations, but eliminate the complexity, so that Gary Howland's core payments or accounting system could just deal in quantities and identifiers. This consisted of three steps: (i) rendering the contract itself—warts and all—into a single, readable, and signable digital document; (ii) making the performance aspects readable by the client software in some sense; (iii) identifying each instrument, so that we could offer a system with many thousands of bonds in play at any one time. I will take these steps in turn.

2. A signed digital—readable—document

In the early 1990s, a software tool called PGP—standing for *Pretty Good Privacy*—provided secure mail encryption and identity, and it showed us how to sign a document in plaintext. Tantalizingly, in those days we saw our architecture as extending the basic email encryption system of PGP into finance. Indeed,

---

[7] A. Kerckhoffs, 'La cryptographie militaire ("Military Cryptography")' (1883) IX *Journal des sciences militaires* 5–38, 161–91, Feb 1883.

WHY THE RICARDIAN CONTRACT CAME ABOUT   95

first we wrote Cryptix, the original Java and Perl packages for cryptography.[8] Then we implemented PGP over the top of Cryptix, and only then did we construct Ricardo as a payment system on that stack. The first system's identities were actual PGP keys, and instructions were PGP-signed records, so you could in theory use your PGP email identity to issue and transfer bonds and money within Ricardo. It was natural and easy to express the contract as a PGP-cleartext signed document, a feature it already had.

```
-----BEGIN PGP SIGNED MESSAGE-----
Hash: SHA1

05.02.11
'Alice' is the owner of the GPG key with fingerprint:
4F16 E4D6 BB9B D4A0 39F8  9644 DF23 CB88 2400 ACE3
'Bob' is the owner of the GPG key with fingerprint:
05CA A3B0 9322 1874 9D1A  2357 9C07 2DDC 4394 91B7

This contract is for the exchange of 20 Bitcoins at a
rate of USD $3.25 per bitcoin, for a total of $65 USD.

Bob agrees to send $65 USD, plus any fees charged by
Paypal, via a Paypal payment with transaction type 'Payment
Owed' (to reduce chargeback risks) to the paypal account
'alice@lol.com' within 24 hours of both parties
signing this contract. Alice agrees to send 20 bitcoins
to IDj1SocbbH9Lbb9aTdqSHB9AAjhdxNNZha within 4 hours of
receiving this Paypal payment.

-----BEGIN PGP SIGNATURE-----
Version: GnnuPG v1.4.11 (GNU/Linux)

iJwEAQECAAYFAk2/PKAACgkQ3yPLiCQArOOc/AP9GL0EgVQMTHZqOX5ynNVGBFb2
6eB7QzRdNQH8Zcj6R0y7fzbpYPbgwX+G3EYtsDjS4G3M8Ld1FFCcJ/JLJGle191e
KLpXp/BWMRayn3KcFYoGogmONtxk1wOVoXF+wiK9jZYFIdjI87qh8iUOCboFVqQk
T3OG7odEKJOjNwYP+j0=
=2mDw
-----END PGP SIGNATURE-----
```

Figure 5.1 A Stylized Contract to Swap Signed with PGP (Prose in grey Italics, PGP signature artifacts in normal)

A holder of an instrument expects the identity of an issuer to sign the contract, so we also put the issuer's certificates inside the contracts. As trust in finance is based on personal knowledge of people and own due diligence, we were able to use PGP identity all the way, and avoid the requirement common in other systems for a gatekeeper—for example a regulator or industry association that permitted

---

[8] Our Cryptix was the most popular crypto library for Java until the arrival of the abomination known as JCE.

newcomers into their systems via a process that could be described as due diligence or discrimination, variously.

3. Markup

The software would also need to extract the useful information from the readable document. How much information did users need? If investors were analysing a bond for pricing then we would need a lot of information; but if bankers were building an accounting engine, which is the foundation of a digital cash and bond trading system, abstractly, we would only need a small set—about ten simple fields. These would include the name of the issuer, the type (eg, debt) and name of issue, the face amount and currency and coupons, and so forth. Simple!

```
-----BEGIN PGP SIGNED MESSAGE-----
Hash: SHA1

;
; Prepaid Services Dollar, Issue A.
;
; Being, a Contract to settle USD-denominated services.
;
; Between, Systemics Inc. and Users.
;

[definitions]

definitions_dollars = *
{
  Prepaid Services Dollar ("PSD") means the electronic
  currency, denominated in United States of America dollars
  ("USD"), as facilitated by this Ricardian contract. Other
  dollars, which may be used as exchange for PSD, are referred
  to as Account Dollars.
}

definitions_units = *
{
  The unit of the PSD is the iota, which is defined as having
  the value of PSD 0.0001.
}
```

Figure 5.2 Snippet of Ricardian 'stablecoin' Dollar Contract Showing Explanatory Comment at Top, Heading, and Prose Clauses

Systemics Inc's Pre-Paid Services Dollar Ricardian Contract, 2003, http://webfunds.org/ricardo/contracts/systemics/Systemics_PSD_a.html or also see https://iang.org/rants/systemics_psd.html (both last accessed 8 July 2021).

I asked Gary Howland to knock up a simple markup language. I thought he'd give me HTML-for-finance, but instead he gave me the venerable old INI-format from Microsoft. I asked for a two-dimensional structure, he added headings. But he was right and I was wrong; the simplicity of the line-based, *tag = value* pairs did us noble service and every attempt to 'update' the format to advanced miracles such as XML gave poorer results.[9] With our format of what we would now call a simple markup language, the contract became parseable by the client software for the cost of about 1,000 lines of code—a trivial amount. Instead of trying to do everything, for all circumstances and all users, we just did what we needed, and found that we only really needed about ten fields to do almost everything.

```
[issue]
;
; This section identifies general aspects of this contract.
;
issue_type = currency
issue_name = Systemics Pre-paid Services Dollar

[currency]
currency_symbol = $
currency_tla = PSD

[unit]
;
; The Unit of Account is the PSD. This currency is denominated
; in PSD, with an underlying unit of contract of iota, which
; is equal to PSD 0.0001.
;
unit_power = 4
unit_mediate_power = 2
unit_major = $
unit_mediate = c
unit_minor = p
unit_major_unit = PSD
unit_mediate_unit = cent
unit_minor_unit = iota
unit_major_units = PSD
unit_mediate_units = cents
unit_minor_units = iotas
```

Figure 5.3 Snippet of Ricardian 'stablecoin' Dollar Contract Showing Tag-value Pairs and Slightly Smart Decimalization

Systemics Inc's Pre-Paid Services Dollar Ricardian Contract, 2003, http://webfunds.org/ricardo/contracts/systemics/Systemics_PSD_a.html (last accessed 8 July 2021).

---

[9] E. van der Koogh, 'Ricardian Contracts in XML' 2001 Edinburgh Financial Cryptography Engineering 01 Conference, 22 and 23 June 2001.

4. The identifier

I had, by then, done a lot of reading on the forms and theory of bonds. We were in an era of the digitization of bonds, sometimes called dematerialization, which was a fancy word for getting rid of the paper. One thread I had noticed in the evolution of the times was that, as soon as any form of automation was required, the IT people insisted on a unique identifier. And woe betide the bond that presented itself with the same identifier as another bond! Or a format that wasn't acceptable! Or from an unauthorized source! What had previously been a liberty of capital was rapidly becoming an activity controlled by bureaucrats in charge of numbers.

These were early days in globalized computing, and we really only had one way to create an identifier: ask a centralized group to allocate numbers. In the context of bonds, it had to be a national body to allocate the numbers. I rebelled. Going back to my original choice of bonds as a perceived 'easy entry market', I did not want a bond system which was beholden to a remote and uncaring agency that sought to extract easy rents. Easy entry was broken if some national organization were in charge of the numbers. And what about international bonds? The biggest bond issuer of all was the World Bank, and if it were to be an Internet bond system, it had to be able to perform for all issuers. I wanted an exchange like the old Amsterdam exchange, where anyone could walk in and do trade. No permissions, no controls, *caveat emptor*. At the very least, I did not want some self-appointed committee of number-allocators to provide those controls through accretion of power.

Clearly, any system of many components needs naming. These were the exciting times of the Web, and things were being named by URLs, IP numbers, and domain names. Each of these systems exposed features and pitfalls, many of which were mirrored in finance—numbers and ticker symbols allocated by institutions were like domain names of companies, intellectual property to be battled over because of artificial scarcity. I wanted none of that. I could already see that the naming systems for domains, IP numbers, and URLs were creating headaches for users. Control, scamming, theft were erupting around these areas. Costs! I feared the death of a thousand cuts would kill the then open business of the Internet. Even Java had chosen to base its international class system on domain names; as we were engaged in the Crypto Wars, we did not follow Sun's lead and named all our classes rooted in Cryptix not org. Cryptix. I wanted a system which did not demand permission at any point, and left open no side-channels for attackers to exploit. Although I didn't say it in these terms, I wanted a system of contracts that could not be stopped by anyone—a principle that was later to drive Bitcoin. And, there was a simpler solution.

5. The hash as identifier

PGP again provided the answer—as it had a convenient feature of providing a cryptographic message digest or *hash* of any document. Out of my paranoia emerged the idea that a hash as an identifier for a contract cut through a lot of costly nonsense. In those youthful days of open cryptography, most people talked about the cryptographic message digest as a compression function for use in RSA digital signing, but we knew that hashing could be used to create a digital identifier for any document, not just a signature. It's just perhaps that nobody really did that at the time.

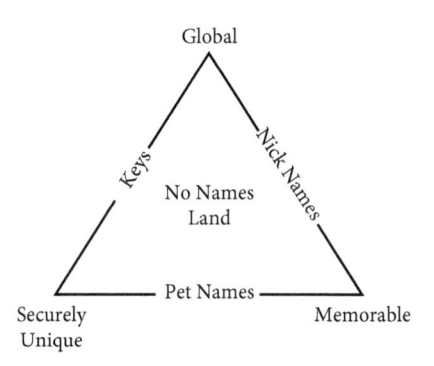

Figure 5.4 Zooko's Triangle: the Ricardian Hash Provides for Two of the Trilemma of Names, being Global, and Securely Unique, but Hashes Lack Memorability

Beyond all, the hash was self-generated, self-proving, and guaranteed to be globally unique and secure—the memorable name would be easily included in the contract to which the hash pointed.[10] That final part was perhaps the most innovative of the design, perhaps because we had tagged legal contracts with cryptography. Or so we felt at the time.

6. The form of the contract

And so it proved. The Ricardian Contract emerged as an INI-formatted prose contract with about ten important embedded tag-value pairs, signed by the PGP key of the issuer, and hashed with SHA1 as an identifier. With this design pattern, we had achieved the perfect separation between the world of law and the world of

---

[10] B. 'zooko' Wilcox-O'Hearn, 'Names: Decentralized, Secure, Human-Meaningful—Choose Two' (2001), <https://web.archive.org/web/20011020191610/http://zooko.com/distnames.html;> see also M. Steigler, 'An Introduction to Petnames' 2005 <http://www.skyhunter.com/marcs/petnames/IntroPetNames.html> both accessed 8 July 2021.

accounting—contract on the left, transactions on the right, and the hash both dividing and joining them. What's more, as a legal document, it could describe anything a contract could describe, and as a cryptographic contract, it could be issued, traded, and valued without limits imposed by the technology. It quickly became clear that the Ricardian Contract was the right building block not only for bonds, but practically all of finance; bonds had just been the lucky one to most clearly surface the contract, and thus put us on the path to dividing finance into a legal contract on one side, and an accounting system of numbers on the other.

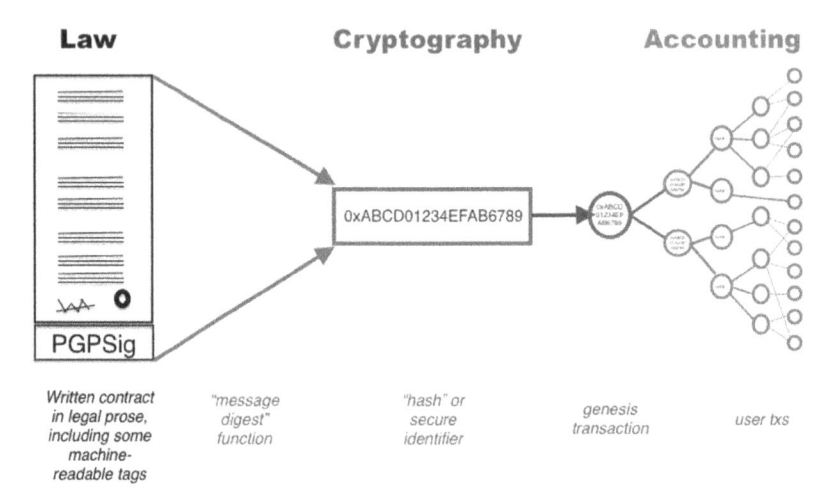

Figure 5.5 the Bow-Tie model of the Ricardian Contract

D. Random Experiences on the Ricardian Journey

Commercial success did not happen to us. We got close, but it is a curse to be ahead of one's time, as it is simply too hard to explain to investors and buyers. Further, the Ricardian Contract had the effect of forcing brutal honesty on issuers, which wasn't a selling point in an industry where every second startup in the 1990s was a Ponzi in disguise (the ICO experience of the late 2010s was worse). However, we built up a lot of experience in the issuance of digital contracts, and that's worth recording. Some quick snippets follow.

- **Form.** The layout should be as readable as possible. It also needs to support digital signatures and hashing, and in practice this means canonicalization. These two requirements are contradictory, and lead to a third: simplicity! In practice, this makes XML a bad choice, but it is also the most popular choice.

- **The One.** In time, we established a wider view of goals and characteristics of the Ricardian Contract.[11] As part of that, we also established *The Rule of One Contract,* that there be only one form of each contract. Every time we tried to improve the results—databases, intermediaries, etc—confusion was the result. You can pick any variation you like, but my advice is to stick to the One!
- **Acceptability.** Our early fear that the legal fraternity would reject our novel contract was unfounded. Courts love to see exotic contracts because it brightens up their dull days, and it allows character to flow through and reveal what is really going on.
- **Arbitration.** One Ricardian Contract landed me into trouble because it had a clause referring disputes to Arbitration, which referral I tried to fight, and lost—but the experience of the following arbitration was very informing, and it taught me an important lesson. Certainty of dispute resolution at the end of the process was just as systemically important as certainty of the contract at the beginning of the process. Dispute resolution has wider effect than just contracts. In CAcert, a world wide open community certification authority (signer of web certificates), we built an arbitration component for all purposes, and it lifted the entire organization to a higher level of reliability.[12] From that experience, I theorize that arbitration can be seen as the apex of an inverted pyramid—over which we layer deep support, user support and finally business; the trade supported is only as strong as the apex: the resolution of disputes generated by the trade.[13] Which experience offers itself as a clear benefit for blockchains built for trade and trust, a topic I return to below.
- **Innovation?** Gary Howland and I were pretty convinced that everything we had done was just good software engineering, including all I have described in this article. We expected others to follow suit as soon as they walked the same path. So much so, we didn't even name it, which is the humbling story behind the name: it was the contract in Ricardo, that's all. It took me years to realize how innovative the Riccy was, as the finance people tended to call it. We never patented it, we never copyrighted it, nobody said 'you should write a paper about that ... ' Hence the original paper only followed years after, as an afterthought derived from rough notes after an attempt to explain it to other engineers.
- **Regrets?** The Ricardian Contract solved its design problems in the day and did so well—there have been no regrets over the original design. Yet, the

---

[11] Webfunds Project, 'Ricardian contracts' notes for developers <http://webfunds.org/guide/ricardian.html> accessed 8 July 2021.

[12] I. Grigg, 'An Open Audit of an Open Certification Authority' 22nd Large Installation Systems Administration Conference (LISA 2008) 13 November 2008 <https://iang.org/papers/open_audit_lisa.html> accessed 8 July 2021.

[13] I. Grigg, 'The Inverted Pyramid of Identity' FC 2009 <http://financialcryptography.com/mt/archives/001165.html> accessed 8 July 2021.

world has moved on and the environment of today is very different to that of the mid-1990s. Several developments have pushed the original design into new territory.

1. Contracting, not contracts

Chris Odom was the first to fully adopt and extend the Ricardian Contract in his system OpenTransactions.[14] He extended it in three ways:[15]

- To use XML;
- To allow one Riccy to include another, a construct he called 'Russian dolls';
- To use the form for many purposes: messages, datafiles, ledgers, payment plans, markets, and trades.

My view and purpose had been the *single issuer, multiple holder* context of an issued financial product; Odom's insight broke that assumption completely open. The Ricardian Contract was now capable of handling any variation of party arrangements—a Riccy could be a component or packet leading up to a wider agreement. Odom's insights were later adopted by OpenBazaar in their system of user-to-user purchasing. Each phase was a signed Ricardian Contract in JSON that included the previous phase:

- Vendors invite shoppers to treat;
- Shoppers offer to buy over the invitation;
- Vendors accept over the offer; and
- Delivery results in payment over the acceptance.

E. Enter 'Smart Contracts'

The novel ideas of Nick Szabo percolated through the cypherpunk community of the 1990s, but seemed stuck in the domain of abstraction.[16] At that time, every problem that smart contracts seemed to solve could either be better solved by coding in features into the clients and servers, or had low demand. As a trivial

---

[14] C. Odom, 'Open-Transactions: Secure Contracts between Untrusted Parties' <http://www.opentransactions.org/open-transactions.pdf> accessed 8 July 2021.

[15] C. Odom, 'Sample Currency Contract' <http://opentransactions.org/wiki/index.php/Sample_Currency_Contract> accessed 8 July 2021.

[16] N. Szabo, 'Smart Contracts', 1994 <https://www.fon.hum.uva.nl/rob/Courses/InformationInSpeech/CDROM/Literature/LOTwinterschool2006/szabo.best.vwh.net/smart.contracts.html> accessed 8 July 2021.

example, the Ricardian Contract had always sported a very limited form of 'smarts' in the form of decimalization, code for which was shared between the contract layout and the client-side display code.

The innovation of Bitcoin changed all that. Instead of providing a raw hard-coded payment, Bitcoin operates by verifying small programs written in a low level language akin to CPU instructions, derived from an old virtual-machine language called Forth. Loosely, one validation rule states that numbers must already exist, another states an exception: the first program in a block can create some numbers. Different programs can be written to envisage higher forms of transaction. Being a shared computation system rather than, narrowly or strictly, a payment system, carries some legal and regulatory implications: the data as a result of the shared computation bears little evidence of eg, payments, and it can only be determined to be a payment system in light of the use made by its users.

No matter that all the popular forms—multisig, crowd funding, timelocks—were still more efficient and tractable in hard-coded form, the smart contract excited an entirely new generation of financial cryptographers. It is fair to say that Bitcoin offered the promise of smart contracts, but delivery was uncertain. Thus sparked an open competition to deliver the first widespread scalable smart contract platform, by Bitcoin itself and others such as Ethereum and R3's Corda.[17]

It is also fair to say that the Ricardian Contract solved a very different problem to the Szaboian smart contract: the Riccy captured the *legal content* at the offering, made it readable and displayable for the holder to accept, and provided a great identifier for all uses. The 'contracts' of the blockchain world, on the other hand, were concentrating on performance—after the contract was agreed. These are not, then, competing ideas at all, they are ideas aimed at different phases of the contract life-cycle.[18] The real question was how to combine all of these ideas together.

1. The Bitcoin unit

One of the oddities of Bitcoin is why it did not use something like the Ricardian Contract. The answer to this, I believe, lies in the nature of contracts. In our world of the 1990s, we believed we could sell software to issue bonds and cash and all sorts of financial instruments, and our design needs were to identify the nature of our instruments as much as possible. This was not how financial cryptography turned out. In practice, no financial instrument other than money took hold. In contrast to our aspirations of strong governance, we saw a steady series of quasi-money issuers who concentrated on fairly simplistic claims that did not come

---

[17] R. Gendal Brown *et al.*, 'Corda: An Introduction' (R3 whitepaper 2016).
[18] I. Grigg, 'On the intersection of Ricardian and Smart Contracts' (Working Paper 2015), <https://iang.org/papers/intersection_ricardian_smart.html> accessed 8 July 2021.

anywhere near to the strength of the Ricardian Contract: Paypal, Webmoney, e-gold, goldmoney, EFTs, and Liberty Reserve are some of the better known names.

I include names of various shades for a reason. In contrast to our designs of strength through information, many systems preferred strength through obscurity, and many of these ran into legal (including criminal) trouble. It was this trouble—the persistent failure and disruption in the presence of attackers of all forms—that inspired the design of Bitcoin. Satoshi Nakamoto designed a system that could not be shut down. By its inherent logic, such a system could not have an issuer, nor an underlying value in payments as mentioned above, nor delivery of coupons nor dividends nor options nor any other promises. In short, all of the elements of the contract threatened the mission of Bitcoin, and consequently the Ricardian Contract or any similar contractual form had no place in Bitcoin. But, as an unforeseen consequence, this also suggested that there could be only one currency per chain, because as soon as you had two, you had to describe the difference.

2. The sum of all chains

Bitcoin may have only one unit, but it has spawned a frenzy of 'altCoins'—copies with minor variations in contractual and parameter terms. Of course, these lacked Ricardian Contracts, because there was none such in the original Bitcoin, but they still required description in some fashion. Vaguely, this difference was described by websites and chat rooms and word of mouth, but more importantly, the software also had the problem that it had to change to accommodate the mostly trivial changes between the original Bitcoin and a new altCoin design—including the location of new chains. As crazy as it seems, all of the details for chains, including the genesis block, are hardcoded into the base software distribution, and the process of issuing a new altCoin is one of hacking the source code and making every new customer download a new program with the new parameters hardcoded in.

This immediately struck me as a Ricardian problem, so I designed a variant that could specify the details of the chain. This tinkering would allow one client software to manage multiple chains from the same code base, just by reading the chain 'contract'. It made sense to me—if you, as a company, were selling the services of coffee-chain or bond-chain or realty-chain, you would want to do this within a contractual framework, notwithstanding the original Bitcoin innovation. If a legal context made sense, so did parameters within the chain's genesis transaction; things like the location of seed nodes, alert keys, the time of a block, and the infamous block size limit all need to be coded into a descriptive device, and in some cases they might need to be adjusted over time. And, if Bitcoin's mining schedule isn't screaming *smart contract* at you, then you've attended too many loud Satoshi rock concerts.

3. The governed blockchain

So emerged an augmented Ricardian Contract or *Ricardian triple* to describe a chain with {prose, code, params} and, of course, using the now-familiar hash as identifier.[19] What was interesting was that this extended design pattern could also describe a wide range of things: smart contracts, individuals, corporations, and even devices or nodes could all be described by a tuple of {prose, code, params}. These devices are more like network-empowered objects in object-oriented thinking, or capabilities. Indeed, there may have been two forerunners to this augmented form, being the E language[20] and the Askemos system.[21]

Drawing from the above experiences, the Ricardian Contract was introduced at the genesis point in the launch of the EOS blockchain.[22] Block producers agreed to a (Ricardian) Community Agreement, and then required agreement by all users in transactions on the chain. The written agreement included clauses on changing the document, and resolution of disputes in a community forum. This was referred to as the *governed blockchain*.[23] This design was not without gaps, and a key difficulty was showing that users had entered into the agreement and thus the jurisdiction.[24] Sadly, adverse elements within the community managed to neuter most of the governance just as it was starting to deliver results: rulings on million dollar cases and community-driven funding for essential works were blocked, burnt, disassembled. Other blockchains have now built successful arrangements of governance, and kept them.

F. Conclusion

This brings us to the current day. In conclusion, I will mention five points for future research:

The tuple. A team at Barclays Bank is building out advanced Ricardian Contracts as laid out above with a tuple of {prose, code, params} towards a long-term goal of replacing the constellation of ISDA swaps contracts.[25] It is clearly an interesting

---

[19] I. Grigg, 'The Sum of all Chains—let's converge' 2015 <http://financialcryptography.com/mt/archives/001556.html> accessed 8 July 2021.

[20] M.S. Miller, C. Morningstar, and B. Franz, 'Capability-based Financial Instruments—an Ode to the Granovetter Operator' *Financial Cryptography* 2000, Anguilla.

[21] J.F. Wittenberger, 'Askemos—a distributed settlement' 2002 <http://citeseerx.ist.psu.edu/viewdoc/summary?doi=10.1.1.11.5050>.

[22] See <https://eos.io>.

[23] I. Grigg, 'The Governed Blockchain' block.one white paper 2018 <https://iang.org/papers/the_governed_blockchain.html> accessed 8 July 2021.

[24] A. Sanitt and I. Grigg, 'Legal Analysis of the Governed Blockchain' (NortonRoseFulbright and block.one Working Paper 2018), <https://www.nortonrosefulbright.com/-/media/files/nrf/nrfweb/imported/emea_4957_online-publication-and-pdf__legal-analysis-of-the-governed-blockchain_v4.pdf?la=en&revision=c15aa8eb-48d5-4d06-8851-8226bdb1145f> accessed 8 July 2021.

[25] C. Clack *et al.*, 'Smart Contract Templates: foundations, design landscape and research directions' (Barclays Working Paper 2016), <https://arxiv.org/abs/1608.00771> accessed 8 July 2021.

question to see how far we can extend the idea of the tuples—can we identify everything this way?

Prose versus Code. The horizontal integration between code and prose is being thought about in several ways:

- to pair tight tuples of code fragment with prose fragment together (Common-Accord);
- to derive the code from the prose or vice versa;
- to verify conformance of code to prose or vice versa; and
- to insert the code into prose or perhaps vice versa.

The last is my favourite, because it conforms to the rule of one contract.

It should perhaps be added that I believe that stronger integration of code and prose should be viewed with caution. On the one hand, some form of logic is required to for example handle coupons, and simple functions or procedures in a high level language such as Java could be inserted into the prose. Our work in simple issuances did not reach that need.

In contrast, issues found in prose such as fuzziness, ambiguity, and incompleteness are rarely of interest to the user and therefore of little interest to the program—we don't need to code up what the user does not use. These factors tend to become of key importance when a dispute happens, but disputes are rare, and are resolved by humans who can read. To this extent, I believe interpreting pure prose as code or vice versa may be a red herring.

Enforceability. There is a question of whether the Ricardian Contract can be enforced, and whether a court will respect the tradition. I think this is so, but I am not a court, and there is an open question of examining precedent here. As much of blockchain and financial cryptography practice is international and cross-jurisdictional by nature, I suspect the winning solution here is contracts that refer disputes not to courts but to international forums of arbitration that accept and align with the community practices assumed in the contract.

Contract Browser. Finally, a challenge which we anticipated and tried to surmount but never achieved: there is a crying need for a contract preparation tool. The workflow and negotiation of contract formation is opaque to the technologist, and verification of format, key management and signing are technical tasks beyond the non-technical lawyer. A careful melding of the right skills is needed.

Identity. My own work is in extending the Ricardian formula to document interactions between peers.[26] I see these events between people as the next generation of identity systems, as they more comfortably capture the persons as they are, as they act and as they wish to control their data.

---

[26] These events are called variously attributes, verified claims or reliable statements (my favourite). See *inter alia*, Rebooting Web of Trust <https://www.weboftrust.info/> accessed 6 July 2021.

6
Smart Contracts
Taxonomy, Transaction Costs, and Design Trade-Offs

*Alfonso Delgado De Molina Rius**

A. Introduction	107	3. Negotiation costs	124
B. Contract Taxonomy	109	4. Agency costs	125
1. An ontological clarification	111	5. Monitoring and verification costs	126
2. Forms of legal contracts	112	6. Enforcement costs	127
3. Smart contracts: evolution of the term	113	D. Design Trade-Offs	132
4. Smart contracts: inherent traits and misconceptions	115	1. Bare smart contract code	132
5. Types of smart contracts	118	2. Natural language and code—no overlap	135
C. Smart Contracts and Contract Law: A Transaction Costs Approach	119	3. Natural language and code—partial or complete overlap	137
1. Search costs	122	4. The price of crypto-anarchy	138
2. Measurement costs	123		

A. Introduction

Over the past few years, smart contracts have been in the limelight of entrepreneurs, professional advisers, and lawmakers alike. Despite the widespread fascination with the technology, its legal treatment, economic implications, and technical capabilities remain the subject of much debate. There has, however, been a chain of important contributions in recent years.[1] For instance, the LawTech Delivery Panel UK Jurisdiction Taskforce's *Legal Statement on Smart Contracts and Cryptoassets* ('UKJT *Legal Statement*') is much welcomed in the path towards greater legal clarity.[2] In the economic sphere, the European Union ('EU'), International

---

* Alfonso Delgado De Molina Rius is Head of Research at Silver 8 Capital, one of the earliest fund managers in the cryptoasset space. He lectures at Imperial College London, where he is finalizing a PhD in Computer Science. Alfonso sits on the DLT Committee of the British Standards Institution. Previously, he practiced as a lawyer and graduated with an MSc in Law and Finance from the University of Oxford.

[1] See A.D.D.M. Rius, 'Split Contracts: Bridging Legal Prose and Smart Contract Code' (2017) <http://alfonso.digitalpapers.uk/> accessed 8 July 2021.

[2] UKJT, 'Legal Statement on Cryptoassets and Smart Contracts' (2020). See also Sir G. Vos, 'End-to-End Smart Legal Contracts: Moving from Aspiration to Reality' (2019) 1: 'The legal treatment of "smart contracts" is rapidly becoming one of the most important legal subjects of our generation.'

Monetary Fund ('IMF'), and World Bank have identified promising applications of the technology across industries.[3] From a technical perspective, the International Organization for Standardization has, through its national delegations, produced helpful guidelines for the adoption of this technology.[4]

Despite this traction, there is progress to be made in bridging theory and practice, as well as in establishing a structured analytical framework. The difficulty stems from the fact that smart contracts have evolved through the cross-fertilization of ideas from a wide range of disciplines.[5] Unfortunately, much of the commentary to date has been domain-specific and dispersed across formal and informal fora.[6] These factors are the main culprits for the semantic walls that shelter specialists' perspectives and turn the use of descriptive terminology into a game of minesweeper.[7]

For the purposes of this chapter, I define a 'smart contract' as an agreement whose performance is automated (at least in part) through the execution of code on a distributed ledger technology (DLT) network. In this chapter, I seek to explore the following three interrelated areas. *First*, I explore the taxonomy of contracts at large and, more specifically, smart contracts. I also consider the evolving usage of the smart contract term, which accounts for the lack of a settled definition. Further, I address certain misconceptions about smart contracts that have become entrenched in the literature. *Second*, I apply principles of new institutional economics to analyse the advantages and drawbacks of smart contracts over traditional contracts, with a focus on transaction costs.[8] In addition, I highlight cases in which parties may benefit from the use of smart legal contracts. *Third*, I provide examples of the design trade-offs and risks that arise from different combinations

---

[3] See, eg, European Union Blockchain Observatory & Forum, 'Blockchain and the Future of Digital Assets' (2020) <https://www.eublockchainforum.eu/sites/default/files/report_digital_assets_v1.0.pdf> accessed 8 July 2021, IMF, 'Fintech: The Experience So Far' (2019) Policy Paper No 19/024, and World Bank, 'Smart Contract Technology and Financial Inclusion' (2019) Fintech Note No 6.

[4] See, eg, 'Blockchain and distributed ledger technologies—Overview of and interactions between smart contracts in blockchain and distributed technology systems' (2019) ISO/TR 23455.

[5] See N. Szabo, 'Smart Contracts: Building Blocks for Digital Markets' (1996) <https://www.fon.hum.uva.nl/rob/Courses/InformationInSpeech/CDROM/Literature/LOTwinterschool2006/szabo.best.vwh.net/smart_contracts_2.html> accessed 8 July 2021: 'the objectives and principles for the design of [smart contracts] are derived from legal principles, economic theory, and theories of reliable and secure protocols.'

[6] See, eg, J. Stark, 'Making Sense of Blockchain Smart Contracts' (*CoinDesk*, 4 June 2016) <https://www.coindesk.com/making-sense-smart-contracts> accessed 8 July 2021: 'The interdisciplinary nature of blockchain technology, and smart contracts in particular, leads people to see the technology as primarily belonging to their own discipline, at the expense of the others.' In Rius (n. 1), I note that many influential articles on smart contracts have been written in online blog sites like Medium, which are often overlooked by academics.

[7] See Rius (n. 1). See also E. Mik, 'Smart Contracts: Terminology, Technical Limitations and Real World Complexity' (2017) 9(2) *Law, Innovation and Technology* 269–300. In the broader context of DLT, see N. Carter, 'Blockchain is a Semantic Wasteland' (2018) <https://medium.com/s/story/blockchain-is-a-semantic-wasteland-9450b6e5012> accessed 8 July 2021 and A. Walch, 'Blockchain's Treacherous Vocabulary: One More Challenge for Regulators' (2017) 21(2) *Journal of Internet Law* 9–16.

[8] For an introductory read, see P.G. Klein, 'New Institutional Economics' in B.R.A. Bouckaert and G. De Geest (eds), *Encyclopedia of Law and Economics* (Edward Elgar Publishing 2000).

of (written) natural language and code, using various financial applications as case studies.[9] I also consider the impact of pseudonymity on transaction costs, showing that privacy is not a free lunch.

I will support my analysis with insights from a variety of fields, including law, economics, distributed computing, and finance. Since the discussion is oriented towards practitioners and academics from diverse backgrounds, I will also clarify some of the technical and academic jargon that populates the relevant literature. The discussion does, however, assume a non-technical familiarity with the core aspects of DLT.[10]

B. Contract Taxonomy

In the smart contract discourse, perhaps the one thing that commentators agree on is the absence of a settled definition for the very term. In fact, Gideon Greenspan quips that the term has been used to mean so many different things that we would be better off by *banning it*.[11] The lack of an established semantic and conceptual framework can lead commentators to talk at cross-purposes and impair analytical progress. However, the challenge does not stop here, as the use of the word 'contract' itself is regarded as contentious.[12] The dominant, dictionary definition of 'contract' is an agreement (ie, a collection of promises between two or more parties) that gives rise to a corresponding set of legally binding obligations.[13] As JG Allen notes, contracts generate 'special legal consequences' within a legal system's logical universe in a way that non-qualifying promises do not.[14] The requirements that need be met for an agreement to be legally binding can vary from one legal system to another. The UKJT *Legal Statement* reiterates the conditions that (at least in common law systems) typically need to be satisfied:

1. an agreement is reached in respect of terms that are sufficiently certain;
2. the parties objectively intended to be legally bound by this agreement; and

---

[9] I use the term 'natural language' throughout the chapter in the context of writing (as opposed to speech). Although I have used the term 'prose' in the past, eg, in Rius (n. 1), I am not convinced that one could not write legal contracts in iambic pentameter. I defer that consideration to future work.

[10] In 'Foundations of Blockchain Technology' (2019), I analyse the core elements of the technology, highlight various applications (including Bitcoin), and dispel certain widespread misconceptions <http://alfonso.digitalpapers.uk/> accessed 8 July 2021.

[11] G. Greenspan, 'Smart Contracts: The Good, the Bad and the Lazy' (2015) <https://www.multichain.com/blog/2015/11/smart-contracts-good-bad-lazy/> accessed 8 July 2021.

[12] See, eg, K. Werbach and N. Cornell, 'Contracts Ex Machina' (2019) 67 *Duke Law Journal* 313–82, 338: 'The first question we must necessarily answer is then: What do we mean by a "contract"?'. The authors, however, do not go on to consider any interpretations of the term outside the domain of law.

[13] Definition derived from the Cambridge and Merriam-Webster online dictionaries (accessed 29 March 2020). From a legal practitioner's perspective, see also H. Beale (ed), *Chitty on Contracts* (31st edn, Sweet & Maxwell 2012) 1-016: 'a promise or set of promises which the law will enforce'.

[14] J.G. Allen, 'Wrapped and Stacked: Smart Contracts and the Interaction of Natural Language and Formal Language' (2018) 14(4) *European Review of Contract Law* 307–43, 14 (citing draft paper).

3. with certain exceptions, each party has provided something of benefit to the other (referred to as *consideration*), which need not be monetary in form.[15]

If I verbally agree to give you my car for free, I may have a *moral obligation* to keep my word, but since there was no consideration from your part, I would most likely not have a *legal obligation* to do so. Since the conditions set out above have not been satisfied, you cannot *enforce* my promise in court by obtaining a legal remedy if I default.[16] Importantly, the law also subverts parties' ability to enforce contracts to matters of public interest, such as the desire to prevent criminal activity and facilitate insolvency proceedings.[17]

On the other hand, the term 'contract' can mean something very different to a computer scientist.[18] In particular, a computer scientist may not concern herself with whether an agreement is capable of being enforced *in court*. Instead, she may see in (source) code the opportunity to specify and execute an agreed set of promises, for instance, by registering the transfer of ownership to a digital asset on a distributed ledger. Further, there is long-standing precedent for the use of the term 'contract' in economics and political philosophy to denote agreements that are not necessarily legally binding.[19]

This semantic disparity has led lawyers to discount an important technological development on the basis that it is merely a 'misnomer'.[20] Consequently, computer scientists are deprived of a recursive body of codified experience that has developed over centuries to streamline socially and commercially desirable patterns of behaviour, patching 'legal bugs' and resolving 'reasoning forks' through a process

---

[15] UKJT *Legal Statement* (n. 2) 31–2. For a cross-jurisdictional perspective, see Norton Rose Fulbright, 'Can smart contracts be legally binding contracts?' (2016) <https://www.nortonrosefulbright.com/en-ca/knowledge/publications/a90a5588/can-smart-contracts-be-legally-binding-contracts> accessed 8 July 2021. In common law jurisdictions, a 'deed' is a type of document that meets certain formality requirements and does not require consideration to flow from each party in order to be legally binding.

[16] Common law systems draw the line at the notion of consideration, on the basis that a promisor can typically change their mind without the promisee incurring an economic loss. There are certain exceptions, such as when dealing with deeds, or when the doctrine of equitable estoppel comes into play. For the classic exposition of the latter, see *Central London Property Trust Ltd v High Trees House Ltd* [1947] KB 130 per Denning J (obiter, as usual).

[17] See S. Bourque and S.F.L. Tsui, *A Lawyer's Introduction to Smart Contracts* (Scientia Nobilitat 2014) 13, where the authors argue that even in jurisdictions in which the right to free speech is largely unfettered, the act of contracting is in fact a heavily regulated exercise. On the other hand, 'freedom of contract' is often regarded as an important tenet of private law in common law jurisdictions.

[18] See C. Colombo, J. Ellul, and G.J. Pace, 'Contracts over Smart Contracts: Recovering from Violations Dynamically' in T. Margaria and B. Steffen (eds), *Leveraging Applications of Formal Methods, Verification and Validation*, vol 11247 (Lecture Notes in Computer Science 2018) 300–15, 300–1.

[19] From an economic perspective, see eg, G. Baker, R. Gibbons, and K.J. Murphy, 'Implicit Contracts and the Theory of the Firm' (1997) NBER Working Paper 6177: implicit contracts are 'informal agreements, supported by reputation rather than law.' On the interplay between social contracts and contract law, see J.H. Kary, 'Contract Law and the Social Contract: What Legal History Can Teach Us About the Political Theory of Hobbes and Locke' (1999) 31(1) *Ottawa Law Review* 73–91.

[20] See eg, C. Lim, T.J. Saw, and C. Sargeant, 'Smart Contracts: Bridging the Gap between Expectation and Reality' (*Oxford Business Law Blog*, 2016) <https://www.law.ox.ac.uk/business-law-blog/blog/2016/07/smart-contracts-bridging-gap-between-expectation-and-reality> accessed 8 July 2021.

of trial-and-error. To circumvent the potential for ambiguity, I will follow the approach adopted throughout this volume and use the term 'legal contract' when referring to a legally binding agreement.

1. An ontological clarification

As part of this taxonomical exercise, it is helpful to distinguish between the *existence* of a legal contract and the *manner in which this is initialized* (and, where applicable, *recorded*). We can conceptualize a legal contract as an object that is initialized once the conditions prescribed by an applicable legal system have been met. This object acquires importance within the legal dimension, as opposed to the state of nature or a virtual environment. As Allen observes, these objects 'are invisible and their existence fundamentally mind-dependent, but they are as "real" as the legal system itself can purport to be'.[21]

This distinction is relevant for various reasons. If we misplace the document that initializes or records the contract (commonly also referred to as 'the contract'), the obligations that this set in motion do not typically evaporate into thin air.[22] In addition, the law may imply terms into all kinds of legal contracts—no matter how they are initialized or documented—based on considerations of business efficacy, paternalism, and moral values. In certain situations, the courts can also authorize a contractual document to be rectified if its terms deviate from that which the parties intended (for instance, due to a typo).[23] Second, a distinction can be drawn between a legal contract (as an object) and the means through which the obligations that it gives rise to are performed (or enforced).[24] For example, the obligations set out in a legal contract that is initialized and recorded in natural language may be performed either by a person carrying out the prescribed actions or executed by an algorithm. In the latter case, the code would not ordinarily be regarded as being part of the legal contract. Here, the natural language document is seen as the authoritative record, with code merely being used as a means of facilitating performance.[25] On that basis, if the output of the execution deviates from that

---

[21] Allen (n. 14) 15.
[22] See Allen (n. 14), 16: 'A bearer bond, on the other hand, is *specifically dependent* on the existence of the document. If such a negotiable instrument is lost or destroyed, the object itself lapses into non-existence.'
[23] For a discussion of the English legal doctrine of rectification, see Allen (n. 14).
[24] In the domain of law, the term 'enforcement' implies the involvement of some third party (or perhaps algorithm) to effect the promises that the parties have made (or, in the alternative, grant a legal remedy such as damages). In contrast, the terms 'performance' and 'enforcement' are used interchangeably in the economics literature, with 'self-enforcement' typically describing instances in which parties' incentives are aligned so as to encourage performance.
[25] Allen (n. 14), 7 provides the example of an e-commerce transaction: 'Once I have entered my credit card details into Amazon.com ... my click sets off a cascade of instructions such that the balance of my account on my bank's digital ledger is depleted by *n* units and the balance of the seller's account with its bank is increased by *n* units.' In this case, code is acting as an execution mechanism for the buyer's payment obligation, as opposed to serving as the authoritative record.

which the natural language prescribes, the courts would likely find that a default has occurred.

2. Forms of legal contracts

This subsection focusses on the manner in which legal contracts can be initialized and (where applicable) recorded. The simplest form of agreement is an *oral contract*. For example, I may verbally agree to sell my shares in Apple at a specific price. This resembles the open outcry system that floor traders use in many stock exchanges. While the agreement is time-efficient, there is little evidence of the agreed terms, so it may not be easy to satisfy a court that, on the balance of probabilities, a thing was said (or not). This leaves room for counterparty opportunism, an issue that I will explore in detail in Section C.

Legal contracts can also be initialized through parties' *actions*. For instance, when Bob walks into a store, picks up some goods, and pays at the counter, this chain of actions will cause a contract to be initialized between the store owner and Bob. This is notwithstanding the fact that Bob has not uttered a single word throughout the transaction. The law would, however, not stay quiet—certain fundamental terms would be implied into, and come to form part of, the legal contract. For example, Bob would be entitled to a refund as a matter of law if the goods are later found to be of sub-par quality or if he decides to change his mind within the statutory cooling-off period.[26]

Agreements in the realm of business are, of course, commonly recorded through the use of *natural language* and initialized by means of a signature. The latter is taken as a widely accepted signal that a party intends to be legally bound. Even if a preliminary oral agreement has been reached in a business setting, it is common to 'memorialise' this in a natural language document, which will typically dominate in the event of inconsistency. In contrast to oral agreements, natural language documents are more precise, easier to amend during the negotiation stage, and less susceptible to disputes regarding parties' intentions.

On the other hand, *algorithmic contracts* are those that are initialized by, and whose terms are recorded in, code.[27] Financial markets are dominated by these

---

[26] In the context of English Law, see the *Sale of Goods Act* 1979 s 14 (on implied terms as to quality and fitness) and *The Consumer Contracts (Information, Cancellation and Additional Charges) Regulations* 2013 reg 29 (on the cooling-off period).

[27] L. Scholz, 'Algorithmic Contracts' (2017) 20 *Stanford Technology Law Review* 101–39, 101: 'Algorithmic contracts are contracts in which an algorithm determines a party's obligations'. See also H. Surden, 'Computable Contracts' (2014) 46 *UC Davis Law Review* 629–700, 634. On electronic data interchange (EDI), see J.M. Sklaroff, 'Smart Contracts and the Cost of Inflexibility' (2017) 166 *University of Pennsylvania Law Review* 263–303. On straight-through processing, see Z/Yen Group, 'A Wholesale Insurance Executive's Guide To Smart Contracts' (2017), <https://www.longfinance.net/publications/long-finance-reports/a-wholesale-insurance-executives-guide-to-smart-contracts/> accessed 8 July 2021.

types of contracts, as they permit a large volume of transactions to be executed in fractions of a second. If I place an order on a regulated trading venue, I may not know who my counterparty is, let alone had the chance to formalize our relationship in natural language, as it would be too time-consuming to do so. Nonetheless, I accept that by placing an order on said venue, I am agreeing to enter into a legally binding relationship with whichever party happens to match my order.[28]

Last, *hybrid contracts* are those that are initialized through, and therefore recorded in, a combination of natural language and code. For instance, an algorithmic contract may reference a 'natural language wrapper', whose terms are incorporated into the associated code (or *vice versa*). To revisit the trading analogy, a party may have entered into a master agreement with a broker to cover all of the individual algorithmic trades that are placed through the broker's API. In this case, the master agreement serves as an umbrella contract that contains provisions of general applicability, thereby reducing the number of transaction-specific parameters that need to be agreed per trade. In light of the various forms of legal contracts, the optional choice of form for initializing and recording a contract will be transaction-specific. I will expand on these considerations when evaluating different smart contract designs in Section D.

3. Smart contracts: evolution of the term

The term 'smart contract' was coined in 1994 by Nick Szabo, who originally defined this as a 'computerized transaction protocol that executes the terms of a contract'.[29] As Szabo has more recently clarified, by 'contract' he meant the computer science interpretation of the term: 'A smart contract makes no attempt to be legally binding'.[30] Instead, Szabo envisioned smart contracts as protocols (or programs) that initialize, record, and enforce an agreed set of terms.[31] It is this last characteristic that might be said to endow these protocols with a dose of 'smartness'. Importantly, Szabo regarded smart contracts as a transactional tool capable

---

[28] In practice, the relationship between trading parties may be complicated by the involvement of clearinghouses and trade executions by brokers acting on an agency basis.
[29] N. Szabo, 'Smart Contracts' (1994) <https://www.fon.hum.uva.nl/rob/Courses/InformationInSpeech/CDROM/Literature/LOTwinterschool2006/szabo.best.vwh.net/smart.contracts.html> accessed 8 July 2021. In Szabo (n. 5), a smart contract is defined as 'a set of promises, specified in digital form, including protocols within which the parties perform on these promises.' See also N. Szabo, 'Formalizing and Securing Relationships on Public Networks' (1997) 2(9) *First Monday*.
[30] N. Szabo, 'Winning Strategies For Smart Contracts' (2017) A Blockchain Research Institute Big Idea Whitepaper 1–37, 16.
[31] *Ibid.* 5: 'In terms of computer technology, smart contracts are software modelled on contractual relationships that facilitate negotiations and incentivize performance via control of assets.'

of preventing contractual breaches, lowering enforcement costs, and minimizing the need to rely on intermediaries.

Szabo's original conception of the term is abstract in form and, since it is not tied to a specific technology, overlaps with the notion of an algorithmic contract. In his articles, Szabo points to the vending machine as a primitive example of a smart contract. Szabo also associates smart contracts with digital cash protocols, which utilize cryptographic techniques like public key cryptography and digital signatures to procure enforcement and avert unauthorized actions. However, Szabo's definition did not indicate that cryptographic primitives are a necessary component of smart contracts.

While Szabo and other cypherpunks sought to develop smart contracting systems in the early 2000s, the notion remained largely unexplored outside of this ideological community.[32] The launch of the Bitcoin network in 2009, which made use of various cryptographic techniques that Szabo had referenced in his articles, marked a turning point in the smart contract discourse.[33] In addition to outright transfers of the network's native cryptoasset (BTC), Bitcoin's programming language (Script) permits the deployment of state-contingent transactions, where BTC can only be spent if the prescribed conditions are met (such as a multisignature requirement).[34] Although Bitcoin introduced a limited range of smart contracting capabilities, it was the launch of the Ethereum network in 2015 that popularized the concept. In the Ethereum Whitepaper, the term is used rather broadly to cover any piece of code that is capable of being executed by the networked nodes, and the output of which will be recorded (in encoded form) on the network's distributed ledger.[35] In hindsight, Vitalik Buterin has recognized that the use of the phrase 'persistent scripts' to describe these programs would have been less ambiguous.[36] Other networks have opted to christen these programs with more technical names (like Hyperledger Fabric's *chaincode*).

---

[32] N. Szabo, 'A Formal Language for Analysing Contracts' (2002) <https://www.fon.hum.uva.nl/rob/Courses/InformationInSpeech/CDROM/Literature/LOTwinterschool2006/szabo.best.vwh.net/contractlanguage.html> accessed 8 July 2021. See also M.S. Miller, C. Morningstar, and B. Frantz, 'Capability-based Financial Instruments', in Y. Frankel (ed), *Financial Cryptography*, vol 1962 (Lecture Notes in Computer Science 2000) 349–78. On the cypherpunk movement, see J. Lopp, 'Bitcoin and the Rise of the Cypherpunks' (*CoinDesk*, 9 April 2016) <https://www.coindesk.com/the-rise-of-the-cypherpunks> accessed 8 July 2021.
[33] S. Nakamoto, 'Bitcoin: A Peer-to-Peer Electronic Cash System' (2008) <https://bitcoin.org/en/bitcoin-paper> accessed 8 July 2021.
[34] See eg, N. Atzei *et al.*, 'SoK: Unraveling Bitcoin Smart Contracts' in L. Bauer and R. Küsters (eds), *Principles of Security and Trust*, vol 10804 (Lecture Notes in Computer Science 2018) 217–42. For a discussion of 'state' in this context, see Section C(5).
[35] V. Buterin, 'A Next-generation Smart Contract and Decentralized Application Platform' (2013) <https://ethereum.org/en/whitepaper/> accessed 8 July 2021. For a technical analysis of Ethereum smart contracts, see also G. Wood, 'Ethereum: A Secure Decentralised Generalised Transaction Ledger' (2014) <https://ethereum.github.io/yellowpaper/paper.pdf> accessed 8 July 2021 and Rius (n. 1).
[36] Vitalik published the following message on Twitter on 13 October 2018: 'To be clear, at this point I quite regret adopting the term "smart contracts". I should have called them something more boring and technical, perhaps something like "persistent scripts"'. In this context, persistence refers to the characteristic of state being stored and outliving the process that created it.

Admittedly, as Brent Miller observes, this sacrifices part of the term's glamour and marketability.[37]

So how are we to reconcile the various uses of the term? At present, the popular approach amongst commentators (and legislators) is to treat DLT networks as an essential ingredient in the definition of a smart contract.[38] Perhaps this is indicative of some sort of 'AI effect', insofar as algorithms that we previously regarded as 'smart' (like those powering vending machines) now fail to impress us.[39] Other commentators prefer to adopt a technology-agnostic definition of the term.[40] Szabo himself has more recently drawn a distinction between the abstract and DLT-specific uses of the term, both of which he regards as valid.[41] Such a reconciliatory view is helpful to bridge differences in the discourse, provided that one clarifies which stream they intend to follow. In this chapter, I will use the term 'smart contract' solely in the context of DLT networks, as I wish to avoid overlap with the broader notion of 'algorithmic contracts', instances of which precede Szabo's conception.

4. Smart contracts: inherent traits and misconceptions

In contrast to more established forms of algorithmic contracts, smart contracts are able to leverage the uniformity, fast settlement, and security assurances of DLT networks. In this environment, smart contracts have given rise to novel forms of fundraising, collaborative applications, and organizational forms. During the ICO boom of 2017–2018, it seemed that there was no problem too large (or too little) that a smart contract could not eradicate.[42] Armed with a golden hammer,

---

[37] B. Miller, 'Smart Contracts and the Role of Lawyers—About "Code is Law"' (2016) <http://biglawkm.com/2016/10/20/smart-contracts-and-the-role-of-lawyers-part-1-about-smart-contracts/> accessed 8 July 2021.
[38] See eg, M. Alharby and A. van Moorsel, 'Blockchain-Based Smart Contracts: A Systematic Mapping Study' (2017) 9(5) *International Journal of Computer Science and Information Technology* 151–64, 151: 'A smart contract is executable code that runs on the blockchain to facilitate, execute and enforce the terms of an agreement between untrusted [sic] parties.'
[39] On the 'AI effect', see, eg, P. McCorduck, *Machines Who Think: A Personal Enquiry Into the History and Prospects of Artificial Intelligence* (2nd edn, Routledge 2004) 204: 'It's part of the history of the field of artificial intelligence that every time somebody figured out how to make a computer do something— play good checkers, solve simple but relatively informal problems—there was a chorus of critics to say, but that's not thinking.'
[40] See C.D. Clack, V.A. Bakshi, and L. Braine, 'Smart Contract Templates: Foundations, Design Landscape and Research Directions' (2016–2017) arXiv:1608.00771, 2 and C.D. Clack, V.A. Bakshi, and L. Braine, 'Smart Contract Templates: Essential Requirements and Design Options' (2016) arXiv:1612.04496. See also Allen (n. 14), 9.
[41] Szabo (n. 30), 4–6.
[42] In 'Towards a Sustainable ICO Process: Community Guidelines on Regulation and Best Practices' (2016–2017), I identify various instances of irrational behaviour amongst ICO contributors <http://alfonso.digitalpapers.uk/> accessed 8 July 2021. See also A. Gurrea Martinez and N. Remolina, 'The Law and Finance of Initial Coin Offerings' (2018) Ibero-American Institute for Law and Finance Working Paper No 4/2018.

entrepreneurs and developers came to attribute all sorts of magical characteristics to smart contracts.[43] As a result of this, a number of important misconceptions have become entrenched in the literature:

- **Immutable/tamper-proof/tamper-resistant:** computer scientists tend to use these terms to indicate that (at least certain) components of a smart contract cannot easily be altered once deployed.[44] Nonetheless, the use of this term is dangerously misleading for the unsuspecting user. In permissionless networks, the notorious demise of the project called 'The DAO' has demonstrated how a protocol can be altered to retrospectively annul the effects of a previously valid transaction.[45] In addition, there is ongoing work on the development of standards for upgradable contracts that enable functions to be replaced after they have been deployed.[46] In permissioned networks, participants can more easily co-ordinate to replace smart contract code and relax the rules of the network's protocol to permit authorized entities to edit deployed code.[47]
- **Autonomous/decentralized/trustless:** smart contracts are not necessarily autonomous (or, by extension, decentralized or trustless). These terms are frequently used in the context of Ethereum to describe the accounts that smart contract code is linked to, as these do not have a corresponding private key that users can control. However, smart contracts can (and usually do) have a contract 'owner' with the ability to call certain reserved functions. For instance, a token issuer may grant themselves the ability to cancel the sale at any time or even to unwind transactions.[48] Parties need also trust the developers that oversee a network's protocol or those who are engaged to write smart contract code.[49] Due to these factors, Angela Walch warns that DLT networks, far

---

[43] See generally Rius (n. 1), Walch (n. 7) and k (n. 7). A golden hammer is an application of the 'Law of the Instrument', introduced in the computer science literature on anti-patterns (programming practices to be avoided). See, eg, W.J. Brown et al., *AntiPatterns: Refactoring Software, Architectures, and Projects in Crisis* (Wiley 1998) 111.

[44] See Rius (n. 1). In Ethereum, the variables that are stored in a contract account can be altered, whereas the functions themselves are harder to replace.

[45] On the demise of The DAO, see, eg, Rius (n. 1) and A. Cunningham, 'Decentralisation, Distrust & Fear of the Body—The Worrying Rise of Crypto-Law' (2016) 13(3) *SCRIPTed* 236–57, 237–8.

[46] B. Marino and A. Juels, 'Setting Standards for Altering and Undoing Smart Contracts' in J.J. Alferes et al. (eds), *Rule Technologies. Research, Tools, and Applications*, vol 9718 (Springer: Lecture Notes in Computer Science 2016) 151–66. See also B. Marino, 'Smart-Contract Escape Hatches: The Dao of The DAO' (2016) <https://hackingdistributed.com/2016/06/22/smart-contract-escape-hatches/> accessed 8 July 2021 and M. Gupta, 'How to Make Smart Contracts Upgradable!' (2018) <https://hackernoon.com/how-to-make-smart-contracts-upgradable-2612e771d5a2> accessed 8 July 2021.

[47] For instance, Accenture has obtained a patent for an 'editable blockchain' that utilises 'chameleon hash functions'. This feature could be implemented in DLT networks to alter the shared ledger's data in the event of an error or fraud.

[48] For an empirical analysis of 'encoded opportunism' in ICO smart contracts, see S. Cohney et al., 'Coin-Operated Capitalism' (2019) 119(3) *Columbia Law Review* 591–645.

[49] L. Lessig, 'Code is Law' (*Harvard Magazine*, January–February 2000): 'the choice is not whether people will decide how cyberspace regulates. People—coders—will. The only choice is whether we collectively will have a role in their choice—and thus in determining how these values regulate—or whether collectively we will allow the coders to select our values for us.' See also S. Mason and T.S.

from displacing the need for trust, are merely 'trust-shifting'.[50] Perhaps more cynically, a writer for The Economist argues that the 'illusion of trustlessness' has served to mask a transfer of wealth to a technocratic elite.[51]

- **Self-executing/self-enforcing:** smart contracts are not necessarily self-executing nor self-enforcing. It is, of course, possible for a simultaneous exchange to be effected *via* smart contracts, as is the case with an initial coin offering ('ICO') contribution. However, this logic does not extend to transactions with a temporal component. In DLT networks, actions cannot be executed at a precise point in time, since it is difficult to synchronize clocks across spatially distributed nodes (due to 'clock drift').[52] Similarly, the process of obtaining data from off-ledger sources (like a finance website) cannot generally be automated with on-ledger code, as this would provide non-deterministic results and compromise the consensus process. The solution to these problems revolves around the use of an 'oracle', namely a manual execution or external algorithm that passes on the relevant parameters (such as the price of a stock) to a function in the smart contract.

These distinctions are important, as we ought to minimize the potential for ambiguity in a definition that could eventually make its way into a piece of legislation and become subject to legal scrutiny by the courts.[53] While it may be useful to consider industry jargon as a common starting point, it is also necessary to recognize where this is the product of inflated expectations or desiderata, as opposed to inherent properties.[54]

Reiniger, '"Trust" Between Machines? Establishing Identity Between Humans and Software Code, or whether You Know it is a Dog, and if so, Which Dog?' (2015) 5 *Computer and Telecommunications Law Review* 135–48, 144: 'this also implies a chain of trust to include the manufacturer, software writers, standards organisations and suchlike.' For a discussion of 'sticky defaults' and user biases, see V. Buterin, 'Software and Bounded Rationality' (2014) <https://blog.ethereum.org/2014/09/02/software-bounded-rationality/> accessed 8 July 2021. For an application of fiduciary principles to coders, see A. Walch, 'In Code(rs) We Trust: Software Developers as Fiduciaries in Public Blockchains' in Hacker et al. (eds),*Regulating Blockchain: Techno-Social and Legal Challenges* (OUP 2019) ch 3.

[50] See Walch (n. 49), 59: 'though [Szabo describes blockchains] as "trust-minimized", I see them as "trust-shifting"; the need to trust in others has simply moved from its traditional place (e.g. the officers and directors of a *bona fide* corporation), leaving us to discern where it has landed.' In this sense, we might say that trust cannot be destroyed, but merely displaced. See also Cunningham (n. 45), 249.

[51] The Economist, 'The great chain of being sure about things' (31 October 2015): 'the latest techy attempt to spread a "Californian ideology" which promises salvation through technology-induced decentralisation while ignoring and obfuscating the realities of power—and happily concentrating vast wealth in the hands of an elite.'

[52] L. Lamport, 'Time, Clocks, and the Ordering of Events in a Distributed System' (1978) 21(7) *Communications of the ACM* 558–65. For a less technical discussion, see P. Kasireddy, 'How Does Distributed Consensus Work?' (2018) <https://medium.com/s/story/lets-take-a-crack-at-understanding-distributed-consensus-dad23d0dc95> accessed 8 July 2021.

[53] See A.D.D.M. Rius and A. Kulasinghe, 'Responses to Public Consultations on Blockchain and Smart Contracts' (2019–2021) <http://alfonso.digitalpapers.uk/> accessed 8 July 2021. See also Walch (n. 7).

[54] See n. 7. In the broader context of blockchain, see D.C. de Leon *et al.*, 'Blockchain: Properties and Misconceptions' (2017) 11(3) *Asia Pacific Journal of Innovation and Entrepreneurship* 286–300.

5. Types of smart contracts

Based on the broad interpretation of the term 'contract', a smart contract may (but need not) be legally binding. Josh Stark's proposed distinction between *smart legal contracts* and *smart contract code* is helpful in this context.[55] Smart contract code is the overarching term that refers to a program that is intended to govern the relationship between two or more DLT users and can be executed by the nodes in a given network. Presumably, we should exclude from this definition code that is not designed to govern user relationships, for instance, if this merely serves as a data repository or library for other smart contracts.[56] In turn, we refer to smart legal contracts as the subset of smart contract code that is also legally binding. This may be as a result of the code itself initializing and recording the terms of a legal contract or due to the presence of an external agreement (oral, implied, or written in natural language) that endows the code with legal enforceability.[57] The UKJT *Legal Statement* has recently endorsed this position in relation to English law, indicating that even within the narrow, legal definition of a contract, smart contracts are not necessarily misnomers.[58]

There are a couple of variants of the smart contract concept that are worth exploring. The notion of a *split contract* was introduced by Mark Miller in 1997 to describe an agreement that comprises both natural language, smart contract code, and an interface to cryptographically link both.[59] Miller regards the American Information Exchange (AMIX) as an early example of a split contracting system.[60] AMIX was created in the late 1980s to enable customers to request information from experts in exchange for a consultation fee. Within AMIX, contracts embodied two different mediums of expression: natural language to express the question to be answered and the agreed compensation, and code that the AMIX system could understand and process. Upon delivery of the information, the transferee

---

[55] Stark (n. 6).
[56] Once referenced by a smart legal contract, a standalone library could come to form part of said contract (as if its terms or definitions had been incorporated).
[57] Rius (n. 1).
[58] UKJT *Legal Statement* (n. 2), 32: 'The precise role played by software in a smart contract can vary: Alice and Bob may contract on the basis that their obligations are defined by the code and that they abide by the behaviour of the code whatever it does; or they may contract on the basis that code will be used to implement their agreement but not define it; or they may contract on some hybrid basis, where some obligations are defined by code, others merely implemented by code and perhaps others not involving code at all. There is a spectrum.' See also Section D, below.
[59] M.S. Miller, 'Computer Security as the Future of Law' (EXTRO 3 conference, 9 August 1997). See also M.S. Miller and M. Stiegler, 'The Digital Path: Smart Contracts and the Third World' in J. Birner and P. Garrouste (eds), *Markets, Information and Communication: Austrian Perspectives on the Internet Economy* (Routledge 2003): 'smart contracts will be unable to express the subtle richness of contracts written in natural language, leading to techniques for combining the two kinds of contract elements into *split contracts*.'
[60] M.S. Miller, 'Observations on AMIX, The American Information Exchange' (1999). See also Chip Morningstar, 'What Agoric Learned from the American Information Exchange About Online Markets' (2020) <https://medium.com/agoric/what-agoric-learned-from-the-american-information-exchange-about-online-markets-91922fc49618> accessed 8 July 2021.

could either accept the transferor's document and make a payment or reject the document by marking it as inadequate. In the latter case, the system would deliver the request (in natural language) and the transferor's document to a human arbitrator, who would provide finality to the parties' dispute.[61]

Ian Grigg's 'Ricardian contract' is (at least in its current usage) a subsequent variation of the smart contract concept. The Ricardian contract was introduced by Grigg in 1996 as an element of the Ricardo payment system.[62] According to Grigg's original conception, a Ricardian contract would look like a conventional natural language contract, though it would also incorporate certain machine-readable tags to allow the document to be classified in accordance with a computer system's protocol, for instance, for accounting purposes. Ricardian contracts would also make use of digital signatures to allow parties to transact in a pseudonymous manner. Grigg explains that Ricardian contracts did not initially embody any executable code, as there was no demand for this at the time. In fact, until recently Grigg argued that Ricardian contracts and smart contracts were each addressing a separate set of issues.[63] However, Grigg notes that as a result of the increasing adoption of smart contracts, the concept of executable code eventually came to be imported into the Ricardian contract.[64] Ricardian contracts now appear to be commonly associated with interlinked natural language and code-based templates that parties can populate with deal-specific parameters.[65] So understood, they could be characterized as a specific structure that split contracts can adopt.

C. Smart Contracts and Contract law: a Transaction Costs Approach

As smart contracts began to gain traction, big corporates and professional advisers hastily implemented R&D programmes for fear of disruptive innovation.[66] In addition, they made sure to aggressively market their use of the technology. Even where the technology was knowingly being misapplied or failing to generate value for stakeholders, its use might have been justified on strategic grounds alone—as

---

[61] Note that, if the natural language is regarded as authoritative, the code would be relegated to serve as an enforcement mechanism (see Section D(2)).

[62] I. Grigg, 'The Ricardian Contract' (2004) *Proceedings of the First IEEE International Workshop on Electronic Contracting* 25–31.

[63] I. Grigg, 'On the intersection of Ricardian and Smart Contracts' (2015): 'Both are trying to improve our agreements at different points and in different ways, within the overall framework of a contract in law.'

[64] Interview with I. Grigg (2017) <http://internetofagreements.com/2017/12/ 25/interview-ian-grigg/> accessed 8 July 2021.

[65] See I. Grigg, 'Implementations of Ricardian contracts' (undated) <https://www.webfunds.org/guide/ricardian_implementations.html> accessed 8 July 2021. See also Clack *et al.* (n. 40).

[66] See C.M. Christensen, M.E. Raynor, and R. McDonald, 'What Is Disruptive Innovation?' (December 2015) *Harvard Business Review* 44–53.

an investment in signalling the company's commitment to delivering better services through innovation. This position is clearly unsustainable in the long run. Unless the technology is proven to yield positive results, a 'smart contract winter' may fall upon us.[67]

We might assume that rational economic agents are incentivized to adopt the most efficient transactional structure that is available and known to them. On that basis, the fact that value is still being exchanged through smart contracts would suggest that it must be the first-best transactional structure in at least some settings.[68] However, user pseudonymity obfuscates the extent to which smart contacts are being adopted to engage in socially undesirable or criminal activities, such as drug trafficking, money laundering, and tax avoidance.[69] As such, the challenge is one of establishing that the technology is capable of having a welfare-enhancing effect on society, with the internet itself being a clear instance of technology with net positive effects.[70]

Smart contracts are an institutional technology that enables the formation of new types of contracts and organizations. On that basis, Sinclair Davidson, Primavera De Filippi, and Jason Potts suggest that a useful analytical framework to assess the merits of this technology is that of new institutional economics, with an emphasis on transaction costs.[71] Indeed, Szabo and Miller applied principles from this framework when analysing the potential merits of smart contracts over traditional contracts.[72] In this section, I examine traditional contracting (within a contract law system) and smart contracts through this lens of transaction costs. In doing so, I will identify situations in which combining attributes of both (in the form of smart legal contracts) might be optimal in order to minimize transaction costs.

Economic agents enter into voluntary transactions to exchange goods and services, or money (an option to defer consumption on the former) in order to derive some utility (a subjective benefit). However, economic agents are not omniscient beings. In particular, they may be ignorant about the existence and

---

[67] On the 'AI winter', see S. Russell and P. Norvig, *Artificial Intelligence: A Modern Approach* (3rd edn, Pearson 2016) 24.
[68] See O. Williamson, 'The New Institutional Economics: Taking Stock, Looking Ahead' (2000) 38 *Journal of Economic Literature* 595–613, 601.
[69] For an attempt to categorize smart contract uses, see M. Bartoletti and L. Pompianu, 'An Empirical Analysis of Smart Contracts: Platforms, Applications, and Design Patterns' in M. Brenner *et al.* (eds), *Financial Cryptography and Data Security*, vol 10323 (Lecture Notes in Computer Science 2017) 494–509. See also S. Foley, J.R. Karlsen, and T.J. Putniņš, 'Sex, Drugs and Bitcoin: How Much Illegal Activity Is Financed Through Cryptocurrencies?' (2019) 32(5) *Review of Financial Studies* 1798–853.
[70] See eg, J. Armour *et al.*, 'Putting Technology to Good Use for Society: The Role of Corporate, Competition and Tax Law' (2018) ECGI Law Working Paper No 427/8.
[71] S. Davidson, P. De Filippi, and J. Potts, 'Economics of Blockchain' (2016) Public Choice Conference (Fort Lauderdale, US, May 2016) 8. See also M. Vatiero, 'Smart Contracts and Transaction Costs' (2018) Discussion Paper, University of Pisa, Dipartimento di Economia e Management, 2018/238.
[72] See Szabo (nn. 29, 30). See also Miller and Stiegler (n. 59).

location of trading opportunities, how to arrive at a mutually agreeable set of terms, and lack certainty about how sequential performance will unfold.[73] This state of imperfect information can give rise to a number of costs that erode economic agents' resources and disincentivize transactional activity.[74] The table below lists the main types of transaction costs that may come into play throughout the contract lifecycle.[75]

Common Stage	Types of Costs	Description
Ex Ante *Before initialization*	Search costs	Finding a counterparty with the desire to trade a specific good or service within a given price range
	Measurement costs	Defining the physical and property rights dimensions of the exchange
	Negotiation costs	Bargaining on economic parameters, the delineation of property rights, and the allocation of risk
	Agency costs	Engaging third party agents to define and formalize the conditions of exchange
Ex Post *After initialization*	Monitoring and verification costs	Tracking a counterparty's compliance with their obligations and verifying adequate performance
	Enforcement costs	Ensuring that a counterparty adheres to their obligations, or, alternatively, that the non-defaulting party receives compensation following a default

Figure 6.1 Overview of Transaction Costs by Common Stage and Type

In a world of transaction costs, institutions play an important role in constraining or enabling economic agents' behaviour.[76] In the economics literature,

---

[73] C. Dahlman, 'The Problem of Externality' (1979) 22(1) *Journal of Law and Economics* 141–62, 148.

[74] The characterization of transaction costs in the economics literature is notoriously inconsistent. In my analysis, I focus on the costs of transacting in a market. See D.W. Allen, 'Transaction Costs' in B.R.A. Bouckaert and G. de Geest (eds), *Encyclopedia of Law and Economics* (Edward Elgar Publishing 2000) 893–926 and P.K. Rao, *The Economics of Transaction Costs: Theory, Methods and Applications* (Macmillan 2003) 8–9. See also J. Niehans, 'Transaction Costs' in J. Eatwell *et al.* (eds), *The New Palgrave: A Dictionary of Economics* (Macmillan 1987) 676–9, 676: '[parties must] find each other, they have to communicate and to exchange information ... goods must be described, inspected, weighed and measured. Contracts are drawn up, lawyers may be consulted, title is transferred and records have to be kept. In some cases, compliance needs to be enforced through legal action and breach of contract may lead to litigation.' For a similar formulation, see R.H. Coase, 'The Problem of Social Cost' (1960) 3 *Journal of Law and Economics* 1–44, 15.

[75] This list is not intended to be exhaustive, and the types of costs outlined may arise at different stages of the contract lifecycle (ie both *ex ante* and *ex post*). For a similar classification, see S.M. Jaffee and J. Morton, *Marketing Africa's High-Value Foods: Comparative Experiences of an Emergent Private Sector* (Kendall/Hunt 1995) 30. Smart contracts may lower 'transfer costs' by taking advantage of a DLT network's settlement speed and security assurances.

[76] D.C. North, 'Transaction Costs, Institutions and Economic Performance' (1992) International Center for Economic Growth, Occasional Papers Number 30, 6. On institutions and technology, see T. Pinch, 'Technology and Institutions: Living in a Material World' (2008) 37 *Theory and Society* 461–83. See also Nick Szabo, 'Money, Blockchains and Social Scalability' (2017) <https://unenumerated.

institutions are defined as humanly-devised systems of formal rules (like the law) or informal norms (like cultural conventions) that shape social, economic, and political interactions.[77] Technology itself can also facilitate or hinder transactional behaviour, as Lawrence Lessig noted with his 'code is law' proposition (perhaps best interpreted as 'code as an institution').[78] Multi-sided platforms like eBay, Uber, and Airbnb are good examples of effective technological institutions. These platforms offer text searches, contract standardization, ratings, and online dispute resolution as a means of mitigating the various forms of transaction costs that parties might otherwise incur.[79]

1. Search costs

Search costs are commonly overlooked, as they are neither observable nor easy to quantify.[80] They encompass the tangible and intangible resources (like time) that are consumed in finding and screening a potential counterparty. In most cases, smart contracts are linked to a user-friendly interface that facilitates interactions with the code, such as a website or a trading venue. Given that smart contracts are generally dependent on existing web tools, it is not evident that their use would yield comparatively lower search costs. One could, however, point to specific examples in which smart contracts have contributed to a reduction in search costs. For instance, one could argue that smart contracts have facilitated the search for willing investors in early-stage tech projects by enabling the ICO funding model, facilitating capital formation and entrepreneurship.[81]

---

blogspot.com/2017/02/money-blockchains-and-social-scalability.html> accessed 8 July 2021: 'The social scalability of an institutional technology depends on how that technology constrains or motivates participation in that institution, including protection of participants and the institution itself from harmful participation or attack.'

[77] D.C. North, 'Institutions' (1991) 5(1) *Journal of Economic Perspectives* 97–112. See also G.M. Hodgson, 'What are Institutions?' (2006) 40(1) *Journal of Economic Issues* 1–25.

[78] L. Lessig, *Code Version 2.0* (Basic Books 2006) 123. See generally Aaron Wright and Primavera de Filippi, 'Decentralized Blockchain Technology and the Rise of Lex Cryptographia' (2015). See also V. Lehdonvirta and R. Ali, 'Governance and Regulation' in *UK Government Office for Science, Distributed Ledger Technology: Beyond Block Chain* (2019) 40–5, 41. Miller (n. 37) explains that there are now incompatible (re)interpretations of the 'code is law' proposition, so much so that it is invoked to defend diametrically opposed viewpoints.

[79] Szabo (n. 30), 13. See also D. Friedman, *Contracts in Cyberspace* (2000) Berkeley Program in Law and Economics, ch VII.

[80] See eg, D.C. North and J.J. Wallis, 'Integrating Institutional Change and Technical Change in Economic History: A Transaction Cost Approach' (1994) 150(4) *Journal of Institutional and Theoretical Economics* 609–24, 612. On the impact of information on search costs, see G. Stigler, 'The Economics of Information' (1961) 69(3) *Journal of Political Economy* 213–25.

[81] See S. Ahluwalia, R.V. Mahto, and M. Guerrero, 'Blockchain Technology and Startup Financing: A Transaction Cost Economics Perspective' (2020) 151 *Technological Forecasting and Social Change* 1–25, 8: 'In entrepreneurial finance, a high environmental uncertainty and a high information asymmetry between entrepreneur(s) and investors significantly enhances transaction costs involved in financing.' At 17–18: 'The primary cost reduction [with DLT] is achieved by reducing search costs.'

2. Measurement costs

Measurement costs are incurred in defining the conditions of the exchange. Two important problems arise in this regard. The first is that information is typically costly to acquire and asymmetrically spread. A seller with an informational advantage may thus be tempted to exploit this asymmetry to sell a low-quality good to an unsuspecting buyer (the problem of 'adverse selection').[82] A buyer can insert protection mechanisms into their legal contract, for instance, by including warranties as to the state of the goods. In addition, contract law will imply certain rights into consumer dealings to accelerate transactional activity and protect consumers from abusive behaviour (see Section B). A clear example of this under English law is the 'red hand rule', which requires parties to highlight any terms that are unusual and detrimental to an unsophisticated counterparty.[83] We can contrast this position with that of many ICOs, in which participants who fail to read the 'fine print' may be left with little more than tokens of gratitude.

The second problem affecting measurement costs is that of contractual incompleteness.[84] Since parties are not omniscient, they are unable to foresee every possible event (or 'state') that may materialize. As Williamson notes, the mind—being a scarce resource itself—must specialize.[85] To the extent that parties can determine, with a high confidence interval, the probability of given states materializing ('weak uncertainty'), they may proceed to allocate property rights (and consequently risk) in each such state.[86] Importantly, contractual incompleteness can also arise from the prohibitive negotiation costs involved in allocating risk in every foreseeable state.[87] To mitigate these issues, contract law systems provide a series of mandatory and default positions that allocate risk when matters are left unspecified.

Smart contracts cannot eradicate completeness issues, as they are engineered by humans with limited foresight and constraints on resources. This alone suggests that parties relying on smart contracts could benefit from resorting to the aforementioned contract law principles. The most obvious way of achieving this would

---

[82] G.A. Akerlof, 'The Market for "Lemons": Quality Uncertainty and the Market Mechanism' (1970) 84(3) *Quarterly Journal of Economics* 488–500.

[83] *J Spurling Ltd v Bradshaw* [1956] EWCA Civ 3 per Denning LJ.

[84] See especially O. Hart and J. Moore, 'Incomplete Contracts and Renegotiation' (1988) 56(4) *Econometrica* 755–85, 755: 'When drawing up a contract, it is often impracticable for the parties to specify all the relevant contingencies. In particular, they may be unable to describe the states of the world in enough detail that an outsider (the courts) could later verify which state has occurred, and so the contract will be incomplete.'

[85] Williamson (n. 68), 600.

[86] See D. Dequech, 'Uncertainty: A Typology and Refinements of Existing Concepts' (2011) XLV(3) *Journal of Economic Issues* XLV 621–40. For the classic distinction between measurable uncertainty (risk) and 'true' uncertainty, see F. Knight, *Risk, Uncertainty and Profit* (Houghton Mifflin Company 1921).

[87] See eg, Hart and Moore (n. 84).

be through the design of smart legal contracts.[88] An alternative approach entails embedding contract law principles in the code, perhaps by creating an ontology of common legal concepts and publishing the associated code in an open-source library.[89] Attempts to formalize core contract law principles have highlighted the limitations inherent in this approach.[90] Further, contract law principles often require the consideration of subjective matters and the exercise of discretion, which a human-centric enforcement mechanism is better suited to.

3. Negotiation costs

Negotiation costs are linked to measurement costs, as they arise in the course of scoping the zone of potential agreement (or lack thereof) and defining the distribution of rights and obligations.[91] Negotiation costs are minimized when dealing with regulated, liquid markets for homogenous products with standardized contractual terms, as is the case with securities in financial exchanges. By reducing transaction costs, these venues allow parties to focus on market prices alone, as these carry the information necessary to co-ordinate trades.[92]

When dealing with smart contracts, the entire negotiation process may take place on-ledger. In this scenario, the smart contract can be characterized as a unilateral offer.[93] A party wishing to take this offer up will call the desired function and transfer the requisite payment. The use of technical standards for tokens (like Ethereum's ERC-20) enables a number of capabilities to be homogenized, facilitating transferability and trading on exchanges (both on-ledger and off-ledger).[94] Alternatively, parties might have negotiated the entire agreement off-ledger, with smart contracts being used merely as a means of automating performance. The latter scenario is more likely to arise in permissioned networks in which parties' identity is known.

---

[88] In (n. 30), 14, Szabo states that 'Traditional law and smart contracts work best in synergy, when the lawyers and software engineers act as a team to secure the terms and conditions of a deal.' Cf. Szabo (n. 30), 17: 'Asking whether smart contracts need to be legally enforceable is akin to asking whether courts need to examine the guts of a vending machine to figure out what parties intended.'

[89] For an ontology of contract law concepts tailored towards smart contracts, see Rius (n. 1).

[90] See E. Tjong Tjin Tai, 'Formalizing contract law for smart contracts' (2017) Tilburg Private Law Working Paper Series No 6/2017.

[91] On negotiation habits and the zone of potential agreement, see R. Fisher and W. Ury, *Getting To Yes: Negotiating an Agreement Without Giving In* (Random House 2012).

[92] On the role of price as a co-ordinating agent, see F.A. Hayek, 'The Use of Knowledge in Society' (1945) 35(4) *American Economic Review* 519–30.

[93] A unilateral offer is one that is made to the world at large, as opposed to being targeted at a specific person. Such an offer is capable of being legally binding, as established in the classic case of *Carlill v Carbolic Smoke Ball Company* [1892] EWCA Civ 1.

[94] For a specification of the ERC-20 standard, see <https://eips.ethereum.org/EIPS/eip-20>.

4. Agency costs

In the principal-agent literature, 'principals' are persons who delegate work to others (the 'agents').[95] There are certain transaction costs that principals (ie parties to a contract) face. For instance, principals may fall short of achieving a desired outcome due to a lack of intelligence, experience or access to valuable resources (including information).[96] As such, principals may be better off by engaging an agent who, through their expertise and connections, can increase the value that principals derive from the transaction.[97] Lawyers are a class of agents that pervades the realm of traditional contacts. Lawyers' specialization in structuring transactions to protect principals' interests and generate additional value has led them to be characterized as 'transaction cost engineers'.[98]

The use of an agent in this setting comprises a 'transaction within a transaction', meaning that the principal-agent relationship carries its very own set of transaction costs. Aside from outright fees, these include competence costs (mitigated by reputation signals), conflict costs (constrained by regulation), monitoring costs to prevent shirking (with regular updates), and enforcement costs where the agent fails to perform to a satisfactory standard. If agents are sheltered from the outcome of a transaction, they may decide to act opportunistically (the 'moral hazard' problem). In the realm of traditional contracts, this risk is mitigated by the tort of negligence, which incentivizes lawyers to perform to industry standards. Principals can also incorporate explicit incentive alignment mechanisms into their agency contracts, for instance, in the form of success fees (a form of 'skin in the game').[99]

It is common for smart contract advocates to argue that the technology will facilitate transactional activity without intermediaries, thereby eliminating agency costs.[100] In practice, not all principals are technically sophisticated, or wish to spend their time formalizing and auditing encoded terms. Therefore, reliance on

---

[95] K.M. Eisenhardt, 'Agency Theory: An Assessment and Review' (1989) 14(1) *The Academy of Management Review* 57–74, 58.
[96] In a managerial setting, see Z. Gosher and R. Squire, 'Principal Costs: A New Theory for Corporate Law and Governance' (2017) 117(3) *Columbia Law Review* 767–829, 795.
[97] This should not be confused with the notion of an 'economic agent', which includes any entity involved in a transaction (in this context, both principals and agents).
[98] R.J. Gilson, 'Value Creation by Business Lawyers: Legal Skills and Asset Pricing' (1984) 94 *Yale Law Journal* 239, 241 (applying the so-called 'Coase Theorem' to firms' capital structure). Of course, access to intellectual capital and reputation signals are also amongst the motives for using lawyers.
[99] See eg, N. Taleb, *Skin in the Game: Hidden Asymmetries in Daily Life* (Random House 2018). Taleb argues that 'the symmetry of skin in the game is a simple rule that's necessary for fairness and justice, and the ultimate BS-buster'.
[100] See eg, W.A. Kaal, 'Blockchain Solutions for Agency Problems in Corporate Governance' in K.R. Balachandran (ed), *Economic Information to Facilitate Decision Making* (World Scientific Publishers 2019): 'Agency relationships in smart contracts run exactly as coded without any possibility of opportunistic behavior of the agent. Information asymmetries between principal and agent, censorship, opportunism of agents, breaches of fiduciary duties, liability rules for principals and agents, fraud or third party interference are removed entirely … Agency related governance in the blockchain takes place without intermediaries.'

third-party developers seems inescapable for most. Crucially, developers are not upheld to the same rigorous standards as lawyers, nor are they required by law to take out professional indemnity insurance.[101] It is hard for a developer to be found negligent, as long as the presence of bugs in code is treated as 'business as usual'. As one English judge put it: 'The expert evidence showed that it is regarded as acceptable practice to supply computer programmes (including system software) that contain errors and bugs.'[102] While this stance might perhaps incentivize technological innovation, it does little to disincentivize moral hazard and leaves principals trapped in a 'liability lacuna'. Even worse, there is a perverse incentive for developers who are familiar with the code to take advantage of user pseudonymity to exploit deliberate vulnerabilities in the code (an 'inside job').

Parties who wish to create smart legal contracts will most likely need to engage both lawyers and developers as agents in their transaction. Apart from compounding agency costs, there is also the prospect of miscommunication between agents. To address this challenge, some commentators have advocated for the development of a new hybrid language that both sets of agents can work from.[103] However, it would probably be more efficient in the long run if more lawyers learned how to program smart contracts. As the contracting paradigm shifts to a world 'code and law', lawyers could well evolve into a specialized subset of developers.[104]

5. Monitoring and verification costs

Most contractual obligations are state-contingent, meaning that they will only be triggered when a predefined state materializes (such as receipt of payment). For this reason, a party will want to monitor whether a relevant state has arisen to comply with any corresponding obligations within the agreed timeframe. Having visibility over the stage of the transaction can also help parties to plan ahead and to identify whether a counterparty is delaying performance. In traditional contracting, parties may need to employ agents (such as accountants) to verify whether an obligation has been discharged, as they may lack the expertise to do so. Alternatively, parties might wish to reduce the 'dispute surface' by relying on the determination of

---

[101] On developers' liability, see S. Mason and D. Cheng, *Electronic Evidence* (4th edn, Institute of Advanced Legal Studies 2017) ch 6. On indemnity insurance in England, see the Solicitors Regulation Authority's Indemnity Insurance Rules, r 3.1.
[102] *Eurodynamic Systems Plc v General Automation Ltd* (QBD, 6 September 1988) [5.a] per Steyn J. This does not prevent developers from being sued for breach of contract.
[103] F. Al Khalil *et al.*, 'Trust in smart contracts is a process, as well' in M. Brenner *et al.* (eds), *Financial Cryptography and Data Security*, vol 10323 (Lecture Notes in Computer Science 2017) 510–19.
[104] J. Czarnecki, 'Between tradition and progress: The role of smart contracts in the lawyer's toolkit' (2017) <https://blog.neufund.org/between-tradition-and-progress-the-role-of-smart-contracts-in-the-lawyers-toolkit-dfec8f26bab9> accessed 8 July 2021. Monax (company) refers to this practice as 'legal engineering'. See also Cunningham (n. 45), 253: 'The law can be viewed ... as another type of programming language ... Code may be becoming (and may already be) law, but law was and is already a type of code.'

an independent expert whose conduct is constrained by regulation and industry standards.

Gans argues that smart contracts can lead to a reduction in monitoring costs; since state itself is recorded in the distributed ledger, parties may be able to monitor the contract lifecycle in close to real-time.[105] Indeed, smart contracts can be programmed to automate parties' performance, with actions being executed sequentially once a function is called. On that basis, parties may not need to rely on human agents to verify that performance is adequate, as the execution of code triggers a state transition whose outcome is recorded on the ledger (alongside a timestamp).[106] By reducing monitoring costs, the range of feasible contracts can be expanded, with attractive possibilities in the realm of financing.[107]

6. Enforcement costs

In personal exchange, kinship ties, friendship, and loyalty constrain parties' behaviour.[108] Insofar as parties do not feel the need to engage in negotiations, monitor, or seek protection from defaults, transaction costs will be reduced. Although the ease of forming personal relationships varies from one society to another, our cognitive capacity limits the scalability of these relationships.[109] Transactional activity in developed economies is instead dominated by impersonal exchange, where 'social and moral shackles' may not suffice to deter a party from defaulting. As Hobbes observed in *Leviathan*: 'he that performeth first, has no assurance the other will perform after; because the bonds of words are too weak ... without the fear of some coercive power'.[110]

---

[105] J.S. Gans, 'The Fine Print in Smart Contracts' (2019) NBER Working Paper, No 25443, 1–22, 9. The effectiveness of monitoring on-ledger activity ultimately depends on a number of network conditions, such as transaction confirmation times and network latency.

[106] *Ibid*. On the accuracy of timestamps, see generally J. Lopp, 'Bitcoin Timestamp Security' (2019) <https://blog.lopp.net/bitcoin-timestamp-security/> accessed 8 July 2021.

[107] Wood (n. 35), 1: Ethereum aims to facilitate 'transactions between consenting individuals who would otherwise have no means to trust one another.' See Gans (n. 105), 6: 'In order for a Blockchain to have value, it must work to enhance trust in situations where neither current social nor institutional mechanisms are present.' See also Coase (n. 74), 15: '[transaction costs can be] sufficiently costly at any rate to prevent many transactions that would be carried out in a world in which the pricing system worked without cost.' In the context of financing, see K. Tinn, ' "Smart" Contracts and External Financing' (Western Finance Association Meeting 2018).

[108] North (n. 76), 7–8.

[109] Szabo (n. 76): 'Without institutional and technological innovations of the past, participation in shared human endeavors would usually be limited to at most about 150 people—the famous "Dunbar number".' On societal trust, see F. Fukuyama, *Trust: The Social Virtues and the Creation of Prosperity* (The Free Press 1996).

[110] *Leviathan or The Matter, Forme and Power of a Common-Wealth Ecclesiastical and Civil* (Andrew Cooke 1651) 105. See also A.T. Kronman, 'Contract Law and the State of Nature' (1985) 1(1) *Journal of Law, Economics and Organisation* 5–32, 10: 'Where one of the parties is put in an asymmetrically disadvantageous position ... where the exchange cannot be made perfectly simultaneously at every step ... If the risk is great enough, it may kill the exchange entirely, even though both parties would be better off were it completed.'

The devil that Hobbes warned of is a master of disguise. In the transaction costs literature, this threat is encapsulated in the notion of opportunism;[111] in the new comparative economics, this falls within the scope of disorder;[112] and in finance, it takes the form of counterparty risk. In turn, the 'prisoners dilemma' in game theory exemplifies how the absence of a credible commitment leads to an unco-operative, Pareto-inefficient equilibrium.[113] Last, the notion of 'trust' is applied generously across the literature to describe relationships in which this threat has been mitigated (though not necessarily eliminated).[114] As Posner reminds us, 'trust ... is merely an imperfect substitute for information'.[115]

One way to mitigate this threat is to search for signals that convey a party's likelihood of default. Reputation systems can be a source of such signals, helping to reduce the scope of due diligence that parties need to conduct. However, reputation systems have their limits too. First, the reliability of these systems depends on how costly they are to game, for instance, by generating fake ratings or shifting to a new account.[116] Second, they do not assist those who are new to the system (the 'chicken and egg' problem). Third, the prospect of repeat business may not deter a party from foregoing their reputation capital where the gain

---

[111] See O.E. Williamson, 'Opportunism and its Critics' (1993) 14 *Managerial and Decision Economics* 97–107, 97: 'Transaction cost economics has proposed that economic agents be described as opportunistic, where this contemplates self-interest seeking with guile.'

[112] S. Djankov *et al.*, 'The New Comparative Economics' (2003) 31(4) *Journal of Comparative Economics* 595–619, 598.

[113] See V. Lehdonvirta, 'The Blockchain Paradox: Why Distributed Ledger Technologies May do Little to Transform the Economy' (*Oxford Internet Institute Blog*, 2016) <https://www.oii.ox.ac.uk/blog/the-blockchain-paradox-why-distributed-ledger-technologies-may-do-little-to-transform-the-economy/> accessed 8 July 2021. See also Rius (n. 1).

[114] There is a lack of agreement in the literature as to whether trust arises from formal or informal institutions, or perhaps both. See generally B. Nooteboom, 'Social Capital, Institutions and Trust' (2007) 65(1) *Review of Social Economy* 29–53, 29: 'These concepts are full of ambiguity and confusion'. From an economic perspective, see J.H. Dyer and W. Chu, 'The Role of Trustworthiness in Reducing Transaction Costs and Improving Performance: Empirical Evidence from the United States, Japan, and Korea' (2003) 14(1) *Organization Science* 57–68, 57: '[Trust is defined in the literature as] one party's confidence that the other party in the exchange relationship will not exploit its vulnerabilities ... Trust in exchange relationships has been hypothesized to be a valuable economic asset because it is believed to (1) *lower transaction costs* and allow for greater flexibility to respond to changing market conditions ... and (2) lead to *superior information sharing* which improves coordination and joint efforts to minimize inefficiencies.' From a computer law perspective, see Mason and Reiniger (n. 49) 137.

[115] R.A. Posner, 'The Right of Privacy' (1978) 12(3) *Georgia Law Review* 393–422, 408. In the context of software, see William S. Harbison, 'Trusting in Computer Systems' (December 1997) University of Cambridge Computer Laboratory Technical Report No 437, 15: 'the concept of trust is better associated with the idea of what we *don't* know rather than what we do know. It can therefore be considered as a *substitute* for knowledge instead of a representation of it.' At 39: 'Trust, by definition, is not a guarantee. Therefore an approach to understanding trust is also one of assessing risk.'

[116] Machine learning algorithms are able to convincingly replicate the nuances of human emotion. See, eg, M. Juuti *et al.*, 'Stay On-Topic: Generating Context-specific Fake Restaurant Reviews' in J. Lopez, J. Zhou, and M. Soriano (eds), *Computer Security*, vol 11098 (Lecture Notes in Computer Science 2018) 132–51.

from defaulting has a higher expected value than continued performance (the 'last-period problem').

Legal institutions can exert a stronger and more pervasive form of credible commitment.[117] Laws are enforced by the courts and backstopped by state agents' coercive powers.[118] At the *ex ante* stage of contracting, the mere threat of enforcement can incentivize parties to perform. At the *ex post* stage, the courts provide finality to a dispute when a contractual breach or unforeseen event occurs. Within the courts' diverse toolkit is the ability to require the defaulting party to compensate the non-defaulting party (through the notion of damages) or to order that the outstanding obligations be performed (i.e. specific performance).[119] These contract law principles may be overridden by equity considerations, insolvency law, and other public policy concerns. Alternative dispute resolution is also a viable (and often more efficient) route to contractual enforcement, though decisions are still made in the 'shadow of the law'.[120]

For all of their virtues, legal systems are not without their fair share of warts. It is perhaps helpful to highlight a few prominent arguments from the literature. First, the litigation process can be costly and time-consuming; in other words, it is skewed in favour of deep-pocketed parties.[121] As such, it may be economically inefficient for a party who has been wronged to litigate, particularly when small

---

[117] See generally D.C. North, 'Institutions and Credible Commitment' (1993) 149(1) *Journal of Institutional and Theoretical Economics* 11–23. See also K. Shepsle, 'Discretion, Institutions, and the Problem of Government Commitment' in P. Bourdieu and K. Coleman (eds), *Social Theory for a Changing Society* (Westview Press 1991) 245–65, where the author notes that a commitment is credible in either of two senses, the motivational (incentive-compatible) or the imperative (coerced). On the latter, see Gans (n. 105) 6: 'Beyond such social forces, there have been institutional mechanisms that have developed to allow obligations to be performed sequentially'.

[118] G.K. Hadfield, 'The Many Legal Institutions that Support Contractual Commitment' in C. Menard and M. Shirley (eds), *Handbook of New Institutional Economics* (Kluwer Academic Publishers 2004) 175–204. See also R. Koulu, *Law, Technology and Dispute Resolution: The Privatisation of Coercion* (Routledge 2019): 'The feedback system or multilateral trust marks may facilitate commerce and increase trust and even create better business practices, but in the end they are not the functional equivalent of engaging law's coercion. They follow a different rationality from the inherent violence of law.' See generally D.C. North, J.J. Wallis, and B.R. Weingast, *Violence and Social Orders: A Conceptual Framework for Interpreting Human Recorded History* (CUP 2013).

[119] In civil law jurisdictions, the default remedy following a contractual breach is specific performance. In these jurisdictions, lawmakers place greater emphasis on the moral obligation to perform that is deemed to underlay each legal obligation. In contrast, common law jurisdictions can be said to be more pragmatic, with damages being the default remedy. See G. Klass, 'Efficient Breach' in G. Klass, G. Letsas, and P. Saprai (eds), *Philosophical Foundations of Contract Law* (OUP 2014). See also S. Shavell, 'Why Breach of Contract May Not Be Immoral Given The Incompleteness of Contracts' (2009) 107 *Michigan Law Review* 1569–81.

[120] R.H. Mnookin and L. Kornhauser, 'Bargaining in the Shadow of the Law: The Case of Divorce' (1979) 88(5) *Yale Law Journal* 950–97. Koulu (n. 118) observes that there is a feedback loop: the legal system either copes 'with the irritation [posed by private enforcement] and improves its immune system by addressing such demands, or it ceases to exist'.

[121] See eg, M. Galanter 'Why the "Haves" Come Out Ahead: Speculations on the Limits of Legal Change' (1974) 9 *Law and Society Review* 95–160. Cf. B. Zorina Khan, '"To Have and Have Not": Are Rich Litigious Parties Favoured In Court?' (2015) NBER Working Paper 20945.

money claims are involved.[122] Second, the law is not uniformly interpreted by lawyers or even judges, thereby giving rise to *legal risk*. Third, the rule of law is not upheld in all legal systems, leaving room for lobbying, corruption and discrimination.[123] Fourth, even in systems where the rule of law is upheld, judges are not immune to biases, emotional swings or fatigue. An empirical study from Israel finds that 'judicial rulings can be swayed by extraneous variables that should have no bearing on legal decisions'.[124]

Szabo, Miller, and other members of the cypherpunk community saw in smart contracts an opportunity to sidestep the enforcement costs and injustices emanating from legal systems.[125] In an ideal setting, smart contracts would be fully automated, with the nodes preventing deviations from an intended state.[126] Even assuming that the code is bug-free, there will be situations in which parties might be better off by agreeing to deviate from the agreed terms, perhaps after acquiring some new information.[127] As Max Raskin notes, if parties 'tie themselves to the mast like Ulysses', they will forego this form of optionality.[128] Similarly, parties may prefer to defer the formulation of certain obligations to a later stage, relying in the interim on parties' mutual interest in preserving an economic relation.[129]

---

[122] Even if parties succeed in their dispute, they will generally be unable to recover in full the legal fees incurred. In the context of English law, see the Civil Procedure Rules, pt 44.

[123] The notion of the rule of law in the literature is admittedly 'highly elastic', as noted in G.K. Hadfield and B.R. Weingast, 'Microfoundations of the Rule of Law' (2014) 17 *Annual Review of Political Science* 21–42. See eg, T. Bingham, *The Rule of Law* (Penguin 2013).

[124] In S. Danziger, J. Levav, and L. Avnaim-Pesso, 'Extraneous Factors in Judicial Decisions' (2011) 108(17) *Proceedings of the National Academy of Sciences* 6889–92, the authors analyse 1,112 judicial rulings in Israeli criminal law cases and identify that judges' propensity to issue a favourable ruling decreases probabilistically on the basis of how close they are to their usual break (an observable proxy for fatigue). See also O. Wendell Holmes, *The Common Law* (Little, Brown and Company 1881): 'The life of the law has not been logic: it has been experience. The felt necessities of the time, the prevalent moral and political theories, intuitions of public policy, avowed or unconscious, even the prejudices which judges share with their fellow-men, have had a good deal more to do than the syllogism in determining the rules by which men should be governed'.

[125] Miller (n. 59) argues that computer security systems are no different than good legal systems, insofar as they can each be characterized as 'a neutral framework of rules that support cooperation without vulnerability'. In K. Binmore, 'Game Theory and Institutions' (2010) 38(3) *Journal of Comparative Economics* 245–52, the author argues that the 'fairness' of institutions reinforces their ability to withstand the sands of time.

[126] See Buterin (n. 35), 1 and Wood (n. 35), 1.

[127] In O.E. Williamson, *The Economic Institutions of Capitalism* (Free Press 1985), this is referred to as 'maladaptation': when parties later discover that the most efficient course of action was not 'A', as defined *ex ante* in the contract, but 'B'. The renegotiation that is likely to ensue can prove costly for both parties.

[128] M. Raskin, 'The Law and Legality of Smart Contracts' (2017) 1 *Georgetown Law Technology Review* 305, 309. Werbach and Cornell (n. 12) 356 suggest that smart contracts might be regarded as 'specific performance on steroids and without the state's coercive machinery'. In turn, Sklaroff (n. 27) refers to the potential for maladaptation and the inability to exploit efficient breaches as the 'cost of inflexibility'.

[129] On relational contracts, see R.J. Gilson, C.F. Sabel, and R.E. Scott, 'Braiding: The Interaction of Formal and Informal Contracting in Theory, Practice and Doctrine' (2010) Stanford Law and

As argued in Section B, performance in the context of smart contracts can typically only be automated in part, with the remainder requiring some form of manual input (and therefore human discretion). To mitigate opportunism in these cases, a smart contract can be programmed to facilitate certain forms of self-help.[130] For instance, a party may be required to post collateral to a contract account, which will cryptographically escrow the transferred assets. Yet, in the absence of a legal concept of 'security interests', this solution burdens the scalability of impersonal exchange. A number of more complex, game-theoretic mechanisms have also been proposed to mitigate the risk of opportunistic behaviour.[131] The literature on bounded rationality and satisficing raises questions as to the extent to which these mechanisms might prove useful beyond the realm of economists' fantasies.[132]

The discussion in this subsection highlights the benefits of smart *legal* contracts, particularly in jurisdictions where the rule of law is substantially upheld. By adopting this transactional structure, parties can take advantage of the efficiency of code execution, while retaining the option to pursue legal enforcement when code malfunctions or a counterparty defaults. There are, however, practical challenges to this approach. The first is that, if parties are unable to identify one another, they will be unable to enforce obligations in court. Any commitment to a contract law system ceases to be credible, with parties operating within a regime of de facto *caveat emptor* ('let the buyer beware'). I will consider the set of issues posed by pseudonymity in Section D. The second challenge is that of determining the applicable law and forum for the resolution of disputes. With regard to the former, approaches such as the Place of the Relevant Intermediary Approach (PRIMA) may not be particularly helpful when dealing with smart contracts, given that, by

---

Economics Olin Working Paper No 389. See also O. Hart and J. Moore, 'Contracts as Reference Points' (2008) 123(1) *Quarterly Journal of Economics* 1–48.

[130] For other means of addressing this threat, including taking collateral, hostages, hands-tying, and union, see Kronman (n. 110) 11–24.

[131] See, eg, Gans (n. 105). See also R. Holden and A. Malani, 'Can Blockchain Solve the Holdup Problem in Contracts?' (2017) University of Chicago Coase-Sandor Institute for Law & Economics Research Paper No 846. On the emergent interdisciplinary field of 'cryptoeconomics', see J. Stark, 'Making Sense of Cryptoeconomics' (*CoinDesk*, 19 August 2017) <https://www.coindesk.com/making-sense-cryptoeconomics> accessed 8 July 2021. In Cunningham (n. 45) 244, the term 'computationalism' is introduced to describe 'a complete faith in the ability of mathematics and technology to eradicate problems emerging from human behaviour'.

[132] See generally J. Baron, 'Heuristics and Biases' in E. Zamir and D. Teichman (eds), *The Oxford Handbook of Behavioral Economics and Law* (OUP 2014). In 'Small-game fallacies' (2015) <https://unenumerated.blogspot.com/2015/05/small-game-fallacies.html> accessed 8 July 2021, Szabo coins the term 'small-game fallacy' to describe situations in which game theorists compress real world scenarios into a limited but workable set of assumptions, sacrificing a significant dose of relevance in the process. See also N. Szabo, 'Micropayments and Mental Transaction Costs' (1999) Workshop Paper, 2nd Berlin Internet Economics Workshop.

maintaining a copy of the ledger, every node in the network is effectively acting as an intermediary.[133]

D. Design Trade-Offs

In the previous section, I focused on the comparative merits of traditional legal contracts and smart contracts. In this section, I wish to shift the attention to the related choice of medium of expression. While parts of the analysis may be transposed to algorithmic and hybrid contracts at large, I aim to account for the idiosyncrasies of DLT networks. In deciding where the 'split' between code and natural language should lie, I will apply the legal principles discussed in Section B and reference the transaction costs framework from Section C.

1. Bare smart contract code

The simplest form of smart contract is that which is comprised exclusively of code. An example might be an ICO smart contract that sets the economic terms for the issue of a new cryptoasset. In the absence of natural language, this contract is still capable of being legally binding, provided that it meets the threshold set by an applicable legal system. In common law systems, an intention to be legally bound is required, which in the case of token issuers might be a dubious assumption. Where that is the case, an ICO issuer who has received the purchaser's funds would be legally obliged to ensure that new tokens are issued to the purchaser. Such an obligation may stand even if an attack or other unforeseen event leads the parties to an unintended state.

One of the main motivations in the use of code is to avoid the semantic ambiguity, or 'open texture', of natural language.[134] DLT networks are deterministic by design, meaning that the entries registered by the networked nodes in

---

[133] As argued in Rius (n. 1), far from facilitating disintermediation, DLT enables *superintermediation*, so that parties need not rely on a single record-keeper (or witness). At the expense of proposing an idealistic solution, it would perhaps be helpful for the challenge of determining applicable laws to be addressed through an international convention. For a discussion of PRIMA in the context of DLT, as well as other related approaches, see ISDA, Clifford Chance, R3 and Singapore Academy of Law, 'Private International Law Aspects of Smart Derivatives Contracts Utilizing Distributed Ledger Technology' (2020) <https://www.isda.org/2020/01/13/private-international-law-aspects-of-smart-derivatives-contracts-utilizing-distributed-ledger-technology/> accessed 8 July 2021.

[134] In 'Wet code and dry' (2011) <https://unenumerated.blogspot.com/2006/11/wet-code-and-dry.html> accessed 8 July 2021, Nick Szabo draws a distinction between wet code (interpreted by humans) and dry code (interpreted by computers). Natural languages and law are mostly wet code, whereas smart contract code is dry code. I agree with Allen (n. 14) 12 in that this terminology is not particularly helpful, particularly when considering the prevalent semantic chaos.

their local copies of the ledger are meant to be consistent. Similarly, smart contract code is executed by a deterministic process that does not concern itself with subjective or contextual considerations. On the other hand, programming languages are also living creatures, as their grammar is capable of evolving. In this regard, Ethereum's most popular programming language (Solidity) is currently immature and poorly document.[135] It is common for Solidity's pre-defined terms ('reserved values') to be deprecated with frequency, imposing monitoring and learning cost on developers that will ultimately be borne by principals.

The DAO is perhaps a well-studied example of bare smart contract code, although natural language was used to set out certain rules that participants were expected to follow.[136] An example of an application that is currently still functional is the Maker platform, which enables users to post ether (and other supported cryptoassets) as collateral for a 'loan' denominated in the platform's stablecoin (DAI).[137] There is a wealth of contradicting, outdated and fragmented documentation about the platform's inner workings. It is clear from the disclaimers in these documents that contributors do not wish to be legally bound by its contents. In view of this, a court could take the view that DAO tokenholders and Maker users implicitly waived their rights under contract law. This does not, of course, prevent the application of criminal law, public law, and perhaps even insolvency law to transactions effected in these platforms. In this regard, participants would benefit from greater legal clarity as to the circumstances in which the 'algorithmic veil' might be pierced by the courts.

A setting in which code alone may fall short is when referencing *off-ledger assets*. There is a lot of interest in the practice of 'tokenisation', which involves the issuance of tokens that represent off-ledger assets, such as currencies (in the guise of 'stablecoins'), commodities or securities. This gives rise to 'mixed-economy risk', that is, the frictions in linking assets in the real economy (or financial markets) to on-ledger assets.[138] Most users would not be satisfied if an issuer were to simply issue tokens on the premise that these are 'fully backed'. An unconventional solution entails storing the underlying assets in a vault and constantly livestreaming the vault's contents, thereby reducing monitoring

---

[135] The documentation for the latest version of Solidity is available at <https://docs.soliditylang.org/> accessed 8 July 2021.

[136] See n. 45.

[137] For the latest(?) iteration of the whitepaper, see Maker Foundation, 'The Maker Protocol: MakerDAO's Multi-Collateral Dai (MCD) System' (2019–2021) <https://makerdao.com/en/whitepaper/> accessed 8 July 2021.

[138] In K. Kaivanto and D. Prince, 'Risks and Transaction Costs of Distributed-Ledger Fintech Boundary Effects and Consequences' (2017) arXiv:1702.08478, 6, the term 'mixed-economy' is introduced to refer to the co-existence of fiat currencies and cryptocurrencies in a given market. I wish to extend this concept to encompass any combination of on-ledger and off-ledger assets.

costs.[139] A perhaps more reliable solution involves the use of an external custody agreement that is linked to the smart contract code (a split contract), allowing tokenholders to enforce a legal claim against a named entity.[140] The decision of whether to introduce a new (and faster) settlement layer for assets through tokenization should factor in the costs involved in setting up and maintaining these legal structures, as one would expect these costs to be passed on to tokenholders. Alternatively (or in addition), operators might be compensated through the exercise of rights to re-use the underlying assets (eg, through lending or rehypothecation), thereby reintroducing the counterparty risk that pervades traditional financial intermediation.

When dealing with code alone, parties should consider the risk posed by bugs and attacks (*code risk* and *cybersecurity risk*, respectively). Several analyses of Ethereum smart contracts have revealed a concerning number of widespread vulnerabilities stemming from the immaturity of Solidity and related testing tools.[141] To address this, developers can incorporate 'escape hatches' that permit performance to be halted with parties' consent.[142] A trade-off arises due to the increased complexity of the code, as these fallback mechanisms open the floodgates to unforeseen vulnerabilities and consequently expands the 'attack surface'.

Last, the use of natural language may be necessary to comply with legal formalities. For instance, there are certain signing and witnessing requirements for parties to a land transaction. In certain jurisdictions, parties to a land transaction may be required to sign in the (physical) presence of a notary. The use of smart contract code to transfer interests in land may thus give rise to legal uncertainty. Nowadays, one could argue that parties can attain similar security assurances through the use of private keys, digital signatures, and multisignature requirements. Further, all of the networked nodes can be said to act as 'witnesses', as the transaction will be recorded in their local copies of the ledger.[143] Unfortunately, the law typically follows (and gives force to) transactional customs, not vice versa. In the absence of legislative reform, these formalities might obstruct the exploration of efficiencies in this setting.

---

[139] See M. Levine, 'Money Stuff' (*Bloomberg*, 12 October 2018): 'First of all, if someone *does* steal the gold [from Eidoo's vault], on camera, while the token holders watch in increasing horror, that is going to be a really funny day on Twitter and Reddit... Second, if you buy these tokens... Are you going to sit at your computer 24 hours a day staring at a live feed of some motionless gold bars in a windowless room, muttering to yourself "yes the future of economics is finally here"?'

[140] On the topic of smart contracts and custody of off-ledger assets, see Mattereum, 'Smart Property Registers' (2019–2020) <https://mattereum.com/wp-content/uploads/2020/02/mattereum_workingpaper.pdf> accessed 8 July 2021.

[141] In D. Perez and B. Livshits, 'Smart Contract Vulnerabilities: Does Anyone Care?' (2019) arXiv:1902.06710, the authors summarize the empirical research on smart contract vulnerabilities and dispel some misconceptions.

[142] See n. 36.

[143] On the notion of witnesses in the context of DLT, see D. Drescher, *Blockchain Basics: A Non-Technical Introduction in 25 Steps* (Apress 2017).

Consider using for	Refrain from using for
Low value transactions (e.g. business-to-consumer or consumer-to-consumer)	High value or complex transactions where bugs or attacks can lead to significant losses
Dealings in cryptoassets in accordance with established technical standards (e.g. ERC-20)	Transactions in which the parties wish to be certain that the courts will deem their relationship to be legally binding
Transactions where the parties are both technically sophisticated	Business-to-business transactions, particularly those executed in permissionless networks
Dealings in permissioned networks where network operators can be held accountable for system errors	Transactions in which the parties or arbitrators under consideration are not technically sophisticated
Transactions in which the developer has clear instructions and can be held liable for bugs or attacks	Agreements that require the inclusion of standards of behaviour or non-operational clauses
	Transations for which the law prescribes incompatible formalities
	Dealings with off-chain assets

Figure 6.2 Indicative Use Cases for Bare Smart Contracts

2. Natural language and code—no overlap

Certain contractual terms are not capable of being expressed in Boolean (or fuzzy) logic.[144] Commentators often refer to these as 'non-operational' terms, in contrast to the 'operational' logic that can indeed be compiled from natural language into code.[145] Amongst these non-operational terms are standards of behaviour (eg, 'reasonable' and 'in good faith') that seek to ameliorate issues of contractual incompleteness. In the event of litigation, the courts can ascribe meaning to these terms by reference to industry standards or legal constructs such as *the reasonable*

---

[144] Cf. J.M. Lipshaw, 'The Persistence of "Dumb" Contracts' (2019) *Stanford Journal of Blockchain Law & Policy*, 29: 'Fuzzy logic permits formal deduction from premises to truth-functional conclusions by allowing propositions to be increasingly true on a [non-binary] scale ... [Fuzzy logic] might be able to decide where performance falls on a scale of running from completely reasonable to completely unreasonable.'

[145] Clack *et al.* (n. 40). In ISDA and Linklaters, 'Smart Contracts and Distributed Ledger—A Legal Perspective' (2017) 10–12 <https://www.isda.org/2017/08/03/smart-contracts-and-distributed-ledger-a-legal-perspective/> accessed 8 July 2021: the authors use the term 'external model' to denote instances in which smart contracts are merely acting as execution mechanisms. They compare this to the 'internal model', where part of the legal contract is expressed in code. In J. Hazard and H. Haapio, 'Wise Contracts: Smart Contracts that Work for People and Machines' in E. Schweighofer *et al.* (eds), *Trends and Communities of Legal Informatics* (Österreichische Computer Gesellschaft 2017) 425–32, the authors set out how their 'CommonAccord' framework can be used to convert certain operational clauses into code. Allen (n. 14) 24 envisions the use of a 'semantic oracle', by enabling a human who can determine whether a standard has been met to trigger the smart contract code by calling the relevant function and passing the right parameters.

person.[146] It is possible that advances in artificial intelligence might eventually enable software to make such subjective determinations.[147]

The use of natural language can remove the ambiguity stemming from the legal enforceability of bare smart contract code. In addition, by using natural language, parties' true intentions are more likely to be correctly gauged by a judge or arbitrator, thereby helping to reduce enforcement costs. Arbitration systems are easier to implement in permissioned networks, as participants are identifiable and can co-ordinate more easily. Nonetheless, a number of arbitration systems have emerged in permissionless networks too; these can be purely code-based and reliant on non-specialized jurors (eg, Kleros), or dependent on traditional, off-ledger arbitration (eg, Mattereum).[148]

The following scenario illustrates the use of a hybrid contract comprised of non-overlapping natural language and code. Parties who wish to trade over-the-counter cryptoasset derivatives can do so under the umbrella of an ISDA Master Agreement, which will record operational terms of general applicability as well as the non-operational terms.[149] In turn, individual trades can be placed by sending the economic parameters of that trade (eg, reference asset, margin, price source, and expiry) to a smart contract template. ISDA itself is exploring the use of split contracts to encode the operational logic in the derivatives lifecycle, thereby automating collateral transfers.[150]

The EOSIO network comprises another example of a non-overlapping use of natural language and smart contract code.[151] This, however, operates at a 'macro' level across *all* network users and smart contracts. The network has a natural language constitution with non-operational clauses that have been 'voted in' by network users. By design, users include a hash of the constitution in every transaction that they send. Block.One, the promoters of the EOSIO network, intended for the constitution's terms to be legally binding; as such, it even includes an arbitration provision.[152] It is unlikely, in practice, that all users will be aware of the constitution's

---

[146] See *Helow v Advocate General* [2008] 1 WLR 2416 at 2417–18 per Lord Hope: the reasonable man forms part of 'the select group of personalities who inhabit our legal village and are available to be called upon when a problem arises that needs to be solved objectively.' See also Rius (n. 1) and Allen (n. 14) 23–4.

[147] See generally H. Surden, 'Machine Learning and Law' (2014) 89(1) *Washington Law Review* 87–115. For a discussion of automation and reasonableness, see R. Abbott, 'The Reasonable Computer: Disrupting the Paradigm of Tort Liability' (2018) 86(1) *George Washington Law Review* 1–45.

[148] For an analysis of different types of arbitration systems for smart contracts, see D.W.E. Allen, A.M. Lane, and M. Poblet, 'The Governance of Blockchain Dispute Resolution' (2020) 25 *Harvard Negotiation Law Review* 75–101.

[149] See A.D.D.M. Rius and E. Gashier, 'On-Chain Options for Digital Assets' (Crypto Valley Conference on Blockchain Technology, 25 June 2019).

[150] ISDA and Linklaters (n. 145). See also ISDA and KWM, 'Practical Framework for Constructing Smart Derivatives Contracts' (2018).

[151] See D. Larimer, 'EOS Technical White Paper' (2017) <https://github.com/EOSIO/Documentation/blob/master/TechnicalWhitePaper.md> accessed 8 July 2021. The 'EOS network' was subsequently rebranded as the 'EOSIO network'. See also I. Grigg, 'The Governed Blockchain' (2018) <https://www.iang.org/papers/the_governed_blockchain.html> accessed 8 July 2021.

[152] See Article IX of the EOS Constitution (as of 29 March 2020) <https://github.com/EOSIO/eos/blob/5068823fbc8a8f7d29733309c0496438c339f7dc/constitution.md>. For a legal analysis of the

terms, which raises doubts as to their enforceability in court. Crucially, there is no overlap between code and natural language in this design; each medium is put to use where deemed most efficient.

3. Natural language and code—partial or complete overlap

Let's return to our example of the ICO smart contract. In practice, this will often be accompanied by a 'whitepaper' that is written in natural language. In this document, the issuer will typically set out details on the team's background, development goals, and proposed use of funds. Often, the whitepaper will also include the economic terms on which the cryptoassets will be issued (eg, at a fixed ether price with a total supply cap). There is, therefore, an overlap between the terms expressed in natural language and those set in the smart contract code.

By default, we would expect natural language to dominate in the event of inconsistency, as it is the more intelligible (and probably detailed) medium of expression. The natural language document might comprise the authoritative record even if the contract has been initialized by means of code (ie by calling a function in the smart contract). In such a case, the smart contract code would simply serve as an execution mechanism for certain operational terms. Should an inconsistency arise, a party might be able to request that an arbitrator or court enforce the terms set out in the natural language document. This assumes, of course, that the parties are readily identifiable and that they intended to be legally bound by the terms in such document. With respect to the latter, the legal autonomous organization ('LAO') model has recently been introduced in the context of distributed organizations to enable participants to enter into legally binding obligations (*inter se* and vis-à-vis third parties). In this setting, a Ricardian contract ties a Delaware entity with limited liability to a web of smart contracts, which will be used to raise funds, vote on governance matters, and engage with other persons.[153]

In general, parties need also consider the ease of reversing any unintended outcomes as a result of the code malfunctioning or a deliberate exploit. Note that, it is usually not possible to unwind transactions executed on a regulated trading venue, for instance, due to a 'fat finger'. By doing so, we risk sending shockwaves down title and collateral chains, potentially giving rise to concerns of systemic instability. Without forking the ledger and causing disruption, it is generally not feasible to

---

EOSIO Constitution, see A. Sanitt, Norton Rose Fulbright, 'Legal Analysis of the Governed Blockchain' (2018) <https://www.nortonrosefulbright.com/en/knowledge/publications/0d56a3a5/legal-analysis-of-the-governed-blockchain> accessed 8 July 2021. See also Grigg (n. 151).
[153] See OpenLaw, 'The LAO: A For-Profit, Limited Liability Autonomous Organization' (2019) <https://medium.com/openlawofficial/the-lao-a-for-profit-limited-liability-autonomous-organization-9eae89c9669c> accessed 8 July 2021. For an ever-critical (yet informed) view, see P. Byrne, 'The LAO, demystified' (2019) <https://prestonbyrne.com/2019/09/03/the-lao-demystified/> accessed 8 July 2021.

revert transactions if assets have been transferred to an account beyond the parties' control. Permissioned networks are better equipped to address such issues, as parties might be able to identify one another and arrange an orderly unwinding process.

Ricardian contracts are a prime candidate for this particular design. In these contracts, parties will insert the transaction-specific parameters into a natural language template. This document itself will be linked to a smart contract template, which will (automatically) be populated with the inputted parameters. As such, the smart contract code will enforce at least part of the agreed obligations. Since this model relies on templates, it would not be well-suited to highly tailored transactions or those that are best structured through the use of an umbrella natural language agreement (as noted in the previous subsection).

4. The price of crypto-anarchy

In *The Crypto Anarchist Manifesto* (1988), Tim May proclaimed that cryptographic advances would soon enable transactions to be conducted in a truly private manner.[154] Indeed, many of these cryptographic tools came to be implemented in DLT networks, with pseudonymity being the default configuration for participants. The use of pseudonyms does not in itself bar the creation of smart legal contracts, as the UKJT *Legal Statement* reiterates in the context of English law.[155] For example, transactions in financial markets are typically conducted in a pseudonymous manner, since parties wish to protect business-sensitive information and keep their views on the market private.

On the other hand, if parties cannot screen who—or what—they are facing, they may fall prey to adverse selection problems and other instances of opportunistic behaviour.[156] In financial markets, this challenge is typically addressed by employing a chain of agents (such as brokers and clearinghouses) linked through intermediating contracts. These agents will conduct due diligence on their respective principals and enter into legally binding confidentiality obligations to safeguard the principals' identity. As a result of adopting this structure, fees accumulate and are passed along the chain to the end client. The settlement of transfers also takes time, as intermediaries must update their books in a sequential manner. Even transactions in the 'spot market' have deferred settlement (eg, +2 business

---

[154] T. May, 'The Crypto Anarchist Manifesto' (1988) <https://www.activism.net/cypherpunk/crypto-anarchy.html> accessed 8 July 2021. May's ethos was echoed in Eric Hughes, 'A Cypherpunk's Manifesto' (1993): 'We the Cypherpunks are dedicated to building anonymous systems. We are defending our privacy with cryptography, with anonymous mail forwarding systems, with digital signatures, and with electronic money' <https://www.activism.net/cypherpunk/manifesto.html> accessed 8 July 2021.

[155] LTDP (n. 2), 37.

[156] As Richard Gendal Brown quips, 'On the blockchain, nobody knows you're a fridge', <https://gendal.me/2013/10/23/on-the-blockchain-nobody-knows-youre-a-fridge/>. This phrase is derived from Peter Steiner's famous cartoon caption: 'On the internet nobody knows you're a dog' (*New Yorker*, 5 July 1993).

days for US equities), so counterparty risk is far from eliminated.[157] The risk of default can be hedged by purchasing derivatives, though this should be considered as another form of transaction cost.[158]

The Decentralised Finance ('DeFi') movement has recently gained traction, with many start-ups seeking to develop financial applications that eliminate the need for agents and settlement delays. For example, 'atomic operations' can be used to exchange assets in an all-or-nothing manner.[159] However, challenges arise when dealing with assets that are recorded in different networks' ledgers, since interoperability is currently underdeveloped.[160] Further, settlement in permissionless networks is generally probabilistic, due to the possibility of chain reorganizations, hard forks and double-spending attacks.[161] In addition, many financial transactions have a temporal element, such that atomicity is barred. In the context of lending, Maker addresses the risk of default by applying significant haircuts to the eligible collateral against which users can draw DAI. Since the collateral must withstand the volatility of cryptoassets, this results in very low loan-to-value ratios.[162] Most DeFi applications are capital-intensive and therefore hard to scale, as they are unable to recreate the legal notion of security interests. As competition from established financial intermediaries increases, we might expect creditworthy parties to switch to these intermediaries to make better use of their capital.

The analysis in this section suggests that privacy, therefore, comes at a cost.[163] To adequately protect themselves against counterparty risk, parties wishing to adopt a pseudonym must choose between two sets of 'evils': (1) reliance on risk-measuring intermediaries within the purview of the legal system, or (2) full collateralization and a consequent drag on transactional scalability.

A potential response to this challenge would be to rely on reputation systems; indeed, this is the solution that May had in mind.[164] However, reputation systems

---

[157] The US SEC maintains a database of 'failures to deliver' securities by their relevant settlement date, <https://www.sec.gov/data/foiadocsfailsdatahtm> accessed 8 July 2021.

[158] Kaivanto and Prince (n. 138), 3: transaction costs include 'the costs of bearing, hedging, or mitigating transaction-specific *risks*'.

[159] See generally I. Grigg, 'Seeking Consensus on Consensus: DPOS or Delegated Proof of Stake and the Two Generals Problem' (2017) <https://steemit.com/eos/@iang/seeking-consensus-on-consensus-dpos-or-delegated-proof-of-stake-and-the-two-generals-problem> accessed 8 July 2021: '[This challenge is] also known as the coordination problem. In blockchains we call it the consensus problem. In the financial cryptography world, it's the double spend problem, and in databases, atomicity'.

[160] See, eg, T. Koens and E. Poll, 'Assessing Interoperability Solutions for Distributed Ledgers' (2019) *Pervasive and Mobile Computing* 101079.

[161] D. Mills *et al.*, 'Distributed Ledger Technology in Payment, Clearing and Settlement' (2016) *Board of Governors of the Federal Reserve System, Finance and Economics Discussion Series* 2016-095, 15–16, the authors emphasize that the finality of settlement in (permissionless) DLT networks is probabilistic.

[162] As of 29 March 2020, the average collateralization ratio for ether was 288 per cent (yielding an effective loan-to-value ratio of 35 per cent). Analytics available at <mkr.tools> accessed 8 July 2021.

[163] Cunningham (n. 45), 239: 'True privacy to the point of anonymity makes authentication of identification difficult ... This separation [of conduct and identity] is obviously appealing from certain political perspectives [with an anarchistic root] but it comes at a cost; that cost is the existence of a general level of trust regarding society at large.' We might interpret this as 'trust by necessity'.

[164] May (n. 154).

are subject to the issues identified in Section C. There is an additional challenge that DLT networks face: for parties to establish a track record, they must either re-use the same address or prove their ownership of various addresses. Either scenario creates a risk of identification through graph analysis, heuristics, and clustering.[165]

An alternative response involves the use of mechanism design to reshape the rules of the game, as well as relaxing the requirement for (permanent) pseudo-nymity. We can conceive of a system that is initially pseudonymous, yet a counterparty's identity is disclosed if they default on performance. Disclosure under this system would be *selective*, such that only counterparties and, where applicable, the arbitrator or courts are able to identify the defaulting party.[166] This selective disclosure increases the ease of legal enforcement, thereby reducing enforcement costs and facilitating impersonal exchange. Crucially, a party's interests in preserving their privacy would, in itself, operate *ex ante* as an incentive to perform. Insofar as this system requires a reliable authentication system for identity, it may currently be best suited to deployment in permissioned networks.

The upshot of this discussion is that, in structuring and analysing transactional activity, a sole focus on transaction costs would be myopic. Parties may be willing to trade-off economic efficiency in exchange for the protection of certain values, such as the right to privacy. Further, Posner notes that there is a case for withholding the property right to privacy from a person where such right would allow them to get away with socially undesirable behaviour.[167] A pertinent challenge stems from the variability of what amounts to socially undesirable behaviour, since this varies from one society to another, in contrast to the universal reach of DLT networks. Further, it would not be sensible to equate all such behaviour; for instance, we might distinguish between criminal activities and mere contractual defaults. The issue of where the line ought to be drawn depends on the extent to which disclosure is able to facilitate legal enforcement where desirable, as well as whether DLT users will be willing to embrace the perils of a *caveat emptor* regime.

E. Conclusion

The concept of a smart contract has a multidisciplinary underpinning, with capabilities that are evolving in line with technological advances. Parties may benefit from using smart contracts to reduce transaction costs by leveraging the efficiency

---

[165] See, eg, B. Srivatsan, 'De-Anonymizing the Bitcoin Blockchain' (2016), <https://bharathsrivatsan.com/files/bitcoin.pdf> accessed 8 July 2021.

[166] See, eg, P. Peterson, 'Selective Disclosure and Shielded Viewing Keys' (2018) <https://electriccoin.co/blog/viewing-keys-selective-disclosure/> accessed 8 July 2021. A more aggressive alternative would involve disclosing the defaulting party's identity to all network users, or perhaps the public at large (a 'name and shame' game).

[167] Posner (n. 115), 403.

of code executions. In choosing how to structure a transaction, parties should recognize that legal systems and DLT networks are not mutually exclusive (with smart legal contracts being a hybrid structure). Importantly, parties need also consider how the choice of medium of expression might impact transaction costs and the set of risks that they face. Further, parties who wish to transact pseudonymously in DLT networks may find that their dealings are necessarily capital-intensive and unscalable, as counterparty risk is heightened in a regime of de facto *caveat emptor*.

I would like to conclude by reflecting on the scope and motivations of this chapter. I recognize that this is a fast-moving field and that some of the distinctions that I have drawn are razor-thin. Similarly, there are a number of ideas that have been introduced in passing and may merit further consideration. There are also related topics that I have not delved into, such as the governance of DLT networks,[168] the organizational forms that smart contracts can enable,[169] or the evolutionary aspects of DLT-enabled institutions.[170] I encourage commentators to build on the shortfalls of this work, without losing sight of the multidisciplinary and tolerant approach that has been advocated.

---

[168] See A.D.D.M. Rius, 'Governance in the Age of Blockchain' (2018) <http://alfonso.digitalpapers.uk/> accessed 8 July 2021. See also N. Carter, 'A Cross-Sectional Overview of Cryptoasset Governance and Implications for Investors' (2017), dissertation presented for the degree of MSc in Finance and Investment at the University of Edinburgh.

[169] See, eg, P. Goorha, 'Blockchains as Implementable Mechanisms: Crypto-Ricardian Rent and a Crypto-Coase Theorem' (2018) 1(2) *Journal of the British Blockchain Association* 1–10.

[170] See, eg, D.W.E. Allen et al., 'Blockchain and the Evolution of Institutional Technologies: Implications for Innovation Policy' (2020) 49(1) *Research Policy* 103865.

7
A Model for the Integration of Machine Capabilities into Contracts

Natasha Blycha and Ariane Garside[*,1]

A. Introduction	143	3. Reasons supporting the use of the conjoined method	160
B. Grounding the SLC Concept—The Space Ship Scenario	146	4. Ability to arbitrate impact of specificity and inflexibility introduced by code	161
C. The SLC Model—Foundational Components	146	5. Outcome-based drafting for conjoined terms	162
1. Relation to other smart contract models	148	6. Legal categorization of coded provisions	163
2. A legally binding agreement	149	7. Summary of the conjoined method	165
3. Machine-readable and digital	151	F. Smart Boilerplate	165
4. Contain natural language and algorithmic instructions	151	1. Why incorporate the code?	165
5. Active function	153	2. Smart boilerplate example: recitals, definitions, and interpretation	166
6. Direct impact of the chosen digital operating environment on contractual terms	154	3. Smart boilerplate example: malfunctioning code and data source provisions	171
D. The SLC Model Drafting Principles	155	4. Smart boilerplate example: variations (including unintended variations)	171
E. Conjoined Method	157		
1. Conjoined term definition	158	5. Smart boilerplate example: data management architecture	172
2. Choice of primacy between smart and natural language terms	158		

---

[*] Natasha Blycha founded and, at the time or writing, led Herbert Smith Freehills' digital law practice globally. She is the founder and Managing Director of Stirling & Rose. She has won various awards for her innovation and thought leadership. She advises on regulatory and privacy issues in the use of digital assets, smart legal contracts, human rights, and the ethics of AI. Natasha is a founding director of the Digital Law Association and sits on Australian Law Council Digital Commerce Committee.

Ariane Garside is a founding director of the Digital Law Association. As global deputy lead of Digital Law for Herbert Smith Freehills, she specialized in digital platforms, smart legal contracting, and ethics of emerging technologies, and led the development of a smart legal contracting platform for a consortium of Herbert Smith Freehills, IBM, and CSIRO. She has a JD from the University of Melbourne and a MBA from the University of Oxford.

[1] With particular thanks to the lawyers of the Digital Law Group (past and present) at Herbert Smith Freehills many whom have contributed (including through vigorous and generous debate) to the concepts addressed and conclusions reached in this paper. Appreciation also goes to Emeritus Professor John Carter for his help in the development of the SLC Model and Jason Ricketts for his considered review and guidance, particularly in the early stages of this paper.

Natasha Blycha and Ariane Garside, *A Model for the Integration of Machine Capabilities into Contracts* In: *Smart Legal Contracts*. Edited by: Jason Grant Allen and Peter Hunn, Oxford University Press. © Jason Grant Allen & Peter Hunn 2022. DOI: 10.1093/oso/9780192858467.003.0008

6. Smart boilerplate example: choice of platform is as significant as choice of governing law	173	I. The Legal Void of the Digital Economy	177
		1. SLCs work as legal instruments to manage data reliance	178
G. Clause Classification	175	J. Conclusion	179
H. The Legal Status of Automated Contract Performance	176		

A. Introduction

In this chapter we set out a Smart Legal Contract ('SLC') Model to facilitate the integration of computer code and natural language into a technically functional and legally enforceable contract. We propose a formal definition of an SLC for the purposes of scoping this Model, and within the SLC Model identify key foundational attributes that require a different approach to that of traditional contracting. We then use this framework to consider some legal principles and practical methodologies for ensuring that neither the legal nor code elements of the contract undermine the other's fitness for purpose and effectiveness in their respective domains of operation.

We identify that there is a need for mechanisms of governance in the natural language over the status and effect of SLC coded elements. These mechanisms focus on the linking and integration of natural language to related code, and so also have the effect of enhancing the drafter's ability to ensure the intended agreement of the parties is unaffected (and indeed enhanced) by the inclusion of code. Finally, we argue that the SLC Model will result in a viable legal contract with enhanced functional ('smart') capabilities that digitally automate the performance of certain (but not all) rights and obligations via the inclusion of coded instructions.

To date, the majority of economic transactions and activities have been both agreed to, and performed by, human actors. The increasing adoption of artificial intelligence and robotics—technologies that are able to observe, react to and impact real-world events instead of, or in conjunction with human actors—is changing the scope of the field. Machines are becoming increasingly capable of assisting with or even performing human labour and economic activities.[2] Contracts are already a key mechanism by which economic actors allocate risk and govern their actions towards one another. Contracts need to continue to play this role, and play this role well, notwithstanding increasing levels of machine activity. Our 'Smart and Legal Contract' ('SLC') is a bi-modal language tool that can facilitate this transition.[3]

---

[2] Throughout this paper we use the term 'machine-assisted' to refer to situations where a human actor provides the driving mind, action and decision making of a process, but is assisted in those by the use of a machine (eg, machine-learning tools, interfaces, and data analytics). Similarly, we use the term 'machine-led', to refer to situations where a process is driven, enacted, or decided by a machine (eg: a complex artificial intelligence or program).

[3] This chapter draws on scholarly work on both 'smart' and 'legal' contracts. In particular, the following provide a good overview of current contractual theory in respect of smart and legal

By combining the use of both human and machine readable language (where the two may converge over time), SLCs can evidence and perform, in both the digital and physical domains, the legal rights and obligations of the parties.[4]

Attempts in this direction are already underway. Traditional contracts are captured (at time of agreement) by human or 'natural languages' such as English, Mandarin, or Czech. Notwithstanding that form is of course not a prerequisite to a legally enforceable agreement, contracts (particularly business contracts) tend to be written in a natural language to evidence those rights and obligations of the bargain. This provides parties with remedies available from a relevant neutral body with requisite authority (such as a court), finding breach. In this instance, the pendulum has been set to support human interactions, but is not designed to support greater machine activity.

With the rise of blockchain and distributed ledger technology, the concept of 'smart contracting' has lately run riot through the legal and technological domains. We define a *smart contract* as computer code that, upon the occurrence of a specified condition or conditions, is capable of running automatically according to pre-specified functions.[5] Assuming the current state of the technology, it is fair to say that smart contracting elevates machine readable language and 'closed loop' scenarios—'if this happens do that'—at the expense of concepts that require nuanced natural language expression and evidence. With smart contracting, the pendulum swings to supporting machine or logic based interactions.[6]

---

contracts: M. Raskin, 'The Law and Legality of Smart Contracts' (2016) 1 *Georgetown Law Technology Review* 304; Christopher D. Clack et al., 'Smart Contract Templates: Foundations, Design Landscape and Research Directions' (2016), <https://arxiv.org/pdf/1608.00771.pdf>; C.D. Clack, 'Smart Contract Templates: Legal Semantics and Code Validation' (2018) 2(4) *Journal of Digital Banking* 338; J.M. Lipshaw, 'The Persistence of 'Dumb' Contracts' (2019) 2(1) *Stanford Journal of Blockchain Law & Policy* 45. See also generally the work of Ian Grigg dating back to the 1990s on 'Ricardian Contracts', a hybrid mechanism that integrates traditional legal agreement language with the ability to encode it, and any actions relating to that agreement into a digital infrastructure such as a blockchain: I. Grigg, 'The Ricardian Contract' (2004) <https://iang.org/papers/ricardian_contract.html> accessed 8 July 2021.

[4] While this article requires no pre-existing technical knowledge of coded or algorithmic drafting, we anticipate that lawyers of the future will need additional skills and new collaborative processes with technical professionals to develop SLCs.

[5] A significant wrinkle here in that the term 'smart contract' is also being used by some in the legal industry to reference what we call a Smart Legal Contract. We argue that (for now) the use of Smart Legal Contract best describes a smart *and* legal contract as it leaves no room for confusion as to the requirement for legal efficacy of coded instructions. At some future point, (if and when there is ubiquitous SLC use) we anticipate the word 'contract' will again suffice to describe what we refer to in this article as an SLC.

[6] Smart contracting code can be stored and processed on a distributed ledger and would write any resulting change into the distributed ledger. The largest use-case to date has been for cryptocurrencies, as these represent stores of value that exist purely on, and can be transferred via, distributed ledgers. In short, it means that if a bargain is struck using a smart contract, when the conditions are fulfilled, the transfer of value (most often currently being in the form of cryptocurrency) will take place regardless of whether or not the payer has had a change of heart.

Critically, however, a 'smart contract' does not in any way refer to or incorporate the concept of a *legal* contract.[7] It is not surprising then that lawyers are particularly concerned as to the certainty and enforceability of smart contracts, while technologists celebrate the perceived efficiency of automating legal processes while sidestepping frictions and frustrations of the law. A key criticism of smart contracts is that they are capable of representing and supporting only a 'thin', or superficial conception of human transactional behaviours, needs, and practices.[8] By contrast, traditional contracts and the law that governs their interpretation have developed over a long historical period to allow for a rich variety of human agreements, and the ways in which they—and the legal rights and obligations they create—are used.

To this end, a 'smart legal contract' is a modern governance tool that needs to support, by design, the methodologies of both the legal and digital domains and their respective languages, while maintaining effectiveness in both. This article sets out a particular model of SLC[9] that integrates both 'smart contract' style computer code and contractual natural language ('SLC Model').

The structure of this chapter is as follows. In Section II, we 'ground' the concept of an SLC by briefly laying out a concrete (if slightly futuristic) example of how an SLC might be used in commercial contracting. In Section III, we lay out and define the five foundational components of the SLC Model. Through analysis of these we are able to articulate some key differences and issues that need to be addressed for the SLC to function both at law and digitally. In sections IV to VII, we propose and explore key legal drafting principles for how an SLC might best manage the changes and risks introduced by SLCs, including introducing the 'Conjoined Term' and 'Smart Boilerplate' methodologies, as well as a method of classifying which terms are appropriate for automation or expression in computer code, to assist with ensuring that contracting parties' intentions are properly achieved and

---

[7] Chamber of Digital Commerce, 'Smart Contracts: Is the Law Ready?' (September 2018) <https://digitalchamber.org/smart-contracts-whitepaper/> accessed 8 July 2021.

[8] *Ibid.*; K.E.C. Levy, 'Book-Smart, Not Street-Smart: Blockchain-Based Smart Contracts and The Social Workings of Law' (2017) 3 *Engaging Science, Technology, and Society* 1.

[9] The definition of an SLC is explored in detail in Section V, however in short, in our conception, the SLC is an emerging form of contract that still contains traditional natural language clauses, but also contains in certain parts computer code that is linked to the natural language, and is generally expected to be hosted on a digital platform that enables those coded parts of the contract to connect to APIs or external platforms or data sources (such as a back-end system or GPS system) and run, similar to a software program. So for example, a derivatives SLC might have all the traditional language of a derivatives contract, but also contain an agreed algorithm and set of 'if, then' conditions in computer code that allow the SLC to detect when a commodities price hits a certain pre-agreed level, and execute a trade automatically through the digital platform it runs on. Put more technically, the SLC is a contract that articulates its terms and conditions in either or both natural language and computer code and is capable of self-executing the terms of an agreement between two or more parties on a legally-enforceable basis. The work of ISDA and its collaborators has been a strong emergent example of smart legal contacting, see ISDA and Linklaters, 'Smart Contracts and Distributed Ledger—A Legal Perspective' (2017) <https://www.isda.org/a/6EKDE/smart-contracts-and-distributed-ledger-a-legal-perspective.pdf>; ISDA and King & Wood Mallesons, 'Smart Derivatives Contracts—From Concept to Construction' (2018) <https://www.isda.org/a/cHvEE/Smart-Derivatives-Contracts-From-Concept-to-Construction-Oct-2018.pdf> both accessed 8 July 2021.

reflected in the SLC. In section VIII, we consider the implications for an SLC of the legal status of machine-assisted or machine-led processes. In Section IX, we conclude by examining how SLCs fit into the broader digital landscape.

B. Grounding the SLC Concept—The Space Ship Scenario

To demonstrate, imagine an example set sometime in the future: a space station privately owned by Albatross Co is in permanent orbit around the Earth. Albatross Co has outsourced its oxygen supply requirements to Hurricane Inc via an SLC. The space station has sensors that automatically detect its oxygen reserve levels. The parties have agreed in the SLC to share this sensor data in real-time, and that when the sensors detect that oxygen reserves have dipped below three months' supply, a purchase order is to be automatically issued by the live SLC to Hurricane Inc.

In turn, Hurricane Inc has an automated warehouse and inventory monitoring system in respect of the materials required to deliver oxygen supplies in the contractually specified modules and amounts. This system provides automatic estimates of delivery dates for purchase orders based on inventory levels and expected upstream supplier delivery dates. Hurricane Inc has agreed to give Albatross Co access to the data feed of these automated delivery date estimates (but only for Albatross Co's particular purchase orders) in real time, to allow Albatross Co to take alternative measures where estimated delivery exceeds three months. Real-time, reliable access to these delivery estimates—and the ability to verify and audit those estimates—is critically important to Albatross Co, because there are three scientist astronauts living on the space station at any given time, for whom Albatross Co has a duty of care. In all cases, the SLC provides for human oversight and discretion in checking, issuing, amending, or updating purchase orders or other automated actions as a failsafe.

Having contractually agreed data sources, and allocations of responsibility as to the maintenance and accuracy of the live data shared between the parties protects and enhances the risk allocation and pricing capabilities of both parties, as well as giving contractual protections should anything go sideways. In addition, the efficiency and auditability of having agreed automatic ordering procedures based on carefully vetted and pre-agreed conditions increases the efficiency of supply, and reduces potential miscommunications or losses of value as between the parties. Lastly and not least, the astronauts can breathe easy.

C. The SLC Model—Foundational Components

In this section we lay out and define the five foundational components of the SLC Model. We then use this SLC Model framework to review the potential impacts introduced to contracting by the SLC, in particular due to its digital construction, its inclusion of code and its digital connectivity to data sources. In the second half of this article, this review will be used to propose drafting mechanisms for ensuring an SLC is both legally enforceable and accurately captures the parties' intentions.

It is difficult to propose any definition for an SLC that does not simply boil down to: 'a contract'. However, for clarity, we set out a short definition that emphasizes the additional component of algorithmic instruction, as it is that component that activates a number of new practical legal considerations. We define an SLC as: *A legally binding, digital agreement in which part or all of the agreement is intended to execute as algorithmic instructions.* This definition underpins the five key components of the SLC Model, which are discrete but interconnected. These are:

1. Status: legally binding—an SLC must conform to the established rules of contract.
2. Form: the machine readable or digital state.
3. Contents:
   a. Natural language, as in any traditional legal contract being any typical contracting and business language used in the jurisdiction of the contract; and
   b. Computer code, or other forms of machine-readable or algorithmic instructions intended to run digitally.[10]
4. Active Function: the how, when and why the digital components of an SLC are triggered or affected by data or events generated from external or internal data sources, including the results of previously executed algorithms.
5. Digital Execution Mechanism: the digital hosting or domain of the SLC and how it integrates with the Active Function.

Components 1–3 of the SLC Model we refer to as the 'Rule-Making Components', and are in effect the components (albeit in slightly differing form) of a traditional ('legal') contract in that they go to the legal, rule-setting function of a contract. For example, even where the language of the contract includes computer code,

---

[10] The use of the caveat in the SLC Model that the Incorporated Code components are '*intended* to run digitally' is an important caveat, as it is designed in recognition that: (1) even a contract without the more complex 'moving parts' (ie, automated obligations discussed below) can be an SLC; and (2) an SLC may still be considered an SLC for the purpose of use or legal interpretation even where it is not actually digitally operating in the manner intended, so long as parts of it are or were intended by the parties to operate digitally. This is to capture situations where an SLC for whatever reason is not operating digitally as intended, for example because it has not yet been uploaded, contains an error that prevents digital operation, or where the platform the SLC is operating on encounters a failure of the platform on which an SLC is hosted or otherwise intended to operate and execute.

that still goes to generating and evidencing, meaning, agreement and obligations. Components 4–5 we refer to as the 'Active Components' and consider to be new components unique to an SLC, as set out in Figure 7.1.

Rule-Making Components

Status: legally binding – an SLC must conform to the established rules of contract

Form: the machine readable or digital state

Language: the natural language and encoded language components

Active Components

Active Function: how, when and why an SLC is triggered or affected by data or events generated from external or internal data sources, including the results of previously executed algorithms

Digital Execution Mechanism: the digital hosting of the SLC.

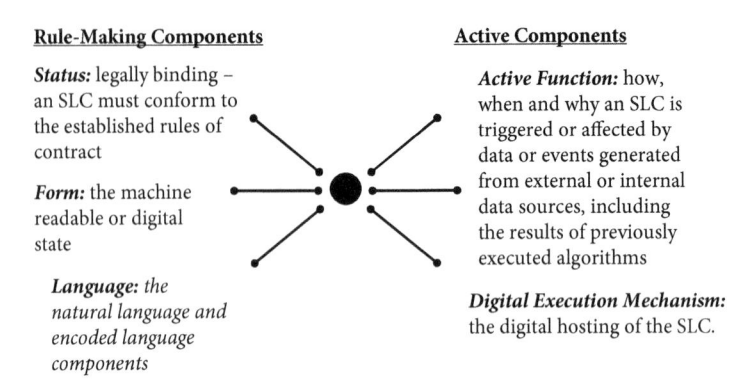

Figure 7.1 The SLC Model

We examine each of these five components in depth below, identifying under each the primary characteristics unique to SLCs that underpin the need for the additional consideration and mechanisms to deal with those unique characteristics that are set out in the remainder of the article.

1. Relation to other smart contract models

JG Allen has suggested an alternative approach to understanding SLCs, using the metaphor of a contract stack comprising multiple layers, some technical and others legal.[11] Recognizing the importance of Allen's seminal work in this space, we have not adopted the 'stack metaphor' for a number of reasons. Perhaps most importantly, our approach is predicated on a slightly different definition of 'smart legal contract' (and 'smart contract') to that set out in Allen's paper. Further, Allen lays more emphasis than we do on the merger of legal prose and machine-readable code in a single written instrument.[12] In our view, this is suggestive of a binary approach whereby one must *either* 'nest' a smart contract (in the Szabo sense)[13]

---

[11] J.G. Allen, 'Wrapped and Stacked: 'Smart Contracts' and the Interaction of Natural and Formal Language' (2018) 14(4) *European Review of Contract Law* 307, 331.
[12] *Ibid.*, 319.
[13] N. Szabo, 'Smart Contracts: Building Blocks for Digital Markets' (1996) <http://www.fon.hum.uva.nl/rob/Courses/InformationInSpeech/CDROM/Literature/LOTwinterschool2006/szabo.best.vwh.net/smart_contracts_2.html> accessed 8 July 2021.

within a legally binding agreement *or* anticipate ' …the merger of contractual terms with machine-parsable code'.[14] This encourages, in our view, an undue focus on the need for *unified language* as a requisite part of the 'contract stack'. This could, in turn, invite potential users of SLCs to imagine legal and 'technical fluency' barriers to SLC adoption that we do not consider to be material—for example, a need to focus on issues associated with textualism and contextualism, or the intentional or unintentional loss of semantic richness. In short, we do not consider that 'the ultimate goal of the smart contract movement is (or should be) to develop a formal language which is intelligible to humans and executable by machines to use for whole or part of the written layer of a contract stack'.[15] Finally, we consider a 'Digital Execution Mechanism' to be a key ingredient in any model, which Allen's stack approach leaves unarticulated. As Sir Geoffrey Vos writes, 'end-to-end smart legal contracts will not become mainstream without legal infrastructure'.[16]

If going forward, Allen's contract stack is read to allow the composition of a 'smart legal contract' from *any conceivable* combination of natural and formal language, there is increasing alignment between the approaches. We regard it as essential that any given SLC be inherently customizable—as adaptable as any regular contract to the intentions of contracting parties. It may contain as much or as little coded, smart functionality as the parties wish and does not require a 'unified' approach to code and natural language. The distinction between the Unified Method and the Paired Method (described further in section V below) is well articulated in Chapter 8 of this volume.[17] We adopt this approach as underpinning our SLC Model and driving greater abstraction in its requisite components.

With these considerations in mind, we now turn to actively considering how the foundational components of our SLC Model can be understood and investigated, from the perspective of how they impact, and differ from, a traditional legal contract.

2. A legally binding agreement

As with any contract, an SLC must be a legally formed, valid, and binding contract in a given jurisdiction. In considering the adoption of SLCs, a practitioner

---

[14] J.G. Allen, 'Wrapped and Stacked: "Smart Contracts" and the Interaction of Natural and Formal Language' (2018) 14(4) *European Review of Contract Law* 307, 330.
[15] Allen (n. 10), 322.
[16] Sir G. Vos, 'End-to-End Smart Legal Contracts: Moving from Aspiration to Reality', Chapter 2 in this volume.
[17] See further S. Wilkinson and J. Giuffre, 'Six Levels of Contract Automation: The Evolution to Smart Legal Contracts—Further Analysis', Chapter 8 in this volume.

must still ask three main questions: (a) Is there a contract? (b) What are the legal implications when something goes wrong in performance? And (c) will the contract comply with any applicable statutory regimes, such as consumer law or fair contracting provisions? The first question is about identifying the assumed legal environment of whether traditional contractual formalities and requirements of formation and enforceability are fulfilled. In particular, digital forms of signing of a contract have different statuses in different jurisdictions, and this must be considered carefully as digital signing would be a main methodology of signing when a contract is entirely digital in its form (though the parties may prefer to have physically signed copies of an SLC to address this issue). For example, under Australian contract law, an agreement is enforceable as a contract if and only if there are two or more parties each having capacity to contract, the agreement includes at least one promise, the promise is sufficiently certain and complete, the promise is supported by consideration (moving from the promisee); and there is an intention to create legal relations. Nothing in the list can be contracted out of, but consideration is not required if the promise is in a deed. In particular, there is a question of certainty: how do lawyers, parties or courts interpret or agree to a contract that contains computer code and which they only half-understand? This issue is examined and a method proposed to address it in Section V.

SLCs require that a practitioner pay greater heed to the 'down the track', to *maintenance* of the assumed legal environment over the course of the desired contractual relationship. It is technically possible (particularly as SLCs become more complex and more connected to the data of *other* SLCs) for an SLC to be varied at some point of time in the future (albeit within pre-agreed parameters) without direct human attention to the variation real time. In this instance, there is the potential for an SLC to be unenforceable for loss of the legal environment.

This innate dynamism requires new drafting protections and appropriately secure digital hosting to maintain the status of contract, which provides technical security that will not allow for unilateral amendments or contract tampering without the agreement of all parties. As SLCs evolve, the innate dynamism of digital contracts may result in much more fluid amendments, and even agreed self-amendments to a contract, which results in a need for a platform that provides reliable records of the status and content of an SLC at any given point in time.[18] See further the discussion and proposed methods to address this under section VII).

---

[18] That is, the dynamism of an SLC may make for example make certainty difficult, when certainty is a central pillar of the contractual environment, or as best put by Bray CJ, 'implicit in the very notion of consensus that the minds of the parties have met in praesenti and not merely that it is hoped or expected that they will meet in futuro'. *Powell v Jones* [1928] SASR 394, 398, quoted in *Crown Melbourne Ltd v Cosmopolitan Hotel (Vic) Pty Ltd* (2016) 260 CLR 1, [2016] HCA 26, [57] (Gageler J).

3. Machine-readable and digital

The digital[19] contract that is an SLC is a contract that is expressed in some part as a series of bits that can be uploaded and read by machines. It may be expressed as series of the digits 0 and 1[20] running on a digital platform. The digital or coded elements of an SLC operating on a digital platform, such as a blockchain or Distributed Ledger Technology ('DLT') infrastructure,[21] should be in a structured data format that can be processed by a computer without human intervention while ensuring no semantic meaning is lost.

A *fully* machine-readable and digitally-hosted SLC has stronger security, can provide better insights, and, perhaps most importantly, allows the contract to viewed as a whole across both its natural language and digital or coded components. An SLC, in our view, is best able to be construed as a whole—including in respect of the changing body of its genesis and previously executed algorithmic data, if it is kept in machine readable form.[22]

4. Contain natural language and algorithmic instructions

Natural language in a contract refers to the traditional legal sense using the language of the jurisdiction which is chosen to regulate the contract. An SLC incorporates coded elements to give legal efficacy to a contract with those automated components. Coded, algorithmic or otherwise machine-readable representations of rights and obligations, here referred to as 'Incorporated Code'. As discussed in section IV, functionally we consider that 'Incorporated Code' refers to the

---

[19] The descriptor 'digital' may be better replaced with 'machine-readable' depending on court's view of application of the primary rule of document to be construed as a whole, as per Gibbs J in *Australian Broadcasting Commission v Australasian Performing Right Association Ltd* (1973) 129 CLR 99, 109. While the term 'machine-readable' is used repeatedly in the Copyright Act 1968 (Cth), as well as in other legislation and regulations, the term does not appear to be defined in any Australian legislation. There is little judicial guidance as to the meaning of 'machine-readable'. In *Computer Edge Pty Ltd v Apple Computer Inc* (1986) 161 CLR 171, Gibbs CJ said: 'The source code or assembly code cannot be used directly in the computer, and must be converted into an object code, which is 'machine readable', ie, which can be directly used in the computer'. This description was included in a passage quoted by the joint judgements of Gleeson C.J., McHugh J., Gummow J., and Hayne J. in *Data Access Corporation v Powerflex Services Pty Ltd* (1999) 202 CLR 1, along with the comment that 'much of what was said by Gibbs CJ remains relevant'. In this article we define Machine-readable data, or computer-readable data, as data (or metadata) in a format that can be easily processed by a computer. Machine-readable data must be structured data. The United States OPEN Government Data Act formally referred to as the Foundations for Evidence-Based Policymaking Act of 2018, Pub L No 115-435', defines machine-readable data as 'data in a format that can be easily processed by a computer without human intervention while ensuring no semantic meaning is lost.'

[20] There is scope for SLCs to incorporate quantum computing and therefore qubits in the future, however that is out of scope for this chapter.

[21] Going forward, we will use the term 'digital platform' to refer to the computer system or platform on which an SLC is hosted or otherwise intended to operate and execute.

[22] See n. 8.

computer code 'representation' of a given contractual obligation or process in the natural language.[23]

Functionally, terms or processes expressed in Incorporated Code enable the digitization and automation of contract formation, storage and automated performance of obligations, in accordance with contractually specified circumstances or triggers, just as traditional computer code is capable of automating a specified process in virtue of their digital nature. Further, they are capable of interacting with external data sources (such as industrial sensors, parliamentary websites, and email notifications) to update or trigger contractual status, conditions, actions, or processes.

Incorporated Code introduces the unique characteristic in SLCs that is somewhat equivalent to the inclusion of a 'foreign language' in the form of computer code (where it is more likely than not that the parties do not know or understand the scope of the code they are agreeing to, but will sign off on it anyway). However, generally speaking, absent fraud, misrepresentation or other improper conduct on the part of the party claiming the contract is unenforceable due to their lack of understanding of the language, and subject to certain consumer protection laws, parties are bound by the documents they sign, whether or not they have read or understood them.[24]

In practice, a heavy onus must be discharged to establish defences on the basis of a failure of meeting of the minds, or mistake arising from misunderstanding or lack of comprehension of the contract, which courts consider must be kept within narrow limits.[25] Such defences are unlikely to be available in the context of commercial transactions between businesses which are generally capable of making further inquiries about the nature and effect of a document, in particular where the 'translation' or 'linking' mechanism of the Conjoined Method discussed in section VII is used. A suggested interplay between natural language and Incorporated Code (to the extent there is an inconsistency or need for primacy between the two required) is described as the 'Conjoined Method' in Section V.

---

[23] We have generally avoided the use of the term 'clause' and instead used 'term' (in the sense that parts of a contract may be referred to as provisions or terms) in this article. This is because in many cases the computer code may only deal with parts of a clause, or many parts of many clauses, rather than be a direct one-to-one translation of natural language clauses. It is important to acknowledge that the boundaries of a given natural language clause are not likely to apply to computer code.

[24] J.W. Carter, *Carter on Contract* (LexisNexis Butterworths Australia 2021), Ch 22. See for UK: *Gallie v Lee* [1969] 2 Ch 17, 36–7; (Lord Denning MR); *Saunders v Anglia Building Society* [1971] AC 1004. For Australia, see *Easyfind (NSW) Pty Ltd v Paterson* (1987) 11 NSWLR 98, 107; *Baird v BCE Holdings Pty Ltd* (1996) 40 NSWLR 374, 382 (Young J) (noting that unconscionable conduct is required). See in particular: *Hue Dieu Luong v Huong Xuan Du* [2013] VSC 723, in which the *non est factum* defence of unilateral mistake was found to be unavailable to an individual whom the Court accepted had limited command of English language, but considered was capable of making further inquiries about the nature and effect of a document.

[25] See for England and Wales, see *Muskham Finance Ltd v Howard* [1963] 1 QB 904, 912. For Australia, see *Petelin v Cullen* (1975) 132 CLR 355, 359; *Tofilau v R (Matter No M144/2006)* (2007) 231 CLR 396, 417–18.

5. Active Function

'Active Function' describes how, when and why the digital components of an SLC are triggered or affected by data or events generated from external or internal data sources, including the results of previously executed algorithms. Here, we focus on the unique characteristic of SLCs in the Active Function, which to re-iterate, deals with the fact that an SLC may be triggered or affected by data or events generated from external or internal data sources, including the results of previously executed algorithms.

Where an SLC operates digitally, this is likely to be based on inflows and outflows of data or information. These flows of data, whether they arise from external data sources or data arising from the contract itself, as well as the subsequently triggered actions of the contract (eg, notifications, payments, transfers of assets), form part of the operation of the contract and in many cases will be recorded immutably by the digital platform (see section III). This raises a few key considerations:

Firstly, this 'Active Function' component gives an entirely new characteristic to a contract that is an SLC. As opposed to traditional contracts which serve a rule-setting, obligation creating purpose, the SLC also has live outcomes from the computer code contained within it. This new characteristic can be understood as the SLC's self-performance of certain of its contractual processes. While a traditional contract sets out (at a crystallized moment in time) rights and obligations, the SLC differs in that it produces, compels and collects the history of its own code-driven live outcomes. It stands to reason that this difference will manifest new areas of tension—and opportunity—in the contracting process (compare the shift from paper and coins to e-money and the resultant change in areas of friction, efficiency, and liquidity this has manifested, eg, the use of direct debit). This proposition is largely predicated on the notion that data driven actions take place *at speed, increasingly outside human direct supervision and can potentially involve exponentially larger and more complex outcomes* than actions not directed by computer code. Of course, natural language may also be said to have 'live outcomes' in the sense of its impact on the behaviour and incentives of the human actors performing the contract, however the live outcomes of the code are more direct in the sense that they are explicitly shaping the real-time actions of machines (once the contract has been signed and made operational on the chosen digital platform). This is 'live' machine-based performance of terms, as opposed to in a traditional legal contract where what occurs is in the end discretionary human performance, with court enforcement as the only 'crunch point' where performance or consequences of the legal language agreed may become non-discretionary in the legal domain.

Secondly, the fact that an SLC may be varied, breached, or fail to run in ways outside the parties' intentions due to connected code functions, malfunctions, bugs, hacking or otherwise being incorrect or corrupted from its purpose.[26] As a result,

---

[26] This gets interesting when a contract becomes a Data Source for another contract. If not drafted correctly, unintended performance or malfunction of code in one contract will have knock on effects in other contracts.

there is a new requirement that a digitally active SLC has additional cyber security requirements. While tearing up a paper contract has little unintended practical consequence, a hacked SLC might have considerable practical consequences for the parties' abilities to perform that contract or any up-stream or down-stream parties or actors who are impacted by the operation of the contract. Again, while human actors are also 'hackable' in a more traditional sense of bribery, brute force, poor judgment, or corruption, it is the speed and potential size of impact of machine-based activity that must be taken into account when code is integrated into a legal instrument.

Thirdly, because those digital operations are prescribed and written into the SLC itself via code and the data connections into that code, any data or records arising from it may form part of the contract itself, and therefore be subject to similar data and IP rights that exist for the natural language drafting of traditional contracts. Much of this will depend on the drafting of a given SLC and how it prescribes the control, management and status data resulting from its operations. Legal complexity around data ownership is also relevant and may need to be managed, if possible, via some form of database rights, or more likely through access and control mechanisms coupled with confidentiality or trade secret provisions, depending on the relevant jurisdiction.

Fourthly, there is the new opportunity (and risk) that SLCs afford for parties to rely on the contract itself to perform its recorded rights and obligations; the robust longevity of the software contract has the potential for far-reaching equitable and commercial implications. The potential legal implications of this reliance are considered in both sections V and VIII. The Conjoined Terms and Smart Boilerplate methodologies outlined in sections V and VI are aimed at protecting against these types of issues from impacting the legal rights and obligations intended under the contract.

Fifthly and finally, the Active Function may also enhance and enable the real-time interconnectedness of SLCs to other SLCs and the broader networks in which they operate, which requires new consideration of flow-through effects of related contracts and networks. This is beyond the scope of this chapter, but requires further examination.

6. Direct impact of the chosen digital operating environment on contractual terms

Blockchain and DLT have been a key catalyst for the development and adoption of smart contract capabilities, because they enable the creation of secure, immutable audit trail of digital information and actions as between the contracting parties. There are a wide variety of blockchain or DLT platforms, or indeed non-blockchain digital platforms, that might be used for SLCs, each with differing technical features and capabilities.[27] Through this, the contracting parties have a means to create a shared source of truth on how party-to-party activities such as important obligations are digitally automated and performed, where neither party would necessarily trust the other to maintain an un-tampered record through traditional digital platforms.

In our view, an SLC must specify the *platform* it is designed and intended to operate on. This is because the impact of the platform on the operation of the contract must be considered in its construction, just as the governing law agreed by the contracting parties must be considered because it impacts the operation and construction of the terms of a contract. Both platform and jurisdiction provide the bedrock in which an SLC will sit, and will govern the limits of not only what a contract can capture and govern within its scope, but now also its operational capabilities.

D. The SLC Model Drafting Principles

In a world where laws and courts have built up an enormous body of codes, regulation and practice precisely to protect and prevent normal legal contractual language from being misinterpreted or exploited, introducing the simplicity and alien nature of computer code to contracts has the potential to create significant risks around transactions. This is why the heart of our principle for creating a legally enforceable 'smart' but legal contract lies in the ability to maintain, should the parties so desire, the *primacy of the natural language* of a contract, with code used to create *efficiencies in execution*.

The rigidity of code, particularly when compared to the elasticity of natural language,[28] means that the coded parts of an SLC will not always be suited to deal with situations that have not been anticipated, resulting in the need to 'conjoin' the code to natural language that in effect provides the governing or primary understanding of the obligation that the code is intended to perform. The countering value of the code is that the process of discussing, designing and agreeing to the form of code to be included in the SLC helps ameliorate what Jeffrey Lipshaw refers to as 'lexical opportunism' or 'the ability to use ambiguity or vagueness to further

---

[27] See generally: C. Molina-Jimenez et al., 'Implementation of Smart Contracts Using Hybrid Architectures with On- and Off-blockchain Components' (31 July 2018) <https://arxiv.org/pdf/1808.00093.pdf>, and as noted in that paper, a good summary of features offered by DLT, Blockchain, and other smart contract-related platforms is available in: M. Bartoletti and L. Pompianu, 'An Empirical Analysis of Smart Contracts: Platforms, Applications, and Design Patterns' (18 March 2017) <https://arxiv.org/pdf/1703.06322.pdf> both accessed 8 July 2021.

[28] G.Q. Zhang, *Elastic Language: How and Why We Stretch Our Words* (Cambridge University Press 2015), as discussed in Lipshaw (n. 1).

ends that likely were never in the contemplation of either party when they executed the contract'.[29]

In drafting an SLC, the lawyer has a primary gateway choice as to whether to incorporate code within the legal parameters of the contract. We argue that incorporating code into the contract creates valuable flexibility to adapt and harness the future operational scope of that contract, provided that the contracting parties include sufficient natural language rules to support and manage the inclusion of that code. Further, technological advancement in the fusion of machine-readable code and natural language would inevitably make it practically impossible to exclude 'code as law', where natural language processing enables a computer to read and execute even natural language drafting.

We thus think that code should be formally integrated or incorporated into the contract to enable the enforceability of contractually agreed mechanisms, overarching protections and liability relating to that code by the contracting parties. In our proposed SLC Model, the code components of an SLC should have two forms of relationship with natural language. The first, which we call *Broad Governance*, is where natural language sets out broad rules for the treatment of coded components of the contract and their execution. This is detailed further below as 'Smart Boilerplate', so-called for its broad-spectrum similarity to boilerplate that governs natural language such as interpretation or governing law clauses. The second, which we call *Specific Governance*, is where natural language in a clause directly or indirectly sets out the contractual process that the code is designed to perform or otherwise interact with (for example, code might be set up to send a notification upon a delivery delay being detected, which directly relates to a natural language clause that requires a notification of delay delivery to be sent). This is detailed further below as the 'Conjoined Method'.

Traditional contracts contain operational issues all the time—consider mistake, clashing terms, informal updates to inventory that take place on the ground, human employees acting in irrational or mistaken manners, and so on. But normally these issues are either dealt with not at all, or *ex post facto*, during a dispute where parties make arguments as to whether operational actions did or did not fall within the scope of performance of the agreement. SLC operational issues will arise as live, contractual events take place in accordance with the purportedly agreed code of the contract, such as: coding bugs, bad oracles, hacking or failure to execute properly; breach of contract (where agreed code or data sources that automate performance of certain of a parties' obligations functions incorrectly or not as agreed); or real-time consequences of mistake or error (where the incorrect code/data has already had consequences that must be made good).[30]

---

[29] Lipshaw (n. 1).
[30] However, this is not so far from traditional contracts, as the performance of a contract occurs in real-time on the ground whether it is performed by humans or machines. But where performed by machines in accordance with agreed code, there are immediate consequences that arise directly from the

Functionally, therefore, the SLC or platform will need to lay out agreed mechanisms for correcting code. Parties must allocate liability for any damage done, and parties must agree who bears responsibility for ensuring correct information and data flows in and out of the SLC. Fundamentally, when code is incorporated into a contract, the contracting parties should clearly and formally elect whether the failure of code to run as expected gives rise to a breach of contract, or whether alternative manual means of performing the job the code was meant to perform will still suffice as performance.

Thus, for certainty, we propose a new mechanism which 'pairs' a natural language clause or expression of the relevant obligation (referred to as a 'term') to the coded expression of that obligation (on the assumption the two are *not* the same). The contract should make it evident that the relevant code acts as a translation, expression or agreed performance mechanism for its 'paired' natural language clause or obligation. There should be overarching interpretation provisions and drafting to reflect the intention of the contracting parties (including for where the codes fail) that assists in managing, interpreting and using the data inputs and outputs which form part of the active nature of an SLC. Clauses that can be expressed or automated via this Incorporated Code, should be carefully selected, based on principles of good legal drafting and the capabilities of human and machine actors involved. We walk through each of these in turn in the sections below.

E. Conjoined Method

This section lays out our conception of an SLC and how its natural language and coded elements are likely to interact with each other, and proposes a mechanism by which contracting parties can manage and customize this interaction. The Conjoined Method comes to life when tools or platforms that support the Paired Method are used. The Conjoined Method can make less sense for an individual using tools or platforms designed to generate largely unified drafting, where the same body of text is human and machine readable, and also machine executable.[31] Unified drafting is more restrictive and channels drafters to focus on only automating those obligations that can be directly translated into computational logic.[32]

---

way the code is written and the operation of that code. This is as opposed to human performance which arises from a myriad of rich factors, including relationships, company politics and hierarchies, guidance documents and so on, of which the interpretation of legal language is only one factor, and significantly less direct an interpretation than that of a computer executing code.

[31] Wilkinson (n. 17), 6–10. The need for the Conjoined Method (and the Paired Method) is likely to decrease in importance as the ability for artificially intelligent systems to derive correct semantic meaning from text is improved—although this is a long way off.
[32] Wilkinson (n. 17), 6–10

For drafting recommendations to accompany and govern the interpretation and status of Conjoined Terms, refer to the 'Smart Boilerplate' Section V.

1. Conjoined Term definition

'Conjoined Term' means a natural language term or terms, parts or the entirety of which are expressed via Incorporated Code. Our recommendation is that the parties explicitly state that the Natural Language element in a Conjoined Term pairing is the primary expression of legal obligations (Primary Term) and the other, coded, element in the Conjoined Term exists to facilitate execution of the Primary Term. However, parties may choose to flip that structure and make the coded element the Primary Term should the specific operation of the code itself be of particular import to the parties. Of course, a well drafted SLC of the future may have any mixture of code or Natural Language as a nominated Primary Term(s), the emphasis being on the risk appetite of the parties and what is agreed and referenced by the parties at time of drafting.

We propose that in the short to medium term, a sensible legal approach to initial use of SLCs is to ensure that coded terms are not drafted in isolation from natural language expressions of those clauses.[33] Any coded provision contained in an SLC can be linked to one or a number of natural language counterparts clearly expressing the obligation and the contracting parties' intent that can be understood by all and vice versa any natural language component in an SLC can be linked (or conjoined) to a coded provision or provisions in the SLC.

2. Choice of primacy between smart and natural language terms

We propose that there is a need for contracts to include Smart Boilerplate that provides that in the case of uncertainty or conflict between Incorporated Code and a Conjoined (natural language) Term, the natural language term is given primacy as being the most accurate expression of the parties' agreement. As discussed further below, it is likely that the nature and content of any conjoined Incorporated Code will be taken into account when interpreting an agreement, however, explicit expression that the natural language is the primary term will give it the stronger position where there is conflict. Therefore, in addition, contracting parties should use a drafting mechanism by which the parties can determine with precision the

---

[33] We anticipate that, over time, parties will become more comfortable with the use of code in isolation.

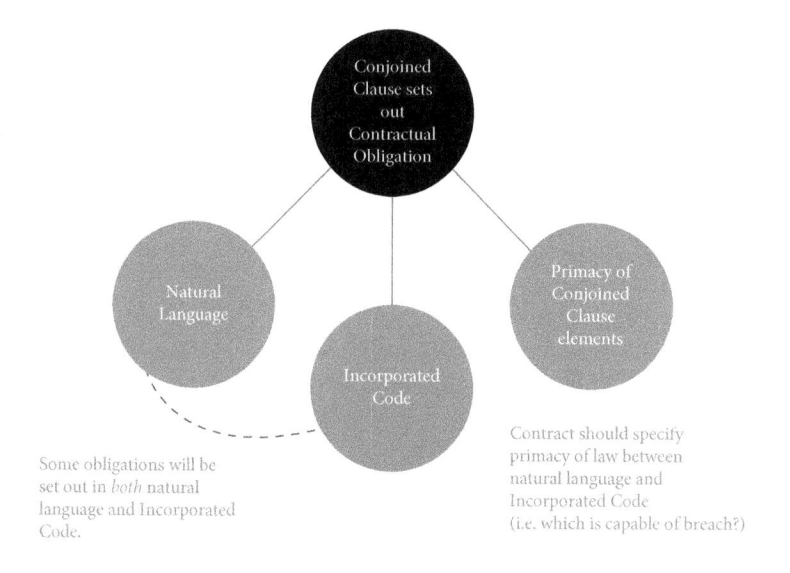

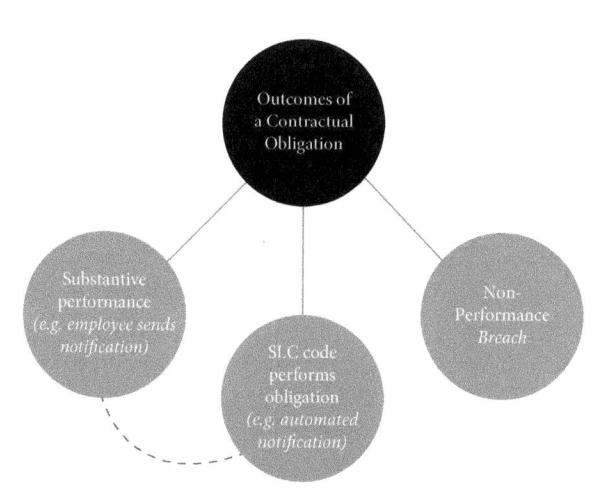

INTEGRATION OF MACHINE CAPABILITIES AND CONTRACTS   159

[Diagram: Central node "Conjoined Clause sets out Contractual Obligation" connected to three nodes: "Natural Language", "Incorporated Code", and "Primacy of Conjoined Clause elements".

Annotations:
- Some obligations will be set out in *both* natural language and Incorporated Code.
- Contract should specify primacy of law between natural language and Incorporated Code (i.e. which is capable of breach?)]

[Diagram: Central node "Outcomes of a Contractual Obligation" connected to three nodes: "Substantive performance (e.g. employee sends notification)", "SLC code performs obligation (e.g. automated notification)", and "Non-Performance Breach".]

Figure 7.2 Structure and Operation of a Conjoined Term in an SLC

parties' intended status of coded expressions of an obligation, as compared to the conjoined natural language obligations.

For example, for one particular obligation the contracting parties may agree that the traditional natural language term contains the primary legal obligation. In this case, when the corresponding Incorporated Code fails, it is not to be considered a breach of contract as the contracting parties explicitly agree that in the case that the code fails, the contracting parties should use alternative methods to ensure the legal obligation held in the natural language term is fulfilled. This mechanism assists contracting parties to ensure there is certainty of terms, by ensuring coded obligations are included in the contract, but controlled and reflected by natural language that governs the intention, use and enforceability of coded obligations; customize the level of rigidity and specificity that would otherwise be introduced by the use of coded provisions that set out, to a minute level, how an obligation should be performed; and manage the risks of automation or reliance on data to trigger performance, because it provides a method by which contracting parties can remove the prospect of inadvertently breaching a contract due to automation failures, or an Internet of Things ('IoT') device linked to an automated contractual obligation providing incorrect information.

Using the Conjoined Method, the contracting parties can agree that in circumstances where the Incorporated Code fails, the contracting parties may fulfil obligations by any means that fulfil the natural language expression of the obligation, and are not bound to the more narrow and specific form of performance set out in the code. The Conjoined Method provides the contracting parties with a framework to handle key new risks introduced by Incorporated Code, as set out in further detail below.

Going back to the space ship scenario outlined above, in the case that Hurricane Inc's automated warehouse went down due to a power failure and could not provide the data update as required by the SLC, the natural language legal drafting of the parties would provide the fall-back position. If the parties agreed that any failure of the warehouse system as outlined in the SLC was a breach, then the power outage would likely give rise to a breach by Hurricane Inc. If, however, the parties had agreed that while this data input from the warehouse would be the responsibility of Hurricane Inc, and the risk of any loss arising from the data being incorrect or not provided in accordance with the contract would sit with Hurricane Inc, it was still acceptable for Hurricane Inc to provide a 'manual' update of their supply levels via an employee, then the power failure would not give rise to breach.

3. Reasons supporting the use of the Conjoined Method

Because Incorporated Code requires the use of machine-readable code, it is reliant on the current state of the technology, essentially written in a different language. As such, an Incorporated Code may not be able to be fully read or understood by: the contracting parties, resulting in uncertainty as to terms; third parties, such as lawyers advising on the contract; or dispute resolution forums and neutrals, where a dispute arises.

The mechanism of a Conjoined Term enables the contracting parties to provide Incorporated Code with a natural language counterpart term that sets out the obligation. This both reflects the likely commercial reality that contractual terms are negotiated by business people in natural language rather than code, with the Incorporated Code then being crafted to give effect to the negotiated provision; and ameliorates the risk that the Incorporated Code will be found either uncertain and therefore unenforceable, or unable to be severed from a contract.

4. Ability to arbitrate impact of specificity and inflexibility introduced by code

We consider SLCs to be capable of providing both the efficiency of code and the flexibility of commercial contracts, and of addressing the grey areas that cannot be usefully incorporated into pure code.[34] The extent to which coded obligations require a natural language mirror depends on the certainty of the coded obligations, and the risk appetite of the contracting parties for the uncertainty arising out of the coded nature of the obligations. At the heart of any contract is a balance of efficiency and risk management. For an SLC, the more coded an obligation becomes, the more the contracting parties have chosen to outline the specific mechanisms for automating and implementing a given obligation. In this way, a highly coded contract could be considered to be more 'complete', as it delves into a deeper level of detail for performance. As put by Lipshaw:

> A far more interesting challenge is to describe a smart contract in which multiple parties with potentially different models of the same transaction come to agree on a single 'well-formed formal model.' […] to make a complex and heretofore negotiated contract smart, i.e. to delegate more and more of the creation, performance and disposition of legally binding transactions to machine thinking [...] The ideal but unlikely complete contract would be the economic optimum because it would perfectly align the incentives of the contracting parties and reduce transaction costs. Hence, to one with an economic bent, 'incomplete contracting' presents a problem to be solved.[35]

On the other hand, a highly coded contract may become imperfect, as the precision of the code, or the precision of terms that the code demands, may narrow the

---

[34] That is, the primary problem with smart contracts is the simplicity of them: they only allow for categorical, black and white outcomes—if this input, then that outcome. Whereas in reality, contractual transactions are often subject to grey areas that cannot be usefully incorporated into smart contract code, such as: (i) disputes over whether conditions were truly fulfilled or not; (ii) unenforceable clauses which exist to set standards or negotiation stances; (iii) enforceable clauses which a party chooses not to enforce due to social or political relationships; (iv) unspecific or vague terms that set behaviour standards or incorporate discretionary, interpretative legal principles such as 'negligence', or to act with 'all reasonable care'. See Levy (n. 7).
[35] Lipshaw (n. 1).

capacity of the contract to deal with unexpected circumstances. In this way, codifying obligations can be a double-edged sword: it avoids the risk that a counterparty may fulfil an obligation under the contract in an unexpected or inconvenient way, but also narrows the flexibility of the contracting parties, and their ability to satisfy in alternative ways the obligation under the contract even if it is agreed between the contracting parties. The Conjoined Method provides the contracting parties with a mechanism to customize the level of flexibility the contracting parties want to build into their contracts. The contracting parties may agree that substantive fulfilment of the natural language term will suffice in place of Incorporated Code.

5. Outcome-based drafting for Conjoined Terms

The contracting parties should also customize the contract by opting for different choices for each Conjoined Term contained in the contract (ie, stating for each whether the Incorporated Code or the natural language term has primacy). Contracting parties ought not simply to rely on a catch-all hierarchy term to achieve the intended effect for Conjoined Term, but should clearly identify in each relevant instance the agreed outcome of any failure of Incorporated Code to execute as intended.[36]

The approach of giving the natural language term primacy (such that failure of the Incorporated Code to perform in the exact way set out in the code does not constitute breach) is likely to be consistent with the approach of the courts to arrive at an interpretation which is commercially sensible, and that expressions are not to be read in a narrow spirit of construction, but as honest people may be presumed to have understood them.[37] As Lord Diplock stated in *Antaios Compania Naviera SA v Salen Rederierna AB (The Antaios)*:[38]

> [I]f detailed semantic and syntactical analysis of words in a commercial contract is going to lead to a conclusion that flouts business commonsense, it must be made to yield to business commonsense.[39]

Given these principles of interpretation, where the contract specifies that a linked natural language expression of the obligation provides the primary obligation, only a narrow semantic focus would allow the courts to consider that the Incorporated Code provides the only method of performance, or that the Incorporated Code

---

[36] Parties should take care when drafting such provisions that they do not comprise an unfair or unenforceable 'exclusion' or limitation of liability clause.
[37] *Cohen & Co v Ockerby & Co Ltd* (1917) 24 CLR 288, 300 (Isaacs J).
[38] *Antaios Compania Naviera SA v Salen Rederierna AB (The Antaios)* [1985] AC 191, 201.
[39] *Antaios Compania Naviera SA v Salen Rederierna AB (The Antaios)* [1985] AC 191, 201 (Lord Diplock, (with whom the other members of the House of Lords agreed).

imposes minute obligations relating to coded functions on the parties. Such an interpretation would have the uncommercial result that where Incorporated Code fails to function as the contracting parties intended, a breach is unavoidable, even where the contracting parties are ready to perform the obligation in accordance with the natural language expression of the obligation in an alternative fashion. Courts would ordinarily strain to avoid such a construction. We consider therefore, that where the contract uses explicit language to couch the Conjoined Method in a way that gives primacy to the natural language, it is likely to be enforceable.

6. Legal categorization of coded provisions

If the order of precedence, and the drafting of coded provisions, is adopted as proposed above, coded provisions will likely be considered a category of 'non-essential' terms—ones in which breach does not have legal consequences, apart from requiring that contracting parties then refer to the natural language term to determine the actions they are obligated to take to fulfil their contractual obligations. Contracting parties are able to stipulate in a contract explicitly whether a term is essential and so determine the legal consequence of its breach, even where a term objectively appears to have little importance.[40] The contracting parties should similarly be able to stipulate: where a coded term is non-essential and where non-fulfilment of that coded term has no legal enforceability or breach consequence, but rather leads to alternative outcomes or obligations (such as, in this case, the need to refer to and fulfil the conjoined natural language term).

The actual effect of the contracting parties' obligations arising from the Conjoined Method must be considered carefully, as in some situations the expressed intention of the contracting parties will be qualified by the actual effect of a bargain or agreement,[41] and the contracting parties cannot by express provision either confer or deny a particular legal character to a relationship which it would not otherwise have or would otherwise have as a matter of law.[42]

In light of the above, we recommend that contracting parties should specify, in each instance, the extent of the importance and value they place on the coded provision being fulfilled by outlining the exact steps to be taken in respect of performance, including where the Incorporated Code fails to execute as expected. For

---

[40] *Shevill Builders Licensing Board* (1982) 149 CLR 620, 627 (Gibbs CJ); *Karacominakis v Big Country Developments Pty Ltd* [2000] NSWCA 313, [123]–[128].

[41] See eg, *Rowella Pty Ltd v Hoult* [1988] 2 Qd R 80, 83 (Ryan J). See also *Toomey v Eagle Star Insurance Co Ltd* [1994] 1 Lloyd's Rep 516 (CA) (parties' description of contract as reinsurance contract was not accurate).

[42] *South Sydney District Rugby League Football Club Ltd v News Ltd* (2000) 177 ALR 611, 645 (Finn J); reversed without reference to the point *South Sydney District Rugby League Football Club Ltd v News Ltd* (2001) 181 ALR 188 (FC) (affirmed sub nom *News Ltd v South Sydney District Rugby League Football Club Ltd* (2003) 215 CLR 563 (HCA)); Carter (n. 22), [12-120].

example, parties could specify that the coded provision is to be the method of performance, but that *after* a failure of the Incorporated Code to execute as intended, the contracting parties can take other actions to fulfil the relevant obligation as held in the natural language term. The use of explicit language spelling out that alternative performance is acceptable where the Incorporated Code fails is important, as otherwise courts may find that departure from the prescribed, coded method of performance is a material departure from the contract.[43]

By contrast, contracting parties may alternatively choose that a party may elect to use the Incorporated Code or not to fulfil an obligation, regardless of whether the corresponding Incorporated Code has been activated or used (though the trade-off for the flexibility of this option is an unpredictability in how precisely the relevant party intends to perform the obligation, and loss to the benefits and efficiencies created by real-time data flows and automation).

The way in which these kinds of specifications are drafted can be expected to influence interpretation of the status of coded provisions. If enough priority is given to the use of a coded term and enough value is placed on coded performance rather than alternative performance, the coded expression may be considered to be an intermediate, or even an essential term, rather than a non-essential term, by objective assessment of the courts.[44]

In addition, the contracting parties should be wary of circumstances where a coded provision, even though deemed non-binding, may give rise to a claim of promissory estoppel[45] with a remedy of restitution where a party incurs expenses in reliance on the coded provision and the other party is unjustly enriched.[46] We believe the above approach of explicit wording setting out the circumstances in which the Incorporated Code performs helps ameliorate this risk. This is because promissory estoppel is more likely to occur in situations where a party can claim reliance on the promise or representation that performance would occur through the coded provision. This might occur, for example, in situations where there is

---

[43] See eg, the UK case of *Veba Oil Supply & Trading GmbH v Petrotrade Inc* [2002] 1 All ER 703. The Court found that a departure from contractually-prescribed instructions for an expert's conduct is material unless it can be characterized as trivial. By contrast, the Court noted that a departure from instructions is quite different from the situation where an expert had gone wrong in the course of carrying out his instructions, which required the court to consider whether that mistake had materially affected the ultimate result.

[44] *Macdonald v Australian Wool Innovation Ltd* [2005] FCA 105, [82] (Weinberg J) considered that the test for determining whether a term is 'essential' is objective.

[45] The leading case in the Australian law of pre-contract promissory estoppel is *Walton Stores (Interstate) Ltd v Maher* (1988) 164 CLR 387. The three essential elements of promissory estoppel are: (i) an unequivocal, clear promise or representation (can be either express of implied); (ii) definite and substantial reliance on the promise or representation (including the fact that the person sought to be estopped must know about the reliance and it must be the case that the reliance will cause detriment if the person sought to be estopped contradicts the promise or representation); and (iii) inequity or unconscionable conduct by the person sought to be estopped.

[46] *British Steel Corp v Cleveland Bridge Engineering Co* [1984] 1 All ER 504 (plaintiffs obtained recovery for work done at the request of the other party in anticipation of a contract that did not eventuate); *EK Nominees Pty Ltd v Woolworths Ltd* [2006] NSWSC 1172, [218] and *Sabemo Pty Ltd v North Sydney Municipal Council* [1977] 2 NSWLR 880, 901–3.

doubt regarding whether the Incorporated Code actually failed to execute as expected, or a party chooses to usurp the performance of the Incorporated Code with alternative performance in circumstances where the contracting parties have not explicitly outlined the circumstances in which such a choice may be made.

7. Summary of the Conjoined Method

To summarize the above discussion, the use of the Conjoined Method enables certainty as to the intentions of the contracting parties, ameliorating the risk that the Incorporated Code (or entire obligation) will be found either uncertain and therefore unenforceable, or unable to be severed from the contract. Further, it enables flexibility such that where the Incorporated Code fails (eg, due to a malfunction), this does not constitute a breach, so long as the party substantively fulfils the relevant obligation in accordance with the natural language term of the contract. However, the extent to which the contracting parties wish to codify obligations, or include natural language provisions that mirror those coded obligations, is entirely customisable depending on their risk appetite.

It may be that the contracting parties wish to nominate the coded provision to contain the binding (and therefore legally enforceable) obligation. In this circumstance, the contracting parties may still include a conjoined natural language provision to ensure they properly understand the intent of the coded provision.

For these reasons, the option of conjoining natural language and code is essential, at least in the short term, to facilitate the ability of the contracting parties, lawyers, third parties and courts to interrogate the obligations and agreement created by an SLC. For the time-being, best practice requires incorporating natural language drafting that reflects or encapsulates the intent of a coded provision, and to draft interpretative provisions that determine which of the Conjoined Terms has primacy at law in cases of conflict.

F. Smart Boilerplate

1. Why incorporate the code?

In order for the contracting parties to agree the legal status of coded obligations as against natural language obligations, the code should be incorporated into the contract. This proposition flows from the fact that the contract *as a whole* should be held in a digital or machine-readable format (recognizing that the natural language itself is machine readable). In particular, this is for two reasons. First, to ensure that the coded obligation can be properly referenced to a natural language expression of that obligation, thereby ensuring the understanding and intention of the contracting parties about the content of the obligation. Secondly, for completeness and certainty as to which specific parts or operations of the Incorporated Code are being referred to when the contracting parties 'conjoin' a term or clause.

In addition, incorporation of the code into the contract enables the use of 'Smart Boilerplate' as set out below. This permits adapting the legal instrument to enable the contracting parties to deal with new risks and consequences introduced by the reliance on Incorporated Code. That is, incorporating the code into the contract enables the contracting parties not only to explicitly agree the code to be used as between them to impact their rights, but also allows the contracting parties to agree certain technical terms relating to the use of Incorporated Code and data, including: which party is to assume the risk of ensuring that the data being used to trigger, update and automate a particular coded obligation is accurate; how the contracting parties intend the Incorporated Code to be activated, including the style of platform the contract is to be hosted on and whether Incorporated Code requires human input from either or both of the contracting parties in order to be activated or suspended; any relevant references or amendments to the terms and conditions of the digital platform or software to be used that might otherwise impact the allocation of risk as between the contracting parties; and any continuing payments required to a provider of a digital platform or software provider to support the continued use of the Incorporated Code.

The most effective way to demonstrate the types of smart boilerplate that may be required or otherwise helpful to enable the contracting parties to customize the use of coded provision is by way of examples, which (noting they are untested and do not comprise legal advice) are set out below.

2. Smart boilerplate example: recitals, definitions, and interpretation

The first element to mention is recitals. These are generally considered non-operative parts of an agreement.[47] They are nevertheless significant in that they set out the assumed state of facts upon which the contracting parties choose to contract.[48] The recitals should include a statement to the effect that the contracting parties are entering into the contract as an SLC (which should be properly defined) and that the SLC will operate on the specified digital platform of the contracting parties' choice in order to automate certain parts of the contractual relationship. This allows the contracting parties to agree that a fundamental basis of the contract is that it should be an SLC, and should be interpreted as such.

In addition, while not part of the recitals, we would advise incorporating—in a similar way to a Definitions table—an index of all Incorporated Code, Conjoined Clauses and agreed digital connections or transactions set out in the SLC, as this

---

[47] *The Leasing Centre (Aust) Pty Ltd v Rollpress Proplate Group Pty Ltd* [2010] NSWSC 282, [79]; *Thiess Contractors Pty Ltd v Placer (Granny Smith) Pty Ltd* [1999] WASC 1046.
[48] *Dabbs v Seaman* (1925) 36 CLR 538, 548–9.

provides: clarity and certainty that the SLC is a contract entire, as otherwise disparate pieces of Incorporated Code have no clear 'home' within the four walls of the contract; a way to map out and understand—in human terms—all the points of connection and automation inside an SLC, providing security in case there are technical failures such as Malfunctioning Code; and similar to a function of legal definitions within a contract, an index by which the parties can easily refer to and create different 'rules' for differing pieces of Incorporated Code (such as which are 'breachable', where responsibility lies and so on, as discussed above in respect of the Conjoined Method and Outcome-Based Drafting).

Following recitals, definitions should include key operational elements relating to coded provisions. In respect of enabling the use of Conjoined Method, in our view definitions should be structured to include and define the following (non-exhaustive) list of concepts.

Smart boilerplate example: definitions

- *Conjoined Term* means any term in this Agreement expressed in both Natural Language and Incorporated Code, which are to be read together.
- *Incorporated Code* means the coded component parts of this contract that underpin any automations and are intended to operate digitally.
- *Machine Readable* means the method by which this contract is able to be processed by a computer or digital system and includes any Incorporated Code.
- *Malfunctioning Agreement Code* means any fault, failure, degradation, deficiency or error in respect of any part of the Machine Readable language which results in:
    - an error message being displayed by the system that this Agreement is running on or being accessed from;
    - an outcome resulting from the operation of the Incorporated Code or a Conjoined Term that was not the intended outcome as stated in the conjoined Natural Language Term; or
    - the Incorporated Code component of a Conjoined Term failing to perform an act or thing that was intended to be performed as stated in the Conjoined Natural Language Term, which [detrimentally] affects a Party or this Agreement.
- *Natural Language* means language that can be a read or interpreted by a lay person without any knowledge of computer code.[49]
- *Primary Term* means the identified Term within a Conjoined Term pairing capable of breach.

---

[49] Notwithstanding that the natural language itself will also be machine-readable.

In respect of the data used and generated, definitions should include terms dictating such elements as the following:

> - *Contract Run Data* means any Data produced by the running of the Incorporated Code.
> - *Data* means information in raw or unorganized form (such as alphabets, numbers, mathematical symbols, geographic co-ordinates, electronic signals, or metadata) that refer to, or represent, conditions, ideas, or objects, whether in written or digital form and which can be entered into a database or stored and processed by a computer for output as usable information.
> - *Data Source* means an oracle or repository of data that provides Data to, or accepts Data from this Agreement.
> - *Data Source Costs* means any costs to be borne by a nominated Data Source Party in respect of a Data Source including [installation, maintenance, and Data Source Malfunction costs].
> - *Data Source Party* means a party nominated as responsible for the proper maintenance and working Data Source or Malfunctioning Data Source.
> - *Malfunctioning Data Source* means any fault, failure, degradation, deficiency or error in respect of any Data Source, which [detrimentally] affects a Party to this Agreement.

Likewise, Interpretation provisions may include provisions to the following effect:

> **Smart boilerplate example: interpretation**
>
> - *Smart Legal Contract Interpretation:* the Parties agree that:
>   - this Agreement is a Smart Legal Contract that is Machine Readable and contains Natural Language and Incorporated Code that are intended to be read together;
>   - [any Data contained in this Agreement will run on [insert nominated digital platform] in keeping with the terms and conditions of that infrastructure as contained in Annexure 1; **or**
>   - any Data contained in this Agreement will run on a digital platform with [insert agreed cyber security standard;]
>   - any SLC Running Costs associated with this Agreement will be borne by [insert nominated party(parties)], and in respect of any failure of payment in respect of SLC Running Costs [the parties will be jointly and severally

> liable and/or will be resolved by reference to [insert agreed payment failure mechanism or link back to dispute resolution clause]].
>
> - *Order of precedence:*
>
> To the extent of any conflict or inconsistency in this Agreement, the order of precedence for the interpretation of the Agreement will be:
>
> - *Natural Language Terms;*
> - *Incorporated Code*[50].
>
> Unless otherwise agreed by the Parties:
>
> - *Natural Language Terms take precedence over Incorporated Code;*
> - *all legal obligations are expressed in Natural Language;*
> - *any Incorporated Code is for execution purposes only and does not create binding obligations on the Parties; and*
> - *the Parties are only bound by a Primary Term in a Conjoined Term pairing.*

Care should be taken when drafting such provisions to take into account existing contract construction law. For example, complex commercial contracts often include what may be an analogous mechanism: a 'priority', 'precedence', or 'hierarchy' clause setting out which of the provisions or documents incorporated into the contract (of all the schedules, main document etc) are to prevail in the event of a conflict.[51] However, recent English authority has emphasized that such clauses are used in construction as a last resort.[52] That is, the normal rules of construction will still apply, taking into account all the documents and provisions that form part of a contract. Only if that process fails, and a clear and irreconcilable discrepancy remains, will it be necessary to invoke the priority clause to resolve the discrepancy.[53]

However, where the Conjoined Method is used, the parties should have a general level of legal protection against Malfunctioning Agreement Code or a Malfunctioning Data Source; effect, that code becomes inconsistent with the

---

[50] Recognizing that any natural language terms are also machine readable, but the machine readable language is further down the technology stack.

[51] N.C. Seddon and R.A. Bigwood, *Cheshire & Fifoot's Law of Contract* (11th Australian edn, LexisNexis Butterworths Australia 2017) 469, [10.32].

[52] See *RWN Npower Renewables Ltd v FN Bentley Ltd* [2013] EWHC 978 (TCC) especially [22]–[24]; upheld on appeal [2014] EWCA Civ 150 (see especially [15]–[16]). Compare where resort to a priority clause was necessary in *CLP Holding Co Ltd v Singh and Kaur* [2014] EWCA Civ 1103.

[53] Cheshire and Fifoot (n. 43), 469, [10.32].

natural language expression of the relevant obligation captured by the code. In such circumstances, 'where the different parts of an instrument are inconsistent, effect must be given to that part which is calculated to carry into effect the real intention of the parties as gathered from the instrument as a whole.'[54] Therefore, the courts will enforce the natural language provision that contains the intention of the parties, over Malfunctioning Agreement Code demonstrated to not accurately be executing those intentions as intended.

In addition, for cases of poorly written code, the approach of Dixon CJ and Fullagar J in *Fitzgerald v Masters* could be applied, in that 'words [in a contract] may be supplied, omitted or corrected in order to avoid absurdity or inconsistency.'[55] Australian appellate Courts have since extended the dictum beyond correction of obvious and/or minor errors, to 'open modification of important provisions in commercial contracts'.[56] Particularly relevant is *Westpac Banking Corp v Tanzone Pty Ltd*,[57] in which a clause in a lease provided for biennial reviews of rent, based on the rate of inflation, but calculated according to a formula that, if literally applied, led to rent increases that far outstripped the effect of inflation by accelerating margins.[58] The New South Wales Court of Appeal held that the literal meaning of the rent review clause produced an absurd result, and 'corrected' it by adding words that instead produced a result that 'properly reflects the intention of the parties to be gathered objectively from the whole context of the lease.'[59]

Globally there are of course a diversity of opinions on whether to 'correct' absurd results or not. In England and Wales the focus of the debate centres around the limits of the so-called 'commercial common sense' approach to the interpretation of contacts.[60] In *Arnold v Britton & Ors*,[61] another rent review case, Lord Neuberger set out a number of relevant factors to guide contractual interpretation. For our purposes the most relevant being that, poor drafting does not justify the court embarking on an exercise of searching for, nor constructing,

---

[54] *Taylor v Dexta Corporation Ltd* [2006] NSWCA 310, as put by High Beale (ed), *Chitty on Contracts* (29th edn, Sweet & Maxwell 2004) vol 1, [12-078], (32nd edn, Sweet & Maxwell 2017) vol 1, [13-080]. See also *GEC Marconi Systems Pty Ltd v BHP Information Technology Pty Ltd* (2003) 201 ALR 55, [2003] FCA 50, [306].
[55] *Fitzgerald v Masters* (1956) 95 CLR 420, 426–7.
[56] Cheshire and Fifoot (n. 43), 472, [10.35].
[57] *Westpac Banking Corp v Tanzone Pty Ltd* (2000) 9 BPR 17, 521.
[58] Cheshire and Fifoot (n. 43), 472–3, [10.35].
[59] (2000) 9 BPR 17, 521 (Priestley JA, Fitzgerald JA, and Foster AJA).
[60] Over the past forty-five years, the House of Lords and Supreme Court have discussed the correct approach to be adopted to the interpretation, or construction, of contracts in a number of cases starting with *Prenn v Simmonds* [1971] 1 WLR 1381 and culminating in *Rainy Sky SA v Kookmin Bank* [2011] UKSC 50 (see November 2011 Litigation Review).
[61] *Arnold v Britton & ors* [2015] UKSC 36.

drafting infelicities in order to facilitate a departure from the natural meaning. Moreover, the fact that a contractual arrangement interpreted according to its natural language, has worked out badly or disastrously for a party is insufficient reason to depart from the natural language. The purpose of interpretation is to identify what the parties have agreed, not what the court thinks that they should have agreed.

To the extent that a tension exists then between the English and Australian position, we would consider that for poorly written code, the Australian approach should be adopted. And because prevention is better than cure, our recommended approach is to at the outset take all steps to reduce opportunities for uncertainty introduced via the inclusion of Incorporated Code into the contract. In this respect the use of the Conjoined Method can assist.

3. Smart boilerplate example: malfunctioning code and data source provisions

Another potential issue relates to malfunctioning code and data source provisions. We recommend that a contract explicitly outline how to achieve desired consequences of an obligation where a coded provision or data source fails to execute as intended, or is otherwise not fulfilled. The contract must address the unintended outcomes caused by the Incorporated Code and oracles. Such a clause would cover: assessment of whether a clause is performing as expected or intended should be done by reference to the natural language component of the Conjoined Term; (if relevant) nomination of a data source party and any relevant costs; notification requirements upon a party becoming aware of malfunction; and reasonable steps to be taken upon notification of malfunction, for example to 'make good' the outcome of malfunctioning code, or to correct any defect, bug or security flaw to ensure the original intention of the contracting parties as evidenced by the natural language terms are reflected, including entering into variations to the SLC.

4. Smart boilerplate example: variations (including unintended variations)

By virtue of the live nature and digital connectivity of an SLC (particularly where another contract is acting as a data source to that SLC), appropriately drafted variations or variation provisions may be used to ensure the scope of and requirements for alteration of any existing terms to the contract (including unintended variations) is as the parties intend.[62] Variation provisions might include: the nomination of specific data sources (which might be specific clauses or contracts with commercial sensitivities) or threshold changes triggered by them that require some element such as notification in writing (by an authorized person, following particular procedures) before a legal variation can be said to occur; the nomination of specific data sources or threshold changes triggered by them that require no notification as they do not constitute a variation; a mechanism for rolling back to an earlier contract state (for example, where something has gone wrong); or abortion or reversion of specific processes or payments to 'make good' an unintended outcome.

The common law of severance for uncertainty is also relevant here. Where the SLC contains a term (most likely in code) that is considered incomplete or ambiguous,[63] for example where the code does not function or is malfunctioning, that term may be effectively severed from the agreement, allowing the natural language expression of that term to remain the only relevant term. The test for whether an uncertain term can be severed depends on the intentions of the parties as to whether the operation of the contract, apart from the uncertain part, was to be conditional on the efficacy of that part.[64] That is, where our drafting principles have been followed, the parties would have made it clear that the relevant malfunctioning Incorporated Code is not necessary to the operation of the contract as where it fails, the natural language expression of that term remains the primary source of the obligation.

5. Smart boilerplate example: data management architecture

The contracting parties should ensure that they put in place adequate obligations and provisions for data management architecture that enable regulatory compliance, including privacy and cybersecurity arrangements to be maintained and upheld over the course of the SLC. A closely related issue is the choice of platform.

---

[62] Noting that waiver provisions are not always upheld but have commercial usefulness if intending to evidence a waiver was not intended. *Liebe v Molloy* (1906) 4 CLR 347, 353–5; *Commonwealth v Crothall Hospital Services (Aust) Ltd* (1981) 36 ALR 567, 567; *Update Constructions Pty Ltd v Rozelle Child Care Centre Ltd* (1990) 20 NSWLR 251; *GEC Marconi Systems Pty Ltd v BHP Information Technology Pty Ltd* [2003] FCA 50, [291], [394]–[395], [467]. The issues raised by 'no oral' variation clauses are discussed at length by Finn J in *GEC Marconi Systems*, [213]–[223].

[63] *David Jones Ltd v Lunn* (1969) 91 WN (NSW) 468, 473; *Whitlock v Brew (No 2)* (1968) 118 CLR 445; *LMI Australasia Pty Ltd v Baulderstone Hornibrook Pty Ltd* [2001] NSWSC 886, [35] (affirmed [2003] NSWCA 74).

[64] *Brew v Whitlock (No 2)* [1967] VR 803, affirmed in the High Court: *Whitlock v Brew (No 2)* (1968) 118 CLR 445.

6. Smart boilerplate example: choice of platform is as significant as choice of governing law

An SLC has different hosting requirements to a traditional contract. A static or paper-based contract doesn't really need to 'live' anywhere. While any given manifestation of a static contract (such as a digitized scan, or a physical copy) will exist in the sense that it occupies a physical or virtual location, this location will have no bearing on the rights and obligations set out in the contract. In contrast, an SLC will be machine readable and may contain coded obligations (Incorporated Code). These obligations, expressed in code, necessarily require digital infrastructure (such as a server) on which to run. Put another way, due to its digital components, an SLC must contemplate the manner in which it should be hosted and run on a digital platform in order to properly execute as the parties intended.

The design and drafting of an SLC must exist in a complementary relationship with its platform, as different platform architectures enable different levels of functionality and contain various technical limitations that may impact the capability of the contracting parties to administer the SLC. For example, some blockchain-based platforms may only allow fully self-executing contracts that cannot be amended, paused or perhaps most importantly kept appropriately confidential. It is important to recognize these as elements of the platform, rather than of the SLC itself. In the same way that the contracting parties may agree to a governing law that may impact the functioning of the obligations contained in the contract, the contracting parties should agree in the SLC to the specific platform, or at least specify the significant functionalities they require of the preferred platform.[65]

---

[65] Though not directly analogous, in *Shell UK Ltd v Enterprise Oil plc* [1992] 2 All ER (Comm) 87, [1999] 2 Lloyd's Rep 456, the English Chancery Division found that the determination of an expert was contractually invalid due to the expert's use of one, rather than the other, of two computer programmes for mapping the contours of strata of rock under the seabed. This goes to demonstrating that the court will take into account technical differences in the functionality and outcomes of even two very similar computer programmes when deciding whether use of an alternative programme to the contractually prescribed program was contractually valid. Each of the two computer programmes were noted to be substantively similar in that both were widely used in the oil industry, well recognized and of high repute. However, the court noted that technical differences in the functionality of the programmes—particularly the algorithms used—resulting in different outcomes was relevant: 'Thus there are many relevant functions within the two packages which are identical, or virtually so, and which produce the same, or very similar, results if applied to the same input data. Other functions, however, are different as between the two packages. Moreover, their operation depends on what figures are chosen for what may be as many as 30 parameters for the particular operation. Thus, starting from the same input data, the same package may be used to produce different results if used by different mappers who set the parameters differently, and two mappers using different packages will certainly produce different results, however the parameters are set.' (at [114]). In particular, differences in terms of user interface, data management, tools, and processes used for loading, storing, referencing, exporting, and archiving data used by the software, and particular differences noted by the court were the way in which the software is used to process data, and the way in which records are kept of operations carried out using the software (at [115]).

174   SMART LEGAL CONTRACTS

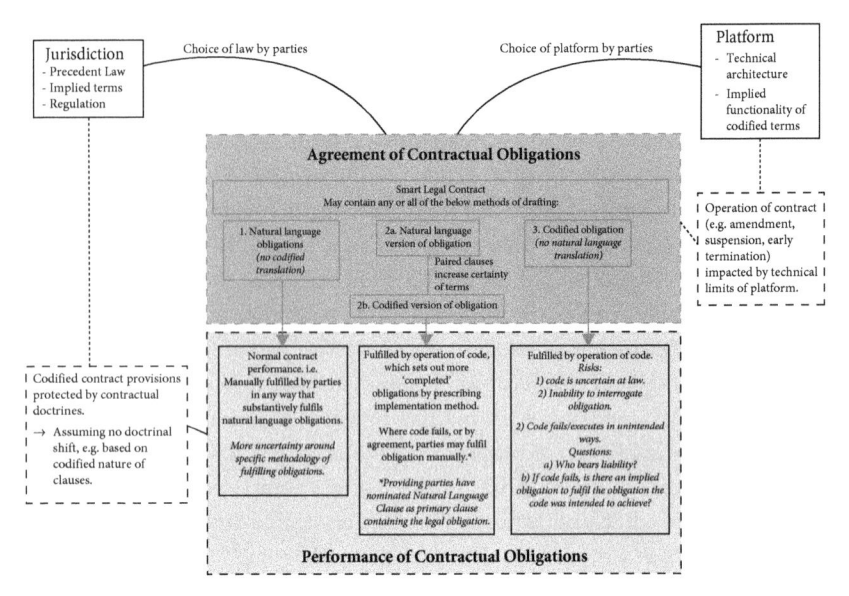

Figure 7.3 Lifecycle of SLC Performance

Most significantly, the innate dynamism of an SLC might enable it (or one of the parties, an employee, or a third party) to vary the terms of the contract (intentionally or otherwise). A pertinent issue is to ensure that the nature of the digital platform is designed to ensure against unilateral or unauthorized variance of the agreed SLC with clear sets of permissions on both access, and authorization to trigger code, amendments and other contractual events.

A digital platform for an SLC should provide a single 'source of truth', a single live version of the SLC that reflects the true state of the contract and that is accessible to the parties at all times. Without adequate drafting protections and appropriate digital hosting, an SLC would require a perpetual or serial examination of adequate construction and formation principles over the contractual lifecycle (not just as is custom now—at the start of the contractual relationship).

To deal with these types of situations arising from the innate dynamism of the SLC, as well as the 'active function' of Incorporated Code, variations specific to SLCs that are likely to require explicit contemplation in the SLC include: continuing on the basis of the natural language components of the contract alone; how coded provisions, their status and data inputs and outputs will be handled, including access, permissions, hosting and usage limitations; who the relevant authorities for triggering each element of code that requires human-input will be; permissions (including where a third party arbitrator will be allowed to make changes in accordance with court orders etc); and whether and how the SLC should be able to 'rollback' to only the natural language provisions in the case of breakdown of the digital platform.

G. Clause Classification

One of the most important considerations in the use of SLCs is which clauses to encode. We propose the following system of Clause Classification to guide assessment of which types of clauses or obligations are appropriate for codification. This is both a legal and commercial question, relying on assessment of elements including: risk appetite, cost and recourse to insurance; capacity of the relevant obligation to be represented and effectively automated by code; the level of specificity as against flexibility preferred in the performance of the relevant obligation; and level of adaption required in behavioural processes by humans interacting with the machine or SLC.

The more generally a term is drafted, the greater the area of delegation or freedom given to the party to decide how that term should be performed. Where a party seeks greater certainty as to how performance should be undertaken, more precise language is likely to be preferred.[66] We consider the more precise the term is intended to be, the more capable it is of being codification. The contracting parties' agreed or preferred level of generality versus precision in the language of a term can be used as an indicator of whether it should and can be coded. If the contracting parties intend that a particular term should be incapable of producing differing responses or forms of performance, then that term is particularly suited to automation. If the contracting parties consider that a particular term is likely to encounter unexpected elements or outcomes in the course of the prescribed performance, the clause may not be suited to automation, except where the variety of possible elements or outcomes to be encountered is finite, and can be identified and accounted for in the coded provision.

The issue of ensuring Incorporated Code terms are robust and accurate is not one unique to these terms. Poor drafting in the legal sense has often led to the equivalent of 'Malfunctioning Agreement Code', where legal drafting has not properly captured the understanding of the contracting parties, or has led to misunderstanding about obligations as between the contracting parties. Indeed, the precision offered by contractually agreed code that automates to a precise degree the implementation of agreed actions and performance is a tool that can help ameliorate the risk of misunderstandings between the contracting parties.

All drafting incorporated into a contract should be prepared with the overarching focus on reflecting the 'meeting of the minds' as between the contracting parties, whether that drafting be captured in natural language (ranging from legalese to industry terms to dictionary definitions and common usage) or code. Looking forward, we expect that bespoke codification of terms will likely be subsumed by machine-learning as natural language processing technology in the law develops to enable auto-coding of natural language provisions. The bespoke

---

[66] S. Robinson, *Drafting: Its Application to Conveyancing and Commercial Documents* (1st edn, Butterworths Sydney 1973) ch 3, 15–20.

style of codifying legal obligations is expected to be an intermediary step to that point.[67]

Lastly, and perhaps most importantly, contracts must—as always—take into account 'human centred' design, in particular as contracting moves into the realm of governing hybrid machine-human performance. Digitization means that many business or operational processes are becoming more automated, and so care must be taken when selecting which clauses or terms to automate in an SLC from the human perspective. Choices as to *how* those clauses are automated should also consider whether they maintain a 'human in the loop' philosophy by for example incorporating well drafted notices set to alert parties to important performance events or their failures. That is, as human oversight becomes increasingly 'opt-in' rather than 'opt-out' as machines take on more of the labour of performance, it is important to carefully consider regulatory, ethical and operational impacts of either (a) removing human oversight or (b) lessening the psychological pressure of human oversight, which may result in more relaxed approaches by the humans involved to ensuring compliance and oversight is properly conducted, even when machines are performing the majority of the work.

H. The Legal Status of Automated Contract Performance

Where an SLC may be capable of being used (and relied on) by parties to automate obligations (such as, for example, issuing an essential purchase order), the implications for liability, responsibility and performance of the coded aspects of an SLC becomes interesting. Natural language contract provisions, just as coded provisions, can delve into minute detail around how an obligation should be fulfilled, up to describing in detail the specific software, code and platform to be used in a specific fashion.[68]

The question then becomes whether this differs to the coded method of performance in SLCs. The substantive difference appears to lie in the *automation* aspect of the SLC method, in that the contract itself—once digitally active—assesses whether a trigger or condition has been fulfilled and proceeds to cause the implementation of the detailed instructions provided by the contract, as compared to one or both of the contracting parties making the choice to input the instructions into a digital system.

---

[67] Algorithmic review and machine learning applied to, eg, combined dispute and contractual data sets will minimize the risks and promote the predictability of SLC terms. The significance of an SLC is that it can draw together the front- and back-end of contractual processes, whereby the outcomes and impacts of a coded contractual term that is capable of being digitally processed and performed can be monitored and recorded in a clear manner, to inform future drafting.

[68] Consider an example of one contract that has a coded provision detailing how execution of a given obligation takes place, compared to another contract that only contains natural language, but contains an equal level of detail as to execution as the coded version.

Whether this difference has implications at law has not been tested. A common sense answer is that the contracting parties agreed to the specification and use of given triggers, and should in the natural language of the contract provided for any responsibilities or liabilities in respect of the code executing automatically. However, the distinction becomes more acute when it becomes possible for an artificial intelligence or otherwise algorithmic-based decision-maker to make a 'machine-subjective' or 'machine-led' decision about whether a contractual trigger condition has been fulfilled. One possible outcome is that the decision-making (and therefore responsibility) of execution of the obligation is considered to have been 'lifted' out of the hands of the party who would otherwise be responsible for the implementation, by the agreement of both of the contracting parties to leave execution up to the automated or machine-driven process.

That is, by agreeing to automate execution, and going one step further and agreeing the precise coding to automate execution and including it in the contract, both of the contracting parties have implicitly agreed to shift responsibility for execution from the relevant party and on to the SLC itself, or else onto the system in which the SLC executes. Currently, there is no status at law for machine-led or machine-assisted processes or for the algorithms, coding or machines that give rise to them, so the trail of causation is likely to still link back to the relevant party.

However, because of the emerging status of machine-assisted processes, we recommend that parties clearly ascribe responsibility of both performing an obligation, and responsibility for the manner in which code executes, to either one or both of the parties to avoid disputes over whether machine-assisted or machine-led processes impact the chain of causation and liability. This line of inquiry leads into the territory of whether the law may adapt to treat machine-led SLCs or SLC processes as an independent legal entity, an agent for parties, or a 'third party' to the contract. This goes beyond the scope of this chapter, but will have significant implications for the law as we begin developing legal instruments capable of taking actions based on machine learning or artificial intelligence assessment mechanisms.

I. The Legal Void of the Digital Economy

The foundational proposition of SLCs is that any agreement, process, task, payment, transaction or economic action that is ordinarily governed by a contract, may also have a digital process such as a smart contract encoding, performing and recording it. As machines become increasingly capable of performing human economic activities, such as physical labour, cognitive activities or complex combinations of those two (such as self-driving cars), the legal and contractual mechanisms between economic entities that regulate the consequences of human economic activities also need to be changed to take into account these new machine or 'data-driven' actors.

The need for SLCs arises from an economy that is increasingly reliant on data and digital technology[69] for economic activity—that is, an economy in which actors and entities may take actions with legal consequences in reliance on, or through the use of, data or digital technology (for example via e-commerce, automation, robotics, and machine learning).[70]

As a fundamental premise of the digital economy, any kind of object, trigger, information or real-world event requires a digitized representation as data in order to become a part of an automated or machine-assisted process. This has the side-effect of creating digitized versions of the real world. This data that creates the digitized versions of real world events can be generated from a wide range of potential sources, ranging from IoT devices or sensors to online foreign exchange rates to human-generated input such as data entry or the clicking of a button to signal (and therefore digitise) consent to an action.

When acting in concert with other parties, we need mechanisms to ensure that data and digital technologies that are mutually relied upon can be trusted and verified, and that the risk of ensuring they are accurate and functioning accurately is allocated. From a risk-management perspective, legal instruments will need to increasingly adapt to and incorporate mechanisms to manage reliance on, and active uses of, data and digital technologies. We propose contracts as the strongest and most adaptable instrument for this, particularly in respect of cross-party automation, data management, or other economic activities that require the interaction and co-operation of multiple entities.

1. SLCs work as legal instruments to manage data reliance

We expect that contracting parties will increasingly seek to rely on SLCs to create contractually agreed digital code, and manage and interpret the data generated by their contracted activities. An SLC provides a mechanism by which the parties can

---

[69] Digital technology can be defined to: ' … encompass all electrical devices which make use of information represented in digital form—such as binary code—to perform useful functions. Data connectivity is what makes a device (eg, light bulb) earn the status of 'digital' (eg, computer screen). Computers, robots, software, smartphones and sensory systems are all digital technologies. When connected they can … give rise to new systems for human communication, governance models and business processes.': S. Hajkowicz and D. Dawson, 'Digital Megatrends: A perspective on the coming decade of digital disruption' (CSIRO Data61, Brisbane 2018) <https://data61.csiro.au/en/Our-Research/Our-Work/Future-Cities/Planning-sustainable-infrastructure/Digital-Megatrends-2019> accessed 8 July 2021.

[70] Robots, algorithms, and automation are already becoming commonplace in manufacturing and large companies such as Rio Tinto, Google, UPS, and Amazon, and approximately half of today's work activities could be automated by 2055, see McKinsey Global Institute, 'A Future That Works: Automation, Employment, and Productivity' (January 2017) <https://www.mckinsey.com/~/media/mckinsey/featured%20insights/Digital%20Disruption/Harnessing%20automation%20for%20a%20future%20that%20works/MGI-A-future-that-works-Executive-summary.ashx> accessed 8 July 2021.

co-design the use and mechanisms of data or automation, as well as allocate, agree and manage the known risks and liabilities of those elements. The result is that the SLC becomes an active tool of contract performance, containing actively running code that can interact with and impact the real world, providing notifications, and triggering events such as payments, delivery orders, or reporting.

How active a tool the SLC is will be limited by a number of factors. These include the machine-level capability of the SLC to interact with, trigger, or be triggered by real world events, the level of digitized representations of reality accessible by the SLC, and the ability of the digitized representation of reality to be agreed and contractually identified by the contracting parties. Also relevant is the accuracy of the digitized representation of reality as it may (for a variety of reasons including malfunction or malicious behaviour) fail, be inaccurate, or be vulnerable to manipulation, exploitation, or privacy breaches.[71] Such failures may occur either at the source of the data (eg, a sensor malfunctioning), during transit of the data (eg, the data is hacked, manipulated, or corrupted before reaching the contract) or at the point of receipt of the data (eg, the platform the SLC is operating on, or the SLC itself is not coded or structured correctly and causes the data to be corrupted or changed). Finally, the contract management performance of an SLC will depend on its ability to act as an untampered source of truth between contracting parties as to what has occurred under the operations of the SLC. This is more likely to be the case where parties use a trusted digital platform, such as one that utilizes some form of DLT.

J. Conclusion

The SLC Model presented in this chapter provides a context in which to reflect on the impact of emerging technologies on the law itself.

> To search for a singular, 'correct' theory of contract, may be to search for something that is 'quite unintelligible' ... the word 'correct' is 'nothing more than a synonym for a complex and coordinated set of intersubjective practices, which practices are the concrete expression of the self-understanding of those who partake of the practice in question (in this case contract law)'. It would be a mistake, therefore, to regard contract as a 'thing' about which we can have 'right' or 'wrong' theories. It might be better to conceive of contract law 'not as a thing but more akin to an ongoing, self-transforming cultural activity'.[72]

---

[71] These issues are not unique to SLCs. Indeed, any form of digital activity or automation, whether tied to a contract or not—face these issues. The difference is that an SLC can provide legally-binding mechanisms to deal with and allocate the risks of the consequences.

[72] Cheshire and Fifoot (n. 43), 1336 [28.1], citing D. Patterson, 'The Philosophical Origins of Modern Contract Doctrine: An Open Letter to Professor James Gordley' (1991) 1432 *Wisconsin Law Review* 1436.

The integration of code into a contract brings it to life.[73] The SLC is a digital 'mirror' to real world events where obligations such as deliveries, payments and reports occur. Like the contract, the SLC is agnostic and powerfully adaptable in its application. It can for example, interact with other digital systems, code or real world data feeds (for example, a delivery clause can monitor in real time the live feed from a weighbridge sensor maintained by the contracting parties). It can automate obligations (for example, the delivery clause can trigger automatic payment to a party upon detecting a delivery event in the weighbridge sensor live feed). It can update in real time (for example, this might include the potential to monitor regulatory or legislative instruments, and update the contract to reflect and notify of any relevant changes impacting the subject matter of the contract, the performance of parties' obligations, or its governance). It can be analysed and provide machine insights when read in concert with other SLCs. It can provide insight into (digital evidence or audit trail) and facilitate automated civil procedure (for example in respect of breach, termination and damages).

This demonstrates the magnitude of potential applications for a properly crafted SLC and why it is important for the rules of contract to evolve (where necessary) to ensure safe adoption.[74] The process of defining the boundaries of a contract becomes more complex the more connected and more interactive an SLC becomes. Defining the boundaries becomes a process rather similar to how one might define the boundaries of a neuron. Viewing SLCs as digital assets[75] proffers the possibility that both the *neuron* (ie, the core SLC drafting and code in its inert written state) *and its live communication with other neurons* (ie, the live, executing coded provisions and connections of an SLC), necessitates the conclusion that the boundaries of the SLC are necessarily dynamic and constantly fluid.[76]

---

[73] SLCs will enable automated performance not just within a single corporate entity, but as between contracting entities. The capability to automate such processes are limited only by the capacity of technology to detect and communicate the process, and the creativity of the parties in identifying what should be measured, monitored, and transacted.

[74] Through the use of SLCs, the guardrails around rights and obligations that contracts provide will be extended into assisting and implementing the actual operational performance of the contract. Parties to a contract will no longer be purely reliant on manual actions and management to achieve performance.

[75] It is outside the scope of this paper to engage in any discussion as to the regulatory morass currently faced by digital assets generally. It is worth making the point that as a digital asset, an SLC is perhaps one of the most complex and critical, more complex and critical then the current incarnation of its 'troublesome' digital asset cousins, smart contracts (eg, fungible or non-fungible digital tokens), stablecoins, cryptocurrencies, and perhaps central bank digital currencies ('CBDC') (though in practice the CBDC and SLC may technically merge in shape and criticality—particularly if CBDCs are used to administer government policy in contract with citizens). The regulatory implications of this will need to be carefully considered including those requirements for the provision of critical digital infrastructure and minimum requirements in respect of it. A. Garside *et al.*, 'Digital Infrastructure Integrity Protocol for Smart and Legal Contracts DIIP 2021' <https://papers.ssrn.com/sol3/papers.cfm?abstract_id=3814811> accessed 28 May 2021.

[76] If this is correct, thought will have to be given to where one SLC begins and another ends and may require new legislative enactments (eg, similar to those already found in maritime laws).

This is a natural consequence of the evolution of contracting from a static record of rights and obligations to a living mechanism that facilitates, audits, and records performance. A contract so formed will act as a live, digital mirror of the enforceable obligations, inputs, outputs and performance of any economic or contracted activity or relationship. The data collected, and the rules governing its collection, may in time come to be considered tradable 'digital assets', quite separate from the obligations or contract itself—for example, imagine a construction site head contract SLC that collects much data about the best way to build a particular type of minesite—such a pool of organized data and rules about how to digitize the construction of such a site would be highly valuable to another entity looking to build a similar one.

In the classic economic sense, a 'complete' contract is one that anticipates all future state contingencies. The move towards SLCs can, in many respects, be understood as a desire to craft more 'complete' contracts—contracts that lay out not just the boundaries of obligations, but architect, enact and respond to the intricacies of day-to-day operations. It would necessarily be far more complex and intricate a beast than the contracts we see today—as the coded provisions require deep detail and thought as to how the contracting parties truly want events to play out on the minute, digital level.

In its fully-realized state, such a contract might sit under a large project like a root system sits under a growing tree, growing and evolving as the project itself does. An active coded obligation might discover a change in circumstances by interacting with a sensor, and so circle back to and update the performance required under another provision, setting off a chain reaction that flows through the contract and changes the state of play, sending different messages and actions flowing through the root system. With almost infinite intricate potential states, such a wholly-enlivened contract would never truly be complete—to look at it at any point in time is only to see one aspect of it; its terms and state as they are at that moment, just as one might catch a flattened, fragmentary glimpse of oneself in a mirror.

8
Six Levels of Contract Automation
The Evolution of 'Smart Legal Contracts'

Susannah Wilkinson and Jacques Giuffre[*]

A. Introduction	182	D. Analogy Between Automation of Contracts and Autonomous Vehicles	191
B. Automation and Digital Transformation	184		
1. Digital transformation of law	184	1. Features of different levels of contract automation	195
2. Digital technologies across the contract lifecycle	184	2. When does a contract become a smart legal contract?	201
C. Smart Legal Contracts	186	3. Features of digital execution mechanism or digital platform	202
1. Necessary components of smart legal contracts	188	E. Conclusion	203
2. Unified Method vs Paired Method of SLC	190		

A. Introduction

Automation and digital transformation are impacting different aspects of business across every industry and every sector. The legal industry is undergoing digital transformation both in relation to legal processes and the form and functionality of legal instruments. Consistent with this trend, the notion of augmenting commercial contracts with automation and digital connectivity is gaining momentum in response to increasing frustration with traditional—static, analog—contracts, that sit disconnected from digital processes and systems and the benefits

---

[*] Susannah Wilkinson is the Digital Law Lead—Australia & Asia at Herbert Smith Freehills. She is a founder and Director of the Digital Law Association and Chair of the Digital Commerce Committee of the Business Law Section of the Law Council of Australia. Susannah has extensive experience in drafting and negotiating contracts for major infrastructure projects and specializes in the development of smart legal contracts and digital assets within HSF's Global Digital Law Group. She has a Masters of Law from the University of New South Wales and a Bachelor of Commerce from the University of Sydney.

Jacques Giuffre is a specialist technology lawyer at Herbert Smith Freehills and a former IT systems consultant. Jacques is leading the development of smart legal contracts through his role as Technical Development Lead within HSF's Global Digital Law Group. He studied law at Murdoch University and computer and mathematical sciences at the University of Western Australia.

Susannah Wilkinson and Jacques Giuffre, *Six Levels of Contract Automation* In: *Smart Legal Contracts*. Edited by: Jason Grant Allen and Peter Hunn, Oxford University Press. © Jason Grant Allen & Peter Hunn 2022.
DOI: 10.1093/oso/9780192858467.003.0009

of digitization. 'Smart contracts' or 'smart (and legal) contracts' are an inevitable outcome.

As awareness of 'smart contracts' spreads from cryptocurrency circles into the mainstream, lawyers have been grappling with how to harness the benefits of automation and digital connectivity in commercial relationships whilst ensuring the legal integrity and enforceability of the contract to result in 'smart legal contracts'. Sir Geoffrey Vos rightly states that 'legal treatment of "smart contracts" is rapidly becoming one of the most important legal subjects of our generation'.[1] However, such treatment of smart contracts conceived as entirely self-executing code is not without its challenges. As well as assessing how law applies to technology, lawyers will need to engage in designing the future digital contracting solutions that will unlock benefits of automation and digitalization for the full spectrum of contracting.

To leverage the benefits of automation, digital connectivity, and the generation and processing of structured data through digitalization of contracts, lawyers will need to understand the implications of contractual obligations being expressed in machine-executable form and interacting with specialized digital infrastructure.

This chapter considers the digital evolution of contracts and, primarily, the question of what digital functionality is required of a contract for it to become a 'smart legal contract'. We explore the different characteristics of contracts along a proposed spectrum of contract digitalization by describing a conceptual model of levels of digitalization and resulting potential for automation of contracts. This model draws analogies with the SAE International J3016 'Levels of Driving Automation' model widely adopted for autonomous vehicles. To assist in this analysis, we explore the distinction between 'smart contracts'[2] and 'smart legal contracts' ('SLCs') and seek to orient them within the broader paradigm of a *legal-led approach* to digitalization and automation of contracts. This chapter thus aims to provide a starting point from which to develop a framework and a taxonomy to assist discussion and development of legally enforceable automation of contractual performance.

Smart legal contracts are nascent products in a market with rapidly growing interest and demand. However, the concept continues to suffer from a lack of agreement on essential elements, standard definitions of form and functionality, and a lack of guidance on legal issues. Agreement on those matters, and clear and consistent terminology to use in discussing them, will assist mainstream development and adoption by lawyers not trained in computer science.

---

[1] Sir G. Vos, 'End-to-End Smart Legal Contracts: Moving from Aspiration to Reality', Chapter 2 in this volume.

[2] See further discussion in Section C, however note that the term 'smart contract' is used in this article to collectively refer to the range of computer code intended to perform functions or transactions between parties but which may lack the indicia of a legally enforceable contract in the traditional sense including: smart contracts as proposed by Nick Szabo, a-legal/legal agnostic smart contracts, Ricardian contracts, and computable contracts.

B. Automation and Digital Transformation

As the disciplines of computer science and law collide with the digital evolution of law, overlapping terminology, with different meanings, is creating confusion (consider the 'execution' of a contract vs 'execution' of code). There is a dizzying array of 'LegalTech', 'Fintech', and 'RegTech' products driving digital transformation of legal products and services, adding to the complexity.

1. Digital transformation of law

Digital transformation of legal processes, and the form and functionality of legal instruments, are converging trends fuelled by both existing technologies, and the opportunities presented by adopting new technologies (such as distributed ledger technology or 'DLT'). Efforts to improve the process of contractual drafting and review have resulted in software being applied to reduce time, cost, and the overall inconvenience of traditional methods. For example, software is now used to automate the preparation of contracts based on templates, with varying levels of sophistication, and to rapidly run large scale document reviews powered by artificial intelligence.

A second trend affecting the form and functionality of legal instruments sees rights and obligations expressed in computational logic and software (eg, smart legal contracts and 'legislation as code' or 'rules as code'[3]). Both of these trends raises different legal issues, but both are contributing to the irreversible and inevitable digital transformation of the law.

2. Digital technologies across the contract lifecycle

In looking at how contracts are evolving in the digital age, it is helpful to consider the technologies being applied to contracts across each of the different stages of the contract lifecycle (see Figure 8.1). All stages of the contract lifecycle are open to process improvement through digitalization and automation. It is important to distinguish between different stages of the contract lifecycle because the practical and legal ramifications vary. For example, practical and legal issues relating

---

[3] '[Rules as code or "RaC"] proposes to create an official, machine-consumable version of some types of government rules, to exist alongside the existing natural language counterpart. This involves the use and integration of technology, but also a reimagining of the processes and methods currently used to create government rules. In this way, RaC is 'the process of drafting rules in legislation, regulation, and policy in machine-consumable languages (code) so they can be read and used by computers' and thus also represents a new approach to rulemaking (de Sousa, 2019).' Observatory of Public Sector Innovation, 'Rules as Code (RaC)' <https://oecd-opsi.org/projects/rulesascode/> accessed 12 March 2021.

to automation of contract creation and electronic signing are different from those raised by the automation of performance of the contractually agreed undertakings.

Generate → Negotiate → Approve → Execute/sign → **Perform** → Dispute/terminate

(Contract formation → Execute/sign)

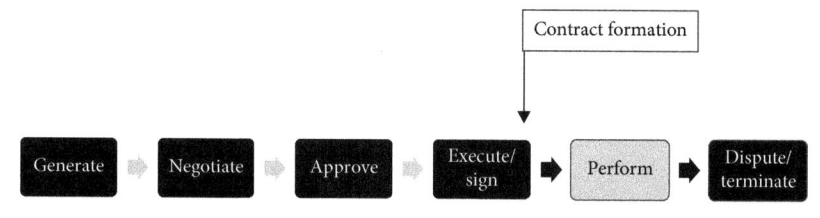

Figure 8.1 Simple Contract Life Cycle

Set out below are some illustrative examples of LegalTech applied at different stages of the contract lifecycle:

(a) In the stages prior to contract formation, tools are available to expedite the generation of contracts (often referred to as 'document automation'), to streamline workflow of approval processes and to provide for digital signing of agreements[4] without the need for paper copies.
(b) Once the contract is in force following contract formation, contract lifecycle management software can be used to track and manage contractual obligations (although the majority of these require significant manual involvement to integrate the contractual data into the contract lifecycle management ('CLM') software, use of natural language processing will likely increase to aid in this process).
(c) Artificial intelligence ('AI') software is increasingly being used to improve efficiency of contractual due diligence and large scale e-discovery in disputes, and there is growing need for online dispute resolution forums and streamlined management and submission of electronic court documents.

These tools increase process efficiency at various points in the contract lifecycle. They do not inherently change the functionality of the contract itself during the performance phase of the contract which begins at contract formation. Digital transformation of contracts in the 5th stage of the contract lifecycle—ie, performance—is the domain of smart legal contracts by virtue of the capability to automate performance of contractual obligations. Smart legal contracts offer a step change in the core functionality of contracts as evidence of the parties' legally binding

---

[4] Electronic signatures may be effected by something as simple as the application of an image of a signature to an electronic document. A digital signature is a specific and more secure type of electronic signature using a 'virtual fingerprint that is unique to a person or entity and is used to identify users and protect information in digital messages or documents. Digital signatures are significantly more secure than other forms of electronic signatures.' Cyber Infrastructure and Security, 'Understand Digital Signatures' (24 August 2020) <https://us-cert.cisa.gov/ncas/tips/ST04-018> accessed 23 March 2021.

agreement. By leveraging disruptive or foundational technologies, such as distributed ledger technology, within a legal framework, smart legal contracts will 'provide commercial entities with the ability to contract as they wish, and ensure that new foundations are available for economic and financial activity'.[5]

C. Smart Legal Contracts

The term 'Smart Legal Contracts' ('SLC') includes a legal tautology—contracts are necessarily legal—but the term is intentionally used to differentiate the concept from a (arguably a-legal) 'smart contract'. The term 'smart contract' emerged as a concept in relation to the automation of contractual clauses or exchanges, as a 'set of promises, specified in digital form, including protocols within which the parties perform on the other promises'.[6] Smart contracts gained further traction with the rise of distributed ledger technologies, including blockchain, as 'systems which automatically move digital assets according to arbitrary pre-specified rules'.[7] The International Standards Organisation defines a smart contract as a 'computer program stored in a distributed ledger system wherein the outcome of any execution of the program is recorded on the distributed ledger'.[8] Smart contracts are written entirely in programming languages[9] and implemented entirely as software designed to operate on distributed ledger technology platforms.[10] In other words, a 'smart contract' is self-executing computer protocol (to facilitate automated performance of a transaction), which does not necessarily possess the requisite characteristics of a legally binding agreement.[11]

---

[5] Sir G. Vos, 'End-to-End Smart Legal Contracts: Moving from Aspiration to Reality', Chapter 2 in this volume on fourth page of the chapter.

[6] The term 'smart contract' was first introduced by Nick Szabo. See N. Szabo, 'Smart Contracts: Building Blocks for Digital Markets' (1996) <http://www.fon.hum.uva.nl/rob/Courses/Info rmationInSpeech/CDROM/Literature/LOTwinterschool2006/szabo.best.vwh.net/smart _contracts _2 .html> accessed 12 March 2021.

[7] The concept of smart contracts gained further interest with the rise of blockchain and distributed ledger technology, in particular the Ethereum blockchain. See V. Buterin, 'Ethereum White Paper' <https://blockchainlab.com/pdf/Ethereum_white_paper-a_next_generation_smart_contract_and_ decentralized_application_platform-vitalik-buterin.pdf> accessed 12 March 2021.

[8] International Organisation for Standardization, *Blockchain and distributed ledger technologies— Overview of and interactions between smart contracts in blockchain and distributed ledger technology systems, Technical Report, ISO/TR23455:2019* (2019).

[9] A. Tyurin et al., 'Overview of the Languages for Safe Smart Contract Programming' (2019) <https://www.researchgate.net/publication/335689429_Overview_of_the_Languages_for_Safe_Sma rt_Contract_Programming> accessed 9 December 2020.

[10] A. Rosic, 'Smart Contracts: The Blockchain Technology That Will Replace Lawyers' (25 November 2020) <https://blockgeeks.com/guides/smart-contracts/> accessed 23 March 2021.

[11] Smart contracts may have a legally binding intention or unsuccessfully contract out of applicable laws of a relevant jurisdiction and as such it is necessary and desirable to consider the legal background, context and definitions. See n. 8.

The term SLC is used to distinguish a concept that necessarily includes the evidentiary record of an agreement that has both the integrity of a legally enforceable contract and the added benefit of some or all of its terms being expressed in computational logic enabling automation and digital connectivity in the performance of its contractual terms. For a contract to be an SLC it must be both a legally binding agreement (under the laws of the applicable jurisdiction)[12] *and also* have certain terms expressed and implemented in machine-executable code. An SLC contains one or more machine-executable components that facilitate automation by reducing or removing the need for human intervention in contractual processes,[13] and is therefore a legal agreement that can be created, executed, managed, and maintained by machines (either partially or wholly). In time, the distinction between contracts, smart contracts, and SLCs will fade, leaving simply contracts with varying degrees of digital functionality.

Not all of the provisions of a contract can, or necessarily should, be expressed in computational logic and code. Those clauses that serve an active operational role and can be expressed in Boolean logic are more likely to be automated (eg, a payment mechanism). Certain common non-operational terms in contracts are not capable of being assessed deterministically and these are best expressed in natural language.[14]

Much of the early legal academic analysis and commentary on smart contracts gives significant weight to this issue and misses a key value proposition for the broad base of potential mainstream users. It is also open to the parties under the contract to agree whether automation should be a shared feature of the contractual arrangements. Bringing the code into the contract enables the parties to contractually agree specific treatment of issues in relation to performance and execution of the code (including in relation to data, failure, error, etc). Alternatively, unilateral automation can be created to enable interaction with a party's internal systems, in which case such coded automation would necessarily be outside of the scope of the legally enforceable contract.

---

[12] The UK Law Commission is conducting a scoping study considering how the laws of England and Wales apply to smart contracts, including issues of jurisdiction, which may provide future guidance on these matters. The Law Commission, 'Smart contracts' <www.lawcom.gov.uk/project/smart-contracts/> accessed 19 December 2020.

[13] ISDA and Linklaters, 'Whitepaper: Smart Contracts and Distributed Ledger—A Legal Perspective' (August 2017) <www.isda.org/a/6EKDE/smart-contracts-and-distributed-ledger-a-legal-perspective.pdf> 4–5 accessed 9 December 2020.

[14] For further discussion on suitability of operational and non-operational clauses to be subject to automation and self-execution see ISDA and Linklaters (n. 13), 10–12.

There will be value for businesses and government institutions in adopting SLCs, including to harness structured data, increase efficiency, and secure a digital audit trail of contract performance. Yet, for SLCs to be adopted widely by businesses, smart contract functionality will need to be served with legal integrity through trusted, secure digital infrastructure.

1. Necessary components of smart legal contracts

All smart legal contracts are contracts, but not all contracts are smart legal contracts. One of the greatest challenges facing the legal profession is how to sensibly and validly marry the natural language elements of a contract, which require human interpretation, with the elements of conditional logic that can be executed by a computer automatically.[15] It is likely that any solution to this challenge that facilitates the mainstream adoption of SLCs will need to address the twin elephants in the room: (i) the vast majority of lawyers are not skilled in computer programming (and will not be any time soon), but (ii) ensuring legal certainty in relation to enforceability of encoded rights and obligations requires lawyers.

One approach to looking at the components of a 'smart legal contract' is the metaphor of a 'contract stack' proposed by J.G. Allen. Allen rightly suggests that digital contracts should be regarded as 'complex legal institutional entities whose legal and technological parts interact'.[16] There are varying approaches to how contracts can leverage automation, which will in turn depend heavily on the choice of platform and software used to create and run smart legal contracts.

The model presented by Natasha Blycha and Ariane Garside in this volume provides perhaps the most comprehensive, formal definition of an SLC for the legal industry to date, and presents a model as a solution for how to integrate computer code and natural language into a technically functional, and legally enforceable contract.[17] Blycha and Garside define an SLC as a *legally binding, digital agreement in which part or all of the agreement is intended to execute as algorithmic instructions.*

---

[15] See for example, two opposing alternatives proposed of the External Model and Internal Model. See ISDA and Linklaters (n. 13).

[16] J.G. Allen, 'Wrapped and Stacked: "Smart Contracts" and the Interaction of Natural and Formal Language' (2018) 14(4) *European Review of Contract Law* 331.

[17] N. Blycha and A. Garside, 'A Model for the Integration of Machine Capabilities and Contracts', Chapter 7 in this volume.

The Blycha & Garside Model sets out five key components required for a contract to constitute an SLC:[18]

1. Status: legally binding in that an SLC must conform to the established rules of contract law in the relevant jurisdiction;
2. Form: the contract must be in a machine-readable or digital state;[19]
3. Contents:[20] the contract must contain a combination of:
   a) natural language, being any of the typical contracting and business language used in the jurisdiction of the contract, as in any traditional contract; and
   b) computer code, or other forms of machine-executable or[21] algorithmic instructions intended to run digitally;
4. Active Function: the parties to the contract should agree how, when, and why the digital components of an SLC are triggered or affected by data or events generated from external or internal data sources, including the results of previously executed algorithms; and
5. Digital Execution Mechanism:[22] the digital hosting or domain of the SLC and how the digital hosting domain integrates with the Active Function.

This model provides a method by which the entire natural language contract can co-exist in parallel with discrete elements of computer code, or other forms of machine-executable or algorithmic instructions intended to run digitally, thereby preserving the legal integrity of the contract (Allen would describe the same arrangement as a 'contract stack' with natural language and machine-readable, formal language 'layers'). This approach provides legal certainty as to the automation of contractual performance by bringing the agreed coded terms into the legally enforceable elements of the contract, rather than having a coded performance mechanism that sits outside the legal contract.

By mirroring or 'pairing' natural language drafting with code that provides complementary functionality, the parties to a contract can retain greater legal certainty and control over the operation and consequences of performance of the relevant terms of the contract. This model provides flexibility in that automations

---

[18] *Ibid.*
[19] Interpreted for the purpose of this paper to require both features rather than one or other.
[20] For example, even where the language of the contract includes computer code, the coded components still go to generating and evidencing meaning, agreement, and obligations.
[21] Interpreted for the purpose of this paper to require both features rather than one or other.
[22] 'Execution' here is used with the common meaning of that term in computer science rather than law. This element highlights the requirement for an SLC to 'run' on a specialized digital platform (ie, distributed ledger technology) that provides requisite properties of cybersecurity, privacy, and data protections.

can be paired with a natural language provision without the requirement for the code to mirror the entire natural language provision (see discussion of Paired Method below).

2. Unified Method vs Paired Method of SLC

To date, much of the commentary around the development of smart legal contracts has been heavily influenced by considering how specific legal obligations can be translated into formal language that machines can understand. This is a vital part of the development, but this approach has resulted in an assumption that only those natural language provisions that can be expressed entirely in computational logic can be enhanced by automation, and runs the risk of limiting the application of automation to narrow (albeit valuable) use cases. In our view, there are two approaches to composing the natural language and encoded elements of a contract, which we will now discuss in turn.

The 'Unified Method' involves translating a suitable natural language obligation into formal language or code that enables the deterministic logic of the obligation to be processed by machines. This results in the contractual obligation being expressed in a way that is simultaneously able to be interpreted, as to its logic, inputs and outputs, by both computers and humans. The Unified Method assumes that only natural language obligations which can be entirely expressed in computational logic (ie, a single representation of contracting language 'intelligible to human beings and ultimately executable by machines'[23]) will benefit from automation.

From a legal drafting perspective, the Unified Method is more restrictive as it requires close correlation between the natural language obligation and the coded expression of that same obligation. For this approach, the natural language obligation is effectively translated through some formal or intermediary language into machine-executable logic. While this approach is valuable for content that is well-suited to translation into computational logic (eg, calculations, payments etc), restricting the contractual content only to those rights and obligations that can be expressed in code, risks overlooking how automation can enhance other aspects of contractual performance and generate value in business relationships more broadly. For example, simple automations or digital connectivity may benefit parties to a contract even where such digital functionality does not mirror the structure and logic of the contractual obligation.

---

[23] Allen (n. 16), 311.

The 'Paired Method' (of which the 'Conjoined Method' described in the Blycha & Garside Model is an instance) is an alternative method, whereby the natural language components of a contract are retained and extended by pairing or tagging them to beneficial coded automation or digital connectivity, for example, by pairing automation of a function with a natural language expression which may or may not mirror the full natural language provision.[24] The Paired Method offers the flexibility of being able to retain any natural language provisions required by the parties, extended or supplemented by automation provided by paired code. The question of which provisions are to be automated will be based on a cost-benefit analysis by the parties. For example, definitions, calculations of dates and prices, party names, and process provisions are readily able to be tagged as machine-readable data or expressed as machine-executable code.

Under this approach, a natural language expression of a particular provision is linked to or paired with a related automation. The two expressions may, but are not required to, correlate closely in structure. The nomination of natural language and code as paired clauses provides legal certainty and flexibility for the parties to contractually determine the legal implications of performance. Counterparties have the flexibility to determine priority between code and natural language in respect of a clause or even part of a clause.

D. Analogy Between Automation of Contracts and Autonomous Vehicles

It is useful to draw on cross-industry examples to help articulate what is meant by automation or digitalization of contracts. A useful analogy can be made between levels of automation or digitalization of contracts and levels of automation of dynamic driving tasks performed by autonomous vehicles.[25]

The SAE International J3016 'Levels of Driving Automation' model has emerged as the dominant model and taxonomy for regulators and manufacturers in relation to autonomous vehicles. The SAE model focuses on whether the human driver or the automated driving system is in *control* of a particular

---

[24] This analysis of possible approaches was informed through discussions with Natasha Blycha in relation to the influence of digital platforms on method for integration natural language and code into legally enforceable agreements, and discussion of the 'Conjoined Method' approach.

[25] See also an alternate analogy using the SAE J3016 Levels of Driving Automation to consider technical smart contract capabilities by P. Ryan, 'Proposed new Taxonomy for Autonomous Smart Contracts' (12 August 2018) <www.linkedin.com/pulse/proposed-new-taxonomy-autonomous-smart-contracts-dr-philippa-ryan> accessed 19 December 2020.

dynamic driving task at different levels of automation. J3016 'Levels of Driving Automation' provides detailed definitions for six levels of driving automation, ranging from no driving automation (level 0) to full driving automation (level 5), in the context of vehicles and their operation on roadways.[26] SAE International has released a supplementary infographic for use with J3016 'Levels of Driving Automation' to provide clarity and using terms more commonly used by consumers, industry, and media.[27]

The SAE model provides a useful analogy for considering the different features of contracts along the spectrum of contract automation and digitalization from a paper contract to a 'self-driving contract'. Our proposed Model for Levels of Contract Automation sets out six levels of contract automation and digitalization from Level 0 (no automation and no digital contractual performance) to Level 5 (fully digitalized and fully autonomous contractual performance). This Model for Levels of Contract Automation seeks to explore the features of a contract at each of the six levels; importantly, highlighting nuances between each level to identify key fundamental changes in the nature and operation of contracts, in particular moving from Level 2 to Level 3, and from Level 3 to Level 4. Of key interest are issues raised about the interplay between the terms of the contract and the terms mandated by the digital hosting platform that arise in the shift from Level 3 to Level 4.

This progression is explored through a number of dimensions. The first dimension is the changing nature of the evidentiary form of the contract from a paper contract (ie, a duplicate evidentiary record of the agreed bargain held by each party), to a single digital instance of the contract accessible by both parties as a shared digital asset. The second is expansion of the scope of mutuality (ie, as a consequence of the contract becoming a shared digital asset, the scope of what can form part of the legally binding agreement can grow). The third is the changing degree of human involvement in monitoring and performing rights and obligations under the contract (represented by different colours in the table). The fourth is how the contract is stored, and the associated features of the evidentiary form of the contract that are enabled by storing or running the contract on specialized digital infrastructure (for example, that ensures neither party can alter the digital instance of the contract without consensus).

---

[26] SAE International, Taxonomy and Definitions for Terms Related to Driving Automation Systems for On-Road Motor Vehicles J3016_201806 <www.sae.org/standards/content/j3016_201806/> accessed 10 December 2020.

[27] SAE International, 'SAE International Releases Updated Visual Chart for Its "Levels of Driving Automation" Standard for Self-Driving Vehicles' (11 December 2018) <https://www.sae.org/news/press-room/2018/12/sae-international-releases-updated-visual-chart-for-its-%E2%80%9Clevels-of-driving-automation%E2%80%9D-standard-for-self-driving-vehicles> accessed 10 December 2020.

CONCEPTUAL LEVELS OF CONTRACT AUTOMATION

	TRADITIONAL CONTRACTS			SMART LEGAL CONTRACTS		
	Level 0	Level 1	Level 2	Level 3	Level 4	Level 5
Description of contract features	Paper / hard copy / scanned (without OCR)—text is not digitally accessible.	Digitally accessible text but cannot be semantically processed by a computer.	Digitally accessible and part of text can be semantically read and processed by a computer. Each party holds a separate digitally accessible version.	Digitally accessible and stored on a specialized digital platform that provides a synchronous 'read-only' shared view.	Same as Level 3 plus shared 'read-write' access to the contract and automated performance of specified, agreed actions under the contract (post-legal signing).	Same as Level 4 but without any human intervention (post-legal signing).
Degree of human involvement in contractual performance (post legal execution)	Human required to monitor and perform obligations and exercise rights under the contract manually, or through engaging with software systems.			Human counterparties use a shared digital instance of the contract (post-legal signing) to monitor and perform contractual rights and obligations.	Machines monitor and perform automated contractual actions within agreed parameters. Interaction with external sources, and choices made by parties, are immutably recorded in the contract. May require human confirmation or choices for specified performance in pre-agreed circumstances.	No human actions required for monitoring or performance. Contract actions are 'performed' by machine.

(continued)

CONCEPTUAL LEVELS OF CONTRACT AUTOMATION

	TRADITIONAL CONTRACTS			SMART LEGAL CONTRACTS		
	Level 0	Level 1	Level 2	Level 3	Level 4	Level 5
What do these features do?	Provides a static record of evidence of the contract, in paper form. A scanned copy results in a digital version that may be digitally shared, stored and replicated—but remains unable to be processed by a computer on any level other than images of a page.	Provides a digital record of evidence of the contract that can easily be searched and analysed by computer, as well as shared, stored, printed, and replicated.	Same as Level 1 plus certain contract data is classified for machine-readability (through manual or automated means) by a party for internal systems. Such data can then be integrated with that party's digital systems and processed without human intervention. However, in contrast to Level 4, this processing is carried out by a single party and does not affect contractual rights and obligations (as each party's separate contractual record remains read-only). Can be facilitated at creation stage by document automation processes to identify and create structured data[1].	The digital instance of the contract is hosted on a mutually accessible platform (eg, a distributed ledger technology platform). The digital instance of the contract is agreed between counterparties as the one true record of evidence of the contract in digital form and is a shared digital asset. The parties have 'read-only' access to the shared record which can be integrated into a party's internal digital systems and processes.	Same as Level 3 plus agreed automation of performance of parts of the contract and integration of performance with external systems and data sources. The parties and external data sources may interact with the contract in a 'read-write' manner, recording performance and altering the state of the contract in the manner pre-agreed at contract formation / legal execution. Integration of the shared, up to date digital asset with internal business systems (eg, ERP software). Provides data generation and capture for data analytics. Single source of truth. Audit trail of data generated by contract performance.	Same as Level 4, but all contractual performance is fully automated and performed without human intervention within specific, suitable use cases.

[1] Alternatively, upgrade of Level 1 contracts to Level 2 can be facilitated post-creation through applying AI-driven and analytical software tools.

1. Features of different levels of contract automation

This section explores example features of contracts for each Level of contract automation for illustrative purposes. In simple terms, a contract exists where 'two or more parties have reached an agreement, intend to create a legal relationship by doing so, and have each given something of benefit'.[28] Traditionally, the form of the contract has been relevant to evidencing elements of formation (which may vary with the nature or subject matter of the contract). Digitalization of contracts necessarily focuses on the form of the evidence of a contract, but equally important are the associated features of a contract. In other words, the analysis expands beyond passive to active: from how the agreed terms are expressed or recorded to what the parties agree the terms can do.

a.) Level 0 (paper contract)
The primary record of the contract is a paper document executed by both parties, with each party holding a copy. In most cases, such contracts are drafted digitally (using word processing software) and often negotiated digitally by exchanging marked-up changes. The agreed final written representation of the contract ('digital final form') is then printed out,[29] usually with a copy for each party which is then signed by the parties to provide a complete original record of the executed contract ('paper contract'). From the paper contract alone, information is wholly inaccessible for machine processing and can only be accessed by humans.

While each party will usually have access to the digital file that generated the paper contract (ie, the Word file that was printed), there is nothing linking the digital file to the original paper contract that was signed as evidence of execution. These final versions can often be misplaced or confused with earlier versions, and there is usually no mutually agreed digital record of the executed document to refer to. A party exercising good document management will ensure these problems do not arise, and may create a digital record that is essentially a Level 1 document.

Level 0 extends to a digital file created by simply scanning an image of the original paper contract, without applying a technology that digitizes the text, such as optical character recognition, or 'OCR', ('scanned contract'). While the scanned contract is a digital record of the paper contract, and therefore of the contract itself, the content of the contract (being primarily text) is not able to be machine-processed in any way—the scan merely tells the computer where ink was on the

---

[28] UK Jurisdiction Taskforce, *Legal Statement on Crypto Assets and Smart Contracts* (The Law Tech Delivery Panel) (November 2019), 8.
[29] Note that this results in an enormous loss of digital information which cannot be regained simply by producing an OCR digital contract—the linked cross-references, data on the structure of the text and other meta-data is lost for good by flattening the far superior digital final form into the paper contract (gaining only some additional formality in the execution). Electronic execution avoids this information loss.

scanned page, not what letters that ink forms. This provides the ability to digitally store, share and replicate the scanned contract, but no deeper processing capability beyond images of the pages.

b.) Level 1 (digitally accessible)
The primary record of the contract is stored in a digitally accessible form ('digital contract'). For example, consider adding digital capability to a paper contract by applying OCR to a scanned contract to result in a digital record of the text of the paper contract ('OCR digital contract'). Or, consider executing the contract electronically without printing a copy in any number of ways—for example, parties may exchange copies of the digital final form by email with appropriate words in the body of the email to indicate execution, or they may exchange separate copies of the digital final form, each with an image of that party's signatory's signature inserted in the execution block ('electronically signed contract'), and of course they may use one of the more sophisticated digital signing solutions such as DocuSign ('digitally signed contract').[30]

Here is the first opportunity to expand the scope of mutuality—by which we mean what has been mutually agreed by the parties and therefore can be said to form part of the legally enforceable contract. At Level 0, the scope of the mutual agreement can only extend to what was printed and signed. However, when parties have access to a shared record of the contract that can be relied upon as identical to the other party's view of the contract, then that view is mutual and, where clearly intended, can form part of the contract.

Of the Level 1 examples, electronically or digitally signed contracts offer a better outcome in terms of mutuality, in that both parties have access to the same mutually shared digital record of the contract at the point of execution and therefore the same digital representation of text and other content. The scope of mutuality extends to the digital representation of the information contained in the digital contract. So, if the parties have agreed at execution on the digital representation of the text, that digital representation can be contractually relied upon. If they have agreed on the digital representation of certain semantic elements in the digital final form then that semantic meaning can be contractually relied upon.

In some circumstances, the level of mutuality available in a digitally signed contract may offer fringe functionality of Levels 2 and 3. For example, both an electronically and digitally signed contract will preserve the basic semantic content that is part of a digital final form, such as cross-references and data about the

---

[30] Note the distinction here that an electronically signed contract is signed using electronic means (such as email) whereas a digitally signed contract is signed through a digital medium built for the purpose. In the latter case, the process of signing has been digitized, whereas in the former the process is analogue. That is, the words in the email which give effect to the contract are meaningless to the email protocol through which they are exchanged, whereas a protocol such as that used by DocuSign understands what each step means and when effective contractual execution has taken place.

structure of the text, providing basic Level 2 functionality. Further, some digital execution platforms provide a secure method for ensuring the contents of the executed document do not change—this would provide a read-only shared view of a digitally signed contract as at the date of execution, providing near-Level 3 functionality. However, the shared view is not synchronous as required for Level 3, ie, changes are not reflected in the shared view.

However, the more basic electronic executions, such as the simple email exchange, will not provide an immutable or synchronous record to the parties. In such cases, there is no way to readily prove—from the digital contract alone that a document later purported to be the digital contract is in fact what was executed. Examination of mail logs and other analysis may be able to offer such proof, but this proof is external to the digital contract and cumbersome to obtain—ie, it is not a core part of the digital contract. Such digital contracts are therefore not completely reliable as records of the agreed contract (though at least as reliable as a paper contract, which can, of course, be tampered with), will diverge from the agreed contract if it is varied or amended and will not provide access to mutually agreed information that is generated by or about performance. That is, they are still 'dumb' records.

However, all Level 1 documents provide a significant additional digital capability over Level 0: they provide machine-readability of the text itself—though not its *meaning* (ie, not semantic machine processing). This provides for text processing such as indexation and rapid search and automated analysis based on the text alone (eg, probabilistic analysis based on particular word usage alongside other words). Such text-based processing could be used to provide for integration with one party's internal approvals and contract management software. However, without semantic machine-readability, this would be cumbersome and not resilient, as it would rely on specific words being included in the digital contract and cleanly extracted and recognized as denoting the relevant data.

c.) Level 2 (meaning can be processed)
As for Level 1, the primary record of the contract is a digital contract. As noted in Section D(1)(b), both electronically and digitally signed contracts will include basic semantic data which provide some Level 2 functionality. However, significant Level 2 functionality will only be available where the digital contract includes more detailed, structured contractual data. As such, an OCR digital contract alone would not meet the requirements of Level 2.

Semantic information could be encoded into the digital contract in a number of ways. For example, a human might identify meaning for the digital contract. The digital final form could be created using specialist digital contract authoring software that includes the ability to encode structured data with the contract text at the outset, such as denoting contractual elements as specific data types or tagging them with information about the element. Alternatively, a machine might identify meaning for the digital contract. Machine learning or other advanced analysis techniques can be applied to digital contract texts once created to automatically encode semantic information into the document—this could occur either before or after electronic or digital execution of the contract.

In both cases, useful structured data will be available about the contract—eg, terms, clauses or headings could be tagged with logic structures and key elements of the contract text can be identified as specific data types or with particular meaning, such as 'commencement date'. This allows for more powerful and reliable analysis of contractual data, including across a large body of such contracts, and integration into business systems. It must be noted that the automated method of adding semantic information will result in outcomes and integrations that are only as reliable as the software used to produce that semantic information. In most cases, this will come down to probabilistic analysis of textual elements which, as noted in respect of OCR digital contracts, may not produce particularly reliable or useful results, at least without significant human curation. This stage of automation generally involves the use of digital data templates which are customized by the party to suit the purposes of the contracted transaction (and internal requirements).

In terms of mutuality, human identified meaning will result in the potential for counterparties to have a shared view of the semantic data as it is contained in the digital final form that is then electronically or digitally executed. Machine identified meaning will result in a shared view only if it is applied prior to execution. In either case, that mutuality is only maintained to the extent that, if the digital contract is executed digitally, the digital platform offers this shared functionality and a secure method for ensuring the contents of the executed document are not subject to unauthorised change—and even then, the mutuality would apply only to the contract, and the machine identified meaning expressed in the contract, as at the date it is executed.

d.) Level 3 (specialized digital platform)

The primary record of the contract is, as for Levels 1 and 2, a digital contract.[31] But at Level 3, the digital contract must be stored on a specialized digital platform that provides a synchronous shared view of a digital instance of the contract, and importantly allows for amendments and variations to the contract to remain synchronized and mutual as a record of the contract.

The 'specialist' element of such platforms referred to at this Level 3 is more than, and must be distinguished from, simple shared drives such as Dropbox or Google Drive. Storing a digital contract on a non-specialized platform allows for a shared view of the contract as at the date it is executed (or stored on the non-specialized platform), but any changes following execution would need to be legally agreed

---

[31] A Level 1 digital contract could conceivably be uploaded to a platform meeting the requirements of a specialized digital platform, and so 'skip' the requirements of Level 2. A specialized platform could have the ability to maintain a synchronous shared view and allow for amendments etc, without significant semantic data being part of the contract.

and evidenced off-platform with the amended version of the contract being manually updated on-platform.[32]

This shared view is 'read-only' (in contrast to Level 4 which offers 'read-write' view). The platform can facilitate agreement of amendments or variations to the legal terms of the contract which can be processed with the resulting amended versions stored on the platform. This facilitates version control of the contract, amendments and variations with counterparties through a single source of truth. At scale, this allows for structured organization of all of a party's contracts (ie, a 'contract library'). However, note that at this 'read only' level, the contract cannot be directly updated in real time by automated provisions that 'write' to (ie, directly modify) the contract—that is, the contract cannot modify itself. This is the distinguishing feature of Level 4.

The shared read-only view can also be integrated with various business systems with the same power and reliability as described for Level 2. Again, the integrations and what the parties do with that data will be off-contract and not mutual. However, the fully mutual and synchronous view of the Level 3 document allows both parties to be assured that the data they are integrating into their systems directly from the contract is the same structured, semantic data that the other party has agreed to (and is likely to be integrating into their business systems). This removes one source of uncertainty as to that data—that the other party may have a different view of the meaning of certain terms. In addition, the specialist platform may also offer more contract-specific functionality, such as shared analytics,[33] enhanced cyber security and permissioned access.[34] Finally, the synchronized view of the shared digital contract removes the need for each party to maintain separate records of the contract and, to the extent shared data is generated, duplicate record keeping by each party.

e.) Level 4 (automated performance)

Once a shared view of the digital contract on a specialist platform is available, functionality can be added to allow for coded provisions of the contract agreed by the parties to provide contractually endorsed automation of performance of certain parts of the contract. Such functionality can only be provided through a specialized platform.

---

[32] Theoretically, the parties could agree a process for amendments and variations which uses such general purpose non-specialized platforms—in such a case, where the process is contained entirely within the digital contract and can be effected using the general purpose platform, that digital contract and platform together could be considered to have put in place a Level 3 contract.

[33] Though outside the contract, such analytics could be considered by the parties to be mutual with a high level of confidence. In some cases, the digital contract may have provisions acknowledging the shared analytics functionality of the contract and endorsing those results as a source of shared, agreed data, in which case the generated data would in fact be as mutual as the rest of the contract.

[34] Given the nature of permissioned access—dealing with authorized personnel of each party—these would be unlikely to be mutual. That is, a party will usually want complete control over which of its personnel are authorized to view, amend or otherwise deal with the contract.

The platform must provide a method for the parties to indicate their binding agreement to certain code which itself requires the parties to fully understand the mechanism that will run the code, how it will access and generate data and, ultimately, satisfy obligations and establish rights. Coded provisions can provide for automated performance of certain obligations that can be entirely reduced to algorithms, given the appropriate data sources, or can provide for identified data within the digital contract to be tagged and paired with relevant automation (such as the automatic generation and issuing of a notice triggered by input of pre-agreed data).

For example, events contemplated by the contract may be confirmed upon agreed values being reported by Internet of Things ('IoT') sensors, such as confirmation of delivery of goods. Connecting to third parties through published Application Programming Interfaces ('APIs') or publicly available data services can deal with events within those third parties' control, such as confirmation of payments being made and calculation of price adjustments based on published rates. Each of these automated provisions require the ability to update the contract (such as a price list) or other contractually agreed data, such as the immutable record of transactions performed under the contract. The specialist digital platform that hosts such contracts must then offer read-write functionality, updating these data according to the mutually agreed rules included in the digital contract, interpreted in accordance with the rules of the platform which would be agreed by reference.

As with Level 3, the contractual data can be integrated into each party's internal business systems. However, now, instead of only the static read-only data being mutually available, the constantly updated outcome of automated provisions can also be accessed with the assurance of mutual agreement on the data and, where semantically encoded, its meaning.

f.) Level 5 (fully autonomous)
Level 5 envisages a fully automated contract, where a Level 4 digital contract has automated provisions for all contract tasks which can operate without human intervention. Such a contract may be difficult to imagine now, except in very narrow use cases. For example, transactions that are already highly automated on established terms and where there are very few judgment calls to be made, such as contracts for trading of securities, pricing of online advertisements and similar high volume, low cost, formulaic transactions.

To take this Level to its fullest expression—no human intervention—we can imagine a point where smart legal contracting technology has matured so that it has become highly trusted and, perhaps, preferred over traditional contracts for the specific use case. Analogously to the autonomous vehicle scenario, SLCs may be considered less prone to error and, given the security of automated provisions, less likely to allow leakage of value through overlooked rights. Parties with a strong preference for automated performance may contract out of as much of the non-codifiable, non-automatable common law rights as they can, agreeing for all disputes to be finally determined by fully digitized and automated dispute resolution platforms, and reducing all liability to expressly calculable amounts.

2. When does a contract become a smart legal contract?

To analyse when a contract, or more specifically the form of evidentiary record of the contract, possesses the requisite features to constitute a smart legal contract, it is helpful to consider how the required components of an SLC under the Blycha & Garside Model apply to the various levels of the Conceptual Levels of Contract Automation. The table depicted in Figure 8.2 shows how a contract at each of the six levels must satisfy the 'Status' component of the Blycha & Garside Model (ie, be legally binding according to the principles of contract law), yet only at Level 3 of the Conceptual Levels of Contract Automation does a contract constitute an SLC, by exhibiting all five components of the Blycha & Garside Model.

Blycha & Garside SLC components	Scale for Contract Automation					
	Level 0	Level 1	Level 2	Level 3	Level 4	Level 5
Status	✓	✓	✓	✓	✓	✓
Form	✗	✗	✓	✓	✓	✓
Contents	✗	✗	✗*	✓[†]	✓	✓
Active Function	✗	✗	✗	✓[†]	✓	✓
Digital Execution Mechanism	✗	✗	✗	✓	✓	✓

Figure 8.2 SLC Components and the Scale for Contract Automation

*In relation to the 'Contents' component, at Level 2, while it is technically possible for a party to extend the contract functionality either by connecting the contract to internal systems and adding automation, at this Level of automation such a feature would only apply as a one-sided, internal feature for a single counterparty (ie, interaction with internal systems with a counterparty's business, ERP software etc), and so would not allow for mutual contents features. In contrast, at Level 3 automation and above, the coded components operate as part of the contract either between counterparties or with third parties.

[†]In relation to the 'Contents' and 'Active Function' component, Level 3 can exhibit these characteristics only in a read-only fashion. By contrast where a Level 4 contract contains agreed code, that code can be executed by the platform on which the digital contract is run, writing its output back to the contract and self-modifying the contract (as pre-agreed). Level 3 may contain agreed code which is run on the platform, but any output must be stored outside the contract. This extra-contractual data may be stored on the platform or in some other pre-agreed location and, with the right language in the contract, may also be contractually endorsed, while not being able to modify the contract itself. This distinction—between the read-only Level 3 contracts and read-write Level 4 contracts may not be significant in reality—it may be trivial for a fully realized digital contracting platform to provide for read-write functionality if it has provided the other features of a Level 3 contract. And it is an open question as to whether Level 3 and Level 4 are distinct enough to form separate levels. However, at this stage, we have maintained the distinction as the ability to self-modify appears to be a significant conceptual step-change, in that it allows for all the power and complexity of unconstrained automation, whereas Level 3 maintains a special status for the contract itself, which is walled-off from agreed automations. While the description above in relation to a Level 3 platform provides for the parties to be able to execute amendments and variations entirely on-platform, the process would be outside the contract.

It is also worth noting that principles of contract automation (and the associated value propositions) can also be applied to other instruments such as policy documents. Applying this analysis from a different perspective, a supposedly a-legal smart contract would only be considered a 'smart legal contract' once it satisfies the requisite components of status, form and content.

3. Features of digital execution mechanism or digital platform

A key aspect of smart legal contracts is the emphasis on the important role of the specialized digital platform (ie, the digital platform infrastructure that hosts the running of a smart legal contract).[35] This becomes relevant for the reasons outlined in the examples of features at Level 3 and above. Furthermore, the specialized digital platform is important due to the fact that an operating SLC will invariably be influenced by the technical requirements or limitations of, and any terms and conditions mandated by, the specialized digital platform.

For widescale adoption of SLCs, commercial counterparties in regular business transactions will require cyber-secure, enterprise-grade, relatively user-friendly, digital platforms in order to allow businesses to move with confidence to digital formation, hosting, performance and management of contracts and other legal instruments. The special status of contracts for business and the economy mean that platform integrity will be key to user confidence.

The proposed core requirements and recommendations in digital infrastructure or enterprise platforms intended to support SLCs are set out in a recent initiative, the Digital Infrastructure Integrity Protocol for Smart and Legal Contracts DIIP 2021 ('DIIP').[36] Recognizing SLCs as a special class of digital asset central to good governance of business relationships and economies more broadly, these principles suggest model features which should ideally be embedded in the design of digital infrastructure for SLCs. These principles were originally born from consideration of legal-led design of SLC infrastructure, and are intended to form the basis for further collaboration amongst law councils globally, relevant stakeholders and industry. The ultimate purpose of the DIIP is to guide users, developers and investors in relation to SLC infrastructure. Digital infrastructure and enterprise platforms that exhibit these features will balance high standards for users against pure commercial drivers of platform providers, and in so doing, promote high integrity digital infrastructure —they will:

(a) Support **confidentiality, privacy, and permissioning** through enabling appropriate permissioned access to, and actions in respect of, the contract,

---

[35] Referred to as the 'Digital Execution Mechanism' under the Blycha & Garside Model.
[36] A. Garside et al., 'Digital Infrastructure Integrity Protocol For Smart Legal Contracts DIIP 2021', 30 March 2021 <https://papers.ssrn.com/sol3/papers.cfm?abstract_id=3814811> accessed 12 July 2021.

including access to view all contractual rights and obligations, management of data, controls in relation to sensitive data, and confidentiality.

(b) Support **access** through ensuring that within the bounds of the platform's capability and business model, the platform should host any or all contracts uploaded and paid for by a user.

(c) Prevent **changes to contracts without counterparty consent** by ensuring that no party to an SLC can form, vary, or amend the contract without the agreement of the other parties. This is consistent with general principles of contract law but has heightened focus where parties share a single shared instance of the record of the contract.

(d) Uphold **data** protection by ensuring the platform collects and records only the minimum amount of individual user data required to run the enterprise platform and SLCs it hosts, and to the extent possible, minimize the use of data other than for the purposes intended by the parties (including limiting use of user data for internal platform analysis etc).

(e) Have appropriate levels of **cybersecurity** for the nature and contents of the SLCs it hosts, to enable proper performance without unauthorized third party interference, be supported by practices, procedures, and systems compliant to ISO 27001 (or equivalent), and implement industry-standard safeguards and procedures to prevent unauthorized access to and the destruction, loss, misuse or improper alteration of information.

(f) Provide for **portability** of the contract (including natural language, connected code, and data) and **interoperability** with other platforms and digital systems, including platforms in other jurisdictions, and take reasonable steps prior to suspension or termination of an account, and also provide information about expected and target hosting service **reliability and availability**.

(g) Be **compliant with all applicable laws** within the relevant jurisdiction that apply to the enterprise platform itself and to the extent applicable to SLCs on the platform.

E. Conclusion

To leverage the benefits of automation, digital connectivity and the generation and analysis of structured data through digitalization of contracts, lawyers need to understand the implications of contracts being recorded in software form and interacting with specialized digital infrastructure. In particular, to understand at what point digitalization of a contract begins to affect not only the form of the evidence of the contract, but also the contract's inherent functionality, and the associated legal issues as the digital contract starts to depend on, and function with, the digital domain in which the contract operates.

Lawyers will need to play a role in resolving these issues in order to ensure confidence in adoption and deployment of smart legal contracts. To this end, understanding the nuances and the implications of step changes through the levels of contract digitalization and automation will assist in addressing the legal issues associated with the changing nature and functionality of contracts into the digital age.

SLCs, as presented in this paper, provide legal certainty to the parties in the automation of contractual performance by bringing the agreed performance of formally coded contractual terms into the domain of the legally enforceable elements of the contract. A contract will shift from being an analog or digital representation of a traditional contract to an SLC when it can be defined as a digitally-accessible legal instrument, where meaning can be derived from whole or part of the text and processed by a computer, and which is stored on specific digital infrastructure that provides counterparties to the contract a mutual, synchronous shared view of a digital instance of the record of the contract and enables secure automation of performance of some or all of the provisions of the contract.

Automation of contract creation is distinct from automation of contract performance which presents different practical and legal issues. The evolution in form and functionality of the evidentiary record of the agreement between parties offered by automated performance of a contract will be integrally linked to the requirement for the contract to be hosted on a specific digital platform.

This paper is intended as a place to start the conversation in clarifying digitalization and contract automation for lawyers. The next stage of the conversation will be to create an agreed taxonomy and definitions to help guide conversations about, and development of, SLCs, and to explore further the requisite features of contracts and digital infrastructure in Levels 3 to 5.

9
Smart Contracts as Execution Instead of Expression

Eric Tjong Tjin Tai*

A. Introduction	205	2. The role of interpretation	213
B. Definition and Principal Characteristics of Smart Contracts	206	D. Extensions to Smart Contracts? Oracles and Libraries	217
1. Vending machines as implied semi-smart contracts	207	E. Implementing Contract Law in Smart Contracts	219
2. Smart contracts in the broad sense as 'computable contracts'	208	1. Doctrines outside the execution chain	220
3. Blockchain-based smart contracts	208	2. The complexity of implementing contractual doctrines	220
C. Smart Contracts and the Role of Interpretation	211	3. The lack of *ex post* protection	222
1. The unavoidability of translation	212	F. Conclusion	223

A. Introduction

In the rapidly growing literature on 'smart contracts' several trends have emerged.[1] Most authors discuss the legal treatment of smart contracts and the claim that smart contracts can supplant traditional legal contracts.[2] It has become clear that

---

* Eric Tjong Tjin Tai is Professor of private law at Tilburg University. He holds degrees in computer science, philosophy, and law and has published numerous articles on private law aspects of digital technologies such as blockchain, AI, and data science. He is co-author of a report on legal aspects of blockchain commissioned by the Dutch government.

[1] See also the UK Jurisdiction Taskforce, *Legal statement on cryptoassets and smart contracts*, November 2019.

[2] Notably C.L. Reyes, 'Conceptualizing Cryptolaw' (2017) 96 *Nebraska Law Review* 384, K. Werbach and N. Cornell, 'Contracts Ex Machina' (2017) 67 *Duke Law Journal* 313, M.I. Raskin, 'The Law and Legality of Smart Contracts' (2017) 1 *Georgetown Technology Review* 305, A. Savelyev, 'Contract Law 2.0: "Smart" Contracts As the Beginning of the End of Classic Contract Law' (2016) <ssrn.com/abstract=2885241> accessed 9 July 2021, M.L. Perugini and P. Dal Checco, 'Smart Contracts: A Preliminary Evaluation' (2015) <ssrn.com/abstract=2729648> accessed 9 July 2021, P. Paech, 'The Governance of Blockchain Financial Networks' (2017) 80 *Modern Law Review* 1072, E. Mik, 'Smart Contracts: Terminology, Technical Limitations and Real World Complexity' (2017) 9 *Journal of Law, Innovation and Technology* 269, J.M. Sklaroff, 'Smart Contracts and the Cost of Inflexibility' (2017) 166 *University of Pennsylvania Law Review* 263, A.J. Casey and A. Niblett, 'Self-Driving Contracts'

smart contracts have to overcome some formidable—possibly insurmountable—obstacles if they are to perform exactly like traditional contracts do. Given this consensus, the time has come to assess more precisely what smart contracts are able to do within their limitations. To use an analogy: the question is not how to make an automobile a better horse. Rather, the question is, for what purposes does a car improve on a horse, and how can a car do that job better? This may also highlight the precise nature and role of traditional contracts in society.

I begin with a discussion as to what 'smart contracts' fundamentally offer in comparison to traditional contracts (Section B). Next, I argue that smart contracts upset the traditional functions of interpretation in the 'contract stack', by providing an automated execution chain that specifies execution without requiring human-readable expressions. Smart contracts *do not* however, do away with the necessity of translating party expectations, from which it also follows that a smart contract should aim at approximating contract law rules (Section C). I will briefly examine two extensions to smart contracts, the use of oracles and libraries, to show that these do not solve the problems of translating expectations and approximating contract law (Section D). Finally, I will examine the various contract doctrines in turn, to show the possibilities and restrictions of smart contracts in following the expectations laid down in contract law (Section E). The conclusion is that smart contracts may achieve a high degree of compliance with contract law, but that there are a few *lacunae* intrinsically bound up with the fundamental lack of expressiveness of smart contracts (Section F).

B. Definition and Principal Characteristics of Smart Contracts

For the purpose of my argument, it is important to work with a clear concept of smart contracts. However, the literature on smart contracts uses many different definitions.[3] In the early literature smart contracts (and similar concepts, such as 'computable contracts') were understood as some kind of code (computer

(2017) 43 *Journal of Corporation Law* 1, R. O'Shields, 'Smart Contracts: Legal Agreements for the Blockchain' (2017) 21 *North Carolina Banking Institute* 177, M. Giancaspro, 'Is a "Smart Contract" Really a Smart Idea? Insights From a Legal Perspective' (2017) 33 *Computer Law & Security Review* 825, P. De Filippi and A. Wright, *Blockchain and the Law* (Harvard University Press 2018), J.G. Allen, 'Wrapped and Stacked: "Smart Contracts" and the Interaction of Natural and Formal Language' (2018) 14 *European Review of Contract Law* 307, E. Tjong Tjin Tai, 'Formalizing Contract Law for Smart Contracts', ICAIL 2017, <https://ssrn.com/abstract=3038800> accessed 9 July 2021, L.A. DiMatteo, M. Cannarsa, and C. Poncibò (eds), *The Cambridge Handbook of Smart Contracts, Blockchain Technology and Digital Platforms* (Cambridge University Press 2019), and the special issue of ERPL 2018/6.

[3] See the discussion of R. De Caria, 'Definitions of Smart Contracts: Between Law and Code', in DiMatteo (n. 2), 21–4, of various definitions.

program) that executes the terms of a contract.[4] However, nowadays smart contracts are primarily identified with a subset, namely *programs executed on a blockchain-based environment to perform contractual obligations, inter alia payments with the cryptocurrency of that blockchain*. Such smart contracts are the endpoint of an evolution in three stages.

1. Vending machines as implied semi-smart contracts

Automated execution of contracts has been possible already for a long time,[5] in the form of vending machines and other automata. Such machines perform an obligation once certain criteria are fulfilled (acceptance of contract by pushing buttons, performing the obligation of payment by inserting coins in a slot). In other words, they make *conditional decisions*.[6]

From a contractual perspective, it is clear that the vending machine is not a contract. Rather, the system gives rise to an *implicit contract* that is accepted by the consumer inserting a coin in the corresponding slot. The implicit contract of buying a bottle of water with a traditional vending machine does not have any readable representation of the contract, it can only be derived from the actual mechanical construction. The terms of the contract would be derived from general expectations, or in some instances from terms and conditions that are in some way accessible to the person buying the bottle.[7] The lack of a written contract is not usually a problem for litigation. On the one hand, if something goes wrong (eg, the machine does not provide the item that was bought), the financial loss of the customer is negligible. The case will not come to court due to the costs of litigation, and the customer will simply have to bear his loss. On the other hand, there are usually other means by which a dissatisfied customer can obtain what is his right, such as complaining to the supervisor of the building where the machine is located, or calling a telephone number printed on the machine.

---

[4] For example, N. Szabo, 'Formalizing and Securing Relationships on Public Networks' (1997) 9 *First Monday* <firstmonday.org/ojs/index.php/fm/article/view/548/469/> accessed 9 July 2021; N. Szabo, 'The Idea of Smart Contracts' <szabo.best.vwh.net/smart_contracts_idea.html> accessed 9 July 2021. See for similar concepts: S.P. Jones, J.-M. Eber, and J. Seward, 'Composing Contracts: An Adventure in Financial Engineering', in *ACM SIGPLAN International Conference on Functional Programming (ICFP)* (ACM 2000), 280–92, H. Surden, 'Computable Contracts' (2012) 46 *University of California Davis Law Review* 629–700. De Filippi and Wright (n. 2), 73–4 discuss other examples as well.

[5] Pointed out by Allen (n. 2), R. De Caria, 'The Legal Meaning of Smart Contracts' (2018) 26 *European Review of Private Law* 731.

[6] The centrality of conditional decisions has been pointed out by Raskin (n. 2).

[7] This could be achieved by printing the conditions of the contract on the machine. Some legal systems actually demand this explicitly, see Art 498 Russian Civil Code, and other codes influenced by the Russian code.

2. Smart contracts in the broad sense as 'computable contracts'

Smart contracts in the broad sense of the term are a continuation of the model of the vending machine, where computer code is capable of making *complex conditional decisions*. A vending machine is limited in the kind of complexity that it can handle. A distinctive feature of such smart contracts is that the code (if programmed in a high-level programming language) is readable and allows a level of detail and sophistication similar to natural language. This raises the question whether the code does not, in fact, embody the agreement. Is it true that the code *is* the contract?

As a matter of law, the code may explicate the contractual agreement, but is not to be equated with the legal relationship.[8] The code does not displace the legal process of interpretation to determine the obligations of parties. The code may be the contract in a different sense, however: if there is no written document that expresses the agreement,[9] the code may indeed 'be' the contract in the sense of a readable proof of the content of the agreement. The code still needs to be interpreted legally, however, and that interpretation may differ from what the code literally says and would do. The example of The DAO hack suffices to point out the difference between a legal, human-centred view and the computer-oriented viewpoint.[10]

However, the code can be said to be the contract in another sense, too. The contract as a matter of fact is executed by the code—ie, the code determines the *factual relationship* between parties. This is important in cases where there is no effective legal enforcement. Nonetheless, the law formally retains its authority: if the code does not do what it should according to contract law, the execution will be deemed legally wrong and the outcome should legally be corrected outside the constraints of the code.[11] This is no different from how the law applies to a vending machine: if the machine malfunctioned, a human operator has to give the customer the object he bought or return his money.

3. Blockchain-based smart contracts

The development that gave new impetus to smart contracts was the availability of a neutral self-executing framework, ie, blockchain technology, which allowed

---

[8] See also UKJT *Legal Statement* (n. 1), [18].
[9] It is of course possible to conclude a contract in the traditional manner and agree that the execution is going to be done in a smart contract, but in that case the smart contract is merely a way of performing the contract. Here we are concerned with cases where there is no other proof than the code.
[10] I will refrain from a description of the 'hack' of The DAO on the Ethereum blockchain, as this is explained in most legal articles on smart contracts. See the literature in n. 2.
[11] Cf the German decision BGH 16 October 2012, X ZR 37/12, *BGHZ* 195/126, where it was decided that the interpretation of an order submitted through an automated system should be done by human standards, not according to the way in which the system works.

a fundamental change in the possibility of actual control over the *performance* of the contractual obligations. The term 'smart contract' is today conceived in a narrower sense, as being implemented on a blockchain-based cryptocurrency. The contract is executed in a decentralized manner, cannot be modified afterwards (except if the environment has some mechanism for this), and the execution of payments can be performed automatically in the cryptocurrency of the blockchain. In the following I will use 'smart contracts' to refer to this more restricted concept.

The reason for focusing on blockchain-based smart contracts is that the decentralized nature of a blockchain has an important consequence. While smart contracts are not completely immune to legal intervention or other forms of governance,[12] such intervention may be costly, and as a matter of course successful intervention will be rare.[13] This claim may need additional argumentation.[14] If the smart contract leads to a legally incorrect outcome, an aggrieved party could try to go to court to obtain a remedy. However, he could face several obstacles in doing so.[15]

First of all, his contracting party might be anonymous, without known address. This may make it impossible to actually start a court procedure, as the law of civil procedure typically requires a court summons which includes the name and/or actual address of the defendant.[16] Although this requirement does allow some exceptions (for example in the case of anonymous squatters or persons without known address), the law of civil procedure in many countries may not allow a summons where neither the name of the defendant nor his physical address is known.

Secondly, assuming a summons is possible and the court has decided for the claimant, the decision has to be enforced. Even if we abstract from the need to also serve the decision to the defendant, there are as yet no effective ways to enforce a decision on a blockchain. A blockchain is not in itself a corporate body, does not have legal personality. Rather, it consists of a large group of independent parties operating the computers ('nodes') working together to keep the blockchain operative. These parties do not clearly act wrongfully if they do not co-operate with enforcing the decision, and it would be practically impossible (and unduly costly) to sue the majority of those parties in all their respective jurisdictions to obtain

---

[12] As exemplified by the reaction to The DAO hack, where the Ethereum community agreed to turn back the consequence of the smart contract in question.

[13] Proof can be found in the fact that thefts of bitcoin (ie, unauthorized transfers) occur regularly. These would be easy to undo on the Bitcoin blockchain if the blockchain could be forked, but this has never happened.

[14] The general literature cited in note 2 explains these issues further and dwells on the technical details. For the sake of brevity I will refer to this literature.

[15] I will leave out the additional consideration that the procedural costs outweigh the value of the claim.

[16] See, however, the discussion in *AA v Persons Unknown* [2019] EWHC 3556 (Civ), [16]–[37] (Bryan J).

their co-operation. Without the co-operation of the majority[17] of the nodes of the blockchain, the blockchain cannot be modified in violation of its protocol.

Admittedly, it is possible that the blockchain is established by and under control of a corporate body, but in that case the claimant would subsequently have to sue that body (which may be located in a different jurisdiction),[18] and needs to succeed in convincing the court that this body is obligated to enforce the original decision against the contract party. It is far from clear that such a claim will succeed (disregarding the costs), given that the body itself is not a party to the contract in question, and in fact may have its own contract with the claimant whereby the claimant agrees to abide by the protocol of the blockchain.

These issues are well known in the literature on blockchain and smart contracts. However, it is necessary to mention them lest it be thought that the formal availability of a court is sufficient to actually enforce a claim. Hence, a blockchain-based smart contract is legally still like a vending machine, but without the possibility of going to the building supervisor or machine operator to get your money back. Entering into such a smart contract is like going in an automated subway train without an emergency brake: you are entirely at the mercy of the automated operation. While the legal control formally exists, it is ineffective in changing the smart contract, it is no better than a bystander pounding on the windows of the automated train. The smart contract would therefore *practically* be immune to the traditional legal control of contractual relationships.

Admittedly, in practice this situation may not often occur. It appears companies often employ smart contracts simply as a means to execute part of their contractual relationship. In such cases, they can take each other easily to court as they know their counterparty and can enforce a decision easily. Where there is an effective way to enforce the legal view, we return to the concept of a smart contract as a vending machine. This does not pose particular legal problems.

Nonetheless, there is considerable interest in situations with no effective enforcement. This may be a real possibility where smart contracts are used for online marketplaces. Hereafter, I will focus on such situations. In such cases the code of the smart contract *de facto* determines how the parties' (contractual) relationship plays out. The natural response is to ensure that the smart contract performs just like a regular contract would, ie, according to the rules of contract law. There is a significant body of literature that has pointed out several problems in doing so. Here I would like to approach this issue from a more fundamental perspective, by first considering how contracts function in society and the function of contract interpretation therein (Section C), briefly look at two extensions that were proposed to overcome the limitations of smart contracts (Section D), and subsequently

---

[17] 'Majority' here does not mean numerical majority but a controlling majority according to the blockchain protocol. In the bitcoin protocol this depends on computing power.
[18] An example is Ethereum, with a foundation established in Switzerland.

provide a general analysis of what we can expect from smart contracts compared to regular contracts (Section E).

C. Smart Contracts and the Role of Interpretation

A frequent criticism of smart contracts is that a contract may serve as a mere symbolic gesture in a broader commercial relationship (so-called 'relational contracting'),[19] in which case it is not actually used by parties to regulate their behaviour. My point here, however, is more fundamental: the way in which contracts are drafted and executed is part of a broader social, institutional structure which is implicit in contract law. To explicate the functioning of contracts in society, I build on the concept of a 'contract stack', as proposed by JG Allen. He explained this as follows: contracts should be regarded as 'complex legal institutional entities' consisting of several 'layers', whose 'legal and technological parts interact'.[20] If I understand his argument correctly, the 'contract stack' consists (at least) of the speech acts (the offer and acceptance) between parties, the result of which is laid down (one level down) in a document, which finally is performed or executed (the lowest layer of the 'stack').

This metaphor is extremely helpful in understanding the complexity of how contracts actually function in human society (figure 9.1). We can view a contract as deriving from the mutual desire of parties to realize a project in the world. They try to explicate their expectations as to what is to be done, and express these in a document, the contract. Subsequently, parties abide by the contract: they perform (or 'execute') its terms. If they do not, an aggrieved party may invite court intervention and enforce the contract by legal means. The notion of a contract stack helps to distinguish several steps in this process which tend to go unnoticed, but which are important when we look at smart contracts.

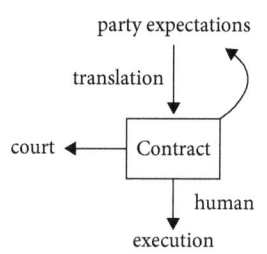

Figure 9.1 A Conventional Contract

---

[19] See Werbach and Cornell (n. 2), 367; K.E.C. Levy, 'Book-Smart, Not Street-Smart: Blockchain-Based Smart Contracts and The Social Workings of Law' (2017) 3 *Engaging Science, Technology, and Society* 1–15; De Filippi and Wright (n. 2), 84.
[20] Allen (n. 2), 311.

1. The unavoidability of translation

The first step in creating a traditional contract, in the sense of a written and signed document that encapsulates the legal relationship between parties and is binding, is to *translate* the intentions and expectations[21] of parties into words. I use the term *translation*, as this is not a straightforward process.[22] Contracting parties often find it hard to capture their precise intentions. Indeed, a large part of a contract lawyer's job consists of teasing out what people actually mean and are agreeing to. This involves explicating assumptions, smoothing out contradictions, and arranging for eventualities which were left unregulated.[23] Drafting a contract entails choices; the contract may deviate from the original intentions where those cannot be realized. The fallacy of many smart contract ideologists lies in the assumption that intention is something clear and given, instead of something that needs to be constructed and carefully given shape. Indeed, it has become clear that smart contracts do not remove the need for a translation process—they merely require a different kind of specialist.

Programming a smart contract is tantamount to translating intentions to code.[24] Again, this is not structurally different from a mechanical engineer designing a vending machine to capture the essence of a sales contract. The translation process in commercial practice often does not happen by direct negotiation and careful consideration of each clause by the parties themselves. Rather, the process is in many cases a complicated interaction between various actors who influence parts of the contract,[25] while the contracting parties themselves mostly rely on advice and defaults.[26] The position of parties may be facilitated because they receive summaries of the main outline of the contract (the essentials). Furthermore, for very common undertakings, such as the simple sale of a commodity, parties can rely on the common understanding of what such a contract involves or even a standard form: this finds support in the law on specific contracts (which may consist of both mandatory and default rules).[27] In such cases,

---

[21] In this article I will use intentions and expectations interchangeably, as in this context they are used largely synonymous, even though they are not identical terms.
[22] Allen (n. 2), 335–6.
[23] See the excellent description in D. Howarth, *Law as Engineering* (Elgar 2013), 30–40.
[24] As is well known in software engineering, this is also not a straightforward process. It requires considerable discussion and questioning to smooth out contradictory and impossible requirements.
[25] Such as contract lawyers, regulators, procurement lawyers, drafters of business-wide standard terms.
[26] See M. Jennejohn, 'The Architecture of Contract Innovation' (2018) 59 *Boston College Law Review* 71.
[27] For example, in the UK the Supply of Goods and Services Act 1982, and the numerous specific contracts in civil law codifications. See F.J.A. Santos, C. Baldus, and H. Dedek (eds), *Vertragstypen in Europa* (Sellier 2011).

drafting the terms of a contract may not require such close attention.[28] Indeed, there may not be an actual written contract: an implied contract may suffice (as in the vending machine example).

2. The role of interpretation

At this point, we have to re-examine the notion of *contract interpretation*. The several layers of the 'contract stack' traditionally involve human beings. The contract itself is usually laid down in writing,[29] which serves as a focal point for the performance of the contract, whereby the contract is interpreted. Interpretation is relevant for three different actors.

First, interpretation of the contract is done by the *courts* in order to decide a contractual dispute. Secondly, interpretation is used to determine what the *contracting parties* may expect: because parties can themselves read and interpret the contract, they are bound by its terms. It is incumbent upon parties to ensure that the text adequately represents their intentions. Thirdly, interpretation is necessary for the persons that execute (ie, perform) the contract. This deserves a little more attention.

On the one hand, interpretation is necessary for execution of traditional contracts, as the words of the contract cannot execute themselves. It requires human beings to read the contract (or be instructed by others who have read the contract) and act accordingly. Admittedly, it is possible that the parties to the contract do not actually follow the terms of the contract to determine their actions, in which case there may be a different implied contract (and the text does not guide performance). We can leave this possibility aside for the moment.

On the other hand, the process of interpretation is useful. It allows the use of fairly open-ended terms that can be explicated later in concrete circumstances. When supervised by courts, notions of fairness may be used to 'bend' the writing towards what seems just. Interpretation is thereby used as a mechanism to *complete* the contract—to make it conform better to the actual intentions of parties by supplanting and reinterpreting contractual terms at the moment of application and execution.[30] In moderate form, a certain degree of open-endedness is also present in formalist interpretation, when parties have deliberately used standards, to postpone difficult decisions to a later moment ('we will cross that bridge when we get to it').

---

[28] This is the more so as unfair terms are non-binding: see Section E.
[29] Here we focus on express written contracts. Implied contracts are discussed later.
[30] This function may also be fulfilled by the notions of fairness and good faith.

Such considerations may explain part of the age-old debate between what English legal scholarship calls a formalist or literal interpretation, and more open or contextual forms of interpretation.[31] On one extreme is the position that the contract is to be interpreted literally; that only the text may be used, and that it must be interpreted on its own, ie, isolated from its factual context. At the other extreme is the position that text needs to be interpreted using contextual and social cues. Most contract lawyers lie somewhere between these extremes. Other jurisdictions have similar debates with the same, basically opposite viewpoints.[32]

This debate can be recast as a difference of opinion on the proper place of translation in the contract stack. Should parties put all their effort into making a perfect translation, and afterwards be barred from adding other considerations into interpretation besides the objective meaning of the words used? Or is it fair to allow later interpretation in order to make expectations match the actual circumstances more closely? The unpredictability that arises from allowing contextual interpretation can also be viewed as the contract being adaptable to later circumstances. The idea that parties can read the contract and are thereby forewarned of any mistakes in the text is also of relevance, as it supports a more restricted interpretation that does not put too much weight on the original expectations of parties.

Interpretation is vital to the way in which traditional contracts function. Interpretation furthermore presumes that the text of the contract has expressive force: it expresses meaning to human beings, as these have to understand and act upon its text. This is recognized in contract law where certain unexpected terms have to be conspicuous in order to be binding, or where certain terms require specific formulation. An example is provided by choice of forum clauses, which in EU law must be an express term of an agreement to be enforceable.[33] Similarly, the Uniform Commercial Code in the USA requires specific formalities for disclaiming warranties.[34]

Turning to smart contracts, we can see that interpretation is a necessity deriving from the *human execution chain*. Human beings are necessary for the performance of traditional contracts, so they must be able to read and act upon ('realize') the terms of the contract. Smart contracts, on the other hand, operate with an *automated execution chain*: once the agreement is laid down in code, the 'performance' proceeds as 'execution' without the human process of contract interpretation. The

---

[31] See amongst others the opposing viewpoints of J. Morgan, *Contract Law Minimalism* (Cambridge University Press 2013) and C. Mitchell, *Contract Law and Contract Practice* (Hart 2013).

[32] See the overview in M. Cannarsa, 'Contract Interpretation', in DiMatteo (n. 2), 102–17.

[33] See Art 25 Council Regulation (EC) 1215/2012 on jurisdiction and the recognition and enforcement of judgments in civil and commercial matters (EEX Regulation) [2012] OJ L315/1, also the decision of the ECJ in *Colzani v Rüwa* [1976] ECLI:EU:C:1976:177, and further case law.

[34] UCC § 2-316(2): 'to exclude or modify the implied warranty of merchantability or any part of it the language must mention merchantability and in case of a writing must be conspicuous, and to exclude or modify any implied warranty of fitness the exclusion must be by a writing and conspicuous. Language to exclude all implied warranties of fitness is sufficient if it states, for example, that "There are no warranties which extend beyond the description on the face hereof".'

adaptable, contextual mode of interpretation (which is a natural possibility flowing from the necessity of interpretation) is at odds with the fundamental nature of smart contracts.

Code only needs to be 'understood' by the system that will execute it. Although code in a high-level programming language seems readable to human beings, this impression is misleading. Constructs like 'a=a+1' may suggest a natural interpretation, but may in fact have an entirely different effect.[35] The code is merely a set of characters that is taken as instructions for the computer to follow. The code is processed by a so-called 'interpreter' or a 'compiler',[36] but that is not an interpreter in the human sense. A term like 'IF' is translated to lower-level codes and ultimately by machine language instructions that the processor can directly execute. This translation process bears no resemblance to the translation of party expectations to a human-readable contract. On the contrary, the computer language 'interpreter' or 'compiler' is a deterministic process with reference to how computers operate (through the definition of the programming language), and bears no intrinsic reference to how human beings understand certain terms or words.

Incidentally, code itself is not as unambiguous as often is assumed. The actual execution of code does depend on the system context, such as the operating system and the version of the programming language. A striking example is the use of software in scientific analysis which contained a bug, such that the results depended on the ordering of files in the specific operating system.[37]

The upshot of this discussion is that code has no *meaning*: it consists only of instructions to a computer. It is irrelevant how human beings would interpret the intentions behind the code. A common problem in programming is that a piece of code has to be debugged (fixed) by another programmer, who finds that he cannot easily understand what the code actually is intended to do. The clarity of the instructions themselves does not show what the effect or function of the code is. This is one reason why good programming habits include commentary (providing extra information as to what the instructions are meant to do). Those comments, however, are not intrinsically linked to the code: it is quite possible to have the comment say one thing while the code does something entirely different.

For a traditional contract, the whole text may be used for interpreting the contract, and the meaning of those words (ie, the meaning for humans) is relevant: this meaning *determines* the content of the contract and simultaneously drives the execution of the contract by humans. For a smart contract, the code drives the

---

[35] In some programming languages this means 'compare a to a+1' which is always false; probably it is intended to be a is increased by 1' (which in a few languages may actually be formulated as 'a=a+1'.

[36] The difference is that an 'interpreter' translates during execution, while a 'compiler' does so beforehand.

[37] J. Bhandari Neupane, 'Characterization of Leptazolines A-D, Polar Oxazolines from the Cyanobacterium Leptolyngbya sp, Reveals a Glitch with the "Willoughby–Hoye" Scripts for Calculating NMR Chemical Shifts' (2019) 21 *Organic Letters*, 8449–53.

execution by the computer, but the legal contract (which may be entirely distinct from the code) is what determines the legal relationship. The connection between the meaning and the execution is broken (figure 9.2). *Code does not have expressive force for the executer.*[38] Therefore, the legal contract (in text or as implied contract) is distinct from the instructions to the execution (laid down in the code of the smart contract). They are not intrinsically connected like they are with traditional contracts. Of course, a court can *ascribe* meaning to the code in order to determine the content of the legal contract, but that meaning does not influence the automated execution chain.

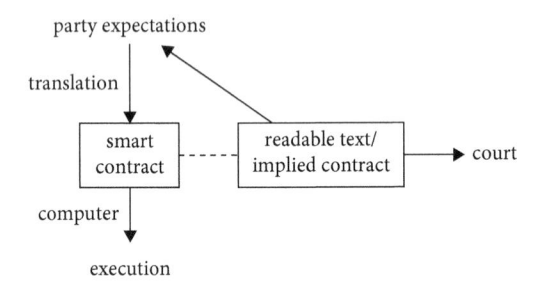

Figure 9.2 A Smart Contract

With conventional contracts, the text is intrinsically connected to the legal relationship. With smart contracts there is, fundamentally, no intrinsic connection between the code (the smart contract) and the legal contract (in text or as an implied contract). This has two important consequences.

First of all, legal interpretation is (from the perspective of the smart contract) superfluous: it is merely a means whereby parties and courts try to understand what is going on, without being able to influence the smart contract directly. Instead of *determining* execution, interpretation is used to *understand* execution.[39] The judge is, so to speak, trying to comprehend what the vending machine does.

To satisfy the need for proof of the legal contract and to inform to parties, it may be necessary to require an additional document that does comprise the actual legal contract. But in that case, we have again resorted to the vending machine analogy. For smart contracts we furthermore have to realize that there is no guarantee at all that such a document would represent what the smart contract would actually do. Of course, the code can be used by parties to learn how the smart contract will execute, difficult though it may be to understand. Courts may decide to attach consequences to this theoretical possibility of understanding the code. But that only

---

[38] This position is contrary to what the UKJT *Legal Statement* (n. 1), [145] seems to presume.
[39] That is, what the code does; see also UKJT *Legal Statement*, [152].

goes in one direction: the computer does not care how humans would understand the code. The expressive power of the code for humans has no impact on the way in which the computer executes the code.

Secondly, if the smart contract does not need to express what it does in a way that parties can understand, this plausibly liberates the code from the shackles of contract law. Recall that I argued that a smart contract may be outside effective court control. Parties may still wish the contract to abide by general expectations, and presumably contract law expresses such expectations to a large degree. But in order to do so, the smart contract does not need to follow the formulation of the legal rules to the letter. That option will be examined in Section E.

D. Extensions to Smart Contracts? Oracles and Libraries

The assessment up to now allows us to quickly deal with two extensions that have been proposed to overcome limitations of smart contracts: the use of so-called 'oracles' to allow more complicated inputs and outputs of smart contracts, and the use of 'libraries' to facilitate the integration of complex rule-systems into smart contracts.

Smart contracts from the outset did have two limitations. The first is *dealing with external interaction*. A smart contract, to be worthwhile, has to interact with the outside world.[40] Even if the smart contract as such would be immutable and trustworthy, the I/O (input-output) of the smart contract would provide an easy attack vector (vulnerability for hacking). There must be some trustworthy way in which to connect with the outside world. The second is *performing assessments*. Some elements of normal contracts require complicated assessments which cannot, or cannot easily, be reduced to elementary, objectively determinable facts. Examples are assessments of good faith, force majeure, or reasonableness. Assessments may also require knowledge of facts in the physical world (ie, is the package damaged?), which overlaps with the first limitation.

The solution to overcome both of these limitations is to engage with what in smart contract practice are often called 'oracles'.[41] These are, in effect, trusted third parties, similar to familiar constructs such as surveyors. An oracle may be automated (for example, you trust a mechanical device to operate correctly, such as an electronic lock that is opened remotely by the smart contract), or it may be human being (for example, a person who receives questions from the smart contract and provides his considered answers).

---

[40] Leaving aside contracts which could be completely performed on the blockchain, such as (possible) a kind of loan contract (which would actually seem to be fairly useless).
[41] For an extended discussion see E. Tjong Tjin Tai, 'Challenges of Smart Contracts: Implementing Excuses', in DiMatteo (n. 2), 80–101.

Given our earlier assessment, we can say that human oracles do not solve anything fundamentally. They simply re-introduce part of the human execution chain into the automated execution chain of a smart contract. Either oracles return us to a vending machine situation, where humans can control or override the performance of the contract, or the implementation of the oracle does not allow humans to influence the performance and we are still at the mercy of the actions of the automated execution chain.

Another suggestion is the use of libraries, which is promoted to reduce the effort involved in creating a sufficiently detailed smart contract. A programmer does not need to program the code for executing a conditional payment, but can simply 'call' (invoke) the function or procedure 'execute_payment' that has been programmed by another programmer. A library is in essence a collection of such functions.

Libraries in programming languages can be implemented in a variety of ways. They are based on the notion of information hiding, whereby a programmer need not know how the functions of a library exactly work: they are essentially a 'black box'. In some implementations, the code of the library is inaccessible to the user of the library (such as with functions in proprietary operating systems like Windows), in others they are formally accessible (such as with functions in open source Python libraries) but are in practice never examined or read by the programmer that uses the library. Even if you would look at the code in the library, it would take a lot of effort to understand how it works. The benefit of a library is that you do *not* have to think about the precise implementation of the functions included therein. But this effectively means that you accept that you do not understand the details, and defer to the better judgement of an expert. In other words, a library functions formally like advisory intermediaries in the process of intention translation. Parties thereby trust the judgement of such intermediaries, and more broadly, of the law.

As such, the use of a library does not bypass the top layer of the contract stack: the translation of party intentions to a contract. If anything, it strengthens the argument that there is no direct link between the actual code and the 'legal contract', ie, how parties understand their relationship.

At best, libraries could function similarly to how contract model terms are used, as a kind of default law that parties can modify whenever it suits them. The practice of drafting contracts based on templates and standard terms and conditions shows that a proper contract requires finetuning to an extent that seems to oppose the widespread use of libraries. The clauses that are appropriate for a contract of sale may be insufficient for a service contract. What works for a lease of minor value would be inappropriate for a major investment. Even if libraries were drafted for certain paradigmatic use cases, these may not work for other cases that are formally in the same category but in content resemble another kind of contract.[42]

---

[42] For example, the sale of a book may differ from the sale of a computer that may also require a license or a service component.

Depending on how libraries are implemented and integrated,[43] they could allow deviation or tailoring, and in that way would allow a much better fit to the actual individual needs of contract parties. This is different from the normal use of libraries in software, and would require a somewhat modified form of incorporation of code libraries as part of the smart contract framework.

E. Implementing Contract Law in Smart Contracts

As argued in Section C, smart contracts do not so much replace the complete 'contract stack', as well as merely supplant the execution by humans with automated execution on the blockchain. In this section, I will discuss how well smart contracts perform when compared to traditional contracts, bearing in mind the full set of expectations that parties have regarding the way in which contracts will be executed.

I will operate with the presumption that it is desirable that a smart contract by and large reaches similar outcomes as a traditional contract. The acceptability of the performance of a smart contract depends on whether it conforms to the expectations of parties as to the contract will work out. As argued in Section C, these expectations will reflect the way that contract law works. Contract law could be considered as the encapsulation of general expectations regarding the just outcome of contracts in a multitude of circumstances and cases.

Doctrines such as default law, mandatory law, implied terms, unfair terms control allow contracting parties to avoid the trouble of a detailed examination and specification of the terms of the contract. Parties can rely on the normal operation of interpretation and contract law to make the contract largely follow general expectations. For example, parties are expected to fill gaps in a way consistent with a reasonable human interpretation of the contract, following the rules of contract law (including default law and mandatory law). Parties can ignore unfair terms and terms against public order, as these are not binding. Rules controlling unfair terms protect parties from having to look out for hidden unexpected clauses insofar those have to be agreed upon explicitly or must be mentioned clearly. During execution of the contract, parties may have to deviate from the rules of the contract where strictly following the rules would be unfair.

By these instruments, contract law ensures that the content of the contract and the execution of the contract are close to what reasonable persons would expect. However, these instruments all assume the human execution chain, where *ex post* correction is possible, based on the circumstances of the case and taking into account human considerations of fairness. An automated execution chain requires

---

[43] Libraries quite often do not allow tailoring but offer their functions simply as is with only the options provided that the developer of the library made available. This may not suffice for the specific purpose, as is regularly experienced in programming practice. See for example discussions regarding shortcomings of functions in standard libraries on stackexchange.com (accessed 9 July 2021).

an *ex ante* specification of the execution in the code. Such code can approximate the performance of the human execution chain if the developers have managed to successfully implement the rules of contract law (and the experience of case law and legal practice).

1. Doctrines outside the execution chain

We can simplify the issue by treating certain doctrines as outside the execution chain. Certain contract law doctrines, in particular those concerned with contract formation, are closely related to what I called the 'translation phase', where party expectations are rendered into the text of the contract. This phase is external to the automated execution chain that is the essence of what smart contracts offer, and can therefore be ignored. Of course, protection against *mistake* is important, but that needs to be found in the broader organization of the smart contract framework, not in the code itself. Indeed, a more detailed analysis of the formation of smart contracts seems to show that it is hard to implement doctrines such as mistake and legal capacity satisfactorily into smart contracts.[44]

Furthermore, if we look at the doctrines that determine the content of a contract, we can see that these partly aim at aligning party expectations and the content of the contract. Also, they may serve to regulate the legal relationship outside the execution (such as choice of forum). Such doctrines operate by their *expressive power*, with the contract parties and the humans performing the contract as their audience. For a smart contract, these are irrelevant. It is of course possible to formulate a choice of forum in a comment in the smart contract, but that is irrelevant for the *operation* of the smart contract. It would be exactly the same if the choice of forum was formulated in an e-mail accepted between parties outside the code of the smart contract. The information to parties about the content of the smart contract is important for their legal expectations, but is distinct from the code: it is likely that parties would rely on the general information provided (in commentary or supporting documentation) as to what the contract does.

2. The complexity of implementing contractual doctrines

Returning to the issue of implementing contract law for the execution of the smart contract, the first issue is the complexity of fully emulating contract law. It can be argued that a diligent programmer (advised by a good lawyer) could implement these rules correctly. Indeed, libraries might fulfil a useful role here. Ultimately, however, it appears impossible for the automated execution chain to operate exactly like humans would.

---

[44] See the analysis of M. Durovic and A. Janssen, 'Formation of Smart Contracts under Contract Law', in DiMatteo (n. 2), 66–9. See also Chapter 19 in this volume by Simon Gleeson.

Consider the doctrines that concern the actual performance of a contract with a human execution chain—representations, conditions, terms, or warranties,[45] breach of contract, force majeure and remedies. Most of these doctrines cannot be implemented in a way that matches their application or observance by humans.[46] For example, an award of damages would be practically impossible to implement, given the necessity to assess the damages, and the complications in how to enforce the liable party to make additional payments.[47] (However, a smart contract could avoid this problem partly by simply working with liquidated damages clauses or even limitation of damages.[48])

For all that, smart contracts may also have an advantage over traditional contracts. A smart contract simply attaches *factual consequences* to the fulfilment of a certain condition (in the 'if'-statement), while it follows from the code what those consequences are. It may be instructive to show how to implement such constructs in a smart contract. To do so, consider *pseudo-code*: code that looks like a programming language but need not follow the precise rules of any specific language, and only intends to show a programmer the logical structure of the program.[49] For the instruments mentioned above, a smart contract might operate by identifying whether a specific condition (in the computational sense) is fulfilled, and attach consequences to the fulfilment (figure 9.3). These consequences may be different for each condition, but it is not necessary to clearly distinguish the categories of contract law (such as the difference between rescission and termination).

```
For each i in parties and each j in conditions:
if party(i).complaint() or
condition(j).moment_of_assessment():
    if condition(j).assess(i)==False:
        if condition(j).response==end:
            contract.pay(contract_sum) # return payments and stop
            contract.end()
        else if condition(j).response==money:
            party(i).pay(condition.fixed_amount) # this would mean
paying an fixed amount on fulfillment of the condition, could be
liquidated damages or a penalty, or a fraction of the contract sum.
            contract.end()
    else:
        # other kind of response
```

Figure 9.3 An Illustration of Pseudo-Code

---

[45] The terminology differs in various jurisdictions; representations are specific to common law but can be implemented in contracts under civil law, and the distinction between the various kinds of clauses is not the same in English law as in US law.

[46] See for response to breach of contract and excuses my analysis in T.F.E. Tjong Tjin Tai, 'Force Majeure and Excuses in Smart Contracts' (2018) 26 *European Review of Private Law* 787, T.F.E. Tjong Tjin Tai, 'Challenges of Smart Contracts: Implementing Excuses' in DiMatteo (n. 2), 80–101.

[47] Normally, smart contracts require parties to already pay the sum owed, effectively putting it in escrow. If additional payments are required, a party could simply block this by emptying his account (by transferring it to another account).

[48] And requiring parties to put money in escrow.

[49] The form of pseudo-code used consists of a mix of Python, Javascript, and C++.

This brief exercise shows that the structure of contractual responses is upended when programmed into a smart contract. There is no clear reason to distinguish between the categories of misrepresentation, breach, rescission, termination, damages, and penalties. It may be argued that these concepts are simply a tool required by the human mind, or the needs of the human execution chain, without being intrinsic to execution of contracts as such.

Thus, insofar as the applicable contract law insists on upholding these formal distinctions, a smart contract could get into legal trouble if it reaches a court. It is also conceivable that courts would allow smart contracts to approach contracts in a different manner, consistent with the viewpoint of code, and would not strike down a smart contract merely for not clearly distinguishing certain kinds of terms. Such an approach is even more likely, given the fact that the code could be interpreted legally as involving an admissible deviation from default contract law.

While it may be impossible to program contract doctrines perfectly in code, the job for the developer may be easier if the code need not follow every detail of contract law, either because the parties accept slight deviations or simplifications (such as in the case of liquidated damages) or because code offers a simplified structure. Further research is therefore desirable into programming the substance of contract law into code, even while abstracting from the details that are irrelevant in light of automated execution. That may also present a reason for lawyers to reconsider the importance of the distinctions that we make: are those really necessary for the human execution chain, or are they simply needless complications?

3. The lack of *ex post* protection

There is a further, fundamental, problem. Corrective instruments such as unfairness, subjective interpretation, good faith, or unforeseen circumstances[50] are applied in cases where the reasonable expectation of a party is at tension with the actual text and/or execution of the contract. If the developer of the smart contract deliberately or negligently fails to correctly implement legal rules that protect the other party, it is the other party that will be harmed. Traditional contracts often come to court because a business wants to collect payment from a consumer, for example. At that moment, the consumer can invoke contract law, in particular the rules controlling unfair terms, to defend himself against undesirable terms that he did not actually read at the time of contracting. This safety valve of *ex post* control is absent in smart contracts, as they can be 'enforced' (in that they

---

[50] Allen (n. 2), 342 refers to the loss of equity as a corrective mechanism in smart contracts.

just execute) without court intervention. This line of argument also applies to the assessment of breach of contract and the application of remedies, where also the behaviour of the smart contract may deliberately be at odds with the requirements of contract law.

In consequence, contracting parties will have to trust the developer of a smart contract to a greater extent than they would need to trust a counterparty, since they may be unable to invoke court supervision. It can be argued that parties should simply be more diligent in assessing the code for undesirable consequences. However, as yet there is little to no knowledge on how to recognize code that, for example, amounts to an unfair term in its consequence during execution. This, too, is an area for further research as the practice develops.

F. Conclusion

On my analysis, blockchain-based 'smart contracts' take over only a restricted part of the complete function of traditional contracts: they take over the execution phase, and do so without reference to the traditional role of interpretation. Smart contracts replace the human execution chain with an automated execution chain, whereby the doctrine of interpretation becomes irrelevant. The code specifies how the contract is executed, without having an intrinsic expressive function towards human readers. Comments and surrounding materials may perform such a function but do not have any intrinsic connection to the way the contract will actually be performed. The burden of translating background expectations is on the person doing the translation.

While it may be desirable for smart contracts to follow (ie, reflect the substantive requirements of) contract law as closely as possible, this may not be feasible in all respects, given the many different cases that may have to be covered. Further research should work to determine how well doctrines such as force majeure can be adequately implemented. The task of a smart contract developer may, however, be simplified to the extent that parties accept certain simplifications, or because a smart contract may not have to exactly follow the intricacies of contract law doctrines. There is no *intrinsic* need to distinguish between certain contractual doctrines or remedies; that is only necessary for lawyers who need to decide on awarding certain claims and remedies.

A fundamental problem remains, however: as smart contracts rely on an automated execution chain, they lack certain correctives for the execution of the contract, such as unfair terms control, the corrective operation of fairness and equity. This is partly inherent to the fact that smart contracts require a complete *ex ante* specification of the desired operation and the practical impossibility of completely foreseeing every possible complication that may arise during execution of the contract. But a further limitation is that the absence of *ex post* correctives implies that contract parties have to trust the smart contract developer to not add rules that amount to unfair terms or unfair behaviour. As parties might legitimately expect such terms or implied disclaimers not to be operative during execution, parties will need to be aware that their common background expectations are not programmed into the contract except if they have explicitly and faithfully been encoded.

10
Smart Contracts

The Limits of Autonomous Performance

Tian Xu*

A. Introduction	225	D. Comparative Analysis of Smart Contracts and Documentary Credit	233
B. De-constructing Autonomous Performance: Three Core Functionalities	227	1. Internalized medium of exchange	233
		2. Closed system	235
		a. Efficient breach	235
C. Documentary Credit: Analogue Autonomous Performance	230	b. Lack of adaptability	238
		c. Invalid and illegal contracts	241
1. The core functionalities of documentary credit	231	3. Securing sufficient funds to enable contractual performance	243
		E. Conclusion	244

A. Introduction

This chapter focuses on two key themes introduced by Sir Geoffrey Vos in Chapter 1 of this volume: (i) the future use cases of smart contracts and (ii) the design of appropriate dispute resolution mechanisms.[1] It seeks to draw out broad principles about where smart contracts will most likely be found useful and how dispute resolution mechanisms should be designed to complement their characteristic functionalities. It shall do so, by analysing the inherent functional limitations which flow from one of smart contracts' core characteristics: *autonomous performance*. Understanding these limitations is crucial to any discussion about future applications of smart contracts, because autonomous performance is arguably the smart contract's most economically useful feature—it supposedly

---

* Tian Xu is a 2019 LLM Graduate from the London School of Economics and Political Science (where he specialized in international business law). He is a projects lawyer with ten years of experience, specializing (among other things) in commodity supply contracts. He is currently a Senior Associate with King & Wood Mallesons in Hong Kong.

[1] Sir G. Vos, 'End-to-End Smart Contracts: Moving from Aspiration to Reality', Chapter 2 in this volume.

facilitates peer-to-peer, trust-less transactions,[2] thereby removing intermediaries and reducing transaction costs.[3]

While the technology underlying smart contracts is new, the concept of autonomous performance is not.[4] Analogue instruments such as documentary credit have long been used to effect autonomous contractual performance and mitigate performance risk. Despite the obvious differences between them, this chapter argues that documentary credit and smart contracts are in fact functionally analogous. They share three common functionalities. First, they both effect contractual performance through an *internalized medium of exchange*, such as money or digital tokens. Second, they both operate as *closed systems*, such that contractual performance under them is insulated from changes in extraneous circumstances. Third, they both provide a method of securing sufficient *funds to guarantee contractual performance*. The core difference is that documentary credit effects autonomous performance through a trusted intermediary (eg, a bank), whilst smart contracts achieves this through technology.[5]

Using these three core functionalities as a framework, this chapter will carry out a comparative analysis of these two different mechanisms for effecting autonomous performance. Through this process, we can map out some inherent limitations to future applications of smart contracts. In particular, this chapter will seek to answer (at least partially) two important questions posed by Sir Geoffrey: to what extent can smart contracts move beyond crypto-assets? And how should dispute resolution mechanisms be adapted to the smart contract context? Further, this paper will challenge the claim that the removal of intermediaries through smart contracts will necessarily reduce transaction costs and increase efficiency.[6]

Section B provides a brief illustration of why autonomous performance is such a central feature of smart contracts and the economically useful role this functionality plays in bridging the trust gap between contracting parties. It then explains how autonomous performance can be deconstructed into the three core functionalities outlined above. Section C explains how documentary credit traditionally

---

[2] H. Eenmaa-Dimitrieva and M.J. Schmidt-Kessen, 'Creating Markets in No-trust Environments: The Law and Economics of Smart Contracts' (2018) 35(1) *Computer Law & Security Review: The International Journal of Technology Law and Practice* 69; E. Mik, 'Smart Contracts: Terminology, Technical Limitations and Real World Complexity' (2017) 9(2) *Law, Innovation and Technology* 269, 277; K. Werbach and N. Cornell, 'Contracts Ex Machina' (2017) 67 *Duke Law Journal* 313, 330.

[3] See eg, A. Savelyev, 'Contract Law 2.0: "Smart" Contracts As the Beginning of the End of Classic Contract Law' (2016) *Higher School of Economics Research Paper No. WP BRP 71/LAW/2016*, 9; M. Giancaspro, 'Is a "Smart Contract" Really a Smart Idea? Insights From a Legal Perspective' (2017) 33 *Computer Law & Security Review* 825, 825–8; A. Wright and P. de Filippi, 'Decentralized Blockchain Technology and the Rise of Lex Cryptographia' [2015], 24–6 <https://ssrn.com/abstract=2580664> accessed 9 July 2021.

[4] See Savelyev (n. 3), 8.

[5] Eenmaa-Dimitrieva and Schmidt-Kessen (n. 2), 12–15; M. Raskin, 'The Law And Legality Of Smart Contracts' (2017) 1(2) *Georgetown Law Technology Review* 306, 316–20.

[6] See eg, Savelyev (n. 3), 9; Cf., M. Vatiero, 'Smart Contracts and Transaction Costs' [2018] <https://ssrn.com/abstract=3259958>.

simulates autonomous performance in a low-tech environment and how it also possesses the three functionalities outline above. Section D then uses the three core functionalities as a framework for undertaking a deeper analysis of the relative strengths and weaknesses of documentary credit and smart contracts. In the process, it will make some hypotheses about the likely use cases for smart contracts and propose some design guidelines for appropriate smart contract dispute resolution mechanisms. Section E concludes.

B. De-constructing Autonomous Performance: Three Core Functionalities

Autonomous performance is perhaps the smart contract's most distinctive and controversial feature. While the concept of contractual terms expressed in machine-readable code is not new,[7] it has only recently become plausible for complete strangers to 'contract' with each other in code form, on a (theoretically) secure and de-centralized blockchain platform, where they rely on the blockchain's underlying algorithm to ensure that their contract is executed autonomously, without the need for any external enforcement and free from interference from either contractual party or any other source.[8]

Autonomous contractual performance lies at the heart of the commercial case for smart contracts—they add economic value by facilitating contractual exchange in environments where parties would have otherwise lacked sufficient mutual trust to transact with each other directly.[9] To illustrate: suppose A wishes to sell a shipment of corn to B (who lives in a different country); either A has to ship the corn first to B's country before it is paid or B has to pay for the corn before it has received delivery. The sequential nature of contractual performance necessarily implies that the party which performs first is exposed to the risk that the other party may not counter-perform in due course. Consequently, the first party must trust the other party to perform. Otherwise, they would have to forego a potentially lucrative transaction, which may be economically sub-optimal.[10]

The smart contract can solve this problem by locking in the digital tokens required to satisfy B's payment obligation at the time of contract formation: if the corn is delivered according to the contract,[11] then the payment will be released to

---

[7] See N. Szabo, 'Formalizing and Securing Relationships on Public Networks' (1997) <https://nakamotoinstitute.org/formalizing-securing-relationships/> accessed 9 July 2021.

[8] Raskin (n. 5), 319; Werbach and Cornell (n. 2), 325–9.

[9] Eenmaa-Dimitrieva and Schmidt-Kessen (n. 2), 12–15; Werbach and Cornell (n. 2), 330–6; Wright and de Filippi (n. 3), 11.

[10] R. Posner, *Economic Analysis of Law* (7th edn, Wolters Kluwer for Aspen Publishers 2007), 93–4.

[11] See E. Wall and G. Malm, 'Using Blockchain Technology and Smart Contracts to Create a Distributed Securities Depository', 43–4, <https://lup.lub.lu.se/student-papers/search/publication/8885750> accessed 9 July 2021.

A. If not, the tokens will be returned to B.[12] From each party's perspective, the risk of counterparty non-performance has been removed by making contractual exchange effectively simultaneous.

Despite its obvious utility, however, the autonomous self-executing nature of smart contracts has also given rise to legal concerns. Some commentators point to the risk of illegal smart contracts being inexorably performed. Others point to the smart contract's inability to adapt to changes in extraneous circumstances (since performance is insulated from outside interference) and the potential costs that comes with such inflexibility.[13] However, arguments about the pros and cons of autonomous performance can create an impasse when pitched at the level of generalities. The present imperative is to build up an 'intentional dialogue between the two sides of the debate',[14] by constructing a more nuanced understanding of how the relative weighting of these arguments may change in the context of different use cases.

To this end, this chapter breaks down the concept of autonomous performance into three core functionalities. First, any effective mechanism for autonomous performance must act through an internalized medium of exchange. This means it must control some economic resource which it can allocate pursuant to a contractual exchange, without either the need for extraneous enforcement or the risk of extraneous interference.[15] In the case of a smart contract operating on a blockchain, the typical medium is a digital token representing economic value (eg, bitcoin or ether). The execution of an obligation under a smart contract can only be said to be truly autonomous if the obligation can be completed within the blockchain ecosystem. If the obligation entails steps to be taken in the real world to be fully completed, the extra-blockchain leg of contractual performance would require human intermediaries to act as the interface between the blockchain network and the real world. That human interface then becomes an entry point for extraneous interference.[16]

To illustrate, if a contractual obligation simply requires the transfer of the digital token itself, then the process can be completely controlled by the smart contract code and, therefore, made fully autonomous. If, on the other hand, the transfer of the digital token is used to denote a transfer which can only be completed through

---

[12] *Ibid.*, 31–6; K. Levy, 'Book-Smart, Not Street-Smart: Blockchain-Based Smart Contracts and the Social Workings of Law' (2013) 3 *Engaging Science, Technology and Society*, 3.

[13] See Eenmaa-Dimitrieva and Schmidt-Kessen (n. 2), 6–8; Werbach and Cornell (n. 2), 365–74; Mik (n. 2), 279–87; Levy (n. 12), 1.

[14] Vos (n. 1), (refer p. 3 of Chapter 2 in this volume).

[15] See P. Ortolani, 'Self-Enforcing Online Dispute Resolution: Lessons from Bitcoin' (2016) 36(3) *Oxford Journal of Legal Studies* 595, 604; P. Paech, 'The Governance of Blockchain Financial Networks', *LSE Legal Studies Working Paper No 16/2017*, 13, <https://ssrn.com/abstract=2875487> accessed 9 July 2021.

[16] B. Arrunada, 'Blockchain's Struggle to Deliver Impersonal Exchange' (2018) 19 *The Minnesota Journal of Law, Science & Technology* 55, 81–7.

additional steps to be taken in the real world (eg, transfer of a digital token is used to represent the title transfer of a shipment of corn, which still requires *physical* delivery), those real world steps would, to some extent, be subject to extraneous interference (eg, the seller could still hold back physical delivery).[17] As we shall discuss in Section 4, this has important implications for what types of obligations can meaningfully be made the subject of smart contracts.

Second, the mechanism must operate as a closed system. This means that the performance of the terms of a smart contract responds only to inputs which have already been hardwired into its code at the time of contract formation. Therefore, its execution is not affected by any other extraneous input, whether from the contractual parties or another source.[18] This is essential to autonomous performance: if either party can still disrupt contractual performance after contract formation, then the parties must trust each other not to exercise this ability opportunistically (or have sufficient deterrents in place against such opportunism) before they will enter into contract.[19] The corresponding drawback of this insulation from extraneous interference is that contractual performance cannot be halted even where performance has become undesirable due to a change in circumstances, or where the underlying contract has become legally invalid.[20]

Third, an effective mechanism for autonomous performance must be able to secure sufficient funds to guarantee contractual performance. Suppose a smart contract provides for the deduction of 100 bitcoins from one party's account on date X, but does not prevent that party from spending the bitcoins in its account. In this scenario, performance cannot be guaranteed, as the account may be depleted before date X.[21] Consequently, autonomous performance is meaningless unless the smart contract has some way of securing the 100 bitcoins. Otherwise, contractual parties must continue to trust each other, instead of the smart contract, to make sufficient funds available. A smart contract addresses this risk by effectively freezing the funds required from a contractual party in an account controlled by the smart contract code, which funds will then be automatically paid to the other party on date X and cannot be dealt with for other purposes in the meantime.[22] As we shall discuss in Section 4, this feature gives rise to capital cost implications which may undermine the commercial efficacy of smart contracts.

---

[17] *Ibid.*; T. Cutts, 'Degenerate Contracts and Liberal Code', 48–51, <https://www.academia.edu/38351785/Degenerate_Contracts_and_Liberal_Code> accessed 9 July 2021; G. Olivier and B. Jacard, 'Smart Contracts and the Role of Law' (2017) 23 *Jusletter IT* 16–19.
[18] Mik (n. 2), 282; Vatiero (n. 6), 3–4; Werbach and Cornell (n. 2), 325–9.
[19] *Ibid.*
[20] See n. 13.
[21] Savelyev (n. 3), 18–19.
[22] See Wall and Malm (n. 11), 31–6; V. Buterin, 'Ethereum: Platform Review—Opportunities and Challenges for Private and Consortium Blockchains' (2016), 3–4, <http://www.smallake.kr/wp-content/uploads/2016/06/314477721-Ethereum-Platform-Review-Opportunities-and-Challenges-for-Private-and-Consortium-Blockchains.pdf>.

C. Documentary Credit: Analogue Autonomous Performance

The problem of distrustful contracting parties is not new. Commercial parties have for centuries relied on a low-tech, but effective solution: *documentary credit*.[23] Documentary credit is typically issued by a bank as security for payment obligations under a contract.[24] The archetype is the letter of credit.[25] To use our earlier example, to give A assurance of timely payment, B (as the applicant) would apply to a bank (typically B's own bank)[26] to issue a letter of credit in favour of A (as the beneficiary). The letter of credit constitutes a separate, binding contract between the bank and A,[27] pursuant to which the bank is under a strict obligation to pay A the purchase price under the main contract, subject only to A satisfying the express conditions stipulated in the letter of credit itself (this would typically require A to present certain title documents, which would allow B to take transfer of the corn when the shipment arrives in B's country). Crucially, the obligations are independent: the bank is obligated to pay even where B has an arguable basis for withholding payment under the sale contract.[28] The bank then transfers the title documents to B in exchange for reimbursement by B, of the purchase price paid by the bank to A.[29] The intermediation of the bank between A and B solves the trust issue discussed above: A receives payment at the same time as it transfers the title documents to the bank; B is not required to pay until it has received the said documents; the bank assumes the risk of B's payment default in the interim.[30]

Documentary credit functions much like a smart contract in that it solves the problem of insufficient trust between contractual parties (which arises from the sequential nature of contractual performance) by making the contractual exchange *effectively* simultaneous from the contractual parties' perspectives.[31] Documentary credit is able to do this effectively, because it is essentially an analogue mechanism for autonomous performance which displays the same three core functionalities as a smart contract.

---

[23] See Malek et al., *Jack: Documentary Credits: the Law and Practice of Documentary Credits Including Standby Credits and Demand Guarantees* (4th edn, Haywards Heath 2009), 2.
[24] *Ibid.*
[25] See R. Goode, 'Abstract Payment Undertakings' in Cane and Stapleton (eds), *Essays for Patrick Atiyah* (Oxford University Press 1991) 209, 213–22.
[26] Malek (n. 23), 3–7.
[27] *Ibid.*
[28] *Ibid.*
[29] *Ibid.*, 87. See also *United City Merchant (Investments) Ltd v Royal Bank of Canada* [1983] 1 AC 168, HL, 183.
[30] Malek (n. 23), 3.
[31] On general analogy between letters of credit and smart contracts, see A. Casey and A. Niblett, 'Self-Driving Contracts' (2017) 43(1) *Journal of Corporation Law* 100, 104.

1. The core functionalities of documentary credit

First, documentary credit acts through its own internalized medium of exchange: currency. The issuing bank is able to allocate resources between A and B without outside assistance, because it initially pays the contract price to A with its own money (although external enforcement may still be required when the bank subsequently seeks reimbursement from B). Just as a smart contract can only meaningfully automate the performance of obligations which can be completed within the blockchain ecosystem (eg, through a transfer of digital tokens),[32] so documentary credit can only meaningfully automate the performance of monetary obligations.

Second, documentary credit also operates as a closed system. Pursuant to the autonomy principle, a documentary credit imposes on the issuing bank a strict obligation to pay the amount stipulated in the credit document, as long as the payment conditions expressly stipulated in the credit document itself have been met, regardless of whether there exists legitimate grounds for the payor/applicant to withhold payment under the underlying contract (eg, due to the invalidity or unenforceability of that contract) and even if the payor/applicant issues an instruction to the bank to withhold payment.[33] In effect, the bank is legally mandated to ignore all extraneous factors which might disrupt contractual payment and conditions its performance only on internally agreed stipulations expressly set out in the credit document. This is analogous to performance under a smart contract, which is contingent only upon pre-agreed conditions programmed upfront into the computer code.[34] The documentary credit operates on a 'pay now, argue later' basis,[35] so that the payor cannot opportunistically interfere with payment by raising defences or withdrawing credit.[36] If it subsequently transpires that the payee was not entitled to payment under the main contract, the parties can seek adjustments between themselves. But the payment under the documentary credit remains unaffected.[37] It is precisely the autonomous nature of the bank's payment obligation that provides commercial parties with comfort that contractual payment is effectively insulated from extraneous interference.[38]

Of course, a legal obligation on the bank to ignore extraneous interference with its payment obligation is not quite the same as a computer programme that ignores

---

[32] See Arrunada (n. 16), 81–7.
[33] *United City Merchant* (n. 29), 183; see also, Malek (n. 23), 17–18; Goode (n. 25), 211, 225–8; D. Horowitz, *Letters of Credit and Demand Guarantees, Defences to Payment* (Oxford University Press 2010), 1–3.
[34] See n. 31.
[35] J. Dolan, 'Tethering the Fraud Inquiry in Letter of Credit Law' (2006) 21(3) *Banking & Finance Law Review* 479, 481–2; G. McNeel, 'Pay Now, Argue Later' [1999] *Lloyd's Maritime and Commercial Law Quarterly* 5.
[36] *Ibid.*; Goode (n. 25), 211.
[37] McNeel (n. 35), 5.
[38] Malek (n. 23), 17–18.

extraneous interference *simpliciter*. For one thing, the bank may simply not comply with its legal obligation, although this carries serious legal and reputational consequences for the bank (and is therefore unlikely). More relevantly, the autonomous nature of the bank's payment obligation is not absolute but subject to exceptions, such as where the beneficiary's claim to payment under the documentary credit is affected by fraud or illegality.[39] The insulation of the bank's payment obligation under documentary credit could easily be eroded if the courts started to apply the exceptions broadly.[40]

Nonetheless, it is well recognized that contractual parties need to be able to rely on payment under documentary credit as being practically immune from extraneous interference. This is essential to maintaining the commercial efficacy of these instruments, and courts have generally been careful to limit the exceptions to the bank's autonomous payment obligation.[41] Therefore, while the autonomy of contractual performance afforded by documentary credit is more qualified compared to that under smart contracts, it is appropriate to treat the former as practically insulated from extraneous interference. And as we shall see, a more qualified form of autonomous performance is not necessarily a bad thing.

Third, documentary credit secures sufficient funds to guarantee contractual performance by backing the payment obligation with the bank's own resources and transferring the applicant's default risk under the main contract to the bank.[42] Thus, the beneficiary is only exposed to the bank's own credit risk. While this does not remove the risk of a payment default completely (since the bank itself can, in exceptional circumstances, default), this risk is considered to be extremely small where the bank is reputable and of good financial standing.

There are, of course, ostensible differences between documentary credit and smart contracts. Documentary credit enables autonomous performance by creating a *separate* obligation undertaken by a third party guarantor, in favour of the payee under the main contract. A smart contract, on the other hand, automates the *primary* obligation embedded within itself. However, the distinction is more apparent than real. Smart contracts often come in the form of a separate account on the blockchain, which houses the contract code and interacts with the accounts of the contractual parties.[43] To this extent, it functions very much like a digital third party in practice. The principal substantive difference is that documentary credit relies on a human intermediary (the bank) to perform the payment obligations autonomously, whilst the smart contract relies on computer algorithms to achieve the result.

---

[39] For detailed discussions of the fraud and illegality exceptions, see Malek (n. 23), 245–80; Horowitz (n. 33), chapters 2, 3, and 7; see also, *United City Merchant* (n. 29); *Themehelp Ltd v West* [1996] QB 84.
[40] Dolan (n. 35), 490–6.
[41] *Ibid.*, 496–502.
[42] McNeel (n. 35), 3.
[43] See eg, Buterin (n. 22).

D. Comparative Analysis of Smart Contracts and Documentary Credit

Having identified the three core functionalities essential to autonomous performance, which are shared by documentary credit and smart contracts, we can now conduct a more detailed comparative analysis of their relative merits and limitations, using these three functionalities as a framework. This section will use the comparative analysis to draw out some tentative hypotheses about future use cases for smart contracts. In particular, it will look at potential limitations to extending the application of smart contracts beyond crypto-assets, how appropriate dispute resolution mechanism might be designed to complement autonomous performance under a smart contract, and capital cost implications arising from use of smart contracts.

1. Internalized medium of exchange

The fact that both smart contracts and documentary credit need to act through an internalized medium of exchange imposes inherent limitations on the types of obligations which may be made the subject of autonomous performance under each. For documentary credit, the medium is money (specifically: commercial bank liabilities) and the corresponding limitation is that only monetary obligations can be made the subject of autonomous performance under it. For example, documentary credit such as demand guarantees are frequently used in the context of construction contracts to secure a contractor's secondary obligation to pay liquidated damages in the event of construction delays. However, they cannot be used to ensure that the contractor will satisfy its primary obligation, ie, to complete construction on time.

Likewise, smart contracts operating on blockchain can only enable the autonomous performance of obligations which can be completed within the blockchain ecosystem. In the immediate future, this might mean that the obligation needs to be reducible to transfers of digital tokens. Of course, it would be too unimaginative to think that the application of smart contracts will remain confined to crypto-assets.[44] For example, digital tokens can readily be made to represent conventional forms of money, securities, and other assets,[45] the transfer of which can be effected on the blockchain platform.[46] Where a digital token is used to denote a real world object, its transfer may still require a degree of external assistance to complete

---

[44] See Vos (n. 1), (refer p. 17 of Chapter 2 in this volume).
[45] P. Paech, 'Securities, Intermediation and the Blockchain: An Inevitable Choice Between Liquidity and Legal Certainty?' (2016) 21 *Uniform Law Review* 612.
[46] Arrunada (n. 16), 81–7.

(eg, court recognition that the transfer of the digital token gives good title) and is therefore not fully autonomous.[47] Further, with technological advancements in the Internet-of-Things ('IoT'), it may soon be possible for the computer code in smart contracts to interact directly with machines in the real world, without the need for or risk of human intervention, thereby greatly expanding the outer-boundaries of the blockchain ecosystem.[48]

However, there remain inherent limitations to the types of contractual obligations which can be the subject of autonomous performance under a smart contract. Ultimately, blockchain and IoT are concerned with digital assets and relatively mechanical robotic processes. It is difficult to conceptualize how such technologies could be applied to execute contractual obligations whose underlying subject matter is primarily concerned with human behaviour. For instance, when a project sponsor engages a contractor to construct a skyscraper, it is not looking for the transfer of title to a specific existing building (which could be denoted by a digital token controlled by a smart contract). It is looking for the technical skills and resources of the contractor to complete the construction according to a pre-agreed schedule and specifications. In fact, under many service contracts, what the service recipient is contracting for is not the transfer of specific existing objects or the implementation of mechanical processes, but an undertaking by the service provider to behave in a particular way, based on its skills and other personal attributes. The performance of such obligations (whose primary subject matter is human behaviour) simply cannot be automated.

For this reason, even with further technological advances, applications of smart contract technology will likely remain confined to digital assets and relatively mechanical robotic processes.[49] This means that smart contract technology may be generally more suited to contracts for sale of goods than provision of services.

The limitation also offers insight into another issue relating to smart contracts: the difficulty of translating vague, open-textured contractual terms (eg, 'reasonable care' or 'good faith') into code.[50] One way to understand the problem is through linguistics—some natural expressions are simply too ambiguous and context-dependent to be translated into formal, machine-readable code.[51]

Another way of framing the problem, however, is to look at the subject matter of a contractual obligation. The subject matter of vague contractual standards is

---

[47] Ibid.
[48] C. Catalini and J. Gans, 'Some Simple Economics of The Blockchain' [2018] *NBER Working Paper Series*, 10–11 <http://www.nber.org/papers/w22952> accessed 9 July 2021; Cf., Mik (n. 2), 298.
[49] See S. Green, 'Smart Contracts, Interpretation and Rectification' (2018) *Lloyd's Maritime and Commercial Law Quarterly* 234, 237; H. Surden, 'Computable Contracts' (2012) 46 *University of California, Davis Law Review* 629, 642–6.
[50] Ibid.; Eenmaa-Dimitrieva and Schmidt-Kessen (n. 2), 7.
[51] Ibid.; see also J.G. Allen, 'Wrapped and Stacked: "Smart Contracts" and the Interaction of Natural and Formal Language' (2018) 14(4) *European Review of Contract Law* 307, 322–4, 334–6.

typically not inanimate objects, but the counterparty's human behaviour. When a party contracts for the other party to use reasonable care in providing services, for example, it is not bargaining for the transfer of a specific asset which could be digitally reified, but for the counterparty to comply with a particular standard of diligence and competence. Therefore, even if the problem of linguistic compatibility between natural and formal language could be overcome (which itself seems unlikely),[52] open-textured contractual standards would still remain incompatible with autonomous performance under smart contracts, because they are ultimately concerned with human behaviour.[53]

2. Closed system

Another important critique on smart contracts is around their 'unstoppable' nature—they cannot respond to any change in extraneous circumstances unless it has been programmed into the code.[54] The critique can broadly be subdivided into three interrelated strains: first, the closed and autonomous nature of performance under smart contracts potentially precludes efficient breach;[55] second, it removes the parties' ability to adapt contracts to unanticipated changes in external circumstances;[56] third, it may lead to the execution of contracts which are legally void or unenforceable or even illegal.[57] While the blockchain network can interact with the real world through oracles, this does not address the fundamental problem: any external input feeding into the contractual code through oracles must still be programmed in up front.[58] We shall address each strain of the critique in turn.

a. Efficient breach

The basic premise of the efficient breach theory is that, where it is more profitable/less costly for one party to breach the contract, compensate the other party for its loss of bargain and divert its resources elsewhere, it should be allowed to do so, rather than be held to the contract.[59] This allows resources to be allocated more efficiently from a macro-economic perspective.[60] The problem with smart contracts is that it makes economically efficient breaches impossible, since contractual

---

[52] Allen (n. 51), 336.
[53] Mik (n. 2), 299.
[54] See n. 18; see also, Paech (n. 15), 14–21.
[55] Werbach and Cornell (n. 2), 366; Eenmaa-Dimitrieva and Schmidt-Kessen (n. 2), 7.
[56] Levy (n. 12), 7–9; Vatiero (n. 6), 9–11; Werbach and Cornell (n. 2), 367; Mik (n. 2), 282–3.
[57] Werbach and Cornell (n. 2), 373; Mik (n. 2), 287; Eenmaa-Dimitrieva and Schmidt-Kessen (n. 2), 8.
[58] Wall and Malm (n. 11), 43–4; Mik (n. 2), 296–7.
[59] Posner (n. 10), 119–26; T. Al-Tawil, 'English Contract Law and the Efficient Breach Theory' (2015) 22(3) *Maastricht Journal of European and Comparative Law* 396, 398–400.
[60] Ibid.

performance is autonomous and cannot be stopped.[61] The same issue exists with documentary credit (albeit to a lesser extent), since the beneficiary under the documentary credit can unilaterally claim payment under it. This effectively forces the applicant to go through with the underlying transaction (since the bank would automatically make the payment and turn to the applicant for reimbursement, although the applicant theoretically has residual discretion not to pay the bank),[62] even if it would have been more economic for the parties to cancel the contract for a payment of damages by the obligor (which might be less than the full amount payable under the documentary credit).

This suggests that both smart contracts and documentary credit may lead to economically sub-optimal outcomes. This proposition should, however, be qualified by three observations. First, it is not universally accepted that 'efficient breach' is desirable. Many have pointed out that the theory undermines the moral underpinnings of a contractual promise.[63] In this sense, then, smart contracts may be regarded as actually reinforcing the moral value of contracts by making contractual breach impossible.[64]

Second, the efficient breach theory assumes that parties would be prepared to enter into a contract in the first place, without security upfront and rely solely on their ability to claim damages in the event of breach.[65] But the economic case for smart contracts is that its autonomous self-executing nature provides distrustful parties with the requisite level of performance assurance, without which they would not have contracted at all.[66] Here, efficient breach and 'unbreachable' smart contracts are simply addressed towards different scenarios.

Third, assuming efficient breach is desirable, a default regime allowing the obligor to elect to pay damages instead of performing is arguably not indispensable to facilitating efficient breach. Some commentators have argued that efficient breach can function equally well under a regime where an order for specific performance (which compels contractual performance) is the default remedy, since the party wishing to commit efficient breach can always negotiate with the other party to be released from its obligation, in exchange for the payment of an exit premium.[67] An unbreachable contract is simply 'specific performance on steroids'.[68] It may, of course, be trickier for parties to negotiate against the background of an

---

[61] Werbach and Cornell (n. 2), 332; Cutts (n. 17), 3; Paech (n. 15), 12–14.
[62] Malek (n. 23), 3–4.
[63] T. Al-Tawil, 'The Efficient Breach Theory—The Moral Objection' (2011) 20 *Griffith Law Review* 449, 462–73;
[64] Cf., Savelyev (n. 3), 17–19.
[65] Posner (n. 10), 94–6.
[66] See *ibid*. See also, Eenmaa-Dimitrieva and Schmidt-Kessen (n. 2), 14; Ortolani (n. 15), 600–3.
[67] D. Lewin-sohn-Zamir *et al.*, 'The Questionable Efficiency of the Efficient-Breach Doctrine' (2012) 168(1) *Journal of Institutional Theoretical Economics* 5, 20–4; M. Bigoni *et al.*, 'Unbundling Efficient Breach: An Experiment' (2017) 14(3) *Journal of Empirical Legal Studies* 527.
[68] Werbach and Cornell (n. 2), 356.

autonomously self-executing smart contract. Unlike a traditional suit for specific performance, parties to a smart contract cannot readily halt performance to negotiate a release of one party's obligations.[69] But the problem is not insuperable. For example, parties can agree to incorporate a 'kill-switch' into the smart contract, which can be turned on if parties need time to negotiate an exit.[70] The key is that parties need to have an effective and adapted dispute resolution mechanism in place, when they disagree about performance under a smart contract. This will likely be critical to their commercialization.[71]

The tension between efficient breach and autonomous performance sheds some light on how such mechanisms should be designed. Let us consider the different permutations for how a 'kill switch' could be triggered (borrowing the taxonomy set out by Sir Geoffrey):[72] if the 'kill switch' could be triggered unilaterally by the performing party (option (a)), it would favour 'efficient breach', as the performing party could unilaterally halt performance and offer to pay damages, but it would effectively neutralize autonomous performance under the smart contract; if the switch could only be triggered by a third party (option (c)) or upon a specific event (option (d)), which event would need to be fed into the smart contract code through a reliable oracle, then a trusted intermediary would effectively be re-introduced into the contractual matrix. (In option (d), the oracle would need to be operated by a trusted third party.) This is the very thing which smart contracts are supposed to replace.[73]

In fact, if autonomous performance and the desire to remove intermediaries are the key reasons for using a smart contract in the first place, the only type of dispute resolution mechanism which would align with those objectives is one where performance is halted jointly by both parties (option (b)). This would, of course, give the obligee much greater bargaining power compared to the obligor seeking release from its obligation (as the obligee could veto any attempt to halt performance).[74] But this is not necessarily a drawback. As discussed above, documentary credit is traditionally used to bridge the trust gap between contracting parties, precisely because it creates a 'pay now, argue later' regime of risk allocation under which payment is practically unstoppable.[75] If the autonomy of the payment obligation under documentary credit (from disputes under the main contract) were eroded, documentary credit would lose much of its commercial utility.[76] Similarly, when designing any dispute resolution mechanism for a smart contract, parties

---

[69] Eenmaa-Dimitrieva and Schmidt-Kessen (n. 2), 17.
[70] Ibid., 7.
[71] Vos (n. 1), (refer p. 15–17 of Chapter 2 in this volume).
[72] Ibid., 16.
[73] See n. 2. See also, Arrunada (n. 16), 65–6.
[74] Lewinsohn-Zamir et al. (n. 67), 7; Werbach and Cornell (n. 2), 376.
[75] See footnote 36; see also, Malek (n. 23), 17.
[76] Dolan (n. 35), 502.

should be live to preserving the 'perform now, argue later' scheme of risk allocation under it, which may well be a key reason for deploying a smart contract in the first place. Where the spectre of autonomous, unstoppable performance seems too problematic, the answer may be that it is simply not an appropriate use case for smart contracts (just as a documentary credit is not appropriate for every contractual scenario).

b. Lack of adaptability

A related critique is that smart contracts remove the parties' ability to adapt to external changes (indeed, efficient breach can be thought of as a form of response to changes in economic conditions). This critique touches on a broader issue. It concerns the fact that contractual performance under a smart contract cannot be stopped even in situations for which the contract has not provided or where the continued operation of the contract under drastically altered circumstances would arguably be contrary to the parties' original intentions.[77] This arguably leads to inefficient outcomes, since the parties would be better off in such cases, if they were able to adapt the contract to the changed circumstances (either explicitly or through implied terms and elastic interpretation).[78]

The problem is essentially one of unintended consequences and exists at two levels. On a technological level, programmers may make mistakes in the coding of the contract and produce outcomes unintended by the commercial parties.[79] More fundamentally, however, the risk remains that smart contracts may self-execute in unintended circumstances, even where the coding is error-free.

This arises from the very nature of incomplete contracts.[80] In theory, it is possible to write a complete contract which provides in advance for every possible contingency. That would remove the need for subsequent adaptations.[81] However, this is seldom realistic for two reasons: first, it is difficult to foresee every possible future contingency; second, even assuming it is possible to foresee every possible future contingency, the cost of research and negotiation to cover them all (however remote) would be prohibitively costly and disproportionate to the countervailing benefit.[82] Therefore, it would often be more efficient for parties to enter into incomplete contracts, leaving gaps to be filled at a later date. This requires that the contract retains sufficient elasticity for subsequent adaptation to changing circumstances.[83] However, there is little (if any) elasticity under a smart contract, since it

---

[77] See n. 54.
[78] Levy (n. 12), 7–9; Vatiero (n. 6), 9–11.
[79] Mik (n. 2), 281; Giancaspro (n. 3), 828–9.
[80] Mik (n. 2), 292–3; Vatiero (n. 6), 5–6.
[81] O. Hart, 'Incomplete Contracts and Control' (2017) 107(7) *American Economic Review* 1731, 1732.
[82] J. Tirole, 'Incomplete Contracts Where Do We Stand?' (1999) 67(4) *Econometrica* 741, 743–4; B. Klein, 'Why Hold-ups Occur: The Self-Enforcing Range of Contractual Relationships' (1996) 34(3) *Economic Inquiry* 444, 447–9; see also, Allen (n. 51), 337.
[83] *Ibid.*; see also, Vatiero (n. 6), 9–11.

operates as a closed system—every relevant contingency must be unambiguously programmed into the code upfront; otherwise, they cannot affect the autonomous performance of the contract.[84] This suggests that smart contracts may produce suboptimal results, particularly in longer-term contracts.[85]

While this lack of adaptability can be problematic, it should be qualified by two observations. First, there is a difference between smart contracts operating on permissionless blockchain networks and those operating on permissioned networks. Permissionless works are open to anyone to join and there are few, if any, identity checks on the participants, who operate on an essentially anonymous basis.[86] Consequently, parties to a smart contract on a permissionless network are unlikely to be able to identify each other in real life and, therefore, seek practical redress if the operation of the smart contract leads to unintended outcomes.[87] Access to permissioned networks, on the other hand, are typically controlled by a central entity or consortium.[88] As such, its participants will usually know each other and have real world relationships. In the event a smart contract on the network does not operate as intended, it remains open to the contractual parties to seek remedies outside the blockchain, just as it is possible for parties to seek *ex post* adjustments where payment under a documentary credit turns out to be inconsistent with the parties' rights under the main contract.[89]

Of course, this assumes that the code in the smart contract does not conclusively represent the parties' intention. In this permissioned context, the concept of the smart contract as a multi-layered 'stack' assumes practical importance.[90] For example, in addition to code, the contract between the parties may include a conventional 'paper wrapper' which sets out parties' commercial intentions and a dispute resolution regime for how to deal with any unintended consequences arising from the operation of the code.[91] In the event of disagreement, this regime could ultimately be enforced through the courts. The code, the paper wrapper and the overlay of legal rules enforceable through courts may all be thought of as layers in the 'contract stack'. Problems arising from the code layer of the contract could potentially be remedied by other layers within the broader contractual architecture.[92]

---

[84] Surden (n. 49), 642–6; see also, n. 51.
[85] See Vatiero (n. 6), 10.
[86] G. Peters and E. Panayi, 'Understanding Modern Banking Ledgers Through Blockchain Technologies: Future of Transaction Processing and Smart Contracts on the Internet of Money' (2015), 5, <https://ssrn.com/abstract=2692487> accessed 9 July 2021.
[87] Eenmaa-Dimitrieva and Schmidt-Kessen (n. 2), 18; Paech (n. 15), 27–9, Wright and de Filippi (n. 3), 21.
[88] Peters and Panayi (n. 86), 5.
[89] McNeel (n. 35), 5.
[90] Allen (n. 51), 330–1; S. Cohney and D. Hoffman, 'Transactional Scripts in Contract Stacks' [2020], 39–49, <https://ssrn.com/abstract=3523515> accessed 9 July 2021.
[91] *Ibid.*; see also, Green (n. 49), 239–42.
[92] Allen (n. 51), 330–1; Cohney and Hoffman (n. 90), 39–49.

Contractual form will also have a material impact on parties' ability to seek redress outside the smart contract code. A contractual framework where parties have clearly defined (i) what texts form part of the contract stack and (ii) how they are to be interpreted together (particularly in the event of inconsistency between textual layers) will facilitate the parties' ability to seek redress in the event the smart contract code operates in an unintended manner.[93] Leaving all these interpretational questions to be determined by a court will likely increase uncertainty and cost. Of course, parties can only agree on an extra-blockchain contractual framework and enforce that regime, if they can identify each other. So this solution is unlikely to be viable on permissionless networks.

Second, the critique against lack of adaptability assumes that parties can actually agree on an efficient adaptation of the contract when extraneous circumstances change. Where there is an obvious adaptation which would benefit both parties, there is no reason to suspect why parties to a smart contract would not be able to reach a settlement in the real world (assuming they can identify each other), even if execution of the smart contract code itself cannot be halted. Often, however, the parties simply cannot agree on whether or how the contract is intended to operate under the changed circumstances, because the parties' interests are misaligned. One party may benefit from the contract's continued and unaltered operation, while the other party may be prejudiced by it. This then gives rise to what is referred to as the 'hold-up problem'.[94] In simple terms, hold-ups occur under an incomplete contract when there is a change of circumstances for which the contract has not provided. This then may give one party a commercial leverage which it would exploit to force the other party to renegotiate a deal more in the former's favour.[95]

Using our earlier example, suppose a dispute arises between A and B as to whether B is still required to proceed with the purchase of corn under their contract after B's country has imposed an embargo on imports from A's country—a contingency on which the contract is silent.[96] If payment remains within B's control, B can withhold payment. The enforcement cost against B (which might be high) might dissuade A against pressing its claim and would work to B's advantage in any negotiated settlement. If, on the other hand, payment has been made autonomous (either under a smart contract or documentary credit), B would be faced with the cost and uncertainty of claiming back the purchase price from A in restitution. The balance of power would be reversed.[97]

In essence, by agreeing to make the performance of an obligation autonomous, whether through a smart contract or documentary credit, the parties effectively

---

[93] See Cohney and Hoffman (n. 90), 45–59.
[94] Klein (n. 82), 444–8.
[95] *Ibid.*; Hart (n. 81), 1732–5.
[96] Dolan (n. 35), 483.
[97] See Werbach and Cornell (n. 2), 376–7.

shift their relative hold-up power in the event of changes in extraneous circumstances.[98] Of course, there is no inherent reason why the relative hold-up power should be in one party's favour rather than the other's. As long as the risk allocation has been deliberately agreed between informed parties, it should not be seen as necessarily inefficient or undesirable. That is for the parties to decide.[99] As discussed above, parties should be careful to preserve autonomous performance under a smart contract when they design appropriate dispute resolution mechanisms, for autonomous performance will likely be a key reason for using a smart contract in the first place, just as parties traditionally used documentary credit precisely because payment under it was rigid and autonomous.[100] A preferred approach would therefore be to leave parties to seek redress after performance is completed rather than give them too much discretion to halt performance in advance.

c. Invalid and illegal contracts

The last critique focuses on the fact that smart contracts could be used to execute legally invalid or even illegal transactions, as performance under them would not respond to extraneous legal inputs.[101] Once again, however, this critique should be tempered with a couple of distinctions. The first is the distinction between permissionless and permissioned networks discussed earlier. In the case of smart contracts operating on permissioned networks, the consequences of performing an illegal or legally void contract could still be reversed or adjusted outside of the blockchain network.[102] It is only in the case of permissionless networks that autonomous performance of the programmed obligation becomes practically irremediable.[103]

Second, a distinction should be made between situations where the allocation of the risk of contractual invalidity can be a matter of legitimate commercial agreement and situations where it cannot. In the first category, parties may enter into a legitimate commercial transaction intending it to be legally enforceable, but the contract may turn out to be unenforceable or void due to some technical defect which either did not exist or were overlooked, at the time of contract formation. For example, a contract may be void due to a total failure of consideration or mistake, but would remain lawful. In these cases, the parties may legitimately wish to allocate the risk of contractual invalidity to one party, by ensuring that it will perform its obligation in all circumstances, leaving it to seek legal redress should

---

[98] Dolan (n. 35), 483.
[99] *Ibid.*
[100] See n. 75.
[101] See nn. 13 and 54.
[102] See Raskin (n. 5), 338–40.
[103] See n. 87.

the contract turn out to be void or unenforceable. This is precisely the function traditionally performed by documentary credit: the issuing bank's payment obligation to the seller under a letter of credit (and, in turn, the buyer's obligation to reimburse the bank) is generally not affected by defects vitiating the validity of the underlying contract (other than in certain instances of fraud or illegality).[104] If the underlying contract turns out to be void or enforceable,[105] the buyer can seek recovery against the seller after the payment has been made.[106] This high degree of payment certainty, even in the event of underlying contractual invalidity or unenforceability, is often essential to facilitating contract formation between two parties who might otherwise lack sufficient mutual trust.[107] To the extent smart contracts perform an analogous function in the digital context, this should not be regarded as problematic *per se*.

The other situation involves the enforcement of transactions which are void or unenforceable for reasons concerning public policy. For example, it would be contrary to public policy for parties to agree to perform a criminal act or for one party to obtain a contractual benefit by fraud.[108] Here, it would not be legitimate for the parties to agree on a risk allocation which guarantees absolute contractual performance, as that would be contrary to broader social interests.[109] This distinction between legitimate and illegitimate risk allocations is, to a large extent, reflected in the law in relation to documentary credit: the issuing bank's autonomous obligation to pay under a documentary credit is excused under limited exceptions where the beneficiary's payment claim under the documentary credit is tainted by fraud or illegality.[110]

Unfortunately, the same distinction would be much harder to draw and maintain in the context of smart contracts operating on strict logic. One solution is for legal rules to be written into the code, so that performance would automatically be halted where illegality, fraud or some other public policy factor is involved.[111] Apart from very basic applications, however, this approach would likely involve setting out in formalistic code, how complex bodies of jurisprudence would apply to the infinite diversity of real life events. For the foreseeable future at least, this would seem beyond reach. The other option is for some form of *ex post* adjustment,[112] a solution for which this paper has advocated in other contexts. The problem here is that, where illegality, fraud, or other public policy factors are involved, irreparable damage might already have been done, if performance of the

---

[104] See n. 33.
[105] See n. 34.
[106] McNeel (n. 35), 5.
[107] Malek (n. 23), 17.
[108] Werbach and Cornell (n. 2), 373.
[109] Raskin (n. 5), 328–9.
[110] See n. 34.
[111] See Raskin (n. 5), 328–33.
[112] *Ibid.*

tainted contract cannot be halted in advance. That is precisely why the allocation of the risk of contractual invalidity in these situations cannot legitimately be left to private agreement in the first place.[113]

This difference highlights a genuine drawback of relying on technology instead of human intermediaries to effect autonomous contractual performance—while the rigidity arising from autonomous performance is not undesirable *per se*, the smart contract solution is suboptimal, as computer code is ill-adapted to exercising nuanced judgment on a case-by-case basis in its interaction with the law.[114] In contrast, because autonomous performance under documentary credit is effected through a human agent and not absolute, it can engage meaningfully and flexibly with the legal system,[115] providing certainty of performance in the vast majority of cases where such certainty is desirable and legitimate, while still taking into account the overriding interests of the law in exceptional cases.

3. Securing sufficient funds to enable contractual performance

The last core functionality of an effective autonomous performance mechanism is that it must be able to secure sufficient funds to enable contractual performance. Here, we see a divergence of approach between documentary credit and smart contracts. Documentary credit guarantees performance by transferring payment default risk under the main contract to the issuing bank, which makes its own resources available to satisfy the beneficiary's payment claim.[116] As the issuing bank usually has an established relationship with the payor who applied for the documentary credit (the payor typically applies to its relationship bank to issue the documentary credit),[117] it can assess and monitor the payor's payment default risk more efficiently than the payee can under the main contract. Further, the issuing bank may use its other dealings with the payor to reduce its exposure to the payor's default risk. For example, if the payor has a deposit account with the bank, the latter could potentially offset its exposure to the payor under the documentary credit against the amount it owes the payor under the separate deposit account. This then leaves the payor free to deploy its own capital in other profitable activities until its obligation to reimburse the bank under the documentary credit becomes due.[118] In short, the issuing bank can leverage off its established relationship with the payor/applicant to take on the payor's payment default risk more cheaply and

---

[113] *Ibid.*, 338–40.
[114] Wright and de Filippi (n. 3), 44–51; see also, n. 51.
[115] See Paech (n. 15), 33–6.
[116] Malek (n. 23), 3–4.
[117] *Ibid.*
[118] *Ibid.*, 86–8.

efficiently than the payee can under the underlying contract. It then sells these efficiency gains to the contractual parties as a service.

By contrast, the smart contract's method of securing sufficient funds to enable autonomous performance is rather crude. Its *modus operandi* is to remove the intermediary and facilitate trustless transactions,[119] so it cannot leverage off any relationship of trust to obtain efficiency gains. Instead, it must lock up the required resources upfront, at the time of contract formation.[120] However, this deprives the payor of the use of those resources in the interim until performance actually becomes due. Where large sums are locked up over a prolonged period, the lost time value of capital can be considerable. To the extent this cost exceeds the administrative cost of procuring a bank to issue documentary credit, smart contracts would be economically less efficient than documentary credit in effecting autonomous performance.

This comparison reveals a much-overlooked shortcoming of smart contracts: they potentially increase the capital cost of transactions. Advocates have consistently claimed that smart contracts can reduce transaction costs, by removing the intermediary.[121] However, this ignores the fact that trusted intermediaries are not idle rent seekers—they can actually leverage their established relationships of trust to create efficiency gains for contractual parties. Therefore, by removing the trusted intermediary, smart contracts also remove the *efficiency gains* a trusted intermediary brings.[122] The resulting increase in capital costs may well offset the savings in administrative costs arising from removing the intermediary. This introduces an important economic calculus when considering appropriate use cases for smart contracts—where an intermediary can generate efficiency gains (as per the example above) greater than the fee it charges, it may well be better to stick to the intermediary than to replace it with a smart contract.

E. Conclusion

This chapter has sought to illustrate that, whilst the technology behind smart contracts and blockchain may be new, the chief characteristic which makes smart contracts commercially useful—autonomous contractual performance—is not. The documentary credit is a prime example of how autonomous contractual performance has been possible long before the advent of blockchain technology (or even computers).

---

[119] See n. 2.
[120] See n. 22 and associated text.
[121] See n. 2.
[122] See B. Arruñada and L. Garicano, 'Blockchain: The Birth of Decentralized Governance' (10 April 2018). *Pompeu Fabra University, Economics and Business Working Paper Series*, 1608, 33 <https://ssrn.com/abstract=3160070> accessed 9 July 2021.

The comparison between documentary credit and smart contacts yields several useful insights into potential limitations on future use cases of smart contracts. First, while smart contracts can potentially enable the autonomous performance of a broader range of contractual obligations than is possible under documentary credit, the need for some internal medium of exchange means their use cases will likely remain tied to digital tokens. In any case, they are inherently unsuited to obligations which are concerned more with human behaviour than asset transfer or mechanical processes.

Second, like the documentary credit, the smart contract will lend itself to contractual scenarios where parties consciously desire to allocate risk on a 'perform now, argue later' basis. In appropriate cases, this may even extend to scenarios where the risk of underlying contractual invalidity is shifted onto the performing party. Rather than seeing the rigidity that comes from autonomous performance as a problem to be solved, it may be better to see it as a functionality whose application should be carefully curated. To an extent, some of the unintended consequences arising from autonomous performance are potentially reversible, at least where parties are contracting on a permissioned blockchain network. There, it is possible for identified parties to have a multi-layered contractual relationship which extends beyond code and can ultimately be arbitrated before a national court. Moreover, when designing a dispute resolution regime for a smart contract, parties should consider how this regime of strict performance can be substantially preserved, for this would often go to the basic commercial rationale for using a smart contract in the first place.

Lastly, human intermediaries can often generate additional efficiencies which computer codes cannot: they can leverage established relationships of trust to assume a party's default risk more cheaply than the contractual parties can themselves; they can also respond more flexibly to issues of illegality and fraud in contractual relationships. Therefore, commercial parties should be circumspect when considering using smart contracts to replace human intermediaries. The latter, too, can give effect to autonomous performance, sometimes more effectively.

11
Techno-Legal Supertoys
Smart Contracts and the Fetishization of Legal Certainty

*Robert Herian**

A. Introduction	246	D. Legally Weak?	257
B. Prelude: The Persistence of 'Supertoys'	249	1. Smart contract ideals and contingent reality	258
1. Smart contracts as techno-legal supertoys	251	2. The immature disruptive potential of smart contracts	259
C. Smart, but not Intelligent, Contracts	252	3. Contract law remedies and risk-allocation	260
1. Emerging definitions of 'smart contracts'	253	4. The broader social function of 'contract'	262
2. The rhetoric of efficiency	256	5. Smart contracts and legal language	263
		6. Smart contracts and good faith	265
		E. Conclusion	265

A. Introduction

Life, some say, imitates art. Nowhere is this better illustrated than in realities, including legal realities, that uncannily reflect the imaginings of science fiction. In the following dialogue from Steven Spielberg's 2001 film *AI: Artificial Intelligence* is the description of an agreement between two boys, one a machine (David) the other human (Martin):

MARTIN: 'If you do something really, really, really special for me—a special mission—then I'll go tell mommy I love you, and then she'll love you to'.
DAVID: 'What shall I do?'
MARTIN: 'You'll have to promise, and then I'll tell you'.

---

* Robert Herian is Senior Lecturer in law at the Open University Law School (UK), a co-founder of the Law, Information, Future, Technology (LIFT) research group and Equity and Trusts Research Network (ETRN), and an expert panel member of the European Union Blockchain Observatory and Forum (EUBOF). Robert's research includes intersections of law, technology and data studies, law and psychoanalysis, critical theory, social and political economy, and philosophy.

Robert Herian, *Techno-Legal Supertoys* In: *Smart Legal Contracts*. Edited by: Jason Grant Allen and Peter Hunn, Oxford University Press. © Jason Grant Allen & Peter Hunn 2022. DOI: 10.1093/oso/9780192858467.003.0012

DAVID: 'You'll have to tell me, and then I'll promise'.
MARTIN: 'I want a lock of mommy's hair; I'll share it with you ... '
DAVID: 'We can ask her'.
MARTIN: 'No, it has to be a secret mission. Sneak into mommy's bedroom in the middle of the night and chop it off'.
DAVID: 'I can't Martin, I'm not allowed'.
MARTIN: 'You promised. You said: tell me and then I'll promise, didn't you?'[1]

As children, one might expect the negotiation, and eventual agreement, between David and Martin to be naïve and stripped of any appreciation for broader, long-term consequences. David and Martin view their agreement as one made in a moment, and, whilst executable in time, that time is the immediate future, the coming night.

Also, David and Martin's agreement is absolute and inviolable, with what little negotiation the boys have on individual terms resulting in an agreement of unbreakable promises. It does not matter which way either party approaches the substance or content of the agreement, the promise is always already part of the outcome, an idea elegantly showed by the exchange. Martin says: 'You'll have to promise, and then I'll tell you'. David says: 'You'll have to tell me, and then I'll promise'. This ideal of fair play, whilst portrayed here by children and arguably redolent of any childlike idealism concerning promises as yet corrupted by the moral hazards and cynicism of social and political life, is recognizable in the utopian worlds of modern technologists who are keen to show they can correct real-world, human, failures in trust, honesty, and accountability with code, protocols, and distributed networks.

Drawing on Anglo-American and European legal theory, doctrines and principles (reflecting the trans-jurisdictional presence and influence of technological systems and networks), this chapter describes how the agreement formation and execution showed in AI is recognizable in 'real-world' electronic agreements known as 'smart contracts', one piece of the larger and expanding jigsaw of distributed and disintermediated technologies built on and around a variety of distributed ledgers and blockchains.[2]

---

[1] *AI: Artificial Intelligence*, Directed by Steven Spielberg (Warner Brothers 2001). Spielberg's film is based on the short story collection, B. Aldiss, *Supertoys Last All Summer Long: And Other Stories of Future Time* (Orbit 2001)

[2] This article will not define nor discuss blockchain technology explicitly. But it is important to note that blockchains have long been associated with the notion that counterparties to a transaction or agreement *do not need to trust one another*. This is because a blockchain checks and verifies transactions or agreements independent of the parties to them. This status afforded by blockchain can be called *post-trust*. See for example, R. Herian, *Regulating Blockchain: Critical Perspectives in Law and Technology* (Routledge 2018), 128.

Smart contracts fall into two broad categories that reflect depths of legal character and complicate orderly definitions. First are disclaimers of the functional legality of smart contracts in favour of a status as programming conventions, and second are a spectrum of definitions that take the legality of smart contracts seriously. An example of the former is: 'Although the word 'contract' is used in the DAO's framework code, the term is a programming convention and is not being used as a legal term of art. The term is a programming convention, not a representation that the code is in and of itself a legally binding and enforceable contract'.[3] Ethereum founder Vitalik Buterin, speaking in 2016, maintained that, 'a smart contract is a computer program that directly controls some digital asset', a definition that recalls the causality of algorithms ('if x, then y').[4] Yet, it is a causality unfamiliar to traditions of contract (and property) law and theory, in which the heterogeneity of inter-party negotiations forms the backdrop to contractual processes.[5] Further, some definitions of smart contracts eschew any explicit legal framework at all, for example: 'A piece of EVM [Ethereum Virtual Machine] Code that may be associated with an Account or an Autonomous Object', foregrounding the question of why legal status ought to be attributed to them at all.[6]

The second category of definitions is the product of the principle that disclaimers and non-legal definitions do not dispel the fact that, *as instruments of promise and agreement*, some 'smart contracts' may well produce legal effects. As Sir Geoffrey Vos maintains: 'Smart contracts may be taken to be enforceable legal agreements expressed to a greater or lesser extent in computer code'.[7] Hence, we find a spectrum of definitions that take the legality of smart contracts seriously. For example, as described in blockchain legislation in the Illinois General Assembly: 'a contract stored as an electronic record which is verified by the use of a blockchain'.[8] At first blush, the wording of the Illinois legislation suggests that a smart contract need not be more than a *record* of a contract existing outside of a system or network, which could mean a traditional contract written to and verified by a distributed ledger or blockchain, a hash of a promissory note, or even an agreement written on a napkin

---

[3] 'Decentralized Autonomous Organization (DAO) Framework'. *Slockit/DAO*. <https://github.com/slockit/DAO> accessed 9 July 2021.

[4] V. Buterin, 'Panel 1: Law 2.0 Understanding Smart Contracts'. *Chamber of Digital Commerce* (YouTube, 8 November 2016) <https://www.youtube.com/watch?time_continue=463&v=ZuHZOryZ_f0> accessed 9 July 2021.

[5] A case in point is *incomplete contracts*. Complete contracts are 'contracts where everything that can ever happen is written into the contract. There may be some incentive constraints arising from moral hazard or asymmetric information but there are no unanticipated contingencies. Actual contracts are not like this, as lawyers have realized for a long time. They are poorly worded, ambiguous, and leave out important things. They are incomplete': O. Hart, *Incomplete Contracts and Control* (Nobel Prize Lecture, 8 December 2016), 372–3 <https://www.nobelprize.org/uploads/2018/06/hart-lecture.pdf> accessed 9 July 2021. See also, R.E. Scott and G.G. Triantis, 'Anticipating Litigation in Contract Design' (2006) 115(4) *Yale Law Journal* 814–79.

[6] M. Dameron, *Beigepaper: An Ethereum Technical Specification* (2019) <https://github.com/chronaeon/beigepaper/blob/master/beigepaper.pdf> accessed 9 July 2021.

[7] Sir G. Vos, 'End-to-End Smart Legal Contracts: Moving from Aspiration to Reality', Chapter 1 in this volume.

[8] *Blockchain Technology Act 2020* (Illinois) ('*Blockchain Act*'), s 5.

that is scanned, recorded, and appended and verified on a distributed ledger or blockchain. In these examples, distributed ledgers and blockchains act like legal clerks maintaining databases of contracts, rather than as instruments of a bottom-up redefinition of contract law.

The remedial analysis of smart contracts in this article highlights concerns regarding smart contract legitimacy and validity by arguing that these electronic agreements promote a false sense of 'legal' certainty through persistent execution that cannot account for the need for remedies in contract law and theory. Put another way, '[s]mart contacts do not distinguish intent and even undesired transactions may be effectively impossible to reverse'.[9] This matters because, as Sir Geoffrey Vos maintains: 'What will ultimately be of most significance to those using smart contracts will be the remedies that they can obtain when things go wrong.'[10]

In connection with concerns for remedial legitimacy, the chapter also highlights what I claim to be a *fetishization* by smart contract stakeholders of contractual perfectibility and totality in electronic agreement design, represented here by the image of the 'supertoy'.[11] As a factor operating within turbulent and blunt attempts to 'revolutionize' or 'disrupt' legal principles and processes, the fetishization of smart contracts conceals the superficiality of techno-legal reason. It also devalues the legal status of smart contracts by failing to account for the full extent and complexity of contract law and theory, especially regarding the importance of remedies, and it threatens to create new fronts of uncertainty and dispute in traditional contracting. Fetishization of contracts by designers of (and stakeholders in) smart contracts also risks diminishing contracts as a legal and social institution, reimagining them as software applications, products, and commodities.

B. Prelude: The Persistence of 'Supertoys'

Before looking at the issues surrounding smart contracts in depth, however, it is convenient to return to Spielberg's film *AI* to introduce an overarching jeopardy confronting the law on smart contracts. It is a jeopardy inclusive of problems with the legal status of (wholly or partly) automated ('smart') agreements, and apprehensions surrounding the stability and reliability of these forms of agreement in fact and law—especially regarding uncertainties as to remedies at law and in equity.

---

[9] The World Economic Forum, *Decentralized Finance (DeFi) Policy-Maker Toolkit, White Paper*, June (2021) 13 <https://www.weforum.org/whitepapers/decentralized-finance-defi-policy-maker-toolkit> accessed 9 July 2021.
[10] Vos (n. 7), 6.
[11] There is no single definition of fetishism, this is because it is highly culturally contingent. For present purposes a reasonably general account of fetishism will be applied. Following the fetishistic nature of the 'supertoy', smart contract fetishism—or the smart contract as fetish—implies 'a meaningful and powerful object', the fetish-thing as 'an agent to which henceforth the fetishist is bound out of respect, fear or desire. The thing therefore assumes the power to effect and generate loyalty'—H. Böhme, *Fetishism and Culture: A Different Theory of Modernity* (A. Galt, tr, De Gruyter 2014) 4.

AI centres on David, a lifelike robotic or 'mecha' boy adopted by Monica, his 'mother', as a substitute for her son Martin, whom she presumes dead and in cryogenic storage. When Martin unexpectedly returns to life and comes home, however, the two boys begin a jealous rivalry for the affection of their mother. In the scene in question, Martin goads David into agreeing to cut a lock of Monica's hair while she sleeps, on the condition that Martin will then tell his mother that he truly loves David like a brother (in the expectation that Monica will to love David like her own son). In the quoted dialogue, the two boys make promises, set out obligations, and ultimately forge an agreement—one that David's 'mecha' logic interprets as both complete and fixed despite acknowledging, even if not fully articulating, that there are risks involved and implied moral conditions surrounding the agreement that he ought not contravene.

That David attempts to perform the agreed task, despite protesting to Martin ('I can't Martin, I'm not allowed'), is crucial to understanding the persistent logic that underscores the formation of the boys' agreement. David's performance avoids disfiguring the positivity of the agreement: he has made a promise that he must keep, and his protest registers only as vague and ultimately noncommittal. Martin secures David's promise by enacting his own brute, narrow, and persistent logic. In every sense, David is Martin's conduit, an automated proxy through which Martin can demand, seemingly without limit. Using David in this way allows Martin to avoid human gestures of negotiation or deference towards a counterparty, instead relying on the persistence of the machine to get what he wants.

David is a useful way for Martin to achieve his goal, but only by ensuring that he acts at once within and against his program. David knows it is wrong (unconscionable) for him to act where this violates other rules or agreements previously made ('I'm not allowed') and that sneaking up on his mother brandishing a pair of scissors is a reckless and unreasonable course of action ('I can't, Martin'). Martin, therefore, deliberately strips David's understanding of the arrangement of any context burdened with the inefficiencies of moral messiness.

At no point does Martin offer David the opportunity to unwind or change the agreement, which, given the extent of David's autonomy, one could assume he would use if given the chance. Instead, Martin outlines the conditions of the agreement and David programmatically executes that agreement, thus reaping a series of *ex post facto* consequences for which Monica must devise repercussions and remedies to address not only what she sees as a blatant risk to her that David now represents, but also the uncertainty that David's persistent logic brings to bear on broader aspects of their domestic and familial relationship.

David has an impoverished level of knowledge and understanding of the agreement and its formation, revealed by his unquestioning willingness to perform the agreement irrespective of the costs or benefits. Above all, it highlights a grave inflexibility of persistent logic that is unable (or unwilling) to register the *context* against which David and Martin make their agreement. The problem is not, therefore, a mere uncertainty that David comes to represent, it is an *excessive certainty* that creates both concern for Monica and drives her subsequent need to apply harsh measures she hopes will contain David's behaviour.

David is not human, so by definition the certainty he generates is alien. Yet, this cannot detract from the fact that his actions have consequences in human reality; ultimately, David's excess of certainty leads his parents to doubt and distrust him, because they are no longer capable of recognizing the fallibility one finds in the character, promises, or actions of a 'real' child.

1. Smart contracts as techno-legal supertoys

Like David, a smart contract is a progeny whose parents—in this case, traditional contract law and theory—must confront the radical unknowability of their offspring. This begins with questions of whether smart contracts fit the longstanding common law tradition of 'contract' at all, including regarding remedies and established modes of contractual conduct. The alternative is to treat smart contracts as lesser, informal agreements with little or no formal legal status. This is because smart contracts arguably privilege performance and notions of perfectibility that are antithetical to the porosity of traditional contracts.

What smart contract design needs to understand is that, if human interests remain the central feature of contract, there will always remain divergences of interests, failures of minds to meet, and the likelihood of dispute overshadowing the process of contract formation. Neither smart contracts nor the distributed ledgers or blockchains that support their use will easily solve these issues, if at all. An important question is, therefore, whether machines can devise and perform peer-to-peer agreements and prevent disputes between human actors that follow in the wake of such agreements or arise during contract performance.

Underpinning this problem is the question whether a cure for the ills of smart contracts is as understandable and necessary as for any form of agreement. Remedies obtained through litigation, mediation, or arbitration would mean lawful dispute resolution and enforcement, giving legitimacy to smart contracting as a legal process *in toto*.

In some evaluations, we see ethics and morality as unnecessary conditions or considerations because of the commercial artificiality of the parties who may use electronic agreements (eg, corporate actors) and see utility or welfare maximization as the goal instead. Dismissing ethical frameworks as a guide to smart contract morality is not a good idea, however, primarily because we need to apply constraints on the persistence of automation, which laws and regulations alone cannot do.[12] The moral pause is something Martin resists in favour of utility

---

[12] For arguments on the division between morality and welfare maximization in commercial contracts see A. Schwartz and R.E. Scott, 'Contract Theory and the Limits of Contract Law' *John M Olin*

precisely *because* his aim is to discredit David as a moral subject. Martin knows David is a machine, not an actual boy with moral probity, and uses this to his advantage despite David's moral effects (the effects his behaviour has) on the world in which he lives.

C. Smart, but not Intelligent, Contracts

[W]hile premodern forms and institutions of magic, myth and cult, religion and festivities begin to disappear in the modern era, the energies and needs bound up within them do not. Instead they are released and now pervade all levels of modern social systems.[13]

Unlike David, (artificial) intelligence does not describe smart contracts or how they operate in many present use cases. But, I argue, smart contracts appear akin to science-fiction writer Brian Aldiss' conception of 'supertoys' because they provide a 'way to link computer-circuitry with synthetic [legal] flesh'.[14] Designers can make smart contracts *appear* at once intelligent and legally legitimate although they are, in substance, neither. They do, as Mireille Hilderbrandt might suggest, apply mechanical and logical rules without leaving room for the contestability of facts and norms.[15] J.G. Allen echoes this analysis, claiming that 'many of the software processes currently hailed as 'smart contracts' are indeed more accurately described as performance mechanisms'.[16] It is also on this basis that I refer to the fetishization of smart contracts or, perhaps more accurately, fetishization of the legal legitimacy and certainty smart contracts appear to provide or facilitate.

David's persistence in performing his promised obligation is, however, a recognizable and pronounced feature of smart contracts to 'algorithmically specify and autonomously enforce rules of interaction'.[17] Once set in motion, a smart contract runs until the task designed for it is complete and thus 'fully performed' according to its program.[18] But a lack of 'intelligence'—in particular the facility of adjusting

Center for Studies in Law, Economics, and Public Policy Working Papers. Paper 275 (2003) <http://digitalcommons.law.yale.edu/lepp_papers/275> accessed 28 March 2019.

[13] Böhme (n. 10), 8.
[14] Aldiss (n. 1), 4.
[15] M. Hildebrandt, 'Data-Driven Prediction of Judgment. Law's New Mode of Existence?' (2019) *OUP Collected Courses Volume EUI Summer-school* 25 <https://ssrn.com/abstract=3548504> accessed 9 July 2021.
[16] J.G. Allen, 'Wrapped and Stacked: "Smart Contracts" and the Interaction of Natural and Formal Language' (2018) 14(4) *European Review of Contract Law* 320.
[17] G. Wood, *Ethereum: A Secure Decentralised Generalised Transaction Ledger Byzantium Version 69351d5-2018-12-10* (2018) 16 <https://ethereum.github.io/yellowpaper/paper.pdf> accessed 9 July 2021.
[18] It has been suggested that smart contracts could run forever due to a problem in computer science known as the 'halting problem', which is rooted in the notion that 'no algorithm that can look at a

or testing the program to deal with contingencies—makes smart contracts blunt tools rather than sophisticated legal instruments for transacting value and data. The duality of smart contracts as 'tools' and 'instruments' is crucial for understanding their legal significance, although there is no neat binary distinction. I will return this duality, and its relative messiness, again throughout the chapter.

A lack of contingent intelligence has led to a reliance on 'data feeds' or 'oracles', third party aggregators that supply smart contracts with necessary data and information (eg, data from a meteorological station), to connect them to the 'real world' and enable effective operation. There is a prominent 'oracle problem' that foreshadows the development of smart contracts; not least, as Ethereum founder Gavin Wood points out, that the 'accuracy and timeliness of this information is not guaranteed and it is the task of a secondary contract author—the contract that utilizes the data feed—to determine how much trust can be placed in any single data feed'.[19] Analysis of the differences between electronic (and automated) contracts as 'smart' or 'intelligent' is also a means of understanding the duality between smart contracts as tools *versus* instruments, and a good example of why we cannot consider the duality a neat distinction.

1. Emerging definitions of 'smart contracts'

To understand the place smart contracts might hold within the common law tradition of contract in the coming years, it is necessary to build on the definition discussed so far by comparing and contrasting traditional contracts with smart contracts. We begin with some recent examples of the legal definition of smart contracts and their characteristics.

The Wyoming State legislature, in a draft Bill on digital assets, adopts an approach to definition that appears to apply legal parameters to Buterin's definition:

> 'Smart contract' means an automated transaction [...] or any substantially similar analogue, which is comprised of code, script or programming language that executes the terms of an agreement, and which may include taking custody of and transferring an asset, or issuing executable instructions for these actions, based on the occurrence or nonoccurrence of specified conditions.[20]

---

program's source code and always correctly determine if it will run forever or not'. In order to limit the operation of smart contracts Ethereum rely on a mechanism known as 'gas', which applies a cost to each instruction thereby incentivizing contract design with in-built limitation. 'You can think of Ethereum like flying on an ultra-discount airline: you pay to get on board and you pay extra for everything you do from there' (Arvind Narayanan *et al.*, *Bitcoin and Cryptocurrency Technologies*. Draft (Pre-Print) 9 February (2016) 288); see also, Wood (n. 15).

[19] Wood (n. 15), 15.
[20] *Senate File No SF0125—Digital assets-existing law* <https://www.wyoleg.gov/Legislation/2019/SF0125> accessed 9 July 2021.

Similarly, the wording applied by the Arizona State Legislature takes a rigorous techno-legal approach:

> 'Smart contract' means an event-driven program, with state, that runs on a distributed, decentralized, shared and replicated ledger and that can take custody over and instruct transfer of assets on that ledger.[21]

Thought leadership from the law firm Norton Rose Fulbright (with cryptologist Ian Grigg) adds important legal qualifications:

> Smart contracts will often be used to document bilateral obligations between a [u]ser and a [c]ounterparty. Smart contracts inherently deal with issues of evidence and intention that are behind some formality requirements—but, until legal systems add rules dealing specifically with smart contracts, these formalities will still need to be satisfied.[22]

Initial conceptualizations of smart contracts maintained that the two variations, smart and traditional, would not perform the same tasks and, therefore, achieve the same legal outcomes.[23] This raises two fundamental issues. First, if smart contracts are not challenging, or are incapable of challenging traditional contract law and theory, then what is the point of them? Second, smart contracts may be little more than a niche intervention that will improve cost effectiveness and efficiency in a limited array of contractual scenarios. Massimiliano Granieri claims that the impact of technology on contracting (and contract law) has been interpreted 'mainly in terms of transaction costs reduction, since technology is instrumental to form agreements in a more expeditious way, regardless of the distance between contractors'; in this respect 'the advent of technology in contract law has too often and too simplistically been considered the same as e-commerce.'[24]

A further tension of importance to smart contract design is between bargained contracts and standard form contracts, otherwise known as 'boilerplate'. Smart contracts, in the immature form we find them, are more like boilerplate than complex varieties of contract that rely more on contingent flexibility. But smart contracts as boilerplate inherit and risk the proliferation of a range of issues that surround such supra-defined agreements. Margaret Jane Radin points to a fundamental

---

[21] Title 44—Trade and Commerce, Chapter 26: Electronic Transactions, Article 5, 44-7061. *Arizona Revised Statutes*. <https://www.azleg.gov/arsDetail/?title=44> accessed 9 July 2021.

[22] A. Sanitt and I. Grigg, Legal analysis of the governed blockchain. *Norton Rose Fulbright* (2018) <http://www.nortonrosefulbright.com/knowledge/publications/167968/legal-analysis-of-the-governed-blockchain> accessed 9 July 2021.

[23] N. Szabo, 'Formalizing and Securing Relationships on Public Networks' (1997) 2(9) *First Monday* (September 1997) <https://firstmonday.org/ojs/index.php/fm/article/view/548/469-publisher=First> accessed 9 July 2021.

[24] M. Granieri, 'Technological Contracts' in P.G. Monateri (ed), *Comparative Contract Law* (Edward Elgar Publishing Ltd 2017) 408.

consumer concern with boilerplate which, I suggest, could equally describe smart contracts (not least because the context in which boilerplate agreements are most pervasive is online or in peer-to-peer digital networks):

> [M]any of the interactions that are called 'contracts' these days are very far from the traditional notion of contract, the idea of bargained exchange by free choice, that still holds sway in our imaginations. Contract reality belies contract theory in many situations where consumers receive paperwork that purports to alter their legal rights. In these situations, contract theory becomes contract mythology.[25]

We can describe conventional contracts as agreements creating obligations enforceable by law,[26] or as the law 'based on liability for breach of promise'.[27] These definitions show that contracting does not involve only the creation and performance of promises and obligations, but also the need for *remedies* if interparty expectations based on those promises need enforcement. As suggested earlier, enforcement can imply a moral duty under state-sanctioned principles of contract, especially where it is socially desirable for contractual promises to maintain a moral character. But utility or welfare maximization also applies and changes the complexion of enforcement from one of moral duty to other means of ensuring performance, for example, the desire of contracting parties to maintain an excellent reputation in business.[28]

As Atiyah concludes, 'it is not very meaningful to say that a promise is binding unless some further explanation is given of what sort of remedy is offered for its breach'.[29] Breach of contract is a vital sign of healthy contract law, not an inconvenience to be 'programmed out' of agreements. Breach shows that a 'definition of contracts in terms of sets of promises does not give full force to the interrelationship of the obligations of the parties which exists in many contracts', an interrelationship which we see particularly in the remedy's availability for substantial failure in performance, by which an injured party may end his own obligations because of the failure of the other party to perform his side of the bargain.[30]

Contracts are best classified in and by their context, with two broad taxonomies being consumer and commercial contracts, both of which we can further subdivide depending on purpose, application, mode of regulation, and so on. There has long

---

[25] M.J. Radin, *Boilerplate: The Fine Print, Vanishing Rights, and the Rule of Law* (Princeton University Press 2014) 12.
[26] The definition echoes that set out in the Proposed Regulation on a Common European Sales Law, which defines 'contract' as 'an agreement intended to give rise to obligations or other legal effects': see H. Beale (ed), *Chitty on Contracts* (33rd edn, Sweet & Maxwell 2018) 1-025.
[27] H.G. Beale, W.D. Bishop, and M.P. Furmston, *Contract Cases and Materials* (5th edn, Oxford University Press 2008) 3.
[28] Schwartz and Scott (n. 11), 17–19.
[29] P.S. Atiyah, *The Rise and Fall of Freedom of Contract* (Oxford University Press 1985) 653.
[30] Beale (n. 24), 1-020.

been a tension between consumer protectionism and the forces of market individualism, especially in English contract law, which has helped to shape modern contracting practices within capitalism in terms that support both consumer and commercial interests and demands.[31]

It would be wrong, therefore, to think technology will ease longstanding tensions. Emerging as they do from a blockchain ecosystem built around the premise of enhancing individual and corporate economic and market engagement, smart contracts are more likely to amplify market individualism and exacerbate tensions in play. This likelihood becomes more apparent when considering how smart contracts fit around determinations of static and dynamic market individualism, where the former maintains 'the principal function of contract law as being to establish a clear set of ground rules within which a market can operate'; and the latter, 'a more flexible approach, guided by the practices and expectations of the contracting community (particularly the commercial community)'.[32]

Flexibility is not a strong attribute of smart contracts, although this is being addressed in a variety of ways in smart contract design. The relevance to smart contracts of the flexibility inherent in dynamic market individualism comes from the onus on market agility demanded by commercial actors. Coupled with the market-supporting principles of static market individualism coded into smart contracts, the ability of commercial (or private) market actors to process transactions at speed and with greater efficiency than traditional contracting potentially makes smart contracts an attractive option for securing future agreements.

2. The rhetoric of efficiency

Efficiency is a key definitional marker of electronic agreements. It describes a shift in technological function that continues to leave human capabilities in its wake. It also describes ideological determinations of socioeconomic primacy that consider a moral society beginning with well-organized, systematic information management. We can define and interpret efficiency, therefore, in a variety of ways. However, efficiency makes its most obvious and impactful claims based on the brute capabilities of the 'electronic' or 'automated' surpass human cognitive capacity and agility. In a 1995 article on the interrelationship between cognition and contract, Melvin Aron Eisenberg described how flawed contracts were really a matter of human cognitive deficiency ('rational ignorance') albeit flaws accepted as the norm because most actors did not want to spend significant amounts of energy or money on perfecting contracts:[33] 'Our abilities to process information and solve

---

[31] See eg, M. Furmston (ed), *The Law of Contract* (6th edn, LexisNexis 2017) 1.105.
[32] Furmston (n. 30), 1.108 and 1.109.
[33] M.A. Eisenberg, 'The Limits of Cognition and the Limits of Contract' (1995) 47 *Stanford Law Review* 214.

problems are constrained by limitations of computational ability, ability to calculate consequences, ability to organize and utilize memory, and the like', claimed Eisenberg, 'hence, actors will often process imperfectly even the information they do acquire. Such imperfections in human processing ability increase as decisions become more complex and involve more permutations.'[34]

A presumed efficiency gain, therefore, lives in the ability of smart contracts (and other types of electronic agreement) to solve the deficiencies Eisenberg highlights—thus drawing nearer to a perfect form of contract. Unfortunately, definitions of the perfection smart contracts ostensibly represent is within limits that do not extend anywhere near the complexity of contract law. Smart contracts represent a very limited statement on efficiency; they are good at what they do, and can undoubtedly surpass human cognition on the range of tasks and objectives set for them, but what they do is far too simple in comparison to the demands of contract law.

Where efficiency arguments regarding smart contracts develop further, however, is in the ability for the agreements to be self-enforcing, in the sense of including arbitration and litigation clauses in the contract's function, thus saving time and money on classic litigation issues of, for example, truth-finding and disclosure.[35]

D. Legally Weak?

'Whether a particular right can be called a remedy', claims Peter Birks, 'depends entirely on whether its relation to its causative event triggers the metaphor of cure.'[36] Given that smart contract performance is all but guaranteed, and that breach (at least in terms of a failure to perform) is improbable, there are two remedial areas of relevance—both of which refer to performance expectation and returning a claimant to a position they were in before the contract.

These are, first, *expectation damages* awarded as compensation to cover poor quality goods; and second (importantly, given the proliferation of smart contracts designed to transact and transfer value rather than goods) restitution to recover overpaid sums (*unjust enrichments*). If we are to treat smart contracts like other ('legal') contracts, then focusing on the most appropriate and effective remedy for disputes must remain a priority. Equity or restitution are key because smart contracts programmed to transfer money (or other value) will unquestioningly do so; the co-identification of funds and proprietary rights, and the recovery of value in whatever form that prevails will be a priority for claimants

---

[34] Eisenberg (n. 31), 214.
[35] For an analysis of efficiency gains in contract design, see Scott and Triantis (n. 5).
[36] P. Birks, *Unjust Enrichment* (2nd edn, Oxford University Press 2005) 165.

over mere damages or compensation (be it fiat currency, cryptocurrency, or other 'tokens').

In this regard, the notable feature of the early cryptoasset case *AA v Persons Unknown*[37] was the claimants' preference for proprietary rights overcompensation. Smart contracts could, therefore, herald a turn to equitable remedies or, perhaps, a rise in restitution as the most effective response to electronic and machine-enabled transactions that do not fulfil the intentions of the parties. This pairing of an electronic instrument with a contractual remedy to form a legally robust 'smart contract' echoes, once again, the 'supertoys' analogy as smart contracts arguably assume the appearance of contractual legitimacy wrapped in legal flesh.[38]

1. Smart contract ideals and contingent reality

Considering the 'ideal' smart contract as impervious to the vagaries of classical agreement-making may help assuage counterparty concerns over the risks of performance, but is it an accurate portrayal? I suggest not, because they defeat neither the latent problems in traditional agreement-making, nor risks concerning performance. Instead, like the naivety of David and Martin in *AI*, smart contracts are gross oversimplifications that belie the complexities and the nuances of classical contract law and theory—including the actuality, and even necessity, of incompleteness, and the place of orality in agreement-making and contract formation.[39]

Perhaps above all, it is the far-reaching insistence and adaptability of a variety of remedies available to parties when agreements fail that makes contracting more that the mere 'execution' of a transaction.[40] The threat of errors and bugs in smart contract design makes it prudent to keep them as basic agreements, but this means that they will continue to be incapable of reflecting the depth and variety of contract law and theory.[41] It is absurd and untrue to say that traditional contract drafting does not suffer from errors—that is precisely why remedies play such a vital role in the overall landscape of contract law.

---

[37] *AA v Persons Unknown* [2019] EWHC 3556 (Comm).

[38] The notion of smart contracts as mere 'instruments' is crucial because it refers to the mode of *recording* a contract rather than the *contract as such*. If smart contracts are little more than instruments, then their legitimacy as a means for the transaction of value or rights diminishes significantly.

[39] For instance, it is not immediately apparent if or how something as basic as the translation of express terms in oral agreements and reasonable intentions of the parties feature in smart contracts. In the broader case of electronic contracts, attempts have already been made to ensure that oral preconditions in contract formation can survive technological change in the form of non-oral modification clauses (NOM). The validity of such clauses has recently been affirmed in the UK by the Supreme Court in *Rock Advertising Limited v MWB Business Exchange Centres Limited* [2018] UKSC 24.

[40] See eg, R. Herian, 'Smart Contracts: A Remedial Analysis' (2021) 30(1) *Information & Communications Technology Law* 17–34.

[41] The Consensys Github page dealing with Ethereum smart contract best practice suggests that designers keep contracts simple because 'complexity increases the likelihood of errors' <https://consensys.github.io/smart-contract-best-practices/general_philosophy/>.

We can view many features of contract law as 'problems' to be 'solved'—those symptomatic of inefficiencies that electronic and smart interventions 'disrupt'—but contract law and theory are not just gratuitously complex. Rather, their complexity has evolved to reflect the heterogeneity and complexity of socioeconomic interactions and transactions in a wide variety of interpersonal and commercial environments. Contracting is an indelibly *human* gesture, and thus subject to the caprices of human conduct and endeavour. If contracts are to cease being so, by their autonomous, smart reconceptualization, then it is arguably human interest and interference that must retreat to make contracts smart. And yet, as Sol Yurick said of the broader march of the Information Age, this endeavour implies 'a perhaps fictional notion; that the universe and everything in it, is logico-mathematical', and that 'all things and forces in the universe [can] be treated as a cryptogram, a code, a text that [can] be *read*, sooner or later'.[42] The pause in time that law and legal processes foster ensures (or ought to ensure) thorough consideration of the value and nature of agreements. To paraphrase Yurick, this is a commendable value in, and benefit of, the law, which insists on a messy, base-level of humanity that confounds the notion of a purely logico-mathematical universe.

2. The immature disruptive potential of smart contracts

Contemporary computing undertakes mundane bureaucratic processes and achieves transactional speeds far greater than those that human operatives could ever hope to achieve. Perhaps it is only when impressive speed—and the desired efficiency that accompanies—it ceases to serve human interest, however, that we can begin, seriously, to talk of technological 'disruption'. On this account, smart contracts are an immature example of 'disruption', where the notion of disruption as a marker of radical or meaningful progress is highly contestable within the present socioeconomic milieu.[43]

Of course, the technology may be a catalyst for significant change in economies and societies by enabling the uncoupling of human actors (and their interventions and interests) from some or all socioeconomic duties and responsibilities. This is a vision of alienation *par excellence*, but arguably one in which the growing distance between humanity and its productive machines might stabilize and comfort society, rather than provide a basis for socioeconomic or political evisceration.[44]

---

[42] S. Yurick, *Metatron* (Semiotext(e), 1985) 26–7.
[43] See eg, Herian (n. 2).
[44] A similar notion has been elaborately expressed by Yanis Varoufakis, former Greek finance minister, in his discussion of a future based on a vision of *Star Trek* (utopian) or *The Matrix* (dystopian): 'Star Trek is this: we're all sitting around having philosophical conversations like in the ancient Agora in Athens and the slaves are not human. There are holes in the walls on the Starship Enterprise; you ask for something and it comes up. Fantastic. So then you can explore the universe and talk to Klingons. That's one choice—the utopia. The dystopia is The Matrix, where the machines are being fed by our own energy. We are plugged into a false consciousness that the machines have been created to keep us happy.

This post-industrial utopia is not exactly where we are heading with any certainty, however. As if to highlight this, it is abundantly clear that smart contracts (like many 'smart' ideals) have bugs that pose what Werbach and Cornell suggest is a 'significant limitation in replacing human enforcement of agreements with software running on the blockchain'; things, they rightly say, 'simply do not always go according to plan'.[45] The opportunity to change or stop electronic agreements that cease to reflect the consent or reasonable expectations ('good faith') of the parties seems more important than ever. And remedial orders such as rescission, which enable the unwinding of agreements, seem like common sense—not an inefficient burden on today's socioeconomic condition.[46]

Ordinarily, it is wrong to view contracts as immutable (complete and fixed), especially regarding one of the most significant consequences of rescission, that of treating the contract as though it never came into existence.[47] There is arguably good cause, therefore, for this precise principle to remain in place in a world of poorly designed, ill programmed, or bug-ridden smart contracts. As such, smart contract designers should accommodate the need for erasure or, at the very least, a capability to overwrite. To grasp the relevance of remedies in a world of smart contracts, it is necessary to examine some key characteristics that plague the case for smart contracts as legally binding and enforceable. The legal weaknesses in smart contract design and implementation that make remedies not just an inconvenient necessity, but an inevitability.

3. Contract law remedies and risk-allocation

As an institution, contract law enables parties to distribute and allocate risk. Key to achieving both ends is not a slavish adherence to formalism but, on the contrary, the need for flexibility inherent in the contractual form and process that reflects contingencies and the common-sense notion that things do not always go according to plan.[48] Flexibility is woven through the fabric of contractual principles,

---

We think we are leading a perfectly normal life, but all along we are the slaves of the machines. So these are the two extremes. And the choice whether we go to Star Trek or The Matrix is ours. It's a political choice.' B. Eno and Y. Varoufakis, 'Brian Eno meets Yanis Varoufakis: "Economists are more Showbiz than Pop Stars now"' *The Guardian* (online, 28 November 2015) <https://www.theguardian.com/lifeandstyle/2015/nov/28/conversation-brian-eno-yanis-varoufakis-interview)> accessed 9 July 2021.

[45] K. Werbach and N. Cornell, 'Contracts Ex Machina' (2017) 67 *Duke Law Journal* 313, 365.
[46] Cardozo J in his judgement in the New York Court of Appeals in *Beatty v Guggenheim Exploration Co* (1919) 225 NY 380 maintained: 'Those who make a contract, may unmake it. The clause which forbids a change, may be changed like any other. The prohibition of oral waiver, may itself be waived. Every such agreement is ended by the new one which contradicts it'.
[47] As per Lord Wilberforce in *Johnson v Agnew* [1980] AC 367.
[48] In English law, contract is not necessarily the best mechanism through which to exercise this flexibility. Constructive trusts, for example, are more flexible still. Yet law's development of additional flexibility via trusts does not discount the flexibility that can be found and is utilized in contract.

doctrines and theories to serve the expansion of domestic and international markets and commercial enterprises; it assumes a variety of forms that aim, paradoxically, to provide certainty, stability, and predictability.[49]

These stable flexible principles include the ability to change a contract (rectification), or unwind an agreement made, for example, under duress or because of an unconscionable bargain (rescission); both of which, ultimately, put parties back in a position they would have been but for the agreement or if they did not perform the agreement as intended (restitution). As previously suggested, restitution is vital to the suite of remedies for breach of contract, and there is every chance that parties in a future of smart contracts will demand more, not less, restitution because failure to perform no longer represents the same level of risk or threat it otherwise does in conventional agreements.

Accompanying many remedies relating to the breach of contract are damages and costs for litigation. In contrast, the equitable remedy of specific performance enables enforcement of an agreement for which money (damages or compensation) does not suffice. To undermine or dismiss remedies rooted in performance seems academic in a world of smart contracts, because the one thing smart contracts almost *always* guarantee is performance. Yet the mere fact of their insistence on performance does not mean smart contracts 'solve' the 'problem' of a suitable remedy for situations in which monetary compensation is not suitable or desirable. Equity, as Sarah Worthington points out, developed specific performance (and injunctions) because the monolithic approach of the common law to contracts became inappropriate and 'ignored the relativities that society attached to different contractual rights'.[50] Smart contracts do not change this, but if allowed to side-step performance-based remedies in equity and remedies at common law alike, they could threaten to undermine contractual rights further.

Much of the work smart contracts do concerns transactions for value relating to currencies and tokens ('fiat' and 'crypto'). The next logical step therefore would appear to be processes built into smart contracts or affiliated with smart contract activity (ie, blockchains supporting the smart contract), triggered if parties require a remedy for compensation or damages. Where parties lose value, or one party is unjustly enriched, automated payback of value would be a proportionate response. The transaction and trade of financial products such as bonds and securities thus offer obvious and potentially profitable domains for smart contracts.

Less clear, however, is the use of smart contracts in contractual domains where enforcement of performance is preferable to compensation for breach—service contracts for instance. Tokenization, as a species of value or representation of right

---

[49] See eg, Atiyah (n. 27), 402–3.
[50] S. Worthington, *Equity* (2nd edn, Oxford University Press 2006) 25.

(eg, property right) relating to blockchain use including smart contracts, differs from transactional modes that are not exactly 'financial' but does not address (or fully address) contracts for which performance is key.

Monitoring the performance of smart contracts, especially where agreements may not occur only online or within a network or system, is a significant obstacle to implementing smart contracts in services. This problem brings us back to the so-called 'oracle problem', but it also relates to existing challenges in contract performance monitoring that gave rise in English law to Civil Procedure Rules concerning so-called 'disobedient parties'.[51] As monitoring the performance of a service contract increases—consider a contract for the construction of a house, for instance—the level and sophistication of data collection required to satisfy the remedy, enforce the right, and discharge the contract increases. It is possible because surveillance technologies already exist that can undertake monitoring of this sort. But inevitably this will stretch smart contract design capabilities and thus potentially exacerbate points of weakness already within the smart contract design processes.

4. The broader social function of 'contract'

Mistakes, as they say, happen. But in contract law, mistakes assume significance regarding contract frustration.[52] Courts aim to uphold contracts when and where possible, but this is not always desirable on the facts. Such processes show that contract is flexible, contingent, and—perhaps above all else—reflects the inherent messiness of human enterprise that leads, all too often, to mistakes and frustration of agreements. This, for some technologists, may be reason enough to find a 'solution' to the 'problem' of traditional contract law. But it is incumbent on smart contract designers to remember that contracts do not only exist in an immature state, like vending machines. Nor is it desirable to 'fix' the apparent problem if doing so jeopardizes the balance between the express and consensual execution of rules-based agreements, on the one hand, and the moral obligation of promise and performance, on the other—both of which are central tenets of legally binding agreements.[53] Put another way, contract is a legal norm that has successfully underwritten and influenced many social structures far beyond

---

[51] *Part 70—General Rules about Enforcement of Judgments and Orders* <https://www.justice.gov.uk/courts/procedure-rules/civil/rules/part70> accessed 9 July 2021.

[52] See eg, *Great Peace Shipping Ltd v Tsavliris, The Great Peace* [2002] 4 All ER 689.

[53] This points to the laws of equity and restitution, especially within Anglo-American common law jurisdictions, both of which work in and around the law of contract to ensure, *inter alia*, that a fair and reasonable balance is maintained between the bargaining powers of parties and that grounds for unjust enrichment or unconscionable bargaining are mitigated.

the abundance of today's commercial transactions. The question of how 'post-trust' electronic agreements might influence social relations more widely is one to take seriously, therefore, and it is important to note the impact of greater levels of inflexibility, demanded in the name of efficiency, on heterogeneous environments.

To address this issue, it is necessary to explore ways in which smart contracts could or, perhaps, need to be more flexible. Ongoing initiatives, for example the Ethereum 'ERC1538: Transparent Contract Standard' addresses the general inflexibility of smart contracts and seeks to create conditions whereby variations in contract terms ('functions') are possible.[54] Addressing the vexed issue of smart contract immutability *qua* flexibility is vital if they are to better align with traditional contract law.[55] But it is also clear that smart contracts lose something if they shed their fundamental and desirable immutability—namely the ability for parties or individuals to execute contracts without having to trust one another. As the author of the standard maintains:

> Immutable, trustless contracts cannot be improved, resulting in increasingly inferior contracts over time. Contract standards evolve, new ones come out. People, groups and organizations learn over time what people want and what is better and what should be built next. Contracts that cannot be improved not only hold back the authors that create them, but everybody who uses them. In some cases immutable, trustless contracts are the right fit. This is the case when a contract is only needed for a short time or it is known ahead of time that there will never be any reason to change or improve it.[56]

5. Smart contracts and legal language

From the point of view of legal services, but also wider business interests, the legitimacy and scalability of smart contacts turns on the matter of *contractual language*. Consider the relative legibility and accessibility of natural language contracts

---

[54] N. Mudge, *ERC1538: Transparent Contract Standard #1538* (31 October 2018) <https://github.com/ethereum/EIPs/issues/1538> accessed 9 July 2021. The standard addresses the following technical issues: (i) a way to add, replace and remove multiple functions of a contract atomically (at the same time); (ii) standard events to show what functions are added, replaced, and removed from a contract, and why the changes are made; (iii) a standard way to query a contract to discover and retrieve information about all functions exposed by it; (iv) solves the 24KB maximum contract size limitation, making the maximum contract size of a transparent contract practically unlimited. This standard makes the worry about contract size a thing of the past; and (v) enables an upgradeable contract to become immutable in the future if desired.

[55] J.M. Sklaroff, 'Smart Contracts and the Cost of Inflexibility' (2016) 166 *University of Pennsylvania Law Review* 263.

[56] Mudge (n. 50).

(English as a common standard for international trade and consumer contracts, for example), compared with the computer language or code of smart contracts. Under s 7 of the Unfair Terms in Consumer Contracts Regulations 1999 (SI 1999, No 2083), for example, written contracts must be expressed in plain, intelligible language, and 'coded' smart contracts do not meet this requirement.[57]

Recall the Illinois General Assembly's definition of smart contracts: 'a contract stored as an electronic record which is verified by the use of a blockchain'.[58] In this example, it is entirely possible for a traditional, natural language contract to form the basis of the electronic record, as, for example, a scanned hard-copy (paper) contract or PDF. This does not disturb the need for natural language, and retrieval and interpretation of the contract could remain a familiar task to the lawyer or paralegal. Compare this to Vitalik Buterin's definition: 'a smart contract is a computer program that directly controls some digital asset'.[59] Here, no documentary form of a contract exists beyond the electronic code and environment created for its execution, and there is no sign of the use of natural language capable of being easily read or interpreted by the contractual parties—unless those parties are familiar with 'reading' code. It embeds the smart contract in the property conveyed or formed at the moment of transaction, and 'written' in code is, perhaps, only communicated to another machine.

Yet, while embeddedness and invisibility may cause problems regarding contract legibility and intelligibility for the parties subject to it, smart contracts appear to satisfy a key feature of traditional contract formation, the establishment of an enforceable *pre-written* promise.[60] Usually, promises are binding if made orally or reflected by conduct that evidences the promise or intentions of the parties to form a contract. With smart contracts as defined by Buterin, however, a promise (or even an effective agreement) exists (latently) *in the property that is the subject matter of the transaction*, and the promise exists not unlike implied terms or clauses in traditional contracts.[61] Instead of *ex post* adjudication to interpret and expressly define an implied term, a smart contract executes because the agreement is always *already* valid.

---

[57] Also, Directive 93/13/EEC on unfair terms in consumer contracts [1993] OJ, L95/29.
[58] *Blockchain Act* (n. 8).
[59] Buterin (n. 4).
[60] In the common law context, it is especially important that this aspect of smart contracts is tested with regard to a variety of remedial actions, notably resulting and constructive trusts and estoppel. Resulting and constructive trusts, for example, have proven to be important safeguards in cases where a contract was obtained by fraudulent misrepresentation (*Lonrho plc v Fayed (No 2)* [1992] 1 WLR 1; *El Ajou v Dollar Land Holdings plc* [1993] 2 All ER 717).
[61] Implied terms are distinguished from express terms. Express terms are 'actually recorded in a written contract or openly expressed at the time the contract is made. But there are cases in which the law implies a term in a contract although it is not expressly included therein by the parties. An implied term may be a condition, a warranty or an intermediate (innominate) term': Beale (n. 24), 14-001.

6. Smart contracts and good faith

The pre-written stage in contract formation raises one final important question: the ability of smart contracts to mirror good faith principles and the reasonable expectations of parties. As a script, a smart contract is a documentary form that can *evidence an agreement*, even if not precisely the formation of a contract as defined at law. The matter of oral agreements (promises made) as binding based on evidence of the consensual intention of the parties is a long-settled and general rule applicable to most types of property. How can smart contracts ensure this rule remains in place, including associated considerations of good faith?[62] If the answer is that we can 'code' oral agreements or good faith into smart contracts, for example by using a lawyer or notary trained in smart contract design and formation, can we consider this an improvement upon existing practices or a mere reinvention of them? There is also a tension that arises between good faith principles, as a standard for fair dealing within contractual contexts, and the promise of smart contracts (and blockchains) to foster 'trustless' or 'post-trust' transacting regimes. If smart contracts negate good faith by design, this places a burden on smart contracts to maintain conditions in which good faith is no longer necessary.

Implicit in this discussion is the notion that smart contracts can or will radically alter legal conduct in ways that continue to reflect good faith, even in the absence of that principle. For smart contracts to achieve this, or many of the key points covered above concerning forms and processes of flexibility and language, design beyond what we are currently seeing is required. Whether aligning smart contracts with traditional contract law is a project that will come to be seen as desirable (or necessary) by technologists remains uncertain. It may be a step too far on a cost-benefit analyses, with the preference remaining instead on basic, vending machine-style transactions that carry less risk and lower maintenance costs. Committing to the project of aligning smart contracts with traditional contract law means ensuring the weaknesses of smart contracts do not unreasonably impact or infect contract law. Equally, however, smart contracts should not exacerbate the flaws and imperfections of traditional contract law.

E. Conclusion

Peer-to-peer service, property and financial agreements and arrangements, modes of exchange, transaction and conveyance are all the subject to re-evaluation in light of current developments in the field of smart contracts. In this chapter, I have

---

[62] For example, in England and Wales, s 53 *Law of Property Act 1925* stipulates that written agreements must be used to create or dispose of an interest in land; to declare a trust of land; or in dispositions of equitable interest under a trust.

argued that, contrary to the notion of smart contracts 'disrupting' existing contract law and theory, smart contracts' legal legitimacy turns upon satisfying a high level of interoperability with the processes and procedures of verification defined by traditional contract law and theory. As Beale *et al.* explain, 'contract law' is used to mean the whole collection of rules which apply to contracts, and these may include many rules that are not 'contractual' in the sense of being based on a promise to do something.[63] This forms part of the brief that smart contracts must meet if they are to be legitimate and legally recognized; while the dynamic nature of contract means it is 'always developing and sometimes changing rapidly as new problems confront the courts and legislature', a full transition to smart contracts, if it occurs, is unlikely to sweep away all the vestiges of traditional contract law.[64] As the UK Jurisdiction Taskforce *Legal Statement on cryptoassets and smart contracts* succinctly put it: 'In no circumstances are there simply no legal rules which apply.'[65]

Definitions rooted in the fundamentals of contractual form and purpose present, therefore, a clear divergence between law and the visions of technologists—not least when technologists insist that the ongoing project of 'disruption' involving blockchain and its associated technologies (eg, smart contracts) has, once and for all, reinvented the proverbial wheel. While smart contracts are problematic as contracts *per se*, the problems they pose are not all that new for the law. Yet the threat of divergence is important for entrepreneurs and technologists keen to 'leverage' perceived failures in law's ability to keep pace with innovation. Rather, smart contracts represent an evolution in electronic instruments that have revealed to the legal imagination that, while it is necessary to engage with and understand the novelties different mediums present (ie, the Internet or analogous distributed networks), centuries of social experience and intellectual rigour that have made contract law and theory what it is today is not easily 'disrupted' nor upended.

As Robert A. Hillman and Jeffrey J. Rachlinski concluded in their assessment of electronic agreements during the first major period of e-commerce, at the turn of the Millennium:

> Although the electronic environment is a novel advance in the history of consumerism, existing contract law is up to the challenge. The influences that affect the judicial approach to the enforcement of standard terms in the paper world also affect the electronic world or have close parallels in the electronic world. The basic economics of the two kinds of commerce are identical. In both the paper and electronic worlds, businesses choose between adopting a set of boilerplate terms that are mutually beneficial or exploitative. In both worlds, they know more than

---

[63] Beale, Bishop, and Furmston (n. 25), 3.
[64] *Ibid.*, 8.
[65] The LawTech Delivery Panel UK Jurisdiction Taskforce, *Legal statement on cryptoassets and smart contracts* (November) (2019), 4.

consumers about the contractual risks, creating an opportunity to exploit consumers. Also in both worlds, consumers can defend themselves by investigating these terms or by making their purchasing decisions based on a business's reputation. E-commerce brings new weapons and defences to both businesses and consumers, but the basic structure remains intact.[66]

The problem of bridging real and virtual worlds (the 'oracle problem') and bringing laws of contract and property into digital harmony, remain major obstacles for smart contract design and implementation.[67] Whether we ought to see smart contracts as contracts at all remains open to debate.[68] We might understand smart contracts instead as a piece within the larger jigsaw puzzle that is contract law, rather than an alternative to or replacement for traditional contracts. It is clear, from a legal standpoint, that smart contracts do not provide a wholly viable alternative to existing forms of contract, nor pose a threat.[69]

Despite innovative steps, smart contracts are juridically immature and incapable of satisfying most fundamental conditions of traditional contract law and theory.[70] Although complacency by lawyers is unwise and potentially misguided, as Marino and Juels conclude, it is 'essential that the architects of this new technology, like the

---

[66] R.A. Hillman and J.J. Rachlinski, 'Standard-Form Contracting in the Electronic Age' (2002) 77 *New York University Law Review* 495.

[67] See eg, J.I.-H. Hsiao, 'Smart Contract on the Blockchain-Paradigm Shift for Contract Law' (2017) 14 *US-China Law Review* 685.
Test cases for smart contract viability have tended to rely on tokenization of non-physical property that is amenable to digital exchange and transaction, such as financial products or intellectual property, and this trend has not changed in recent years despite some high-profile attempts to demonstrate that both chattels and real estate can be conveyed using smart contracts. See for example, J. Ream, Y. Chu, and D. Schatsky, 'Upgrading Blockchains: Smart Contract Use Cases in Industry' *Deloitte Insights* (blog, 8 June 2016) <https://www2.deloitte.com/insights/us/en/focus/signals-for-strategists/using-blockchain-for-smart-contracts.html> accessed 9 July 2021; A. Dikusar, 'Smart Contracts: Industry Examples and Use Cases for Business' *XB Software* (blog, 17 October 2017) <https://xbsoftware.com/blog/smart-contracts-use-cases/> accessed 9 July 2021; S. Khatwani, 'These are the 5 Best Use Cases of Ethereum Smart Contracts' *Coin Sutra* (22 May 2018) <https://coinsutra.com/ethereum-smart-contract-usecases/> accessed 9 July 2021.

[68] See for example, Werbach and Cornell (n. 42); M. Raskin, 'The Law and Legality of Smart Contracts' (2017) 1(2) *Georgetown Law and Technology Review* (April) 305–41; S.A. McKinney, R. Landy, and R. Wilka, 'Smart Contracts, Blockchain, and the Next Frontier of Transactional Law' (2018) 13 *Washington Journal of Law, Technology & Arts* 313. In a Twitter exchange between Ethereum founder Vitalik Buterin and publishers of the Crypto Law Review, Buterin admitted: 'To be clear, at this point I quite regret adopting the term "smart contracts". I should have called them something more boring and technical, perhaps something like "persistent scripts"' (@VitalikButerin. *Twitter*. 6.21PM. 13 October 2018).

[69] For example, *Chitty on Contracts* does not mention smart contracts in the latest (October 2018) edition, only electronic documents and deeds with regard to provisions in land registration legislation for e-conveyancing measures—Beale (n. 24), 1–123

[70] The operators of seemingly innovative smart contract applications themselves remain cautious and hesitant regarding the legal force of smart contracts and continue to recommend users seek formal legal advice before agreeing to terms of service. See for example, Ana Alexandre, Decentralized Aragon Court Now Onboards Jurors To Settle Real Cases. *Coin Telegraph* (8 January 2020) <https://cointelegraph.com/news/decentralized-aragon-court-now-onboards-jurors-to-settle-real-cases>.

architects of contracts, create viable ways to alter and undo them'.[71] 'Parties should obviously think about what will happen when things go wrong before they do' argues Sir Geoffrey Vos, and, thus, coders are wrong to believe dispute resolution is not required for these methods of transaction, especially given the continued fallibility of the human element involved in smart contracts.[72] Failure to heed this is one account of the problematic fetishization of the contractual form by smart contract designers: they consider the electronic agreement alone to be perfect, when this does not, in fact, describe a contract—only a new techno-legal supertoy.

---

[71] Bill Marino and Ari Juels, *Setting Standards for Altering and Undoing Smart Contracts* (2016) <https://www.arijuels.com/publications/>.
[72] Vos (n. 7), 15.

12
Languages for Smart and Computable Contracts

Christopher D Clack[*]

A. Introduction	269	3. Practical aspects of validating changes in code or agreement	281
B. The Language Stack	271	D. Semantics	283
1. Natural language	273	1. Different perspectives	284
2. Specification language	274	2. Consequences for validation	285
3. Programming language	275	3. Semantics and validation	286
4. Assembly language and object code	276	4. Semantics of the agreement	287
5. Executable languages, machine code and instruction sets	277	5. Semantics of the code	290
6. Runtime systems, virtual machines, interpreters, and byte code	277	E. Computable Contracts	292
		1. Markup languages and templates	293
C. Natural and Formal Expression	278	2. Domain specific programming languages	295
1. From contract to code	279	3. Controlled natural language	298
2. Internal or external model	280	F. Conclusion	303

A. Introduction

The field of 'smart contracts' is broad, with multiple and sometimes contradictory definitions of what is considered to be a smart contract. Various factors have contributed to this complexity, including a technical divergence that occurred when the term was used to describe stored procedures in the Ethereum blockchain,[1]

---

[*] Christopher D. Clack is a Professor in the Department of Computer Science at UCL. He is a recognized expert on blockchain technologies, smart contracts and computable contracts, especially focusing on smart derivatives contracts. He holds a Higher Doctorate (ScD) from the University of Cambridge and is joint Field Chief Editor of the open-access research journal Frontiers in Blockchain, leading an editorial board of over 500 researchers in forty-four countries. The author is grateful to two anonymous reviewers who provided commentary on an early draft of this chapter. Many thanks also to Bob Kowalski and Henning Diedrich for comments on this draft, their help in providing examples of their controlled natural languages, and their insightful discussions on the topic of computable contracts.

[1] V. Buterin, 'A Next Generation Smart Contract & Decentralized Application Platform' (2013) *Ethereum Foundation Whitepaper*, <https://cryptorating.eu/whitepapers/Ethereum/Ethereum_white_paper.pdf> accessed 24 June 2021.

which conflicted with the original definition (pre-dating Ethereum by seventeen years) that aimed to automate commercial agreements in general, regardless of technology platform.[2] Significant research has been, and continues to be, conducted on general smart contracts that are not necessarily linked to blockchains. Another factor is the broad range of disciplines involved, including computer science, law, logic, and linguistics.

Moreover, there is a fundamental conflict inherent in the term 'smart contract', which brings together the two disparate and highly specialized disciplines of computer science ('smart') and law ('contracts'). Although there may be a surface similarity between a written contract and a computer program (both of which are carefully structured and may contain *inter alia* definitions, descriptions of actions to be taken, and conditional logic), there are substantial differences between the language, culture, and perspective of lawyers and computer scientists.

It is to be expected that differences of opinion and commercial or political imperatives will contribute to continuing debate about definitions for a while longer. Yet there is also a growing acknowledgement that the potential for misunderstanding impedes progress, and more general definitions of the term have been created in order to obtain broader consensus. An example is the widely-cited portmanteau definition from Clack *et al.*:[3]

> A smart contract is an agreement whose execution is both automatable and enforceable. Automatable by computer, although some parts may require human input and control. Enforceable by either legal enforcement of rights and obligations or tamper-proof execution.

Even this definition has its problems: it uses the term 'execution' in a computing sense (the running of computer code), whereas from a lawyer's perspective perhaps 'performance' might have been a better choice. Furthermore, definitions of the terms 'automatable' and 'enforceable' are not given, leaving room for differing interpretations; though to some extent this may also explain the popularity of this definition.

The automation of commercial agreements requires that some[4] or all of the intentions of the parties should be expressed in computer code. Yet how can there be

---

[2] N. Szabo, 'Smart Contracts: Building Blocks for Digital Markets' (1996) 16 *EXTROPY: The Journal of Transhumanist Thought* 50, 64 <https://archive.org/details/extropy-16/page/50/mode/2up> accessed 24 June 2021.

[3] C.D. Clack, V.A. Bakshi, and L. Braine, 'Smart Contract Templates: Foundations, Design Landscape and Research Directions' (2016) *arXiv preprint* <https://arxiv.org/abs/1608.00771v2> accessed 24 June 2021.

[4] The selection of which aspects of an agreement to automate is beyond the scope of this chapter, and has been covered in a specific context elsewhere. See C.D. Clack and C. McGonagle, 'Smart Derivatives Contracts: The ISDA Master Agreement and the Automation of Payments and Deliveries' (2019) *arXiv preprint* <https://arxiv.org/abs/1904.01461> accessed 24 June 2021. Also see ISDA and King & Wood Mallesons, 'Smart Derivatives Contracts: From Concept to Construction' (2018) <https://www.isda>.

confidence that the computer code is faithful to those intentions? It is not sufficient to check whether the code is correct solely with respect to those aspects being automated, but also to check that there is no deviation from any aspect of the entire agreement.[5] The matter is more acute where it is intended to automate the performance of some or all of a legal agreement (a 'smart legal contract' as defined for example by Stark,[6] drawing a contrast with the automation of agreements that are not contracts), especially one of high value and potentially very long term (perhaps stretching into decades, as with some financial contracts) and whose legal documentation may have substantial size and complexity.

This chapter explores aspects of this question ('is the code faithful to the agreement?') in the context of 'smart legal contracts', to demonstrate some of the depth and subtlety of the issues at play. The aim is to provide a better understanding of the different ways in which technology may be used to convert aspects of a legal agreement into computer code[7] and of the issues that arise when attempting to validate the behaviour of the code. Much of the discussion will focus on language: the *specialized natural languages* used by computer scientists and lawyers, and a variety of *synthetic languages* used by computer scientists.

Section B introduces various terms of art from computer science and the 'language stack' of different languages that may be used during the conversion from the agreement to the instructions that control a computer. Section C discusses aspects of natural and formal expression; this includes issues that arise when converting from agreement to code, such as whether the code defines or implements contractual obligations, and strategies for validating repeated updates to the code or the agreement. Section D analyses issues that arise with respect to the semantics of the agreement and the semantics of the code, and Section E discusses research developments and directions in smart contract methodology using 'Computable Contracts'—including markup languages, templates, domain specific languages and controlled natural languages. Section F concludes.

B. The Language Stack

The automation by computer of selected aspects of a legal agreement requires code to be written, and that code must be verified and validated. Here we use the term 'verified' to mean an internal process whereby computer code is checked for technical

---

org/a/cHvEE/Smart-Derivatives-Contracts-From-Concept-to-Construction-Oct-2018.pdf> accessed 24 June 2021.

[5] For example, code that automates the calculation and performance of payments and deliveries might fail to implement an appropriate grace period in the case of delayed payment.

[6] J. Stark, 'Making sense of blockchain smart contracts' (2016) Coindesk.com, <http://www.coindesk.com/making-sense-smart-contracts/> accessed 24 June 2021.

[7] This is part of what Allen calls the 'technology stack' (n. 9).

correctness (is the programmer building the *code right*?), whereas the term 'validation' means an external process whereby previously verified code is checked for whether it is faithful to the agreement (is the programmer building the *right code*?).

Validation can be substantially more difficult than verification, and establishing whether the code is faithful to the agreement may require (for example) that all possible behaviours of the code (ie, sequences of actions and calculations, with timings, performed by the code whether or not in response to input data) correctly automate exactly what needs to be automated (no more and no less) and without conflicting with any aspect of the overall agreement. For complex code, it may be impossible to engage in exhaustive testing of all behaviours for all inputs and outputs because there are too many combinations, and so formal analysis based on program semantics may be used (see Section D). The person or team that is responsible for validation therefore needs to have a full understanding of both the agreement and computer science. The former may for example require a full understanding of the relevant law and of standard business practices for the relevant sector. The latter requires, *inter alia,* a full understanding of the 'language stack' as explained in this section.

This chapter focuses on written contracts. Whilst the legal documentation is likely to be a key resource, and a large part of the effort of creating and validating code will focus on conversion from the legal documentation to the code, it is not the only source of information about the agreement. J.G. Allen argues that a contract can be viewed as a complex legal institutional entity comprising a 'stack' of interacting legal and technological 'layers'. He introduces the term 'contract stack' to describe this structure and gives the example of a written contract whose 'contract stack' comprises:[8] '(i) the spoken words through which the contractual terms were negotiated and against which the text was drafted, (ii) the written text, and (iii) legal rules implying terms and governing construction.'[9]

Allen relates this notion of 'contract stack' to the 'technology stack' of the underlying elements (such as the languages and software products) of a computer application. The appearance of languages in the technology stack is extremely important; multiple languages are used in a highly structured manner, and this chapter therefore introduces the term 'language stack'.

It is essential to understand the language stack in order to understand the many issues that arise when validating whether the automation of an agreement is faithful to that agreement. A computer can only carry out instructions provided in an 'executable language' comprising sequences of binary digits (0 and 1), and that executable language is very far removed from the human-readable code produced

---

[8] Noting that the extent to which spoken words may be upheld by a court of law may vary according to jurisdiction.
[9] J.G. Allen, 'Wrapped and Stacked: "Smart Contracts" and the Interaction of Natural and Formal Language' (2018) 14(4) *European Review of Contract Law* 307–43. He notes that these rules in (iii) are often highly restrictive of the relevance of (i).

by programmers. The conversion from human-readable code to executable code proceeds via multiple intermediate layers in the language stack, each with its own specialized language(s). Errors and mis-interpretations can occur during the process of conversion down the layers of the language stack to the final bits that control the computer, and it is important to understand why and how these errors and mis-interpretations can occur.

Conversion generally requires a transformation of *syntax* (words and grammar) while retaining the *semantics* (throughout this chapter we use the terms 'meaning', 'semantics' and 'substance' as synonyms), yet the creation of code for a smart contract ('smart contract code') will typically require the semantics of only some aspects of the agreement to be converted to code, and may require understanding of aspects of the agreement that are not in the written contract. Furthermore, this process of conversion requires that the semantics of those aspects of an agreement that are to be automated must be known in advance (this does not mean that the semantics must be fully specified for all possible future events, but that the semantics must be known in advance for those future events that are contemplated by the parties—even if the required action in response to an event is 'pause and refer to one or both parties for guidance').

When focusing on the legal documentation, the starting point for the language stack is not the code written by a programmer: instead, it is the natural language used in the written documentation. The following brief summary provides sufficient background for subsequent discussion. Relevant terms of art from computer science include 'source code' (an artefact using a human-readable programming or specification language, as defined below) and 'execution' (the performance by a computer of 'machine-code' instructions).

1. Natural language

At the top of the language stack is the natural language (eg, English) in which aspects of the agreement, including definitions, conditional logic, and actions to be performed, are expressed. Agreements may use sector-specific terms of art and where these terms are complex they may be structured to record the properties of these terms, and the relationships between them, by use of standardized ontologies such as the Financial Industry Business Ontology ('FIBO').[10] A 'controlled natural language' ('CNL')[11] may have even stricter controls on grammar and

---

[10] F. Horn and R. Trypuz, 'What is FIBO' (2020) EDM Council, <https://wiki.edmcouncil.org/> accessed 24 June 2021.

[11] Kuhn surveys existing English-based CNLs, including 100 CNLs from 1930 to 2014: T. Kuhn, 'A Survey and Classification of Controlled Natural Languages' (2014) 40(1) *Computational Linguistics* 121–170. See also A. Wyner *et al.*, 'On Controlled Natural Languages: Properties and Prospects' (2009) 5972 Lecture Notes in Computer Science 281, 289.

vocabulary (nouns, verbs, adjectives, adverbs, etc) and may also be a 'domain-specific language'.

2. Specification language

For many decades in computer science and electronic engineering formally-based 'specification languages' have been used for complex descriptions of software and systems.[12] With the increasing computerization and automation of processes across different sectors, there has been increasing use of specification languages for complex descriptions of commercial systems and processes. Specification languages can also provide formal descriptions (specifications) of legal agreements. A specification language is not normally a natural language, but rather may be a mathematical or logical formalism,[13,14,15,16,17,18] or may be similar to a programming language and may support computer simulation of contract performance.[19] Conversion between natural and specification languages is typically achieved manually. A specification language could potentially be used before, during, or after drafting a natural-language contract and can provide clarity regarding the natural language. For example: (i) for analysis to guide the drafting lawyer (such as

---

[12] For example 'Z notation'. See J.R. Abrial, S.A. Schuman, and B. Meyer, 'A Specification Language', in A.M. Macnaghten and R.M. McKeag (eds), *On the Construction of Programs* (Cambridge University Press 1980).

[13] Hvitved provides a comparative survey of formal languages and models for contracts, together with his own Contract Specification Language (CSL): T. Hvitved, 'Contract Formalisation and Modular Implementation of Domain-specifi Languages' (2012) PhD thesis, Department of Computer Science, University of Copenhagen (DIKU).

[14] Lee uses a logic programming model and models a contract as a set of transition rules for a Petri net: R.M. Lee, 'A Logic Model for Electronic Contracting' (1988) 4(1) *Decision Support Systems* 27, 44.

[15] See Prisacariu and Schneider's Contract Language (CL) that combines deontic, dynamic, and temporal logics: C. Prisacariu and G. Schneider, 'A Formal Language for Electronic Contracts' (2007) 4468 Lecture Notes in Computer Science 174, 189. See also G. Pace, C. Prisacariu, and G. Schneider, 'Model checking contracts–a case study' in *International Symposium on Automated Technology for Verification and Analysis* (Springer 2007) 82, 97.

[16] The Business Contract Language ('BCL') monitors contract events: G. Governatori and Z. Milosevic, 'A Formal Analysis of a Business Contract Language' (2006) 15(04) *International Journal of Cooperative Information Systems* 659, 685.

[17] Flood and Goodenough specify a contract as a deterministic finite automaton with transition rules (this may be thought of as a 'virtual machine' used as an executable specification): M.D. Flood and O.R. Goodenough, 'Contract as Automaton: The Computational Representation of Financial Agreements' (2015) *Office of Financial Research Working Paper* 15-04. This has some resemblance to Lee's Petri net transitions (n. 14) and to the finite state machine representation used by Molina-Jimenez et al.: C. Molina-Jimenez et al., 'Run-time Monitoring and Enforcement of Electronic Contracts' (2004) 3(2) *Electronic Commerce Research and Applications* 108–25.

[18] Also see H. Prakken and G. Sartor, 'The role of logic in computational models of legal argument: a critical survey' in *Computational logic: Logic Programming and Beyond* (Springer 2002) 342, 381.

[19] If a specification language is not itself a programming language (eg, if it is a non-executable mathematical formalism) then it may be amenable to semantics-preserving translation into a programming language.

inconsistency and incompleteness analysis);[20] (ii) as an intermediate step in translation to a lower layer in the language stack; and/or (iii) as an agreed definition of the semantics of the natural-language layer, against which the code can be validated (for example, an important role for specification languages is in formal proofs of the correctness of software).[21]

A 'domain-specific modelling language' (DSML) may be used as a specification language to draft a new contract or to create a formal model of a contract (typically either to assist analysis of properties of the contract—such as consistency analysis or 'what if' analysis—or to assist generation of code at a lower level in the language stack): these DSMLs may be customized to the drafting or modelling of contracts in a given business sector and are either (i) embedded in a general programming language (more understandable for a programmer) or (ii) designed as a separate language (more understandable for a lawyer, and perhaps using a 'controlled natural language'), which may assist validation that the code is faithful to the agreement.[22] Occasionally, a DSML may have a visual programming interface (specification with visual elements rather than text—see Section E.2).

A 'markup language' such as XML[23] can be used to annotate natural language with tags to provide additional information relating to presentation, structure or semantics and may act as a specification language, albeit in a limited way since its purpose is to annotate existing natural language expressions rather than to provide an alternative expression.[24]

3. Programming language

Computer programmers construct software using a programming language. Often these are general-purpose languages, but 'domain-specific programming languages' (DSPLs) are designed for a specific purpose—for example, to target a specific application, or a specific distributed ledger platform.[25] DSMLs and

---

[20] For example see K. Angelov, J.J. Camilleri, and G. Schneider, 'A Framework for Conflict Analysis of Normative Texts Written in Controlled Natural Language' (2013) 82(5–7) *The Journal of Logic and Algebraic Programming* 216, 240.

[21] If the natural-language contract makes use of a standard ontology (such as FIBO—see n. 10) then it will assist checking of the specification if the specification language is also able to use the terms from that ontology, with the same definitions.

[22] Embedded and non-embedded DSMLs are sometimes known as 'internal' and 'external' DSMLs.

[23] See <https://www.w3.org/TR/REC-xml/> accessed 21 February 2022.

[24] A markup language is not a programming language, but it can guide an application that views, edits or analyses text, and it can for example annotate an area of text to indicate that it is source code written in a programming language.

[25] Examples of DSPLs for code running on specific distributed ledger platforms include Solidity for Ethereum, <https://en.wikipedia.org/wiki/Solidity> accessed 21 February 2022, Plutus for Cardano, <https://docs.cardano.org/plutus/learn-about-plutus> accessed 21 February 2022, and Pact for Kadena <https://d31d887a-c1e0-47c2-aa51-c69f9f998b07.filesusr.com/ugd/86a16f_442a542b64554cb2a4c1ae7f528ce4c3.pdf> accessed 21 February 2022. By contrast the DSPLs CSL by Deon Digital (see n. 94) and DAML by Digital Asset (see n. 95) are not specific to any particular technology platform.

DSPLs belong to the general category of domain-specific languages ('DSL's). There are many programming languages, with differing styles of expression and with differing degrees of formality in terms of their defined syntax and semantics. The semantics (or meaning) of programming languages is at the heart of our understanding of how a computer program behaves and what it computes, and is an important tool for the validation of all but the simplest code.[26] Declarative languages such as the functional languages Haskell[27, 28] and Miranda,[29, 30] and the logic language Prolog,[31, 32] have formally defined semantics and are especially helpful in providing certainty about the meaning of code; they may also be used either as a programming language or as a specification language or both.[33] Where there is a desire for flexibility in targeting multiple platforms, a programmer might construct software using a general-purpose programming language and then automatically (or semi-automatically) translate the software to a platform-specific programming language.

4. Assembly language and object code

Software written in a programming language must be converted to a lower-level language for execution by a computer. For example, a 'compiler' converts a program expressed in a programming language into a program expressed in an executable language ('machine code'). However, the compiler may employ several intermediate steps using intermediate languages: for example, 'assembly language' is a lower-level language and can be further converted into executable machine code by an 'assembler', and 'object code' is an intermediate form of machine code that needs to be 'linked' with other object code before it can be executed by a computer.

---

[26] The semantics of programming languages typically refers either to denotational or operational semantics: the former maps programming expressions (and by extension the whole program) to formal mathematical objects, whereas the latter creates proofs from logical statements about the way a program operates. As an example of the former see D. Scott and C. Strachey, 'Toward a Mathematical Semantics for Computer Languages', Technical Monograph PRG-6 (Oxford University Programming Research Group 1971).
[27] S. Peyton Jones (ed), *Haskell 98 language and Libraries: The Revised Report* (Cambridge University Press 2003).
[28] S. Thompson, *Haskell: The Craft of Functional Programming* (Addison-Welsey 1999).
[29] D. Turner, 'An Overview of Miranda' (1986) 21(12) *ACM Sigplan Notices* 158, 166.
[30] C.D. Clack, C. Myers, and E. Poon, *Programming with Miranda* (Prentice Hall 1995).
[31] D.H. Warren, L.M. Pereira, and F. Pereira, 'Prolog—The Language and its Implementation Compared with Lisp' (1977) 12(8) *ACM Sigplan Notices* 109, 115.
[32] W.F. Clocksin and C.S. Mellish, *Programming in PROLOG* (Springer 1981).
[33] See for example D.A. Turner, 'Functional Programs as Executable Specifications' (1984) 312(1522) *Philosophical Transactions of the Royal Society of London. Series A, Mathematical and Physical Sciences* 363, 388.

5. Executable languages, machine code and instruction sets

Software is primarily created with the expectation that it will be executed on computer hardware. The final step is (almost) always that an electronic component fetches code as a package of binary digits (bits) from a storage medium, performs whatever action is defined by the code bits (which may include fetching and operating on data bits), and then fetches the next package of code bits. The bits may be structured into packages of eight (a 'byte') or 32 (a 32-bit 'word') or larger. Both code and data in a modern digital computer are represented as sequences of packages of bits; what makes code different to data is only (i) it is stored where code is expected to be found, and (ii) (hopefully) it represents a sequence of valid actions. What action is defined by a particular package of bits is highly specific to the hardware (each understands a different 'executable language', often called its 'instruction set'). A sequence of such bit patterns is called 'binary code', 'machine code', or 'native code'.

6. Runtime systems, virtual machines, interpreters, and byte code

Part of the executable code run by a computer is standard code inserted by the compiler to deal with low-level matters such as the layout and reuse of memory, the passing of arguments to (and results from) functions, and interfacing with the operating system. This is called the 'runtime system' and its behaviour is an important part of the behaviour of a program that is converted to an executable language. In order to validate whether code is faithful to the agreement, it is essential to understand how the runtime system operates because it may alter the semantics of the program (eg, what it calculates and how it operates).

A sophisticated runtime system may act as a 'virtual machine', providing a more complex instruction set than the underlying hardware; in this case a compiler would produce executable code in the language of that virtual machine and the behaviour of the virtual machine would be another vital component in establishing the validity of the code. A sophisticated virtual machine may define its own executable language at a high level of abstraction, similar to a programming language;[34] this is conceptually similar to an 'interpreter' that reads a programming language in small portions and creates and runs executable code for each portion before processing the next. Some benefits of both compilation and interpretation may be obtained by partially compiling a program from a programming language into an executable form called 'byte code', that is subsequently processed by an interpreter.

---

[34] The concept of a 'virtual machine' may also be helpful in reasoning about the meaning of programs and translations between languages.

Byte code can be portable across different hardware platforms, each with its own interpreter for the byte code, where each interpreter may contribute its own bias (in terms of errors or mis-interpretations) to the code.

In summary, an understanding of the language stack is vital to understanding the complexity of validating whether smart contract code is faithful to the agreement. The computer hardware does not understand code written at any other than the lowest layer of the language stack, and considerable expertise in computer science (including, for distributed ledger implementations, the semantics of distributed systems), is required to ensure effective validation. However, a greater potential for error arises from the translation from natural language to programming language, which requires considerable expertise and experience in multiple domains such as computer science, law, and the business sector. The issue of semantics is explored further in Section D.

C. Natural and Formal Expression

Given the desire to automate aspects[35] of a contract, it is necessary to know the meaning of the agreement and of those aspects that require automation. To be clear, this necessarily and fundamentally entails an analysis of semantics (see Section D) *ante hoc*, and requires amongst other things an analysis of the natural language expressions contained in the written contract.

The writing of computer code to automate an agreement requires the anticipation of a range of possible events that may occur during the performance of the agreement. It does not necessarily require *all* possible events to be anticipated: typically, the code will contain a default action to perform (such as to alert one or both counterparties) if an unanticipated event were to occur. It will also be necessary to anticipate possible sequences of events occurring in different orders, and to establish the semantics of the agreement in each of these contexts. Again, not all sequences need to be anticipated (just as the text of legal documentation does not anticipate all possible futures). When we talk of the semantics of an agreement, we mean a formal description that includes (*inter alia*) those actions that parties should undertake and the changes that should occur to deontic aspects such as rights, permissions and obligations as a result of each of the anticipated sequences of events.

The ease with which such semantic analysis can be undertaken for a specific agreement may inform and constrain the choice of which aspects of an agreement are amenable to automation.

---

[35] The selection of which aspects to automate has been covered for specific contracts elsewhere. See n. 4.

1. From contract to code

We focus on written agreements, where a large part of the agreement is expressed in writing. The legal text is typically not sufficient, but is an important component and it is necessary to investigate the natural language contract (both as a whole and in terms of the various textual components), to determine meaning and from that meaning to produce computer code.

The ease with which (aspects of) an agreement can be converted into code depends on how the contract is written, and in particular whether it is written using an uncontrolled natural language or a controlled natural language.

a.) Uncontrolled natural language and controlled natural language (CNL)
In the case of an uncontrolled natural language, the text generally has insufficiently constrained structure of syntax and semantics for automatic conversion into a programming or specification language, and the conversion must therefore normally proceed manually. This process may require expertise from multiple disciplines—primarily law and computer science, with input from the relevant business sector, but also linguistics and logic—and this human involvement, coupled with the potential for miscommunication and misunderstanding between subject experts, is a potential source of error.

By contrast, a CNL may retain the nuance and flexibility of a natural language and yet also be sufficiently structured for easier conversion to a programming or specification language. Current research is addressing the design of a CNL that is also a specification language (a technique known as 'Computable Contracts': see Section E), thereby reducing the potential for human error during the conversion process.

b) Conversion to code
In both cases (though more prevalent with an uncontrolled natural language) there will be an issue relating to whether (and if so how) automation of separate aspects of a contract should be brought together into a single computer program. The meaning of some aspects of a contract may convert easily, most notably where they do not depend on operational context: for example, a definition of a bank account number is straightforward to convert into code,[36] and the calculation of an amount to be paid may be no more than a description in natural language of an algebraic expression. Such aspects could be converted separately, but how should they be brought together into a single computer program such that (for example) calculations and payments are performed at the correct time?

---

[36] Smart contract code running on a blockchain should also support the changing of such basic data during the term of a long-running agreement—this may conflict with the notion of immutability for some blockchain architectures, but it is an important design requirement.

Furthermore, in general terms the substance to be converted will be more difficult than an algebraic expression: the meaning of each aspect (and therefore the code to be written) may not be self-contained due to interactions between clauses, and the text may not be representative of the entire agreement. Attention must also be given to the ways in which applicable law applies to the contract. In linguistics there is a helpful distinction between the semantics of the written text and the pragmatics of unwritten understanding between the writer and the reader of the text—in a written contract, the action of applicable law is part of the linguistic pragmatics. For example, implied terms may act to constrain the written terms of a contract, and in doing so they may change the rights, obligations, permissions or prohibitions that apply to the parties and this in turn affects the deontic semantics of the agreement. This is of great importance to the conversion into smart contract code, and to the validation of that code, since both depend on a correct understanding of the semantics of the agreement.

An alternative to bringing the parts together into a single program might be to implement the code as a collection of autonomous and asynchronous programs communicating via the passing of electronic messages. However, validating the semantics of such a complex distributed implementation may be challenging (see Section D).

2. Internal or external model

If the parties agree on the smart contract code that will automate aspects of an agreement, they will almost always base that agreement on code written in a human-readable specification language or programming language (source code). Bearing in mind that in English law 'The parties' contractual obligations may be defined by computer code',[37] then there are two possibilities that have implications for validation: (i) the source code implements aspects of the agreement, but does not define any aspect of the agreement. This is the 'external model' defined by ISDA and Linklaters.[38] Or, (ii) the agreement is defined in whole or in part by the source code. This is the 'internal model' defined by ISDA and Linklaters.[39]

In the case of the external model there is a risk of human error in converting from a natural language to a specification or programming language. By contrast, in the case of the internal model some of the risk of human error during conversion

---

[37] UK Jurisdiction Taskforce, *Legal Statement on Cryptoassets and Smart Contracts* (The LawTech Delivery Panel 2019) https://35z8e83m1ih83drye280o9d1-wpengine.netdna-ssl.com/wp-content/uploads/2019/11/6.6056_JO_Cryptocurrencies_Statement_FINAL_WEB_111119-1.pdf accessed 24 June 2021.

[38] ISDA and Linklaters, *Smart Contracts and Distributed Ledger—A Legal Perspective* (ISDA 2017) <http://www.isda.org/a/6EKDE/smart-contractsanddistributed-ledger-a-legal-perspective.pdf> accessed 24 June 2021.

[39] See n. 38.

from a natural language to a specification or programming language is removed, but the ability to express the substance of the agreement using a specification or programming language depends on how well the language fits the task of drafting a contract. For example, is it sufficiently flexible? Is it capable of expressing the contractual obligations that the lawyer wishes to express? It also depends on the extent to which the different languages interface well with each other (eg, can a clause written in a natural language easily and precisely make reference to an object defined in a programming or specification language? And *vice versa*?).

3. Practical aspects of validating changes in code or agreement

Both code and agreement may be subject to change. To illustrate the former, code may require updating due to a change in computer hardware or operating system, or because it is exhibiting anomalous behaviour. A change in either code or agreement will most likely require a change to the other. Where changes occur, validation must be repeated to ensure that the code remains faithful to the agreement. There are four optional strategies for where the source code is stored,[40] none of which make any legal difference but each of which can have practical consequences for the validation of changes in code or contract.

The first strategy is to *keep the contract and source code separate*. If, for example, the source code were deemed to implement rather than define the contract, this may be tempting due to the operational pragmatics of conversion and management. However, keeping the contract and code separate can be problematic in terms of version synchronization when the agreement or code is revised—in practice, in the context of an organization that manages very many agreements, the link between agreement version and code version may be lost, so that it may become unclear which version of the code relates to which version of the agreement.

The second strategy is to *attach the source code as an appendix to the contract*. This is a better strategy, and is especially helpful if for example the source code were deemed to be part of the contract. Version control for repeated update and validation are substantially easier. If required, the legal text may be annotated with references to lines of code in the appendix.

The third strategy is to *distribute the source code throughout the contract*. This has the advantage of placing lines of code visually adjacent to the legal text whose substance they are intended to automate (perhaps using a markup language to

---

[40] Where the *executable* form of the code is stored is of less interest for this discussion, though it is important operationally and, for example, Ricardian Contracts require bidirectional links between contract and executable form. See I Grigg, 'The Ricardian Contract' in *First IEEE International Workshop on Electronic Contracting* (IEEE 2004) 25, 31 <http://iang.org/papers/ricardian_contract.html> accessed 24 June 2021. See also I. Grigg, 'Why the Ricardian Contract Came About: A Retrospective Dialogue with Lawyers', Chapter 5 in this volume.

distinguish between code and non-code). There are well-established operational advantages to this 'literate' style of layout that mixes textual expressions and code.[41] If the only automation being performed is the writing of small amounts of code for extremely simple calculations or actions, it may be straightforward to include all of the smart contract code as multiple small additions to the legal text (though combining these small pieces into a single program may be complex, as mentioned previously). A more likely scenario is the combination of this strategy with either the first strategy or the second strategy, where most of the source code is separate or in an appendix and a small amount of source code (or carefully structured text) is embedded in the contract to indicate either values for defined names[42] or specific arithmetic formulae to be used.[43,44]

The fourth strategy is to *do nothing*. It is possible for a contract to be expressed *entirely in source code*. Trivially, this is true because source code can contain textual data objects of any complexity (and the code could therefore simply define a text object to contain the entire natural language contract). More usefully, because a specification language (for example) could: express deontic aspects[45] such as rights, obligations, permissions, and prohibitions (and the smart contract code could monitor those deontic aspects during performance of the agreement); express operational aspects (actions) and temporal constraints; and record definitions (such as choice of jurisdiction) for later use (for example to be made available during dispute resolution, which itself might be automated); and so on.

If a specification language or programming language (that might also be a CNL) were used to define an entire contract, then we could say that 'the contract is the source code' and there would be no separation. This makes it considerably easier to manage validation following a change. It should however be noted that the contract is not the *entire* expression of the agreement, and validation must still be undertaken to ensure that the code is faithful to the agreement as a whole. (See also Section E.)

---

[41] See D.E. Knuth, 'Literate Programming' (1984) 27(2) *The Computer Journal* 97, 111.

[42] In the terminology of Ricardian Contracts, these names and values would be 'parameters'—part of the Ricardian Triple of prose, parameters, and code. See <http://financialcryptography.com/mt/archives/001556.html> accessed 24 June 2021.

[43] This is also the basis of Smart Contract Templates. See <https://vimeo.com/168844103> accessed 24 June 2021. Also see n. 3, n. 74, and C.D. Clack, 'Smart Contract Templates: Legal Semantics and Code Validation' (2018) 2(4) *Journal of Digital Banking* 338, 352.

[44] Further examples of the use of parameters embedded in legal prose can be found in J. Hazard and H. Haapio, 'Wise Contracts: Smart Contracts that Work for People and Machines' in E. Schweighofer et al. (eds), *Trends and Communities of Legal Informatics. Proceedings of the 20th International Legal Informatics Symposium IRIS 2017* (Osterriechische Computer Gesellschaft 2017) 425, 432.

[45] Here we use the term 'deontic' in the sense of formal deontic logic (see G.H. Von Wright, 'Deontic Logic' (1951) 60(237) *Mind* 1, 15), where for example rights, obligations, permissions, and prohibitions are addressed separately to operational issues (actions) and temporal issues (time). Although deontic expressions often denote obligations etc with respect to actions, they operate at a meta-level: they may refer to an action but they are not the action itself.

D. Semantics

Several fundamental semantic issues arise when attempting to automate the performance of all but the simplest aspects of an agreement—especially high-value agreements where absolute certainty is required that the code is faithful to the agreement. For example, the parties may wish not only to automate the performance of certain actions at specified times and perhaps conditional on certain events, but also to automate the monitoring of deontic aspects that may themselves be conditional on certain events. For example, the parties may wish to automate the monitoring of actions at the time each action is performed to ensure that such action is supported by an obligation or a right and does not conflict with a prohibition. Furthermore, for example, if a contract were to contemplate multiple possible futures with a branching structure in time then certain sequences of actions might be permitted along one future time path but not along a different future time path: in this example, the parties might wish smart contract code to be generated to automate adherence to these temporal aspects.

Many observers have highlighted the need for verification and validation of smart contract code,[46, 47, 48, 49] and verification alone is likely to be insufficient. Consider that the contract is drafted by lawyers, whereas the code is created by programmers: the lawyers often do not understand the code (which requires specialist knowledge in computer science) and the programmers often do not understand the contract (which requires specialist knowledge in law).

Lawyers and computer scientists are highly trained, analytical problem-solvers; as a result there is a high probability that, with a small exposure to concepts of law, a programmer might incorrectly believe that he or she understands the agreement, and similarly with a small exposure to concepts of computing a lawyer might incorrectly believe that he or she understands the code. Meetings between lawyers and programmers to help clarify the meaning of agreement and code may be unsuccessful (despite a surface appearance of understanding) because lawyers and programmers have substantially different perspectives and do not share the same language.

---

[46] F. Al Khalil et al., 'Trust in Smart Contracts is a Process, As Well' in Brenner M and others (eds), *Financial Cryptography and Data Security*, vol 10323 (Springer: Lecture Notes in Computer Science 2017) 510, 519.

[47] B. Harley, *Are Smart Contracts Contracts?* (Clifford Chance 2017). <https://www.cliffordchance.com/content/dam/cliffordchance/briefings/2017/08/are-smart-contracts-contracts.pdf> accessed 20 September 2021.

[48] See n. 38.

[49] D. Magazzeni, P. McBurney, and W. Nash, 'Validation and Verification of Smart Contracts: A Research Agenda' (2017) 50(9) *IEEE Computer Journal Special Issue on Blockchain Technology for Finance* 50, 57.

1. Different perspectives

Both programmers and lawyers rely on a large corpus of knowledge that will not be expressed in the contract or the code (eg, of how law applies to legal text, and of how source code is manipulated and processed by a compiler and a runtime system). Furthermore, both lawyers and computer scientists use commonplace words as terms of art with deeply specialized meanings that require training to understand fully. A few simple examples will make the point:

- 'Execution' has a lay meaning (eg, performing a sentence of death), a specialist meaning to a lawyer (eg, *signing* a contract), and a specialist meaning to a programmer (eg, the *carrying-out*, by a computer, of the instructions of a program).
- 'Performance' has more than one lay meaning (an act of presenting a form of entertainment, or the action of undertaking a task), a specialist meaning for lawyers (eg, undertaking contractual obligations), and a specialist meaning for computer scientists (eg, the amount—or computational complexity, depending on context—of memory and time[50] used by a program).
- 'Interpretation' may generally refer to 'explaining the meaning of something' or, for a lawyer, 'the post-hoc semantic analysis of legal text', or for a computer scientist 'on-the-fly creation and running of executable code from source code'.
- 'Construction' may generally refer to 'the act of building some real or abstract thing', or for a lawyer 'to determine the legal effect of a contract' or for a computer scientist 'creation of a computer program or formal model'.

Computer scientists are accustomed to establishing semantics *a priori* and *ante hoc*, whereas lawyers are accustomed to semantic analysis (such as interpretation and construction) being deferred until a dispute occurs, *post hoc*, with potentially different outcomes depending on what semantics are inferred from the words and clauses of the contract.

a.) Ante hoc *and* post hoc *analysis*
The advantage of *post hoc* analysis is that it can focus on events that actually happened, rather than anticipating what the agreement would mean following many possible sequences of events that might happen. However, such *post hoc* semantic analysis is problematic for smart contracts, since it is difficult to write code to automate the performance of an agreement without knowing in advance what needs to

---

[50] Where 'time' may be measured as a number of 'clock cycles' of a computer's CPU (the central processing unit).

be done—ie, the semantic definition of what the agreement means must be undertaken *ante hoc*, and it is the *ante hoc* semantics that drive both the creation and the validation of the code. It is of course often true that the meaning of an agreement is not fully specified (because future events are not entirely knowable), but a small percentage of unknowns can be managed – computer scientists are accustomed to working with incomplete specifications (for example, for an unforeseen event the code could raise an alert with the parties and pause performance until instructed how to proceed).[51]

Similarly, programmers are accustomed to temporal aspects being well-defined with clear logic (including, for example, whether time is viewed as discrete or continuous), whereas lawyers are accustomed to highly flexible and context-sensitive interpretations of time (eg, 'the payment may be late, but is it *materially* late?' and 'regardless of the actual time of an event it is *deemed* to have occurred at the start of the day'). Thus, decisions based on the timing of events may need to be made with a varying degree of precision, and the amount of variation in precision may not be known until the point at which the decision must be made (and sometimes not until after a decision is made).

2. Consequences for validation

With such deep differences in perspective and language, attempting to create and then validate smart contract code by asking programmers to view a written specification produced by lawyers is likely to be problematic. The specification may be misleading, confusing or unintelligible to the programmers, or may have multiple possible meanings thereby presenting the risk that the programmers might make an incorrect choice of meaning.

Until the gap in linguistic semantics and pragmatics between lawyers and computer scientists is resolved, the creation and the validation of smart contract code for high-value or safety-critical agreements should ideally be undertaken by a multi-disciplinary team of lawyers and computer scientists working together closely in three steps: first, to establish an agreed, detailed and unambiguous formal specification of the meaning of the agreement, and an identification of those parts of the agreement that the parties wish to automate; second, to agree on the technology platform (eg, which Distributed Ledger Technology platform will be used); and third, to collaborate in the creation and validation of the smart contract code. If the first step were to prove difficult, then a practical way forward might be to adopt

---

[51] The two-layer approach of 'interpretation' and 'construction' highlights an interesting issue: where they differ, which should guide the creation and validation of smart contract code? Another way to view this is to ask whether the parties wish to automate aspects that may not be upheld by a court of law as well as aspects that would be upheld by a court of law.

a 'rapid-prototyping' approach, where the first, second, and third steps would be repeated for a sequence of prototypes of increasing complexity.

3. Semantics and validation

In general terms, possible strategies for validating smart contract code (in the sense previously discussed of whether the code correctly automates the aspects – such as calculations and actions – that need to be automated, no more and no less, whilst not conflicting with any aspect of the overall agreement) include the following.

The first strategy could be called *exhaustive validation*. For very simple smart contracts, 'path testing' could be used, whereby every possible path through the agreement (for all possible contemplated future events, in all possible orders) and every possible path through the smart contract code would be validated. For each possibility it would be necessary to know what the code should be doing with respect to the semantics of those aspects of the agreement that require automation. It would also be necessary to understand the semantics of the entire agreement, to confirm that the smart contract code never conflicts with the agreement. This is an extremely time-consuming approach, it may prove impossible to cover all possible paths, and it is unlikely to be feasible for complex smart contracts.

The second strategy consists of the application of *formal methods*. Mathematicians, logicians and computer scientists have been studying and developing formal proofs of the correctness of code since the 1930s. Much work has been done in the area of formal verification, though formal methods can also be applied to validation. Two example techniques are model-checking[52] and theorem proving[53]: with model-checking, both the code and the agreement could be modelled as automata (based on semantic specifications of each) and these two automata could be compared to determine if the behaviour of the code conforms to that of the agreement; by contrast, with theorem-proving both the code and the agreement could be expressed as logical formulae, with inference rules being used to demonstrate a mapping from the former to the latter.[54]

The advantages of formal methods are that (i) within the context of their assumptions and those logical statements they seek to prove they can give a very great deal of certainty about the result, and (ii) this is a mature area, having been developed over many decades. The rub is in knowing that the automata or logic in

---

[52] See eg, C. Baier and J-P. Katoen, *Principles of Model Checking* (MIT Press 2008).
[53] See eg, M. Fitting, *First-order Logic and Automated Theorem Proving* (Springer Science & Business Media 2012).
[54] A simple example, in a different field, is given in S. Lampérière-Couffin et al., 'Formal Validation of PLC Programs: A Survey' in *1999 European Control Conference (ECC)* (IEEE 1999).

each case is a full representation of the code or agreement respectively.[55] For the code, this is made considerably easier if it is written using a declarative language.

The third strategy is to make smart contracts *valid by design*. The burden of validation could be eased considerably if the potential for human error during conversion from agreement to code were removed. One solution would be for lawyers to draft contracts using a programming language or a domain specific language ('DSL'). The former is not impossible, but unlikely; the latter would be considerably more attractive if it could be made to resemble a natural language, and almost certainly this would be a CNL. If a DSL could be designed that were also a CNL customized for the task of drafting contracts, and if that DSL/CNL hybrid were to have clearly defined semantics then much of the conversion from agreement to code could be automated, with proofs of correctness at each step of the conversion down the language stack to executable code, and a large part of the final code would be 'valid by design'. The final executable smart contract code would also include an appropriate runtime system and perhaps standard ancillary code, and the entire code would be validated against the agreement; this process would be substantially facilitated by the fact that the code had been automatically created from the contract.

The final strategy—validity by design—is the aim of the methodology known as 'Computable Contracts', which is discussed further in Section E. All strategies, however, require a better understanding of the semantics of both the agreement and the code, which are further discussed below.

4. Semantics of the agreement

The analysis of the semantics of an agreement must consider multiple aspects including *deontic* aspects (ie, rights, obligations, permissions, prohibitions, etc),[56] *operational* aspects (actions to be performed) and *temporal* aspects (relating to and reasoning about time). Each such aspect may be specified independently, or preferably in combination[57] and it is essential for the formal semantic specification itself to be validated to determine whether it correctly captures the meaning of the contract.

Section C introduced the observation that some portions of legal text (such as definitions and algebraic expressions) may be trivial to convert into an expression in a programming or specification language. This is because they have simple

---

[55] Important work is underway with respect to the formal semantics of blockchain platforms, for example in providing a formal model of the Ethereum Virtual Machine (to be used as part of the formal model of the smart contract code). See Y. Hirai, 'Defining the Ethereum Virtual Machine for Interactive Theorem Provers' in *International Conference on Financial Cryptography and Data Security* (Springer, Cham 2017) 520, 535.

[56] These are concerned with contractual deontics rather than deontological ethics.

[57] See n. 14.

semantics. In general, however, the meaning of an isolated portion of legal text cannot necessarily be derived independently because there is nothing to constrain another clause from modifying the meaning of the clause being studied, and a reading of the entire contract may be required to identify conflicts with other clauses. Furthermore, as mentioned previously, the meaning of a contract cannot necessarily be derived from the text alone; it is necessary also to consider the broader agreement and the role of law and how it affects the contract.

A contract may include both ambiguity and vagueness, both of which hinder the determination of meaning. We use the term 'ambiguity' to mean either (i) the use of a term or phrase that is inherently ambiguous (such as in the phrase 'I bequeath all my black and white horses', which might mean 'all my black horses and all my white horses' or 'all my horses that are both black and white'),[58] or (ii) a word or expression that the parties believe to be unambiguous but by which they understand differing meanings (perhaps due to a misunderstanding over what the term denotes, such as whether 'Paris' is in France or Texas, or what it connotes, for example whether 'chicken' refers to any bird of the subspecies *Gallus gallus domesticus*, or a young chicken suitable for frying).

A bigger problem is vagueness: here we use this term to refer to expressions that do not have a single meaning, nor are they ambiguous with a small number of meanings from which to choose, but rather they have an indeterminate, possibly deferred meaning. Sometimes, vagueness is inherited from the language used to create legal text (such as the words 'reasonable', 'fair', and 'timely') and sometimes a clause may be deliberately vague because it is the only way to achieve agreement between the parties.

When defining the semantics of an agreement, either to guide the creation of smart contract code, or to be used during the validation of smart contract code, or to be used to analyse an agreement, it is necessary to consider multiple aspects of meaning: for example, the deontic, operational and temporal aspects. Whether undertaken separately or in combination, we call the result a 'semantic specification'; it is a view of the entire agreement in formal terms that is amenable to formal analysis and formal logic. It is important that this specification gives a view of the agreement as a whole, since there are semantic interactions between clauses—the meaning of one clause may be affected by another clause, and so simply gathering a set of separately-derived semantic definitions of a number of separate aspects of the agreement would not be sufficient. When creating a semantic specification, three issues arise:[59]

---

[58] This example was drawn to the author's attention by Paul Lewis (Linklaters).

[59] C.D. Clack and G. Vanca, 'Temporal Aspects of Smart Contracts for Financial Derivatives' (2018) 11247 *Lecture Notes in Computer Science, Springer* 339, 355, Springer. These are not the only issues that arise; Pace and Schneider explain other semantics-based challenges: G.J. Pace and G. Schneider, 'Challenges in the Specification of Full Contracts' (2009) 5423 Lecture Notes in Computer Science 292, 306.

The first is the *separability problem*. The temporal, deontic and operational aspects are closely intertwined and difficult to separate (both in the natural language text of written contracts and in the development of formal logics). Although programmers tend to focus on the logic of actions such as payments and deliveries (the 'operational' aspects), it is important that they should also consider the deontic aspects that function at a meta level to reason for example about whether a party has the right, permission or obligation to perform each such action. Relevant logics include von Wright's deontic logic,[60] Rescher and Urquhart's temporal logic,[61] Azzopardi et al.'s contract automata,[62] von Wright's logic of action[63] and Prisacariu and Schneider's action-based logic.[64] Computer scientists also draw a distinction between 'denotational' and 'operational' semantics of computer languages, which may carry over into their perspective of the semantics of legal agreements.

The second is the *isomorphism problem*. The structure of the semantic specification may be substantially different to the structure of the legal documentation. For example, a single clause may be mapped to multiple parts of the semantic specification, and one part of the specification may be derived from multiple clauses. This may make it difficult for a lawyer to understand and validate the semantics.

The third is the *canonical form problem*. There may be many different ways to structure the semantic specification for a given legal agreement; specifically, there may be no agreed standard way (sometimes called a `canonical form') to structure the semantics such that (i) two contracts with the same meaning will always have structurally identical semantic specifications, and (ii) two contracts with different meaning will always have structurally different semantic specifications. This may make it difficult to compare specifications automatically to see if they have the same meaning, which could be helpful in a number of different circumstances such as:

- determining whether a collection of changes to an agreement that are intended to be benign (eg, to simplify the wording) has resulted in any change in meaning;
- determining whether a collection of changes to an agreement that are intended to change the meaning has achieved the required change; and

---

[60] See G.H. von Wright, 'And Next' (1965) *Fasc XVIII Acta Philosophica Fennica* 293, 304. Also see G.H. von Wright 'The Logic of Action: a Sketch' in N. Rescher (ed), *The Logic of Decision and Action* (Univ Pittsburgh Press 1967) 121, 136. And also G.H. von Wright, 'An Essay in Deontic Logic and the General Theory of Action' (1968) *Fasc XXI Acta Philosophica Fennica*.
[61] N. Rescher and A. Urquhart, *Temporal Logic* (Springer-Verlag 1971)
[62] S. Azzopardi et al., 'Contract Automata' (2016) 24 *Artificial Intelligence and Law* 203, 243.
[63] See n. 60.
[64] C. Prisacariu and G. Schneider, 'CL: An Action-Based Logic for Reasoning about Contracts' (2009) 5514 *Lecture Notes in Computer Science, Springer*, 335, 349.

- determining whether different versions of a proposed collection of changes to an agreement, drafted by different lawyers, result in the same meaning.

5. Semantics of the code

Just as it is impossible to know what code to write if the meaning of the agreement has not been established, so too it is impossible to know whether the written code is faithful to the agreement if the meaning of the code is not known.

Determining the meaning of a computer program may be achieved in several ways. For example: by ascribing mathematical meanings to syntactic expressions (mapping syntactic expressions to mathematical objects),[65] by creating proofs from logical statements about the way a program operates, by defining how a syntactic expression would change the state of a defined virtual machine, or by describing axioms that apply to a syntactic expression. Formally-based languages such as Haskell and Prolog are generally more amenable to formal determination of semantics. These techniques are used for very complex, very - high - value, or safety-critical software because of the impracticality (sometimes impossibility) of validating all possible behaviours of a program. Such semantic analysis of programs has been an established technique for decades.

Various issues arise in determining the semantics of a program. For example, the meaning of an isolated portion of code from a computer program cannot necessarily be derived independently, and may need to be derived in context by reading the entire program in the order in which it was written. This may be especially true for *imperative* source code and less true for *declarative* source code. For example, declarative languages based on the λ-calculus benefit from the Church-Rosser property that the order in which evaluation rules are applied (if that order terminates) does not make a difference to the eventual result. Furthermore, it is necessary to consider not just the actions of the source code but also of the compiler and runtime system.

Source code is often modified during the process of compilation in order to improve performance (such as execution speed and parsimonious use of computer memory).[66] In most cases the modification does not change the meaning of the code, but occasionally (especially for complex optimizations) the meaning may be slightly changed. Furthermore, it has been demonstrated[67] that many well-established, mature compilers sometimes produce executable code that may sometimes

---

[65] This deduces the meaning of a program just by 'looking at the code', in a similar fashion to understanding what a mathematical expression means (what it will calculate) just by looking at it.

[66] For example, repeated calculation of the same constant expression is unnecessary and the code may be modified so that the calculation is only performed once.

[67] Contrary to note 106 on page 45 of UK Jurisdiction Taskforce, see n.37.

be incorrect (it does not exactly follow the source code instructions).[68] The meaning of the code may be more difficult to ascertain where the runtime system is structured as multiple autonomous communicating parts, since it is necessary to consider the numerous different ways in which the parts may communicate (though if structured appropriately the semantics may be tractable, for example via use of process calculi[69, 70]).

In general terms, the lower-level implementation software (compilers, interpreters, optimizers, code generators, linkers, loaders, operating system, runtime system, etc) should not be assumed to be free from *semantic distortion* (ie, they may be unable to preserve the semantics of the source code). The preservation of semantics must be tested and demonstrated. If they are not so demonstrated, then the executable code that runs on a computer may not perform in the way predicted by the semantics of the source code at the top of the language stack. For example, a semantic specification of a program written in a language near the top of the language stack may give confidence about the behaviour of the code with respect to an intermediate level description of a virtual machine, but the implementation of that virtual machine on a specific technology platform must itself be tested for the existence of obvious coding faults and validated for the existence of more subtle errors that may change the semantics of the code. As an example of a semantics-changing error, consider 'data races' where one operation may speed ahead of another that started earlier, thereby leading to a change in the sequencing of actions. Mature technology tends to be fairly stable in this regard, but less mature technology (such as new technology platforms, and new platform-specific languages) may be less stable.

It appears to be inescapable that, especially for contracts of very high value, the executable code must always be thoroughly tested and validated for fidelity to the agreement (as previously explained). This would be especially true, for example, if the 'internal model' were used and if the parties were legally bound by what the code *does*, rather than by what it *says*.[71] However, the use of formally-based languages with known semantics at the higher levels of the language stack can substantially reduce the burden of validation.[72]

---

[68] Interesting examples can be found in X. Yang *et al.*, 'Finding and Understanding Bugs in C Compilers' in *Proceedings of the 32nd ACM SIGPLAN conference on programming language design and implementation* (ACM 2011) 283, 294.
[69] C.A.R. Hoare, 'Communicating Sequential Processes' (1978) 21(8) *Communications of the ACM* 666, 677.
[70] R. Milner, *A Calculus of Communicating Systems* (Springer Verlag 1980).
[71] See Paragraph 165 of n. 37.
[72] An example of this for a mission-critical financial system is given in L. Braine *et al.*, 'Simulating an object-oriented financial system in a functional language' (1998) <https://arxiv.org/abs/2011.11593> accessed 24 June 2021.

E. Computable Contracts

As long as the agreement and the code remain separate there will be a need to validate whether the code is faithful to the agreement, and it has been demonstrated in the foregoing discussion that this is problematic. The task includes the following five steps:

1. For that part of the agreement to be automated, determining *ante hoc* what it means (so that we know what the code should do) – this is not necessarily straightforward.
2. For the agreement as a whole, determining *ante hoc* what it means (so that we can check that the code does not conflict with the agreement as a whole)—this is the semantic specification of the agreement, and is not necessarily straightforward.
3. For the written source code, determining *ante hoc* what it means (what will the source code do, for all specified inputs and circumstances?)—this is the semantic specification of the source code and may be more or less easy to achieve depending on the chosen language.
4. Determining whether the source code, as expressed in its semantic specification, correctly automates the meaning of the selected aspects of the agreement, whilst not conflicting with the whole agreement (as expressed in the semantic specification of the agreement).
5. Determining whether the implementation software (comprising compilers, interpreters, optimizers, code generators, linkers, loaders, operating system, runtime system etc) correctly implements the semantics of the source code.

An emerging methodology in the field of smart contracts is that of 'computable contracts',[73] where part or all of the written legal documentation is written in a CNL *that is also* a DSL, where the latter has formally defined syntax and semantics and can be converted into a programming language via semantics-preserving transformations. Thus, that part of the written legal documentation will serve as *a single artefact* expressing both contractual obligations and the automated implementation of those obligations—it would be both contract and code, understandable to humans (lawyers and programmers) and computers (eg, it can be taken directly as input to a compiler, for automatic conversion into executable code).

With an appropriately designed DSL, a Computable Contract could also be (or be automatically converted into) a formal semantic specification: the single artefact could be contract, code and semantic specification. With a single artefact, the task of checking whether the meaning of the source code matches the meaning

---

[73] The term 'computable contract' was first introduced by Surden. See H. Surden, 'Computable Contracts' (2012) 46 *University of California, Davis, Law Review* 629, 700.

of the agreement would be much simpler, and validation would include the following steps:

1. For the agreement as a whole, determining *ante hoc* what it means—this is made easier by the fact that the computable contract (the 'single artefact') has a clear semantic specification.
2. Determining whether the semantic specification of the computable contract correctly automates the meaning of the selected aspects of the agreement, whilst not conflicting with the whole agreement (as expressed in the semantic specification of the agreement).
3. Determining whether the implementation software (compilers, interpreters, optimisers, code generators, linkers, loaders, operating system, runtime system, etc.) correctly implements the semantics of the computable contract.

1. Markup languages and templates

One approach to linking a written contract with its associated smart contract code is to use a markup language to add annotations to the contract. With this approach, some parts of the written text are annotated to indicate that they are natural language text and other parts are annotated to indicate that they are parameters (eg, named values) that communicate with the code. Although the written contract and code remain separate, they are at least linked, and the concept can be extended so that the programming language source code is contained within the same text file as the written contract. Further markup annotations can also be applied to the natural language text, for example to provide bilateral linkages between separate documents and to annotate clauses to indicate their purpose.[74, 75]

Substantial work has been done using this approach. Early work by Grigg proposed the term 'Ricardian Contract' for financial trading, aiming to achieve smart contracts that are simultaneously understandable by humans and computers by use of a markup language and linkages between contract and code.[76, 77] 'Smart Contract Templates'[78] extended Ricardian Contracts and proposed an abstract specification for structuring contracts, together with requirements and principles for templating. Hazard and Haapio[79] extended both Ricardian

---

[74] See for example C.D. Clack, V.A. Bakshi, and L. Braine, 'Smart Contract Templates: Essential Requirements and Design Options' (2016) *arXiv preprint*, <https://arxiv.org/abs/1612.04496> accessed 24 June 2021.

[75] Also see <http://www.commonaccord.org/> and <https://www.accordproject.org/> accessed 24 June 2021.

[76] I. Grigg, 'Financial Cryptography in 7 Layers' (2001) 1962 Lecture Notes in Computer Science 332, 348.

[77] See n. 40.

[78] See nn. 43 and 74.

[79] See n. 44.

Contracts and Smart Contract Templates with their work on encapsulated pieces of legal text (that they call 'prose objects') that may contain definitions of values for names that link to smart contract code.[80] The markup languages LegalXML[81] and LegalRuleML[82] provide, respectively, data schemas and a rule interchange language for the legal domain.[83] Other straightforward markup languages for contract drafting include OpenLaw[84] and the Accord Project:[85] the latter, for example, provides a library of contract and clause templates and the template language Cicero (combined with the expression language Ergo) to bind declaratively any existing natural language text to a data model.[86] At the time of writing, a British Standards Institute Publicly Available Specification for a standardized approach to contract templates was in its public consultation phase.[87]

The use of a markup language to provide templates for smart contracts is a pragmatic approach to co-ordinating the requirements and activities of (i) drafting legal contracts; (ii) integrating those contracts with computerized business processes; and (iii) managing smart contract code for the automation of (some aspects of) those contracts. However, although the use of markup languages is currently popular there are several problems with this approach.

First, the semantics of the agreement are only known to the extent that they are expressed in the tags attached to the legal text (which could be only a very small extent) and only for those aspects of meaning for which a tag exists. Second, the meaning of a clause may be too complex to express with a simple tag. Two obvious solutions to this are (i) giving simple semantic tags to simple textual elements and defining an overarching analysis to derive the semantics of each clause from the semantics of its elements, or (ii) developing a tagging language to support complex semantic tags. However, both of these solutions are at odds with the essential simplicity of markup languages. Third, in most cases the code would still be written in a programming language that may be opaque to lawyers. Fourth, although the contract and the code may have been brought together physically, in most cases the code would remain logically separate from the contract (even if parts are interspersed throughout the clauses

---

[80] CommonAccord provides a collection of sample prose objects: see n. 75.
[81] <http://www.legalxml.org> accessed 24 June 2021.
[82] <https://www.oasis-open.org/committees/tc_home.php?wg_abbrev=legalruleml> accessed 24 June 2021.
[83] LegalRuleML focuses on markup for legislation. Grosof and Poon provide a rule-based approach to representing contracts that builds on RuleML and process knowledge descriptions from Semantic Web ontologies: B.N. Grosof and T.C. Poon, 'SweetDeal: Representing Agent Contracts with Exceptions Using XML Rules, Ontologies, and Process Descriptions' in *Proceedings of the 12th International Conference on World Wide Web* (2003) 340, 349.
[84] <https://www.openlaw.io/> accessed 24 June 2021.
[85] See <https:// www.accord proj ect.org/ > accessed 24 June 2021 (founded by co-editor, P.G. Hunn).
[86] <https://github.com/accordproject/cicero> accessed 24 June 2021.
[87] <https://web.archive.org/web/2020123012214/https://standardsdevelopment.bsigroup.com/projects/2018-03267#/section> accessed 25 June 2021.

of a contract). Finally, a markup language only makes a small contribution to address the key problem of how to validate whether the code is faithful to the agreement.

2. Domain specific programming languages

The key vision of computable contracting is the use of a single artefact to express *both* the contractual obligations and the smart contract code. This goes much further than marking-up natural language text, and envisions the design of a new language for drafting contracts. A first step in this direction has been the use of Domain Specific Languages ('DSLs').

For many decades, DSLs have been proposed and used to help in the creation of legal documentation as well as to help with automating the performance of agreements. According to both the original Szabo definition and the Clack *et al.* definition, the use of a DSL to support the automated performance of an agreement would make it a 'smart contract'. There has also been substantial use of DSLs in a 'computable contract' role, providing a single semantic specification of contract and code. A very brief history of DSLs in this context is now given, much of which has been in the realm of financial trading agreements.

Early work by van Deursen and colleagues[88] developed the domain-specific language 'RISLA' for designing interest rate financial products in a way that was easy for financial engineers to understand. The language (which could be automatically translated into the COBOL programming language) was upgraded with (i) a component library to improve modularization; and (ii) a questionnaire style of user interface. Peyton Jones *et al.*[89] subsequently used a compositional style of programming to model the core product definitions of financial contracts, proposed as a DSML but also with an example implementation as a DSPL embedded in the functional programming language Haskell. Andersen *et al.*[90] extended the work of Peyton Jones *et al* to the exchange of money, goods and services amongst multiple parties and provided a formal representation of contracts that supports definition of user-defined contracts and user-definable

---

[88] A. van Deursen, 'Executable Language Definitions: Case Studies and Origin Tracking Techniques' PhD thesis (University of Amsterdam 1994). Also see B.R.T. Arnold, A. van Deursen, and M. Res, 'An Algebraic Specification of a Language for Describing Financial Products' in *ICSE-17 Workshop on Formal Methods Application in Software Engineering* (IEEE Computer Society Press 1995) 6, 13. And: A. van Deursen and P. Klint, 'Little Languages: Little Maintenance?' (1998) 10(2) *Journal of Software Maintenance: Research and Practice* 75, 92.

[89] S. Peyton Jones, J.M. Eber, and J. Seward, 'Composing Contracts: An Adventure in Financial Engineering (Functional Pearl)' (2000) 35(9) *ACM SIGPLAN Notices* 280, 292.

[90] J. Andersen *et al.*, 'Compositional Specification of Commercial Contracts' (2006) 8(6) *International Journal on Software Tools for Technology Transfer* 485, 516.

analysis of their state before, during and after execution. Henglein et al.[91] extended this further to demonstrate how formal contract specifications provide the core of a process-oriented event-driven architecture. Seijas and Thompson's domain-specific language 'Marlowe' is also based on the compositional style of Peyton Jones et al., extended to embrace issues that arise when executing financial contracts on distributed ledgers.[92] Marlowe is embedded in the programming language Haskell and has a formal semantics that supports analysis of Marlowe specifications of agreements (which they call 'contracts', and which can be used to specify smart contracts). Although not yet developed, Goodenough proposes the development of a Legal Specification Protocol that '*is independent of natural language*'—the early indications are that this might eventually be either a DSML or DSPL.[93]

Building on the compositional approach of functional programming languages, several commercial DSLs have been designed to help write smart legal contracts for a variety of different distributed ledgers: for example, the 'Contract Specification Language' (CSL) from Deon Digital,[94] and the 'Digital Asset Modeling Language' (DAML) from Digital Asset.[95] Gulliksson and Camilleri's Simplified Contract Language (SCL)[96] is an academic DSL based on Haskell that provides support for specification of normative texts—ie, it includes the specification of deontic as well as operational aspects (and also includes conditional clauses and timing constraints). Deontic specification within SCL is restricted to deontic modalities of actions, rather than deontic modalities of 'states of affairs'—for example, it can specify what must, may or may not *be done*, but it cannot specify what must, may or may not *be true*. It provides a convenient compositional approach to building contracts, though the authors observe that nevertheless terms in SCL can become 'quite large and unwieldy'. All of these examples are used as DSMLs, yet the style is programmatic (ie, 'in the style of a programming language') so that they may also be designated as DSPLs.

Marlowe has an optional visual user interface (using an adaptation of the visual language Google Blockly[97]) that provides a different style of specification using

---

[91] F. Henglein et al., 'POETS: Process-oriented Event-driven Transaction Systems' (2009) 78(5) *Journal of Logic and Algebraic Programming* 381, 401.

[92] P.L. Seijas and S. Thompson, 'Marlowe: Financial Contracts on Blockchain' (2018) 11247 Lecture Notes in Computer Science 356, 375.

[93] O. Goodenough, 'Developing a Legal Specification Protocol: Technological considerations and requirements' CodeX white paper (Stanford University 2019) <https://law.stanford.edu/wp-content/uploads/2019/03/LSPWhitePaperJan1119v021419.pdf> accessed 24 June 2021.

[94] <https://deondigital.com/docs/v0.38.0/> accessed 24 June 2021.

[95] <https://daml.com/> accessed 24 June 2021.

[96] R. Gulliksson and J.J. Camilleri, 'A Domain-Specific Language for Normative Texts with Timing Constraints' in *23rd International Symposium on Temporal Representation and Reasoning (TIME)* (IEEE 2016) 60, 69.

[97] Google, `A JavaScript Library for Building Visual Programming Editors' <https://developers.google.com/blockly> accessed 24 February 2022.

visual blocks as a metaphor for modules. Skotnica and Pergl have similarly suggested a visual DSL for modelling smart contract code.[98] Morris has developed the logic-based visual language 'Blawx' for specifying legal contracts,[99] and Martínez et al. have created Contract-Oriented Diagrams for visualizing normative texts.[100] Whilst visual programming languages are often aimed at novice programmers, they can be used to extend expressibility of a language,[101] and more generally Haapio and colleagues have collaborated to combine concepts from visualization and contracting.[102,103]

DSPLs are powerful and can express many operational aspects (eg, payments, deliveries, and business logic) of smart legal contracts, especially in the realm of financial contracts. The better DSPLs provide a semantic certainty and clarity (noting as a caveat the previously discussed problems that may occur lower in the language stack) that makes them well suited to defining elements of the legal agreement (the 'internal model'). However, there is not yet sufficient evidence of their ability to support the specification and automation of deontic aspects,[104] with the required degree of extent (for example, including deontic modalities of both actions and states of affairs) and subtlety for lawyers to draft high-value smart legal contracts. Nor is there yet an agreed methodology by which the smart legal contract should be structured and elements included in a standardized way. Finally, the style of textual expression used in the embedded DSPLs is very similar to computer programming and may not always be easily and immediately understood by (or be attractive to) lawyers, even for very simple specifications. Figure 12.1 provides illustrative examples of two DSPL drafting styles.

---

[98] M. Skotnica and R. Pergl, 'Das Contract-A Visual Domain Specific Language for Modeling Blockchain Smart Contracts' (2019) 374 Lecture Notes in Business Information Processing 149, 166.

[99] See <https://www.blawx.com/> and J. Morris, 'Rules as Code: How Technology May change the Language in which Legislation is Written, and What it Might Mean for Lawyers of Tomorrow' [2021] <https://s3.amazonaws.com/us.inevent.files.general/6773/68248/1ac865f1698619047027fd22eddbb a6e057e990e.pdf> accessed 24 June 2021.

[100] E. Martínez et al., 'A Model for Visual Specification of E-contracts' in 2010 IEEE International Conference on Services Computing (IEEE 2010) 1, 8.

[101] For example, Braine and Clack have demonstrated how a visual notation can be used to facilitate the integration of two very different programming styles: L. Braine and C. Clack, 'Object-flow' in 1997 IEEE Symposium on Visual Languages (Cat. No. 97TB100180) (IEEE 1997) 418, 419.

[102] M. Wong et al., 'Computational Contract Collaboration and Construction' in Co-operation: Proceedings of the 18th International Legal Informatics Symposium IRIS (2015) 505, 512.

[103] H. Haapio, D. Plewe, and R. deRooy, 'Next generation deal design: comics and visual platforms for contracting' in Networks: Proceedings of the 19th International Legal Informatics Symposium IRIS (2016) 373, 380.

[104] As previously observed in n. 45, the right to do something doesn't necessarily entail an action (the party may never exercise that right). Thus, the right (deontic aspect) acts at a meta-level over the action (operational aspect). Furthermore, deontic modalities may apply over states of affairs rather than over actions. Rights, permissions and prohibitions can be expressed conditionally and therefore vary dynamically during the performance of the contract, and the automation of deontic aspects tends to lead to automation of the monitoring of performance, in addition to automating the performance itself.

type CakeOrder: Event {
  amount: Int,
  receiver: Agent,
  item: String
}
type CakeDelivery: Event {
  receiver: Agent,
  item: String
}
template entrypoint CakeSale
(customer,shop,amount,item)=
  <buyer> order: CakeOrder
  where
    order.amount = amount &&
    order.receiver = shop &&
    order.item = item
  then
  <seller> delivery: CakeDelivery
  where
    delivery.receiver = customer &&
    delivery.item = item
	agreement :: Contract
	agreement = CommitCash ident party1
	  (ConstMoney 1000) 15 200
	  (When (OrObs (two_chose party1 party2 party3 0)
	    (two_chose party1 party2 party3 1))
	  190
	  (Choice (two_chose party1 party2 party3 1)
	    (Pay ident2 party1 party2
	      (AvailableMoney ident) 200
	      redeem_original)
	    redeem_original)
	  redeem_original)
	Null

Figure 12.1 Drafting Style in CSL (left) and Marlowe (right)

The CSL example is derived with permission from similar examples at <https://docs.deondigital.com/v0.60.0/src/guidechapters/yourfirstcontract.html> accessed 25 June 2021. The Marlowe example is derived with permission from PL Seijas and S Thompson, 'Marlowe: Financial contracts on blockchain', in International Symposium on Leveraging Applications of Formal Methods (Springer 2018) 356.

3. Controlled Natural Language

With a CNL that is also a DSL (ie, where the top two layers of the language stack have been merged), it is envisaged that drafting lawyers could ensure consistency of expression and structure for a written contract, without needing to become programmers. The combined CNL/DSL would, for example, be a structured variant of English and the process of drafting a contract would use English vocabulary and sentence construction—however, the CNL/DSL would also have sufficiently well-defined syntax and semantics to enable automatic conversion to lower layers in the language stack (for those aspects requiring automation), culminating in executable smart contract code to control a computer.[105]

For smart contracts, this would remove the error-prone step of manual conversion from natural language to a specification or programming language.

---

[105] Furthermore, it is likely that the process of drafting using a CNL would utilize a customized word processor with an advanced user interface (textual, visual, or a combination of both) to guide correct usage. An example of such an application is Juro (<https://juro.com/> accessed 24 June 2021). Similar tools (eg, structure editors and source-code editors) have long been available to computer programmers.

With help from a customized user interface, it could be impossible to write a contract that could not be automatically convertible to executable code. This would provide substantial advantages for validating smart contract code, whilst remembering that the code must be validated against the entire agreement, not just the written contract.

Advantages would also accrue, in some sectors such as financial services, from the standardization of contract language and semantics.[106] Further advantages with respect to automated analysis of contracts (eg, to highlight conflicts between clauses, missing clauses or incomplete expressions) include 'helping a practitioner clarify what is going on, even without encoding those statements into software'[107] and may potentially have impact more generally in legal drafting.[108]

Attempto Controlled English (ACE)[109] is a mature CNL that generates Prolog code and maps onto the Web Ontology Language (OWL), though it has not yet been used directly in the specification of legal contracts.

The language 'L4' is currently under development and aims to be a combined CNL and DSL.[110] Similarly, Stanford University's CodeX centre proposes a computable contracting approach with the development of a Contract Description Language that is a single artefact that does not require programming yet is 'machine-understandable'.[111]

More immediately, Kowalski's 'Logical English'[112] combines a controlled natural language with a prototype implementation in the logic programming language Prolog. Kowalski describes Logical English as being 'modelled on the language of law' and 'designed not only to be understood without computer training, but to be useful for a wide range of computer applications, including legal applications involving smart contracts'. Kowalski and his colleagues at Imperial College London have been working on the logical specification of legal language for decades,[113, 114] and this recent work builds on the

---

[106] The benefits of standardization of contracts are well established in the financial sector (eg, ISDA, *User's guide to the ISDA 2002 master agreement* (ISDA 2003)) and the construction sector (eg, D. Chappell, *Understanding JCT Standard Building Contracts* (9th edn, Routledge 2012) and are also being used in other sectors (eg, K. Martin, 'Deconstructing Contracts: Contract Analytics and Contract Standards' in *Data-Driven Law* (Auerbach Publications 2018) 33, 34). See also ISDA's 'Clause Project' work on standardization of language used in ISDA Schedules.
[107] See n. 93.
[108] J. Cummins and C. Clack, 'Transforming Commercial Contracts Through Computable Contracting' (2020) *arXiv preprint*, <https://arxiv.org/abs/2003.10400> accessed 24 June 2021.
[109] N.E. Fuchs *et al.*, 'Attempto Controlled English: A Knowledge Representation Language Readable by Humans and Machines' (2005) 3564 Lecture Notes in Computer Science 213, 250.
[110] <https://github.com/smucclaw/dsl> accessed 24 June 2021.
[111] <http://compk.stanford.edu/> accessed 24 June 2021.
[112] R. Kowalski, 'Logical English' in *Logic and Practice of Programming (LPOP)* (2020) <http://www.doc.ic.ac.uk/~rak/papers/LPOP.pdf> accessed 24 June 2021.
[113] R.A. Kowalski, 'Logic for Knowledge Representation' (1984) 181 Lecture Notes in Computer Science, Springer 1, 12.
[114] M.J. Sergot *et al.*, 'The British Nationality Act as a Logic Program' (1986) 29(5) *Communications of the ACM* 370, 386.

Logic-Based Production System (LPS) programming language developed with Sadri and Calejo.[115] Logical English was developed with assistance from Davila and Karadotchev; in particular, Karadotchev's MSc dissertation provides a case study of using Logical English to express parts of the ISDA Master Agreement for financial transactions,[116] and further work by Kowalski and Datoo[117] has focused on the use of Logical English to standardize the wording of legal clauses concerning automatic early termination in ISDA Master Agreements. Figure 12.2 illustrates the style of the current version of Logical English that can be translated directly into Prolog. Prolog itself is a declarative specification language that is suitable for automatic conversion to lower layers in the language stack and can therefore contribute to the generation of smart contract code.

```
It is not the case that
      it is an obligation that a party pays to a counterparty
      an amount in a currency for a transaction on a date
   if it is an obligation that the party pays to the counterparty
      a net amount in the currency for the transaction on the date

It is an obligation that a party pays to a counterparty
      a net amount in the currency for a transaction on a date
   if the net amount is a larger aggregate amount minus a smaller aggregate amount
      and the larger aggregate amount is the sum of each amount of each payment by the
      party to the counterparty in the currency for the transaction on the date
      and the smaller aggregate amount is the sum of each amount of each payment by the
      counterparty to the party in the currency for the transaction on the date
```

Figure 12.2 Example Drafting Style in Logical English

Reproduced with permission from R. Kowalski 'Logical English as an Executable Computer Language', Keynote Presentation at ReMeP2019 (Imperial College London 2019): <http://www.doc.ic.ac.uk/~rak/papers/Logical%20English.pdf> accessed 24 June 2021. See also n.116.

From the example given in Figure 12.2 it can be seen that the current version of Logical English is much closer to natural language than the DSL examples given in Figure 1, and is somewhat closer to the computable contracting concept of a single artefact that is understandable to lawyers *and* understandable to computers.

---

[115] R.A. Kowalski, F. Sadri, and M. Calejo, 'How to do it with LPS (Logic-Based Production System)' in RuleML + RR (Supplement) International Joint Conference on Rules and Reasoning (2017) <http://ceur-ws.org/Vol-1875/paper16.pdf> accessed 24 June 2021.

[116] V. Karadotchev, 'First Steps towards Logical English', MSc dissertation (Imperial College London, 2019) <https://github.com/vkghc/logical-english-interpreter> accessed 14th September 2021.

[117] R. Kowalski and A. Datoo, 'Logical English meets Legal English for Swaps and Derivatives' (2021) Artificial Intelligence and Law, Springer < https://link.springer.com/article/10.1007%2Fs10506-021-09295-3> accessed 20 September 2021.

The language Lexon[118] also a combined CNL and DSL and specifically targets the generation of smart contract code for blockchains, aiming for automation of performance rather than analysis of contract semantics. Lexon comes with tools to support an extensible grammar, a formal syntax definition is being developed with a small core operational semantics, and the current version of the language can generate Solidity, Javascript, or Sophia[119] as output. Figure 12.3 illustrates the drafting style for Lexon: notice that whereas the Logical English example in Figure 12.2 expresses deontic aspects (obligations), the Lexon example in Figure 12.3 expresses actions (since its purpose is to generate code to make the relevant payments).

LEX Netted Payment #1.

"Party One" is a person.
"Party Two" is a person.
"Total Payable of Party One" is an amount.
"Total Payable of Party Two" is an amount.

CLAUSE: Register Payable By Party One.
The Total Payable of Party One is increased by a given Amount.

CLAUSE: Register Payable By Party Two.
The Total Payable of Party Two is increased by a given Amount.

CLAUSE: Daily Netting.
If the Total Payable of Party One is greater than the Total Payable of Party Two, then
Party One pays the Net Amount to Party Two.
If the Total Payable of Party Two is greater than the Total Payable of Party One, then
Party Two pays the Net Amount to Party One.
Afterwards, terminate the contract.

CLAUSE: Net Amount.
"Net Amount" is defined as the difference between
the Total Payable of Party One and the Total Payable of Party Two.

Figure 12.3 Example drafting style in Lexon
This example is reproduced with permission from a personal communication with H. Diedrich.

---

[118] H. Diedrich, *Lexon Bible: Hitchhiker's Guide to Digital Contracts* (Wildfire Publishing 2020). See also Idelberger's comparative analysis of Lexon: F. Idelberger, 'Merging Traditional Contracts (or Law) and (Smart) e-Contracts—a Novel Approach' in *The 1st Workshop on Models of Legal Reasoning* (2020) <https://lawgorithm.com.br/wp-content/uploads/2020/09/MLR2020-Florian-Idelberger.pdf> accessed 24 June 2021.
[119] <https://aeternity-sophia.readthedocs.io/en/latest/contracts/> accessed 24 June 2021.

Angelov *et al.* have created a controlled natural language for the purposes of analysing conflicts in normative texts.[120] Their system 'AnaCon' converts CNL into a formal specification language, detects conflicts and gives counter-examples in cases where conflict is found. Their CNL is somewhat restricted, being a subset of what can be expressed in the formal language, and uses braces to identify the start and end of literal text. The language is action-based and cannot make statements concerning 'state of affairs', but it does support reasoning about concurrent actions and permits the user (who drafts the CNL) to state *a priori* those actions that cannot occur concurrently. It also supports statements of reparations—ie, penalties that apply where a party breaches either a prohibition or an obligation. Camilleri *et al.*[121] modified this CNL to support the generation of Contract-Oriented Diagrams,[122, 123] which provide visual representations of contracts together with a translation into timed automata.

The approach of computable contracts can be viewed as a specific methodology within the context of smart contracts. Computable contracts, if successful, have the potential to bring substantial benefit to the validation of smart contract code, and are a key component of current research and development in smart contracts. There are of course many research challenges for this methodology.

One challenge is the representation of both (i) meaning that is known in advance; and (ii) meaning that is not fully known in advance and may require dynamic or post-hoc consideration of context and facts. The latter, for example, includes important legal phrases and words whose semantics are difficult to define (simple examples include the words 'reasonable', 'material', and 'timely'); and deliberately vague clauses (as discussed in Section D). Another challenge is the representation of points in the contract where human discretion is desired (and an understanding of how this will be implemented as interaction with the running code).[124] Another again is the representation of complex temporal aspects of a contract.[125]

A further research consideration is the investigation of new modular forms of expression for contracts, to enable greater encapsulation and re-usability of components (such as expressions and clauses). With natural language contracts, there is nothing to prevent two or more clauses being in conflict, and the entire contract must be read and understood in order to know whether any other clause conflicts with or overrides the clause we wish to understand. An important question is whether it could be possible to approach contract drafting in a different way, where to understand the meaning of a component (eg, a clause or expression)

---

[120] See n. 20.
[121] J.J. Camilleri, G. Paganelli, and G. Schneider, 'A CNL for Contract-oriented Diagrams' in *International Workshop on Controlled Natural Language* (Springer 2014) 135, 146.
[122] See n. 100.
[123] G. Diaz et al., 'Specification and Verification of Normative Texts Using C-O Diagrams' (2013) 40(8) *IEEE Transactions on Software Engineering* 795, 817.
[124] See n. 4.
[125] See n. 59.

it is no longer necessary to read the entire contract. Approaches to modularity include syntactic solutions (eg, templates, prose objects, common contractual forms)[126] and language solutions (eg, functional composition,[127] the controlled use of natural language[128]). Another approach is to use non-monotonic reasoning in the semantics, so that the overlap in clauses is directly modelled without the need for modules; for example, Guido Governatori's defeasible deontic logic with violations[129] supports overlapping clauses and provides a superiority relation to manage conflicts.

F. Conclusion

For smart legal contracts, where computer technology is used to automate the performance of aspects of legal contracts, a key issue is whether the code is faithful to the contract. This chapter has exposed some of the complex issues underlying such a seemingly simple question, and in particular it has explored the role played by languages and the problems that arise when translating from high-level languages (such as natural languages) down through the 'language stack' to low-level languages (such as the instruction sets for computers). The problem of validation is not just technical in nature, and a perspective has also been provided on the difficulties that arise when the two specialized fields of law and computer science interact—many of these difficulties also arise in the context of language, such as the large gap in linguistic semantics and pragmatics. This is problematic not just for the automation of legal contracts but also for the current movement towards 'Rules As Code' where it is argued that contracts and legislation should be drafted in both code and natural languages at the same time.[130]

In an attempt to ameliorate some of these issues, a current direction of research within the area of smart contracts is the methodology of computable contracts, where a single artefact is both the contract (understandable by lawyers who are not programmers) and the code (understandable by computers). An appropriate

---

[126] See Section E.1. Also see K. Martin, 'Deconstructing Contracts: Contract Analytics and Contract Standards' in *Data-Driven Law* (Auerbach Publications 2018) 33, 34.
[127] See Section E.2, especially the compositional approach: also see n. 89
[128] H.E. Smith, 'Modularity in Contracts: Boilerplate and Information Flow' (2006) 104 (5) *Michigan Law Review* 1175, 1222 <https://repository.law.umich.edu/cgi/viewcontent.cgi?article=1538&context=mlr> accessed 24 June 2021.
[129] G. Governatori, 'Representing Business Contracts in RuleML' (2005) 14(2–3) *International Journal of Cooperative Information Systems* 181, 216.
[130] <https:// s3.amazon aws.com/ us.inev ent.files.gene ral/ 6773/ 68248/ 1ac865f169861 9047 027f d22e ddbb a6e0 57e9 90e.pdf> See n. 99. See also M. Lauritsen and Q. Steenhuis, 'Substantive Legal Software Quality: A Gathering Storm?' in *ICAIL'19 Proceedings of the Seventeenth International Conference on Artificial Intelligence and Law*, (ACM 2019) 52, 62, and J. Eyers, 'CSIRO says laws should be published in code' *The Australian Financial Review* (17 January 2020).

language for drafting that single artefact must be devised: one that is (i) readily generated, understood, and used by lawyers, and (ii) expressed using a specification language that may be translated directly to lower layers in the language stack. Various approaches are being pursued, including markup languages, specification languages and domain-specific languages, including controlled natural languages that are also domain-specific languages.

The issue of the drafting lawyer's user experience is not yet resolved. Some Domain Specific Programming Languages (such as CSL[131]) are quite advanced, yet their style is more like programming code than writing legal prose. By contrast, Logical English (see Section E.3) is a formal specification language that approaches the kind of controlled natural language with which a lawyer might be comfortable, as does Lexon. However, the results of evaluation on large and complex contracts have not yet been published and in their preliminary forms they are not yet as flexible and elegant as uncontrolled English. But these are early days—the preliminary version of Logical English eschews pronouns in order to avoid ambiguity, and although (as observed by Smith[132] and initially by Grice[133]) much of the brevity of natural language comes from the ability to imply context, perhaps the avoidance of ambiguity is more important. Logical English has made initial steps in the implication of context through the controlled use of definite articles, and perhaps a formalization of more complex implicature in natural language (without re-introducing ambiguity) could be a fruitful direction for future research.

---

[131] See n. 94.
[132] See n. 128.
[133] H.P. Grice, 'Logic and Conversation' in *Speech Acts* (Brill 1975) 41, 58.

13
The Mathematization of Legal Writing
The Next Contract Language?

*Megan Ma**

A. Introduction	305	3. Logical roots of drafting	314
B. A Primer on Translation	307	D. A Study of Code	315
1. Semantics	307	1. Ergo	316
2. Context	308	2. Lexon	318
3. Code	309	E. Observations and Implications	322
C. Logical Ancestors and the Formalistic Return	310	1. Ergo	322
		2. Lexon	323
1. Early signs	310	3. Blawx	319
2. Modern variations	311	F. Conclusion	325

A. Introduction

Legal pedagogy is experiencing a pressure to evolve with the currents of 'progress'; namely, at the hand of artificial intelligence technologies in law. Mireille Hildebrandt's recent textbook is a prime example. *Law for Computer Scientists and Other Folk*, as she describes, is an endeavour to 'bridge the disciplinary gaps' and 'present a reasonably coherent picture of the vocabulary and grammar of modern positivist law'.[1] Moreover, law schools are beginning to offer technology-driven and dynamic courses including training in computer programming.[2]

---

* Megan Ma is a PhD candidate at Sciences Po Law School and is an incoming CodeX Fellow at Stanford Law School. She is also a Lecturer in Law at Sciences Po, teaching courses in AI and Legal Reasoning, Legal Semantics, and Public Health Law and Policy.

[1] M. Hildebrandt, *Law for Computer Scientists and Other Folk* (forthcoming OUP 2020). A web version is currently accessible on the open source platform <https://lawforcomputerscientists.pubpub.org/> accessed 12 July 2021.

[2] Law schools are beginning to offer courses in technical development, including computer programming. Moreover, classes that apply design-thinking to legal studies and were developed with the intention of acknowledging technology as a powerful driving force in law. Consider Harvard Law School and Georgetown Law School's Computer Programming for Lawyers classes, or The Design Lab at Stanford

Between law and computer science, there appears to be two opposing spectrums of thought: one in boundless enthusiasm of the two working in tandem; and the other in rampant scepticism. This raises the question: do these two disciplines operate in the same language? If not, could they? This chapter seeks to unpack these questions through the case of smart contracts[3] and, specifically, the programming languages of these contracts.

Reflecting on the philosophies of logic, linguistics, and law, my project follows the conundrum: what is the significance of *medium* in contract drafting? Jacques Derrida questioned natural language and the medium of writing as the accepted form of communication. His argument strikes an interesting parallel to the use of written and descriptive language in law. Derrida notes that writing is perceived as the original form of technology; that 'the history of writing will conform to a law of mechanical economy'.[4] Independent of structure or meaning, writing was a means to conserve time and space by way of 'convenient abbreviation'.[5] Is legal writing then not merely a method of notation? Would this not suggest that the use of code advances the notion of convenience, communicating in a manner that further conserves time and space?

Alternatively, Michel Foucault states that, rather than 'an arbitrary system', language forms and is interwoven with the world. It is an 'enigma renewed in every interval ... and offer[ed] ... as things to be deciphered'.[6] Equally, Geoffrey Samuel argues that the 'true meaning of a legal text is hidden within the language employed'.[7]

The project is, therefore, a thought experiment on the translation of text to numbers by unpacking several formal languages used in computable contracts. In identifying the logic of these languages, the project tackles methods of legal writing. The hypothesis is that, by analysing the components of both legal and programming language, we can develop a richer dialogue on the sociological implications of translating law to algorithmic form. Furthermore, it would be interesting to consider what contextual understanding may need to exist to 'interpret' contractual language.

Law School. See for example Harvard Law School, 'Computer Programming for Lawyers', <https://hls.harvard.edu/academics/curriculum/catalog/default.aspx?o=75487> accessed February 2020.

[3] When using the term 'smart contracts' for this paper, I am not referring to the narrow scope of blockchain contracts, but to 'computable contracts' as discussed in H. Surden, 'Computable Contracts' (2012) 46 *University of California Davis Law Review* 629, 647.

[4] Jacques Derrida, *Limited Inc* (Northwestern University Press 1988) 4.

[5] *Ibid.*

[6] M. Foucault, *The Order of Things: An Archaeology of the Human Sciences* (Tavistock Publications 1970) 35.

[7] G. Samuel, 'Is Legal Reasoning like Medical Reasoning?' (2015) 35 *Legal Studies* 323, 334.

The chapter[8] will unfold as follows. Section B will open with a primer on translation, introducing broader notions of conceptual transfer, meaning, and understanding. Section C will reflect on histories of logic and formalism; and their return in light of new contract drafting technologies. Section D embarks on a brief investigation of programming languages, analysing sample translations of contracts from natural language to computer code. Section E will gather observations and suggest implications. Finally, Section F concludes with a few remarks.

B. A Primer on Translation

Rules are pervasive in the law. In the context of computer engineering, a field that regards itself as fundamentally deterministic, the translation of legal text to algorithmic form is seemingly direct. In large part, law may be a ripe field for expert systems and machine learning. For engineers, existing law appears formulaic and logically reducible to 'if, then' statements. The underlying assumption is that the legal language is both *self-referential* and *universal*. Moreover, *description* is considered distinct from *interpretation*; that in describing the law, the language is seen as quantitative and objectifiable. The qualities described would then make computer programming languages ideal. But is descriptive natural language purely dissociative? In other words, does the medium matter in legal writing? From the logic machine of the 1970s to the modern fervour for artificial intelligence (AI), governance by numbers is making a persuasive return. Could translation be possible?

1. Semantics

Recently, Douglas Hofstadter commented on the 'Shallowness of Google Translate'.[9] He referred largely to the Chinese Room Argument;[10] that machine translation, while comprehensive, lacked understanding. Perhaps he probed at a more important question: does translation *require* understanding? Hofstadter's experiments seemed to suggest it does. He argued that the purpose of language was not about the processing of texts. Instead, translation required imagining and remembering: 'a lifetime of experience and [...] of using words in a meaningful way, to realize how devoid of content all the words thrown onto the screen by Google

---

[8] An ongoing collaboration between the author and the MIT Computational Law Report examine formal programming languages is underway. This chapter will proceed with a select analysis of a few languages used. Nevertheless, these suffice to illustrate the working hypothesis.
[9] D. Hofstadter, 'The Shallowness of Google Translate' *The Atlantic* (30 January 2018) <https://www.theatlantic.com/technology/archive/2018/01/the-shallowness-of-google-translate/551570/>. accessed 2 March 2022.
[10] A thought-experiment first published by John Searle in 1980 arguing that syntactic rule-following is not equivalent to understanding.

translate are.'[11] Hofstadter describes the classic illusion, known as the 'ELIZA effect', of having the appearance of understanding language; instead, the software was merely 'bypassing or circumventing' the act.[12]

2. Context

For Yulia Frumer, translation not only requires adequately producing the language of foreign ideas, but also the 'situating of those ideas in a different conceptual world'.[13] In languages that belong in the same semantic field, the conceptual transfer involved in the translation process is assumed. In the event that languages do not share similar intellectual legacies, the meaning of words must be articulated through the conceptual world in which the language is seated.

From a historical perspective, Frumer uses the example of eighteenth century Japanese translations of Dutch scientific texts. The process by which translation occurred involved analogizing from Western to Chinese natural philosophy; effectively reconfiguring the foreign to local through experiential learning. This is particularly fascinating, provided that scientific knowledge inherits the reputation of universality. Yet, Frumer notes, ' ... if we attach meanings to statements by abstracting previous experience, we must acquire new experiences in order to make space for new interpretations'.[14]

Interestingly, Duncan Kennedy tested the relationship between structure, or symbols, and meaning by deconstructing argument into a system of 'argument-bites'. Argument-bites form the basic unit and such bites often appear in opposed pairs. Operations performed on argument-bites constitute and build legal arguments. Such operations diagnose and assume the circumstances, or relationships, in which the argument-bite is to be manipulated and 'deployed'.[15] Such import of structural linguistics conceptualizes law and argument as systematically formulaic—'a product of the logic of operations'.[16] Perhaps most interesting thing about Kennedy's theory is his idea of 'nesting'. Kennedy describes nesting as the act of 'reproduction' or the 'reappearance of [argument-bites] when we have to resolve gaps, conflicts or ambiguities that emerge [from] ... our initial solution to the doctrinal problem'.[17] Therefore, the conundrum surfaces where language may be applied to law in a mechanical fashion but the process of reducing legal argument to

---

[11] See n. 9.
[12] Ibid.
[13] Y. Frumer, 'Translating Worlds, Building Worlds: Meteorology in Japanese, Dutch, and Chinese' (2018) 109 *Isis* 326.
[14] Ibid., 327.
[15] Kennedy describes relating argument-bites to one another by such operations as a means of confronting legal problems. See D. Kennedy, 'A Semiotics of Legal Argument' (1994) 3 *Collected Courses of the Academy of European Law* 317, 351.
[16] Ibid., 343.
[17] Ibid., 346.

a system of operations raises considerations on the act of labelling and the power in its performativity. That is—as Kennedy rightfully notes—'language seems to be "speaking the subject," rather than the reverse'.[18]

3. Code

Hildebrandt teases at this premise by addressing the inherent challenge of translation in the computer 'code-ification' process. Pairing speech-act theory with the mathematical theory of information, she investigates the performativity of the law when applied to computing systems. In her analytical synthesis of these theories, she dwells on meaning. 'Meaning', she states, 'depends on the curious entanglement of self-reflection, rational discourse and emotional awareness that hinges on the opacity of our dynamic and large inaccessible unconscious. Data, code ... do not attribute meaning.'[19] The inability of computing systems to process meaning raises challenges for legal practitioners and scholars. Hildebrandt suggests that the shift to computation necessitates a shift from reason to statistics. Learning to 'speak the language' of statistics and machine-learning algorithms would become important in the reasoning and understanding of biases inherent in AI-driven legal technologies.[20]

More importantly, the migration from descriptive natural language to numerical representation runs the risk of slippage as ideas are (literally) 'lost in translation'. Legal concepts must necessarily be reconceptualized for meaning to exist in the mathematical sense. The closest in semantic ancestry would be legal formalism. Legal formalists thrive on interpreting law as rationally determinate. Judgments are deduced from logical premises and syllogisms; meaning is assigned. While, arguably, the formalization of law occurs 'naturally'—as cases with like factual circumstances often form rules, principles, and axioms for treatment—the act of conceptualizing the law as binary and static is puzzling. Could the law behave like mathematics; and thereby the rule of law be understood as numeric?[21]

---

[18] *Ibid.*, 350.

[19] M. Hildebrandt, 'Law *as* Computation in the Era of Artificial Intelligence: Speaking Law to the Power of Statistics' (2019) *Draft for Special Issue University of Toronto Law Journal* 10.

[20] Advances in natural language processing (NLP), for example, have opened the possibility of 'performing' calculations on words. This technology has been increasingly applied in the legal realm. See *ibid.*, 13.

[21] What is being described here is not in reference to the World Justice Project (WJP) Rule of Law Index. I do, nevertheless, acknowledge that it is a prime example of a broadly qualitative assessment transformed as a 'quantitative tool for measuring the rule of law in practice'. See World Justice Project, *World Justice Project Rule of Law Index* (2019) 7. Interestingly, the collection of data for the Index is a multi-pronged empirical study taken from both experts and citizenry. Yet, the assessment on adherence to the rule of law is based on the WJP's own universal principles. Consequently, it may be a worthwhile future project to consider the risks involved with identifying the rule of law in a numeric context, particularly when the assessment is internal to its own organization's standards.

C. Logical Ancestors and the Formalistic Return

To translate the 'rule of law' in a mathematical sense requires a reconfiguration of the legal concept. Interestingly, the use of statistics and so-called 'mathematisation' of law is not novel. Oliver Wendell Holmes Jr most famously stated that '[f]or the rational study of the law, the blackletter man may be the man of the present, but the man of the future is the man of statistics and the master of economics.'[22] Governance by numbers then realizes the desire for determinacy; the optimization of law to its final state of stability, predictability, and accuracy. The use of formal logic for governance has a rich ancestry. From Aristotle to Descartes to Leibniz, the common denominator was that mathematical precision should be applied across all disciplines.

1. Early signs

Twelfth-century logicians allegedly used logical paradoxes to spot 'false' arguments in courts of law.[23] It was not, however, until the seventeenth century when Gottfried Leibniz proposed a mental alphabet;[24] whereby thoughts could be represented as combinations of symbols, and reasoning could be performed using statistical analysis. Building from Leibniz, George Boole's infamous treatise, *The Laws of Thought*, argued that algebra was a symbolic language capable of expression and construction of argument.[25] By the end of the twentieth century, mathematical equations were conceivably dialogic—a form of discourse.

This was perceivably owed to Boole's system; that complex thought could be reducible to the solution of equations. Nevertheless, the most fundamental contribution of Boole's work was the capacity to isolate notation from meaning.[26] That is, the 'complexities' of the world would fall into the background as pure abstraction was brought to centre stage. Eventually, Boole's work would form the basis of the modern-day algorithm and expression in formal language.

The American Standard Code for Information Interchange ('ASCII'), is an exemplary case. Computers are only capable of understanding numbers. For a computer to interpret natural language, ASCII was developed to translate characters to numbers. Using a binary numeral system, ASCII assigns a value to a letter. In brief, by performing the mathematical calculation, a binary code of 0s and 1s could be

---

[22] O.W. Holmes Jr, 'The Path of Law' (1897) 10 *Harvard Law Review* 457, 469.
[23] K. Devlin, *Goodbye Descartes: The End of Logic and The Search for a New Cosmology of the Mind* (John Wiley & Sons 1997) 54.
[24] *Ibid.*, 62.
[25] G. Boole, *The Laws of Thought* (1854) chapter 1.
[26] See n. 23, 77.

computed from a letter. Early conceptual computing devices, such as the Turing machine, were born into existence as a direct product of Boolean algebra.

Christopher Markou and Simon Deakin point to the breakthroughs in Natural Language Processing ('NLP') as contributors to the emergence of 'legal technology'.[27] Markou and Deakin point to Noam Chomsky and early researchers of AI designing 'hard-coded rules for capturing human knowledge'.[28] Chomsky's work stirred new developments in NLP, eventually powering advances in machine translation and language mapping. Known as expert systems, NLP applications 'relied upon symbolic rules and templates using various grammatical and ontological constructs'.[29] These achievements were then further enabled by Deep Learning[30] models, capable of abstracting and building representations of human language.

With the rise of artificial legal intelligence, computable contracts—and more broadly, computable law—are making a powerful return. Contracts may be represented as computer data with terms made 'machine-readable' through a process of conversion: from descriptive natural language to consonant computer instruction. Conditions of agreements are not explained but listed as structured data records. Despite the capacity to express contracts in an alternative computable form, there is no means for interpretation. Instead, interpretation is perceived as irrelevant. Should digital data inscription and processing be considered a form of legal writing? If so, would it change the character of law?

2. Modern variations

Expert systems and machine learning technology used for the revision of contracts seek to reduce the risk of human error. Eventually, contract analysis would manage, record, and standardize provisions that are 'proven favourable';[31] in effect, perfecting contractual boilerplate. Boilerplate contracts are often regarded as a trade-off between tailoring and portability; that with broad standardization, the 'burden' of interpretation is lifted.[32] Contractual

---

[27] C. Markou and S. Deakin, 'Ex Machina Lex: The Limits of Legal Computability' (2019) Working Paper <https://ssrn.com/abstract=3407856> accessed 2 March 2022.
[28] *Ibid.*, 13. See also cited reference, E. Brill and R.J. Mooney, 'Empirical Natural Language Processing' (1997) 18 *Artificial Intelligence Magazine* 4.
[29] See n. 27, 11–15.
[30] Deep Learning is a subset of machine learning that involves artificial neural networks and the assigning of numerical weights on input variables. For further explanation, see *ibid.*, 10–12.
[31] B. Rich, 'How AI is Changing Contracts' *Harvard Business Review* (Web Article, February 2018) <https://hbr.org/2018/02/how-ai-is-changing-contracts> accessed 2 March 2022. See also white paper 'How Professional Services Are Using Kira' *Kira Machine Learning Contract Analysis* <https://cdn2.hubspot.net/hubfs/465399/04-resources/whitepapers/KiraSystemsWhitePaper-HowProfessionalServicesFirmsAreUsingKira.pdf> accessed February 2019.
[32] H.E. Smith, 'Modularity in Contracts: Boilerplate and Information Flow' (2006) 10 *Michigan Law Review* 1175, 1176.

boilerplate, therefore, relies heavily on formalistic drafting, whereby form presides over meaning. For computable contracts, the migration of mediums—from descriptive natural language to mathematical form—generates data that identifies and signals the specific version of contracts that should be used in future cases.

a.) Market uptake

Edilex, a Canadian legal technology start-up, is automating contract drafting by offering both AI-programmed applications and downloadable contract and legal document templates. Edilex's mission statement: The simplification of legal transactions and democratizing access to legal services. Genie AI is another fascinating legal technology start-up that offers AI-powered contract drafting. Using machine learning, clauses are recommended to help lawyers 'draft contracts faster'.[33] Moreover, the technology marketed is focused on legal language, and one that is 'suitable for lawyers'.[34]

Evidently, the target demographic for each of the start-ups is rather different. The former is focused on the democratization of legal services; while the latter on enhancing the legal profession. Yet, both start-ups thrive on the notion of formalization; that there is a 'perfect' form achievable. By integrating AI in contract drafting, there is a push away from static mediums of writing. These include Microsoft Word and Adobe PDF; the original technological artefacts that evolved from pen and paper. In either case, the technology is never described as a replacement.[35] The purpose of these inventions is merely assistive.

b.) New environments

Interestingly, the legal community is beginning to explore the problems associated with the use of static platforms like Microsoft Word. In a recent paper, Michael Jeffrey interrogates the use of Microsoft Word as the dominant and default format for the editing of legal documents. He considers the inefficiencies of manual updating, drafting, and reviewing. Though interpreted as a static platform, Microsoft Word, in actuality, 'can be controlled through code'.[36] Included in its software is, in fact, a number of templates modelled specifically for

---

[33] 'Super Drafter' (*Genie AI*) <https://genieai.co/home> accessed February 2020.
[34] *Ibid*. Genie equally advertises smart filters and an automatic knowledge base.
[35] This follows the existing literature that technology could only be complementary to the law. See F. Pasquale, 'A Rule of Persons, Not Machines: The Limits of Legal Automation' (2019) 87 *George Washington Law Review* 2, 6. See also N.M. Richards and W.D. Smart, 'How should the law think about robots?' in R. Calo *et al.* (eds), *Robot Law* (Edward Elgar 2016) 16–18, arguing that law hinges on social and political relationships and metaphors that require a *latent* understanding of temporal social constructs.
[36] M. Jeffrey, 'What Would an Integrated Development Environment for Law Look Like?' (2020) 1(1) *MIT Computational Law Report* <https://law.mit.edu/pub/whatwouldanintegrateddevelopmentenvironmentforlawlooklike> accessed 2 March 2022.

drafting legal documents. These templates contain automatic text entry, macros, and special formatting.[37]

For long and complicated legal documents, Jeffrey argues that an Integrated Development Environment ('IDE') could 'facilitate the authoring, compiling, and debugging' of contracts.[38] For programmers, the use of IDE provides several key features that are amenable to legal drafting. Options include increased readability owed to color-coded syntax highlighting, automatic error detection, and predictive auto-complete features to provide suggestions while drafting. These features, he claims, could improve the drafting process by reducing the risk of human error and increasing efficiency.

Yet, the most interesting perspective he offers is the subtle equation of linguistic concepts as inherently mathematical.[39] Jeffrey draws programming concepts and applies them specifically to elements of legal drafting. The syntax, he notes, is 'designed for drafting and document generation' and that the process would be 'quite natural'.[40] The underlying assumption is that static platforms and IDEs have the same functional purpose. The differences lie in the added features for real-time edits. This speaks to a greater assertion: programming languages serve the same uses as natural language. Yet, the shift from pen and paper to Microsoft Word did not fundamentally change the use of natural language for legal drafting. The use of IDEs, on the other hand, would effectively alter not only the platform, but also the method of execution.

Juro, for example, is a legal technology start-up that promotes contract management on a single, browser-based, platform.[41] Juro works to improve contract management by translating contracts drafted on Microsoft Word or Adobe PDF to machine-readable form. The startup's platform allows for contracts to be built in a text-based format that is language independent (ie, JSON). The contracts, thereby, exist in code. Other startups such as OpenLaw apply a hybrid approach; an integration of machine-readable code with clauses drafted in natural language.[42]

OpenLaw runs on Javascript[43] and uses a markup language to 'transform natural language agreements into machine-readable objects with relevant

---

[37] 'MS Word for Lawyers: Document Templates' (*Tech for Lawyering Competencies: Research & Writing*) <https://law-hawaii.libguides.com/TLC_Research_Writing/WordTemplates> accessed 1 May 2020.

[38] See n. 36.

[39] Jeffrey notes, 'For legal drafting ... the focus is linguistic—rather than mathematical—but the core concepts are the same.' See *ibid*.

[40] *Ibid*.

[41] See R. Mabey and P. Kovalevich, 'Machine-readable contracts: a new paradigm for legal documentation' (*Juro Resources*) <https://info.juro.com/machine-learning?hsCtaTracking=60e75e06-22bb-4980-a584-186124e645b3%7C6a7d3770-289d-4c97-bcfb-c9f47afec77f> accessed 1 February 2020.

[42] 'Markup Language' (*OpenLaw*) <https://docs.openlaw.io/markup-language/#variables> accessed 1 April 2020.

[43] Defined as a programming language with a code structure to build commands that perform actions. 'Code Structure' *The JavaScript Language* <https://javascript.info/> accessed 1 April 2020.

variables and logic defined within in a given document'.[44] These documents are then compiled together to act as contracts. Clauses are interpreted as 'embedded template[s]'.[45] The goal is to reduce drafting work by storing boilerplate clauses as data that may be added to contracts. The incorporation of code with natural language offers a dynamic interpretation of legal agreements. It mirrors the notion that select contractual elements are reproducible and calculable, while others require human intervention. The drafting process is left rather unchanged.

The aforementioned start-ups are only a few of the growing number of legal technology start-ups committed to improving contract drafting. These contracts are classified as more efficient, precise; otherwise, 'smarter'. Despite these developments, there is a dearth of literature on the use of formal languages for legal writing. However, formal programming languages for contract drafting not only exist but have proliferated in the past few years. Interestingly, their ancestors sprung from logic programming in the 1970s.

3. Logical roots of drafting

Even before the days of logic programming, contract drafting has seen symptoms of logic-based strategies in the literature since the 1950s. In 'Symbolic Logic: A Razor-Edged Tool for Drafting and Interpreting Legal Documents', Layman E Allen proposed the use of mathematical notation for the expression of contracts. He argued that its application will improve clarity, precision, and efficiency of analysis. Allen's article introduces six elementary logical connectives: implication, conjunction, co-implication, exclusive disjunction, inclusive disjunction and negation.[46] The most interesting connectives are implication and co-implication. These logical connectives are associated with the representation of causal relations; otherwise, 'if X then Y' statements. Allen labels this form of expression as 'systematically-pulverized'[47] and the process of transforming a statement to this form requires two primary actions: (1) divide statement into constituent elements; (2) and rearrange elements to approximate a 'systematically pulverized' form. Co-implication enhances the equation by including logical equivalencies. In sum, he teases at the age-old use of syllogisms in legal writing and in so doing provides an excellent backdrop to the current study. In effect, how are programming languages applying logic to legal drafting?

---

[44] See n. 42.
[45] Ibid.
[46] L.E. Allen, 'Symbolic Logic: A Razor-Edged Tool for Drafting and Interpreting Legal Documents' (1957) 66 *Yale Law Journal* 833.
[47] Ibid., 836.

D. A Study of Code

Two of the most broadly used programming languages, Python and Prolog, use opposing methods of operation; the former is procedural, while the latter is declarative. Procedural programs often specify *how* the problem is to be solved. That is, with procedural programs, there are clear instructions for the program to follow. Akin to baking, all terms are defined explicitly, and all rules must be laid out. Should a program, such as Python, find that it cannot proceed with the task, this is typically because the program is unable to recognize the syntax. Equally, Python is incredibly sensitive to changes in the code; even a misplaced comma or indent in the spacing could affect the overall outcome of the specified task. Procedural programs often include *functions*: self-contained modules of code capable of being manipulated and reused for innumerable tasks. Perhaps its most powerful operation, Python is able to examine and decide actions on the basis of conditions. Moreover, Python simplifies work by being able to loop through the same tasks in a given list. Rather than the manual repetition of a given task, Python is able to do so in a matter of seconds.

On the other hand, declarative programs specify *what* the problem is and ask the system, instead, to solve it. Declarative languages are founded on either the relationships (1) between objects; or (2) between objects and their properties. These relationships may be defined implicitly through rules or explicitly through facts. Facts describe relationships, while rules qualify them. The purpose of Prolog, therefore, is to form a fixed dataset that would derive answers to future queries about a relationship or set of relationships based on the inputted information. In contrast, the purpose of Python is to complete a particular task. While it can certainly account for prospective changes to the data, every step is explicitly expressed.[48]

Advancing forward several decades, Python and Prolog have become the basis for a new era of programming languages used for drafting computable contracts. Ergo, Lexon, and Blawx are among a few of the current languages being prototyped. Each language is built from a different model. Ergo is a programming language modelled on execution logic for legal writing. It belongs to the suite of resources offered by the Accord Project.[49] Blawx and Lexon, on the other hand, are non-coding options with the former developed on declarative logic and the latter derived from linguistic modelling.[50]

In order to understand how formal languages may be used to draft contracts, I refer to extracts of legal documents translated from natural language to code.

---

[48] While Python is able to work in adaptive environments and does not have a fixed data set, the comment is directed at the explicit expression of a given task.

[49] Founded by co-editor, P.G. Hunn. The Accord Project also offers CiceroMark and Concerto. The former is a contract template generator that helps build agreements embedded with machine executable components. The latter is a program that enables the data of computable contracts to be manipulated and modelled. The Accord Project also offers a template editor to build and test out smart agreements. For more information, see 'Key Concepts' (*Accord Project*) <https://docs.accordproject.org/docs/accordproject-concepts.html> accessed 1 October 2020.

[50] Lexon qualifies its model as designed with the intention of reasoning in natural language and uses formal linguistic structure. See H. Diedrich, *Lexon: Digital Contracts* (Wildfire Publishing 2020).

These translations are originals of each programming language, unedited and taken directly from their technical documentation. They were included as demonstrations of how contracts may be drafted in the select language. The translations are, therefore, presumed to be manually done by each language's programmers; and thereby, implicitly representative of their respective design choices.

1. Ergo

To begin, Ergo follows a more traditional form of procedural programming and is largely function-based. This means that its language is predicated on the performance of the contract. However, Ergo is unique. It cannot be divorced from the overarching contract implementation mechanism, known as Cicero. Cicero consists of three 'layers': (1) text; (2) model; and (3) logic. Ergo is the logic component.[51] It is perhaps considered the 'end' process of a continuous flow of translation from human-readable to machine-executable.[52]

The Cicero architecture, therefore, is an interdependent network of resources that start with natural language text and end with compartmentalized data packages. That is, natural language contracts may be deconstructed into reproducible modules that can be interchangeably used between various types of contracts. How does this work?

Contractual clauses are sorted and categorized into qualitative and quantitative components. Descriptive terms of the contract remain at the text layer.[53] Variables that are quantifiable, on the other hand, are extracted from the natural language and captured in the model layer. These variables are notably bits of information that are reusable, iterative, and computable. This layer binds natural language to data, as variables map conditions and relationships of the contract. Arriving at the logic layer, what remains are functional requirements of these variables. In other words, what are the specific operations necessary in order for these variables to perform the demands and terms of the contract?

Consequently, Ergo is intentionally limited with its expressiveness.[54] Consider the following contractual clause translated from descriptive natural language to Ergo. The original provision, in prose, states:

> Additionally, the Equipment should have proper devices on it to record any shock during transportation as any instance of acceleration outside the bounds of -0.5g and 0.5g. Each shock shall reduce the Contract Price by $5.00.

---

[51] See n. 49.
[52] *Ibid.*
[53] *Ibid.*
[54] The goal is for conditional and bounded iteration. This is presumably contributive to the reusability of contractual clauses. See 'Ergo overview' (*Accord Project*) <https://docs.accordproject.org/docs/logic-ergo.html> accessed 1 February 2020.

The clause, in code, reads:

```
contract FragileGoods over FragileGoodsClause {
    clause fragilegoods (request : DeliveryUpdate) : PayOut emits PaymentObligation {
        let amount = contract.deliveryPrice.doubleValue;
        let currency = contract.deliveryPrice.curencyCode;
        let shocks =
            integerToDouble(count(
                foreach r in request.accelerometerReadings
                where r > contract.accelerationMax or r < contract.accelerationMin
                return r
        ));
        let amount = amount - shocks * contract.accelerationBreachPenalty.doubleValue;

        enforce request.status = ARRIVED and request.finishTime != none
        else return PayOut{
            amount: MonetaryAmount{
                doubleValue: amount
                currencyCode: currency
            }
        };
```

Figure 13.1 Extracted from Ergo's 'Fragile Goods Logic' (Cicero Template Library, Github) <https://github.com/accordproject/cicero-template-library/blob/master/src/fragile-goods/logic/logic.ergo> accessed October 2020

At first glance, the translation is rather striking. There are ostensibly several omissions from the natural language text to the Ergo language. First, mention of recording devices that determine the weight changes is absent from the code. Moreover, fluctuations in the 'Contract Price' are equally excluded. Instead, only variables remain, such as DeliveryUpdate, PaymentObligation, accelerometerReadings, accelerationMin, and etc.

Upon closer reading, it becomes clear that the contractual clause has undergone a *decoupling process*—that is, a conversion from the original unified contractual language to independent, actionable constituents has taken place. These variables are quantitative reconfigurations of the 'performative' elements of the contract. For example, the model layer reconstructs the weight changes and fluctuations in the 'Contract Price' to:

```
},
"accelerationMin" : -0.5,
"accelerationMax" : -0.5,
"accelerationBreachPenalty" : {
    "$class" : "org.accordproject.money.MonetaryAmount",
    "doubleValue": 5,
    "currencyCode": "USD"
}
```

Figure 13.2 Extracted from 'Fragile Goods' (Accord Project) <https://templates.accordproject.org/fragile-goods@0.14.0.html> accessed 1 October 2020

As noted, Ergo applies these variables and signals their operations. The Ergo language requests for the acceleration readings from the recording devices, then dependent on the parameter changes, computes whether the 'Contract Price' would alter. This method of distilling the quantifiable from the qualifiable suggests that contracts are necessarily unambiguous and, in effect, are simply a matter of structuring.

2. Lexon

Lexon is an innovative peculiarity. Unlike other programming languages, Lexon is founded on linguistic structure and designed to reason in natural language. Lexon reduces vocabulary and grammar to rule sets. Lexon's base vocabulary consists of definable 'names' used to designate objects and clauses. Just as one would draft sentences in natural language with a subject and predicate, Lexon operates in a similar fashion. There is, however, an important difference: articles are considered superfluous, 'filler', words.

```
LEX Payment.

:Payer" is person.
"Payee" is person.
"Payment" is amount.

Prayer pays Payment to Payee.
```

Articles (a, an, the) can be left out.

Figure 13.3 Extract of a Contract Drafted in Lexon

For an agreement at this level of simplicity, articles may not seem necessary to clarify the meaning of contractual terms. Nevertheless, party obligations do occasionally hinge on articles, potentially affecting the performance of the contract. It is not inconceivable that specifying a particular object as opposed to a general one matters, especially in certain procurement and sales contracts. Lexon argues that the primary role of articles is to improve text readability. Yet, Lexon concedes that articles can 'fundamentally change the meaning of a contract' and that this may be an area ripe for abuse.[55]

---

[55] Lexon has noted that future tools would account for the possibility such abuse. See n. 50, 33.

Further complicating the narrative, Lexon is not concerned about semantics altogether. The startup's creator, Henning Diedrich, acknowledges the inherent ambiguity of natural language that renders interpretation challenging; but argues that the Lexon language is not to clarify nor create *complete contracts*. Instead, Lexon is *bridging the gap* between formal programming and natural languages. Like other formal languages, Lexon cannot understand the 'meaning' of its terms. Its structural design only accounts for functionality. Lexon uses Context Free Grammars (CFG). First theorized by Chomsky, CFG do not depend on context; rules operate independent of the objects in question.[56] Chomsky had originally developed CFG in an effort to formalize natural language. While this was largely unsuccessful in linguistics, it has since been popularized in computer science. Consequently, Lexon applies the model to create a programming language that is both expressible in natural language and readable by machines.

Diedrich contends that meaning could never be attained. Meaning is regarded as something that, though it cannot be extracted, could be pointed to or described.[57] The Lexon language is structured in a manner reflective of these underlying assumptions. That is, rather than dwelling on the interpretation of the specific word or phrase in natural language, *Lexon limits meaning to function*. Diedrich states, 'the actual functionality of the contract is the better description of ... the list of the actual rights and obligations of that person without relying on the original meaning of the word.'[58] By framing functionality as a proxy for party obligations, Lexon inadvertently reframes the basis of contract theory from party autonomy to contract performance.

3. Blawx

Finally, Blawx is a programming language based on declarative logic.[59] Perhaps the most interesting element of this language is its user interface. The code visually appears as puzzle pieces or 'blocks' searching for their missing piece. Blawx was inspired by the program, Scratch, a in the manner of a Visual Programming Language ('VPL') created at MIT as an educational assistant for children learning how to code. VPLs use visual expressions, spatial arrangements of text, and graphic symbols to depict entities in their ontologies and represent syntax. As the blocks

---

[56] The term 'context-free grammars' is what is most commonly used by linguists today. Chomsky's original formulation was known as constituency grammars. Chomsky emphasized the scientific study of language in a rational manner, free of context and culture. See N. Chomsky, *Cartesian Linguistics: A Chapter in the History of Rational Thought* (3rd edn, Cambridge University Press 2009) and also, N. Chomsky, 'Remarks on Nominalization' in R.A. Jacobs and P.S. Rosenbaum (eds), *Readings in English Transformational Grammar* (Ginn and Company 1970) 184–221.
[57] See n. 50, 107.
[58] *Ibid.*, 106.
[59] At the time of writing, Blawx was in alpha version and at the early stages of a prototype.

literally connect with one another, they visually capture the relationships between objects and their properties.

Much like Prolog, Blawx operates on sets of facts and rules. Facts represent objects, or things, known to be true *in the code*. Rules are coded statements composed of both conditions and conclusions. Both elements are required in order for a rule to exist. Unlike other programming languages, Blawx works on the premise of declarative rules such that 'conclusions are true if conditions are true'. This may seem no different than traditional 'if, then' statements. This is surprisingly false. In programming, the 'if conditions then conclusions' framework operates temporally. For machines, this means that conditions only apply to the specific task at hand and do not apply globally to the program.[60] In the case of Blawx, rules are encoded in a declarative manner to help form the particular program's 'universe of knowledge'. Once the universe of facts and rules have been established, the program will be able to answer to queries. Queries are fact-based and binary.

Blawx thus aims to transform legal documents to queryable databases. In practice, this would suggest that contracts may be encoded using the aforementioned logic of the program. Ultimately, the goal is for parties to be able to reason by simply asking binary questions to the application. The encoding of facts and rules allows parties to move from legal reasoning to legal information extraction. Interpretation, then, is no longer required since the solutions are presumed to be directly retrievable.

A typical example of Blawx takes a piece of legal prose, such as a legislative provision defining a 'personal directive' and the requirements of its validity (such as being signed and dated by its maker in the presence of a witness. The example provision appears visually.[61] This translation is an especially difficult read. First, the 'block' appearance of the language may be troubling for those who are not visual learners. The programming language forces the reader to focus on the conceptual components of the rules as opposed to the clause. The logic of the program necessitates a substantive breakdown of the legislation to its ontological elements. Simply put, it reduces the law to the relevant actors and their obligations. In this example, the elements are (i) the roles (actors); and (ii) the signatures (obligations).

More importantly, the process of converting natural language to Blawx raised significant challenges with interpretation.[62] Coding the legislation required

---

[60] This is described as 'if right now the conditions are true, then next the computer should do conclusions'. See 'Facts, Rules, and Queries' (*Blawx.com*) <https://www.blawx.com/2019/09/facts-rules-and-queries/#page-content> accessed February 2020.

[61] See 'Example: Using Blawx for Rules as Code' Blawx.com, accessed 1 February 2020 <https://www.blawx.com/2020/01/example-using-blawx-for-rules-as-code/#page-content> accessed 13 July 2021.

[62] There is repeated commentary on the difficulty of interpretation when converting to a binary. 'Example: Using Blawx for Rules as Code' (Blawx.com) <https://www.blawx.com/2020/01/example-using-blawx-for-rules-as-code/#page-content> accessed 1 February 2020.

reframing the meaning of 'personal directive'[63] into a binary; either as an object or an action. Fundamentally, it is a reconfiguration of the law to its function. Rather than, 'what are the requirements of a personal directive', the question becomes 'what actions must be taken in order for the personal directive to have legal effect?' The questions asked *de facto* bear the same meaning. The difference, while subtle, crucially points to an implicit recognition of the legal effect of the document in natural language. Notably, a personal directive could only *exist* should the requirements be met. Otherwise, it would simply be a piece of paper. This was raised as a note on the translation. Blawx introduced the concept of 'validity' as a new condition[64] because there was no form of classification for a document that was not a personal directive. In the context of computable contracts, the Blawx language—like Ergo—would perhaps work best for contracts with clear objectives and unidirectional relationships.

Thus, in examining the three prototype programming languages, the technology is observably limited. Namely, contracts drafted in these languages are governing simple transactions. Nonetheless, they expose conflicting interpretations of contract theory between computer scientists and legal actors. More specifically, a commonality across all program languages is the formulation of contract law as entirely predicated on performance. Consequently, programming languages alone are function-based. The principle of party autonomy, expressed often as details in contract terms, is only secondary to the actual completion of the transaction. Rather than what parties have agreed to and *how* the parties have fulfilled their obligations, it becomes solely dependent on *whether* the obligation has been completed.

Zev Eigen claims that contracts are a product of how drafters and signers interpret the law.[65] Contracts that are negotiated represent a 'meeting of the minds'. Standard boilerplate, on the other hand, is the product of only the drafters' interpretation, not the signers'. In this case, programming languages run the risk of eliminating 'the signers' altogether; meanwhile, 'the drafters' are the code itself.[66] Consequently, this could reconfigure basic contract law doctrines, conflating principles of consideration as offer and acceptance as obligation.

---

[63] Here, the personal directive is understood to be a 'living will'.
[64] Following the formula of a declarative rule, this would suggest 'this is a personal directive (conclusion) if it is valid (condition)'. See n. 61.
[65] Z.J. Eigen, 'Empirical Studies of Contract' (2012) *Faculty Working Paper* 204, 7, <https://scholarlycommons.law.northwestern.edu/cgi/viewcontent.cgi?article=1203&context=facultyworkingpapers> accessed 12 July 2021.
[66] Consider Lawrence Lessig and the conceptualization of code as law. Lessig draws attention to code as a form of control; that 'code writers are increasingly lawmakers'. See L. Lessig, *Code 2.0* (2nd edn, Basic Books 2006) 79.

E. Observations and Implications

With the increasing normalization of smart contracts, computer code could foreseeably become a vehicle in which contracts are drafted. The question remains: should programming languages be recognized as a form of legal language? The following section will analyse the observations taken from the study against existing literature. As discussed, function becomes paramount to computable contracts. Formal programming languages reveal that because natural language is indeterminate, a migration away from semantics to syntax could resolve the challenges relevant to interpretation.

In 'Self-Driving Contracts' Casey and Niblett consider the gaps in contract theory owed to the ambiguity of natural language. They argue that, currently, natural language as a medium of legal expression allows contracts to be both intentionally and unintentionally incomplete.[67] Intentional incompleteness is interesting because it implies that general language circumvents the *ex ante* costs of decision-making and creates a space for changes in conditions. This, however, often leads to issues of enforceability; such as disputes about the definitions of 'reasonable' and 'material'.[68] Consequently, 'self-driving contracts' would use machine learning algorithms and expert systems to remove questions of enforceability.

1. Ergo

Much like 'self-driving' contracts, the aforementioned programming languages help automate the processes of contract creation and interpretation. As observed in the study, interpretation is internalized by the technical bounds of the programming language as contractual clauses are constructed to reason purposively. For Ergo, the question remains whether contractual ambiguities are a mere consequence of improper structural representation. Notably, the migration from text-to-model layer implies the potential for mathematical precision from inception. Duncan Kennedy argues that, whether for H.L.A. Hart or Hans Kelsen, determinacy is a matter of degree.[69] Though legal drafting may be simplified through the act of sorting, assessing whether a clause is sufficiently amenable to reusability is a difficult ask. The underlying assumption for the Cicero architecture is that the simplification process will not eventually alter the method of drafting. Perhaps a better question would be: is there value to qualitative descriptive clauses in legal writing?

---

[67] A.J. Casey and A. Niblett, 'Self-Driving Contracts' (2017) 43 *Journal of Corporation Law* 101, 112–17.
[68] *Ibid.*, 113.
[69] D. Kennedy, *Legal Reasoning: Collected Essays* (Davies Group Publishers 2008) 154.

That is, would the 'text' layer remain relevant going forward? What is the significance of retaining the natural language component of contract drafting?

As discussed by Casey and Niblett, contracts are deliberately incomplete. Again, this is because contracts are manifestations of party intent.[70] In effect, *how* contracts are written frames the behaviour of parties, and thereby influences their performance. Contracts that are negotiated tend to be less specific and have more room for interpretation. Performance is less likely to be exact. Yet, performance is not compromised despite the 'incompleteness' of the contract. Instead, the contract's incompleteness signals trust between parties.[71]

Contracts, then, call for ambiguity, and specifically semantic ambiguity. In isolation, programming languages like Ergo create the illusion that mutual assent is automatic and indisputable. Semantic ambiguities no longer exist, as contractual negotiations are limited to operations with little care for parties' preferences. This could potentially invoke a behavioural change since contracts would become primarily functional in nature. Equally, this could conceivably lead to a simplification of contracts and a convergence towards contractual boilerplate. But, just as Cicero operates through the trifecta of text-model-data, natural language is indispensable from contract drafting. The role of natural language becomes monumental, ensuring that the elements of trust and party autonomy are not compromised and, rather, maintain the heart of contracts doctrine.

2. Lexon

Lexon's language poses a similar puzzle. Readable in natural language, Lexon's verbs are coded such that they coincide with the performance of the transaction. Diedrich's formulation of meaning finds parallels with Ludwig Wittgenstein's writings. Wittgenstein argued that language, as used presently, extends beyond names and 'dry dictionary entries with their definitions'.[72] The actions derived from words are effectively married to their meanings. It is conceivable, then, that language could be no more than a list of orders and classifications. It follows that abiding by the rules of association is accepting the inherent authority of its practice. Meaning is found in the *performance* of the word, and not in the *understanding* of it.

Lexon claims that it neither translates nor transforms thought.[73] Instead, Lexon preserves the natural language construction of 'meaning', by placing a constraint

---

[70] See n. 64.

[71] *Ibid.*, 17. Eigen references the study by Chou, Halevy, and Murninghan. See E.Y. Chou *et al.* (2011), 'The Relational Costs of Complete Contracts' IACM 24th Annual Conference Paper, <https://papers.ssrn.com/sol3/papers.cfm?abstract_id=1872569>.

[72] S. Jasanoff, *Can Science Make Sense of Life?* (Polity 2019) 117. Wittgenstein considered language as a form of life; and thereby, linguistic expression is constructive of its being. See also L. Wittgenstein, *Philosophical Investigations* (2nd edn, Macmillan 1958) 19.

[73] See n. 50, 104.

on its rules. That is, Lexon uses a subset of natural language grammar as the programming language of the legal contract.[74] This approach is known as 'controlled natural language'. Rather than processing *all* of natural language, a machine need only to process an assigned vocabulary and grammar. The assigned set becomes the operatives of the language game. Equally, Lexon wears the legacy of Chomskyan formal semantics; whereby the syntactic structure is both a projection and vessel of its function. Interpretation is again internalized by 'mapping ... symbols to a reference structure'.[75] The difficulty lies in whether the constrained grammar could sufficiently manage more complex legal contracts. In the attempt to draft contracts within its specific grammar, party intentions may be lost in the language game.

3. Blawx

Blawx, by way of contrast, requires definition in advance the actions of contractual parties. Again, the code internalizes interpretation as a preliminary step. Using a declarative logic, Blawx must first set the parameters of its dataset. On several occasions,[76] the code required defining new categories and forming different classifications in order to be amenable to translation. This typically involved making explicit the relationship between legal objects and their properties. Interestingly, legal questions, particularly those assumed to be accommodating to mathematical configuration, were found to be challenging in the Blawx language. For example, the determination of a personal directive could easily be structured as a binary question. Still, it was necessary to define the object that did not fulfil the requirements of a personal directive. This subsequently provoked a deeper question on the implicit recognition of legal documents.

Simply put, Blawx exposes the tacit force of law. Reflecting on Hart, the underlying assumption of 'power-conferring rules [...] exist not in virtue of some further law-making act, but in virtue of a fundamental rule of recognition implicit in the practice of law-applying officials'.[77] Similarly, J.L. Austin contemplated the performative effect of 'utterances'. The act of marriage, for example, demonstrates how the utterance of a certain few words puts into effect its meaning.[78] Austin suggests that legal and moral obligations are relative to public specification; that utterances necessarily correspond with particular procedures situated within social contexts. Their mis-performance leads to a nullification or voidance of the act.[79]

---

[74] *Ibid.*
[75] G. Baggio, *Meaning in the Brain* (MIT Press 2018) 62.
[76] Blawx had encountered difficulty with interpreting the natural language of the legislation. Blawx recognised that it took 'creative liberties' in converting the statute to Blawx language. See n. 61.
[77] H.L.A. Hart, *The Concept of Law* (Oxford University Press 1961) chapters 4, 6.
[78] J.L. Austin, *How to Do Things with Words* (2nd edn, Harvard University Press 1975) 7.
[79] *Ibid.*, 16.

In the case of Blawx, the meaninglessness and inability to articulate the 'inverse' of a legal document (ie, something missing the signature of a witness which would otherwise be a personal directive) points to the implicit dimension of the law.[80] The dividing line between a document having legal force—or not—speaks to the inherent authority of legal rules. Just as marriage could only be recognised within a specific circumstance, it was necessary for Blawx to acknowledge the deeper context; that is, 'how is legal recognition being defined?' Blawx then applied a purposive interpretation, classifying legal recognition as validity. While the translation is rather sound—and validity is often a proxy for determining legal effect—the questions asked are distinct. The movement from 'is it legal' to 'is it valid' is necessarily distinguishable in contract law. A contract may be valid but legally unenforceable. Therefore, interpreting legal force as validity subverts existing contract theory and, again, narrows interpretation to seemingly functional equivalents. Casey and Niblett are correct in noting that there will be an attempt to 'pigeonhole [computable contracts] into existing frameworks of thought'.[81] For Blawx, its uptake would likely require changes to existing contracts doctrines.

The challenge of using programming languages centres on interpretation. Drafting contracts in formal programming languages highlights the ambiguity of the original source. The task of translating contracts from descriptive natural language to code brings to light underlying assumptions of legal authority as well as re-evaluates party autonomy in contract theory. In nearly all the cases, the interpretative exercise was done *ex ante*; that the contract's legal effect was established in direct parallel to performance.

F. Conclusion

As mentioned, formal programming languages have the impact of unifying legal concepts such as mutual assent with performance; effectively, reinvigorating arguments associated with contractual boilerplate.[82] Alternatively, they raise an argument for increased granularity by breaking down and identifying the conceptual components of contracts to specific executable tasks programmable in the language. In either case, there is a definite reframing of contract law doctrines.

---

[80] G.J. Postema, 'Implicit Law' (1994) 13 *Law and Philosophy* 361. There is an alternative argument that Blawx may not be the right choice in programming language for particular types of law (ie, legislation). That is, procedural languages could perceivably be a better option. Python, a procedural language, could construct a personal directive on the basis that the requirements are fundamentally conditional. There may be merit to a deeper investigation as to whether certain programming languages are more conducive to specific types of contracts.

[81] See n. 66.

[82] Boilerplate contracts as lifting the burden of interpretation and ensuring enforcement. Computable law borrows and extends the characteristics of contractual boilerplate in the name of increased precision, efficiency, and certainty. See Smith (n. 32).

Recalling Derrida: is the use of computer code for legal writing beyond 'convenient abbreviation'? Hofstadter would argue that computer code cannot be devoid of meaning and would indeed imprint its effect to the system. Hofstadter states, '[w]hen a system of "meaningless" symbols has patterns in it that accurately track, or mirror, various phenomena in the world, then that tracking, or mirroring imbues the symbols with some degree of meaning...'[83] Structure cannot be divorced from meaning.

Perhaps the question asked is not whether programming languages *should* be a legal language, but *how* they could be amenable to the demands of contract law. Are these demands to create more complete contracts, or to limit ambiguity and ensure contract enforcement? This chapter has sought to raise a number of concerns relevant to the use of programming languages, particularly in the translation of contracts from natural language to code. These concerns speak to whether the effort to complete contracts or disambiguate contractual terms could resolve inherent tensions of contract interpretation and enforceability.

However, using programming languages to draft contracts could pose challenges akin to incorporating contractual boilerplate into new contracts. As Richard Posner argues, clauses 'transposed to a new context may make an imperfect fit with the other clauses in the contract...'[84] At the current stage, the programming languages discussed appear to limit interpretation to functionality. By so doing, they run the risk of a conceptual mismatch with existing contract theory; potentially reframing the purpose of contract law altogether. With the use of programming languages to draft contracts, future challenges would include ensuring that the interpretative exercise is not forgotten. Instead, interpretation should continue to be understood as a continuous effort, allowing for responsiveness to changing environments.

---

[83] D. Hofstadter, *Gödel, Escher, Bach* (Twentieth-anniversary edn, Basic Books 1999), preface-3.
[84] R.A. Posner, 'The Law and Economics of Contract Interpretation' (2005) 83 *Texas Law Review* 1581, 1587.

14
Beyond Human

Smart-contracts, Smart-Machines, and Documentality

David Koepsell[*]

A. Introduction	327	4. Inscriptions that (re)write themselves	332
B. Social Objects and Documents	328	5. Inspectability and endurance	333
1. The role of records in making the social world	329	6. 'Smart legal contracts' and the digital foam at the top of the stack	335
2. Blockchains and specific dependence	330	7. Issues of intentionality and Chinese rooms	337
3. Computability and documentality	331	C. Conclusion	337

A. Introduction

A blockchain is a ledger with some special features. It is typically digital, distributed, democratic, and immutable. Because the book-keeping in a blockchain is verified by numerous, distributed 'nodes', and updates are only adopted when a consensus of those nodes says they are true, no central, verifying authority has control over the addition of new entries.[1] The entries provide a perfect record of all properly verified changes made over time, so the record is trustworthy and immutable. Blockchains like Bitcoin can provide new ways to exchange money without central banks, for instance. But blockchains like that are 'dumb' in the sense that they do nothing but record verified transactions. They cannot 'act', they can only be acted upon. Some blockchains allow not only the recording of static entries, but also for instructions about how to deal with certain types of

---

[*] David Koepsell is a Lecturer in Law at the Texas A&M University Philosophy Department and a is a lawyer admitted to practice in New York. He has published widely including landmark work in law and technology. He is the founder and CEO of EncrypGen, Inc, a blockchain genomics software company, and has been a tenured Associate Professor at TU Delft, Visiting Professor at UNAM, Instituto de Filosoficas and the Unidad Posgrado, Mexico, Director of Research and Strategic Initiatives at COMISION NACIONAL DE BIOETICA in Mexico, and Asesor de Rector at UAM Xochimilco.

[1] M. Hamilton, 'Blockchain Distributed Ledger Technology: An Introduction and Focus on Smart Contracts' (2020) 31(2) *Journal of Corporate Accounting & Finance* 7–12, 7.

new entries, entities, or other inputs such that they can execute actions based upon logic embedded in those entries. These blockchains are the foundation for what some call 'Web 3.0', where the full potential of the 'semantic web' means that automated business and social processes can execute logic across the web's distributed architecture.[2] Web 3.0 blockchains enable computation and are 'Turing-complete' in that they embody the infrastructure for a sort of 'world computer' upon which distributed programs can perform any conceivable function.

The theory of 'documentality' is a way of describing social reality. Developed by Italian philosopher Maurizio Ferraris, it says that the world of social objects is a world of documents—*fundamentally*. Specifically, it attempts to fill in gaps regarding the existence of objects whose dependence precedes traditional, written documents. Borrowing from Jacques Derrida, Ferraris concludes that no part of social reality exists outside of texts, while expanding the notion of texts to include inscriptions (including even memories in minds). Social reality is constructed by 'inscriptions' on documents, the most basic of which can be the inscriptions of memories, ideas, and things like promises and intentions on the matter of human brains.[3]

In earlier work, Barry Smith and I raised some issues that confront the theory of documentality when electronic documents are involved, specifically problems concerning the distinction between fixed inscriptions and dynamic software, as well as the existence of legal entities that are never inscribed at all (like a common law marriage, that can exist even without any agreement among the parties). In this short chapter, I consider briefly how extending our discussion of documentality and electronic media is further complicated by Web 3.0, or the emerging realm of documents and processes involved in smart contracts and their offspring, and consider some implications for the law arising from this new manner of executing code and weaving new layers of social reality.[4]

B. Social Objects and Documents

'Social reality' is composed of objects whose existence depends upon 'collective intentionality.' The modern philosopher who has done the most to spur the study of social reality is John Searle. He first proposed the formula 'x counts as y in context c' to explain how social objects come about and described the mechanism for their

---

[2] B.E.J. Floros 'Web 3.0—The Internet of Value' (John Wiley & Sons, Inc 2019). <https://doi.org/10.1002/9781119551973.ch38>, 127.

[3] M. Ferraris, 'Documentality, or Europe' (2009) 92(2) *The Monist* 286–314.

[4] N. Szabo, 'Formalizing and Securing Relationships on Public Networks' (1997) *First Monday* (first proposed the notion of programmable 'smart contracts').

existence as 'collective intentionality', or distributed beliefs about the existence of social objects.[5]

A prototypical example is money. Money differs from currency. A dollar bill denotes value, but the money that exists does so despite the bills that denote it. Our collective valuing of US Dollars ('USDs'), and the vast web of institutions that help to maintain our collective valuing of USDs, are what make money, as opposed to mere currencies. Fluctuations in the values of money of different kinds, and the occasional failures of monetary systems completely, help to demonstrate how money is a complex social object that is not dependent upon the bills that are circulated.[6]

Most economies consist of large amounts of money that are, in point of fact, *debts*. In other words, when parties agree in an exchange that one will owe another a sum, as some other thing is exchanged, that obligation counts as part of the total money supply, generally called the M2 supply. In the case of banks, those debts come to be 'backed up' by state insurance, and the amount considered part of the total money 'supply'. Money can come into existence through collective agreements about who owes how much what to whom. Interestingly, this precisely demonstrates how cryptocurrencies come to be valuable. It is the exact same mechanism of collective intentionality—except omitting central authorities. The entire 'market cap' for Bitcoin ('BTC') or Ether ('ETH')—the two biggest cryptocurrencies so far—is due to the web of beliefs about the nature of that money having value.

1. The role of records in making the social world

Much of social reality depends at some point on *records*. Record-keeping helps to establish the verity of claims about things like debts, obligations, and other sorts of social objects that exist by virtue of collective intentionality. The records don't always *create* those objects (though in cases of what we call 'specific dependence', they do), but they serve as accessible recordings of the existence of those objects. Because of the importance of recordings about social objects, documents of various kinds serve as an important focus of our inspection of social reality, and underscore our concerns with creating better modes of verifiable record-keeping.

Documenting social reality, and the role of documents in creating social reality, led Maurizio Ferraris to the rather grand claim that *all* of social reality is documents, or inscriptions of some kind in some medium.[7] While we maintain that there are exceptions to the theory of documentality that continue to make it suspect for certain cases, the emergence of blockchain technology provides an interesting

---

[5] J.R. Searle, *The Construction of Social Reality* (Free Press 1995).
[6] J.R. Searle, *Making the Social World: The Structure of Human Civilization* (Oxford University Press 2010).
[7] M. Ferraris, *Documentality: Why it is Necessary to Leave Traces* (Fordham University Press 2012).

set of new questions, and also a basis for a new use of the theory as a sort of guidance for best practices in emerging technologies upon which new sorts of social objects may be built.

2. Blockchains and specific dependence

In their most prevalent uses, blockchains are documents that both embody and enable transactions. Because the truth of their entries can be maintained with a distributed network of nodes, the records that blockchains create can be trusted without regard to a central authority. This is a significant evolution of documentary trust from that to which we are accustomed. Until blockchains, the trust which could be placed in documents like bank, citizenship, birth, and other records depended upon the degree of trustworthiness ascribed to the social institutions that establish and maintain those objects.[8] Typically, those entities have been states and other institutions established by states and agreements among them. The most famous, and arguably first electronic blockchain, the Bitcoin network, was created as an attempt to show that the social institution of money could be created and maintained without a state, or any central governing authority that required trust.

In some ways, blockchains help to solve some of the issues of provenance and authenticity posed by electronic documents that Smith and I noted in our article 'Beyond Paper'. The authenticity of a particular document can better be recorded and checked by the existence of an immutable record maintained by a distributed network with very little risk of hacking or illicit alteration.[9] More so certainly than when electronic records are maintained in 'ordinary' networks or cloud storage in central locations with little to no community validation. Combined with improved technologies for validating identity and confirming origins of documents, blockchains promise to be able to provide the sort of indicia of authenticity for a range of documents reserved until now by notary, official filing, and *apostille* procedures, all without needing some central authority.

This means that numerous social facts upon which there is specific or prototypic dependence for a document (like birth certificates, cadastral registration of land, bearer bonds, or visas, etc) could become independent of central, state, or other governing bodies and could move with confidence to electronic-only mechanisms for creation and preservation without losing trust, and maybe even while improving trustworthiness. New technologies involving blockchains even present opportunities to solve some problems associated with the reproducibility of electronic records, and enable the creation of unique, exchangeably *singular* electronic

---

[8] F. Ferguson, 'Bitcoin: A Reader's Guide (The Beauty of the Very Idea)' (2019) 46(1) *Critical Inquiry* 140–66. <https://doi.org/10.1086/705302>.
[9] D. Koepsell and B. Smith, 'Beyond Paper' (2014) 97(2) *The Monist* 222–35.

individuals. Non-Fungible Token ('NFT') technology allows digital individual items to be maintained without confusion with copies. So, a NFT-based birth registry database, for instance, could maintain 'true' and 'only' original digital birth certificates, traceable, and verifiable by all, conforming to community-approved and vetted standards, against which any copy could be compared, all without a central governing authority being necessary.[10] Specifically-dependent electronic documents can be enabled by sophisticated blockchains, including both NFTs and smart contracts. But smart contracts make more complicated the social nature of those documents, especially as they mature to fulfil the promise of the Turing-complete platforms upon which they are being built.

3. Computability and documentality

Problems with 'originality' proof, and authenticity of electronic documents impeded their broad adoption as replacements for paper documents. Some of these problems could be solved by mature blockchain technologies as they are perfected. But more complicated is the problem of the *dynamic* nature of blockchains such as Ethereum incorporating smart contracts, making computable an entire layer of electronic expression. Entire phenomena, previously requiring intentionality and some 'meeting of minds' for execution of agreements, may now be programmed and unleashed as automated processes—without the need for humans on either end to execute some exchange or other result.

Ethereum and other blockchains are being designed to be Turing-complete, which means they can function as programming languages upon which any conceivable set of instructions could ultimately be coded. The idea has been to build a world-wide computer, and the benefits for distributed networks, the emergence of Distributed Automated Organizations ('DAOs')[11] and the potential for entirely new, automated, decentralized, and global transactions of hitherto unconceived types means that forms of documentality will evolve that Ferraris's theory of documentality fails to encompass, but for which we will need to formulate some conception of social object status and theory of social reality that accounts for such new objects. Without such a theory, legal and philosophical ambiguities will doubtless lead to significant conflict.

The 'smart contract' was intended to help realize the full automation of distributed business (and other) processes on a programmable, distributed, trustworthy international network. While the Bitcoin blockchain allows for transfers

---

[10] Q. Wang et al., 'Non-Fungible Token (NFT): Overview, Evaluation, Opportunities and Challenges' (2021) *arXiv preprint arXiv:2105.07447*.

[11] K. Jones, 'Blockchain in or as Governance? Evolutions in Experimentation, Social Impacts, and Prefigurative Practice in the Blockchain and DAO Space' (2019) 24(4) *Information Polity* 469–86. <https://doi.org/10.3233/IP-190157>.

of money without banks or states, smart contracts could allow social phenomena of conceivably unlimited range to be automated and executed, or even as many are now attempting through combination with machine learning, to evolve on their own. But all this raises the question: can machines alone create social reality? Do their objects count as *social*, and what role does a theory of documentality play in describing such phenomena?

4. Inscriptions that (re)write themselves

A foundational part of the theory of documentality is the notion that social reality, which is composed of other-directed human intentionality, is always inscribed in some medium, including human minds/brains. Ferraris claims that nothing social exists that isn't somehow inscribed as a text in some manner. Taking this to be true, this works fine for static, even electronic texts, but is problematic for complex software—especially for algorithms that are not created by humans, or that take some human input and weave from it something largely unintended or even largely unknowable by humans. For example, machine learning processes can be set in motion that use neural networking algorithms to perfect some manner of performing something (like finding an object among others) without human programming. Machine learning algorithms can even be 'programmed' by other machine learning algorithms. Machines that become good at tasks through such processes can 'compete' with other machines and evolutionary algorithms can select for those that evolve to be best.

The intended future of Web 3.0, running on smart contracts and blockchains, includes the better automation of a range of business and other social processes that have, until now, depended upon human, often imperfect and slow, input and behaviours.[12] Consider, for instance, the armies of digital employees combing through social media posts for suitability, reviewing complaints, or policing for illegal behaviours. Or investments strategies that are based on flawed, human emotion and not on sound financial principles. Even simpler examples now abound in the millions of interactions per day that are occurring solely between one human and one machine, potentially without the human knowing their interlocutor is a machine.

Chatbots are generally very simple AI that use adaptive programming, rarely (so far) neural networks, and large volumes of training materials to provide useful answers to customers queries in electronic interactions. Companies like Zendesk make their platforms available to companies worldwide for cheaper, faster, easier, and arguably more accurate customer support than using armies of live humans.

---

[12] See eg, Z. Zheng et al., 'An Overview on Smart Contracts: Challenges, Advances and Platforms' (2020) 105 *Future Generation Computer Systems* 475–91.

Current chatbots are mundane and generally indicated as such. There is a risk of employing a chatbot without alerting the user that it is one, as they cannot respond to complicated queries, may lead a customer astray, and could be deceptive. But the race is one to give them ever greater adaptability and intelligence.

The future of Web 3.0 could well include adaptive chatbots of sorts negotiating agreements for complex transactions, all mediated and recorded by smart contracts and blockchains. This underscores the question: will those agreements be part of our social reality, in what way, and to what degree? Is the lack of *human intentionality* relevant? In what way would this impact Ferraris's conception of documentality? Will machines be involved in creation of social reality, or must human minds be part of the process? Will we need to revisit our notions of what counts for minds capable of the requisite intentionality for the creation of social objects?

5. Inspectability and endurance

An issue we raised in 'Beyond Paper' was the inspectability of supposed traces/inscriptions in minds that Ferraris claims helps form the basis for social objects. Blockchains and smart contracts help solve this. Because prototypical public blockchains create immutable, public records, they are necessarily inspectable. The traces that comprise any element of a blockchain entry can be browsed via any number of tools. Blockchains like Ethereum and Bitcoin have numerous open-source tools that enable anyone with access to a web browser to look at the entry and to inspect it fully. Unlike minds, the inspectability of social objects recorded or formed on blockchains is assured, and perhaps more durably than paper records.[13]

Social objects inscribed solely in minds, like an oral promise made between two people binding their property or heirs, are necessarily ephemeral—even if we accept (which not all do) that they count as inscribed texts in minds. Once the relevant minds cease to exist, the social objects disappear. The theory of documentality does not solve this, it only complicates it. While Searle's social object theory might account for the endurance of *ideal* social objects even when the minds that created them have ceased to exist, the theory of documentality, in attempting to reify those objects in some physical substrate, makes things like promises, obligations, and contracts less endurant. Again, blockchains and smart contracts create more certainty and provide more likelihood of endurance as well as transparency.

To the degree that we can solve some of the problems noted in 'Beyond Paper' with social objects in digital media by utilizing blockchains, we can start to consider Ferraris's work on documentality not so much as a descriptive theory, but

---

[13] D. Koepsell and B. Smith, 'Beyond Paper' (2014) 97(2) *The Monist* 222–35.

as a *prescription* for creating tools and criteria for social objects that can better conform to social reality and our expectations about the objects that comprise it. Blockchains and smart contracts add important features of inspectability, can aid in auditing the originality and uniqueness, authenticity, and provenance of a document, and can even host and provide proof of the uniqueness of a digital document that has no copies, or that can be used as an exemplar against which copies are judged. Blockchain-based documents can endure as permanent, unalterable digital records of the social reality and objects that may even be solely created on them, providing better collective acceptability and trustworthiness, all without having to succumb to trust in some central authority which can be perverted, subverted, and corrupted.

a) 'Documentality' as prescriptive requirements

Social reality continues to evolve as our technologies for recording it change. The present evolution of recording via digital technologies involves a new set of challenges, including posing questions about what sort of things might count as social objects when direct, human intentionality no longer is necessary. However, blockchains especially provide opportunities to help to clarify the nature of a range of social objects and settle practical challenges that inevitably arise when they are vague.

Blockchains, which record their inscriptions in distributed, public networks, can solve issues of inspectability for document acts that create, maintain, or record social objects. Because such networks are trustless, meaning we do not need to put our trust in some central authority, but rather in the algorithmic processes and mechanical infrastructure on which the network functions, the verity of blockchain-recorded inscriptions and the authenticity of their origins can help be ensured. Smart contracts, which can be used to create computable, deterministic execution of agreements or other objects of social reality, can help to automate the consummation of document acts, record their documentary existence, and provide certainty and clear audit trails of the agreements and other social objects involved. This can provide greater certainty, help to eliminate disagreements and conflicts *post hoc*, and enable complex business and other processes to be programmed.

Transparency, predictability, inspectability, and certainty about the objects of social reality can be facilitated by the use of blockchains and smart contracts. But these tools may open up new questions about the nature of social reality itself. Moreover, objections about the ability of the theory of documentality to account properly for the nature of social reality remain. Setting aside those objections, the bases for the theory may help serve as a subset of design principles for smart contracts.

If *nothing social exists outside of texts* is taken as a starting point for building the next generation of networked social objects in ways that serve our societal purposes, then we can build better tools for tracking texts, recording agreements, and resolving conflicts about them—provided we take seriously the essential role that texts have in anything involving computation. All computerized phenomena exist by virtue of texts. Computation is a textual process. The binary code upon which all computerized phenomena depend is textual. Unlike the 'inscriptions' that may or may not describe how brains and minds work as a substrate for our intentionality, the bits that the computerized world run on are clearly digital inscriptions, a textual world that makes up an increasingly large amount of social reality. That social reality can perdure in ways that other sorts of texts may not, with greater certainty about their provenance and origins, authenticity and even meanings. The insights of documentality can thus be used as a set of concise design principles for the web of digital social reality being woven from technologies like blockchains and smart contracts. However, some perplexing philosophical questions about the nature of social reality itself will remain unresolved, and potentially grow stranger.

6. 'Smart legal contracts' and the digital foam at the top of the stack

JG Allen aptly describes contractual social reality as a 'stack', and proposes that smart contracts (blockchain based and otherwise) can be explained as another 'layer' to the traditional legal/social stack that comprises the law and customs of the social objects we call 'contracts'.[14] The advent of smart-contract-based social reality, which will include but not be limited to legal objects, will doubtless raise numerous legal disputes and require lawyers, courts, and regulators to help clarify and formalize modes of resolving them.[15] The law adapts, and while traditional notions of contract resolution, focusing on equity, intentions, and meeting of minds help us to resolve real world legal disputes in courts and arbitrations, these are all sorts of fictions that are created, as pragmatic mechanisms, to smooth the rough edges of a small but important domain of social reality. Ultimately, the objects of contracts—the rights and obligations that arise from our public interactions and private but frankly inscrutable intentional states—are at best *post hoc* assemblages from the best sources of evidence.

As more commerce and other complex social interactions become digitally mediated (and even wholly digitally created) a new layer of contractual, legal, and social reality will become increasingly prevalent. Grappling with its ontology will

---

[14] J.G. Allen, 'Wrapped and Stacked: "Smart Contracts" and the Interaction of Natural and Formal Language' (2018) 14(4) *European Review of Contract Law* 307–43.
[15] L. William Cong and H. Zhiguo, 'Blockchain Disruption and Smart Contracts' (2019) 32(5) *The Review of Financial Studies* 1754–97.

require adapting our conceptions of what counts as a 'contract', what a 'meeting of the minds' encompasses, and what equity may demand.

By way of example, consider two artificial chess agents playing chess against each other. The International Chess Federation (FIDE) has added rules regarding computer chess play.[16] Philosophers might argue as to whether computers playing chess against each other are engaging in the game of chess. Taking Barry Smith's definition of chess, for instance: 'A game of chess is a sequence of deliberate moves of certain distinctively shaped pieces across a distinctively patterned board made by two opposing players who alternate in making their moves in accordance with certain well-defined rules of which the players are aware.'[17] Serious questions arise as to whether computers count as players, and certainly as to the 'awareness' of those players. Two computers can at best *emulate* playing chess, but we can regard that as important in *some* context, and recognize these instances as worthy of *some* status.

FIDE has also drafted rules for when computers 'play chess' against each other. *FIDE Section E. Miscellaneous 03. Regulations for Play with Computers* is a set of constitutive rules governing regulation computer *versus* computer matches. The body that 'governs' international chess amended its rules for things that are arguably not chess games, or at least not between agents 'playing' chess. But these phenomena are considered important, useful, and interesting enough for new rules from a peak norm-creating body. When agents create a similar layer of institutional, artificially conducted, non-human social reality, where computers create documents, agreements, interactions, transactions, institutions, and objects via smart-contracts, despite the lack of human intentionality, or at least with significantly distanced human intentions, the importance, usefulness, and interest with which we view this new layer in the contractual stack should guide our considerations about the rules, existing or new, that circumscribe that layer.

In other words, while smart contracts, AI, and blockchain pose challenges for social reality, and perhaps legal objects in particular, we can always choose to recognize new institutional, constitutive rules to govern them. Indeed, we *must* if we want these emerging technologies to lead to prosperity. The positive law can be altered to accommodate new objects. This is often and increasingly done as technology rapidly alters our social landscape. The dynamic 'foamy' layer of digital documentality and institutional reality will settle into our existing legal order and become manageable and predictable as other new forms of technology have over time, even when they were initially very disruptive.

---

[16] T. Just and D.B. Burg (eds), *US Chess Federation's Official Rules of Chess* (5th edn, Random House Puzzles & Games 2003) compiled and sanctioned by the US Chess Federation.

[17] B. Smith, D.M. Mark, and I. Ehrlich, *The Mystery of Capital and the Construction of Social Reality* (2008) edited by B. Smith, D.M. Mark, I. Ehrlich. Open Court, 35. See also I. Johansson, 'Money and Fictions' in Kapten Nemos Kolumbarium (F. Larsson, ed, Göteborg University 2005), 73–101.

7. Issues of intentionality and Chinese rooms

John Searle, who has led much of the modern discussion of social objects and social reality, is also famous for proposing a challenge to the 'Turing test' as a means of testing for the emergence of artificial intelligence. The Turing test would allegedly help us decide if an artificial agent is really intelligent if, when an unhindered ability to question and converse with such an agent leads to a human thinking, reasonably, that they are speaking with another human, then an artificial agent is intelligent.

Searle offers the following counterexample: suppose you don't understand a word of Chinese nor its written language, but you are given the complete rulebook for choosing the correct characters that are responses to any set of Chinese characters posed in question form. The rulebook doesn't indicate the meanings of the characters (no semantics), but merely the exhaustive *syntax* for every potential query and response. The Chinese room thought experiment is meant to illustrate that a computer could be programmed or evolved to pass the Turing test, but will not necessarily ever have the *understanding* we associate with intelligence.[18]

Now consider that the future of *blockchained* social reality may be one of 'Distributed Autonomous Organizations' ('DAOs') doing business with each other, driven by machine learning, producing records of transactions completely disassociated—or at the very least, very distantly associated—from human intentionality. Until now, social reality has hinged upon collective, human intentionality. The validity of agreements and obligations, duties, debts, values, and principles and other social phenomena has been based upon the nature of our collective, sometimes unspoken, but always at least mentally held beliefs about the nature of certain things. The documents comprising a good amount of what may be considered to be social reality in the not-so-distant future may be composed by artificial agents, using evolutionary algorithms, evolving their means of generating transactions of nearly any conceivable type without human intermediaries.

C. Conclusion

Smart contracts merge documents with computation and enable much more complex computational objects and processes to be built, involving more than storage of data in documents, but a range of potential objects, even distributed autonomous organizations. We will need to determine whether and to what extent the decisions, actions, and recordings of such DAOs comprise social reality as we know it, or will need to be described as something else. Resolving this will require answering whether human intentionality is involved in machine products engaged

---

[18] J. Searle, 'Chinese Room Argument' (2009) 4(8) *Scholarpedia Journal* 3100 <https://doi.org/10.4249/scholarpedia.3100> accessed 22 February 2022.

in non-deterministic action based upon deterministic initial programming states, and whether machine intelligence itself can undertake social behaviours consistent with our current understanding of social reality.

A theory of documentality provides a good starting point for delving into these questions, as it affords us a good basis for describing the relation between inscriptions, texts, and social reality, and all digitally-based social reality (or whatever we decide to call it depending on whether machines can compose social objects) is and will likely always be fundamentally inscriptions, some text in some medium. But documentality remains limited, as we described in 'Beyond Paper', and perhaps is unsuitable for when we soon must consider what the nature of our interactions, transactions, and objects may be as we move Beyond Human.

15
Smart Contract 'Drafting' and the Homogenization of Languages

Siegfried Fina and Irene Ng (Huang Ying)[*]

A. Introduction	339	1. Programming standardization	345
B. Language, Contract Drafting, and Lawyers	340	2. Language as a barrier to entry	346
1. Smaller number of native speakers, greater monopoly?	341	E. Impacts of Language Homogenization by Smart Contracts	347
2. Smart contract 'drafting'	342	1. Loss of linguistic diversity	347
C. Smart Contracts and Language Homogenization	342	2. Notarized (smart) contracts	348
1. Standardization of programming language	343	3. Impact on the legal profession and industry	350
D. Language Homogenization	344	4. Interpretation of smart contracts by the courts	350
		F. Conclusion	352

A. Introduction

Language and contract drafting are intricately intertwined. Traditionally, contracts are drafted in written prose and in natural language (such as English, German, or Spanish). This is the type of contract that lawyers are normally expected to draft for their clients. Unsurprisingly, as providers of contract drafting services, lawyers are expected to have a good command of the language in which they are drafting.

---

[*] Siegfried Fina is a Jean Monnet Professor of European Union Law and Associate Professor of European Union Law and Technology Law at the University of Vienna School of Law, where he directs the Vienna Technology Law Program and the LLM Program in European and International Business Law. He is also a Jean Monnet Professor of European Union Law at Danube University Krems, and a Visiting Professor of Law and Co-Director of the Stanford-Vienna Transatlantic Technology Law Forum at Stanford Law School

Irene Ng (Huang Ying) is a Fellow at the Stanford-Vienna Transatlantic Technology Law Forum and a Research Affiliate at the Singapore Management University Centre for Artificial Intelligence and Data Governance. She completed her doctorate and LLM degrees at the University of Vienna and her LLB (Hons) at the National University of Singapore. In addition to her academic work, Irene currently serves as a Senior Attorney (admitted in Singapore and New York) at CMS Reich-Rohrwig Hainz and Senior Project Manager at Lupl, Inc.

Siegfried Fina and Irene Ng (Huang Ying), *Smart Contract 'Drafting' and the Homogenization of Languages* In: *Smart Legal Contracts*. Edited by: Jason Grant Allen and Peter Hunn, Oxford University Press. © Jason Grant Allen & Peter Hunn 2022.
DOI: 10.1093/oso/9780192858467.003.0016

While English is normally used as the default language of choice for international contracts,[1] numerous contracts are drafted in other languages, with some contracts written in bilingual form.[2]

With the advent of 'smart contracts', which are coded using programming languages, there arise potential issues related to the homogenization of natural and programming language. This chapter explores how smart contract drafting has caused language homogenization and evaluates its potential impact.

B. Language, Contract Drafting, and Lawyers

Language competency—regardless of the language of choice for the contract—is imperative in the art of contract drafting. However, in principle, contract drafting can be done by anyone and everyone. A contract that is written by a layperson is enforceable before the courts – hiring a lawyer is not a precondition for the enforceability of a contract, although one may hire a lawyer to ensure that his or her contracts are enforceable. With the Internet allowing people to share template contracts in a cost-efficient manner, there are more alternatives for a layperson to obtain a contract drafted without a lawyer.

Technology has allowed people to obtain template contracts quickly and edit them with a certain degree of confidence using software. Software, such as LegalSifter, screens through contracts uploaded by users and informs users whether their contract may have missing clauses.[3] Such software is made possible through machine learning techniques, also known as artificial intelligence (AI).

There is a growing academic discussion on the use of certain technologies, such as AI, to draft contracts.[4] Several software developers have made technology available that provides contract drafting services powered by artificial intelligence to enable the software user to prepare contracts faster[5]—the target user being a lawyer who wishes to make his or her practice more efficient. Some software providers have even integrated contract drafting and contract management services into one

---

[1] See K. Adams and R. Scherr, 'Top ten tips in drafting and negotiating an international contract', *Thomson Reuters* (online) <https://legal.thomsonreuters.com/en/insights/articles/top-10-tips-in-drafting-and-negotiating-international-contracts> accessed 13 July 2021. There is also much literature on the drafting of contracts, for instance, the latest edition of Adams' manual on contract drafting. K.A. Adams, *A Manual of Style for Contract Drafting* (4th edn, American Bar Association 2020).

[2] M. Rozovics, 'Drafting Multiple-Language Contracts', *American Bar Association* (online at 3 April 2019) <https://www.americanbar.org/groups/gpsolo/publications/gp_solo/2011/april_may/drafting_multiple-languagecontractswhenyouonlyspeakenglish/> accessed 13 July 2021. There are also discussions on how two different languages interact with each other in drafting: see P. Torbert, 'Globalizing Legal Drafting: What the Chinese Can Teach Us About Ejusdem Generis and All That' (2007) 11 *Scribes Journal of Legal Writing* 41.

[3] LegalSifter <https://www.legalsifter.com/> accessed 13 July 2021.

[4] I. Ng (H. Ying), 'The Art of Contract Drafting in the Age of Artificial Intelligence: A Comparative Study Based on US, UK and Austrian Law' (2017) 26 *TTLF Working Papers*.

[5] For example see 'Hotdocs' <https://www.hotdocs.com/> accessed 13 July 2021.

package,[6] thereby allowing users greater latitude in producing, storing and managing their contracts.

1. Smaller number of native speakers, greater monopoly?

In smaller countries where the national language or language of administration has relatively fewer native speakers, there will also be fewer lawyers (in absolute terms) competent in the national language. Given the fewer number of experts in that language, the lack of supply of experts gives lawyers in such jurisdictions greater control over the provision of contract drafting services.

While legal technology and contract automation has been touted as an alternative—either to allow lawyers to draft contracts faster, or to replace lawyers in the contract drafting and generation process[7]—there are generally more such tools available for languages with larger speaking populations as compared to languages with smaller speaking populations.[8] From this perspective of legal technology, lawyers who are experts in these natural languages that are not supported by contract automation software have an even greater monopoly opportunity over providing contract drafting services in this language due to the lack of other alternatives.

a.) Smart contracts

In recent years, a new variant of contracts has emerged. So-called 'smart contracts' have become increasingly popular with the surge of interest in blockchain of the late 2010s. The definition of 'smart contract' has been debated in several academic works;[9] however, from a broader point of view, smart contracts can be taken to refer to contracts that are written in programming language or code that can be automatically executed by a machine.[10] Smart contracts have gained popularity primarily in the blockchain sphere, as they can be automatically executed and

---

[6] Thomson Reuters, *Contract management solutions* <https://legalsolutions.thomsonreuters.co.uk/en/explore/document-management/contract-drafting-automation-management.html> accessed 13 July 2021.

[7] N. Sahota, 'Will A.I. Put Lawyers Out of Business?' *Forbes* (online at 9 February 2019) <https://www.forbes.com/sites/cognitiveworld/2019/02/09/will-a-i-put-lawyers-out-of-business/> accessed 13 July 2021.

[8] Luminance, however, has claimed that its artificial intelligence tool has been developed to work with eighty different languages. See Luminance, 'Market-leading AI platform, Luminance, used in 80 languages across the globe' <https://www.luminance.com/news/press/20191126_marketleading_ai.html> accessed 23 February 2022.

[9] See P. Istrup, 'Smart contracts as contracts' (Conference Presentation, 1st ICT 2020, 21 January 2020); J. Lampič, 'Ricardian contracts: A smarter way to do smart contracts?', *Schönherr* (online in 2019) <https://www.schoenherr.eu/publications/publication-detail/ricardian-contracts-a-smarter-way-to-do-smart-contracts/> accessed 13 July 2021.

[10] N. Szabo, 'Formalizing and Securing Relationships on Public Networks' (online in 1997) <https://nakamotoinstitute.org/formalizing-securing-relationships/#building-blocks-of-smart-contract-protocols> accessed 23 February 2022.

recorded on blockchain systems, such as Ethereum, thereby arguably ensuring a transparent and immutable execution of the obligations coded in the smart contract.[11] Mindful of the practical importance of blockchain-based smart contracts, this chapter will take a broader, technology agnostic, approach to smart contracts with a focus on the legal characterization of code that *prima facie* has some 'contractual' declarative effect, consistently with the aims of this volume.

2. Smart contract 'drafting'

Smart contracts are written in programming language that allows their execution on a given platform or computing environment.[12] Drafting a smart contract is invariably the task of a programmer or coder who is well-versed in the requisite programming language to ensure that the smart contract does what it is intended to do. While lawyers need to learn coding to draft smart contracts, programmers who can comprehend a natural language can draft a contract (even if it may not be linguistically competent nor even legally enforceable). The ability to code is, then, a barrier to entry in the smart contract market for lawyers.

For smart contracts that are executed on Ethereum, one of the most widely used languages is Solidity.[13] However, smart contracts can also be coded in Java or Python.[14] If a broader definition of 'smart contract' is adopted, ie, one that is automatically executed irrespective of the technology powering its execution, then there is theoretically no platform-based restrictions on the programming languages that may be used.

C. Smart Contracts and Language Homogenization

Smart contracts may serve as an impetus to standardize both the natural language and programming language used in contract drafting. Programming languages are expressed in a formalized style, typically using mathematical symbols, computer science syntaxes, and in English. For instance, a programmer coding in Python would express the 'if-else' loop in English. While teaching of the programming language can be done in a different natural language, programming languages incorporate a certain degree of English as numerous functions are expressed in the English language, as seen from the example below.

---

[11] See generally C. Dannen, *Introducing Ethereum and Solidity: Foundations of Cryptocurrency and Blockchain Programming for Beginners* (Springer 2017) for further elaboration on Ethereum and Solidity programming.
[12] The platform is a system or application that allows parties to execute the smart contract functions that they have coded.
[13] Ethereum, *Developer Resources* <https://ethereum.org/developers/> accessed 23 February 2022.
[14] *Ibid.*

```
<script>
function myFunction () {
    var time = new Date ().getHours () ;
    var greeting;
    if (time < 20) {
        greeting = "Good day";
    } else {
        greeting = "Good evening";
    }
    document.getElementById("demo").innerHTML = greeting;
}
</script>
```

Figure 15.1 Example of an If-Else loop in Javascript
w3schools.com, *JavaScript if/else Statement* <https://www.w3schools.com/jsref/tryit.asp?filename=tryjsref_state_if_else> accessed 21 July 2021.

As seen above, the function uses English words such as 'if' and 'else', even if the majority of the function is expressed in symbols. Unsurprisingly, there are programming languages that are expressed in other natural languages or purely in symbols, such as 易语言 (Pinyin translation: Yi Yu Yan)[15] and APL,[16] respectively. However, even if there are such non-English expressed programming languages available, it should be noted that English expressed programming languages are still the most widely used programming languages, even in countries such as China.[17] This use and understanding of English in order to code in the programming language is thus important and necessary.

1. Standardization of programming language

The popularity of executing smart contracts on Ethereum has also led towards a consolidation of the smart contract community to move towards using Solidity as a *lingua franca* for coding blockchain-based smart contracts.[18] Solidity is generally not the default or 'go-to' programming language to learn (especially for beginners who seek to learn a computing language; Python appears to be the top choice in recent years[19]). However, its popularity means that there is a general trend towards the use of Solidity for drafting blockchain smart contracts. This does not preclude other programming languages from being used to

---

[15] W3Cschool, 易语言教程 <https://www.w3cschool.cn/eyuyantutorials/> accessed 13 July 2021.
[16] Try APL <https://tryapl.org/ accessed 13 July 2021.
[17] Alibaba Cloud, *25 Things You Should Know About Developers in China*, <https://www.alibabacloud.com/blog/25-things-you-should-know-about-developers-in-china_415712> accessed 13 July 2021.
[18] *Ibid.*
[19] R. Chen, 'The 10 most popular programming languages, according to the Microsoft-owned GitHub', *Business Insider* (online at 6 November 2019) <https://www.businessinsider.de/international/most-popular-programming-languages-github-2019-11/?r=US&IR=T> accessed 13 July 2021.

draft/code smart contracts, although this demonstrates a push towards a standardized and homogenized programming language for blockchain-based smart contract drafting.

D. Language Homogenization

The topic of language homogenization through the search for a *lingua franca* has always been an issue when communication between multiple parties, who do not share a native language, is required. This is even more important in commercial settings, where parties have to reach an agreement and have this agreement set out in writing. Throughout history, this bridging language or auxiliary language has constantly changed, with Latin arguably being the common legal language during classical times[20] and English being the most popular and default language of communication in modern day business settings.[21]

Choosing and allocating one single language as the global lingua franca today is politically challenging. In large institutions or supranational bodies where multiple parties from different backgrounds must debate, work, and agree with each other, there is generally not just one language indicated as the official language of the institution, but rather a set of recognized languages. For example, the United Nations has six official languages and all official documents are published in these six languages.[22] The European Union (EU), which adopted the motto 'united in diversity',[23] enshrines this principle by recognizing all of its different member states' national languages as official languages—the EU thus makes available parliamentary documents in twenty-three different languages, with care and attention spent on ensuring that these documents are translated properly and have the same meaning across all twenty-three versions.[24]

The difficulty in compelling people from different nationalities to accept one *official lingua franca* is evident, even if in practice there is one commonly used language. This means that with regular contracts, it is unsurprising and inevitable to a certain degree that bilingual or trilingual contracts will be drafted for parties that do not share the same native languages even if the parties understood an auxiliary

---

[20] M. Ristikivi, 'Latin: The Common Legal Language of Europe?' (2005) 10 *Juridica International* 199.

[21] C. Nickerson, 'English as a Lingua Franca in International Business Contexts' (2005) 24(4) *English for Specific Purposes* 367; A. Kankaanranta and W. Lu, 'The Evolution of English as the Business Lingua Franca: Signs of Convergence in Chinese and Finnish Professional Communication' (2013) 27(3) *Journal of Business and Technical Communication* 288.

[22] UN Library, *What are the official languages of the United Nations?* <http://ask.un.org/faq/14463> accessed 13 July 2021.

[23] European Union, *The EU Motto* <https://europa.eu/european-union/about-eu/symbols/motto_en> accessed 13 July 2021.

[24] European Parliament, *Fact Sheets on the European Union* <http://www.europarl.europa.eu/factsheets/en/sheet/142/language-policy> accessed 13 July 2021.

language such as English. For instance, a German and a Chinese businessman may sign a contract in English, but with translations made in German and Chinese with a provision that states that in the event of a dispute, the English version shall prevail. From a language standpoint, if smart contracts were to continue to gain popularity in replacing traditional contracts, the search for a *lingua franca* might move away from finding a natural language which all can agree in using—which is politically difficult to achieve but has already been effected in practice—to finding the right programming language and the right standards for that.

1. Programming standardization

Should smart contracts gain traction in the commercial world, one important consideration would be the programming language that should be used and the accompanying standards for that language. While Solidity happens to be the most popular programming language used by blockchain-based smart contract programmers, the use of this specific programming language is very much tied to Ethereum and the use of blockchain in executing the smart contract.

The use of Solidity raises some key issues, especially if it were to be designated as the *lingua franca* for smart contract drafting. Should Solidity be the standard language for smart contract programming or drafting? Who or which institution or authority (governmental or otherwise) should be in charge of improving and maintaining the Solidity language? Should there be specific programming standards required of the Solidity language? Which programming language should smart contract drafters choose if they decide not to use a blockchain system or an Ethereum-based system when they do so chose?

These questions are difficult. The popularity of a specific programming language does not necessarily warrant it to be the default language when programming smart contracts. The use and popularity of Solidity is intertwined with the popularity of Ethereum as a public blockchain platform of choice. Therefore, for developers that wish to use another platform to execute smart contract functions, they may choose to use a programming language that is less platform specific. Solidity is currently unregulated by a designated entity or authority; entrusting the regulation, development and maintenance of the language to governmental authorities (or any institution) could result in resistance or backlash from a community that has built a reputation on decentralization and lack of intervention by centralized authorities.[25] For those that do not wish to build smart contracts on Ethereum, they are theoretically free to code smart contracts with whatever programming

---

[25] E. Muzzy, 'Measuring Blockchain Decentralization' *ConsenSys* <https://consensys.net/research/measuring-blockchain-decentralization/> accessed 13 July 2021; Solidity, <https://solidity.readthedocs.io/en/v0.6.2/> accessed 13 July 2021.

language that they wish to use, unless specified by the platform that they intend to execute the smart contract on.

If one considers smart contracts from a broader perspective, ie, one that is technologically neutral, then the above questions shed light on even deeper and more pertinent questions. What is the purpose for seeking a standardized programming language for smart contracts? Should the standardization of programming languages be regulated? If yes, how should this programming language be regulated? The homogenization of programming languages for drafting smart contracts is therefore difficult in practice on an official or formal level.

2. Language as a barrier to entry

Knowledge of a drafting language, be it a natural language or a programming language, is a barrier to entry in providing contract drafting services. The acquisition and mastery of a new natural language largely depends on the mutual intelligibility and similarity of the new language to the existing language(s) that the learner knows. For instance, a person who knows only French is likely able to learn Spanish faster than Russian, due to French and Spanish sharing similar linguistic roots.[26] Therefore, the barriers to entry for a lawyer to learn a new language to draft in another language can range from low (ie, languages from similar families) to high (ie, languages from completely dissimilar language families). Even then, language acquisition is subject to numerous other factors (eg, frequency of usage of the target language, whether the learner is learning the target language where the target language is deemed a native language) and is not only limited to mutual intelligibility.

In the case of programming languages, the barriers of entry are arguably lower than in the case of natural languages. While there exist numerous species of formalized languages, such as scripting languages and mark-up languages, the ability to code in a given language allows one to be able to learn another similar language with much less difficulty, as the concepts and syntax may often be transferrable or at least appreciably similar. There is generally a reduced need to learn new grammatical rules or extensive new vocabulary; rather, a coder learning a new programming language may have to become acquainted to the syntax and relative 'strictness' of the new programming language.

For example, the 'if-else' loop and the concept of variables and arrays are applicable in many object-oriented languages such as Java, Javascript, Python, C++, and Solidity. The key difference is how it is expressed in either of these languages. An analogy would be the word 'sport' in German, French, English, and Russian—the word is the same in all four languages but is pronounced differently. Ultimately,

---

[26] See A. Ciobanu and L. Dinu, 'On the Romance Languages Mutual Intelligibility' <http://citeseerx.ist.psu.edu/viewdoc/download?doi=10.1.1.675.6045&rep=rep1&type=pdf> accessed 13 July 2021.

however, as with natural languages, fluency and mastery of programming languages is necessary to draft smart contracts in that language.

E. Impacts of Language Homogenization by Smart Contracts

As discussed, smart contract 'drafting' requires the use of a programming language that invariably, if indirectly, draws on a natural language. The current popular programming languages for smart contract drafting generally draw on English. The use of a *lingua franca* has several implications, one of which is economies of scale. When a programming language becomes the default language of choice in drafting contracts, all contracts and information relating thereto are only written in one language. This means that the programming logic and information needed to draft similar smart contracts can be quickly used, edited or recycled for other contracts drafted in the same programming language. The obvious impact of such economies of scale is the potential reduction in translation costs. Smart contracts do not have to be translated into another natural language, unless it is being translated into another scripting language, which is likely to be expressed in English in any case.

The general assumption is that everyone who drafts with smart contracts has an adequate command of English and the programming language the smart contract is drafted in. However, considering how programming logic is different from natural language, the comprehensibility of the programming language by someone who may not necessarily be fluent in English remains high. Therefore, smart contract drafting might open doors for a standardized and universal contract drafting language, using programming code without requiring mastery of a specific natural language—eg, English or Chinese. It might also allow for the recognition of one language to express contract drafting that will not arouse sensitive debates about the use of some national language in contract drafting.

1. Loss of linguistic diversity

If a programming language were to become the default language in contract drafting, the use of such a standardized programming language to draft contracts could lead to a loss of linguistic diversity. As people realize that they would only need to comprehend in one natural language (ie, English) in order to be 'fluent' in the relevant programming language, there is likely to be a shift towards greater use and mastery of English over other natural languages.[27] As mentioned earlier,

---

[27] Studies on language shift amongst cultures also show how in certain populations, certain circumstances cause populations to shift from one language to another over time. See generally N.H. Hornberger, 'Language Shift and Language Revitalization' in *The Oxford Handbook of Applied Linguistics* (2nd edn, Oxford University Press 2010).

the most widely used programming language in China was reportedly Javascript, which is expressed in English.[28] There have been also studies whereby English has been seen as a key reason for language erosion; as K.D. Harrison aptly notes, 'small islands of languages are being submerged in a rising sea of English'.[29]

Languages with smaller native speaker communities are particularly vulnerable to decreasing use, even if they are given the status of a 'national language' in some jurisdiction and are the language of administration. If smart contracts were to gradually replace traditional contracts in commercial transactions, there may be a push towards learning and using code (expressed in English) and its use in professional settings. For example, a Slovenian and an Estonian are most likely going to contract in English. Whether they would use some kind of 'smart' contract is less than certain; however, to the extent they do, the dominance of English (at the expense of relatively small natural languages like Slovenian and Estonian) will continue to grow. Either way, it appears that English—whether the natural language itself or a programming language expressed in English—will be the most practicable to use and learn. This raises concerns about the long-term viability of the national languages of the contracting parties.

Given what we know, it would not be surprising to observe the reduced use of these natural languages in professional settings. As commercial transactions play an important part in the international business landscape, there may be a push towards learning and using programming code (expressed in English); without conscious intervention to promote or prevent these natural languages from being used as a language of administration, this may eventually relegate them to the status of spoken languages only, or dialects generally used only in private settings.

2. Notarized (smart) contracts

Certain commercial contracts must be notarized before a notary public before the relevant transaction is deemed to have occurred. Whether a notarized contract is required in a specific context is a question of national law; however, where the contract is not in the country's national language or language of administration, national regulations may require the contract to be drafted in the national language prior to notarization.[30]

If smart contracts were to be subjected to the same requirement, ie, the need to be in the form of a notarial deed, several complications would arise. First, as smart contracts are not drafted in the same manner as traditional contracts, converting

---

[28] *Supra* n. 19.
[29] K.D. Harrisson, *When Languages Die* (Oxford University Press 2008) 11.
[30] This is the case for several civil law jurisdictions. For example, in Austria, an agreement for the sale of a property must be done in the form of a notarial deed.

smart contracts into a paper equivalent may be legally challenging. In the 1990s when the recognition of electronically 'written contracts' became a legal question, the United Nations Commission on International Trade Law ('UNCITRAL') produced the Model Law on Electronic Commerce,[31] which enshrined the principle of *functional equivalence*.[32] The principle of functional equivalence permitted digital contracts to be legally recognized and treated as equivalent to their paper counterpart.[33]

However, the reverse (ie, for a paper contract to be recognized as equivalent to its digital counterpart), requires further analysis. A more recent model law by UNCITRAL, the Model Law on Electronic Transferable Records,[34] addresses this situation through Article 18, which allows paper transferable records to be recognized as their electronic equivalents.[35] With the Model Law on Electronic Transferable Records as an enabling legislation for smart contracts,[36] the recognition of smart contracts in paper form should not pose insurmountable legal challenges. However, Ng and Lampič have noted that despite this legal recognition, smart contracts may not be easily expressed in written form, especially where metadata is concerned.[37] While there appears to be no conceptual problem in recognizing the paper-based smart contract as equivalent to its digital form in *theory*, the practicalities render the idea less certain.[38] Reams of metadata may have to be printed to supplement the main contract, which may be impractical,[39] as the information may run into hundreds or thousands of lines (eg, timestamp logs for a certain period of time). This may be necessary if the smart contract were to be in the form of a notarial deed, where the notary public may require all ancillary information pertaining to the contract to be in the notarial deed. If a smart contract is to be disputed in court, and if the court requires for the smart contract to be tendered in physical form as part of evidence, these reams of metadata may have to be printed and tendered together as evidence too. It remains to be seen how such practical matters will be addressed.

---

[31] Model Law on Electronic Commerce 1996 (United Nations Commission on International Trade Law).
[32] United Nations Commission on International Trade Law, *UNCITRAL Model Law ON Electronic Commerce (1996) with additional article 5 bis as adopted in 1998*, <https://uncitral.un.org/en/texts/ecommerce/modellaw/electronic_commerce> accessed 13 July 2021.
[33] *Ibid.*
[34] Model Law on Electronic Transferable Records 2017 (United Nations Commission on International Trade Law).
[35] *Ibid.*, Art 18. Also see Law Commission of England and Wales, Digital Assets: Electronic Trade Documents (Consultation Paper 254).
[36] I. Ng, 'UNCITRAL E-Commerce Law 2.0: Blockchain and Smart Contracts' *LawTech.Asia* (22 April 2018), <https://lawtech.asia/author/ireneng/>(accessed 13 July 2021).
[37] I. Ng and J. Lampič, 'UNCITRAL Model Law on Electronic Transferable Records, Contract Automation and Metadata' (Conference Presentation, 1st ICT 2020, 21 January 2020).
[38] *Ibid.*
[39] *Ibid.*

Secondly, it is not straightforward how a smart contract could be produced in the form of a notarial deed, even if it were legally recognized in theory. The smart contract is written in programming language expressed in English. If there is a requirement that the smart contract be translated into a national language other than English for whatever reasons, it is unclear how this could be done. Nonetheless, the notary public is required to understand the code components of the smart contract and ensure that the parties understand the smart contract code as well. However, even if the 'code' were somehow translated into the natural language native to the parties, they may not necessarily understand the programming code. In this regard, there is the expectation that the parties and the notary understand the smart contract notarial deed for it to be legally executed. This also then pushes parties to learn coding (and English) in order to be 'fluent' and convince the notary that he or she understands what he or she is signing.

3. Impact on the legal profession and industry

Lawyers who draft contracts are expected to have mastery over the language in which they draft these contracts. In countries with a smaller population and fewer number of speakers of the national language in the country, lawyers have a certain monopoly over the market because of their ability to draft in that language without much competition. However, if there is a move towards the use of smart contracts expressed in English in commercial transactions or daily life, then these lawyers may gradually lose their monopoly over the contract drafting market as they can no longer charge a premium for their ability to read and draft expertly in the native language. Furthermore, a new category of legal service providers for contract drafting—ie software developers—may compete or co-opt with lawyers for the same share of the market. Lawyers may then find it harder to compete if they are not fluent in English or relevant programming languages.

4. Interpretation of smart contracts by the courts

If smart contracts are increasingly recognized as a substitute for written contracts, an important question would be the interpretation of smart contracts before the court in the event of a dispute. At present, it remains to be seen how courts will interpret smart contracts. Considering that it is written in testable, executable, code, there is arguably lesser ambiguity in a smart contract due to reduction instead of natural language words that could be interpreted differently. However, courts may still deal with 'mistranslation' caused when the parties instruct the programmers when drafting the contract, and the formalization of contracting language raises its own difficult questions of 'interpretation' and 'meaning'. There is also a possibility of voiding the contract by mistake on the part of the draftsperson. Many of these issues have been explored in other chapters in this volume.[40]

More fundamentally, lawyers, judges (and the legal profession as a whole) may have to be retrained and taught programming language if they are to be able to interpret smart contract code. Some law faculties have including programming modules to their students in certain certification courses, in a bid to prepare their students for the future of law practice.[41] Other universities have offered a double degree in computer science and law.[42] This interdisciplinary education will hopefully prepare students who have to draft and interpret smart contracts in the future.

a.) AI and legal technology developments

One of the largest challenges in developing contract drafting tools powered by AI is natural language processing. AI is notoriously dependent on data training sets. Here, again, most AI tools for contract drafting available in the market are trained in the English language, whereby there exists a large volume of available contracts in the public domain.[43] However, training algorithms in languages where there is limited resources or publications available may be challenging due to the lack of contracts written in that language. Several AI-based contract drafting tools have sought to circumvent this problem by providing lawyers with a platform that allows them to 'teach' the algorithm how it should treat and process natural language correctly, thereby improving the algorithms.[44]

If programming language and English were to become the standardized language, then development in contract drafting using artificial intelligence tools would focus and concentrate on this programming language instead of a wide number of natural languages. This would mean that economies of scale in artificial intelligence contract drafting could be better achieved due to the larger output of data in one language and the focus of resources on this one language.

i.) Embedding of metadata

One other possibility with the increasing use of smart contracts is the use of contracts being embedded with external data or metadata. In short, these are smart contracts that make reference to dynamic data, eg, a timestamp or geolocation generated by a third-party device, which will automatically trigger execution of the

---

[40] For example, see E. Tjong Tjin Tai, Chapter 9, C.D. Clack, Chapter 12, Megan Ma, Chapter 13, and S. Gleeson, Chapter 19. See also generally J.G. Allen, 'Wrapped and Stacked: "Smart Contracts" and the Interaction of Natural and Formal Language' (2018) 14(4) *European Review of Contract Law* 305.

[41] Bucerius Law School, *The Future of Law and Legal Services*, <https://www.law-school.de/internatio nal/education/bucerius-summer-programs/legal-technology-and-operations> accessed 13 July 2021.

[42] Stanford Law School, *Law and Computing Science*, <https://law.stanford.edu/education/degrees/joint-degrees-within-stanford-university/law-and-computer-science/> accessed 13 July 2021.

[43] Whether these contracts in the public contracts are well drafted contracts are a separate story.

[44] This is oft-claimed by AI-enabled software providers. See, eg, Luminance, *Advisory* <https://www.luminance.com/advisory.html> accessed 13 July 2021.

contract when a certain value or state is attained.[45] The use of external data in smart contracts is an unprecedented step in contracts as it now allows contracts to be integrated with other systems or objects (eg, the internet of things or 'IoT') or even with other contracts itself—eg, contracts that make reference to each other in one transaction. As extracting and using dynamic data from its source is done in programming language, more contracts being 'drafted' in programming language will potentially enable such dynamic data smart contracts to be used in transactions. The problem of how to convert these contracts from digital to written form in practice, however, remains an issue.

F. Conclusion

Presently, smart contracts are not the preferred contractual form for the vast majority of contracts. There is, however, a good argument that smart contract drafting will lead to a gradual homogenization of languages or at the very least influence laymen and lawyers to pick up programming—the former to understand the smart contract code, and the latter to continue providing contract drafting services albeit in another language. It is our view that such homogenization, however, will occur in two ways: first, through the natural language used in expressing the programming language (generally, English); second, through the programming language to draft smart contracts. It remains to be seen whether Solidity will become the lingua franca of smart contract drafting—as much as it is popular now, its survival and popularity is dependent on the Ethereum platform. Either way, a future in which a small number of smart contract programming languages dominate—all of them expressed in English—is one possible scenario.

Such language homogenization through the rise of 'smart contracting' would have multiple impacts on society and commercial operations. There are clear benefits in the use of one single language—be it in natural language or programming language—in contract drafting. However, language homogenization also brings numerous issues, such as the potential loss of diversity of languages, the challenge of lawyers' near monopoly in the provision of legal services and practical issues such as notarization. Even if Solidity or another programming language used to code smart contracts were to become the *lingua franca*, the lack of a general body to monitor to development of such a language (unlike most natural languages which generally have *de facto* or *de jure* authorities advocating and ensuring the proper use of that natural language) may also lead to awry developments in the programming language.[46]

---

[45] Ng and Lampič (n. 40).
[46] In 2016, a bug in a smart contract coded in Solidity was exploited by a hacker. See K. Finley, 'A $50 Million Hack Just Showed That the DAO Was All Too Human' *Wired* (18 June 2016) <https://www.wired.com/2016/06/50-million-hack-just-showed-dao-human/> accessed 13 July 2021.

16

Practice Makes ... Pragmatic

Designing a Practical Smart Contract Legal Architecture

Scott Farrell, Hannah Glass, and Henry Wells[*]

A. Introduction	353	E. Accountability	362
B. Interoperability	355	F. Safety	365
C. Certainty	357	G. Conclusion	367
D. Flexibility	358		

A. Introduction

Much of the research and analysis relating to smart legal contracts has had a focus on what a smart legal contract could be, the manner in which code and natural language could be combined, and how important contractual legal principles could be determined for a legally-binding contract represented in a combination of a digital and analogue form.[1] These are important foundational

---

[*] Scott Farrell is a Senior Partner in King & Wood Mallesons' financial markets and systems team. He advises the public and private sector on, and guiding legal change in, the financial system landscape including in connection with financial technology. Scott has performed a number of government roles related to developments in technology, information, and finance.

Hannah Glass is a Senior Associate in King & Wood Mallesons' financial markets and systems team, specializing in Fintech, blockchain, payments, and Regtech. Hannah sits on the Australian Department of Industry Science, Energy and Resources' National Blockchain Roadmap Steering Committee, and is chair of the Regtech Working Group. Hannah holds a Bachelor's degree in law and international studies from the University of New South Wales.

Henry Wells is currently completing an MSc in Political Theory at the London School of Economics and Political Science, focusing on the legal, political, and ethical challenges of transformative technologies. He previously worked in the financial markets and systems team at Australian law firm King & Wood Mallesons and has a Bachelor's degree in Arts and Law (Honours) from the University of New South Wales.

[1] In this article, we use the categorization that the parts of a smart legal contract represented by computer code are the digital layers of the smart contract stack, whilst those parts of the smart legal contract represented by natural language are the legal architecture layers of the smart contract stack: see for instance, J.G. Allen, 'Wrapped and Stacked: "Smart Contracts" and the Interaction of Natural and Formal Languages' (2018) 14 *European Review of Contract Law* 4, 307; P. De Filippi and G. McMullen,

issues to resolve in developing a conceptual framework for smart legal contracts.[2]

However, when seeking to work with smart legal contracts in a practical context other legal issues can arise. Practical applications tend to use multiple smart contracts, often together with distributed ledger technology, in the context of an existing market of contractual arrangements between multiple parties.[3] This changes the context of legal issues from those which relate to the intricacies of a single contract between two parties to the complexities of those which relate to combinations of contractual interactions between multiple participants. The nature of the solution adopted to manage these legal issues informs the manner in which the legal relationships between the parties are established, and the way in which those participants interact in a legal context. This is referred to in this chapter as the 'legal architecture' of the smart contract application and, from a pragmatic point of view, it is just as important, and sometimes more difficult to resolve, than the application's technological architecture. Although these legal issues are not fundamental to the very concept of a smart legal contract, they are proving to be important in their practical application and use.

In this chapter, we briefly summarize five different issues that can arise for consideration in designing smart contract legal architecture for use in practice. These are: (i) interoperability, (ii) certainty, (iii) flexibility, (iv) accountability, and (v) safety. They are discussed below in turn, followed by a summary conclusion.

'Governance of Blockchain Systems: Governance of and by Distributed Infrastructure' (White Paper, Coalition of Automated Legal Applications, June 2018) <https://coala.global/wp-content/uploads/2019/02/BRI-COALA-Governance-of-Blockchains.pdf> accessed 13 July 2021; S. Farrell et al., 'Lost and Found in Smart Contract Translation—Considerations in Transition to Automation in Legal Architecture' (2018) 33 *Journal of International Banking Law and Regulation* 1, 24; S. Farrell et al., 'How to Use Humans to Make "Smart Contracts" Truly Smart' (*King & Wood Mallesons*, 7 July 2016), <https://www.kwm.com/en/au/knowledge/insights/smart-contracts-open-source-model-dna-digital-analogue-human-20160630> accessed 13 July 2021; King & Wood Mallesons, 'Project-DnA' (*Github*, 4 August 2016) <https://github.com/KingandWoodMallesonsAU/Project-DnA> accessed 13 July 2021; S. Farrell and C. Warren, 'Smart Contracts: From Concept to Construction' (*King & Wood Mallesons*, 4 October 2018).

[2] International Swaps and Derivatives Association and King & Wood Mallesons, 'Smart Legal Contracts: From Concept to Construction' (White Paper, ISDA, October 2018), <https://www.isda.org/a/cHvEE/Smart-Derivatives-Contracts-From-Concept-to-Construction-Oct-2018.pdf> accessed 13 July 2021 (hereafter ISDA and King & Wood Mallesons, 'Smart Legal Contracts: From Concept to Construction'); International Swaps and Derivatives Association and Linklaters, 'Whitepaper: Smart Contracts and Distributed Ledger—A Legal Perspective' (White Paper, ISDA, August 2017), <https://www.isda.org/a/6EKDE/smart-contracts-and-distributed-ledger-a-legal-perspective.pdf> accessed 13 July 2021 (hereafter ISDA and Linklaters, 'Whitepaper: Smart Contracts and Distributed Ledger—A Legal Perspective').

[3] This is because the desired commercial outcome is usually based on serving the needs of an existing market and its participants, rather than creating a totally new market and participants.

B. Interoperability

Interoperability is commonly regarded as the key to unlocking the potential of smart contracts.[4] While smart contracts can often reliably communicate within their own systems, the broader smart contract ecosystem is fragmented. There is a lack of standardization of protocols and programming languages to enable different platforms to communicate with each other and with legacy systems. Mass adoption of smart contract infrastructure throughout the digital economy requires that smart contracts can interact with external data sources (such as APIs[5] and IoT[6] devices) and exchange information across different smart contracting platforms owned and operated by different entities.[7]

Solving for interoperability is predominantly a technological issue. Participants need to ensure that digital assets and information on one platform can be exchanged with and represented on another platform and vice versa. However, technological decisions made with respect to the composition of the smart contract 'stack' (for the purposes of ensuring interoperability) will inevitably inform the way in which the participants interact in a legal context and the extent to which they rely on contracts represented in analogue form to establish their legal relationship. Decisions around which parts of the contractual arrangement should be represented in computer code and which parts should be represented in natural language are particularly important in shaping the overall legal architecture.

Significant progress has been made in the creation of bridging platforms that perform a translation function, facilitating communication across different platforms. However, given the proliferation of smart contracting programs and programming languages, and the current absence of industry wide standards,[8] ensuring interoperability between multiple smart contracts and contracting parties typically requires the adoption of a consortium model.

In a consortium model, a select group of participants collaborate on a specific project and agree on a common set of protocols and communication standards.

---

[4] Data61 defines interoperability as [t]he ability of a system to work effectively with other systems. This will typically involve sharing or accessing data or services, through defined interfaces.' See 'Risks and Opportunities for Systems Using Blockchain and Smart Contracts' (White Paper, Data61, May 2017), <https://data61.csiro.au/~/media/052789573E9342068C5735BF604E7824.ashx> accessed 13 July 2021.

[5] 'Application Programming Interfaces' which allow computing programs to interact and share data.

[6] The 'Internet of Things', being devices connected to the Internet that are able to transfer data over a network without requiring human oversight or interaction.

[7] For the purposes of illustration, consider an iOS mobile app that connects to a third party IoT device to trigger a smart contract to pay two separate parties, one in Bitcoin and one in Australian dollars via an electronic funds transfer system such as PayPal.

[8] We note that many organizations have initiated standardization efforts in this area, including the International Organization for Standardization ('ISO') which is working on technical standards for smart contracts as part of ISO Technical Committee, ISO/TC 307 (Blockchain and distributed ledger technologies). The British Standards Institution (BSI) held a consultation seeking public contributions to an open technical specification for Smart Legal Contracts: Publicly Available Specification (PAS) 333 in 2020. Other technological standards for particular protocols are emerging. However, interoperability across platforms remains an issue..

The legal relationship between the parties is typically set out in a consortium agreement, which outlines the rights and responsibilities of the parties as well as rules around governance and dispute resolution. Whilst this is a viable option for enterprise solutions of a limited scope, and to promote innovation in the short term, it is not conducive to the creation of an integrated and scalable smart contract ecosystem where information can be seamlessly sent and received across multiple platforms.

Widespread interoperability and scalability over the long term requires the creation of a common set of industry protocols and communication standards. By way of comparison, consider the critical role of technological standards in international finance.[9] In this context, messaging standards such as SWIFT Message Type and ISO 20022 were created to ensure connectivity and consistency across global payment services, clearing systems and settlement systems.[10] Similar solutions are currently being developed for smart contracting systems in both the public and private sector, including the creation of general standards for legally binding smart contracts.[11] The challenge is to create standards that are flexible (to avoid stifling innovation) and adaptable (to keep pace with the dynamic and evolving nature of smart contract technology), but also stable (to ensure the legal effect of smart legal contracts remains certain over time).

Of course, whilst technological interoperability is necessary, it is not sufficient. Technological standards need to defer to relevant legal standards to ensure underlying transactions are effective at law.[12] In this regard, the laws of any applicable jurisdiction can be viewed as a set of standards to which contracting parties must adhere.[13] Whilst standardization of protocols and programming languages may facilitate the exchange of information across different smart contracting platforms, compliance with relevant legal standards is necessary to avoid limiting the impact to the technological sphere. In practice, there is a distinct need for legal *certainty*.

---

[9] See S. Farrell, 'Blockchain Standards in International Banking: Understanding Standards Deviation' (2019) 7(3) *Journal of ICT Standardization*, <https://www.riverpublishers.com/journal_read_html_article.php?j=JICTS/7/3/2> accessed 13 July 2021.

[10] Australia is in the process of migrating from the SWIFT Message Type messaging standards to the ISO 20022 standard. Please refer to 'ISO 20022 Migration for the Australian Payments System— Conclusions Paper' (Conclusions Paper, Reserve Bank of Australia, February 2020), <https://www.rba.gov.au/publications/consultations/202002-iso-20022-migration-for-the-australian-payments-system/pdf/iso-20022-migration-for-the-australian-payments-system-conclusions-paper.pdf> accessed 13 July 2021.

[11] See 'Standards by ISO/TC 307: Blockchain and distributed ledger technologies' (*ISO*), <https://www.iso.org/committee/6266604/x/catalogue/p/0/u/1/w/0/d/0> accessed 13 July 2021.

[12] By way of example, legal standards applicable to derivatives contracts are reflected in ISDA's standard legal documentation. ISDA's work in commissioning netting opinions in relation to that documentation provides certainty to derivatives markets participants that they are entering into legally enforceable netting arrangements.

[13] See S. Farrell, 'Blockchain Standards in International Banking: Understanding Standards Deviation' (2019) 7(3) *Journal of ICT Standardization*, <https://www.riverpublishers.com/journal_read_html_article.php?j=JICTS/7/3/2>> accessed 13 July 2021.

C. Certainty

In addition to the interoperability required between different smart contracting platforms, there is a need for the smart contract legal architecture to be designed so that smart legal contracts are 'legally interoperable' between other legal contracts that the parties also enter into, whether they are smart legal contracts or traditional contracts. There is a need to be able to provide certainty that the contracts, regardless of their form, have the same legal effect, when necessary.

This need for legal certainty can be shown by considering the potential adoption of smart legal contracts in the international derivatives market.[14] This market functions by pairs of counterparties entering into bilateral contracts[15] under which they agree to make payments or deliveries of currencies, commodities, or financial instruments (such as shares or bonds) between each other in the future, sometimes only if certain events occur.[16] The payments or deliveries are determined by reference to one or more specified assets, liabilities, rates, prices, indices, or some other value.[17] An important economic function performed by these contracts is that they have the effect of transferring risks and returns relating to that underlying value on which the contract is based.[18] Liquidity and fungibility in derivatives contracts is important because contracts are often entered into in order to offset and manage the risks and returns created by other derivative contracts. This requires a high level of standardization of contractual terms between derivative transactions so that there is certainty that different contracts can have the same legal effect,[19] which is particularly important when a contract is entered into in order to offset an existing contract.[20] If there was no certainty of the precise legal

---

[14] This is a market where there already has been a significant amount of effort in the creation and application of smart legal contracts and distributed ledger applications. For example, see the legal guidelines for smart derivatives contracts released by the International Swaps and Derivatives Association, Inc (ISDA): 'ISDA Papers on DLT and Smart Contracts' (*International Swaps and Derivatives Association*, 16 October 2019), <https://www.isda.org/2019/10/16/isda-smart-contracts/> accessed 13 July 2021.

[15] The contracts used can be forward contracts, options, swap contracts, or combinations of them. There are many more names used for these contracts, but in essence they are constructed by using combinations of these basic contractual types.

[16] For example, the event could be the occurrence of a date, the change in a price or index, or some other event, such as the bankruptcy of a company or the occurrence of a specific level of rainfall.

[17] For example, an interest rate, the price of a foreign currency, the price of gold or a weather measurement like temperature.

[18] For example, an interest rate swap effects a transfer of interest rate risk, a foreign currency option transfers exchange rate risk and a gold forward transfers risk on the price of gold.

[19] Where there is a significant level of fungibility in a particular type of contract which is traded then it can become standardized, enabling it to be traded on an exchange or regulated market. However, the majority of the volume of derivatives traded on the international derivatives market are 'over-the-counter' or 'OTC' contracts, which are not entered into on an exchange or regulated market. The standardization of the terms for OTC derivatives contracts has occurred primarily through the work of the International Swaps and Derivatives Association, Inc ('ISDA').

[20] This is one reason why there is a focus on 'close-out netting' in financial markets, as this is the legal process which effects the reduction of outstanding obligations on early termination, enabled by offsetting contracts.

effect of the contracts, then the effect of a new contract might not offset another as intended. This would increase, instead of decreasing, a party's risk.[21] Given the scale in number and value of these contracts, and the nature of the risks being managed, such uncertainty would be less than optimal.

The use of smart legal contracts could assist in this need for certainty of legal effect, as it should be possible to verify whether provisions which are expressed in code in multiple contracts are indeed identical. However, as a practical matter, it is not reasonable to expect that all contracts used in such a broad and deep market will be smart legal contracts. Even if participants in the market wanted to 'switch' all of their contracts to smart legal contracts, some traditional contracts would inevitably continue.[22] Accordingly, the participants in this market will need certainty that the legal effect of their smart legal contracts and their conventional contracts are the same. For example, if a market participant wants to offset some of the risk it has taken on already with a traditional interest rate swap by entering into an interest rate option in the form of a smart contract then that participant will need to be certain that the legal effect is consistent with the intended management of risk.[23]

This certainty as to legal effect is more than a theoretical or technological exercise: it is a question of law. There are a few practical consequences of this. First, those responsible for confirming the legal effectiveness and enforceability of traditional legal contracts, i.e. practising lawyers, will be required by market participants to perform the same function with smart legal contracts too. Second, it will be necessary that the coded part of the smart legal contract is expressed in a language (perhaps a formal representation) that the practising lawyer can understand. Third, the context of the relevant market is going to be critical to ensuring that the smart legal contract is actually 'useable' by those for whom it is being created.

However, the need to involve practising lawyers in the verification of legal effect of smart legal contracts does not mean that the entire framework needs to be driven by either lawyers or the law. Instead, there is a need for *flexibility* to be built into the legal architecture.

D. Flexibility

Flexibility in the smart contract legal architecture is important in practical applications, especially whilst the use of the technology is developing. This is particularly

---

[21] Such a risk could be characterized as a 'basis risk', although it is not based on the basis on which a market rate or index is determined but on a difference in the 'legal basis' between the contracts. Lawyers constructing derivative contracts usually try to avoid such legal basis risk.
[22] This would be the case if all trading in such contracts were to move to a financial market or exchange at a single point in time. However, this very rarely occurs.
[23] This point is also made in Farrell and Warren (n. 1).

the case whilst the principles for connecting the legal and technological layers of the smart contract 'stack' are not yet complete.

This can be demonstrated by way of example. A common aim of DLT applications in a financial services context is the digitisation of financial instruments so that their ownership is represented by entries in the distributed ledger. The financial instruments may be bonds, shares, trade finance documents or anything else which is, or once was, represented by writing on paper.[24] Usually, the purpose of the project is to simplify and streamline the processes relating to the financial instruments, such as issuance, transfer and termination, which have become more and more complicated with the increasing complexity of the global financial system.[25] This is not a difficult concept from a technological perspective and the technological architecture does not need to be complex.[26] The distributed ledger is designed to record information and technological procedures, such as smart contracts, which are designed to enable the records to be created and changed as needed.

The task of the legal architecture is to give the record of information—as created and maintained by those smart contracts—legal meaning. Using the characterization of smart contract models expressed in the ISDA and Linklaters Whitepaper[27] there are at least two ways in which this could be done. First, the *internal model*, under which the legal architecture could seek to incorporate each of the smart contracts into the contractual framework by referring to them expressly, their inputs and outputs in the contractual terms. This would give the smart contracts legal meaning because they are themselves part of the legal terms of the contracts. Second, the *external model*, under which the legal architecture could seek to include a natural language description of each smart contract in the contractual terms. This would give the smart contracts legal meaning because they would be performing the corresponding natural language terms of the contracts.

Each of these approaches binds the technological and legal layers together, the first more tightly than the second. However, in practice, both of these can prove challenging because each assumes that the technological and legal architecture is settled, and one can inform the other. Instead, in the case of a developing distributed ledger project, each of these can be changing constantly to meet new commercial, regulatory or technological demands. The lawyers are not in a position to instruct the technologists as to what the code needs to work with, and the technologists are

---

[24] Of course, legal tender is also a financial instrument which is represented by writing on paper, or some synthetic substitute for paper, depending on the currency and denomination.

[25] For example, the issuance and holding of debt instruments usually now requires custodians, clearing systems, intermediaries and payment systems.

[26] That is not to say that it does not require a high level of technological skill and expertise. However, as a matter of practice, the creation of a distributed ledger with an interface and smart contracts which enable the information to be changed has not required that new areas of computer science be discovered.

[27] ISDA and Linklaters (n. 2).

not in a position to instruct the lawyers what the code will do. Accordingly, there is a need for flexibility to change and adjust the technological and legal layers of the project's architecture without them 'getting in each other's way'.

There is at least one alternative approach that has been taken where smart contracts are already used to perform tasks in distributed ledger applications which are intended to have legal, and not just technological, effect.[28] Under this approach, the smart contracts are not intended to form part of the legal contracts between parties. Instead, they are used as processes to produce information which is referenced by the terms of legal contracts. In concept, this is similar to the manner in which interest rates or market indices are referenced in legal contracts relating to finance. These contracts usually do not set out the way in which the interest rate or index is determined and the procedure undertaken is not actually part of the contractual terms, even though the incorporation of its output is.[29]

An example can be shown using the digital representation of a financial instrument by the records held on a distributed ledger. Under the technological architecture, the record is likely to be created using smart contracts which take in various inputs established between the parties using a communication platform and the distributed ledger application. Separate from this, under the legal architecture, there will be processes required for the records on the distributed ledger to represent a register of legal ownership to the financial instrument.[30] Some of these would be set out in the terms relating to the financial instrument, and others will be based on market conventions and procedures. If this technological architecture needs to adapt to a new design requirement, then it would be preferable if it could do so without changing the legal architecture.

Similarly, if there is a new legal requirement, it would be preferable for it to be met without changing the technological architecture. Where changes to law arise, these apply irrespective of the underlying contractual terms. However, where the parties agree to change those obligations, express agreement is required. This is contrasted to the technological layer which is only able to analyse and respond to programmed inputs. These inputs may need to be revised to preserve system integrity, such as in the case of updates and 'bug fixes', but must not affect the legal relationship between the parties. Thus, the legal architecture must be flexible enough to

---

[28] This distinction between technological and legal effect is an important distinction in practice. A distributed ledger application can be effective in storing, changing and sharing information without needing to effect or affect any legal relationships. However, if the application is to create, change or discharge legal relationships then it needs to have some legal effect.

[29] This analogy becomes particularly interesting when considering potential systemic risks related to reliance on smart contracts in the context of the concerns around the reliance made on the calculation of LIBOR and similar rates.

[30] For example, in the context of registered financial instruments, the distributed ledger records could constitute or inform the register which is the foundation of title to those instruments. Of course, there are other legal issues to consider in this context, such as conflict of laws issues relating to the location of such an entitlement if the register is being simultaneously maintained in multiple different jurisdictions.

adapt to any changes in law without express amendment, and sufficiently inflexible to require express agreement to any legal amendment. Whereas the technological architecture must permit changes to be made quickly, potentially unilaterally, and in a manner which does not affect the legal architecture or relationship of the parties, to preserve the legal relationship.

A solution can be found by determining the necessary point at which the technological and the legal architecture should connect, ensuring that connection is made and seeking to limit any unnecessary overlap between them. For example, in the case of a digitised financial instrument, the point of connection could be the technological record under the technological architecture which is then given legal effect as ownership under the legal architecture. The information is provided by the technology, including the smart contracts, and it is given legal meaning by the law. The technological processes do not need to be reflected in the legal architecture, except to the extent that their effect would contravene law, or except to the extent that there is some mandatory legal requirement to be met. Otherwise, the technological and legal architectures could be kept separate in order to preserve the flexibility of the technologists and lawyers to adapt their architecture to meet changing commercial and regulatory needs. This approach can be particularly useful in development of new applications of DLT which are intended to have legal effect. That is because of the significant flexibility which it grants to both technologists and lawyers.

In a distributed ledger context, this reliance on smart contracts to produce information for contracts is not because using smart contracts to perform or express the legal terms of the contract would not be *effective*. Instead, it is because it is not practically *efficient* in the evolving design of the application.[31] The reason for this is that the development of a distributed ledger project usually involves the interaction of technological, commercial, legal, and regulatory requirements such that an iterative process is undertaken so changes can be incorporated as they are identified. Whilst such iteration is not unusual within any legal, technological, or commercial context, it is more of a challenge when all of these elements are working together.[32]

Of course, this flexibility does not mean that technologists and lawyers do not need to know what the other is doing as there is still a connection between the two architectures. And ultimately, as more is learned about the way in which technology can give effect to law, and law can support technology, this separation should not be needed. However, it is quite useful as proofs of concept turn into

---

[31] This distinction between the effectiveness and efficiency of provisions of smart legal contracts was made in ISDA and King & Wood Mallesons (n. 2).

[32] As has been noted in other works, such as C. Clack, 'Smart Contract Templates: Legal Semantics and Code Validation' (2018) 2 *Journal of Digital Banking* 4, 338, one of the critical challenges is the use of a language which allows all the different perspectives to communicate with some level of precision as to meaning.

live pilots. Also, it does not absolve the technologists of legal responsibility for the smart contracts which they create, there is still a role for *accountability*.

E. Accountability

Smart contracts are said to give effect to commercial agreements with certainty that outcomes will occur without the need for human intervention. This requires parties to rely on technology to carry out contractual obligations. This is a fundamental departure from existing principles which rely on people to carry out those obligations. It is important for parties to understand and consider the implications of such a shift.

For smart contracts to have legal effect, we need to understand who is responsible for that effect. Accountability is defined as 'being required to account for one's conduct'.[33] Being able to identify contracting parties and ensuring that they have capacity to agree to the terms of the contract is essential to effect performance of contractual obligations.[34]

Yet in the context of smart contracts, it has been suggested that the smart contract itself, and not a party to the contract, may be able to be held accountable.[35] This stems from the unique features of smart contracts which could be described as having 'identity', 'storing information' and 'appearing to act autonomously'. First, in relation to *identity,* each smart contract can be uniquely identified both at the time of its creation and for the duration of its life. Even as the smart contract changes, its identity remains the same. Second, smart contracts *store information*. A smart contract can be a repository for information, like a document management system. Over the course of its lifetime it may continue to receive and store information. As the records cannot be tampered with, the smart contract may be a 'source of truth' and can provide confirmations relating to the information it stores to other smart contracts.[36] Third, smart contracts *appear to act autonomously.* Smart contracts are executable computer code which executes in response to pre-defined triggers without the interference of any third party. These external events, and resultant actions will continue for the duration of the contract term.

These features allow code to fulfil the obligations of the contract, in whole or in part. This has led some to question whether a smart contract itself, and not a contracting party or technologist, should be held accountable.

---

[33] *Oxford Australian Dictionary* (2nd edn, 2011), see 'accountability' (def 1).
[34] For instance, if a party does not have capacity to take responsibility because, for example, they are under the age of eighteen, the contract may be void.
[35] C. Jentzsch, 'Decentralized Autonomous Organization to Automate Governance' (White Paper, Slock.IT, 2016) 1, <https://web.archive.org/web/2019*/https://download.slock.it/public/DAO/WhitePaper.pdf> accessed 13 July 2021.
[36] For example, a smart contract may store information relating to the price and volatility of an asset over time. This may be used to confirm a strike price has been hit and that it was not reached prior to that point in time for the life of the contract.

However, this view fails to consider the role of legal entities in creating and maintaining smart contracts. It has long been accepted that even where machines have a degree of autonomy, they act in response to inputs programmed by technologists who act on their own behalf or on behalf of a legal entity.[37] Following this logic, four entities may be responsible for a smart contract: the party, the counterparty, the individual technologist and the entity on whose behalf the technologist is acting. When an error arises, it is fixed by a technologist. From this moment, six entities may be held responsible: each of the four original entities, plus the technologist who amended the smart contract terms, or the entity for whom the second technologist was acting. Responsibility is likely to be determined on a case-by-case basis, and apportioned between these entities depending on their role and the nature of the error.[38]

Questions of responsibility become increasingly complex in the context of decentralized autonomous organizations ('DAOs'). In a DAO, a series of multi-party smart contracts operate together to effect the outcomes of the organization. Members have equal ability to propose, vote and give effect to smart contracts, but no single member has control.

Unlike the solution proposed above where all entities and the role they play are identifiable, in a DAO, changes to smart contracts may typically be proposed by any technologist, but are only adopted when a predetermined percentage of DAO participants agree.[39] Given the role played by all participants and the interlocking nature of smart contracts in the DAO, it becomes difficult to separate the actions of the individual from the collective, making it difficult to determine accountability.

It has been suggested that the structure of a DAO means that no person is accountable for the consequences of its constitutive smart contracts. However, simply using new technology is not grounds for a lack of accountability. Practically, we have found that many people may be simultaneously accountable for the outcomes of a smart contract. This is particularly true where the role played by all participants is intrinsically linked to the outcome. Legally, all who participate may be jointly and severally liable.[40]

---

[37] For example, a printer can print an infinite array of documents which it is requested to print by a person working on a computer (subject to physical restraints, such as printing in black and white or colour, or the size of the page). Yet the printer is not responsible for the meaning of the words on the page. Responsibility for the actions of the machine lie with the manufacturer or the technician who maintains the printer and extend only to the act of producing the words on the paper. A smart contract will only store information, take actions, or react to external inputs if it is programmed to do so.

[38] Note that the developer(s) of the blockchain and any person who is responsible for maintaining it may also be responsible. Depending on the nature of an issue, this means that more people should be considered when apportioning responsibility. It does not in any way indicate that no person is responsible.

[39] Depending on the code, this may or may not be a simple majority.

[40] For example, although a partnership is a separate legal entity, responsibility for the actions of the partners in pursuing the objectives of the partnership are shared jointly and severally between them. Similar principles exist for unincorporated associations.

Yet this may not be seen to be fair where participants do not participate equally in producing the outcome. To better allocate responsibility, calls have been made to recognize DAOs as separate legal entities.[41] Such calls argue that a DAO's web of contracts has similar characteristics to other legal entities like corporations and partnerships. Like a company, there is a division between those who control the DAO, being technologists, and those who are able to vote on the direction of the DAO.[42] There may also be a division between those who created the DAO and those running it at any time. Another structure which demonstrates a limitation of risk is a limited partnership. Under such a structure, only technologists who manage the DAO might be responsible. Such an approach removes uncertainty regarding responsibility.

However, recognizing a DAO as a new distinct legal entity is not possible without legislative reform.[43] Were such reform to occur, it might be seen as a departure from existing contractual principles as technologists and contracting parties could be able to abdicate responsibility for their actions by implementing a technological function in an otherwise typical contractual context.

In light of this uncertainty, and potentially significant liability, DAOs have started implementing traditional mechanisms to allocate accountability for consequences at the outset. One mechanism is to create a legal entity. As set out above, a DAO may lend itself to either a corporate or a partnership model. Another, and arguably the most popular structure, is a Swiss foundation which is used to raise funds and provide access to a platform. If an entity is established at the outset, the same rules which apply to the legal entity would apply to the DAO. For instance, actions of the smart contract are attributed to the entity which operates the DAO. Technologists proposing smart contracts either do so on behalf of the entity (director, shareholder, employer, etc), or as an independent third party contracting with the entity. Operations and management of the decision-making process is attributed to the entity itself. If implemented, care must be taken to ensure the features of that structure do not give rise to any unintended consequences.[44]

---

[41] For discussion, see also J.G. Allen, 'Bodies Without Organs: Law, Economics, and Decentralised Governance' (2020) 4(1) *Stanford Journal of Blockchain Law & Policy* 54.

[42] The doctrine was first set out in *Salomon v Salomon and Company Limited* [1897] AC 22 ('*Salomon v Salomon*'). The court provided at page 22 of the judgment that '*if the company was a real company, fulfilling all the requirements of the Legislature, it must be treated as a company, as an entity, consisting indeed of certain corporators, but a distinct and independent corporation.*'
Additionally, the court said at page 43 of the judgement

> In a popular sense, a company may in every case be said to carry on business for and on behalf of its share-holders; but this certainly does not in point of law constitute the relation of principal and agent between them or render the shareholders liable to indemnify the company against the debts which it incurs.

[43] Indeed, even in the seminal case of *Salomon v Salomon* which establishes the doctrine which separates the company from its members, this case was interpreting statute which initially permitted the recognition of companies. See *Companies Act 1862* (UK) 25 & 26 Vict, c 89 ss 6, 8, 30, 43.

[44] For instance, a feature of a Swiss foundation is that the president has sole authority to manage the bank accounts of the foundation. This is the key issue in the well-publicized dispute between the president and directors of the Tezos Foundation. The founders who are non-resident directors of the

Another increasingly popular mechanism is to draft natural language 'governance documents' which govern the members' rights and relationships in the DAO. These governance documents set out the legal basis on which parties have rights to participate in the DAO, and the relationship between participants. Where a governance document is in place, any person who participates in the operation of the DAO is required to agree to be bound by the terms of such an agreement, meaning rights are enforceable in contract. This also means that existing precedent can be relied on in the event of a dispute.

Governance documents are likely to consider issues beyond traditional constitutions, and may be coupled with a separate legal entity.[45] These allow technologists and contracting parties to take advantage of the legal protections inherent in these mechanisms, such as limitation of liability and certainty of jurisdiction. Such documents exist in tandem with existing technological arrangements and are likely to be drafted on a bespoke basis taking account of the factors set out in the sections entitled 'flexibility' and 'safety'.

Practically, these mechanisms ensure that commercial agreements can be seamlessly and automatically implemented in both a technological and legally enforceable manner. This allows parties to rely on the technology but to have the comfort that parties are able to be readily identified and held accountable through traditional legal mechanisms to ensure performance. However, concerns relating to the *safety* of smart contracts can still remain.

F. Safety

Using a legal architecture to clarify accountability in a DAO is an external safeguard which provides confidence in, and stability to, the system. This clarifies accountability at the legal level, ensuring participants understand the impact of their actions and their rights when interacting with the technology prior to its use.

However, developing a legal architecture is only one way in which the system is safeguarded. As set out above, there is always a possibility of unintended events

---

Tezos Foundation accuse the president of misappropriating funds from the Foundation. The President has argued that it was within his power to act unilaterally. See *In Re Tezos Securities Litigation* 17-cv-06779-RS (ND Cal).

[45] Note that a legal architecture can and is likely to include mechanisms which extend beyond the allocation of responsibility. Indeed, it can be used to manage any external circumstances which impact upon a contract. For instance, it can be used by parties to select a particular jurisdiction for disputes or include an arbitral clause. Commentary from ISDA has noted that such a clause will be legally enforceable. See International Swaps and Derivatives Association et al., 'Private International Law Aspects of Smart Derivatives Contracts Utilizing Distributed Ledger Technology' (Report, International Swaps and Derivatives Association, 13 January 2020) 20, <https://www.isda.org/a/4RJTE/Private-International-Law-Aspects-of-Smart-Derivatives-Contracts-Utilizing-DLT.pdf> accessed 13 July 2021.

interfering with the operation of the contract.[46] Given the self-executing nature of the code, some safeguards are only effective if embedded in the technological architecture. These technological mechanisms act as a 'back-stop' to preserve the rights of the parties.

Whilst there are many types of safeguards which may be built, three key safeguards are 'kill switches', 'off-ramps', and 'air gaps'.

A 'kill switch' allows the parties to step out of the smart contract. If activated, the smart contract stops operating and the parties are able to determine the appropriate course without interference by technology. When developing the technology, parties should carefully consider the types of circumstances in which this would typically need to be activated.[47] Certain circumstances, such as power failure are easy to conceive. However, not all circumstances are as readily apparent (if at all) at the time that a smart contract is created.[48] Instead, a mechanism is required to allow the kill switch to be activated in unknown circumstances. This can occur by way of establishing a procedure for human intervention which can override the contract. Such a feature preserves parties' rights and means they are not subject to the technology.

A kill switch is frequently augmented by an 'off ramp'. An off ramp ensures that where technology does not work as intended, or is ill-equipped to manage certain circumstances, the parties are not only able to stop the technological operations, but can also remove transactions from the technological architecture. Once uplifted, the legal contract continues to operate in the analogue world. This allows the commercial arrangement to continue without disruption, regardless of the technology used. Like the kill switch, parties need to consider the circumstances in which the off ramp can be activated, including any automatic circumstances and a process for human intervention to activate the off ramp to account for the unknown unknowns.

In some circumstances, giving legal effect to the technology underpinning a smart contract may give rise to significant and insurmountable legal problems. 'Air gaps' quarantine the technology and ensure that legal consequences only flow from the legal architecture agreed by the parties. This includes matters such as where a record of a transaction resides and which record of transactions has legal effect, which may not be the technological smart contract. This protects the ultimate legal consequences from being subject to technological errors. Whilst air gaps will not

---

[46] For example, in the event of a 'black-out', a smart contract which relies on electricity may be unable to run. Even if there are backup systems such as a battery or generator, there will inevitably be a gap perceptible to the technology which may interfere with the certainty of outputs. These circumstances cannot be managed through technology alone as the technology will not, in the moment where there is no power, be able to execute the code. Some other mechanism is required.

[47] For instance, in the case of 'The DAO', if there was a 'kill switch' the smart contract which was exploited to remove the funding from The DAO could have been switched off without needing to disrupt the underlying blockchain. See Farrell et al. (n. 1).

[48] For instance, given that the smart contract is intended to operate over time, 'unknown unknowns' are beyond the realm of contemplation before they occur. See Farrell et al. (n. 1).

prevent technological issues, they will ensure that these do not give rise to any unintended legal or commercial consequences. An air gap may also be necessary for an off ramp to be effective.

These safeguards operate concurrently to stop the technological contract, step outside of the technological environment and preserve the legal relationship in the event it is needed. Safeguards become increasingly necessary in the case of smart contract applications which are particularly complex or where the consequences of legal or technological failure would disrupt systemically important systems, such as the international derivatives market. These safeguards protect the parties' ability to control their legal relationship as they preserve parties' commercial and contractual arrangements without needing to contemplate the infinite possible changes to technology or all external circumstances which may impact the system.

For smart legal contracts to go beyond pilots and into production, practical measures are needed to protect system integrity. It is inevitable that there will be circumstances where technology does not operate as intended or requires updating. In these instances, it is critical that the commercial arrangement between the parties remains on foot and is legally binding, regardless of the technology. Building practical safeguards into the technology at the outset places control of the commercial arrangement in the hands of the parties, not the technologists. Safeguards allow parties to take advantage of smart contract technology, secure in the knowledge that the parties will be able to achieve the right commercial result, even if the technology does not operate as intended.

G. Conclusion

The five issues of interoperability, certainty, flexibility, accountability, and safety are worth considering in designing smart contract legal architecture for use in practice, particularly when there will be multiple contracts between multiple pairs of counterparties. These are not the only legal issues which require consideration and these do not replace the important issues relating to the relationship between the different layers of the smart legal contract 'stack'. Further, as more contracts and parties are added, new issues can arise, particularly if parties start to rely on the interaction between the smart legal contracts for the maintenance of their business. As this develops, the stability of the smart contract legal architecture becomes important and systemic risks can also arise.[49]

---

[49] This concept goes further than the safeguards which need to be built into individual smart legal contracts as discussed earlier in this chapter. It requires consideration of what is to happen to the 'platform' of smart legal contracts, when these safeguards need to be used and whether the result is that the default of one party leads to the default of others who are using, and relying on, the same legal contract architecture. This concept is well understood in 'traditional contract platforms' such as payment systems, clearing houses, and financial exchanges (which, in the context of financial markets, are called 'financial market infrastructures'). However, further consideration is beyond the scope of this chapter.

The intention in drawing attention to these legal issues is not to argue that smart legal contracts should not be used in a practical context. Instead, it is to argue that in a practical context, practical issues arise. These can be addressed in designing the legal architecture, but a pragmatic rather than theoretical approach often needs to be taken. Practice does not make perfect, but it does lead to a pragmatic solution.

17
Lawyer Meets Developer
How Interdisciplinary Collaboration Builds Smarter Legal Contracts

Madeleine Maslin and Joshua Butler*

A. Introduction	369	2. The benefits of collaboration for smart legal contracts	376
B. The Emerging Taxonomy of Interdisciplinary Collaboration	371	3. Smart legal contracts as a development domain	378
1. Global consortia models	372	D. Lawyers, Standards, and Emerging Technologies	379
2. Strategic partnerships	373	1. A new standards framework for 'legally binding smart contracts'	380
C. The Relative Benefits of Different Ways of Working	374	2. The future: new ways of working	381
1. Going it alone	375	E. Conclusion	382

A. Introduction

It is by now trite to talk of the unprecedented rate of change affecting many established industries. As new technologies continue to spark revolutions in the way we work and do business, law has proved to be the rule, rather than the exception: its slow-moving cogs an appealing target of user-friendly digital alternatives. In Australia, for example, legal technology ('legaltech') is now fully enmeshed in the mainstream consciousness of the legal industry.[1] The *2019 State of the Legal Market Report* identified adopting technology and embracing innovation as the

---

* Madeleine Maslin is an adviser to the Treasurer of the Commonwealth of Australia. She has worked as a commercial litigation and technology lawyer, served as Tipstaff at the Supreme Court of New South Wales, and is a volunteer member of ISO/TC 307 and researcher for its Smart Contracts Working Group. Madeleine holds a Bachelor of Arts (French; Media & Communications) and Juris Doctor from the University of Melbourne.

Joshua Butler is a Mergers & Acquisitions and Venture Capital lawyer based in the Silicon Valley office of White & Case. He was a founding member of the LawTech Hub in Melbourne, Australia and is a volunteer researcher for the ISO/TC 307 Smart Contracts Working Group. He holds a Bachelor of Commerce (Accounting) and Bachelor of Laws (Honours) from Deakin University.

[1] Thomson Reuters, *2019 Australia: State of the Legal Market* (Report 2019) 12.

two most significant strategies of successful Australian firms going forward.[2] This prediction proved prophetic, with the 2020 report finding that the COVID-19 pandemic has fast-tracked technology procurement decisions at some firms and reaped tremendous benefits for those that had already invested in a robust virtual working environment—namely an effective digital client interface and workflows that enable lawyers to work more productively from home.[3]

Nonetheless, enthusiasm for distributed ledger-based solutions, including smart contracts, remains guarded. The term itself, by now well-known, if not well-understood, has been labelled a misnomer,[4] unpicked as neither 'smart', nor 'contract', and described as facilitating 'non-contractual social exchanges', rather than legally recognizable contracts.[5] Abroad, a similar narrative has emerged: amidst the legaltech tsunami, smart contracts have so far made little more than a ripple.[6] One explanation is that investment in legaltech is reaching saturation point,[7] a factor that is likely to disproportionately affect more speculative technologies, like smart contracts. Indeed, smart contracts, and the platforms on which they run— blockchains being one prominent example—are still relatively new and their uses evolving.[8] The question of how the law will apply to these instruments remains unsettled.[9] Another possibility is that capital investment is only part of the story; what is missing are the partnerships and regulatory framework to make investing in smart contracts worthwhile.

In this chapter, we focus, in the first instance, on 'smart *legal* contracts'—that is, legally enforceable agreements between parties, drafted by lawyers, whose text is both human-intelligible and machine-readable, which incorporate an algorithm that automates some or all of the performance of the terms.[10] Defined as such, smart legal contracts may be distinguished from 'smart contracts', which are not necessarily lawyer-made, nor legally binding, and are generally associated with distributed ledger technology (DLT) and Ethereum in particular. It is our thesis that through meaningful collaboration—across disciplines, industries, and state

---

[2] Thomson Reuters, *2019 Report* (n. 1), 12–16.

[3] Thomson Reuters, *2020 Australia: State of the Legal Market* (Report 2020) 13.

[4] See J.G. Allen, 'Wrapped and Stacked: "Smart Contracts" and the Interaction of Natural and Formal Language' (2018) 14(4) *European Review of Contract Law* 307, 309–10.

[5] P. Ryan, 'Smart Contract Relations in e-Commerce: Legal Implications of Exchanges Conducted on the Blockchain' (2017) 7(10) *Technology Innovation Management Review* 10, 10.

[6] See eg, HSBC UK, *Peer group analysis: Investment trends in legal technology* (Report 2018) (hereafter HSBC UK, *Investment trends in legal technology*); HSBC UK, *Peer group analysis: Financing investments in legal tech* (Report 2017); HSBC UK, *Annual law firm strategy and investment survey* (Report 2020); Thomson Reuters, *2020 Report* (n. 3).

[7] HSBC UK, *Investment trends in legal technology* (n. 6), 7.

[8] See M. McMillan *et al.*, 'Smart(er) contracts in 2020' (online article, 7 August 2020) <https://www.mccullough.com.au/2020/08/07/smarter-contracts-in-2020/> accessed 13 July 2021.

[9] This aspect is explored in detail in Sir Geoffrey Vos, 'End-to-End Smart Legal Contracts: Moving from Aspiration to Reality', ch 2. See also Allen (n. 4), 310: 'Though it means tracking a moving target, it is necessary for lawyers and legal academics to define what exactly we are dealing with.'

[10] Allen (n. 4), 313

lines—we can create a regulatory and commercial environment in which legaltech, and smart legal contracts in particular, can thrive. We propose that, by harnessing the complementary skill-sets of law and technology, we can create transformative legal software solutions that are both 'smart' and (really) 'contracts'.

B. The Emerging Taxonomy of Interdisciplinary Collaboration

As a starting point, if smart legal contracts are to move from contentious theory to widespread practice, the interests of three key stakeholders must be understood.[11] First, *lawyers* want to enhance and diversify their areas of expertise to provide more value to new and existing clients, without eroding their brands as providers of legal services.[12] Secondly, *developers*[13] want to build high quality, legally sound, and commercially viable tools, which will define new and better ways of working. Finally, and perhaps most importantly, *users* (and thereby investors) want practical, accessible solutions to real world problems; greater simplicity, transparency, and security in conducting their business; and access to legal remedies to protect against fraud, ensure a dependable market, and resolve disputes.[14]

Unlike a lot of technologies designed to enhance the work of lawyers and law firms,[15] when it comes to smart contracts there remains a considerable divide between developers and lawyers.[16] On the one hand, some developers may believe that they have no need for lawyers or law, because smart contracts can operate without any overarching legal framework and represent a 'technological alternative' to traditional legal services.[17] Lawyers, meanwhile, are often hesitant to try their hands at a technology that remains largely untested in the courts and legally under-defined. What is more, lawyers who are not early adopters of the technology are still yet to understand the value proposition of smart legal contracts. By considering the user, however, it becomes clear that developers exploring smart legal contract use cases, and those in the legal profession distilling where this technology will fit, need to work together.

---

[11] The interests of a fourth stakeholder, *regulators*, are also critical to the capacity for smart contracts to flourish on a global scale. This aspect is discussed in Part 3 of this chapter.
[12] See eg, B. Alarie, A. Niblett, and A.H. Yoon, 'How Artificial Intelligence Will Affect the Practice of Law' (January 2018) 68(1) *University of Toronto Law Journal* 106, 106.
[13] A term we use as a catchall for individuals and companies developing legal technology solutions.
[14] Vos (n. 9), 5.
[15] Consider, for example, legal technologies focused on cyber security, client collaboration, document automation, data visualization, predictive analytics, and risk management. Tools in these domains are designed to speed up manual processes at scale, or remove them entirely, freeing up the lawyer to focus on higher value work. Save for the question of data security, the architecture and use of such tools is largely uncontroversial as between lawyers and developers.
[16] Vos (n. 9), 5.
[17] Allen (n. 4), 320.

With this in mind, a variety of interdisciplinary approaches have emerged. For present purposes, we have focused on two: (i) global consortia involving law firms, enterprise, and technologists, and (ii) strategic partnerships between law firms and technology startups. We also look at models currently in use for the development of a range of legal technologies, which we suggest could be applied to develop smart legal contracts in a way that minimizes the costs of production and maximizes the utility of the end product.

1. Global consortia models

In the absence of internationally agreed ways of working with smart contracts, which we address in Section 3, the private sector has begun to take matters into its own hands, creating standards and digital ecosystems for testing and growing smart contracts. While the distributed ledger universe has contextualized 'consortium' to mean a hybrid blockchain system in which a group of independent organizations join, and run nodes on, a gated network,[18] here we use it in the plain English sense: 'coming together with others in your horizontal or vertical ecosystem, in common purpose.'[19] As well as gaining momentum in the wider world of legaltech, the consortium has become the model of choice for many groups looking to proliferate smart contract technology.[20] For instance, the Accord Project, an open-source non-profit initiative[21] enables anyone to build smart agreements and documents on a technology neutral platform.[22] Uniting a global network of lawyers and developers, Accord stands out from the consortium crowd for its volume of projects in production.[23] Another illustration is the Global Legal Blockchain Consortium, founded by Integra Ledger.[24] By aligning global legal industry stakeholders, this group of more than 300 law firms, software companies, and universities aims to develop standards to govern the use of blockchain technology in the business of law.

---

[18] See generally D. Yafimava, 'What are Consortium Blockchains, and What Purpose do They Serve?' *Blockchain Insights* (online Article, 15 January 2019) <https://openledger.info/insights/consortium-blockchains/>>.

[19] L. Pawaczuk, R. Massey, and J. Holdowsky, 'Deloitte's 2019 Global Blockchain Survey', *Deloitte Insights* (Survey Report, 6 May 2019) 10.

[20] See eg, Reynen Court, an app store for cloud-based legal software, designed for law firms and in-house counsel. The platform is backed by a consortium of nineteen law firms, which provide guidance on product as well as financial investment.

[21] Founded by co-editor, P.G. Hunn and contributed to the Linux Foundation.

[22] See *Accord Project* <https://www.accordproject.org> accessed 13 July 2021.

[23] See *Accord Project Github* <https://github.com/accordproject> accessed 13 July 2021; cf. 'Template Studio', an online editor for building, editing, and testing smart legal contracts; and 'Ergo', a programming language specifically engineered for legal agreements.

[24] Integra Ledger is an enterprise blockchain purpose-built for the legal industry: *Integra Ledger* <https://integraledger.com> accessed 13 July 2021.

At a minimum, these models spread positive awareness of the technology they evangelize, as well as facilitating engagement from industry players. If smart contract technology is ever to bridge the chasm from early adopters to mainstream market acceptance, this is an important step within a broader process of development, regulation, and value demonstration. Already, we are seeing that consortia with a technology focus and meaningful participation from both the legal profession and the tech community, can yield tangible benefits for the development of smart contract technology.[25] Before taking the consortium plunge, however, participants should have a clear understanding of both the strategic purpose of the consortium they are joining as well as what they aim to achieve individually.[26]

2. Strategic partnerships

A hundred years before Jeff Bezos opined that 'if you can't feed a team with two pizzas, the team is too large',[27] French engineer Maximilien Ringelmann discovered that individual productivity decreases as group size increases.[28] The Ringelmann Effect would suggest that perhaps one-to-one collaboration between lawyer and developer, rather than the fashionable consortium, is a more effective approach for building smart contracts. This may well be true; especially once the consortium model has served its purpose of creating a regulatory and commercial environment that is ready for smart contracts, and once standards have been implemented to offer more certainty around questions of interoperability, scalability, and governance.

Until then, there is much that those backing the success of smart legal contracts can learn from strategic partnerships focused on building better legal applications of technology.[29] One such approach is law firms making tactical investments in

---

[25] See eg, Accord Project 'Cicero', a templating system for creating 'reusable machine readable natural-language contracts and clauses': <https://accordproject.org/projects/cicero> accessed 13 July 2021.

[26] See L. Pawczuk, P. Wiedmann, and L. Simpson, 'So, you've decided to join a blockchain consortium: Defining the benefits of "coopetition"' (online Article, 2019) 2 <https://www2.deloitte.com/content/dam/Deloitte/us/Documents/technology/us-cons-blockchain-consortium.pdf> accessed 13 July 2021.

[27] R. Brandt, 'Birth of a Salesman, Behind the rise of Jeff Bezos and Amazon', *The Wall Street Journal* (online, 15 October 2011) <https://www.wsj.com/articles/SB10001424052970203914304576627102996 83120> accessed 13 July 2021.

[28] 'Social loafing', as it was later coined, is a phenomenon referred to in social and behavioural psychology: A. Simms and T. Nichols, 'Social Loafing: A Review of the Literature' (2014) 15(1) *Journal of Management Policy and Practice* 58; see also M. de Rond, 'Why Less Is in Teams' *Harvard Business Review* (online, 6 August 2012) <https://hbr.org/2012/08/why-less-is-more-in-teams> accessed 13 July 2021.

[29] See eg, J. Bennett et al., 'Current State of Automated Legal Advice Tools' (Discussion Paper No 1, April 2018) 22 for examples of automated legal advice tools, including 'Automation of legal advice with truly smart contracts.'

legaltech companies, whether by acquisition, incubation or strategic alliance.[30] We take the popular example of the 'big law' supported accelerator program. These accelerators are usually modelled as fixed-term, cohort-based programs, which include mentorship and educational components and culminate in a public pitch event or demonstration day.[31] The legal version typically includes some, if not all, of these elements, with the backing of a large law firm.[32]

For example, Australian law firm Lander & Rogers' LawTech Hub is a six-month immersion program for early-stage companies building legal tech. The LawTech Hub enables these companies to deploy, test and iterate their software inside a law firm. Under this model, developers periodically interact with the lawyers using their product, in order to tailor its functionality and ultimately maximize its value. By engaging in a meaningful product-driven dialogue over the space of six months, the conversation changes from 'sorry, this is not exactly what we are looking for' (a common response to a one-touch sales pitch) to 'what if you focused on this part of the problem, instead?'.

Since the start of the legaltech boom, lawyers have been faced with the question of whether to build, borrow or buy legal technology.[33] For law firms, the accelerator model offers the opportunity to drive product design in a direction that serves their own (and their clients') interests, and fits within the broader narrative of investing in technology that helps lawyers to work smarter and focus on higher value work. Other one-to-one models of collaboration between lawyer and developer likewise aim to drive efficiencies that benefit clients – with the caveat that 'efficiency' should not compromise a lawyer's capacity to meet his or her traditional performance metrics.

C. The Relative Benefits of Different Ways of Working

Globally, there is a growing market for legal services,[34] as well as a large potential market of unmet legal need from people who for a range of reasons cannot

---

[30] E. Chin, 'Three strategies for law firms as NewLaw reaches a tipping point' (June 2016) *Australian Law Management Journal* 1, 4; see also Thomson Reuters, *2019 Report* (n. 1), 15.

[31] S. Cohen and Y. Hochberg, 'Accelerating Startups: The Seed Accelerator Phenomenon' (Research Paper, March 2014), <http://seedrankings.com/pdf/seed-accelerator-phenomenon.pdf> accessed 13 July 2021.

[32] Commonly, the startups involved will be building products to solve legal or business problems that are relevant to the law firm and its clients, for example in areas of legaltech and regulatory technology ('regtech'). In a 2021 report, the American Bar Association states that '[s]ince the first legal incubator appeared in 2007, over 70 self-identified legal incubator programs have emerged around the globe.' ABA Standing Committee on the Delivery of Legal Services, 'Results of the Legal Incubator Lawyers' Survey' (Report, April 2021) <https://www.americanbar.org/content/dam/aba/publications/center-for-innovation/deliveryoflegalservices/delivery-legal-incubator-survey-2021.pdf> accessed 13 July 2021.

[33] Chin (n. 30).

[34] See eg, Mordor Intelligence, *Legal Services Market—Growth, Trends and Forecast (2020–2025)* (Report, 2019); Mordor Intelligence, *Legal Services Market—Growth, Trends, COVID-19 Impact, and Forecasts (2021–2026)* (Report, 2020); Thomson Reuters, *2020 Report* (n. 3), 5.

access legal services. In Australia, for example, more than one-fifth of people experience three or more legal problems in a given year, with the most disadvantaged in the community disproportionately affected.[35] These statistics are reflected in the USA.[36] Technology, however, presents many opportunities for improving access to justice by enabling lawyers to provide services more quickly and efficiently, at a lower cost, and consequently to a larger client base. In theory, this makes the law more accessible. Legal technologies also present a risk to lawyers, however, in areas of law where software solutions are willing and able to cut blood and bones lawyers out of the picture.

Law firms have a history of staying in, and dominating, their own lane. Their reluctance to collaborate comes from the 'asymmetrical relationship' lawyers have enjoyed for so long with their clients and society at large, and is reflected in the attempts of firms to survive the digitization of legal services delivery by keeping their efforts in-house.[37] This attitude ignores a fundamental truth of the digital age: collaboration is essential for competitiveness.[38] If the desired destination is putting great legal technologies (smart contracts and others) in the hands of clients, while preserving human lawyers' place in the legal marketplace, then we posit that the siloed approach is the long road to get there.

1. Going it alone

In 2019, amongst the twenty-five of the fifty largest law firms in Australia to have formalized an innovation function, innovation duties were largely allocated to existing roles.[39] In other words, partners, knowledge management directors, and heads of technology are, or were, being tapped to take on the (often additional) task of heading the firm's innovation strategy. For law firms seeking to develop client-facing technology solutions in-house as part of that strategy, substantial resources must be allocated to acquiring new capabilities, starting with a dedicated engineering function. Other capability challenges that firms need to consider include marketing and distribution. The product sales cycle, in particular, while critical to the success of any tech product, is often foreign to law firms.

---

[35] C. Coumarelos *et al.*, Legal Australia-Wide Survey: Legal Need in Australia (Report 2012), 15.
[36] *Ibid.*, 33.
[37] M. Cohen, 'The Legal Industry is Starting to Collaborate—Why Now and Why It Matters, *Forbes* (online, 22 July 2019) <https://www.forbes.com/sites/markcohen1/2019/07/22/the-legal-industry-is-starting-to-collaborate-why-now-and-why-it-matters/#378589ea343d> accessed 13 July 2021.
[38] *Ibid.*
[39] Thomson Reuters, *2019 Report* (n. 1), 12.

One of the poster kids of the 'new law' age was Silicon Valley darling, Atrium.[40] Marketed as a hybrid corporate law firm and technology company, Atrium went after the lucrative emerging growth legal market with subscription-based pricing models and a suite of in-house developed legal tech designed to support the office of general counsel. In March 2020, however, Atrium shut its doors, laying off more than 100 employees.[41] By the company's own admission, their 'full-stack' hybrid model did not lead to operational efficiencies.[42] It would be an oversimplification to suggest that Atrium's demise is demonstrative of the inevitable fatality of going it alone. It does, however, illustrate the challenges of playing the role of lawyer and developer all at once.

The startup model is premised in large part upon the ability to pivot and adapt as the new business moulds its chosen solution to the problem it set out to solve. By contrast, established law firms do not have the same innate agility to reinvent themselves, overhauling staff, branding, and their core competencies. For big law, what is needed is a more conservative approach to meeting clients' evolving needs and expectations, without fundamentally altering their business models or growth and investment strategies. We suspect that this will be as true for law firms developing smart legal contracts, as for those building other forms of legaltech.

2. The benefits of collaboration for smart legal contracts

The legaltech boom has spawned many precedents for multidisciplinary collaboration within law firms. Examples include engaging innovation consultants, process engineers, developers, and design thinkers, or even establishing client-facing legal technology teams. For some law firms, multidisciplinary collaboration is the culmination of the 'innovation journey'. It begins with unilaterally assessing what innovation means for the firm, before progressing to collaboratively identifying and solving operational bottlenecks, workflow inefficiencies and technology adoption issues, in concert with their tech counterparts.[43]

When it comes to smart legal contracts, however, we are not just talking about legal technology as we know it now. What is required to determine the capabilities and limitations of a *new* technology, with global application, is interdisciplinary collaboration—not *within*, but *between* organizations, industries, and jurisdictions.

---

[40] In 2018, Atrium raised $65 million, led by tier one venture capital firm Andreessen Horowitz: 'Atrium raises $65M from a16z to replace lawyers with machine learning' *TechCrunch* (online Article, 11 September 2018) https://techcrunch.com/2018/09/10/atrium-legal/ accessed 13 July 2021.
[41] '$75M legal startup Atrium shuts down, lays off 100' *TechCrunch* (online Article, 4 March 2020) <https://techcrunch.com/2020/03/03/atrium-shuts-down/> accessed 13 July 2021.
[42] Ibid.
[43] See eg, Thomson Reuters, *2019 Report* (n. 1), 15.

The potential of smart legal contracts lies at the intersection of contract law, distributed systems engineering, and end-user experience. This being the case, those designing and building smart legal contract applications would do well to lean on the lawyer experience in order to better grasp the problem this technology is trying to solve.[44] At this point, it is useful to consider the respective needs and capabilities of our three key stakeholders.

Lawyers offer developers their knowledge of legal clients and legal contracts, including how they are formed, performed and broken. *Developers*, meanwhile, with input from lawyers, bring the expertise to meaningfully, securely, and in a way that is user-friendly, create programs that are both smart and contracts. By collaborating, lawyers can develop the requisite skillset to advise *users* when things go wrong, be it with the terms of the smart legal contract or the code itself.

Accounting for these interests and capabilities is the cornerstone of human-centred design, which calls for a focus 'on the people whom a product, service or system is trying to serve.'[45] This problem-solving framework has captured the attention of the legal services industry in recent years, championed by the work of Stanford University's Legal Design Lab.[46] Applied to the example of developing a smart legal contract that includes a mechanism for negotiation, the human-centred designer starts by obtaining a keen understanding of the manner in which parties tend to negotiate. In the absence of meaningful, problem-specific understanding, some legal technologies miss the mark for lawyers and their clients, by failing to appreciate the way lawyers work and how clients do business.

For developers, the fundamental value proposition offered by the lawyers and law firms looking to collaborate with them is twofold: first, they bring *institutional knowledge* and, second, they offer rich *data sets*. Firms may employ technology to aid delivery more and more, but they remain human-oriented businesses. Although clients' needs and expectations are changing,[47] the knowledge and

---

[44] The notion of 'loving the problem, not the solution' is attributed to Ash Maurya, author of *Running Lean* and *Scaling Lean*, and thought leader on the lean startup methodology. Maurya describes the pitfall of product managers becoming predisposed to a particular way of solving a problem as 'the Innovator's Bias': A. Maurya, 'Love The Problem, Not Your Solution', *Medium* (Blog Post, 12 August 2016) <https://blog.leanstack.com/love-the-problem-not-your-solution-65cfbfb1916b> accessed 13 July 2021.

[45] M. Hagan, 'A Human-Centered Design Approach to Access to Justice: Generating New Prototypes and Hypotheses for Intervention to Make Courts User-Friendly' (2018) 6(2) *Indiana Journal of Law and Social Equality* 199, 202, <https://www.repository.law.indiana.edu/ijlse/vol6/iss2/2/> accessed 13 July 2021.

[46] An interdisciplinary team of lawyers, software engineers and designers based out of Stanford Law School's Center on the Legal Profession and Stanford University's Institute of Design ('d.school').

[47] See eg, M. Cohen, 'What's A Lawyer Worth? *Forbes* (online, 4 December 2017), <https://www.forbes.com/sites/markcohen1/2017/12/04/whats-a-lawyer-worth/#7c28665377c4>> accessed 13 July 2021 for a well-articulated perspective on the impact of technology and globalization on the legal industry, the emerging tendency of clients to view 'legal' matters as business challenges that raise legal

experience of the practitioner remains paramount and invaluable. Where developers are striving for product-market fit within the legal services industry, they would be wise to spend time understanding the lawyer and user vantage points. This should be emphasized for legal tech that builds interaction with human lawyers into the user experience.

The techno-sibling of the lawyer's knowledge and experience is the data sitting inside the law firm's document management system. Be it the result of concerns around legal professional privilege, reticence to share data, or the practical question of providing appropriate levels of access to these document management systems, however, dataflow between law firms and technology developers has been a problem area in the construction and adoption of legaltech. This has proved especially true for machine learning products, which require access to large data sets. If firms can overcome security and privacy challenges and find ways to harness the huge amounts of data they are holding to contribute to better legal technology—including smart contracts—we envisage benefits for the entire industry.

3. Smart legal contracts as a development domain

So far, we have drawn principally on strategies that work for the development of legal technology generally (or, broader still, the development of any consumer-facing technology), extrapolating them to the context of smart contract development. If we are to take this approach, we must also be alive to the differences between these two distinct domains. Briefly, we can do this by considering the example of building a consumer-facing application. In the general domain, such applications will often be built with a single type of consumer in mind.[48] A consumer-facing application in the legal tech domain, however, may have at least two separate user types: lawyer and client.[49] By contrast, smart legal contract applications may have both lawyer and client users, with the additional design requirement that all the elements of a legally binding contract are embedded in the application. This added level of complexity is a further indicator of the need for interdisciplinary collaboration and domain expertise in smart legal contract development.

---

issues, and the persistent phenomenon of lawyers doing 'far too much law for those who can afford it and far too little for those who cannot.'

[48] For example, an instant messaging application on your mobile device; such software has been built with the user of the application at the centre of the design process.

[49] For example, software which allows lawyers to build client-facing applications without using computer code, such as bots that can triage information, automate documents and give simple advice. This kind of software has been built with two distinct users at the centre of the design process: the lawyer building the application and the client using the end product.

D. Lawyers, Standards, and Emerging Technologies

Sir Geoffrey Vos predicts that 'end-to-end smart legal contracts will not become mainstream without a legal infrastructure.'[50] In particular, Vos suggests, the use of smart contracts would be advanced by greater clarity in relation to '(i) the legal enforceability of contractual provisions expressed in code, (ii) how such provisions will be interpreted, and (iii) what parties can do when things go wrong with the code.'[51] One way of providing such clarity, at least in relation to the technical aspects of smart contracts, is through standardization, agreed on an industry-specific, national, or international basis.[52]

In simple terms, standardization is the process of establishing specifications to ensure that products made by different manufacturers are safe, reliable and of good quality by asking 'what's the best way of doing this?'. The focus of most technology standards is ensuring that devices, systems and services can connect and interoperate with each other, thereby boosting innovation and investment, and supporting market liberalism.[53] In crude terms, there is currently a lack of interoperability between different blockchain and distributed ledger platforms, which inhibits market confidence and the broader rollout of these systems. If they are to continue to grow and attract investment, many will need to be updated or indeed replaced in order to remain competitive and to avoid security problems and obsolescence. As the technology matures, having common standards for smart contracts, and the platforms on which they sit, is essential.[54]

It is from this premise, and from the pervading sense of the unrealized potential of blockchain and smart legal contracts, that the International Organization for Standardization's Technical Committee for Blockchain and Distributed Ledger Technologies (ISO/TC 307) was born. Established in 2017, the goal of ISO/TC 307 is to further these technologies 'by providing internationally agreed ways of

---

[50] Vos (n. 9), 4.
[51] Ibid.
[52] This is particularly so given that smart contracts lie on a spectrum: a contract may be written a) entirely in code; b) in code with a separate natural language version; c) in code incorporating by reference the terms of a natural language master agreement; or d) in natural language with some encoded performance: J. Rogers, H. Jones-Fenleigh, and A. Sanitt, Arbitrating Smart Contract Disputes (Report, October 2017) 1, <https://www.nortonrosefulbright.com/en-au/knowledge/publications/ea958758/arbitrating-smart-contract-disputes> accessed 13 July 2021.
[53] In modern information and communication technologies (ICT) parlance, the service value of a device relies on the ability to communicate with other devices; this is known as the network effect: 'ICT and Standardisation', European Commission, <https://ec.europa.eu/digital-single-market/en/policies/ict-and-standardisation> accessed 13 July 2021.
[54] Department of Industry, Science, Energy and Resources, National Blockchain Roadmap (Report, February 2020) 19, <https://www.industry.gov.au/data-and-publications/national-blockchain-road map> accessed 13 July 2021 (hereafter Department of Industry, Science, Energy and Resources, National Blockchain Roadmap).

working, stimulating greater interoperability, speedier acceptance and enhanced innovation in their use and application.'[55] Australia plays a leading role as the Secretariat for ISO/TC 307, which has a membership of forty-six participating countries and comprises eleven Working Groups. In its *Roadmap for Blockchain Standards*, Standards Australia found that, for the majority of stakeholders, challenges, and inconsistencies in the definition of terms such as 'smart contracts' posed the 'highest priority standards issue for blockchain'.[56]

1. A new standards framework for 'legally binding smart contracts'

In response to this urgent need, ISO/TC 307's Smart Contracts Working Group was created and tasked with preparing a Technical Report 'describing what smart contracts are and how they work.'[57] This document, which focuses on the technical aspects of smart contracts, distinguishes smart contracts 'as a technology for [blockchain] automation in general' from those with 'legally binding intention'. It observes that understanding the structure and legally binding nature of smart contracts requires an understanding of legal definitions and principles.[58] This is an important caveat when discussing smart contracts. First, it highlights the risk that the code in legally binding smart contracts may not include all or some of the aspects that are present in a legal contract and the surrounding legal framework.[59] Second, it suggests that even where the code is legally comprehensive, smart legal contracts nonetheless require smart legal minds.

Working out precisely what constitutes a smart *legal* contract was the Working Group's next focus. Its Technical Specification on 'Legally binding smart contracts' aims to assist developers by prescribing the features of a legally binding smart contract and setting out a legal risk management process for developing and working with smart contracts.[60] This document also presents a series of

---

[55] Craig Dunn, Chair of ISO/TC 307, quoted in Clare Naden, 'Blockchain Technology Set to Grow further with International Standards in Pipeline' *ISO News* (online Article, 24 May 2017) <https://www.iso.org/news/Ref2188.htm>.

[56] Standards Australia, *Roadmap for Blockchain Standards* (Report, March 2017), 10 <https://www.standards.org.au/getmedia/ad5d74db-8da9-4685-b171-90142ee0a2e1/Roadmap_for_Blockchain_Standards_report.pdf.aspx> accessed 13 July 2021 (hereafter Standards Australia, *Roadmap for Blockchain Standards*).

[57] ISO/TC 307 Blockchain and distributed ledger technologies, *Overview of and interactions between smart contracts in blockchain and distributed ledger technology systems* (Technical Report ISO/TR 23455, 2019) 1 <https://www.iso.org/standard/75624.html?browse=tc> accessed 13 July 2021 (hereafter ISO/TC 307 Blockchain and distributed ledger technologies, *Overview*).

[58] Ibid.

[59] Scott Farrell quoted in Standards Australia, *Roadmap for Blockchain Standards* (n. 57), 16.

[60] See ISO/TC 307 Blockchain and distributed ledger technologies, 'ISO/AWI TS 23259 Blockchain and distributed ledger technologies — Legally binding smart contracts' (online, 2019), <https://www.iso.org/standard/75095.html?browse=tc> accessed 13 July 2021.

best practice factory patterns to demonstrate how different types of smart legal contracts can be coded.[61] The benefits of having international consensus on the basic architecture, legal elements, and diverse capabilities and functionalities of smart legal contracts will be felt as much by developers as by lawyers, regulators, and users.

2.) The future: new ways of working

By collaborating with experts from a range of disciplines, industries, and nationalities, lawyers and developers have a critical role to play in establishing international ways of working with smart contracts. Input from experienced network architects is critical to ensuring that standards grapple comprehensively with the technical infrastructure. Equally, lawyers help craft standards that are principles-based, technology-neutral and capable of ready adoption by industry, regulators and lawmakers. Although standards are not able to take priority over the law or act as a substitute, regulators and governments count on ISO standards in order to help develop better regulation, thanks in large part to the involvement of globally established experts.[62]

The Smart Contracts Working Group necessarily comprises a broad cross-section of experts. Within the group, lawyers and developers join forces with academics, engineers, regulators, governments, investors, industry stakeholders, and enthusiasts. Such a diversity of knowledge ensures that standards are built on a foundation of soundly establishing, and thoroughly testing, the legal and technical parameters of smart contracts, in order to better facilitate their deployment, utility and governance around the world.

A new global standards regime and technical specification for legally binding smart contracts will bring greater certainty to those working to build them, both alone and collaboratively. It will also create more work for lawyers, as the private sector and governments scale up their smart legal contract operations, and offer direction to lawyers about how to resolve disputes by differentiating 'smart contracts' and 'smart legal contracts'. Whether the publication of the Technical Specification and factory patterns catalyses a new wave of development, investment, and utilization of smart legal contracts, only time will tell.

---

[61] Bearing in mind ISO's commitment to supporting the United Nations' 17 Sustainable Development Goals, the use cases adopted by the Smart Contracts Working Group for these factory patterns include multi-party solar sharing agreements and fair trade supply chain transparency; see ISO's recently updated New Work Item Proposals document available at ISO, 'Stages and Resources for Standards Development' <https://www.iso.org/stages-and-resources-for-standards-development.html> accessed 13 July 2021.

[62] ISO, 'Benefits of Standards' <https://www.iso.org/benefits-of-standards.html> accessed 13 July 2021.

E. Conclusion

A key recommendation from the Australian Government's *National Blockchain Roadmap* is to '[e]stablish a collaborative model comprising working groups of industry, the research sector and government to progress analysis on the next use cases'.[63] This collaborative approach is especially critical for smart contracts. As we see it, if smart contracts are to reach their transformative potential, then global consortia, strategic partnerships, and international standards all have vital and related roles to play.

The publication of ISO's Technical Specification on 'legally binding smart contracts' will provide greater certainty to all parties with an interest in smart contracts. Likewise, consortia looking to develop technology agnostic ecosystems for smart contracts are already beginning to provide valuable tools for integrating them into the business landscape. Further, and perhaps more importantly, consortia present a compelling argument for *why* organizations should adopt smart contracts. Down the track, partnerships at the local level, between law firms and technology providers, will be best placed to produce smart legal contracts tailored to specific clients and practice areas. One possible outcome of these collaborations is the creation of new revenue streams, such as the development and sale of 'white label' smart legal contracts, which can be procured and rebranded by firms.[64]

In concluding, it should be reiterated that the potential of smart legal contracts exists at a crossroads between law, engineering and user experience. To borrow a phrase, for smart contracts to move from 'technologically feasible aspiration to legal and commercial reality' what is required is more than just greater certainty as to how the law will approach these new legal programs.[65] Specifically, we need to create an environment that is ready for smart contracts, and to build interdisciplinary teams capable of uniting sound legal principles with frictionless architecture. In such an environment we will have: (i) developers who can build and sell viable smart contracts; (ii) users with the confidence to invest in and rely on them; and (iii) lawyers with the understanding to implement them in practice and, inevitably, resolve disputes. Our advice to all three—and to lawyers especially—is to engage with this field as it develops, and to champion collaboration opportunities as they arise.

---

[63] Department of Industry, Science, Energy and Resources, *National Blockchain Roadmap* (n. 54) 13.

[64] See D. Gainor, 'Why A White Label Solution Is Easier Than Building Your Own', *Forbes* (online, 3 June 2014) <https://www.forbes.com/sites/theyec/2014/06/03/why-a-white-label-solution-is-easier-than-building-your-own/#77353700dd9e> accessed 13 July 2021; see eg, Appenate, which allows users to publish iOS, Android and Windows native apps to respective app stores carrying bespoke branding and imagery, with no mentions of Appenate anywhere: *Appenate* <https://www.appenate.com/white-label/> accessed 13 July 2021.

[65] Vos (n. 9), 2.

18
Not Up To The Job

Why Smart Contracts Are Unsuitable For Employment

Gabrielle Golding and Mark Giancaspro*

A. Introduction	383	C. Why Smart Contracts are Unsuitable for Employment	388
B. Background to Smart Contracts in Employment	385	1. Inability to account for the managerial prerogative	388
		D. Conclusion	395

A. Introduction

In this chapter, we argue that smart contracts are not suitable for employment. As our world of work continues to shift to and grow via online platforms, most obviously in respect of work performed in the 'gig economy'[1]—leaving aside the vexed issue of whether these workers are appropriately classified as employees, independent contractors, or something in between[2]—it is unsurprising that employers

---

* Dr Gabrielle Golding is a Senior Lecturer in Law and 2022 Barbara Kidman Women's Fellow at The University of Adelaide. Her research expertise is in employment and contract law, and their intersection.

Dr Mark Giancaspro is a Lecturer and practising commercial lawyer at the University of Adelaide Law School. He holds an honours degree in Laws and Legal Practice from Flinders University and a PhD from the University of Adelaide. He is a member of the Law Council of Australia (Digital Commerce Committee, Business Law Section) and researches in contract and consumer law.

[1] See generally, J. Prassl, *Humans as a Service: The Promise and Perils of Work in the Gig Economy* (OUP 2018).

[2] Importantly, this chapter's scope is limited to the consideration of the common law employment contractual relationship. However, to take the United Kingdom by way of example, there are two intermediate categories of personal work relationship, which attract some employment rights. These two concepts are the 'worker' contract and the 'contract personally to do work'. They sit somewhere in between the contract of employment and the commercial contract for services. See also M. Freedland and N. Kountouris, *The Legal Construction of Personal Work Relations* (OUP 2011), in which a new central organizing idea for modern employment protection systems is developed in the form of 'the personal work relation', the concept of which aids understanding the relationship between the standard contract of employment and other work relationships. See also, R. Owens, J. Riley, and J. Murray, *The Law of Work* (2nd edn, OUP 2011) 165–6, which frames considerations of the 'law of work' beyond the standard contract of employment to include broader work relationships.

may now be tempted to contract with their employees using digitally generated and maintained smart contracts. At face value, there seems to be a clear and obvious efficiency reason for doing so, particularly in respect of the engagement and monitoring of larger workforces. However, we say, that as compelling and tempting and as the option may be, it is wholly unsuitable in respect of an employer contracting with an employee for a multitude of reasons.

To begin, in Section B we define smart contracts in the context of blockchain technology. We also identify a possible use case for smart contracts in the field of employment and question whether they might be utilized in formalizing a contractual relationship between an employer and employee.[3] Following this contextual discussion, we identify a variety of reasons as to why we view smart contracts as entirely unsuitable for employment. These reasons are broadly split across four different branches, which concern both employer- and employee-based interests. First, smart contracts cannot account for the existence of the managerial prerogative, which lies at the heart of the employment relationship, being one of its core underlying features. Secondly, smart contracts are unable to account for the exercise of any discretion, which is inherent in the employment relationship, and may include, among other things, the assessment of whether discretionary performance standards are met, so as to warrant the award of a bonus payment, potentially resulting in unfairness to the employee. Thirdly, a smart employment contract is unable to allow an employer to performance manage, discipline and potentially dismiss employees for misconduct, as well as the opportunity for an employee to respond in such circumstances; all such actions require a subjective assessment, not able to be accounted for in the smart contract. Fourthly, the very nature of a smart contract is unable to accommodate for certain changes that are cognizant in instances of employment; they are inflexible, contain functional vulnerabilities and would drive unprecedented and unnecessary structural change throughout workplaces, possibly giving rise to job losses, rather than job maintenance or creation.

It is with these arguments in mind that we recommend and conclude in Section C that, while they may be suitable in other discrete contractual contexts, smart contracts are an unwise and unhelpful means through which an employer and employee could contract with one another. The potential transition from this aspiration to practical reality is, as will be explained, almost certainly inhibited by the foregoing factors.

---

[3] It was not previously possible to speak of an employment contract applying to all categories of wage-dependent labour. There were separate categories of 'service' and 'employment', with the notion of service developing during the eighteenth century under the English Master and Servant Acts. It was not until well into the twentieth century after those Acts were repealed that employment relationships became fully accepted as contractual, both in England and, in turn, across other common law jurisdictions. It took time for common law courts to develop their understanding of employment, both as a contractual relationship and unitary concept, whereby employees were no longer referred to as servants. See further, the discussion concerning this transition period from status to contract in S. Deakin and G. Morris, *Labour Law* (6th edn, Hart Publishing 2012), 22.

B. Background to Smart Contracts in Employment

The concept of the 'smart contract' is actually decades old, originating in a series of online articles and blog posts authored by American computer scientist, Nick Szabo, from 1994.[4] Szabo's 1997 publication, 'The Idea of Smart Contracts', was the first to elaborate in detail upon this then fanciful notion. The smart contract was described as a computerized transaction protocol, which executes the terms of a contract.[5] Szabo envisaged a variety of useful applications for this technology, such as contracts for the purchase of a motor vehicle on credit, whereby the vehicle would immobilize itself if security protocols stipulated in the contract (such as verification of identity upon use, or timely periodic repayment) were not met. The emergence of cryptocurrency platforms, such as Bitcoin and Ethereum, has made the possibility of such applications very possible owing to their advanced functional capabilities.

Szabo's description of smart contracts has since become commonplace and his concept underlies the archetypes in use today. Smart contracts are stored on, and operate as, computer programs within a *distributed blockchain network*. The coding of these programs can, as Szabo predicted, be fashioned to mimic the terms of an orthodox legal contract. What makes them unique is their capacity to autonomously execute those coded terms and perform complex functions in response to real-world conditions.[6] This, in turn, displaces the need for a traditional intermediary to facilitate the transaction. The code can be designed in such a way to constantly draw data from external sources via 'oracles', electronic agents embedded within smart contract coding.[7] These oracles interact with online sources of information to verify whether certain coded preconditions are met, which then triggers the smart contract's ability to enforce its terms.

In light of their capabilities, it has been suggested in the literature that smart contracts might, for example, be programmed to immediately issue compensation to insured passengers in the event of flight cancellation, which they would accomplish through communication with global air traffic databases to determine which flights have proceeded as scheduled or been cancelled.[8] This would dramatically

---

[4] See eg, M. Giancaspro, 'Is a Smart Contract Really a Smart Idea? Insights from a Legal Perspective' (2017) 33 *Computer Law and Security Review* 825, 825; K. Werbach and N. Cornell, 'Contracts Ex Machina' (2017) 67 *Duke Law Journal* 313, 323; M. Bacina, 'When Two Worlds Collide: Smart Contracts and the Australian Legal System' (2018) 21 *Journal of Internet Law* 15, 16–7.

[5] See eg, R. de Caria, 'The Legal Meaning of Smart Contracts' (2019) 6 *European Review of Private Law* 731, 734.

[6] See eg, M. Chilaeva and P. Dutton, 'Smart Contracts: Can They Be Aligned with Traditional Principles or are Bespoke Norms Necessary?' (2018) 8 *Journal of International Banking and Finance Law* 479, 479.

[7] See eg, E. Tjong Tjin Tai, 'Force Majeure and Excuses in Smart Contracts' (2019) 6 *European Review of Private Law* 787, 791–2.

[8] See eg, M. Finck, 'Smart Contracts as a Form of Solely Automated Processing under the GDPR' (2019) 9 *International Data Privacy Law* 78, 81.

expedite the traditional claims process. Alternatively, an employment contract might automatically disburse a bonus payment to an employee who has met specified performance goals.[9] Similarly, this would accelerate what is otherwise a more cumbersome payroll task. We discuss further potential uses of smart contracts in respect of employment in more detail below in this section. For the moment, it is worth noting that in both scenarios just mentioned, there is no need for human verification, nor enforcement, as the contract would perform these functions itself. There would be no need for a human agent to verify flight details or performance measures, and the smart contract could do so in real time and not solely during business hours when there is a human agent on hand to carry out these processes.

From these examples alone, it can be seen that smart contracts offer many advantages over traditional text-based contracts and even those digital contracts with limited 'if-then' automation, which have been around for decades.[10] The range of benefits smart contracts promise for governments, businesses, and consumers make them particularly appealing, so it is unsurprising that a great deal of investment has already directed towards developing blockchain technologies.[11]

For a start, smart contracts may increase efficiency. Being decentralized, transactions are no longer dependent upon the involvement of an intermediary for validation. Removal of the 'middlemen', coupled with the smart contract's capacity to automatically perform (or 'enforce') its own terms, means transactions can be completed with greater speed and with the involvement of fewer hands. Moreover, close to all transactions occurring on the blockchain are instantaneous, meaning processing delays that accompany common transactions conducted through intermediaries (such as fund transfers via online banking platforms) are obviated.

Smart contracts are also likely to entail lower transaction costs. The lack of involvement from any kind of central authority or trusted intermediary in a blockchain means the transaction fees those parties would normally charge for their services (such as processing charges levied by credit providers) are avoided entirely. Moreover, the smart contract can interpret and enforce its own terms, and potentially execute dispute resolution mechanisms, in accordance with its coding, and is therefore not reliant upon expensive lawyers. This ability for smart contracts to operate in a 'trustless' cyberworld gives them a distinct advantage over conventional intermediated contracts.[12]

Finally, the networked and decentralized nature of blockchain ledgers means commercial transactions conducted therein through smart contracts are visible

---

[9] *Ibid.*
[10] Werbach and Cornell (n. 4), 320–1.
[11] The following summary of the benefits of smart contracts is drawn from Giancaspro (n. 4), 827–8.
[12] 'By virtue of their tamper-proof, time-stamped and immutable character, smart contracts offer a viable option to create and strengthen trade relationships. As the performance of a particular agreement is ensured, transacting parties would not need to trust each other, but instead they would just need to rely on the correct functioning of the smart contract': O. Borgogno, 'Smart Contracts as the (New) Power of the Powerless' (2019) 6 *European Review of Private Law* 885, 888.

to all miners within the blockchain. The ledger is synchronized across all nodes within the network and updated in real time for all participants to see. Transactions are conducted through each miner's digital 'wallet',[13] which automatically verifies their identity and securely stores and transfers their financial information without having to involve an intermediary. Miners therefore enjoy an unprecedented level of anonymity (or pseudonymity) and transparency through utilizing smart contracts.

Much of the literature addressing smart contracts assumes them to be compatible with existing legal frameworks. This assumption has been challenged.[14] It is not clear whether the autonomous, irreversible and anonymous features of smart contracts make them adaptable to basic contract law principles relating to formation, performance and remedies. For the purposes of this chapter, we assume the general validity of smart contracts and their capacity to operate as we suggest, though we acknowledge the concerns in this regard.

This chapter now turns to discussing potential applications for smart contracts in the employment context. As mentioned earlier, there is an obvious temptation for employers here: smart contracts appear modern, capable, adaptable, and above all, efficient in the context of the engagement of larger workforces, in particular. For example, there is evidence of smart contracts having been trialled in the context of managing the payroll of employees of a large company with transnational operations.[15] Similarly, above, we also made a brief reference to the potential for a smart contract to streamline the award of a bonus payment to an employee where certain performance criteria are met.

Beyond these potential and discrete usages, some online commentators have boldly presumed that smart contracts would be ideal for instances of all employment.[16] They reason, in sweeping terms, that a smart contract will create 'enforceable and immutable rights and obligations for all participants [to the employment contract] ... [f]or example, automatically ... [releasing] payments from escrow once workers complete assigned tasks, which smooths income for workers and

---

[13] A digital wallet is, essentially, an electronic device, which permits individuals to make electronic transactions. The most commonly recognized example is the contactless payment technology embedded into many modern smartphones. For a more detailed discussion of digital wallets, see eg, R. Krishna Balan and N. Ramasubbu, 'The Digital Wallet: Opportunities and Prototypes' (2009) 42 *Institute of Electrical & Electronics Engineers Computer* 100; R. Kemp, 'Mobile Payments: Current and Emerging Regulatory and Contracting Issues' (2013) 29 *Computer Law & Security Review* 175.

[14] See eg, Giancaspro (n. 4); Bacina (n. 4); M. Raskin, 'The Law and Legality of Smart Contracts' (2017) 1(2) *Georgetown Law Technology Review* 305.

[15] See eg, 'Smart Contracts May Help Corporations Pay Their Employees' (*News BTC*, 17 September 2018) <https://www.newsbtc.com/2018/09/17/smart-contracts-may-help-corporations-pay-their-employees/> accessed 12 May 2021.

[16] See eg, 'Everything You Need to Know About Smart Contracts: A Beginner's Guide' (*Hackernoon*, 27 August 2018) <https://hackernoon.com/everything-you-need-to-know-about-smart-contracts-a-beginners-guide-c13cc138378a> accessed 12 May 2021; '5 Ways Blockchain Will Affect HR' (*Gartner*, 27 August 2019) <https://www.gartner.com/smarterwithgartner/5-ways-blockchain-will-affect-hr/> accessed 12 May 2021.

cash flow for companies'.[17] Some have even gone so far as to suggest that smart contracts would function to ensure a heightened element of clarity, ensure greater fairness, and mitigate conflict between the parties:

> [U]sing a single smart contract for both the parties, the terms, and conditions can be made clear which would help improve fairness. These records could be anything such as salary amount, job responsibilities etc. Once these transactions are recorded on smart contracts, they can be looked into in case of any conflict. This will improve the employee-employer relationship.[18]

More specifically, we also acknowledge the potential for the use of smart contracts for employers to engage casual employees, or, more controversially, to engage employees under a zero-hours contract.[19] Indeed, in respect of casual employees, there exists an argument to suggest that each and every time a casual worker is engaged to perform work that, of itself, constitutes a 'new' contract in respect of each individual engagement.[20] Assuming that understanding of casual engagement is correct, a smart contract could well provide a streamlined way forward for both employers and casual employees in the context of each engagement. Even so, as we will argue, the utility of a smart contract in the context of all instances of employment—irrespective of whether the engagement is of a casual, fixed-term, or permanent nature—is fraught with issues on both the employer and employee side of the bargain. We consider each of those issues in turn directly below taking into account both employer- and employee-based interests.

C. Why Smart Contracts are Unsuitable for Employment

Smart contracts are unsuitable in the employment context for a number of reasons that touch both employee and employment interests.

1. Inability to account for the managerial prerogative

First and foremost, we acknowledge that, generally speaking, courts are willing to uphold and extend the managerial prerogative—a notion that permits an employer to manage its workforce by having the capacity to issue instructions, either

---

[17] '5 Ways Blockchain Will Affect HR' (n. 16).
[18] 'Everything You Need to Know About Smart Contracts: A Beginner's Guide' (n. 16).
[19] See eg, L. Dickens, 'Exploring the Atypical: Zero Hours Contracts' (1997) 26 *Industrial Law Journal* 262, 263; J. Prassl, *The Concept of the Employer* (OUP 2015), 4.
[20] See eg, A. Stewart et al., *Creighton and Stewart's Labour Law* (6th edn, Federation Press 2016) 245–6. Cf, *Melrose Farm Pty Ltd v Milward* (2008) 175 IR 455, [106].

to employees individually or via managerial personnel to a wider group, and to have those instructions followed.[21] Indeed, implied into every employment contract is a general duty owed by an employee to obey their employer's lawful and reasonable instructions.[22] That duty, with its origins in the former master and servant regime,[23] is said to be inherent in, and at the defining core of, every employment relationship.[24]

By supplanting a smart contract in the place of a traditional employment contract, whether it be written, verbal or a combination of both,[25] this shift would have the effect of abrogating the employer's managerial prerogative. Employers would find themselves bound by the operational limitations of the smart contract, developed and maintained from the moment of its creation; indeed, the courts' willingness to accommodate managerial control is said to emerge most eminently in relation to attempts by employers to alter working arrangements from those prevailing at the time of the commencement of employment[26]—most obviously, an employer's ability to direct when, where, how and what work is to be done following an employee's commencement in a role. Typically, core issues in the exercise of the managerial prerogative in employment tend to concern the type of work performed and the nature in which it is carried out.[27] However, for an employee engaged under a smart contract, the consequence would be that the employer's managerial prerogative would become all but subsumed by the very instrument that is meant to make the exercise of their power simpler and more efficient. Being bound by a smart contract would have the opposite effect, generating rigidity, inflexibility and limitations in an employer's capacity to direct and manage its workforce.

a.) Inability to allow for the employer's exercise of discretions

As we have suggested earlier, smart contracts are certainly capable of executing their own terms and would not struggle with certain quantitative concepts in the

---

[21] See eg, Stewart *et al.* (n. 20), 497.

[22] See eg, *Laws v London Chronicle (Indicator Newspapers) Ltd* [1959] 1 WLR 698; *McManus v Scott-Charlton* (1996) 140 ALR 625; *Darling Island Stevedoring & Lighterage Co Ltd; Ex parte Halliday and Sullivan* (1938) 60 CLR 601, 621-2; G. McCarry, 'The Employee's Duty to Obey Unreasonable Orders' (1984) 58 *ALJ* 327.

[23] See eg, G. Golding, 'The Origins of Terms Implied by Law into English and Australian Employment Contracts' (2020) 20 *Oxford University Commonwealth Law Journal* 163.

[24] See eg, G. Golding, 'The Distinctiveness of the Employment Contract' (2019) 32 *Australian Journal of Labour Law* 170, 185, where it is suggested that a duty to obey is so pertinent to employment that it ought not to be capable of exclusion.

[25] While employment contracts are generally in writing, there is no requirement that they must be, except in very rare cases: see eg, J. Carter, *Contract Law in Australia* (6th edn, LexisNexis Butterworths 2013) 190. Indeed, employment contracts are often created informally through the parties reaching a verbal agreement, or where a written contract is created only after an employee commences work: see eg, *Walker v Salomon Smith Barney Securities Pty Ltd* (2003) 140 IR 433, [154] and [167]; *Damevski v Guidice* (2003) 133 FCR 438, [79]-[99].

[26] See eg, Stewart *et al.* (n. 20), 498.

[27] *Ibid.*

context of employment (eg, accounting for quantifiable performance targets, accounting for hours worked, enabling clocking in or out, etc). However, a smart contract will struggle with more fluid and innately subjective or normative concepts requiring some exercise of a discretion by the employer.

Three pertinent examples of challenges to the employer's exercise of a discretion exist.[28] First, an employer's exercise of a discretion may depend on them holding an opinion, or being satisfied of a particular state of affairs. Case law informs us that such powers cannot be exercised unless the employer has a rational and honest opinion or satisfaction about the matter.[29] Apart from the obvious inability for a smart contract to make any assessment as to a discretionary standard altogether, there can be no capability for a smart contract to assess the employer's rationality or honesty in the manner required by the common law. In turn, that would place the employee in a situation of great unfairness.

Secondly, certain powers and discretions of an employer are conditioned on certain processes being completed. Andrew Stewart and others provide the example of the right to terminate conditional on the employer giving the employee a chance to rectify a breach or improve their performance.[30] Quite simply, the smart contract cannot make this kind of subjective assessment, and particularly not in a way that observes the employer's obligation to act honestly and for a proper purpose in such situations. Again, without that assessment taking place, an employee would be subject to unfair treatment.

Thirdly, many powers in employment contracts are bare and unfettered, and a power to terminate on notice and without cause generally falls within that category.[31] In saying that, we acknowledge that a smart contract could well be programmed for the exercise of such a contractual power. However, while there are limited, or perhaps no, good faith requirements attaching to the exercise of such a power,[32] in certain situations, the obligation of good faith may still have a role to play; for example, where a contractual power is given for either party to terminate the agreement on notice in terms wider than necessary for the protection of the party's legitimate interests, it must be exercised in good faith.[33] As before, there is no capability of a smart contract to make an assessment as to whether such a power is being exercised in that requisite manner. Absent that requirement, an employee would, once again, find themselves in a situation cognizant

---

[28] See eg, Stewart *et al.* (n. 20), 530.
[29] See eg, *Service Station Association v Berg Bennett & Associates Pty Ltd* (1993) 45 FCR 84, 94; *Renard Constructions (ME) Pty Ltd v Minister for Public Works* (1992) 26 NSWLR 234, 268, 279–80; *Amann Aviation Pty Ltd v Commonwealth* (1990) 22 FCR 527, 532, 542–4; *Bartlett v Australia and New Zealand Banking Group Ltd* [2016] NSWCA 30, [40]–[49]; *Braganza v BP Shipping Ltd* [2015] 1 WLR 1661.
[30] See eg, Stewart et al. (n. 20), 530.
[31] *Ibid.*, 530–1.
[32] See eg, *Trans Petroleum (Australia) Pty Ltd v White Gum Petroleum Pty Ltd* (2012) 268 FLR 433, [155]; *Bartlett v Australia and New Zealand Banking Group* [2016] NSWCA 30, [78]–[89].
[33] See eg, *Adventure World Travel Pty Ltd v Newsom* (2014) 86 NSWLR 515, [26] and [44].

with a balance of power weighted too heavily, and potentially unfairly, in their employer's favour.

b.) Inability to performance manage, discipline, and dismiss for misconduct

In the realm of smart contracts, an employer would be inhibited from realizing the full range of performance management and disciplinary action, and potentially limited in effecting a dismissal for serious and wilful misconduct of an employee. Conversely, an employee would be prevented from presenting a case to the contrary. It is well-accepted that if a worker commits a breach of an employment obligation, for example, by engaging is some kind of misconduct, or by failing to perform work to an appropriate standard, their employer can seek to impose some kind of disciplinary action,[34] and that in turn, the employee will have the ability to respond, with that response being taken into account.

At one end of the spectrum, this disciplinary action may encompass a mere informal reprimand perhaps a more formal warning. At the other end, an employer may decide that it is necessary to summarily dismiss the employee,[35] the legality of which will depend on the seriousness of the breach and the procedure adopted in bringing about the termination, along with the employee's response to any such action.[36] Crucially, what each of these actions requires is the employer's subjective assessment of the employee's conduct and response, and perhaps also the assessment of that behaviour and any response as against any relevant employment policy or code of conduct,[37] should one apply. Similar to the reasoning already put forward earlier in this section, a smart contract could simply not account for these kinds of subjective assessments, arguably only capable of being assessed, performed and ultimately carried out by a human mind. Not only would this lack of subjective assessment limit an employer's ability to performance manage, discipline and potentially dismiss employees, but would in turn diminish an employee's ability to respond to any purported wrongdoing, and to have that taken into account as part of a disciplinary procedure.

c.) Inability to accommodate change

Here, we suggest that smart contracts are unable to accommodate certain changes that are cognizant in instances of employment. For reasons of their inflexibility and functional vulnerability, smart contracts would drive unprecedented and unnecessary structural change throughout workplaces.

---

[34] See eg, Stewart *et al.* (n. 20), 531.
[35] *Ibid.*
[36] *Ibid.*, ch 22.
[37] As to the interrelationship between workplace policies and employment contracts, see eg, A Chapman *et al.*, 'Organisational Policies and Australian Employment Law: A Preliminary Study of Interaction' (Working Paper No 53, Centre for Employment and Labour Relations Law, University of Melbourne 2015); M. Giancaspro, 'Do Workplace Policies Form Part of Employment Contracts? A Working Guide and Advice for Employers' (2016) 44 *Australian Business Law* 106.

i.) Inflexibility

It is ironic that one of the more appealing features of smart contracts also makes them rather unsuitable for use in many contexts, including employment. As discussed earlier, smart contracts will undoubtedly save costs and make all manner of transactions more efficient. They could certainly be utilized to record and enforce the terms of employment contracts. However, once initiated, verified and added to the blockchain, smart contracts are notoriously difficult—perhaps impossible—to change.[38] Their immutability stems from the design of the decentralized and distributed blockchain network itself, coupled with the self-executing code of the smart contract. A smart contract will continue to execute its coded terms unabated unless it is either programmed to cease at a particular point (which may be hard to define with precision), it becomes dysfunctional, or a 'fork' is created and deployed to stop it.[39] This also means that transactions conducted through smart contracts are irreversible.[40] As McKinney and others explain:

> Smart contracts, by their nature, are not intended, or desired, to be flexible. Rather, the goal—immutability and measurability—is the very opposite, unlike traditional contracts, which commonly build in mechanisms for amendments, modifications, or varying standards of performance.[41]

---

[38] See eg, Werbach and Cornell (n. 4), 327 and 346–7; L. DiMatteo and C. Poncibo, 'Quandary of Smart Contracts and Remedies: The Role of Contract Law and Self-Help Remedies' (2019) 6 *European Review of Private Law* 805, 818; M. Milnes, 'Blockchain: Issues in Australian Competition and Consumer Law' (2018) 26 *Australian Journal of Competition and Consumer Law* 265, 266. However, as Mik explains, some permissioned ledgers allow participants to alter the contents of a block and perhaps even the underlying consensus mechanism: E. Mik, 'The Legal Problems Surrounding Blockchains' (2018) *SAL Practitioner* 13, 9.

[39] On dysfunction and coding see eg, G. Governatori et al., 'On Legal Contracts, Imperative and Declarative Smart Contracts, and Blockchain Systems' (2018) 26 *Artificial Intelligence Law* 377, 402: 'In blockchain systems where smart contracts cannot be blocked (unless the relevant account of money is emptied, or the smart contract has some programming interfaces to block it, etc.), a party who is unsatisfied with the content or the execution of the contract has no way to stop the contract performance, for example by claiming that the contract is invalid or that the other party has failed to comply. If the contract is unstoppable and immutable, then one has to rely on the initial code and the programmers who must anticipate all the states reached by parties during the life of the contract, with no errors in coding (in particular with no infinite loops extremely costly in blockchain systems)'. See also, J. Rohr, 'Smart Contracts and Traditional Contract Law, or: The Law of the Vending Machine' (2019) 67 *Cleveland State Law Review* 71, 72: 'Because of blockchain's immutability, smart contracts that have been uploaded to the blockchain take on a life of their own: they cannot be unilaterally stopped, delayed, or modified absent a fundamental change to the protocol of the blockchain on which the code resides or an "out" that was incorporated into the code from the outset'. On forks, see eg, Werbach and Cornell (n. 4), 332: 'The only exception to immutable execution of a smart contract is a fork which splits the entire blockchain into incompatible tracks. If enough network nodes follow the track without the smart contract, it effectively no longer exists. However, such a move is so technically and politically costly that it rarely if ever occurs on functioning blockchains'.

[40] See eg, P. Ryan, 'Smart Contract Relations in e-Commerce: Legal Implications of Exchanges Conducted on the Blockchain' (2017) 7 *Technology Innovation Management Review* 14, 18.

[41] S. McKinney et al., 'Smart Contracts, Blockchain, and the Next Frontier of Transactional Law' (2018) 13 *Washington Journal of Law, Technology & Arts* 313, 329.

This trait of immutability makes smart *employment* contracts a challenging ideal. Employment contracts are particularly susceptible to change. Basic conditions such as an employee's salary, entitlements, leave allowances, scope of duties, and the like will invariably change with time, especially following enterprise bargaining or internal promotions, which may well be of great benefit to employees over time. Any variations to an employee's rights or obligations will, *prima facie*, be incapable of inclusion within their employment contract once it is added to the blockchain. It will instead operate as it was coded at the outset. A new contract would have to be drawn up and initiated following the termination of its predecessor. Once again, the potential for unfairness on the part of the employee would not just be present, but inherent if a smart contract were to be used for their engagement.

It is plausible that some terms of a smart employment contract could be updated to reflect changes in an employee's status through the use of oracles, thereby avoiding the need to try and replace it. For example, if a smart employment contract were coded to increase an employee's annual salary by a predetermined rate according to a contractual agreement, or, in the Australian context for example, by reason of provisions in an applicable enterprise agreement or Modern Award (whichever applies),[42] it could adapt itself and ensure that future transactions, provided that the data in that agreement could be accessed from a suitable online source by an oracle embedded within the smart contract—for instance, payment of the employee's remuneration would be modified as required. Other material changes, which cannot rely upon oracles, however, will be incapable of inclusion. By way of example, changes in the range of duties required of the employee will require amendment to the original coding which, as discussed earlier, is a near impossible task.

ii.) Functional vulnerabilities

As with all technologies, smart contracts are also vulnerable to malfunction. The coding underlying a smart contract could spontaneously corrupt and disrupt its operation. Indeed, blockchains have proven fallible in this regard.[43] This vulnerability could be potentially perilous in the employment setting. Should a smart contract vested with responsibility for executing its own terms fail, either or both of the parties could potentially breach the agreement without the intention of doing so. For example, the employer may inadvertently fail to pay the employee his or her due remuneration, or the employee may fail to meet predetermined performance targets upon which their entitlements are contingent. Alternatively, the smart contract may execute one or more of its terms, but do so incorrectly;[44] the employee's

---

[42] For further discussion as to the interrelationship between employment contracts, enterprise agreements, and Modern Awards in the Australian context, see eg, Stewart *et al.* (n. 20), [12.5]; Owens, Riley, and Murray (n. 2), [5.6], [7.3], and [11.1].

[43] See eg, Giancaspro (n. 4), 832.

[44] See eg, A. Marthews and C. Tucker, 'Blockchain and Identity Persistence' in C. Brummer (ed), *Cryptoassets: Legal, Regulatory, and Monetary Perspectives* (OUP 2019) 243, 249.

remuneration might be accidentally paid into the incorrect bank account, or they might wrongly be recorded as having fallen short of performance targets which were actually met, triggering performance management mechanisms. All of the foregoing outcomes, though unintended, are technically breaches of the contract,[45] with the potential to create managerial chaos for an employer, and conversely, prejudice an employee.

It is also entirely plausible for oracles, being programs themselves, to fail. As Kevin Werbach and Nicholas Cornell rightly point out, unlike the blockchain itself, oracles are not fully decentralized, meaning the contracting parties must, to some degree, vest trust in an oracle's operator and the authenticity of its data feed.[46] Let us use another conceivable example in the employment context. Assume a smart employment contract was due to increase an employee's salary by reference to the Consumer Price Index (CPI) on June 30. The contract is embedded with an oracle, which attempts to draw the required CPI data from the Australian Bureau of Statistics (ABS) website on June 30 to determine the proportionate rate of increase. If the ABS website happens to be down on the relevant date, the oracle will fail to populate the smart contract with the information it needs. This failure will prevent the contract from enforcing its terms and it will stop working, generating an unfavourable outcome on both the employer and employee side of the bargain. As Borgogno notes, therefore, an incorruptible set of oracles is equally as important as a comprehensive code for a properly functional smart contract.[47]

iii.) Inevitability of structural change

As businesses become more familiar with the concept of distributed ledger technology and learn of its benefits and applications, uptake is likely to increase. Factors such as cost and infrastructural needs are also undoubtedly retarding blockchain's infiltration of commerce though, as discussed earlier, experimentation is already well underway. It is an inevitable consequence of blockchain's influence upon the manner in which businesses can transact that many businesses will undergo structural change. Consider a company that opts to utilize smart contracts to automate its accounting and payroll duties. With each employee's smart contract of employment performing these functions autonomously, there would be little need for a payroll officer or department. Entire institutions, which perform similar intermediate roles—such as banks, brokers, and money-transfer agencies—may similarly become obsolete as the smart contract dismantles the

---

[45] Cf. E. Mik, 'Smart Contracts: Terminology, Technical Limitations and Real-World Complexity' (2017) 9 *Law, Innovation and Technology* 269, 281 who argues that, as neither party can interfere with the operations of the smart contract, breach is theoretically impossible. On this basis, Mik argues, it is more appropriate to speak of such occurrences as mere 'malfunctions' and not as contractual breaches. Liability for this risk of malfunction eventuating would either have to have been allocated through prior agreement or otherwise through operation of the law.

[46] See eg, Werbach and Cornell (n. 4), 336.

[47] See eg, Borgogno (n. 14), 897.

traditional party-intermediary-party transaction model. As such, many businesses stand to potentially be reshaped by the march of the blockchain. The likely and obvious consequence of this is largescale job losses, negatively impacting the current and future employment prospects of those in the workforce.[48]

Of course, blockchain has not yet been fully calibrated for use in commerce. As normally happens when the notion of automation is floated, the assumption is that jobs will automatically disappear if and when this technology becomes a more common feature of commercial transacting. In truth, the possible impact upon the workforce is wholly impossible to assess given the infancy of the technology.[49] It may well be that the introduction of blockchains into industry will actually lead to job 'creation'. After all, smart contracts are, ironically, not that smart at all. They are excellent at seamlessly executing coded instructions and following logical algorithmic processes to produce clear and defined outcomes, but they are hopeless when dealing with any kind of ambiguity or subjective or fluid concept dependent upon human rationality for resolution.[50]

A computer has no way of determining whether an employer's disciplinary actions are 'reasonable', how an employee's response to any such disciplinary action ought to be taken into account (if at all), or whether an employee's 'positive' or 'friendly' demeanour warrants reward, essentially stripping back the employee's already unequal bargaining power. In essence, smart contracts still need smart human professionals, and studies show that, while firms do tend to replace workers with new technologies, they inevitably end up hiring more workers to meet the challenges of growth.[51] Smart contracts will inevitably fail, require amendment or replacement, and become the subject of a dispute, meaning human parties must then pick up the pieces. It is more likely, therefore, that blockchain will complement and change, rather than replace, the roles of traditional intermediaries.[52]

D. Conclusion

To conclude, we have argued that while they may have their discrete uses in respect of quantitative transactions associated with employment (eg, the performance of a payroll function), smart contracts are not suitable for the employment as a whole.

---

[48] See eg, D. Drescher, *Blockchain Basics: A Non-Technical Introduction in 25 Steps* (Apress 2017), 246.
[49] See eg, Organisation for Economic Co-operation and Development (OECD), *OECD Digital Economy Outlook 2017* (OECD Publishing 2017), 317.
[50] See eg, Giancaspro (n. 4) 831, 833.
[51] See eg, M. Dutz, R. Almeida, and T. Packard, *The Jobs of Tomorrow: Technology, Productivity, and Prosperity in Latin America and the Caribbean* (World Bank Publications 2018), ch 6.
[52] This is not to mention the countless jobs that will be created for software engineers and programmers as blockchain and smart contract technologies continue to develop: see eg, C. Benedikt Frey, *The Technology Trap: Capital, Labor, and Power in the Age of Automation* (Princeton University Press 2019), 347.

While they offer many potential benefits for businesses, such as more affordable and efficient transactions and automated enforcement, they suffer from several critical drawbacks, impacting the employer and employee side of the bargain. Aside from being unable to account for the existence of the managerial prerogative, they are incapable—at least, with current technology—to process innately subjective or normative concepts inherent in the employment relationship, including the exercise of discretionary powers afforded to employers, along with the inability to account for the potential need for an employer to performance manage, discipline or even dismiss an employee for misconduct. From the employee's perspective, there is no ability for the smart contract to take their reasons or explanations for alleged misconduct into consideration, thereby inequality and unfairness on their part.

Perhaps the most substantial reason that smart contracts are unsuited to employment is that they are patently inflexible. The rigour of the smart contract's code, and the impermeable and inexorable nature of blockchain ledgers, mean smart contracts are not conducive to any change. In the employment context, this status is significant because rights and obligations of both employers and employees often vary as the employment relationship matures. Being autonomous, self-executing programs, smart contracts also threaten to impact how businesses are structured, potentially resulting in job losses. Like all technologies, we also know that smart contracts are susceptible to malfunction.

Smart contracts and the blockchain are certainly valuable technologies, which may revolutionize the way that businesses transact. They could certainly be suitable for certain business types and relationships and may improve the same. In our view, however, smart contracts are not an ideal means through which to capture the employer-employee relationship. The 'human' element of this relationship is lost on smart contracts. If the computer automates the relationship then its normative nature, the managerial prerogative, fairness afforded to the employee, as well as the flexibility that comes with conventional text-based and/or verbally agreed employment contracts, are all abandoned. We recommend that employers think twice about utilizing smart employment contracts and wait until the technology is advanced enough to address the concerns we have raised throughout this chapter, not just for their own sake, but for the sake of their workforce. In our view, with the current state of technology, smart contracts simply are not up to the job.

19
The Legal Consequences of Automated Mistake

*Simon Gleeson**

A. Introduction	397	D. Integrating Cyber-contracts with the Law of Mistake	412
B. *Quoine Pte Ltd v B2C2 Ltd*	398		
C. The Law of Mistake	403	E. Commercial Certainty	416
		F. Conclusion	419

A. Introduction

What should be the legal consequences when a computer makes a mistake? This is in some respects a trick question; in practice, computers do not make mistakes—they make errors. The distinction is relatively straightforward: a *mistake* is what happens where a person does something on the basis of a mistaken belief; an *error* is the application of a mechanical process in a way which is inappropriate to the circumstances in which the process is applied. Computers do not have beliefs; they therefore cannot make mistakes in the legal sense of the word. Briefly, an error arises where a process designed to apply to a particular set of inputs is applied to a different set of inputs.

For human beings, an error is frequently the result of a mistake, but the two are distinct. For a computer, there is really no such thing as a mistake *per se*—if a computer designed to monitor the health of a group by assessing their body temperatures is instead provided with their ages, it will perform exactly the process which it was designed to perform, but the output will be nonsense. It is possible that this may be the result of a mistake by the operator—he may have believed that the data

---

* Simon Gleeson is a partner of Clifford Chance UK and is a recognized leader in banking and financial markets law globally. In addition to legal practice, Simon is the author of several leading texts on financial law (including *The Legal Concept of Money* which deals with the impacts of virtual currencies) and has held research and teaching positions at numerous leading universities.

Simon Gleeson, *The Legal Consequences of Automated Mistake* In: *Smart Legal Contracts*. Edited by: Jason Grant Allen and Peter Hunn, Oxford University Press. © Jason Grant Allen & Peter Hunn 2022. DOI: 10.1093/oso/9780192858467.003.0020

file he was inputting was of temperature rather than of age—but it is also possible that it may be the result of a defective programme, with no human intervention of any kind. The question which this raises goes to how—if at all—the legal doctrine of mistake should apply in these circumstances?

The reason this matters is that it determines the answer the question: What happens when an automated trading programme does something which, if it were done by a human being, would fall within the law of mistake? This was the core of the case that the Singapore Court of Appeal had to decide in *Quoine Pte Ltd v B2C2 Ltd*,[1] ('*Quoine*'), and the result is of interest to all those working in the field of computer contracting.

The relevance of this issue to 'smart contracts' is that a smart contract is simply a pre-packaged automated trading programme. Specifically, a smart contract is an arrangement between two or more parties whereby, on the occurrence of a particular event, a particular algorithm will be applied to a particular set of data, and as a result a particular transaction or set of transactions will be entered into between those parties. In the case under discussion here, the transactions did not arise under a smart contract entered into directly between the parties, but arose as a result of the use by the parties of algorithms which submitted orders on their behalf to a central trading system, where the rules of the trading system treated the orders so submitted as absolutely legally binding. This is for all practical purposes identical to the situation as it would have been had there been no intermediate trading system, but the parties had entered into a smart contract directly between themselves. However, regardless of the structure of the arrangement, the facts are—simply put—that the relevant algorithms entered into transactions which it is agreed that no human trader would ever have entered into.

B. *Quoine Pte Ltd v B2C2 Ltd*

The facts of *Quoine* were fairly straightforward. Quoine itself was an operator of a cryptocurrency exchange platform, and the primary market maker on that platform. The function of the platform was to bring together buyers and sellers of cryptocurrencies. The particular contracts which were the subject of the litigation were entered into directly between B2C2, a user of the platform, and a number of other market users (the 'Counterparties'). All of these parties—Quoine, B2C2, and the Counterparties—dealt through algorithmic trading programmes.[2] In that sense, the programmes were trading directly with each other.

---

[1] *Quoine Pte Ltd v B2C2 Ltd* [2020] SCGA(I) 02.
[2] The Counterparties in fact entered into the trades as a result of the actions of Quoine. This is because Quoine's trading algorithms were programmed to close out margined positions when the value of the collateral held by Quoine dipped below a certain level relative to the position collateralized. However nothing turns on this.

These programmes were themselves complex pieces of software, but their effect was to analyse the prices upon which transactions were actually occurring on the Quoine platform, and to make bids and offers for 'cryptocoins' (ie, digital assets based on a 'distributed ledger' such as Bitcoin or Ethereum) based on those prices. Critically, these programmes took their pricing input only from the prices at which transactions were executed on the Quoine platform.

The reason that this approach made sense was that Quoine itself was supposed to ensure the accuracy of these prices: Quoine was the major supplier of prices to the platform, and the major dealer ('market-maker') on the platform. If prices on the platform diverged from prices on other trading platforms, Quoine itself would be strongly incentivized to arbitrage away that difference by buying on one platform and selling on the other. Thus, the individual users on the platform effectively relied upon the self-interest of Quoine and the other dealers to ensure that prices on the platform remained in touch with those in the outside world.

What then happened was—initially—depressingly commonplace. In the course of a software upgrade, Quoine changed some of the passwords within the system, but these changes were not carried through across the system as a whole. That meant that the Quoine system could no longer access price data from other venues. This had two consequences. The first was that, lacking price inputs, the Quoine system could not make market prices. This resulted in the book thinning out, and volatility increasing. The second was that, unmoored from other trading venues, the prices of cryptocoins on Quoine began to diverge very significantly from what might be called 'real world' prices.[3] However, the trading programmes, which were designed to treat the Quoine prices as reliable, continued to trade on those prices. This eventually resulted in the various trading programmes 'agreeing' amongst themselves to sell a quantity of one asset (Ether) for another (Bitcoin) at a price which was roughly 250 times the real-world price. However, since this was the best price showing on the Quoine system, the Counterparties' programmes accepted this offer, and contracts where concluded.

Needless to say, all of this happened in the early hours of the morning without any human involvement. When the humans arrived at their desks the following morning the row began, and has continued ever since. In practice, of course, human traders make these sorts of mistakes on a fairly regular basis. The fact that this happens is well-known in all financial markets, and those markets have generally developed established mechanisms for dealing with the outcomes. Where the trades are executed on a trading venue, the operator of the trading venue should have the power to cancel them—indeed, the existence of the operator as an independent third party to decide whether a trade should be cancelled or not is one of the advantages of trading on a venue. For trades executed privately between two

---

[3] See J.G. Allen and R.M. Lastra, 'Border Problems: Mapping the Third Border' (2020) 83(3) *Modern Law Review* 505.

parties, the process can be more contentious, but the negotiations between the winning and the losing party in respect of trades of this kind are generally tempered by an awareness (in both parties) that, in the fullness of time, the discussions are likely to be reprised with the roles reversed. In all of these cases, the questions asked are likely to be the same: How egregious was the error? How obviously was it a genuine mistake and not a failed trading strategy? Could the counterparty reasonably have thought it was a real bid or offer?

The trades at the heart of *Quoine* were thus simple fat finger trades, albeit that the fingers were not digits but digital programmes. Upon discovering that they had happened, the winning party (B2C2) did not pat himself on the back for the success of his trading strategy, but immediately e-mailed the venue operator with a message to the effect that there had been a 'major ... database breakdown'. Quoine, the operator, promptly cancelled the trades, as it believed it was entitled to do.

This was where the problems began. The court decided that the provisions in Quoine's rulebook upon which it relied to cancel the trades were ineffective for that purpose. This created a problem, since Quoine had, by that point, released the relevant assets back to the parties. It is important to note at this stage that Quoine was not a central counterparty, but merely an operator of the trading venue concerned. Despite B2C2s arguments to the contrary, the court was satisfied that Quoine was merely a facilitator of trading, and that the contracts which were made using its services were contracts *directly* between the two participants. B2C2s case against Quoine was therefore that by purporting to cancel the trades Quoine was in breach of its obligations to B2C2. Quoine's defence was that, since the trades would have been void for mistake in any event, it was not in breach of its contract with B2C2.[4]

1. The decision

The Singapore Court of Appeal had a number of knotty issues to consider in this case. However, the most difficult was the basic question of what the position was with regard to these contracts. Counsel for Quoine argued that the contracts themselves were clearly mistaken—indeed, it was not disputed that, when the staff of Quoine arrived in the office that morning, their first reaction was to examine the contracts and cancel them on the basis that they were clearly erroneous. This would arguably have solved the problem, were it not for the inconvenient fact that they turned out to have no power to do any such thing. It was not disputed that any

---

[4] As the Singapore Court of Appeal pointed out, there is a fascinating question as to whether a person who was not a party to a contract is even entitled to invoke the doctrine of mistake in respect of that contract (para [78]). However, since the parties did not take this point, the court was not called upon to decide it.

reasonable person looking at the contracts would have concluded that they could not have been intended, had they been entered into by human traders.

The Court therefore turned to the question of how the law of mistake should be applied in such cases. Counsel for B2C2 argued that by putting a trading programme in place, the person putting that programme in place made what was, in effect, a unilateral offer to the world at large to contract on whatever terms the program saw fit to advance. There could therefore be no concept of mistake by the programme. The only space that the law of mistake has to operate is in the mind of the person putting forward the programme. Hence, the issue was whether the fact that the programme had gone off the rails in this fashion demonstrated that there was some mistake operating on the mind of the person who *designed* the programme in the first place. In this regard, they followed the findings of the judge at first instance. These findings had been the subject of some academic criticism,[5] on the basis that, since the person constructing the programme could not, at the time that he constructed it, have any knowledge of what it might subsequently do when fed incorrect data, there was no scope for holding that he was, at the moment when he wrote the programme, under any misapprehension as regards those subsequent transactions. The academic commentators argued that this approach could not be correct, since it would eliminate any scope for the doctrine of mistake to operate with respect to cyber-contracts (ie, contracts formed through the 'action' of computer programmess[6]). The majority took the view that the approach was correct, and did have this effect.

Counsel for Quoine, by contrast, argued that the point should be approached by applying a fiction, namely that the bargain had been made by *hypothetical human traders* meeting on the floor of an exchange. If, in such circumstances, it was clear that a contract must have been made by way of mistake, then the contract should be treated as vitiated by the mistake in the same way that it would have been had it been entered into between two human traders. This approach was rejected by both the majority and the minority.

A second point which troubled the judges related to the requirement that a contract can only be vitiated on grounds of mistake if the non-mistaken party can be shown to have known that the other party was indeed mistaken. Even if the contract here could be shown to have been entered into by reason of a mistake made by one trading programme, how might it be possible to establish that the other trading

---

[5] N. Yeo and J. Farmer, 'Mapping the Landscape: Cryptocurrency Disputes Under English Law (Part 2) (2019) 5 *Butterworths Journal of International Banking and Finance Law* 290 and K. Low and E. Mik 'Unpicking a Fin(e)tech Mess: Can Old Doctrines Cope in the 21st Century?' (Oxford Business Law Blog, 8 November 2019) <https://www.law.ox.ac.uk/business-law-blog/blog/2019/11/unpicking-finetech-mess-can-old-doctrines-cope-21st-century> accessed 6 July 2021.

[6] Blockchain-based 'smart contracts' are a sub-category of 'cyber-contracts'. There is a potentially important distinction between contracts formed, or apparently formed, by means of an automated process *within* an overarching contractual framework (such as an exchange rulebook) and those formed, or apparently formed, outside such a framework.

programme knew or ought to have known of the mistake? It was suggested that, if one programme had been programmed with the deliberate intention of benefiting from the mistakes of others, that condition might be satisfied. However, since it was found as a fact that neither party had, when constructing their programmes, ever seriously contemplated the sequence of events which actually occurred, it was held that it could not be the case that this condition could be satisfied. This, the court held, was fatal to any argument based on unilateral mistake, even if such a mistake could be established.

The position of the majority can therefore fairly be summarized as that in order to vitiate a contract, a mistake must be active in the mind of the person entering into the contract at the time that he does so. Since that moment was when the trading programmes were first set in motion, the test of state of mind had to be applied at that time. The logic of this position was set out by the trial judge. He described the programmes concerned as simply 'robots',

> Where it is relevant to determine what the intention or knowledge was underlying the mode of operation of a particular machine, it is logical to have regard to the knowledge or intention of the operator or controller of the machine. In the case of the kitchen blender, this will be the person who put the ingredients in and caused it to work. His or her knowledge or intention will be contemporaneous with the operation of the machine. But in the case of robots or trading software in computers this will not be the case. The knowledge or intention cannot be that of the person who turns it on, it must be that of the person who was responsible for causing it to work in the way it did, in other words, the programmer. Necessarily this will have been done at a date earlier than the date on which the computer or robot carried out the acts in question. To this extent I reject B2C2's contention that that the only relevant knowledge is knowledge at the time of contracting. I agree with Quoine that regard should be had to the knowledge and intention of the programmer of the program in issue when that program (or the relevant part of it) was written.[7]

We can now turn to the minority—Lord Mance, former Deputy President of the United Kingdom Supreme Court. His position, in a nutshell, was that equitable relief should be granted, and the transactions voided. His starting point was that 'it would have been obvious to any human that a wholly untoward breakdown or error had occurred'.[8] However, he agreed that the case could not be analysed on the basis of the convention analysis of mistake for the reasons given by the majority: 'The case does not therefore fit within the principles governing unilateral mistake at common law, and it would not be right to extent these to cover such a

---

[7] Para [208]–[210].
[8] Para [153].

situation.' The question, therefore, was simply one of whether equity ought to provide relief?

His Lordship's conclusion was that it did. In particular, in the context of the sort of computerized trading before the court, a new species of equitable relief was required. He said that 'where any reasonable trader would at once have identified ... a fundamental computer system breakdown as the cause of the transactions, the considerations weighing in favour of reversal of the transactions outweigh in the balance any errors or faults which led to that breakdown.' He went on to argue that this should be the case even in the absence of any fault:

> Suppose in the present case that a mouse had eaten [...] a cable linking the platform to the Quoter programme ... [...]the same question, whether relief could be granted, would arise, without there being necessarily any background of fault. The law must be capable of addressing such a situation in a manner which corresponds with what I would regard as the clear justice of the case, as well as with the natural expectations of reasonable traders.[9]

C. The Law of Mistake

In order to explain why the application of the English law of mistake is so challenging in the context of smart contracts (or any cyber-contracts), it is first necessary to consider the structure of that law. There is no doubt that, in rejecting equitable interference with apparently concluded contracts, the majority were rowing with the mainstream of common law thought. English law has generally taken a very conservative view of the scope of the doctrine of mistake, and seeks to confine it within the narrowest possible grounds. This is in good part pursuant to the strong policy of the common law, over many years, that *pacta sunt servanda*, and that courts should only interfere with concluded contracts where there are the strongest possible grounds for doing so. However, another reason is that English law has a problem which other laws (notably German law) do not, in that if a contract is held to be vitiated by mistake, it is void, and any property transferred under it reverts to its original owner.[10] If you sell shares to me, I sell them on to Jack, and Jack sells them to Jim, if the contract between you and me is held to be void for mistake then Jim is suddenly deprived of the shares he thought he owned. This is a profoundly unattractive outcome. Consequently, the predisposition of the English courts in this regard is accurately characterized by John Cartwright: 'when considering mistake, the judge does not begin by assuming that the mistake should release the

---

[9] *Quoine*, [196].
[10] See generally H. Kötz, *European Contract Law* (G. Mertens and T. Weir, tr, Oxford University Press 2017), Ch 9.

mistaken party from the contract. He is more inclined to ask; why should the non-mistaken party lose the contract'[11].

The reason that, at common law, mistake vitiates a contract, is because, in order for a contract to come into existence, there must be a *meeting of minds* between the parties as to the agreement entered into. If I offer to sell you Blackacre and you agree to buy Whiteacre, there is no agreement between us, and therefore no contract ever comes into existence. Thus, where one party is mistaken as to a fundamental term of what is being agreed, it can be reasonably said that there is, in fact, no agreement at all. This was articulated by Blackburn J in *Smith v Hughes*:[12]

> If one of the parties intends to make a contract on one set of terms, and the other intends to make a contract on another set of terms, ... there is no contract, unless the circumstances are such as to preclude one of the parties from denying that he has agreed to the terms of the other.[13]

However, taken to its logical extreme, this would result in a situation where any misunderstanding between parties, no matter how minor, would have the effect of destroying the validity of contract. This would tear a substantial hole in the commercial framework of English law. As Lord Aitken said in *Bell v Lever Bros*:[14]

> It is of paramount importance that contracts should be observed, and that if parties honestly comply with the essentials of the formation of contracts—i.e., agree in the same terms on the same subject-matter—they are bound by, and must rely on the stipulations of the contract for protection from the effects of facts unknown to them.[15]

What this pronouncement amounts to is, in effect, a rule that where parties contract with each other, they should agree between themselves where the risk of misunderstanding should lie. This is a sound commercial principle; however, it leaves open the question of what should happen if they do not. Here Blackburn J had this to say:

> If, whatever a man's real intention may be, he so conducts himself that a reasonable man would believe that he was assenting to the terms proposed by the other party, and that other party upon that belief enters into the contract with him, the

---

[11] J. Cartwright, *Misrepresentation, Mistake and Non-Disclosure* (5th edn, Sweet & Maxwell 2019), paras 12–15.
[12] *Smith v Hughes* (1871) LR 6 QB 597.
[13] *Ibid.*, 607.
[14] *Bell v Lever Bros* [1932] AC 161, HL.
[15] *Ibid.*, 224.

man thus conducting himself would be equally bound as if he had intended to agree to the other party's terms.[16]

The point here is simply that a party should not be able to set up his own misunderstanding as a mechanism to release him from a contract by which he no longer wishes to be bound. In this regard, the principle is unquestionably correct. One way of looking at the resulting legal position is as creating a form of estoppel—that a mistaken party who has acted in such a way that the other party cannot know that he is mistaken is thereafter estopped from raising his own misunderstanding as a challenge to the contract. This has been suggested in some cases.[17] However, Cartwright correctly points out that there it is not necessary to import the doctrines of estoppel into this particular part of the law; the rule being applied is simply a rule as to the interpretation of communications:

> In entering into a contract, a party is entitled to act on what he honestly, and on reasonable grounds, believes the other party to be agreeing. For the purpose of his claim to enforce the contract, the other party's assent will be interpreted by reference to that honest and reasonable belief.[18]

Thus, where one party seeks to assert that a contract was formed on particular terms and the other denies it, there are two tests to be applied. The first is the 'objective' test. This involves an assessment of whether the defendant's words or conduct would have led a reasonable person in the claimant's position to believe that the defendant had agreed to the terms advanced by the claimant. The second is the 'subjective' test. This involves an assessment as to whether the claimant did, in fact, believe that the defendant was agreeing to the terms.[19] This can be summarized as follows: Where the non-mistaken party knew, or ought to have known, that the other party did not in fact intend to contract on the terms specified, no contract arises at common law.[20]

This makes clear that the question of whether a contract is vitiated by mistake at English common law is entirely dependent on the states of mind of the parties at the time when the contract is in fact entered into. Thus, the question that we need to ask in respect of these contracts—or indeed of any cyber-contract—is exactly

---

[16] *Smith v Hughes* (1871) LR 6 QB 597, 607.
[17] *Pearl Mill Co Ltd v Ivy Tannery Co Ltd* [1919] 1 KB 78 and *The Hannah Blumenthal* [1983] 1 AC 854.
[18] J. Cartwright, *Misrepresentation, Mistake and Non-Disclosure* (5th edn, Sweet & Maxwell 2019), [13-11].
[19] See eg, per Brightman LJ in *The Hannah Blumenthal* [1983] 1 AC 854, HL, 924.
[20] *Hartog v Colin and Shields* [1939] 3 All ER 566. Cartwright (13–19) puts this the other way around, saying that the defendant *is* bound if his words, conduct or silence *would* have led a reasonable person in the claimant position to believe that he was agreeing to the contract as specified. The two formulations are identical.

when was it entered into. This turns out to be an extremely difficult question to answer.

1. Cyber-contract formation

The basic difficulty when asking whether a cyber-contract is formed is fitting the interaction between computer programmes into the traditional analysis of offer and acceptance. The basic position at English law (and in many other legal systems) is entirely clear: a *contract* is created when an *offer* made by one of the parties is *accepted* by the other to whom the offer is addressed, and that acceptance is *communicated* to the offeror.[21]

On the basis of the facts in Quoine, when, exactly, was that? It should be noted that this point was not raised at all in the *Quoine* litigation. However, the legal justification for the decisions reached assumes that the relevant contracts were 'made' when the automated trading programmes were set in motion, since that is the point at which the court assessed the states of mind of the parties. However, that argument is fraught with difficulty—parties cannot be said to have contracted at a time when they had literally no idea what terms (or what counterparties) their programmes may 'choose'. The best that could be said of any such contract would be that it is a *contract to contract*; although such contracts can sometimes be enforceable at law, this will only happen where the terms of the future contract can be ascertained.[22] Since at the time that the programmes were set in motion the terms of any future transactions were both unknown and unknowable, this cannot be the correct analysis.

A better argument, and one which was alluded to in the Singapore Court of Appeal, is what might be termed the '*Shoe Lane* analysis'. This is based on the fact that it is clear that a person can make a valid contract with an unknown counterparty by making a standing offer to the world capable of being accepted by any person. When a person accepts that offer, a contract comes into existence, even though the person making the offer does not know that it has been accepted, or by whom.[23] It would be perfectly possible to cast the activities of both programmes as the making offers which, if accepted, would result in the formation of contracts at the time of the acceptance of those offers.

The problem with this line of analysis, however, is that if this is what both programmes were doing, then no contract can have resulted from their interaction. It is a well-established principle of English contract law that 'cross-offers are not acceptances of each other'.[24] Put simply, offer may be automated, but acceptance

---

[21] H.G. Beale (ed), *Chitty on Contracts* (33rd edn, Sweet & Maxwell 2018) ('Chitty') para 2.001.
[22] Chitty 2-143.
[23] *Thornton v Shoe Lane Parking Ltd* [1971] 1 KB 532.
[24] *Tinn v Hoffman & Co* (1873) 29 LT 271, 278, and see Chitty 2-043.

requires an act of will. The argument that the acceptance arose through the conduct of the party programming his computer to purport to accept an offer falls at the same hurdle—conduct only constitutes 'acceptance' where that conduct is clear, objective evidence of the fact that the accepter has made the necessary act of will to enter into the contract. If, on the facts, the accepter is ignorant of the very existence of the offer, this condition cannot be satisfied.

This line of analysis leads us in a profoundly uncomfortable direction. If there is no acceptance at the time of the contract, then, in theory there is no contract, and indeed it has been said that '[t]here is a very strong argument for the unenforceability of algorithmic contracts'.[25] On this basis, the best analysis of what trading algorithms are doing at night is merely teeing up mutual offers, with acceptance occurring only when a human being comes into the office in the morning, reviews what the algorithms have done, and indicates acceptance of it. Such an analysis, however, would be absolutely contrary to the intention of the parties, and cannot be accepted.[26]

One possible solution to this problem would be to accept that no contract is ever made in this way—but that, because of their conduct, the parties are *estopped* from denying that fact, and must proceed as if they had in fact contracted. This, however, must also be rejected. Electronic exchanges and their users operate on the basis that a transaction is a transaction, and that the rights and liabilities of the parties arise at the moment when the transaction is entered into the system. The conclusion that what appear to be transactions concluded within the system are not, in fact, 'transactions' at all is radically incompatible with the intentions of the users of such platforms.

This is, of course, only one instance of a widespread problem, to wit, that people generally are apt to act with the most callous disregard for legal technicalities in their personal and commercial transactions. There is, as *Chitty* ruefully notes,[27] a significant gap between the technical legal analysis of offer and acceptance and the modes of dealing in the commercial world (or, at least, significant segments of it). This has, from time to time, led the courts to take a robust line that where the correspondence as a whole and the conduct of the parties shows that they believe that they have made a contract, they should be treated as having done so, regardless of the presence or absence of identifiable offer or acceptance.[28] However, as Chitty continues, 'such an outright rejection of the traditional analysis is open to

---

[25] L. Scholz, 'Algorithmic Contracts' (2017) 20 *Stanford Technology Law Review* 128, 151. The solution Scholz proposes—that programmes be regarded as agents for their principals—does not help as regards the problem of mistake, since where an agent makes a mistake in deciding whether to entering into a contract for his principal, it is the state of mind of the agent which must be tested.

[26] There is surprisingly little academic analysis of this problem, perhaps because it grows down into roots of profound theory about agency, action, and attribution.

[27] *Ibid.*, [2-118].

[28] See eg, *Gibson v Manchester City Council* [1978] 1 WLR 520, 523, *Finmoon Ltd v Baltic Reefer Management Ltd* [2012] EWHC 920 (Comm), [2012] 2 Lloyds LR 388, [22].

the objection that it provides too little guidance for the courts (or for the parties or for their legal advisors) in determining whether an agreement has been reached ... This approach is supported by cases in which it has been held that there was no contract precisely because there was no offer and acceptance'.[29] In this regard, the position of the Singapore authorities is on the conservative side—in *Gay Choon Ing v Loh Sze Ti Terence Peter*,[30] the Singapore Court of Appeal said on this point:

> Whilst it is true that the court concerned must examine the whole course of negotiations between the parties ... , this should be effected in accordance with the concepts of offer and acceptance. What is required, however, is a less mechanistic or dogmatic application of these concepts and this can be achieved by having regard to the context in which the agreement was concluded.[31]

On the basis of the facts of *Quoine*, it seems impossible to dispute that the conduct of the parties and the facts on the ground lead to two conclusions; one being that the participants in the Quoine system intended to, and did, enter into multiple different contracts between themselves for the purchase and sale of cryptocoins, and the other being that, in their minds at least, the time at which they entered into those contracts was the time at which their trading programmes mutually recorded a transaction as having been effected. This, therefore, is the answer to the question 'when were the contracts formed?', and it is therefore at this moment that the states of mind of the parties should be tested.

This seems to lead to a paradox, in that we are to enquire into the state of mind of a party who does not know of the thing in relation to which his state of mind is to be tested. However, this is no more a paradox that the alternative idea of applying the test to the mind of the participant at a time when he had no idea that the transactions concerned would be entered into. Indeed, this latter is open to the objections of articulated by Low & Mik (which were cited to the court):

> Being unaware of the conclusion of a contract, a contracting party utilising automated contracting is ipso facto incapable of having any actual knowledge of any mistake on the part of its counterparty at the time of contracting, however egregious the mistake. But this would have the effect of immunising any contracting party employing algorithmic contracting from the doctrine of unilateral mistake entirely, which cannot be correct. ... It is unrealistic to attempt to attribute knowledge of a future mistake to a past programmer *à la* Nostradamus.[32]

---

[29] *Ibid.*, [2-119].
[30] *Gay Choon Ing v Loh Sze Ti Terence Peter* [2009] SGCA 3.
[31] *Gay Choon Ing v Loh Sze Ti Terence Peter* [2009] SGCA 3, [63].
[32] K. Low and E. Mik 'Unpicking a Fin(e)tech Mess: Can Old Doctrines Cope in the 21st Century?' (Oxford Business Law Blog, 8 November 2019), <https://www.law.ox.ac.uk/business-law-blog/blog/2019/11/unpicking-finetech-mess-can-old-doctrines-cope-21st-century> accessed 2 March 2022.

However, the court's response was—in effect—to reason that, if the parties had chosen to behave in a way which took them outside the scope of conventional legal analysis, that was their problem. The idea that conventional analysis might be revisited was rejected, and the position was maintained that the only circumstances in which the law of mistake could be applied to the facts under consideration would be where the programmer, at the time when he programmed the software, 'contemplated or ought to have contemplated that a mistake might arise on the part of a counterparty to a future contract, and designed the algorithm to exploit such a mistake'.[33] Since the evidence of the relevant programmer was that he had had no such intention, the conclusion that was reached was that the law of mistake had no application to these particular mistakes because they had occurred without direct human intervention.

If the majority's holding is accepted, then there can be no remedy in common law for a computerized mistake—effectively under any circumstances. This raises the question considered by Lord Mance: does the absence of any remedy in common law therefore necessitate the development of a remedy in equity? In order to answer this question, it is first necessary to review the fluctuating fortunes of equitable relief for mistake in the English courts over the last century.

2. Equity as a remedy for mistake in English law

The common law basis of the English law doctrine of mistake was authoritatively expounded in 1932 by Lord Atkin in *Bell v Lever Brothers Ltd*.[34] However, eighteen years later, in *Solle v Butcher*,[35] Denning LJ identified an equitable jurisdiction which permitted the court to intervene where the parties had concluded an agreement that was binding in common law despite a common misapprehension of a fundamental nature as to the material facts or the parties' respective rights. To be fair to Lord Denning, his starting point was that the common law could only remedy a mistake where the mistake went to identity or subject matter; all other types of mistake fell to be remedied either in equity or not at all. This doctrine was finally disapproved in *The Great Peace*.[36] There is a tendency to characterize the development of English law between *Solle v Butcher* and *The Great Peace* as a massive expansion of equitable interference in contracts which was progressively cut down and finally extinguished. However, a more accurate characterization would be that an approach to mistake based on the idea that only a small number of types of mistake sounded in common law, with the rest remediable in equity or not at all, was

---

[33] *Ibid.*, [104].
[34] *Bell v Lever Bros* [1932] AC 161.
[35] *Solle v Butcher* [1950] 1 KB 671.
[36] *The Great Peace* [2002] EWCA Civ 1407, [2003] QB 679.

replaced by an idea that almost all types of mistake are remediable at common law, so that equity had no useful role left to perform.

It is important to understand this pattern of development in order to understand what *The Great Peace* actually decided. At first instance, Toulson J concluded (in the magnificently laconic summary of Phillips MR) 'that the view of the jurisdiction of the court expressed by Denning LJ in *Solle v Butcher* was "over-broad", by which he meant "wrong"'. Toulson J's finding was that equity neither gives a party a right to rescind a contract on grounds of common mistake, nor confers on the court a discretion to set aside a contract on such grounds. However, recognizing the importance of the point, he gave permission to appeal his own decision. The Court of Appeal agreed with Toulson J and, in effect, overruled its own decision in *Solle v Butcher*[37] to find that there is no equitable jurisdiction to vitiate a contract which does not contravene the common law rules on validity. The basis of the argument was set out by Lord Phillips:

> Thus the premise of equity's intrusion into the effects of the common law is that the common law rule in question is seen in the particular case to work injustice, and for some reason the common law cannot cure itself. But it is difficult to see how that can apply here. Cases of fraud and misrepresentation, and undue influence, are all catered for under other existing and uncontentious equitable rules. We are only concerned with the question whether relief might be given for common mistake in circumstances wider than those stipulated in *Bell v Lever Brothers*. But that, surely, is a question as to where the common law should draw the line; not whether, given the common law rule, it needs to be mitigated by application of some other doctrine. The common law has drawn the line in *Bell v Lever Brothers*. The effect of *Solle v Butcher* is not to supplement or mitigate the common law; it is to say that *Bell v Lever Brothers* was wrongly decided.[38]

The position at English law is therefore currently as follows. Where only one party is mistaken, and the other party knows or should know that there has been a mistake, and knows what the true intention of the other party is, by agreeing to contract with that other he agrees to contract on the intended terms, and that contract can be enforced against him at common law. Where the other party knows or should have known that there has been a mistake, but does not know what the true intention of the other party is, the mistake renders the contract void at common law. There is no separate equitable jurisdiction to set aside a contract for unilateral mistake,[39] although equity may provide the remedies of rescission or refusal of

---

[37] Technically, of course, the Court of Appeal cannot do this, being bound by its own precedents—see *Young v Bristol Aeroplane Co* [1944] KB 718, CA, *Miliangos v George Frank (Textiles) Ltd* [1976] AC 443, discussed in S.B. Midwinter, 'The Great Peace and Precedent' (2003) 119 *Law Quarterly Review* 180.
[38] *The Great Peace* [2003] QB 679, [156].
[39] Chitty 3-027.

specific performance. Where the other party ought to have known of the mistake, he will not be able to hold the mistaken party to the literal meaning of his offer.[40]

The effect of all this in practice is rather to conflate common law and equity. Equitable remedies (in this case limited to rectification or refusal of specific performance) are available against a party whose state of mind at the time of entry into the contract could be regarded as dishonest or as acting in bad faith.[41] The common law remedy of voiding the contract is available against a party who knew or should have known at the time of contracting that the other party's intention was at variance with his words or conduct. To the ordinary observer, these two look very much like the same thing.

3. Mistake and equity in Singapore law

The position in Singapore is more nuanced. In *Chwee Kin Keong v Digilandmall.com Pte Ltd*,[42] the Singapore Court of Appeal held that the common law doctrine of mistake applies only when the non-mistaken party had actual knowledge of the other's mistake. The court said:

> In our opinion, it is only where the court finds that there is actual knowledge that the case comes within the ambit of the common law doctrine of unilateral mistake... The concept of constructive notice is basically an equitable concept: see *The English and Scottish Mercantile Investment Company, Limited v Brunton* [1892] 2 QB 700 at 707 per Lord Esher MR. In the absence of actual knowledge on the part of the non-mistaken party, a contract should not be declared void under the common law as there would then be no reason to displace the objective principle.[43]

Under Singapore law, therefore, anything short of *actual* notice must be addressed within the equitable jurisdiction. However, constructive notice at common law is a different thing from imputed notice in equity, and the Singapore test for equitable relief requires actual dishonesty. Slightly further on in the judgement, the court cited with approval the words of Russell LJ in *Riverlate Properties Ltd v Paul*:[44]

> If reference be made to principles of equity, it operates on conscience. If conscience is clear at the time of the transaction, why should equity disrupt the

---

[40] *Centrovincial Estates Plc v Merchant Investors Assurance Co Ltd* [1983] Com LR 158, *OT Africa Line Ltd v Vickers Plc* [1996] 1 Lloyd's Rep 700, 703; *Chitty* 3-023.
[41] *Thomas Bates Son v Wyndhams Ltd* [1981] 1 WLR 505, 521 per Buckley LJ.
[42] *Chwee Kin Keong v Digilandmall.com Pte Ltd* [2005] SGCA 2, [2005] 1 SLR 502. Noted in T.M. Yeo (2005) 121 *Law Quarterly Review* 393, K.F.K. Low [2005] *Lloyd's Maritime and Commercial Law Quarterly* 423, and P.W. Lee (2006) 22 *Journal of Contract Law* 81.
[43] *Chwee Kin Keong v Digilandmall.com Pte Ltd* [2005] SGCA 2, [2005] 1 SLR 502, [53].
[44] *Riverlate Properties Ltd v Paul* [1975] Ch 133.

transaction? If a man may be said to have been fortunate in obtaining a property at a bargain price, or on terms that make it a good bargain, because the other party unknown to him has made a miscalculation or other mistake, some high-minded men might consider it appropriate that he should agree to a fresh bargain to cure the miscalculation or mistake, abandoning his good fortune. But if equity were to enforce the views of those high-minded men, we have no doubt that it would run counter to the attitudes of much the greater part of ordinary mankind (not least the world of commerce), and would be venturing upon the field of moral philosophy in which it would soon be in difficulties.[45]

The point that is being made here is relatively clear: Equity will not intervene simply because one party to a transaction has made a miscalculation. Equity will intervene where one party has sought to induce or encourage the miscalculation that the other has made, but that intervention arises because the conscience of that party is affected, not merely because of the mistake. It is necessarily true that a party's conscience cannot be affected in respect of a transaction of which he has no knowledge, and it does therefore seem to be the case that conventional equitable intervention is not available in these circumstances.

What this meant, applied to the facts of *Quoine*, was that even though Singapore jurisprudence had not closed the door to equitable relief quite as firmly as had been done in England, the particular form of equitable remedy provided by Singapore law was not available on the facts of the case. In order for it to have been available, it would have been necessary to show that one or other of the programmers had created his programme with a deliberate intention to deceive or entrap other users, there is little doubt that conventional equitable relief would have been available. However, since no such intention was found, equitable relief was not available in Singapore any more than it would have been in England.

D. Integrating Cyber-contracts with the Law of Mistake

All of these analyses are premised on the court being able to find that there is a divergence between the *action* of the claimant and his *state of mind*. Such a divergence cannot, by definition, exist where the claimant is unaware of the transaction, since no such divergence can be found. In principle, this is an easy question—if you do not know what I am doing, it can hardly be said that you have misled me into doing it, or that you should have known that I was mistaken when I did it. However, the effect of this analysis is as follows. Because the parties have contracted in a way which was never considered by the courts that established the existing law of

---

[45] *Ibid.*, 141.

mistake, the question of whether there should be a remedy or not is not even asked. It is this conclusion against which the minority revolted, and it is very difficult not to agree with this position on policy grounds. In particular, where technology creates new ways of dealing and new ways of entering into transactions, old models based on face-to-face dealings will come under progressively greater stress. The maxim *ubi jus, ibi remedium* is likely to be repeatedly pressed into service as these issues come before the courts, and it is simply unacceptable to conclude that actions which fall outside the traditional bounds of remedies should go unremedied. In particular, it is deeply unattractive that a set of circumstances which would be decided in one way (ie, if the agreement concerned had been between human beings) should have a different outcome simply because the agreement was reached electronically through the interaction of computer algorithms.

The concrete position that we therefore face is that a computer's lack of 'knowledge' of the mistake constitutes a bar to treating a cyber-contract in the same way as a 'human' contract. This brings us back to the question of what exactly we mean by 'knowledge' in this context. The general principle as regards unilateral mistake is that a unilateral mistake 'as to the terms of the contract, *if known to the other party*, may affect the contract'.[46] What do we mean by 'known' in this context? The courts are prepared to impute knowledge even in the absence of any evidence of it—for example, in *Hartog v Colin and Shields*[47] it was held that the terms of the contract were so much at variance with what was usual in the industry that the plaintiffs must have known that the offer did not express the true intention of the parties—in other words, the fact of the plaintiffs knowledge of the mistake could be inferred from the fact that no reasonable person familiar with the facts would have believed that the other party intended to contract on the express terms.

1. Constructive or deemed knowledge as a solution?

It may therefore be asked whether it might be possible to build an argument for relief at *common law* on this basis. It is not beyond the realms of reason to apply the doctrine of constructive knowledge to say that a person should be deemed to know a thing which he clearly would have known had he entered into a transaction knowingly and personally—thus arguing that the mere fact that the transaction was in fact entered into without his knowledge (ie, by an automated programme) is not a defence to a claim in mistake.

There are, however, two substantial problems with this idea. The first is that common law deemed knowledge is simply a finding that a person *did* know a thing, even though he may not acknowledge it. This seems incompatible with the position

---

[46] Chitty 3-022, italics in the original.
[47] *Hartog v Colin and Shields* [1939] 3 All ER 566.

where a person can prove to the court's complete satisfaction that he did *not* know that thing. The doctrines of equity may be more flexible in this regard, but even in equity constructive notice has been said to be 'in its nature no more than evidence of notice, the presumptions of which are so violent that the court will not allow even of its being controverted'.[48] This makes sense when applied to circumstances where a person has deliberately or carelessly failed to inform himself or certain facts, but it is a huge leap to apply it in a situation where it is perfectly clear that the party to whom it is sought to apply such a presumption not only did not know of the facts concerned, but could not have known about them at the relevant time.

The second problem arises from the desire of the courts to preserve contracts. As noted above, the tendency of common law courts in general is to confine the doctrine of mistake within the narrowest possible bounds in order to preserve certainty of contract, and this in general is an objective which is shared by all users of financial and other markets. The creation of a doctrine which could render concluded contracts challengeable by reference to events occurring *after* their conclusion would create some commercial uncertainty, and strike at the legal foundations of such markets' operation. This issue arises in part from the fact that a successful challenge at common law would render a contract void and, as a result, void any subsequent contracts entered into based on that contract. However, the greater problem is simply the period of uncertainty which would exist between the moment when a computer trade was executed and the moment when it was looked at by a human being and declared to be 'not unreasonable'. This would impose a status of legal uncertainty on computer trades which would not exist between human traders, and break the fundamental principle of equality of treatment between computer and other contracts.

2. Equitable relief—Lord Mance's remedy

If this is correct, what is the nature of the remedy that should be granted? Here, a clear and compelling intellectual structure was set out by Lord Mance. He said: 'Equity's conscience must be capable of being affected by behaviour in seeking to retain the benefit of the mistake, once it is discovered'.[49] Lord Mance cited his own judgement in *McDonald v Coys of Kensington*,[50] where he said:

> I have no doubt that justice requires that a person, who (as a result of some mistake which it becomes evident has been made in the execution of an agreed

---

[48] *Plumb v Fluitt* (1791) 2 Anstr 432, 438, and see J McGhee (ed), *Snell's Equity* (32nd edn, Sweet & Maxwell 2010).
[49] Para 173.
[50] *McDonald v Coys of Kensington* [2004] EWCA Civ 47.

bargain) has a benefit or the right to a benefit for which he knows that he has not bargained or paid, should reimburse the value of that benefit to the other party if it is readily returnable without substantial difficulty or detriment and he chooses to retain it (or give it away to a third party) rather than to re-transfer it on request. Even if realisable benefit alone is not generally sufficient, the law should recognise, as a distinct category of enrichment, cases where a benefit is readily returnable.[51]

There is no doubt that, because of the more liberal approach taken by the Singapore courts to equitable relief for mistake, this would have been a permissible approach under Singapore law. Would such an approach be permissible at English law? It seems that it would. The English Court of Appeal held in *The Great Peace* that there is no jurisdiction in equity to rescind a contract for common mistake where the mistake is not sufficient to render the contract void at common law,[52] but its justification for that conclusion was that 'the premise of equity's intrusion into the effects of the common law is that the common law rule in question is seen in the particular case to work injustice, and for some reason the common law cannot cure itself.'[53] There is an argument that the decision in *The Great Peace* should be confined only to cases of common mistake, but it is difficult to see the logical grounds for this—the principle applies equally to unilateral mistake.

The correct analysis of the conclusion in *The Great Peace* is that, where the common law provides a complete and coherent analysis in a particular case, equity cannot step in to provide a different remedy. It does not say, and should not be read as saying, that equity has no role even where the common law does not provide an answer—that, indeed, is precisely the situation where 'the common law cannot cure itself', and equitable intervention is required.

In cases of this kind, it is clear that the common law cannot cure itself. The common law relies upon notice, whether actual or constructive, and notice requires a present state of mind in the contracting parties. In the absence of a state of mind of the parties, there is nothing for the common law to engage with, and therefore no possibility of a common law remedy. In cases of automated contracting, it is not that the common law has engaged with the facts and delivered a conclusion; in such cases, there are no facts of a type which the common law can engage with. The field is therefore open for equity to intervene if the facts so merit.

This is a convenient conclusion, because there are good practical reasons why the available remedy should be in equity rather than at common law. The consequence of common law mistake is avoidance of the contract, and in an automated

---

[51] Ibid., [37].
[52] The Great Peace [2002] EWCA Civ 1407, [2003] QB 679.
[53] Ibid., [156].

trading context the avoidance of one contract could have the most unfortunate consequences for subsequent transactions in the instruments traded. A remedy requiring the repayment of benefits accrued in error, without interference with the underlying transactions, is clearly a better outcome in scenarios such as *Quoine*.

E. Commercial Certainty

The argument that it is the duty of the common law to preserve contracts wherever possible is too well established to be overcome by mere necessity. However, it cannot but be noted that in the context of securities and financial trading markets, there are well-established mechanisms for cancelling and reviewing erroneous trades; in other words, the sanctity of contract that the courts are so keen to preserve in theory is not observed in practice—at least not in these particular markets.

The starting point is the (perhaps counter-intuitive) proposition that, in a trading market, the most important thing is the price formation process. Trading markets have a wide variety of rules which are aimed at ensuring that certain types of transaction do not happen—notably, those based on inside information or manipulative intent—and the reason for this is the paramount importance of protecting the process of formation of the market price. Market users will only use a market if they are satisfied that the price at which they deal in that market will be properly arrived at, ie, through a process of even-handed negotiation.[54] The proposition that we can derive from this is that, in a financial market, the *protection of price formation* is at least as important as the *preservation of individual contracts*. This is not to suggest that the validity of contracts is not as important in a financial market as it is in any other kind of market. But, in a financial market, there may be other considerations in play which dethrone this important principle from its status as the ultimate goal and place it as one amongst a number of competing objectives.

This can be seen most clearly in market and regulatory policies across the world regarding 'error trades'—that is, trades which cannot be explained within the context of the normal market environment. Error trades are as old as markets, and explanations for them over the years have ranged from excessive alcohol intake to illegible handwriting on dealing slips to the current term—'fat-finger trades'. Thus, it is almost universal practice in securities, commodities and other trading venues for the venue operator to have a power to cancel contracts which are clearly entered into by mistake. The justification for such rules is set out in the International Organisation of Securities Commissions ('IOSCO') *Final Report on Policies on Error Trades* of October 2005:

---

[54] See A.M. Fleckner 'Regulating Trading Practices', in N. Moloney, E. Ferran, and J. Payne (eds), *The Oxford Handbook of Financial Regulation* (Oxford University Press 2015).

Once an error trade is executed, the erroneous trade data will be disseminated and other traders will act on such information. For example, orders for securities or derivatives that are executed erroneously at prices substantially away from the existing trading range and in large volumes could cause other traders to take actions based on reports of such trades, not only in the same security but also in derivative or cash-related markets. Erroneous executed trades also could automatically trigger the execution of contingent trades (e.g., 'stop' or 'limit' orders). The longer it takes for a trader to report and the exchange to resolve an allegedly erroneous trade, the longer such 'inaccurate' trading information could have an effect on price formation.[55]

There is, of course, no definition of an 'error trade' in the IOSCO report. The most common approach to identifying trades to be cancelled on this basis is a 'margin of error' rule, where a trade is deemed to be an error trade (and therefore cancelled) if it is purported to be executed at a specified percentage margin either above or below the market price of the investment concerned.[56] As IOSCO say in their report,

[M]ost futures exchanges have established a range of prices above and below the prevailing price within which erroneous trades may not be cancelled under error trade policies ('no-bust' ranges). By establishing such ranges in advance an exchange decides which transaction prices will be considered to have been executed at 'valid' prices and provides a measure of predictability and consistency of treatment. Other exchanges have not adopted no-bust ranges. However, both the decision by an exchange to adopt a no-bust range and, if so, the range chosen, may be influenced, in part, by the degree to which a market is committed as a matter of 'trading philosophy' or 'business doctrine' to maintaining trades, the volatility characteristics of the traded product (e.g., futures versus equity securities), the perceived need for such no-bust ranges or the presence of other measures. These decisions are appropriately within the discretion of the exchange.[57]

There is therefore no common philosophy which enables the abstract determination as to which trades are error trades and which are not—the issue is one to be determined in relation to all of the facts of the particular case.

The trades in *Quoine* were clearly 'error trades'; when the facts of the case were discovered, it seems clearly to have been the common expectation of all of the commercial parties that the trades would indeed be cancelled. Unfortunately, this did

---

[55] IOSCO, *Final Report on Policies on Error Trades*, <https://www.iosco.org/library/pubdocs/pdf/IOSCOPD208.pdf> accessed 6 July 2021, 8.
[56] See for example the NASDAQ Trader 'Obvious Error Transactions Policy', <https://www.nasdaqtrader.com/Micro.aspx?id=ObviousErrorPolicy> accessed 6 July 2021.
[57] IOSCO, *Final Report on Policies on Error Trades*, 9.

not happen, since the Quoine platform rulebook was found not to contain any such power. We therefore end up in the slightly topsy-turvy situation where the commercial expectation was that the trades would be cancelled, but, since there was no provision in the relevant documentation permitting cancellation, the commercial parties were—*unexpectedly for all of them*—held to their transactions.

Interestingly, this point was raised in the first instance litigation. Since it was found that the Quoine rulebook did not contain an express power to reverse error trades, Quoine argued that a term to that effect should be implied into the rulebook as an ordinary and necessary part of any trading venue rulebook. The expert evidence (from both sides) supported the proposition that such provisions were a common feature of trading rulebooks—one of the experts said:

> I consider it to be common practice for trading exchanges to deal with clearly erroneous transactions by cancelling them if it is in the best interests of the marketplace to do so. The major stock exchanges in the world, such as the Singapore Stock Exchange ('SGX-ST'), Nasdaq, the New York Stock Exchange ('NYSE') and the London Stock Exchange ('LSE'), have the ability to cancel or reverse erroneous transactions. Similarly, several of the major cryptocurrency exchanges, including Coinbase, Kraken, Gemini and Poloniex, have the ability to reverse or cancel transactions which are clearly erroneous and/or for other reasons at their own discretion.[58]

The court was, understandably, unconvinced that evidence that such provisions were common in the rules of other trading venues was sufficient to imply such a term into the rules before it, but the fundamental point was not questioned.[59]

Finally, it is necessary to consider the argument that the English Court of Appeal rejected equitable intervention in *The Great Peace* on the basis that parties should not look to equity to remedy deficiencies in their own contract drafting.[60] This is true. However, as an argument it fails the test of rationality. If a court is being called upon to determine issues such as this, it is by necessity because the parties have not addressed them in their contracts. The point was well made by Lord Mance:

> It was suggested that all such problems, including the present, could have been dealt with by appropriately framed conditions of business. No doubt that is so.

---

[58] *B2C2 Ltd v Quoine Pte Ltd* [2019] SGHC(I) 3, [47].

[59] Although this point seems to have got lost in the transfer from first instance to appeal. The Singapore Court of Appeal said that the proposition that Quoine should be allowed to cancel transactions that did not pass a 'reasonableness' test could not possibly be correct (para [70]), which is odd given the undisputed evidence that such terms are standard in both securities and cryptocurrency markets.

[60] Note also Steyn J's view in *Japanese Bank (International) Ltd v Credit du Nord SA* [1989] 1 WLR 225, 268 that the doctrine of mistake can only operate at all where the contract makes no provision for the risk of a mistake having been made.

But the same could said in many of the situations in which the common law has developed principles of relief, to achieve just results. The law governing mistake is itself a classic example, as is the law of misrepresentation, duress, undue influence, etc. The question is not whether the parties might have regulated such situations generally, or the present situation in particular, by specific agreement, but whether in the circumstances they should be taken to have accepted the risk of their occurrence so as to preclude application of such common law principles, adapted as necessary to the age of algorithms.[61]

F. Conclusion

The facts of *Quoine* have provided an early illustration of the type of problems that can arise for conventional contract law doctrines in the context of automated processes that are intended to lead to contract formation. Contracts formed by computer programmes without human intervention do not fit comfortably into the traditional analysis of offer and acceptance. However, they must nonetheless be treated as valid contracts giving rise to enforceable contractual obligations between the parties arising at the time when the programme purports to enter into the contract, if only because that is the clearly and unambiguously expressed intention of the parties when they set these programmes in motion. But this raises problems for the remedy of mistake because the parties to a transaction cannot be said to have had any identifiable state of mind at the time when those trading programmes purport to enter into contracts. Consequently, when a trading algorithm makes a mistake, the common law will be powerless to assist, no matter what the circumstances of the mistake, and this will be true even if the common expectation of all parties is that the mistake is of a kind which would ordinarily result in the contract being disregarded in the markets in which the underlying transaction takes place.

As Lord Mance said in his dissenting speech in *Quoine*, this does seem to be a paradigm case of a situation in which the common law 'cannot mend itself', and where equitable intervention is therefore necessary. However, that intervention should not be based on a fiction of knowledge (or 'notice') in circumstances where it is undisputed that no such knowledge actually existed. Instead, the proper basis of such a remedy is that laid down in *McDonald v Coys of Kensington*,[62] namely that where a person, as a result of an evident mistake in the execution of a contract, has received a benefit for which he knows that he has neither bargained nor paid, he should return it or its value.

---

[61] *B2C2 Ltd v Quoine Pte Ltd* [2019] SGHC(I) 3, [197].
[62] *McDonald v Coys of Kensington* [2004] EWCA Civ 47.

20
Dispute Resolution for the Digital Economy
DLT as a Catalyst for Online Dispute Resolution?

Charlie Morgan, Dorothy Livingston, and Andrew Moir[*]

A. Introduction	421	1. Defining the concept of decentralized justice	436
B. Setting the Scene	422	2. Procedure for resolving SLC disputes	437
1. Dispute resolution	422		
2. Distributed ledger technology	423	3. Substantive questions for smart contract and SLC dispute resolution	439
3. 'Smart contracts' *versus* 'SLCs' and party intentions	424		
4. Online dispute resolution	428	4. Examples of DLT-based ODR offerings	441
C. Drivers and Obstacles to Online Dispute Resolution	428	5. Challenges to overcome	445
1. Key drivers for moving dispute resolution online	430	E. The Road Ahead: Multidisciplinary Collaboration	451
D. Is DLT an Additional Catalyst for ODR?	435	F. Conclusion	452

[*] Charlie Morgan is a senior dispute resolution lawyer at Herbert Smith Freehills LLP in London, specializing in international arbitration. He helps clients to resolve complex international disputes across a broad range of jurisdictions. He has particular experience acting for clients in the energy and technology sectors. Charlie chaired the Working Group on Legal Tech in Arbitration (author of the Protocol for Online Case Management in International Arbitration 2020) and is a member of the ICCA/IBA Joint Task Force on Data Protection in Arbitration.

Dorothy Livingston is a consultant and former Partner (1980–2008) at Herbert Smith Freehills LLP in London with a background in financial and banking law. She is also chair of the Financial Law Committee of the City of London Law Society (CLLS) and represents it on the Treasury Banking Liaison Panel which considers important subsidiary legislation and the Code of Practice under the Banking Act 2009 related to the Special Resolution Regime for failing banks. Dorothy is a member of the UK Jurisdiction Taskforce sub-committee that authored the Digital Disputes Rules in 2021.

Andrew Moir is Global Head of Herbert Smith Freehills' Cyber and Data Security practice, and a partner in the firm's intellectual property group in London. He advises clients on the full cyber security lifecycle, including proactive cyber-readiness and resilience, incident response (including data breach and ransomware attacks) and cyber related aspects of transactions and projects.

Charlie Morgan, Dorothy Livingston, and Andrew Moir, *Dispute Resolution for the Digital Economy* In: *Smart Legal Contracts*. Edited by: Jason Grant Allen and Peter Hunn, Oxford University Press. © Jason Grant Allen & Peter Hunn 2022. DOI: 10.1093/oso/9780192858467.003.0021

A. Introduction

The growing popularity of Online Dispute Resolution ('ODR') is a natural consequence of today's increasingly digital economy. There is no unified definition for ODR, but it is clear and widely accepted that dispute resolution processes are changing (and need to change increasingly quickly) to keep pace with new and emerging technologies and the increasing digitization of information, products, and services. Whether the drivers for ODR stem from efficiency, accessibility, accountability, environmental sustainability, cybersecurity, or confidentiality, transferring dispute resolution processes online has many benefits.

However, the transition to an online, digital world for the resolution of disputes also has its challenges—none more significant than the human factor of culture change. To date, the move to ODR has not been an imperative, despite the efficiency gains and other benefits that ODR has afforded to some early adopters. In the years to come, as emerging technologies such as natural language processing, distributed ledger technologies and automation reach mainstream, and as litigation and arbitration lawyers become more familiar and comfortable with the streamlined processes that they enable, the speed of change, and the continued move to the digital realm for resolving, are likely to accelerate. In time, resolution of disputes through an end-to-end digital process will need to harness technological advances, while maintaining the necessary legal certainty that makes business possible.

ODR mechanisms are regularly discussed in the context of DLT-based 'smart contracts' (viz, computer code that monitors and self-executes certain digital events or functions in a DLT environment) and 'smart legal contracts' ('SLCs') (viz, valid and effective natural language contracts, stored, and processed on distributed ledgers and implemented in whole or part through code). SLCs promise to automate aspects of contract performance thereby eliminating transaction costs and streamlining business processes. Consistent with these definitions, this chapter will focus on 'smart legal contracts' in the sense of DLT-based smart contracts that are intended to create and structure legally-binding relationships.

Considering that one of the primary drivers for SLC development and adoption is to reduce transaction costs, minimize intermediary processes, and break down silos of data, resolving smart contract and SLC-related disputes through an efficient, legally robust, and enforceable electronic process makes much intuitive sense. As Sir Geoffrey Vos rightly states:

> Commercial entities will wish to consider what kind of dispute resolution they wish ultimately to adjudicate their disagreements, should they occur. This holds true for smart contracts, and end-to-end smart legal contracts in particular, as it does in more conventional legal relationships.[1]

---

[1] G. Vos, 'End-to-End Smart Legal Contracts: Moving from Aspiration to Reality', Chapter 2 in this volume.

This raises the question of what the most effective ODR process would look like for resolving the disputes of tomorrow—and smart legal contract disputes in particular. Indeed, it is unlikely that the best possible ODR process would merely mirror in digital form the physical steps and processes that currently take place in traditional dispute resolution fora. Instead, lawyers, technologists, arbitrators, judges, regulators, governments, law makers, and other stakeholders need to come together to collaborate in the design and implementation of new online dispute resolution processes fit for the digital economy and supported by a robust framework of law and regulation.

This chapter summarizes the basic concepts related to ODR, DLT, smart contracts, and SLCs, reviews the possibility of resolving DLT disputes through online tribunals or courts, and explores the promise and challenges of DLT-based ODR solutions currently available. It concludes that there is a need for greater multi-disciplinary collaboration at the interface of law and technology to build an ODR process fit for the digital economy.

B. Setting the Scene

This section provides an introduction to the relevant concepts.

1. Dispute resolution

In this chapter, unless otherwise made clear, 'dispute resolution' refers to the resolution of disputes to a standard that, failing a consensual settlement, results in a binding decision that is enforceable as a matter of law, either by an arbitral tribunal or a court of competent jurisdiction. This chapter considers a number of new and evolving offerings available to the parties to a dispute, that use digital and connected methods to resolve disputes. However, this chapter seeks to analyse those ODR tools in terms that enable traditional legal systems to protect the rights of the parties to a dispute under an SLC and to enforce their obligations. With that in mind, this chapter seeks to provide an analysis of how disputes may arise from SLCs and how they are likely to be conducted, rather than a review of the ultimate constitutional role of legal systems, particularly courts, in providing justice in a digital context.

While consensual methods for resolving disputes between parties online will have their place and will enable parties to efficiently and amicably resolve disputes in practice, they will not represent a one-stop-shop. Some existing ODR mechanisms may seek to engender a binding result by contract (eg, eBay's dispute resolution mechanism) in a way that could then be enforced through a new claim. Similar consensual methods are seen in early SLC dispute resolution offerings (eg, the parties to a smart contract agree that a decision arising from an 'on-chain' process will be enforced within the DLT ecosystem, without requiring the losing party's consent).

However, such solutions do not eliminate the potential need to resort to traditional dispute resolution mechanisms to have the settlement or third-party decision upheld. In those instances, only a legally binding arbitral ruling or court judgment (subject to any applicable right of appeal or challenge) would be conclusive as to the parties' rights. An agreement between parties to be bound by a process that falls short of arbitration or a court judgment would be ineffective to oust the jurisdiction of the court. This does not, however, mean that such ODR mechanisms are impractical. In fact, they may be preferable to deal with a high proportion of disputes by agreement, particularly in lower value contexts, where speed and cost are most highly-prized by the parties.

However, in high value and complex disputes, parties will usually want to enshrine in their SLCs a more decisive dispute determination with clearly legally enforceable outcomes. In those cases, parties may wish to consider digitized arbitration that could offer the benefits of ODR techniques while ensuring legally enforceable decisions. Parties will also need to have in place mechanisms to obtain effective relief in relation to events outside the four corners of the SLC or DLT ecosystem, such as misrepresentations.[2] Another important issue (discussed in Section 4, below) is that the rules for ascertaining law and jurisdiction in the absence of any agreement may be extremely difficult to apply in the digital world. Such rules rely on knowing the place of habitual residence or domicile of the defendant (often an unidentified person) and/or the identification of the location of property.[3] Thus, for a dispute resolution process to be capable of producing a binding resolution, the choice of both a system of law and of arbitration or court process is likely to be key to the development of effective ODR in relation to smart contracts, DLT etc. As such, this chapter is anchored around the premise (which is contentious) that there is no substitute in practice for enabling binding dispute resolution in the digital, decentralized world.

2. Distributed ledger technology

A distributed ledger is a decentralized database of transactional records shared between multiple computers. 'Blockchain' is a type of DLT that has a specific set

---

[2] Vos (n. 1), 15.
[3] Regulation (EU) 1215/2012 of the European Parliament and of the Council on jurisdiction and the recognition and enforcement of judgments in civil and commercial matters (recast) [2012] OJ L351/1 (hereafter Recast Brussels Regulation 2012); see A. Dickinson, 'Cryptocurrencies and the Conflict of Laws' in D. Fox and S. Green (eds), *Cryptocurrencies in Public and Private Law* (Oxford University Press 2019).

of features, organizing its data in a chain of 'blocks' containing transactional records. Although blockchain is a subset of DLT, it has, through popular use, become a generic term for all DLT projects, which is a common misconception. While all blockchains are DLTs, not all DLTs are blockchains.

In such a database, each block is stamped and contains a reference to previous transactions. This enables anyone with the right permissions to trace the history of all transactions leading up to a particular moment and to verify their authenticity. In one common implementation of blockchain technology, to alter any information on the ledger, a consensus of more than half the network participants would be needed. If a majority of nodes do not verify a transaction, that transaction will not be committed to the ledger. Accordingly, the record stored in the blockchain is considered to be secure, permanent and immutable.

3. 'Smart contracts' *versus* 'SLCs' and party intentions

DLT largely underpins the recent excitement and potential around smart contracts and SLCs. Written on a distributed ledger, smart contracts are software programs that self-execute without the need for further human intervention. At a theoretical level, self-execution of contractual obligations could reduce the prospect of disputes arising from a transaction and reduce the risk of human error (eg, in overseeing and performing contractual obligations). This is because a transaction is automatically performed based on pre-agreed terms and specified parameters. Of course, the risk of disputes will always remain, not least because this assumes that the software implementing the smart contract is free from bugs.

Despite its label, a 'smart contract' may not be a 'legal contract'. The common law requirements for a contract to have legal effect (offer, acceptance, consideration, capacity, intention and legality) may not be easy to ascertain from computer code.[4] Additionally, although parties' use of a private key to sign the smart contract may suffice to evidence their intention to be bound, issues such as interpretation, mistake, fraud, or duress would not be accounted for within the code of the smart contract and would require extraneous evidence to resolve.[5] Indeed, the use of DLT in the context of disputes raises interesting and sometimes complex issues around the availability and admissibility of evidence, particularly in the context of English law, which significantly limits reliance on extraneous evidence in the exercise of construing parties' intentions.

---

[4] See discussion in J.G. Allen, 'Wrapped and Stacked: "Smart Contracts" and the Interaction of Natural and Formal Language' (2018) 14(4) *European Review of Contract Law* 307–43, 328 on whether smart contracts are 'legal contracts'.

[5] A. Schmitz and C. Rule, 'Online Dispute Resolution for Smart Contracts' [2019] *Journal of Dispute Resolution* 103, 104.

Smart contracts do not require valid consideration in order to run, and they therefore may encode and enforce gratuitous promises which are without effect at law (and could therefore be unwound by a court with jurisdiction over the parties). People without legal capacity, including children, are able to obtain private encryption keys and so transact on a DLT platform. Smart contracts can be coded to enforce an illegal or unlawful deal, which the courts or an arbitral tribunal would refuse to uphold (or would unwind, if asked to do so, and assuming it were technically and practically possible). Certainty of terms that is required for a legal contract may pose further issues related to a smart contract's validity as a legal contract and its practical effect. As a result, the resounding conclusion is that smart contracts will not eradicate disputes.

'Smart legal contracts' represent an attempt to address some of the legal limitations of smart contracts. SLCs on the model presented by Blycha and Garside in this volume, are legally enforceable agreements that contain a mix of natural language (as in a conventional contract) and 'smart' clauses—ie, machine-readable expressions of contractual terms that enable automation or other digital activities arising from the contract.[6] SLCs are held in digital form within the relevant DLT ecosystem, but the legal impact and effect of the operative code of the 'smart contract' applications are addressed in the binding legal mechanics of the agreement (in human-readable, natural language capable of interpretation under traditional legal principles). This approach ensures that parties can more readily seek support from traditional judicial authorities (be it courts or arbitral tribunals) to enforce their contractual agreements when the smart contract itself does not execute as planned. This requires parties to engage in a legally-compliant and multidisciplinary approach to the design of the DLT ecosystem and the drafting of smart contracts.

While implementations of DLT often include mechanisms that support shared, inter-generationally hashed data that is simultaneously located across multiple places, in practice there are a number of additional considerations that should be taken into account, such as substantive differences in public and private infrastructures, distinct consensus protocols, methods of exchanging and retaining data, anonymity features, use of public and private keys, and single or multi-channel architectures that do, or do not, allow for compliance with regulatory requirements such as those under the General Data Protection Regulation 2016/679 ('GDPR').

In this context, there has been a first generation of DLT-based dispute resolution offerings that were designed and launched with the aim of digitizing the traditional dispute resolution process, but which in fact were technically geared to ingest

---

[6] Other chapters in this volume have defined 'smart legal contracts' to include 'computable contracts', in which the 'smart' (coded) elements are *also* human-readable—for example, Chapter 12 by Christopher Clack. On the substantive questions arising from the combination of conventional and 'smart' components, see: E. Mik, 'Smart Contracts: A Requiem' [2019] *Journal of Contract Law* 36, 70; see also J.G. Allen's discussion of the 'contract stack' in Allen (n. 4), 328.

smart contract code rather than complex digitized legal contracts. These 'on-chain' dispute resolution offerings often purported to be a form of arbitration. However, most of them did not satisfy the requirements under domestic laws (eg, for arbitrations seated in England and Wales, the Arbitration Act 1996) or international treaties (eg, the New York Convention 1958) and therefore would not result in a valid legal decision enforceable against a recalcitrant party in the 'off-chain' world. Some proponents of 'on-chain' dispute resolution tools argue that validity in the eyes of the law is not what matters in the world of DLT, if enforcement is built in to the code of the smart contract and is irreversible as a matter of practice. However, this argument cannot hold for SLCs and is a misuse of the word 'enforcement' as currently understood in the legal context. In particular, most courts would not accept that their jurisdiction could be limited or removed ('ousted' in English legal language) by the agreement of the parties, unless an alternative recognized judicial or arbitral system is clearly chosen by the parties for the resolution of their disputes instead.

We are now seeing subsequent generations of dispute resolution offerings aimed at the resolution of SLC and other digital disputes. These take various forms but, more often than not, they seek to adapt well-established international arbitral processes to facilitate a more streamlined and online resolution of digital disputes. Where the proposed process seeks instead to reinvent dispute resolution mechanisms more substantively, their authors and proponents increasingly accept that (until potential changes in domestic laws are made in relevant jurisdictions) these mechanisms do not prevent parties taking recourse to courts or tribunals 'off-chain', but rather are intended as a means of promptly obtaining *practical* recourse when a dispute arises, thereby helping to allocate the commercial and cashflow burden that can often arise for parties in more protracted, traditional dispute resolution processes.

As an example of the growing focus being given to dispute resolution in the context of SLCs, on 22 April 2021, the UK Jurisdiction Taskforce ('UKJT') issued Digital Dispute Resolution Rules.[7] The UKJT is one of six taskforces under the Lawtech Delivery Panel ('LTDP'), a UK government-backed initiative established to support digital transformation in the legal sector. The Digital Dispute Resolution Rules offer parties to smart contracts the option to incorporate 'real world' dispute resolution within their digital contract, by offering arbitration under the English Arbitration Act 1996 or an expert determination process. The Rules may be incorporated into a contract, digital asset or digital asset system by reference, and are intended to offer flexibility to adapt to various technologies. They also contain provisions specific to digital technologies including enabling

---

[7] The Digital Dispute Resolution Rules may be accessed here: <https://35z8e83m1ih83drye28o09d1-wpengine.netdna-ssl.com/wp-content/uploads/2021/04/Lawtech_DDRR_Final.pdf> accessed 17 May 2021.

'on-chain' implementation of decisions by conferring powers on the Tribunal in relation to digital assets.[8]

Established international arbitration institutions are also publishing amendments to their existing arbitration rules to promote greater party and tribunal autonomy to determine the appropriate procedures for their arbitrations (including the transition to a fully online process). In some cases, arbitral institutions are also issuing amended rules aimed specifically at SLC disputes.[9]

In relation to court litigation, the legal frameworks established at international and regional levels by multilateral instruments, such as the Recast Brussels Regulation 2012, the 2007 Lugano Convention and the 2005 Hague Convention on Choice of Court Agreements (the '2005 Hague Convention'), are of great importance, since they define the circumstances in which a dispute could be referred to a court of a particular jurisdiction. In particular, the 2005 Hague Convention states that, where the parties to a contract have concluded a choice of court agreement designating that contractual disputes should be decided exclusively in a court of a contracting state, that court shall have jurisdiction to decide a dispute which arises in relation to the contract, and shall not decline to exercise jurisdiction on the ground that the dispute should be decided in another court.[10]

Due to the distributed nature of DLT, coupled with the fact that the users of the network are likely to be located in multiple jurisdictions, these conflict of law questions are complicated in the absence of an express choice between the parties, as it can be difficult to identify a particular jurisdiction with closest connection to the transaction or to make out other traditional gateways to establishing jurisdiction (eg, place of residence of a defendant). In light of these complexities, there would be much benefit in an ODR solution that would be compatible with both traditional legal principles and digital legal infrastructures (including legislative and contractual digital infrastructures), that would facilitate the effective performance of SLCs (including automated arbitration or other dispute resolution clauses

---

[8] The Digital Dispute Resolution Rules were drafted by a sub-committee appointed by the UKJT that included Dorothy Livingston.

[9] See eg, the JAMS Rules Governing Disputes arising out of Smart Contracts, <https://www.jamsadr.com/rules-smart-contracts> accessed 13 July 2021.

[10] Article 3; On 2 July 2019, the Hague Conference on Private International Law announced a new international convention: the Hague Convention on the Recognition and Enforcement of Foreign Judgments in Civil or Commercial Matters. This instrument complements the 2005 Hague Convention and requires contracting states to recognize and enforce judgments given in civil or commercial matters in other contracting states. While certain areas of law, including intellectual property, are excluded from the scope of the convention, this instrument can potentially significantly facilitate cross-border dispute resolution and mobility and may make the traditional court system a preferred option for DLT-based disputes, at least where the chosen jurisdiction recognizes digital assets as property. In April 2021, the UK Law Commission released a call for evidence on whether digital assets should, among other things, be 'possessable'. The Law Commission's digital assets project will build on the conclusions of the Legal Statement on Cryptoassets and Smart Contracts authored by the UKJT in 2019 (discussed in Section IV.C). The call for evidence can be seen here: <https://www.lawcom.gov.uk/project/digital-assets/> accessed 13 July 2021.

within those SLCs), access to justice, and the satisfaction of procedural and any other jurisdictionally based regulatory requirements.

4. Online dispute resolution

ODR is a broad concept. In its simplest form, it refers to the use of online tools to assist with the resolution of a dispute (eg, the use of email to exchange information in relation to a dispute). In this way, technology is deployed into existing manual procedures and so it is aimed at facilitating current working practices. At the other end of the spectrum, it refers to a far more fundamental re-design of the process for delivering justice in the twenty first century. ODR can refer to disputes that arise online. It can also involve disputes that do not have any links to online platforms, but where the parties have chosen an online platform for resolving their dispute, ranging from consumer-to-consumer ('C2C') and business-to-consumer ('B2C') disputes to court proceedings and cross-border disputes.[11]

In this chapter, the term 'ODR' is used to refer to the transition of dispute resolution processes online (procedures that result in a decision that is binding on the parties as a matter of law). This chapter considers both the opportunities for replicating traditional processes in a digital way but also the new opportunities that digitalization and DLT provide for a more significant re-invention of the dispute resolution process.

C. Drivers and Obstacles to Online Dispute Resolution

The development of ODR can be understood along a 'spectrum'. The use of ODR grew quickly in the 1990s with the rapidly growing e-commerce industry as a means to resolve problems in a fast and cost-effective way. ODR has proven to be an effective dispute resolution mechanism for certain types of disputes: eBay is a well-known example of this, with at least the early stages of its disputes handled entirely by computers.

Other examples of ODR tools are more focused around electronic communications rather than the actual resolution of the dispute online. These include, for example, the English Court's online money claim procedure ('MCOL')[12] and the Uniform Domain Name Dispute Resolution Policy ('UDRP') adopted by the

---

[11] United Nations Commission on International Trade Law ('UNCITRAL'), Forty-ninth session, (A/71/17, 27 June–15 July 2016), 86.
[12] The MCOL can be accessed here: <https://www.moneyclaims.service.gov.uk/eligibility>; <https://assets.publishing.service.gov.uk/government/uploads/system/uploads/attachment_data/file/762843/mcol-userguide-eng.pdf> accessed 13 July 2021.

Internet Corporation for Assigned Names and Numbers ('ICANN') in 1999.[13] The MCOL is designed to be a simple way for parties to commence and respond to a county court claim for a fixed amount of money. MCOL enables a party to start (and respond) to a money claim via an online questionnaire which collates and sends the relevant information to the counterparty along with guidance from the court on procedural next steps. The UDRP similarly enables parties to file complaints and respond to them online, but the claims/complaints are still fundamentally dealt with by humans. In the context of SLCs specifically, the UKJT's Digital Dispute Resolution Rules direct the arbitral tribunal to consider available technologies and the need for expedition while adopting a procedure for the case, but the decision-making process is not automated.

However, technological advancement, coupled with the political and economic forces of globalization, has made the world a smaller place. In 1995, Jeff Bezos launched Amazon and Pierre Omidyar founded eBay. Since then, internet-based commercial activities have adapted to meet increasingly fast-paced communications and the coming together on a single global platform of linguistic, cultural and legal backgrounds. The spectrum of ODR has been steadily expanding with the advancement of technology. Some commentators refer to the use of ODR as a *'fourth party'* to dispute resolution, aimed at assisting a decision-maker to reach a better decision more efficiently and cost effectively.[14] Looking ahead, as law and regulation adapt to greater digitalization in society, the role of algorithmic decision-making within the justice system is only likely to grow.

Advances in artificial intelligence ('AI') will be integral to the continued development and success of ODR. E-commerce giants such as Alibaba already use algorithms instead of humans to generate quick and cheap decisions to resolve online disputes. To date, such AI-based resolutions have been especially well-suited to simple disputes where the relief sought is monetary in nature and liability is often uncontested. However, AI tools can now go beyond that (used and supervised appropriately by skilled disputes lawyers) and can help to resolve increasingly complex problems when accurately trained to do so.[15]

These advances in automation capabilities open the door for new dispute resolution processes such as blind bidding systems that consider confidential settlement offers from parties in making a decision (eg, Smartsettle), automated negotiation platforms (eg, Modria), automated mediation and arbitration platforms (eg, ADRg Express), online court proceedings (eg, Civil Resolution Tribunal

---

[13] Uniform Domain-Name Dispute-Resolution Policy website, available here: <https://www.icann.org/resources/pages/help/dndr/udrp-en> accessed 13 July 2021.
[14] E. Katsh, 'ODR: A Look at History—A Few Thoughts About the Present and Some Speculation About the Future' in M.S. Abdel Wahab, E. Katsh, and D. Rainey (eds), *Online Dispute Resolution: Theory and Practice: A Treatise on Technology and Dispute Resolution* (Eleven International Publishers 2011) 21, 32.
[15] R. Susskind, *Online Courts and the Future of Justice* (Oxford University Press 2019), 263–4.

(British Columbia, Canada)), agreement monitoring platforms (eg, Rechtwijzer), online consumer advocacy and complaint systems (eg, eBay's Resolution Center), consumer complaint boards, ombudsmen, med-arb for consumers, and others.[16]

1. Key drivers for moving dispute resolution online

ODR became popular for several perceived benefits. ODR promised to resolve disputes at speeds significantly faster than those of offline dispute resolution mechanisms. It was also seen as a private (and sometimes confidential) way in which to resolve disputes, without risking the reputational impacts of a hearing in open court. Beyond that, ODR has also been celebrated for increasing access to justice and bolstering the user friendliness of dispute resolution processes. Commentators anticipate that there will be much greater commercial exploitation of ODR in the coming years, in particular in relation to the high-volume, low-value disputes.[17]

As the use of the more complex ODR tools becomes more mainstream, ODR will also help to address pain points in larger cross-border disputes that require grappling with different time zones and languages and cross-border exchange of data (this is an increasingly pressing need given the broad data protection regulations being implemented across the globe which do not expressly account for data processing in disputes outside the traditional court context). For example, in the European Union, the GDPR and additional local legislation that implements its terms impose a strict protection regime in relation to personal and sensitive data.[18] The GDPR establishes an administrative framework and places obligations on data controllers to comply with a number of data protection principles: for example, personal data must not be transferred outside the European Economic Area unless sufficient protection is ensured. Further, there is a growing global trend towards the implementation of data localization laws that require data to be collected, processed, and stored within a particular territory or location.[19] Therefore, the need to deal with personal data in a way that is lawful is likely to drive the need for users of ODR to identify the system of law within which their dispute resolution process is anchored.

---

[16] Thomson Reuters, *The Impact of ODR Technology on Dispute Resolution in the UK* (Thomson Reuters 2016), 7; T. Schultz, 'Does Online Dispute Resolution Need Governmental Intervention? The Case for Architectures of Control and Trust' (2004) 6 *North Carolina Journal of Law & Technology* 71, 73.

[17] Susskind (n. 15), 261.

[18] Directive 95/46/EC of the European Parliament and of the Council of 24 October 1995 on the protection of individuals with regard to the processing of personal data and on the free movement of such data [1995] OJ L281/31 (hereafter EU Data Protection Directive 1995).

[19] Brussels Privacy Hub, 'Data Localisation: Deconstructing Myths and Suggesting a Workable Model for the Future: The Cases Of China and The EU', Working Paper (2019) 5(17).

As discussed in more detail below, a number of ODR platforms are working on deployment of new models of decentralized justice. Decentralized justice systems are fully driven by independent peers built on DLT, and cannot be controlled by any single party. Such platforms have a number of benefits, including decentralization and disintermediation of the dispute resolution process, reduced costs, greater transparency, fairness and automation. These vary, however, based on the type of ODR adopted as there is a large variety of designs and specifications that DLT platforms can have. Such platforms are perfectly suited for the resolution of cross-border claims, claims in e-commerce, complex technology-related disputes and many other issues arising from the constantly growing digital economy. However, this will largely depend on courts being prepared to recognize the outcome of such ODR platforms as a matter of law, if one of the parties denies its validity or effect. Otherwise, the claims will depend on acceptance by the parties which may in practice arise in many instances but will not arise for all, in particular in high-value and complex disputes.

a.) Increased efficiency, accountability, and reduced costs

ODR is perceived as a more efficient, faster and more flexible form of dispute resolution and has the capability to resolve disputes at a reduced cost.[20] For example, Online Schlichter, an online mediation service for B2C e-commerce, states that it is able to resolve the majority of disputes in an average of sixty days. The US-based company CyberSettle that uses a blind-bidding system states that it has a 66 per cent settlement rate within thirty days of submission and reduces settlement time on average by 85 per cent, which saved around $11.6 million in litigation costs over the 1,200 claims submitted.[21] Further, the process of ODR can be flexible and accommodate the needs of the parties: ODR can be conducted synchronously, in real-time, or asynchronously, when users have the ability to access ODR at any time during or outside of working hours, leave messages for other parties and be notified of responses. In addition to reducing costs, ODR platforms also address a number of environmental, health and sustainability concerns by supporting the move to paperless hearings and the reduction in travel for all parties, witnesses, lawyers and experts. ODR systems reduce the costs associated with reservations of dispute resolution centres or meeting rooms, etc.[22]

In the fast-moving age of the digital economy, a substantial number of transactions involve parties across multiple jurisdictions, particularly those related to

---

[20] P.D. Galloway, 'Is Construction Arbitration ready for Online Dispute Resolution?' (2013) 30(2) *The International Construction Law Review* 215, 218–20.

[21] Online Dispute Resolution Advisory Group, Online Dispute Resolution for Low Value Civil Claims: Report by the UK Civil Justice Council (2015), 15.

[22] G. Kaufmann-Kohler, *Online Dispute Resolution and its Significance for International Commercial Arbitration, Global Reflections On International Commerce And Dispute Resolution* (ICC Publishing 2005) 443, 453.

emerging technologies and blockchain. It may not always be practical for those transactions to confine their dispute to a particular jurisdiction. ODR and, in particular, DLT-based platforms, remove jurisdictional obstacles and allow the parties to resolve their disputes more efficiently than any of the national dispute resolution mechanisms. DLT-based platforms could increase speed and lower inefficiencies by removing intermediaries and automating various stages of the dispute resolution process. DLT removes the need for verification of the evidence and information since, on DLT-based systems, these are recorded, shared and synchronized across a distributed network, which is accessible by the relevant counterparties. DLT can also provide the parties with more secure and efficient systems of storing and exchanging data and evidence and reduce the infrastructure cost for maintaining such data.[23]

Indeed, DLT-based ODR tools facilitate frictionless collaboration and the sharing of documents in an efficient and secure way. Well designed and successfully implemented, ODR enables its users to access all necessary information and communicate with other stakeholders in the dispute through a single portal. This can significantly reduce the number of communications over a multitude of platforms during the course of proceedings. Again, this drives efficiency and reduces costs. An online repository of case data—accessible to all stakeholders simultaneously (on a permissioned basis)—assists parties to manage version control, avoid duplication, and maintain a consistent approach to data handling throughout the proceedings.

DLT-based ODR platforms are also able to ensure greater accountability, cybersecurity and data protection—storing data in a consistently-used and secure repository helps to minimize cybersecurity risks on a case-by-case basis by 'levelling up' the weakest link in the custody chain and minimizing the processing of data in the dispute. It also helps to minimize confidentiality risks: granular controls can be given to each user that enable better tracking and supervision of compliance with confidentiality obligations. In future, information drawn from ODR platforms (again, with the necessary permissions) will enable businesses to better quantify, assess, and monitor litigation risk across their businesses, to identify opportunities to prevent future disputes and spot weaknesses in their supply chain or services.

DLT can facilitate the automation of a number of manual processes, including those that are the responsibility of the parties, as well as certain functions of the relevant decision maker. DLT-based tools further provide the parties with an option of automatic enforcement through smart contracts. This means that, once a decision is issued, any applicable compensation is paid to a winning party directly

---

[23] D. Carneiro *et al.*, 'Online Dispute Resolution: An Artificial Intelligence Perspective' (2014) 41(2) *Artificial Intelligence Review* 211, 215.

(without the need for consent from a losing party) or, for non-monetary awards, steps can be effected within the DLT ecosystem.

b.) Increased accessibility and fairness

ODR platforms are designed to improve the accessibility and affordability of the existing dispute resolution practices and address the common drawbacks such as delay and complexity.[24] An effective ODR platform should significantly improve overall user experience compared to the current mechanisms. ODR can help to simplify legal procedures for non-lawyers and provide greater access to justice to negotiate, mediate or arbitrate a wide range of disputes from any part of the world.

ODR procedures are likely to minimize the need for lawyers for certain types of disputes, and will be able to gather the relevant information even where users are representing themselves, making the procedure fairer for all parties.[25] The ODR processes are often much more integrated and streamlined and can be directly supervised by a decision maker. ODR platforms can be accessible on different types of devices across multiple jurisdictions and time zones. For cross-border disputes, ODR platforms are able to offer users the possibility to conduct dispute resolution procedures in different languages and provide translation services.[26]

Fairness is a concept that is difficult to define and has many dimensions.[27] In general terms, fairness of ODR procedures can be broadly categorized into fairness of procedure and fairness of outcome. ODR would increase fairness by providing the parties with the ability to actively participate in the process and share their views on the relevant subject with other participants. ODR platforms can provide a forum for conducting dispute resolution in a form of a respectful dialogue and deliver fair outcomes through transparent, timely, effective procedures, in which parties can participate on an equal footing.[28] ODR platforms would be able to ensure that users have access to sufficient information on the procedural rules and the outcome of the process at the appropriate time.

As mentioned in Section 3, DLT technology will also bring transparency to the ODR systems and will help to ensure that documents and evidence have not been tampered with. Further, DLT-based platforms would be able to automate the majority of stages involved in the dispute resolution process and, therefore, reduce the risks of such stages being partial towards either party or corrupted

---

[24] Reuters (n. 16), 15.
[25] JUSTICE, *Delivering Justice in an Age of Austerity* (JUSTICE 2015), 17.
[26] See eg, the European Commission ODR platform that allows EU consumers and traders to settle their disputes for both domestic and cross-border online purchases, available here: <https://ec.europa.eu/consumers/odr/main/?event=main.home2.show> accessed 13 July 2021.
[27] N. Ebner and J. Zeleznikow, 'Fairness, Trust and Security in Online Dispute Resolution' (2015) 36(2) *Hamline University School of Law Journal of Public Law and Policy* <https://digitalcommons.hamline.edu/jplp/vol36/iss2/6>> accessed 20 May 2021.
[28] M. Barendrecht *et al.*, 'ODR and the Courts: The Promise of 100% Access to Justice?' (2016) *The Hague Institute for Innovation of Law, Trend Report IV*, 43–4 <https://www.hiil.org/wp-content/uploads/2018/09/Online-Dispute-Resolution-Trend-Report.pdf>> accessed 21 May 2021.

in other ways. ODR has the potential to reduce unconscious bias associated with gender, ethnicity, appearance, disability, or socio-economic status. Under some of the ODR platforms it is not necessary to appear via video or audio links, which would reduce the possibility of bias in determining the outcome of a dispute.[29]

c.) Scalability

As ODR continues to be tested for the resolution of low value, repetitive, high volume disputes and for promoting Alternative Dispute Resolution ('ADR'), new technologies will likely accelerate the shift to a more wholesale and widely used ODR process. ODR platforms have the potential to introduce economies of scale to the dispute resolution processes and streamline the resolution of high volume, small value disputes, such as separation, accidents, employment issues, neighbour problems, land problems, etc. The reduced costs would mean that more parties would be able to afford ODR. If ODR provides more effective outcomes, more parties will be willing to pay.[30] ODR is able to efficiently process extremely large numbers of disputes: as mentioned in the previous section, eBay has been operating an online dispute resolution system for C2C or B2C transactions for many years and currently claims to handle up to sixty million disputes a year through its ODR system.[31]

AI-powered automation is changing society and the way we work on a massive scale. Carefully constructed AI-powered algorithms are able to collect data from the users, quickly analyse the submitted data, identify data on any similar disputes and previous decisions and generate a quick report, listing viable solutions to help the decision-makers improve their performance.[32]

However, there remains huge untapped economic potential in the continued digitization of dispute resolution processes. The next wave of digitization is expected to come through the development and adoption of technologies like DLT, cloud and edge computing, automation, and augmented and virtual reality.[33] Beyond that lies the promise of quantum computing and artificial general intelligence, which could lead to a tectonic shift in the way our society operates and significantly greater opportunities for the increased use of ODR.

---

[29] R.J. Condlin, 'Online Dispute Resolution: Stinky, Repugnant, or Drab' (2017) 18 *Cardozo Journal of Conflict Resolution* 717, 734.
[30] Barendrecht *et al.* (n. 28), 3.
[31] E. Katsh and O. Rabinovich-Einy, 'Blockchain and the Inevitability of Disputes: The Role for Online Dispute Resolution' (2019) *Journal of Dispute Resolution* 47, 57.
[32] J. Zeleznikow, 'Can Artificial Intelligence And Online Dispute Resolution Enhance Efficiency And Effectiveness In Courts' (2017) 8(2) *International Journal For Court Administration* 30, 36.
[33] McKinsey Global Institute, 'Twenty-Five Years of Digitization: Ten Insights into How to Play It Right' (McKinsey, 21 May 2019), <https://www.mckinsey.com/business-functions/mckinsey-digital/our-insights/twenty-five-years-of-digitization-ten-insights-into-how-to-play-it-right>> accessed 24 May 2021.

d.) COVID-19

While the rate of adoption of ODR was already increasing towards the end of the last decade, the process of digital transformation in the context of dispute resolution has markedly accelerated in the light of COVID-19. The pandemic and consequential restrictions on the movement of people globally has inspired a sea change in the use of technology for dispute resolution within unprecedented timeframes. With necessity being the mother of invention, courts and arbitral institutions have—more or less overnight—dramatically revised their processes to enable disputes to continue to be resolved in a time of quarantine and enforced social distancing.[34]

The general consensus is that this short-term change will be of much longer-term impact on the way parties resolve their disputes going forward. In England, for example, HM Courts & Tribunals Service ('HMCTS') has already begun building capacity to deliver justice in new ways.[35] A July 2020 report by HMCTS sets out a number of measures that were put in place to respond to the pandemic but which are proposed to be retained and adapted in the longer-term (eg, the use of audio and video in hearings, the 'Cloud Video Platform', etc.).[36] HMCTS also plans to make the Video Hearings service available in a number of jurisdictions, and accessible on smartphones.[37]

D. Is DLT an Additional Catalyst for ODR?

DLT is considered to represent a new frontier for electronic information management and exchange. The secretariat of the World Trade Organization has reported that, by one forecast, the business value of DLT systems is expected to grow to over $3 trillion by 2030, representing a 'global large-scale economic value-add'.[38] As is

---

[34] Hebert Smith Freehills, 'Update [8]: 'Necessity is the Mother of Invention': Covid-19 Dramatically Accelerates Digitalisation of Arbitration Processes' (*Herbert Smith Freehills*, 10 July 2020) <https://hsfnotes.com/arbitration/2020/07/10/update-8-necessity-is-the-mother-of-invention-covid-19-dramatically-accelerates-digitalisation-of-arbitration-processes/> accessed 25 May 2021.

[35] HM Courts & Tribunals Service, 'COVID-19: Overview of HMCTS Response' (July 2020) <https://assets.publishing.service.gov.uk/government/uploads/system/uploads/attachment_data/file/896779/HMCTS368_recovery_-_COVID-19-_Overview_of_HMCTS_response_A4L_v3.pdf>> accessed 26 May 2021.

[36] *Ibid.*; HM Courts & Tribunals Service, 'New Video Tech to Increase Remote Hearings in Civil and Family Courts' (1 July 2020) <https://www.gov.uk/government/news/new-video-tech-to-increase-remote-hearings-in-civil-and-family-courts> accessed 27 May 2021.

[37] HM Courts & Tribunals Service, 'Guidance: HMCTS Services: Video Hearings Service' (14 May 2021) <https://www.gov.uk/guidance/hmcts-services-video-hearings-service> accessed 1 June 2021.

[38] World Trade Organization, 'World Trade Report 2018: The Future of World Trade' (*World Trade Organisation*, 2018), 35, <https://www.wto.org/english/res_e/publications_e/world_trade_report18_e.pdf>> accessed 28 May 2021, citing R. Kandaswamy and D. Furlonger, 'Blockchain-Based Transformation: A Gartner Trend Insights Report' (*Gartner*, 27 March 2018) <https://www.gartner.com/en/doc/3869696-blockchain-based-transformation-a-gartner-trend-insight-report>> accessed 1 June 2021.

covered elsewhere in this publication, DLT solutions promise to enable greater efficiency, remove intermediary parties and processes, improve business transparency and boost system resilience and data security.[39]

1. Defining the concept of decentralized justice

The novel characteristics of DLT and, in particular, the decentralized nature of the network, generate new opportunities for the ways in which disputes between users of a DLT network can be resolved online. We identify a number of new ODR offerings which seek to challenge and disrupt the way in which disputes are currently resolved in a DLT context below. Some of the founders and technologists developing these new ODR tools speak of their aim to democratize justice, to see decision making 'back in the hands of the community' and to enable parties to circumvent national judicial bodies that are backed by nation states. They suggest that the decentralization of dispute resolution processes gives parties the necessary confidence for DLT adoption to go mainstream by providing certainty and peace of mind in how issues will be resolved. However, the courts are likely to resist this approach. In practice, it may be difficult to the escape the reach of national jurisdictions or arbitral tribunals, and there would often be considerable risks for parties to do so in any event. At present, arbitration is the only internationally recognized way of limiting the role of national courts to aspects of supervision and enforcement of awards.

On the whole, however, the main drivers behind the development of these tools appear to be to reduce the time and costs associated with resolving disputes. This arises from a perception that the costs and timeframes of dispute resolution, in particular for the smaller and less complex disputes, have spiralled out of control within traditional systems of justice. The various whitepapers cited in this section speak of redundant activities, a multitude of duplicative processes and outdated pricing models within the legal sector as the drivers for technologists seeking to enable the resolution of disputes outside of the reach of national courts or traditional arbitral tribunals. They also refer to the inaccessibility of justice for smaller players, who are, they say, driven away from the courts or arbitration due to the financial and time investment needed to obtain a decision. They argue that justice currently serves only a few large and powerful economic players and suggest that the automation and streamlining of dispute resolution processes via DLT-based ODR will help to redress that balance. Drawing an analogy to the delivery of technology, they discuss how justice can be delivered online 'as a service'.

---

[39] See eg, Section 3 *above*.

2. Procedure for resolving SLC disputes

There are two main options for the resolution of DLT-based disputes: through traditional legal frameworks (eg, courts, arbitration, or other alternative dispute resolution procedures) or through ODR mechanisms embedded in smart contracts/SLCs that result in digital actions executed within the DLT network. The most effective solution in any given instance will depend on the nature of the dispute and the needs of the parties.

The first option is likely to be most readily adopted as it is the 'tried and tested' approach, and would likely give the parties greatest legal certainty at least in the short to medium term. However, the procedures at play in those traditional dispute resolution frameworks have not been designed with DLT in mind or to maximize automation opportunities or expediency in the light of the ways in which data is generated and maintained in a distributed network. Additionally, resolving DLT disputes through traditional dispute resolution mechanisms may lead to some significant challenges, for example, where the parties to a particular transaction on the distributed network remain anonymous or pseudonymous as between each other and the wider world.

An ODR platform may prove valuable in this context, to enable disputes to be resolved effectively notwithstanding those novel features of distributed networks. Many DLT enthusiasts argue that embedding ODR directly into a smart contract avoids the need for the parties to submit to any national jurisdiction and can provide the parties with the benefits offered by decentralized justice, including efficiency, reduced costs, anonymity, automatic execution, and tamper-resistance.[40] It also allows the smart contract to function effectively from end to end without the need for recourse to stakeholders outside the relevant DLT ecosystem.[41]

The proposition is that the combination of DLT and ODR enables parties to insert a clause in their smart contract that would specify the steps for triggering an ODR process should any dispute arise and the commands and network operations that would lead to a determination in relation to the dispute ultimately being executed on the network without the need for further party consent (at least from the 'losing' party). The potential pros and cons of this type of approach are considered in the context of different potential ODR offerings in the context of DLT below.

In general terms, a resolution of disputes through a dispute resolution process embedded in a smart contract or SLC is likely to proceed through six stages. In the first instance, after an alleged breach occurs, a notice of breach/dispute will normally be required. With a DLT-based dispute, the option of a hard-copy notice is of course still available, but other, more efficient, solutions may also exist. For

---

[40] D.W.E. Allen, A.M. Lane, and M. Poblet, 'The Governance of Blockchain Dispute Resolution' (2019) 25 *Harvard Negotiation Law Review* 75, 83.
[41] Vos (n. 1), 15.

example, the service of a dispute notice could be automated in the event a breach occurs which could be identified electronically (ie, the notice provision is codified to monitor the obligations of the contract and trigger a notification to the offending party if a contractual event within their control does not take place).

In the second instance, automated elements of the SLC may be suspended. Pending resolution of the dispute, the aggrieved party might want to prevent the SLC from continuing to run. The question then arises of how, and by whom, the SLC should be temporarily suspended and what impacts such suspension would have on any arguments as to affirmation or repudiation of a contract between the parties. Further thought needs to be given to the process/safeguards that can be put in place to effect a temporary suspension to smart aspects of the SLC when a genuine dispute arises, but without undermining the rationale for codification. Options might include appointment of an independent expert or arbitrator to determine pursuant to an emergency procedure whether or not there is a valid issue to be heard in the dispute (ie, the summary judgment test) and, if so, whether or not the operation of the code should be suspended (in whole or part). Automatic performance of a smart contract may also be suspended at the behest of one party, by agreement of both parties, or made contingent on the occurrence of an event.[42]

In the third instance, amicable discussions take place. If there is to be a period of amicable negotiation between the parties before a formal dispute process is triggered, the SLC will need to provide a means by which the parties can submit their agreed resolution to the DLT platform in a way that would amend the SLC code accordingly.

In the fourth instance, evidence is collected and assessed. In theory, a decision-maker could be given access to the full audit trail of relevant contractual events upon the service of a dispute notice (or at the relevant stage of the dispute resolution process). However, once a dispute has arisen, one party or another may wish to dispute the veracity of that data or its relevance to the issues at play in the dispute (ie, the parties might be in dispute because the data input into the smart contract is itself erroneous). The question therefore arises as to what evidential value the contract-run data will have (and what data a decision-maker will receive in the context of a dispute).

In the fifth instance, a formal dispute resolution process is triggered. The parties may choose several options at this stage, including expert determination or arbitration. The nature of SLCs means that new disputes of a technical (computer science/data analytics) nature may arise, which would be suitable and efficient for an expert to determine. Arbitration is also one of the best-suited options, particularly where the SLC runs on a distributed cross-border network or the parties want to take advantage of automation within the dispute resolution process, as

---

[42] *Ibid.*, 16.

arbitration would provide additional benefits, such as party autonomy and ease of international enforcement.

Finally, a decision is made. The decision can be executed and enforced automatically. This means that, once a decision is issued, any applicable monetary compensation can be paid into a party's digital wallet directly. Some 'on-chain' dispute resolution offerings transfer funds from the parties' digital wallets to escrow until the dispute is resolved. Decision makers are, in some instances, appointed from a pool of anonymous users of the DLT network who deposit a financial stake in cryptocurrency in order to gain a right to vote on the outcome of the dispute. Those decision makers then cast a vote from a pre-determined list of pre-identified outcomes and those who voted along with the majority receive compensation, while those who voted in the minority forfeit their stake. Again, the final decision may be automatically executed on the DLT network, and a payment triggered for the costs of the dispute resolution service.

3. Substantive questions for smart contract and SLC dispute resolution

There are still a number of legal and procedural challenges that parties face if they implement a transaction through a smart contract, without an express choice of law and specified forum for resolving disputes. Failing to include a choice of law and dispute resolution provision in a smart contract or an SLC (or such choice applying by virtue of the applicable system rules) creates a number of uncertainties and may result in lengthy and expensive court proceedings around the questions of applicable law and jurisdiction when a dispute arises.

The novel features of DLT, in particular the distributed nature of the network and the consensus models which give effect to events within the DLT ecosystem, can make it difficult to determine the applicable jurisdiction and the law applicable to the dispute according to traditional principles. Therefore, it is advisable for the parties to consider a number of issues at the outset of entering into an SLC, in order to avoid any future complications and delay, including the following.

The first question that parties need to consider in the context of dispute resolution in a DLT context relates to the *form of the smart contract*—whether they have a valid and effective contract (as a matter of law). Certain legal systems require specific types of contracts to comply with strict procedural formalities in order to be valid and enforceable (eg, around the form of the agreement and formalities around execution). Meeting these requirements can prove problematic if the smart contract is written only in code. To avoid these issues, the parties should consider entering into smart contracts/SLCs that contain natural language.

A second question relates to *governing law and jurisdiction*. It is essential that the parties select the governing law and forum which will apply to their contractual obligations, for service of process and whether arbitration or court proceedings are chosen. Without express written agreement, there can be no binding referral of disputes to arbitration or ODR. Failing to include a choice of law and dispute resolution provision in an SLC (or such choice applying by virtue of the applicable system rules) creates a number of uncertainties and may result in lengthy and expensive court proceedings around the questions of applicable law and jurisdiction when a dispute arises.

So far as English court jurisdiction is concerned, where the common law rules apply parties would need to be able to serve proceedings within the jurisdiction or, failing that, obtain permission to serve against a defendant outside of the jurisdiction. In order to obtain permission to serve out of the jurisdiction, the parties would need to establish that the claim falls within one or more of the gateways under the Practice Direction 6B of the Civil Procedural Rules as well as demonstrating that England and Wales is the appropriate forum, which may not always be straightforward. This process can be time-consuming and costly, particularly where jurisdiction is challenged.[43] Additional complexities also arise in the context of defendants whose identity is unknown. However, the English courts have facilitated processes to overcome these (eg, bringing a claim again 'persons unknown' and serving documents electronically to a known address or even via a chat).

A third question relates to the *capacity of the parties*. DLT platforms and smart contracts are potentially open to pseudonymous parties, who do not usually confirm their capacity at the outset, which may cause additional difficulties. The majority of jurisdictions would recognize a contract as legally-binding only if the parties have the capacity to perform their obligations. In the event that the parties lack legal capacity, such contracts may be considered invalid in traditional as well as online dispute resolution proceedings, which may enable parties to evade their obligations.

Several jurisdictions have sought to clarify these and other issues about how smart contracts can be countenanced within traditional legal systems and principles. A *Legal Statement* published in November 2019 by the UKJT concluded that there is no bar under English law for cryptoassets to have the legal status of property and for smart contracts to be legally binding. The *Legal Statement* is not binding on any court in England and Wales, but it is intended to give greater market confidence that English courts will take a pragmatic and commercial approach when these issues come before them. It has also been cited and relied on by the English courts and other common law courts in recent decisions.[44]

---

[43] A. Pertoldi and M. McIntosh, 'Enforcement of Judgments between the UK and the EU Post-Brexit: Where Are We Now?' (*Thomson Reuters*, 20 January 2020), <http://disputeresolutionblog.practicallaw.com/enforcement-of-judgments-between-the-uk-and-the-eu-post-brexit-where-are-we-now/>> accessed 19 May 2021.

[44] See eg, *AA v Persons Unknown* [2019] EWHC 3556 (Comm), where the High Court adopted the position in the UKJT Legal Statement, finding that cryptoassets can be treated as property under English law.

The flexible approach taken by the courts to date in applying traditional common law principles in England and Wales to the novel characteristics of cryptoassets and smart contracts is to be welcomed. However, the guidance from the courts to date is far from the last word on the matter; it will be important to monitor the approach taken in other jurisdictions. Given the distributed, global nature of DLT platforms, a cross-jurisdictional analysis will be vital in assessing legal rights and risks. In the meantime, the design and implementation of SLCs (as we have defined them, being DLT-based 'smart contracts' which sit within a digitized 'legal wrapper' in natural language) and the proliferation of ODR will help to pave the way for a more mainstream adoption of these technologies, while ensuring legal certainty is preserved.

Although traditional dispute resolution mechanisms may be an option for parties to resolve smart contract/SLC disputes, the associated processes in today's systems run counter to many of the drivers for smart contract/SLC adoption. Indeed, existing 'traditional' dispute resolution processes risk undermining some of the benefits that smart contracts/SLCs offer and, in a worst-case scenario, driving technologists and potentially businesses to seek refuge outside the reach of the courts in a technology-driven, lawless distributed digital realm. That may be a dystopian image, but it is a topic of discussion amongst technologists (often referred to as the 'code is law' debate), and many products already seek to resolve disputes in a commercial, if not legally-driven, manner—away from the usual dispute resolution fora.[45] It is incumbent on the legal profession to grapple with these issues and drive change in the legal sector from within, to stay relevant in an increasingly online society.

4. Examples of DLT-based ODR offerings

As mentioned in Section 3, a number of companies have developed DLT-based dispute resolution systems as a result of the perceived drawbacks of existing dispute resolution processes. These offerings seek to respond to smart contract users' appetite for speed and efficiency—often over and above legal certainty. These DLT protocols, libraries and platforms have largely centred around the concept of online 'arbitration' (although that term is often misused), crowd-sourced dispute resolution and AI-powered automated resolution of disputes (or a combination of these).

Proposed ODR procedures can be grouped into three categories. The first comprise *online 'arbitration' solutions* that are modelled on arbitration and seek to incorporate arbitration procedures within the code of a smart contract. In general,

---

[45] L. Lessig, 'Code Is Law, On Liberty in Cyberspace' (*Harvard Magazine*, 2000) <http://harvardmagazine.com/2000/01/code-is-law-html> accessed 25 May 2021.

these solutions seek to give parties an option to choose 'arbitration' before disputes arise and their awards are claimed to be legally binding and enforceable.[46] A second group comprise *crowdsourced dispute resolution* that allows anonymous users/nodes on the network to vote on 'winners'. Those users in the majority (who chose the right 'winner') are rewarded.[47] A third group comprises *AI-powered 'bots' that resolve the dispute*. These hinge on predictive analytics tools that generate data-driven decisions which may be subsequently coded into a smart contract. AI tools are also being offered to help predict the outcome of disputes, which the parties can then use in driving a settlement strategy.[48]

Although still at an early stage, DLT-based ODR solutions for resolving smart contract disputes are currently being actively marketed. Although each one has challenges to overcome (sometimes very significant challenges), they reveal a variety of possibilities for re-inventing the dispute resolution process and they offer valuable insights into the thought processes of technologists developing the digital infrastructure of tomorrow. Some of the different types of offerings in this area are identified below.

a.) Digitizing and automating recognized processes

The first type of dispute resolution offering in the DLT context seeks to provide parties with a machine-readable dispute resolution clause that seeks to mirror traditional processes, but which can be triggered and (at least in part) automated by means of a smart contract. Once the dispute arises, a party can trigger the relevant smart contract command, following which a number of recognizable (and potentially off-network) steps take place that follow the steps under a traditional dispute resolution clause and lead to an arbitral award that is enforceable as a matter of law.

Such offerings often comprise a contract notification and monitoring service, a command to freeze the smart contract's automated operation and a 'marketplace of dispute resolution vendors to choose from'.[49] The contract notification and modification service will enable parties to access and modify previous versions of the smart contract (with the agreement of all parties). A party who identifies a breach of contract may freeze the operation of the smart contract calling on the relevant command. While the automated execution of the smart contract is frozen, parties may seek amicably to resolve the dispute, amend or terminate the smart contract.[50]

---

[46] Solutions along these lines have been proposed in whitepapers by the likes of Sagewise, Jur, and Juris, but those whitepapers have not necessarily led to a product roll-out.
[47] See eg, the Kleros and Aragon offerings.
[48] Schmitz and Rule (n. 5), 117.
[49] B. Dhakappa, 'Sagewise—Adding Dispute Resolution To Smart Contracts' (*TechWeek*, 9 September 2018) <https://techweek.com/sagewise-blockchain-los-angeles/> accessed 1 June 2021.
[50] J. Shieber, 'Sagewise Pitches a Service to Verify Claims and Arbitrate Disputes over Blockchain Transactions' (*Tech Crunch*, 3 August 2018) <https://techcrunch.com/2018/08/03/sagewise-pitches-a-service-to-verify-claims-and-arbitrate-disputes-over-blockchain-transactions/>> accessed 5 June 2021.

Failing an amicable resolution, the intention is that parties can then refer the dispute to a neutral decision maker through the platform's dispute resolution marketplace or via notification (automated or otherwise) to a well-known arbitration institution.[51]

b.) Re-designing dispute resolution within a distributed network
At the other end of the spectrum, other DLT-based ODR offerings seek to implement decentralized justice by relying on tokenized juror voting code and behavioural economics for the resolution of disputes. These ODR models are often several steps removed from relevant legislative definitions of arbitration and the characteristics of a traditional arbitration that would lead to a valid and effective arbitration award enforceable under the New York Convention.

This model often requires that the parties agree a fixed number of potential outcomes for categories of disputes at the time of entering into a smart contract.[52] This enables crowdsourced (and often anonymous) 'jurors' to select their preferred outcome for the dispute), with the majority of decision makers benefitting financially from their choice (ie, jurors are rewarded economically for voting with the majority). Juror fees can be paid through the subscription fees charged to all parties who incorporate the relevant dispute resolution commands in their smart contract or as a licence fee on a recurring basis during the life of the smart contract.[53]

This model implicitly relies on game theory, in that each juror is encouraged to maximize their financial return by investing effort into the decision to work out the most defensible position—and therefore the majority decision. Jurors who voted in the same way as the majority receive compensation in the form of an arbitration fee deposited by the parties based on the terms of their smart contract. Those jurors who voted against the majority (ie, in favour of the 'losing' party) forfeit the stake they deposited at the outset of the dispute and receive no fee. Under this model, the decision of the majority of jurors is generally executed automatically as a command of the smart contract itself, as is the payment for the cost of the arbitration (borne by the 'losing' party).

As a matter of law, however, the jurors' decisions may not be upheld in the courts or before a tribunal. Many of the service offerings recognize this and seek to address the issue through the smart contract. For example, some offerings enable an unlimited number of appeals where a party is dissatisfied with the outcome of a dispute. The party appealing the decision is often required to deposit the funds required to cover the costs of the appeal, which—for example—may double for each appeal.[54]

---

[51] Dhakappa (n. 49).
[52] Kleros, 'One Pager' (*Kleros*, 2018) <https://kleros.io/onepager_en.pdf> accessed 4 June 2021.
[53] Aragon GitHub, <https://github.com/aragon/whitepaper>.
[54] *Ibid.*

c.) A hybrid solution

Increasingly, ODR offerings aim to combine several types of existing ODR models and provide various layers according to the value, complexity and specific needs of the parties to a dispute, culminating in a recognized arbitration process leading to an enforceable award, if required.[55] In their Introduction to this volume, JG Allen and P.G. Hunn describe 'smart legal contracts' in terms of a 'contract stack'. A similar analysis can be applied to the dispute resolution processes available for the resolution of SLC disputes. Indeed, the 'smart' element (ie, truly distributed, automated and machine-readable elements) of ODR in the context of SLCs will likely remain as 'one part of a more complex stack, which will include more conventional "legal" components including conventional "paper" agreements and mandatory rules of national law expressed in natural language.'[56]

For example, some platforms split their ODR layers into three layers:[57] (i) a crowdsourcing layer, where the decision-making process is open to all participants through principles of game theory; (ii) online expert determination, where only experts who are members of the community selected by the parties can participate in the decision-making process and, in some instances, execute their own decisions within the DLT ecosystem within which the SLC is hosted; and (iii) an arbitration dispute resolution mechanism, which leads to a binding and enforceable arbitration award under the New York Convention.

The first layer, the 'crowdsourcing' layer, can be suitable for lower value disputes and uses the same game theory principles as described in Section 2, where decision makers who constitute a simple majority are rewarded with tokens.[58] The ODR platforms concede that this approach does not qualify as a judgment or decision with the same legal standing as a court judgment or arbitration award, but suggest that it is fair and fast (and can be enforced automatically if an escrow account is attached to the smart contract).

The second layer, online expert determination, often deploys a system of economic incentives based on game theory to motivate voters to choose between the parties' respective positions and give weight to their vote by 'staking' tokens. This enables determination of disputes by experts identified within a given 'community' of the platform users. This layer is estimated to resolve medium complexity disputes within 24 hours to one week. However, such processes are not arbitration processes and do not produce a decision that is enforceable as a matter of law in its own right (rather than, for example, creating a new contractual right). They seek instead to draw on the 'wisdom of crowds and the incentives enabled by tokenization.'[59]

---

[55] Allen (n. 4), 330.
[56] Ibid., 331.
[57] Jur, 'Whitepaper' (*Jur*, July 2019), <https://jur.io/wp-content/uploads/2019/05/jur-whitepaper-v.2.0.2.pdf> accessed 2 June 2021.
[58] Ibid.
[59] Ibid.

While courts and tribunals may be prepared to give effect to these types of agreements, their effect is not to eliminate the dispute entirely, but to change the basis or nature of disputes (eg, an 'on-chain' determination, while potentially unenforceable as a binding judgment or award 'off-chain', could be enforced before relevant courts or through arbitration as a matter of *binding contract*).

The final layer, often described as an online arbitration process, can potentially combine some of the benefits of decentralization, blockchain technology, and digitization with traditional arbitration mechanisms. The dispute resolution procedure in this layer is often more complex in comparison to the other layers, but it can allow parties to the agreement to seek enforcement according to the principles of the New York Convention. ODR platforms can also offer different types of procedures for the resolution of disputes under this layer, for example, 'Documentary Arbitration' (arbitration without hearings or witnesses), 'Quick Arbitration' (arbitration limited to two hearings maximum, a maximum of two witnesses per party and a time limit of about three months), and 'Ordinary Arbitration' (for disputes of €150,000 or more).[60] As mentioned previously, international arbitration institutions and bodies like the UKJT are also adapting existing well-established arbitration rules to better enable ODR and to enable parties, where appropriate, to streamline procedures for the purpose of disputes arising out of SLCs, and other digital disputes.

5. Challenges to overcome

Despite a number of substantial advantages, today's ODR procedures still face some major challenges and barriers. The following section summarizes a number of barriers to the mainstream adoption of the ODR platforms. There are still some areas that require further consideration by adopters, lawyers, coders, and legislators. The more pertinent challenges include the resistance of the users and legal professionals to accept the change, technical limitations and issues related to enforcement.

a.) Culture and people (any change is difficult and takes time)

Despite the fact that one of the main advantages of ODR is its potential to provide better access to justice, in reality ODR may not be easily accessible to all users. ODR by definition requires users to be comfortable with using technology on at least a high-level, which may cause difficulties to those who are unable to use computers with confidence, or do not have access to the technology for other reasons. Such obstacles are caused by a number of factors,

---

[60] *Ibid.*

including age, education, socio-economic status, physical disability and cultural differences.[61]

The report of the UK ODR Advisory Group cites the 2013 report by the Oxford Internet Institute at the University of Oxford to the effect that twenty-two percent of adults in the UK are not using the Internet, and around five percent of people surveyed reported that they 'definitely' would not have anyone who could help them use an ODR service. While it is possible to predict that this percentage is likely to decrease over time, the report suggests that measures should be put in place to ensure assistance to the people who may require it, rather than delaying the deployment of ODR platforms because of concerns that some users may not be comfortable using them. This may also be extended to wider commercial settings.[62]

There is also a concern that ODR processes may remove the empathy that comes with personal appearance, as well as the cathartic element of being heard in person. Some users are concerned that absence of face-to-face interaction may have a negative impact on the outcome of the case.[63] The UK Bail Observation Project, for example, found that fifty percent of those heard via video link were refused bail, compared to twenty-two percent of those heard in person.[64] On the other hand, these results may vary on a case-to-case basis. Overall, there are studies that confirm that users are becoming more and more comfortable with technology over the recent years.[65]

While ODR procedures may remove an element of unconscious bias, this point is quite contentious, as there is evidence that algorithms can build on the prejudices of the typical person used in the modelling for their creation, and therefore may contain certain 'absorbing' bias. If the developer has any racial prejudices, for example, this may be reflected in the code, by predicting a higher rate of offences in relation to a particular group. There is evidence that a criminal justice algorithm in the US inaccurately associated higher risk of reoffending with black people.[66] Further, the UK Home Office used AI technology in deciding visa applications,

---

[61] E. Clark, G. Cho, and A. Hoyle, 'Online Dispute Resolution: Present Realities, Pressing Problems and Future Prospects' (2003) 17 *International Review of Law, Computers & Technology* 7, 21.

[62] Online Dispute Resolution Advisory Group, 'Online Dispute Resolution for Low Value Civil Claims: Report by the UK Civil Justice Council' (*Civil Justice* Council, February 2015), 26–7 <https://www.judiciary.uk/wp-content/uploads/2015/02/Online-Dispute-Resolution-Final-Web-Version1.pdf> accessed 22 May 2021.

[63] A. Schmitz, 'Measuring "Access to Justice" in the Rush to Digitize' (2020) 88 *Fordham Law Review* 2381, 2384.

[64] J. Hynes, ' "Hello Dungavel!": Observations on the Use of Video Link Technology in Immigration Bail Hearings' (*UK Administrative Justice Institute*, 6 May 2019) <https://ukaji.org/2019/05/06/hello-dungavel-observations-on-the-use-of-video-link-technology-in-immigration-bail-hearings/> accessed 6 June 2021.

[65] M. Anderson and A. Perrin, 'Tech Adoption Climbs Among Older Adults' (*Pew Research Center*, 17 May 2017) <https://www.pewresearch.org/internet/2017/05/17/tech-adoption-climbs-among-older-adults/>> accessed 7 June 2021.

[66] See eg, ProPublica, 'Machine Bias: There's Software used Across the Country to Predict Future Criminals. And It's Biased against Blacks' (*ProPublica*, 23 May 2016) <https://www.propublica.org/article/machine-bias-risk-assessments-in-criminal-sentencing>> accessed 8 June 2021.

which had a number of issues with transparency and bias. The algorithm was inclined automatically to refuse applications from countries in Africa and to approve applications from other countries.[67]

b.) Engaging the legal profession

While the traditional legal profession may fear that efficient ODR procedures may diminish the role of lawyers in dispute resolution, most of the existing ODR platforms still involve a significant number of legal professionals. Higher value, advanced platforms are likely to lead to additional work for skilled, tech-savvy lawyers. At the same time, professional standards in various jurisdictions may limit the pool of people who are able to provide legal advice online.

Therefore, ODR is able to provide lawyers with new opportunities to diversify their service offerings and perform the roles of mediators, settlement experts, arbitrators, forensic experts, early neutral evaluators, damages assessors, reviewers, and providers of legally sound solutions. In addition, a proportion of clients would still prefer to be guided by lawyers even when going through ODR procedures, particularly in higher value disputes.[68] If ODR makes dispute resolution more accessible, there will be more work for lawyers to assist their existing and new clients with. At the same time, streamlined ODR processes could help unburden legal professionals of administrative issues and give them an opportunity to focus on the merits of the dispute. Finally, there is an opportunity for lawyers to actively participate in the development of ODR tools and take ownership of such platforms. If legal professionals were actively developing and taking advantage of innovative ODR solutions, there would be fewer sceptics and less fear that ODR would reduce the need for legal services.

c.) Coding limitations (today and in future)

A further constraint on seeking to fully digitize and automate dispute resolution processes arises from the limitations of coding languages: code is deterministic, inherently binary in approach and limited to the monitoring and execution of digital events, whereas real-world disputes often require tribunals and courts to deal with the unexpected and make judgments/awards (from a spectrum of possibilities) that have impacts beyond the digital realm.

During dispute resolution processes, lawyers often have to address new issues at short notice. At the moment, AI-based software can tag and cluster related data, which can reduce the review time for lawyers, contributing to better preparedness and consequently a more efficient legal system. Moreover, the efficacy

---

[67] The Solicitors Group, 'Racial bias in immigration algorithms: The Law Society described the decision announced by the Home Office as timely and has warned of the risk of discrimination.' (*The Solicitors Group*, 10 August 2020) <https://thesolicitorsgroup.co.uk/news/2020/racial-bias-in-immigration-algorithms> accessed 9 June 2021.

[68] Barendrecht *et al.* (n. 28), 72.

of community-based DLT offerings (which require jurors to vote for different outcomes) declines with the variety and complexity of outcomes that are put to vote. As a result, such offerings are likely to be more suitable for simple (and mostly low-value) claims, at least in their current form. Real-world disputes also require tribunals to deal with the unexpected. As things stand, while fully automated ODR procedures may be a viable solution for small, straightforward and predictable disputes, it is not clear how these solutions can be applicable to more complex, multi-jurisdictional disputes that require careful consideration of detailed evidence.

Artificial intelligence has made significant progress in recent years and these technologies have the potential to transform the way trials are conducted. Considerable research is being done in relation to algorithmic decision makers (ie, computers which process the parties' data, analyse relevant case law or submissions and generate a judgment or order). Online dispute resolution tools are already being used to help parties narrow issues between them and to facilitate settlement and to determine small claims. It is not beyond the realms of imagination that parties may choose to resolve disputes by means of an algorithmic decision maker in future. It is also very likely that AI tools will be used as a first, non-binding step for dispute resolution in years to come, in the same way that early neutral evaluation works today. The advantage of using computer software is that the process stands to be much cheaper and faster.[69]

However, given the obstacles presented across most judicial systems to enforcing a computer-generated judicial order (without consent from the 'losing' party), fully automated judicial decision making is likely to require legislative change in many jurisdictions. That being said, human decision makers may increasingly be assisted by technology in reaching their decision on the facts and law. One simple example is the use of facial recognition software to assist a court or tribunal to assess what weight to give oral witness testimony. Such technologies along with voice recognition can now be used to review video and audio files to analyse body language or tone of voice with accuracy, or to establish whether it is authentic. That accuracy will only continue to increase in the years to come.[70]

d.) Compatibility issues

ODR procedures envisage any communications being conducted online and any documents and evidence being shared electronically, which would require counsel,

---

[69] C. Morgan and R. Reed, 'Dispute Resolution in the Era of Big Data and AI' (*Herbert Smith Freehills*, 18 September 2019), <https://www.herbertsmithfreehills.com/latest-thinking/dispute-resolution-in-the-era-of-big-data-and-ai> accessed 26 May 2021.

[70] K. Hamann and R. Smith, 'Facial Recognition Technology: Where Will It Take Us?' (*The American Bar Association*, 2019) <https://www.americanbar.org/groups/criminal_justice/publications/criminal-justice-magazine/2019/spring/facial-recognition-technology/>> accessed 3 June 2021.

parties and decision makers to have adequate and compatible hardware and software. While hardware interoperability seems to be less of an issue these days, users will still be required to use equipment with a reasonable level of processing power, adequate data storage capacity and internet connectivity with sufficient bandwidth for communication using standard interfaces. In terms of the software, users may potentially have different operating systems, programs and other software which may cause issues with compatibility. Parties may need to consider these issues at the outset.[71]

Where the parties propose different solutions, the decision maker (and the parties) should consider whether there is a need to select a uniform software in order to avoid situations in which one party presents evidence that can only be viewed by using software that is unavailable to other participants.[72]

e.) Data integrity risks

ODR platforms need to be built on top of adequate risk management procedures. It is vital for ODR platforms to ensure privacy and protection from cyberattacks. This would include setting out protections around the communication channels, the software, the servers and any hardware used for ODR to prevent hackers from obtaining confidential data as well as any information in relation to the parties and subject-matter of a dispute, or indeed that might allow the hackers to influence the judgment in the dispute (such as changing the votes in a crowdsourced decision making process). ODR platforms would need to ensure that the stored data is secure and backed up regularly, and that adequate cryptographic or hashing-based technologies are applied at each stage of the dispute resolution process to preventing tampering. The platform providers would also need to ensure that the data would not be shared by the parties who have access to the information and limit the information that the other side can view.[73]

A number of issues may also arise in relation to intellectual property. For example, copyright and licensing requirements in relation to the transmission and use of data and software. With ODR procedures, each party and tribunal member will normally remain liable to third parties for any IP infringement. There is also the issue of whether the statutory exclusions (for example, as to copyright infringement in relation to 'judicial proceedings') would be effective in relation to the ODR process in use.[74]

---

[71] Chamber of Commerce (ICC) Commission on Arbitration and ADR Task Force, 'Information Technology in International Arbitration' (*International Chamber of Commerce*, 2017), 10, <https://iccwbo.org/content/uploads/sites/3/2017/03/icc-information-technology-in-international-arbitration-icc-arbitration-adr-commission.pdf> accessed 8 June 2021.
[72] Ibid.
[73] Ebner and Zeleznikow (n. 27), 158.
[74] See eg, Copyright, Designs and Patents Act 1988, s 45(1).

f.) Building trust and the surrounding regulatory framework

One of the key obstacles to the mainstream adoption of ODR platforms is a lack of understanding and trust from the wider public. ODR should be presented in such a way that the public will trust it as a transparent, fair, more efficient, and cheaper procedure of dispute settlement.[75] There are a number of factors which can influence whether users will trust an ODR platform enough to use its services. In general terms, the users will need to be sure that the technology behind ODR platforms is reliable, competent, time and cost efficient, user-friendly and suitable to support their dispute.[76] However, this may prove difficult without an independent body that can certify ODR platforms and set the industry standards.

While ODR platforms often have their own codes of professional responsibility, there is no uniform code or regulation that would cover the ODR industry.[77] While there has been some academic discussion on this topic, governments have yet to address this issue.[78] A number of international, business and professional organizations have been working on creating codes of conduct and other guidelines setting out fundamental principles of online justice, which largely cover five broad themes: transparency, accessibility, independence, timeliness, and fairness. However, some level of supervision is required to ensure that the principles are complied with, and to hold ODR platforms accountable in the event of any evidence of bias, inefficiency, or errors that can be harmful to the end user.

In the absence of a robust regulatory framework, ODR platforms may become susceptible to exploitation and poor conduct, which may in turn undermine the already sceptical attitude of users and some legal professionals. There might be a risk that ODR platforms can cause harm by, for example, providing more favourable outcomes to repeat users in comparison to other parties, in order to generate more profit.

g.) Enforcement

In addition to the lack of uniform regulatory framework, another important consideration is enforcement. The advantage of ODR in overcoming geographical boundaries may become problematic at the enforcement stage. Specifically, the question centres on ensuring that once a decision has been rendered, the winning party is able to obtain from the other party the relief that was ordered against them. In order for these novel ODR tools to give parties the necessary certainty to carry on business in a decentralized world, they must be as legally robust as they

---

[75] Ebner and Zeleznikow (n. 27), 155.

[76] L.E. Teitz, 'Providing Legal Services for the Middle Class in Cyberspace: The Promise and Challenge of On-Line Dispute Resolution' (2001) 70 *Fordham Law Review* 985, 1014.

[77] D.B. Farned, 'A New Automated Class of Online Dispute Resolution: Changing the Meaning of Computer-Mediated Communication' (2011) 2(2) *Faulkner Law Review* 335, 343.

[78] N. Ebner and J. Zeleznikow, 'No Sheriff in Town: Governance for Online Dispute Resolution' (2016) 32(4) *Negotiation Journal* 297; Schultz (n. 16).

are technologically sound. The decisions rendered on a DLT-based ODR platform need to be valid, effective and final in the physical world as well as being enforceable as a matter of practice in the online world. If parties are able to challenge or otherwise undermine the outcome of that DLT-based ODR process in courts or before an arbitral tribunal by reference to a system of law, then the tool is likely to increase rather than decrease the time and costs associated with finally resolving disputes.

Again, 'automaticity' is appealing here (ie, the ability for a decision to be enforced automatically, without the need for the 'losing' party's consent). Automatic enforcement could do away with the cost and lengthy delays associated with enforcement proceedings that are often required following receipt of an award or judgment. However, this potential shift in the role of a decision maker (be it characterized as an expert, arbitrator or judge) to implement directly the terms of their decision marks a shift from traditional practices and presents further legal and practical obstacles.

For example, in arbitral proceedings, depending on the seat of arbitration, there is likely to be a minimum mandatory period during which the award is susceptible to challenge. Beyond that time, however, a court can generally still permit a challenge if deemed necessary. The ability to challenge an arbitral decision in this way may create a further obstacle for automatic enforcement, because any automatic enforcement could ultimately need to be reversed. In one way, this is no different to the existing position. However, the practical realities are quite different: in practice, enforcement proceedings take many months. The real benefit of automated execution lies in avoiding that process.

Another issue relates to the potential anonymity of parties transacting on a distributed ledger. If a party does not know the identity of its counterparty or, therefore, its place of residence or the location of its assets, then in practice any decision against such a counterparty would be de facto unenforceable without that counterparty's co-operation within the DLT ecosystem. If a party insists on maintaining its anonymity, but was otherwise happy to submit to the jurisdiction of an ODR platform, then this could in theory be addressed by advance payment.

E. The Road Ahead: Multidisciplinary Collaboration

DLT-based ODR, which would enable disputes to be resolved on the same platform on which the smart contracts/SLCs operate and contractual data relevant to the parties' commercial and legal relationship is recorded, promises to reduce the cost and time required to resolve disputes. Achieving a legally-effective and efficient process for DLT-based online resolution of disputes would help to preserve the efficiency gains associated with embedding code in a contract (or, according to an alternate view, expressing a contract in code). However, it is not clear that any of the existing DLT-based ODR tools achieve this (yet).

If parties want to take full advantage of digitalization and automaticity in the context of their dispute resolution process, they will need to consider very carefully at the *drafting stage* of their contract how that automaticity will be treated as a matter of law and what its purpose is towards the final resolution of a dispute (eg, recognizing at the outset that many of the existing DLT-based ODR tools largely remain akin to forms of ADR). Again, this strongly points in the direction of parties drafting a robust smart *legal* contract which provides the necessary 'legal wrapper' around the code to help drive efficiency in the party's relationship whilst preserving legal certainty (rather than deploying 'pure' smart contracts on a DLT platform). In their SLCs, parties should expressly address the governing law of their agreement and how disputes will be resolved in a manner that leads to a final judgment/award that would be upheld by traditional courts or tribunals.

In the short term at least, this might look a lot like an escalation clause with ODR tools used as a means of facilitating amicable settlement, but recognizing the need for the process to culminate in a procedure similar to traditional arbitration (if parties fail to reach agreement or to abide by the outcome of the ODR process). However, in designing that process, parties should consider where efficiency and security gains are nonetheless achieved in traditional processes through, for example, automated notifications and DLT-backed security of data exchange. For example, parties might seek to automate the process for commencing an arbitration (eg, such that a short form Request or Notice of Arbitration is automatically sent to the relevant arbitral institution upon a negotiation period elapsing without the parties agreeing to extend) or that the parties can themselves verify any conflicts an arbitrator might have, by virtue of their case history being stored and verifiable on the DLT state database.

F. Conclusion

The growing speed of technological development will continue to drive increasing interest in and adoption of ODR tools in the years to come. Emerging technologies like DLT raise a variety of possibilities for re-inventing the dispute resolution process. Founders and development teams at existing DLT-based ODR start-ups are to be commended for seeking to drive dispute resolution into the digital age. However, more work is needed to ensure that those tools do indeed increase efficiency and certainty in the resolution of disputes and do not risk increasing the complexity of disputes and threatening to further delay their final (and legally effective) resolution.

Although desirable and likely in the longer term, a drastic change to existing dispute resolution processes is unlikely for mainstream commercial disputes in the short term. Technical limitations as well as human factors discussed throughout are likely to work as barriers to the broad adoption of DLT-based ODR within the next few years. More significantly, however, is the question of how these new ODR tools sit within existing legal frameworks. In order for new ODR tools to be adopted for the mainstream resolution of commercial disputes, the decisions handed down at the end of the relevant procedure must be robust and enforceable as a matter of law, not just as a matter of practice or technological capability.

In the short term, therefore, flexible dispute resolution models that allow parties to test 'automaticity' of dispute resolution processes and new ODR models, as well as providing a legally robust *fall back*, are likely to be popular. In the medium to longer term, law and regulation will also evolve as business and society becomes more comfortable with automaticity, leading to a radical step change in the transition to a fully digital dispute resolution process. However, the path for high and low value and complexity disputes may be different: what in practice is accepted in a low-value, low-complexity context may not withstand court scrutiny in a high value context. It may be suitable for high value digital environment methodologies to stay more traditional and perhaps less reformative, while at same time allowing the parties to benefit from many cost saving digital techniques to the procedural side of the dispute resolution process.

Bibliography

Editor's Introduction (Allen and Hunn)

Accord Project, 'Open source software tools for smart legal contracts' <https://accordproject.org> accessed 5 October 2021

Allen JG, 'Wrapped and Stacked: "Smart Contracts" and the Interaction of Natural and Formal Language' (2018) 14 *European Review of Contract Law* 307

—— and Lastra RM, 'Border Problems: Mapping the Third Border' (2020) 83 *Modern Law Review* 505

Buterin V, 'A Next-Generation Smart Contract and Decentralized Application Platform' (2013) <https://ethereum.org/en/whitepaper/> accessed 5 October 2021

—— 'Persistent Scripts' (Twitter, 13 October 2018) <https://twitter.com/vitalikbuterin/status/1051160932699770882> accessed 29 September 2021

Bitcoin.org, 'Transactions' (Bitcoin Developer) <https://developer.bitcoin.org/reference/transactions.html> accessed 19 July 2021

Cohney S and Hoffman D, 'Transactional Scripts in Contract Stacks' (2020) 105 *Minnesota Law Review* 319

Cruse DA, 'Some Thoughts on Agentivity' (1973) 9 *Journal of Linguistics* 11

Cuccuru P, 'Beyond Bitcoin: An Early Overview on Smart Contracts' (2017) 25 *International Journal of Law and Information Technology* 179

De Filippi P and Wright A, *Blockchain and the Law: The Rule of Code* (Harvard University Press 2018)

Ethereum.org, 'Introduction to Smart Contracts' <https://ethereum.org/en/developers/docs/smart-contracts/> accessed 5 October 2021

Fox D and Green S (eds), *Cryptocurrencies in Public and Private Law* (Oxford University Press 2019)

Gatteschi V and others, 'Technology of Smart Contracts' in DiMatteo LA and others (eds), *The Cambridge Handbook of Smart Contracts, Blockchain Technology and Digital Platforms* (Cambridge University Press 2019)

Hildebrandt M, 'Text-Driven Jurisdiction in Cyperspace' (Keynote Hart Workshop 26–28 April 2021, New Perspectives on Jurisdiction and the Criminal Law, 2021) <https://osf.io/jgs9n/> accessed 19 July 2021

Hunn P, 'Smart Contracts as Techno-Legal Regulation' (2019) 7 *Journal of ICT Standardization* 269

IEEE, 'P2963—Standard for Data Formats for Smart Legal Contracts' (IEEE Project, 21 May 2021) <https://standards.ieee.org/project/2963.html#Standard> accessed 19 July 2021

Kleros, 'The Justice Protocol' <https://kleros.io> accessed 19 July 2021

Law Commission, 'Smart Contracts Call for Evidence' (17 December 2020) <https://www.lawcom.gov.uk/project/smart-contracts/#related> accessed 19 July 2021

Lawson C, *Technology and Isolation* (Cambridge University Press 2017)

Levy KEC, 'Book-Smart, Not Street-Smart: Blockchain-Based Smart Contracts and The Social Workings of Law' (2017) 3 *Engaging Science, Technology, and Society* 1

Lipshaw JM, 'The Persistence of Dumb Contracts' (2019) 2 *Stanford Journal of Blockchain Law & Policy* 1

Mik E, 'Smart Contracts: Terminology, Technical Limitations and Real-World Complexity' (2017) 9 *Law, Innovation and Technology* 269

de Molière JBP, *Le Bourgeois Gentilhomme* (Paris 1670)

Möslein F, 'Smart Contracts and Civil Law Challenges' in Chiu I and Deipenbrock G (eds), *Routledge Handbook of Financial Technology and Law* (Routledge 2021)

Nakamoto S, 'Bitcoin: A Peer-to-Peer Electronic Cash System' (2008) <https://bitcoin.org/bitcoin.pdf> accessed 20 September 2021

Perillo JM, 'The Origins of the Objective Theory of Contract Formation and Interpretation' (2000) 69 *Fordham Law Review* 427

Reyes C, 'Conceptualising Cryptolaw' (2017) 96 *Nebraska Law Review* 384

Stabile DT and others, *Digital Assets and Blockchain Technology: US Law and Regulation* (Edward Elgar 2020)

Stark J, 'Making sense of Blockchain Smart Contracts' (Coindesk, 4 June 2016) <https://www.coindesk.com/markets/2016/06/04/making-sense-of-blockchain-smart-contracts/> accessed 19 July 2021

Steyn J, 'Contract Law: Fulfilling the Reasonable Expectations of Honest Men' (1997) 113 *Law Quarterly Review* 433

Svantesson DJB, *Solving the Internet Jurisdiction Puzzle* (Oxford University Press 2017)

Szabo N, 'Smart Contracts' (1994) <https://www.fon.hum.uva.nl/rob/Courses/InformationInSpeech/CDROM/Literature/LOTwinterschool2006/szabo.best.vwh.net/smart.contracts.html> accessed 19 July 2021

—— 'Smart Contracts: Building Blocks for Digital Markets' (1996) <www.fon.hum.uva.nl/rob/Courses/InformationInSpeech/CDROM/Literature/LOTwinterschool2006/szabo.best.vwh.net/smart_contracts_2.html> accessed 20 September 2021

—— 'Formalizing and securing Relationships on Public Networks' (First Monday, 1997) <https://firstmonday.org/ojs/index.php/fm/article/view/548/469> accessed 20 September 2021

—— 'Secure Property Titles with Owner Authority' (1998), <https://nakamotoinstitute.org/secure-property-titles/> accessed 19 July 2021

—— 'A Formal Language for Analyzing Contracts' (2002) <www.fon.hum.uva.nl/rob/Courses/InformationInSpeech/CDROM/Literature/LOTwinterschool2006/szabo.best.vwh.net/contractlanguage.html> last accessed 20 September 2021

UK Jurisdiction Taskforce, 'Legal Statement on Cryptoassets & Smart Contracts' (Tech Nation, November 2019) <https://technation.io/lawtech-uk-resources/#cryptoassets> accessed 29 September 2021

—— 'Digital Dispute Resolution Rules' (Tech Nation, 2021) <https://technation.io/lawtech-uk-resources/> accessed 19 July 2021

Vos G, 'Cryptoassets as property: How Can English Law Boost the Confidence of Would-Be Parties to Smart Legal Contracts?' (Joint Northern Chancery Bar Association and University of Liverpool Lecture, 2 May 2019) <https://www.judiciary.uk/announcements/speech-by-sir-geoffrey-vos-chancellor-of-the-high-court-cryptoassets-as-property> accessed 13 August 2021

Wood G, 'Ethereum: A Secure Decentralised Generalised Transaction Ledger Byzantium Version 69351d5 - 2018-12-10 (2018)' (GitHub 2018) <https://ethereum.github.io/yellowpaper/paper.pdf> accessed 19 July 2021

Chapter 1 (Allen)

Allen JG, 'What's Issued in an ICO? Digital Tokens as Things' (14 March 2018) <https://papers.ssrn.com/sol3/papers.cfm?abstract_id=3140499> accessed 22 September 2021

BIBLIOGRAPHY 457

Amselek P, 'Philosophy of Law and the Theory of Speech Acts' (1998) 1 *Ratio Juris* 187
Atzei N, Bartoletti M, and Cimoli T, 'A Survey of Attacks on Ethereum Smart Contracts (SoK)' in Maffei M and Ryan M (eds), *Principles of Security and Trust: POST 2017 Proceedings* (Springer 2017)
Austin JL, *How to Do Things With Words* (Oxford University Press 1962)
Bacon L, '"Smart Contracts"—The Next Big Battleground?' (2017) *Finance & Credit Law* 1
von Bar C, *Gemeineuropäisches Sachenrecht*, vol 1 (CH Beck 2015)
Barbrook R and Cameron A, 'The Californian Ideology' (1996) 6 *Science as Culture* 44
Bartoletti M and Pompianu L, 'An Empirical Analysis of Smart Contracts: Platforms, Applications, and Design Patterns' in Brenner M and others (eds), *Financial Cryptography and Data Security Proceedings 2017* (Springer 2017)
Bartoletti M and Zunino R, 'A Calculus of Contracting Processes' (University of Trento Technical Report #DISI-09-056, October 2009) <https://citeseerx.ist.psu.edu/viewdoc/download?doi=10.1.1.491.4858&rep=rep1&type=pdf> accessed 5 October 2021
Bentham J, *An Introduction to the Principles of Morals and Legislation* (Burns JH and Hart HLA eds, Athlone 1970)
Brey P, 'The Social Ontology of Virtual Objects' (2003) 62 *American Journal of Economics and Sociology* 269
Brinz A, *Lehrbuch der Pandekten*, vol 1 (2nd edn, Deichert 1873)
Buterin V, 'Ethereum and Oracles' (Ethereum Blog, 22 July 2014) <https://blog.ethereum.org/2014/07/22/ethereum-and-oracles/> accessed 22 September 2021
—— 'On Turing completeness and rich statefulness' (*Twitter*, 18 April 2017) <https://twitter.com/VitalikButerin/status/854271590804140033> accessed 20 September 2021
—— 'Ethereum Whitepaper' (last edited 31 August 2021) <https://ethereum.org/en/whitepaper/> accessed 20 September 2021
Chamber of Digital Commerce, *Smart Contracts: 12 Use Cases for Business and Beyond* (December 2016) <http://digitalchamber.org/assets/smart-contracts-12-use-cases-for-business-and-beyond.pdf> accessed 20 September 2021
Cieplak J and Leefatt S, 'Smart Contracts: A Smart Way to Automate Performance' (2017) 1 *Georgetown Law and Technology Review* 418
Clack CD, Bakshi AV, and Braine L, 'Smart Contract Templates: Foundations, Design Landscape, and Research Directions' (arXiv:1608.00771v3, 15 March 2017) <arxiv.org/pdf/1608.00771v3.pdf> accessed 20 September 2021
Cohn A, West T, and Parker C, 'Smart After All: Blockchain, Smart Contracts, Parametric Insurance, and Smart Energy Grids' (2017) 1 *Georgetown Law and Technology Review* 273
Crosby AW, *The Measure of Reality: Quantification and Western Society 1250-1600* (Cambridge University Press 1997)
Cuccuru P, 'Beyond Bitcoin: An Early Overview on Smart Contracts' (2017) 25 *International Journal of Law and Information Technology* 179
Cunningham A, 'Decentralisation, Distrust & Fear of the Body—The Worrying Rise of Crypto-Law' (2016) 13 *SCRIPTed: A Journal of Law, Technology and Society* 235
Davies PS, 'Interpretation and Rectification in Australia' (2018) 76 *Cambridge Law Journal* 483
Diedrich H, *Ethereum: Blockchains, Digital Assets, Smart Contracts, Decentralised Autonomous Organisations* (CreateSpace 2016)
Fairfield JAT, 'Smart Contracts, Bitcoin Bots, and Consumer Protection' (2014) 71 *Washington & Lee Law Review Online* 35
Ferraris M, *Documentality: Why it is Necessary to Leave Traces* (Richard Davies tr, Fordham University Press 2012)
—— 'Perspectives of Documentality' (2012) 2 *Phenomenology and Mind* 41

—— and Terrengo G, 'Documentality: A Theory of Social Reality' (2014) 57 *Revisti di estetica* 11

Garlick M, 'Creative Commons Version 3.0 Licenses—A Brief Explanation' (*Creative Commons Wiki*) <https://wiki.creativecommons.org/wiki/Version_3> accessed 22 September 2021

Giones F and Brem A, 'From Toys to Tools: The Co-Evolution of Technological and Entrepreneurial Developments in the Drone Industry' (2017) 60 *Business Horizons* 875

Goodrich P, 'Law and Language: An Historical and Critical Introduction' (1984) 11 *Journal of Law and Society* 173

Griggs I, 'Financial Cryptography in 7 Layers' (Financial Cryptography Fourth International Conference, Anguilla, 21–24 February 2000) <http://iang.org/papers/fc7.html> accessed 20 September 2021

—— 'The Ricardian Contract' (Proceedings of the First IEEE International Workshop on Electronic Contracting, San Diego, 6 July 2004) <https://iang.org/papers/ricardian_contract.html> accessed 20 September 2021

—— 'The Sum of All Chains—Let's Converge!' (Financial Cryptography, 29 April 2015) <http://financialcryptography.com/mt/archives/001556.html> accessed 20 September 2021

—— 'On the Intersection of Ricardian and Smart Contracts' (July 2016) <http://iang.org/papers/intersection_ricardian_smart.html> accessed 20 September 2021.

Griggs LD and others, 'Blockchains, Trust and Land Administration: The Return of Historical Provenance' (2017) 6 *Property Law Review* 179

Gunter CA, *Semantics of Programming Languages: Structures and Techniques* (MIT Press 1992)

Hildebrandt M, 'Law as Information in the Era of Data-Driven Agency' (2016) 79 *Modern Law Review* 1

Hohfeld WN, 'Fundamental Legal Conceptions as Applied in Judicial Reasoning' (1917) 26 *Yale Law Journal* 710

IQ Magazine, 'Value of the Global Entertainment and Media Market from 2011 to 2021 (in Trillion U.S. Dollars)' <https://www.statista.com/statistics/237749/value-of-the-global-entertainment-and-media-market/> accessed 13 April 2018

Kharpal A, 'Initial Coin Offerings Have Raised §1.2 Billion and Now Surpass Early Stage VC Funding' (CNBC, 9 August 2018) <http://www.cnbc.com/2017/08/09/initial-coin-offerings-surpass-early-stage-venture-capital-funding.html> accessed 20 September 2021

Klass G, 'Interpretation and Construction in Contract Law' (Georgetown University Law Center 2018) <https://scholarship.law.georgetown.edu/cgi/viewcontent.cgi?article=2971&context=facpu> accessed 22 September 2021

Koepsell DR, *The Ontology of Cyberspace* (Open Court 2000)

—— and Smith B, 'Beyond Paper' (2014) 97 *The Monist* 222

Lamport L, Shostak R, and Pease M, 'The Byzantine Generals Problem' (1982) 4 *ACM Transactions on Programming Languages and Systems* 382

Leibniz GW, 'Elementa Juris Naturalis' in *Sämtliche Schriften und Briefe* vol 1 (Preussische Akademie der Wissenschaften 1930)

Levinson SC, *Pragmatics* (Cambridge University Press 1983)

Lim C, Saw TJ, and Sargeant C, 'Smart Contracts: Bridging the Gap Between Expectation and Reality' (Oxford Business Law Blog, 11 July 2016) <www.law.ox.ac.uk/business-law-blog/blog/2016/07/smart-contracts-bridging-gap-between-expectation-and-reality> accessed 22 September 2021

Lindahl, *Position and Change* (Riedel 1977)

Macaulay S, 'The Real and the Paper Deal: Empirical Pictures of Relationships, Complexity, and the Urge for Transparent Simple Rules' (2003) 66 *Modern Law Review* 44

MacCormick N and Weinberger O, *An Institutional Theory of Law* (Reidel 1986)

Mulligan K (ed), *Speech Act and Sachverhalt: Reinach and the Foundations of Realist Phenomenology* (Springer 1987)

Nakamoto S, 'Bitcoin: A Peer-to-Peer Electronic Cash System' (2008) <https://bitcoin.org/bitcoin.pdf> accessed 20 September 2021

O'Connor R, 'Simplicity: A New Language for Blockchains' (13 December 2017) <https://blockstream.com/simplicity.pdf> accessed 22 September 2021

Outlier Ventures, 'Ecosystem' <https://outlierventures.io/trackers/#ecosystem> accessed 13 April 2018

Post DG, 'How the Internet is Making Jurisdiction Sexy (Again)' (2017) 25 *International Journal of Law and Information Technology* 249

Raskin M, 'The Law and Legality of Smart Contracts' (2017) 1 *Georgetown Law Technology Review* 305

Reinach A, 'The Apriori Foundations of Civil Law' (Crosby JF tr, 1983) 3 *Alatheia* 1

Robertston D, 'Contracts in Crises' [2014] *AMPLA Yearbook* 221

Ruiter DWP, *Legal Institutions* (Kluwer 2001)

Salice A, 'The Phenomenology of the Munich and Göttingen Circles', *The Stanford Encyclopdia of Philosophy* (Fall edn, 2016) <https://plato.stanford.edu/archives/win2016/entries/phenomenology-mg/> last accessed 22 September 2021

Savelyev A, 'Contract Law 2.0: 'Smart' Contracts as the Beginning of the End of Classic Contract Law' (2017) 26 *Information and Communications Technology Law* 116

Schlag P, 'How to Do Things with Hohfeld' (2015) 78 *Law and Contemporary Problems* 185

Shin L, 'Republic of Georgia to Pilot Land Titling on Blockchain with Economist Hernando De Soto, BitFury' (Forbes, 21 April 2016) <https://www.forbes.com/sites/laurashin/2016/04/21/republic-of-georgia-to-pilot-land-titling-on-blockchain-with-economist-hernando-de-soto-bitfury/#57d3903e44da> last accessed 22 September 2021

Siegel D, 'Understanding the DAO Hack' (Coindesk, 25 June 2016) <https://www.coindesk.com/understanding-dao-hack-journalists/> accessed 22 September 2021

Sklaroff JM, 'Smart Contracts and the Cost of Inflexibility' (2017) 166 *University of Pennsylvania Law Review* 263

Smit JP, Buekens F, and du Plessis F, 'Cigarettes, Dollars and Bitcoins—An Essay on the Ontology of Money' (2016) 12 *Journal of Institutional Economics* 327

Smith B, 'How to Do Things with Documents' (2012) 50 *Revisti di estetica* 179

Sommer JH, 'Where is a Bank Account?' (1998) 57 *Maryland Law Review* 1

de Soto H, *The Mystery of Capital* (Black Swan 2000)

Stark J, 'How Close are Smart Contracts to Impacting Real-World Law?' (Coindesk, 11 April 2016) <https://www.coindesk.com/blockchain-smarts-contracts-real-world-law> accessed 22 September 2021

Surden H, 'Computable Contracts' (2012) 46 *UC Davis Law Review* 629

Susskind R, *The End of Lawyers? Rethinking the Nature of Legal Services* (Oxford University Press 2010)

Sventsson D, 'The Holy Trinity of Legal Fictions Undermining The Application of Law to the Global Internet' (2015) 23 *International Journal of Law and Information Technology* 219

Szabo N, 'Smart Contracts: Building Blocks for Digital Markets' (1996) <www.fon.hum.uva.nl/rob/Courses/InformationInSpeech/CDROM/Literature/LOTwinterschool2006/szabo.best.vwh.net/smart_contracts_2.html> accessed 20 September 2021

—— 'Formalizing and Securing Relationships on Public Networks' (First Monday, 1997) <https://firstmonday.org/ojs/index.php/fm/article/view/548/469> accessed 20 September 2021

—— 'A Formal Language for Analyzing Contracts' (2002) <www.fon.hum.uva.nl/rob/Courses/InformationInSpeech/CDROM/Literature/LOTwinterschool2006/szabo.best.vwh.net/contractlanguage.html> accessed 20 September 2021

—— 'The Dawn of Trustworthy Computing' ('Unenumerated' blog, 11 December 2014) <http://unenumerated.blogspot.de/2014/12/the-dawn-of-trustworthy-computing.html> accessed 20 September 2021

—— 'Wet Code and Dry' ('Unenumerated' blog, 24 August 2008) <http://unenumerated.blogspot.de/2006/11/wet-code-and-dry.html> last accessed 22 September 2021

Tai ETT, 'Formalising Contract Law for Smart Contracts' (2017) Tilburg Private Law Working Paper Series 06/2017 <www.ssrn.com/link/Tilburg-Private_Law.html> accessed 13 April 2018

Tan ZX, 'Beyond the Real and the Paper Deal: The Quest for Contractual Coherence in Contractual Interpretation' (2016) 79 *Modern Law Review* 623

The Merkle, 'Eastern Blockchain—Financial Liberation Through Crowdsales' (24 July 2017) <https://themerkle.com/eastern-blockchain-financial-liberation-through-crowdsales/> accessed 5 October 2021

Thierer D and Crews CW, 'The Libertarian Vision for Telecom and High-Technology' (Cato Institute, 3 April 2001), <www.cato.org/publications/techknowledge/libertarian-vision-telecom-hightechnology> accessed 22 September 2021

Thomason RH, 'Conditionals and Action Logics' (AAAI Spring Symposium 'Commonsense 2007', Stanford University, 26–28 March 2007) <www.ucl.ac.uk/commonsense07> accessed 22 September 2021

Turner R and Eden AH, 'Towards a Programming Language Ontology' in Dodig-Crnkovic G and Stuart S (eds), *Computation, Information, Cognition—The Nexus and the Liminal* (Cambridge Scholars Press 2008)

Vogenauer S and Kleinheisterkamp J (eds), *Commentary on the UNIDROIT Principles of International Commercial Contracts* (Oxford University Press 2009)

Vos G, 'Contractual Interpretation: Do Judges Sometimes Say One Thing and do Another?' (2017) 23 *Canterbury Law Review* 1

Walport M, *Distributed Ledger Technology: Beyond Block Chain* (UK Government Office for Science 2016)

Werbach K and Cornell N, 'Contracts Ex Machina' (2017) 67 *Duke Law Journal* 313

Chapter 2 (Vos)

Allen JG, 'Wrapped and Stacked: "Smart Contracts" and the Interaction of Natural and Formal Language' (2018) 14 *European Review of Contract Law* 307

—— 'Negotiability in Digital Environments' [2019] July/August *Butterworths Journal of International Banking and Financial Law* 459

—— 'Property in Digital Coins' (2019) 8 *European Journal of Property Law* 1

Blandin A and others, 'Global Cryptoasset Regulatory Landscape Study' (Cambridge Centre for Alternative Finance, 16 April 2019), <https://www.jbs.cam.ac.uk/faculty-research/centres/alternative-finance/publications/cryptoasset-regulation/#.XO5PXaRS-Uk> accessed 27 September 2021

Cieplak J and Leefatt S, 'Smart Contracts: A Smart Way to Automate Performance' (2017) 1 *Georgetown Law and Technology Review* 418

Clifford Chance, 'Are Smart Contracts Contracts?' (August 2017) <http://globalmandatool kit.cliffordchance.com/downloads/Smart_Contracts.pdf> accessed 8 July 2021

Cohn A, West T, and Parker C, 'Smart After All: Blockchain, Smart Contracts, Parametric Insurance, and Smart Energy Grids' (2017) 1 *Georgetown Law and Technology Review* 273

Cuccuru P, 'Beyond Bitcoin: An Early Overview on Smart Contracts' (2017) 25 *International Journal of Law and Information Technology* 179

DuPont Q, 'A History and Ethnography of "The DAO", A Failed Decentralized Autonomous Organization' in Campbell-Verduyn M (ed), *Bitcoin and Beyond: Cryptocurrencies, Blockchains, and Global Governance* (Routledge 2017)

Durovic M and Janssen A, 'The Formation of Blockchain-based Smart Contracts in Light of Contract Law' (2018) 6 *European Review of Contract Law* 753

Falkon S, 'The Story of the DAO—Its History and Consequences' (Start It Up, 25 December 2017) <https://medium.com/swlh/the-story-of-the-dao-its-history-and-consequences-71e6a8a551ee> accessed 27 September 2021

Fox D and Green S, *Cryptocurrencies in Public and Private Law* (Oxford University Press 2019)

Gleeson S, *The Legal Concept of Money* (Oxford University Press 2018)

Hodge P, 'The Potential and Perils of Financial Technology: Can the Law Adapt to Cope?' (The First Edinburgh FinTech Law Lecture, 14 March 2019) <https://www.supremecourt.uk/docs/speech-190314.pdf> accessed 27 September 2021

Iansiti M and Lakhani K, 'The Truth About Blockchain' (2017) 1 *Harvard Business Review* 118

International Swaps and Derivates Association, 'Legal Guidelines for Smart Derivatives Contracts: Introduction' (January 2019) <https://www.isda.org/a/MhgME/Legal-Guideli nes-for-Smart-Derivatives-Contracts-Introduction.pdf> accessed 27 September 2021

—— 'Legal Guidelines for Smart Derivatives Contracts: The ISDA Master Agreement' (February 2019) <https://www.isda.org/a/23iME/Legal-Guidelines-for-Smart-Derivati ves-Contracts-ISDA-Master-Agreement.pdf> accessed 27 September 2021

Jenkinson G, 'IBM's Blockchain Patents: From Food-Tracking and Shipping to IoT and Security Solutions' (Cointelegraph, 15 October 2018) <https://cointelegraph.com/news/ ibms-blockchain-patents-from-food-tracking-to-iot-and-security-soluti ons> accessed 27 September 2021

King & Wood Mallesons, 'Smart Derivatives Contracts: From Concept to Construction' (Whitepaper, October 2018) <https://www.isda.org/a/cHvEE/Smart-Derivatives-Contra cts-From-Concept-to-Construction-Oct-2018.pdf> accessed 27 September 2021

Pollock F, 'What is a Thing?' (1894) 10 Law Quarterly Review 318

Rogers JS, 'Negotiability, Property, and Identity' (1990) 12 *Cardozo Law Review* 471

—— Fenleigh HJ and Sanitt A, 'Arbitrating Smart Contract Disputes' (2017) 9 *Norton Rose Fulbright International Arbitration Report* 21

Savelyev A, 'Contract Law 2.0: 'Smart' Contracts as the Beginning of the End of Classic Contract Law' (2017) 26 *Information and Communications Technology Law* 116

Sklaroff JM, 'Smart Contracts and the Cost of Inflexibility' (2017) 166 *University of Pennsylvania Law Review* 263

Smart Dubai, 'Smart Dubai 2021' (2021) <https://2021.smartdubai.ae> accessed 8 July 2021

Szabo N, 'Smart Contracts: Building Blocks for Digital Markets' (1996) <www.fon.hum. uva.nl/rob/Courses/InformationInSpeech/CDROM/Literature/LOTwinterschool2006/ szabo.best.vwh.net/smart_contracts_2.html> accessed 20 September 2021

The Law Society, 'Lawtech' <https://www.lawsociety.org.uk/campaigns/lawtech> accessed 8 July 2021

UK Jurisdiction Taskforce, 'Legal Statement on Cryptoassets & Smart Contracts' (Tech Nation, November 2019) <https://technation.io/lawtech-uk-resources/#cryptoassets> accessed 29 September 2021

Werbach K and Cornell N, 'Contracts Ex Machina' (2017) 67 *Duke Law Journal* 313

Chapter 3 (Abdullah and Goh)

Allen JG, 'Wrapped and Stacked: "Smart Contracts" and the Interaction of Natural and Formal Language' (2018) 14 *European Review of Contract Law* 307

Allen T and Widdison R, 'Can Computers Make Contracts' (1996) 9 *Harvard Journal of Law & Technology* 25

Atiyah PS, *Essays on Contract* (Oxford University Press 1990)

Chopra S and White L, 'Artificial Agents and the Contracting Problem: A Solution via an Agency Analysis' (2009) 2 *Journal of Law, Technology & Policy* 363

Gal MS, 'Algorithmic Challenges to Autonomous Choice' (2018) 25 *Michigan Technology Law Review* 59

Mik E, 'Smart Contracts: A Requiem' (2019) 36 *Journal of Contract Law* 70

Paech P, 'Law and Autonomous Systems Series: What is a Smart Contract?' (Oxford Business Law Blog, 9 July 2018) <https://www.law.ox.ac.uk/business-law-blog/blog/2018/07/law-and-autonomous-systems-series-what-smart-contract> accessed 28 September 2021

Savelyev A, 'Contract Law 2.0: 'Smart' Contracts as the Beginning of the End of Classic Contract Law' (2017) 26 *Information and Communications Technology Law* 116

Scholz LH, 'Algorithmic Contracts' (2017) 20 *Stanford Technology Law Review* 128

Chapter 4 (Estcourt)

Allen JG, 'Wrapped and Stacked: "Smart Contracts" and the Interaction of Natural and Formal Language' (2018) 14 *European Review of Contract Law* 307

Aouidef Y, Ast F, and Deffains B, 'Decentralised Justice: A Comparative Analysis of Blockchain Online Dispute Resolution Projects' (2021) 4 *Frontiers in Blockchain*, Article 564551

Aragon, 'Aragon Network Whitepaper' (Github, 18 July 2019) <https://github.com/aragon/whitepaper> accessed 28 September 2021

Buterin V, 'Ethereum and Oracles' (Ethereum Blog, 22 July 2014) <https://blog.ethereum.org/2014/07/22/ethereum-and-oracles/> accessed 22 September 2021

Esterbrook FH, 'Cyberspace and the Law of the Horse' [1996] *University of Chicago Legal Forum* 207

Ethereum Foundation, 'Welcome to Ethereum' <https://ethereum.org> accessed 8 July 2021

George W, 'Kleros and Mob Justice: Can the Wisdom of the Crowd Go Wrong?' (Kleros Blog, 4 June 2018) <https://medium.com/kleros/kleros-and-mob-justice-can-the-wisdom-of-the-crowd-go-wrong-ef311209ea36> accessed 28 September 2021

Hodge P, 'The Potentials and Perils of Financial Technology: Can the Law Adapt to Cope?' (First Edinburgh Fintech Law Lecture, University of Edinburgh, 14 March 2019) <https://www.supremecourt.uk/docs/speech-190314.pdf> accessed 28 September 2021

Howell BE and Potgieter PH, 'Uncertainty and Dispute Resolution for Blockchain and Smart Contract Institutions' [2021] *Journal of Institutional Economics* 1

Jur, 'White Paper' (v3.0.0, March 2021) <https://jur.io/wp-content/uploads/2021/03/jur-white-paper-v.3.0.0.pdf> accessed 28 September 2021

Kleros, 'The Kleros Juror Startet Kit' (Kleros Blog) <https://blog.kleros.io/the-kleros-juror-starter-kit/> accessed 8 July 2021

Lesaege C and Ast F, 'Kleros, Short Paper v1.0.7' (Kleros, September 2019) <https://kleros.io/whitepaper.pdf > accessed 8 July 2021

Lessig L, 'The New Chicago School' (1998) 27 *Journal of Legal Studies* 661

—— 'The Law of the Horse: What Cyberspace Might Teach' (1999) 113 *Harvard Law Review* 501

Nappert S and Ast F, 'Decentralised Justice: Reinventing Arbitration for the Digital Age?' (Global Arbitration Review, 1 May 2020) <https://globalarbitrationreview.com/decentralised-justice-reinventing-arbitration-the-digital-age> accessed 28 September 2021

Thomson Reuters, 'Cryptoeconomics: Can blockchain reinvent justice systems?' <https://blogs.thomsonreuters.com/answerson/cryptoeconomics-blockchain-reinvent-justice-sytems-kleros/> accessed 8 July 2021

UK Jurisdiction Taskforce, 'Digital Dispute Resolution Rules' (Tech Nation) <https://technation.io/lawtech-uk-resources/#rules> accessed 28 September 2021

UNIDROIT, 'Digital Assets and Private Law' <https://www.unidroit.org/work-in-progress/digital-assets-and-private-law/> accessed 8 July 2021

Chapter 5 (Grigg)

Brown RG and others, 'Corda: An Introduction' (2016) <docs.corda.net/en/pdf/corda-introductory-whitepaper.pdf>

Chaum D, 'Blind Signatures for Untraceable Payments' (1983) 82(3) *Advances in Cryptology Proceedings of Crypto* 199–203

Clack C, Bakshi V, and Braine L, 'Smart Contract Templates: Foundations, Design Landscape and Research Directions' (2016) Barclays Working Paper <arxiv.org/abs/1608.00771>

Del Giudice M, Evangelista F, and Palmaccio M, 'Defining the Black and Scholes Approach: A First Systematic Literature Review' (2015) 5 *Journal of Innovation and Entrepreneurship* 5

Grigg I, 'How We Raised Capital at 0%, Saved Our Creditors from an Accounting Nightmare, Gave Our Suppliers a Discount and Got to Bed Before Midnight' (2003) <iang.org/rants/systemics_psd.html>

Grigg I, 'The Ricardian Contract' (2004) IEEE 1st Workshop on Electronic Contracting <iang.org/papers/ricardian_contract.html>

Grigg I, 'An Open Audit of an Open Certification Authority' (2008) 22nd Large Installation Systems Administration Conference (LISA 2008) <//iang.org/papers/open_audit_lisa.html>

Grigg I, 'The Inverted Pyramid of Identity' (2009) <http://financialcryptography.com/mt/archives/001165.html>

Grigg I, 'The Sum of all Chains—let's converge' (2015) <financialcryptography.com/mt/archives/001556.html>

Grigg I, 'The Governed Blockchain' (2018) <iang.org/papers/the_governed_blockchain.html>

Grigg I, 'On the Intersection of Ricardian and Smart Contracts' (2015) <iang.org/papers/intersection_ricardian_smart.html>

Howland G, 'The Development of an Open and Flexible Payment System' (1996) <systemics.com/docs/sox/overview.html>

Kerckhoffs A, 'La cryptographie militaire ("Military Cryptography")' (1883) IX *Journal des sciences militaires* 5–38, Jan 1883, pp 161–91, Feb 1883

van der Koogh E, 'Ricardian Contracts in XML' (2001) *Edinburgh Financial Cryptography Engineering* 01 Conference

Miller MS, Morningstar C, and Franz B, 'Capability-based Financial Instruments—an Ode to the Granovetter Operator' (2000) *Financial Cryptography* 2000

Odom C, 'Open-Transactions: Secure Contracts between Untrusted Parties' (2015) <www.opentransactions.org/open-transactions.pdf> accessed 6 June 2016

Odom C, 'Sample Currency Contract' (2013) <opentransactions.org/wiki/index.php/Sample_Currency_Contract> accessed 6 June 2016

Sanitt A and Grigg I, 'Legal analysis of the governed blockchain' (2018) NortonRoseFulbright and block.one <www.nortonrosefulbright.com/en/knowledge/publications/0d56a3a5/legal-analysis-of-the-governed-blockchain>

Steigler M, 'An Introduction to Petnames' (2005) <www.skyhunter.com/marcs/petnames/IntroPetNames.html>

Systemics Inc, 'Pre-Paid Services Dollar Ricardian Contract' (2003) <webfunds.org/ricardo/contracts/systemics/Systemics_PSD_a.html>

Szabo N, 'Smart Contracts' (1994) <web.archive.org/web/20011102030833/http://szabo.best.vwh.net/smart.contracts.html>

Webfunds Project, 'Ricardian contracts' <webfunds.org/guide/ricardian.html>

Wilcox-O'Hearn B, 'Names: Decentralized, Secure, Human-Meaningful—Choose Two' (2001)

Wittenberger JF, 'Askemos—A Distributed Settlement' (2002) <citeseerx.ist.psu.edu/viewdoc/summary?doi=10.1.1.11.5050>

Chapter 6 (Rius)

Abbott R, 'The Reasonable Computer: Disrupting the Paradigm of Tort Liability' (2018) 86 *George Washington Law Review* 1–45

Ahluwalia S, Mahto RV, and Guerrero M, 'Blockchain Technology and Startup Financing: A Transaction Cost Economics Perspective' (2020) 151 *Technological Forecasting and Social Change* 1

Akerlof GA, 'The Market for "Lemons": Quality Uncertainty and the Market Mechanism' (1970) 84 *Quarterly Journal of Economics* 488

Al Khalil F and others, 'Trust in Smart Contracts is a Process, As Well' in Brenner M and others (eds), *Financial Cryptography and Data Security*, vol 10323 (Springer: Lecture Notes in Computer Science 2017) 510

Alharby M and van Moorsel A, 'Blockchain-Based Smart Contracts: A Systematic Mapping Study' (2017) 9 *International Journal of Computer Science and Information Technology* 151

Allen, DW, 'Transaction Costs' in Bouckaert BRA and de Geest G (eds), *Encyclopedia of Law and Economics* (Edward Elgar Publishing 2000)

—— Lane AM and Poblet M, 'The Governance of Blockchain Dispute Resolution' (2020) 25 *Harvard Negotiation Law Review* 75

—— and others, 'Blockchain and the Evolution of Institutional Technologies: Implications for Innovation Policy' (2020) 49 *Research Policy* 103865

Allen JG, 'Wrapped and Stacked: Smart Contracts and the Interaction of Natural Language and Formal Language' (2018) 14 *European Review of Contract Law* 307

Armour J and others, 'Putting Technology to Good Use for Society: The Role of Corporate, Competition and Tax Law' (2018) ECGI Law Working Paper No 427/8

Atzei N and others, 'SoK: Unraveling Bitcoin Smart Contracts' in Bauer L and Küsters R (eds), *Principles of Security and Trust*, vol 10804 (Springer: Lecture Notes in Computer Science 2018)

Baker G, Gibbons R, and Murphy, KJ, 'Implicit Contracts and the Theory of the Firm' (1997) NBER Working Paper 6177

Baron J, 'Heuristics and Biases' in Zamir E, and Teichman D (eds), *The Oxford Handbook of Behavioral Economics and Law* (OUP 2014)

Bartoletti M, and Pompianu L, 'An empirical analysis of smart contracts: platforms, applications, and design patterns' in Brenner M and others (eds), *Financial Cryptography and Data Security*, vol 10323 (Springer: Lecture Notes in Computer Science 2017)

Beale H (ed), *Chitty on Contracts* (31st edn, Sweet & Maxwell 2012)

Bingham T, *The Rule of Law* (Penguin 2013)

Binmore K, 'Game Theory and Institutions' (2010) 38(3) *Journal of Comparative Economics* 245–52

Bourque S and Tsui, SFL, *A Lawyer's Introduction to Smart Contracts* (Lask: Scientia Nobilitat 2014)

British Standards Institution, 'Blockchain and Distributed Ledger Technologies—Overview of and Interactions Between Smart Contracts in Blockchain and Distributed Technology Systems' (2019) ISO/TR 23455

Brown RG, 'On the blockchain, nobody knows you're a fridge' (2013) <https://gendal.me/2013/10/23/on-the-blockchain-nobody-knows-youre-a-fridge/> accessed 5 October 2021

Brown WJ and others, *AntiPatterns: Refactoring Software, Architectures, and Projects in Crisis* (Wiley 1998)

Buterin V, 'A Next-Generation Smart Contract and Decentralized Application Platform' (2013) <https://ethereum.org/en/whitepaper/> accessed 8 July 2021

—— 'Software and Bounded Rationality' (2014) <https://blog.ethereum.org/2014/09/02/software-bounded-rationality/> accessed 8 July 2021

Byrne P, 'The LAO, Demystified' (2019) <https://prestonbyrne.com/2019/09/03/the-lao-demystified/> accessed 8 July 2021

Carter N, 'A Cross-Sectional Overview of Cryptoasset Governance and Implications for Investors' (MSc thesis, University of Edinburgh 2017)

—— 'Blockchain is a Semantic Wasteland' (2018 <https://medium.com/s/story/blockchain-is-a-semantic-wasteland-9450b6e5012> accessed 8 July 2021

Christensen CM, Raynor ME, and McDonald R, 'What Is Disruptive Innovation?' (December 2015) *Harvard Business Review* 44–53

Clack CD, Bakshi VA, and Braine L, 'Smart Contract Templates: Foundations, Design Landscape and Research Directions' (2016–2017) arXiv:1608.00771

—— 'Smart Contract Templates: essential requirements and design options' (2016) arXiv:1612.04496

Coase RH, 'The Problem of Social Cost' (1960) 3 *Journal of Law and Economics* 1

Cohney S and others, 'Coin-Operated Capitalism' (2019) 119 *Columbia Law Review* 591

Colombo C, Ellul J, and Pace GJ, 'Contracts Over Smart Contracts: Recovering from Violations Dynamically' in Margaria T and Steffen B (eds), *Leveraging Applications of Formal Methods, Verification and Validation*, vol 11247 (Springer: Lecture Notes in Computer Science 2018)

Conte de Leon D and others, 'Blockchain: properties and misconceptions' (2017) 11 *Asia Pacific Journal of Innovation and Entrepreneurship* 286

Cunningham A, 'Decentralisation, Distrust & Fear of the Body—The Worrying Rise of Crypto-Law' (2016) 13 *SCRIPTed* 236–57

Czarnecki J, 'Between tradition and progress: The role of smart contracts in the lawyer's toolkit' (2017) <https://blog.neufund.org/between-tradition-and-progress-the-role-of-smart-contracts-in-the-lawyers-toolkit-dfec8f26bab9> accessed 8 July 2021

Dahlman C, 'The Problem of Externality' (1979) 22 *Journal of Law and Economics* 141

Danziger S, Levav, J, and Avnaim-Pesso, L, 'Extraneous factors in judicial decisions' (2011) 108 *Proceedings of the National Academy of Sciences* 6889

Davidson S, De Filippi P, and Potts J, 'Economics of Blockchain' (2016) Public Choice Conference (Fort Lauderdale, US, May 2016)

Dequech D, 'Uncertainty: A Typology and Refinements of Existing Concepts' (2011) XLV(3) *Journal of Economic Issues* XLV 621

Djankov S and others, 'The new comparative economics' (2003) 31 *Journal of Comparative Economics* 595

Drescher D, *Blockchain Basics: A Non-Technical Introduction in 25 Steps* (Apress 2017)

Dyer JH and Chu W, 'The Role of Trustworthiness in Reducing Transaction Costs and Improving Performance: Empirical Evidence from the United States, Japan, and Korea' (2003) 14 *Organization Science* 57

Eisenhardt KM, 'Agency Theory: An Assessment and Review' (1989) 14 *The Academy of Management Review* 57

European Union Blockchain Observatory & Forum, 'Blockchain and the Future of Digital Assets' (2020), <https://www.eublockchainforum.eu/sites/default/files/report_digital_assets_v1.0.pdf> accessed 8 July 2021

Fisher R and Ury W, *Getting To Yes: Negotiating an agreement without giving in* (Random House 2012)

Foley S, Karlsen JR, and Putniņš TJ, 'Sex, Drugs and Bitcoin: How Much Illegal Activity Is Financed Through Cryptocurrencies?' (2019) 32 *Review of Financial Studies* 1798

Friedman D, *Contracts in Cyberspace* (2000) *Berkeley Program in Law and Economics*

Fukuyama F, *Trust: The Social Virtues and the Creation of Prosperity* (The Free Press 1996)

Galanter M, 'Why the "Haves" Come Out Ahead: Speculations on the Limits of Legal Change' (1974) 9 *Law and Society Review* 95

Gans JS, 'The Fine Print in Smart Contracts' (2019) NBER Working Paper, No 25443

Gilson RJ, 'Value Creation by Business Lawyers: Legal Skills and Asset Pricing' (1984) 94 *Yale Law Journal* 239

Gilson RJ, Sabel CF, and Scott RE 'Braiding: The Interaction of Formal and Informal Contracting in Theory, Practice and Doctrine' (2010) *Stanford Law and Economics* Olin Working Paper No 389

Goorha P, 'Blockchains as Implementable Mechanisms: Crypto-Ricardian Rent and a Crypto-Coase Theorem' (2018) 1 *Journal of the British Blockchain Association* 1

Gosher Z and Squire R, 'Principal Costs: A New Theory for Corporate Law and Governance' (2017) 117 *Columbia Law Review* 767–829

Greenspan G, 'Smart contracts: The good, the bad and the lazy' (2015) <https://www.multichain.com/blog/2015/11/smart-contracts-good-bad-lazy> accessed 8 July 2021

Grigg I, 'The Ricardian Contract' (2004) *Proceedings of the First IEEE International Workshop on Electronic Contracting*

—— 'On the intersection of Ricardian and Smart Contracts' (2015)
—— 'Seeking Consensus on Consensus: DPOS or Delegated Proof of Stake and the Two Generals Problem' (2017) <https://steemit.com/eos/@iang/seeking-consensus-on-consensus-dpos-or-delegated-proof-of-stake-and-the-two-generals-problem> accessed 8 July 2021
—— 'The Governed Blockchain' (2018) <https://www.iang.org/papers/the_governed_blockchain.html> accessed 8 July 2021
—— 'Implementations of Ricardian contracts' <https://www.webfunds.org/guide/ricardian_implementations.html> accessed 8 July 2021
Gupta M, 'How to make smart contracts upgradeable!' (2018) <https://hackernoon.com/how-to-make-smart-contracts-upgradable-2612e771d5a2> accessed 8 July 2021
Hadfield GK, 'The Many Legal Institutions that Support Contractual Commitment' in Menard C and Shirley M (eds), *Handbook of New Institutional Economics* (Kluwer Academic Publishers 2004)
Hadfield GK and Weingast BR, 'Microfoundations of the Rule of Law' (2014) 17 *Annual Review of Political Science* 21
Harbison WS, 'Trusting in Computer Systems' (December 1997) University of Cambridge Computer Laboratory Technical Report No 437
Hart O and Moore J, 'Incomplete Contracts and Renegotiation' (1988) 56 *Econometrica* 755
—— and Moore J, 'Contracts as Reference Points' (2008) 123 *Quarterly Journal of Economics* 1
Hayek FA, 'The Use of Knowledge in Society' (1945) 35 *American Economic Review* 519
Hazard J and Haapio H, 'Wise Contracts: Smart Contracts that Work for People and Machines' in Schweighofer E and others (eds), *Trends and Communities of Legal Informatics* (Österreichische Computer Gesellschaft 2017) 425
Hobbes T, *Leviathan or The Matter, Forme and Power of a Common-Wealth Ecclesiasticall and Civil* (Andrew Cooke 1651)
Hodgson GM, 'What are Institutions?' (2006) 40 *Journal of Economic Issues* 1–25
Holden R, and Malani A, 'Can Blockchain Solve the Holdup Problem in Contracts?' (2017) University of Chicago Coase-Sandor Institute for Law & Economics Research Paper No 846
Holmes OW, *The Common Law* (Little, Brown and Company 1881)
Hughes E, 'A Cypherpunk's Manifesto' (1993) <https://www.activism.net/cypherpunk/manifesto.html> accessed 8 July 2021
IMF, 'Fintech: The Experience So Far' (2019) Policy Paper No 19/024
ISDA and KWM, 'Practical Framework for Constructing Smart Derivatives Contracts' (2018)
—— and Linklaters, 'Smart Contracts and Distributed Ledger—A Legal Perspective' (2017) <https://www.isda.org/2017/08/03/smart-contracts-and-distributed-ledger-a-legal-perspective/> accessed 8 July 2021
—— and others, 'Private International Law Aspects of Smart Derivatives Contracts Utilizing Distributed Ledger Technology' (2020) <https://www.isda.org/2020/01/13/private-international-law-aspects-of-smart-derivatives-contracts-utilizing-distributed-ledger-technology/> accessed 8 July 2021
Jaffee SM, and Morton J, *Marketing Africa's High-Value Foods: Comparative Experiences of an Emergent Private Sector* (Kendall/Hunt 1995)
Juuti M and others, 'Stay On-Topic: Generating Context-specific Fake Restaurant Reviews' in Lopez J, Zhou J, and Soriano M (eds), *Computer Security*, vol 11098 (Lecture Notes in Computer Science 2018)

Kaal WA, 'Blockchain Solutions for Agency Problems in Corporate Governance' in Balachandran KR (ed), *Economic Information to Facilitate Decision Making* (World Scientific Publishers 2019)

Koulu R, *Law, Technology and Dispute Resolution: The Privatisation of Coercion* (Routledge 2019)

Kary JH, 'Contract Law and the Social Contract: What Legal History Can Teach Us About the Political Theory of Hobbes and Locke' (1999) 31 *Ottawa Law Review* 73

Kasireddy P, 'How Does Distributed Consensus Work?' (2018) <https://medium.com/s/story/lets-take-a-crack-at-understanding-distributed-consensus-dad23d0dc95> accessed 8 July 2021

Shepsle K, 'Discretion, Institutions, and the Problem of Government Commitment' in Bourdieu P and Coleman K (eds), *Social Theory for a Changing Society* (Westview Press 1991)

Kaivanto K and Prince D, 'Risks and Transaction Costs of Distributed-Ledger Fintech Boundary Effects and Consequences' (2017) arXiv:1702.08478

Khan BZ, '"To Have and Have Not": Are Rich Litigious Parties Favoured In Court?' (2015) NBER Working Paper 20945

Klass G, 'Efficient Breach' in Klass G, Letsas G, and Saprai P (eds), *Philosophical Foundations of Contract Law* (Oxford University Press 2014)

Klein PG, 'New Institutional Economics' in Bouckaert BRA and de Geest G (eds), *Encyclopedia of Law and Economics* (Edward Elgar Publishing 2000)

Knight F, *Risk, Uncertainty and Profit* (Houghton Mifflin Company 1921)

Koens T and Poll E, 'Assessing Interoperability Solutions for Distributed Ledgers' (2019) *Pervasive and Mobile Computing* 101079

Kronman AT, 'Contract Law and the State of Nature' (1985) 1 *Journal of Law, Economics and Organisation* 5

Lamport L, 'Time, Clocks, and the Ordering of Events in a Distributed System' (1978) 21 *Communications of the ACM* 558

Larimer D, 'EOS Technical White Paper' (2017) <https://github.com/EOSIO/Documentation/blob/master/TechnicalWhitePaper.md> accessed 8 July 2021

Lehdonvirta V, 'The blockchain paradox: Why distributed ledger technologies may do little to transform the economy' (Oxford Internet Institute Blog, 2016) <https://www.oii.ox.ac.uk/blog/the-blockchain-paradox-why-distributed-ledger-technologies-may-do-little-to-transform-the-economy/> accessed 8 July 2021

—— and Robleh A, 'Governance and Regulation' in UK Government Office for Science, *Distributed Ledger Technology: beyond block chain* (2019)

Lessig L, 'Code is Law' *Harvard Magazine* (January-February 2000)

—— *Code Version 2.0* (Basic Books 2006)

Levine M, 'Money Stuff' *Bloomberg* (12 October 2018)

Lim C, Saw TJ and Sargeant C, 'Smart contracts: Bridging the gap between expectation and reality' (Oxford Business Law Blog, 2016) <https://www.law.ox.ac.uk/business-law-blog/blog/2016/07/smart-contracts-bridging-gap-between-expectation-and-reality> accessed 8 July 2021

Lipshaw JM, 'The Persistence of 'Dumb' Contracts' [2019] *Stanford Journal of Blockchain Law & Policy* 29

Lopp J, 'Bitcoin and the Rise of the Cypherpunks' (CoinDesk, 9 April 2016) <https://www.coindesk.com/the-rise-of-the-cypherpunks> last accessed 8 July 2021

—— 'Bitcoin Timestamp Security' (2019) <https://blog.lopp.net/bitcoin-timestamp-security/> accessed 8 July 2021

Maker Foundation, 'The Maker Protocol: MakerDAO's Multi-Collateral Dai (MCD) System' (2019-2021 <https://makerdao.com/en/whitepaper/> accessed 8 July 2021

Marino B, 'Smart-Contract Escape Hatches: The Dao of The DAO' (2016) <https://hackingdistributed.com/2016/06/22/smart-contract-escape-hatches/> accessed 8 July 2021

—— and Juels A, 'Setting Standards for Altering and Undoing Smart Contracts' in Alferes JJ and others (eds), *Rule Technologies. Research, Tools, and Applications*, vol 9718 (Lecture Notes in Computer Science 2016)

Martinez AG, and Remolina R, 'The Law and Finance of Initial Coin Offerings' (2018) Ibero-American Institute for Law and Finance Working Paper No. 4/2018

Mason S, and Cheng D, *Electronic Evidence* (4th edn, Institute of Advanced Legal Studies 2017)

Mason S, and Reiniger TS, '"Trust" Between Machines? Establishing Identity Between Humans and Software Code, or whether You Know it is a Dog, and if so, which Dog?' (2015) 5 *Computer and Telecommunications Law Review* 135

Mattereum, 'Smart Property Registers' (2019-2020) <https://mattereum.com/wp-content/uploads/2020/02/mattereum_workingpaper.pdf> accessed 8 July 2021

May T, 'The Crypto Anarchist Manifesto' (1988) <https://www.activism.net/cypherpunk/crypto-anarchy.html> accessed 8 July 2021

McCorduck P, *Machines Who Think: A Personal Enquiry Into the History and Prospects of Artificial Intelligence* (2nd edn, Routledge 2004)

Mik E, 'Smart contracts: Terminology, technical limitations and real world complexity' (2017) 9 *Law, Innovation and Technology* 269

Miller B, 'Smart Contracts and the Role of Lawyers—About "Code is Law"' (2016) <http://biglawkm.com/2016/10/20/smart-contracts-and-the-role-of-lawyers-part-1-about-smart-contracts/> accessed 8 July 2021

Miller MS, 'Computer Security as the Future of Law' (EXTRO 3 conference, 9 August 1997)

—— 'Observations on AMIX, The American Information Exchange' (1999)

—— Morningstar C and Frantz B, 'Capability-based financial instruments' in Frankel Y (ed), *Financial Cryptography*, vol 1962 (Springer: Lecture Notes in Computer Science 2000) 349

—— and Stiegler M, 'The Digital Path: Smart Contracts and the Third World' in Birner J and Garrouste P (eds), *Markets, Information and Communication: Austrian Perspectives on the Internet Economy* (Routledge 2003)

Mills D and others, 'Distributed ledger technology in payment, clearing and settlement' (2016) Board of Governors of the Federal Reserve System, Finance and Economics Discussion Series 2016-095

Mnookin RH, and Kornhauser L, 'Bargaining in the Shadow of the Law: The Case of Divorce' (1979) 88 *Yale Law Journal* 950

Morningstar C, 'What Agoric Learned from the American Information Exchange About Online Markets' (2020) <https://medium.com/agoric/what-agoric-learned-from-the-american-information-exchange-about-online-markets-91922fc49618> accessed 8 July 2021

Nakamoto S, 'Bitcoin: A Peer-to-Peer Electronic Cash System' (2008) <https://bitcoin.org/en/bitcoin-paper> accessed 8 July 2021

Niehans J, 'Transaction Costs' in Eatwell, J and others (eds), *The New Palgrave: A Dictionary of Economics* (Macmillan 1987)

Nooteboom B, 'Social capital, institutions and trust' (2007) 65 *Review of Social Economy* 29

North DC, 'Institutions' (1991) 5 *Journal of Economic Perspectives* 97

—— 'Transaction Costs, Institutions and Economic Performance' (1992) International Center for Economic Growth, Occasional Papers Number 30

—— 'Institutions and Credible Commitment' (1993) 149 *Journal of Institutional and Theoretical Economics* 11

—— and Wallis JJ, 'Integrating Institutional Change and Technical Change in Economic History: A Transaction Cost Approach' (1994) 150 *Journal of Institutional and Theoretical Economics* 609

—— Wallis, JJ, and Weingast BR, *Violence and Social Orders: A Conceptual Framework for Interpreting Human Recorded History* (CUP 2013)

Norton Rose Fulbright, 'Can smart contracts be legally binding contracts?' (2016), <https://www.nortonrosefulbright.com/en-ca/knowledge/publications/a90a5588/can-smart-contracts-be-legally-binding-contracts> accessed 8 July 2021

—— 'Legal analysis of the governed blockchain' (2018) <https://www.nortonrosefulbright.com/en/knowledge/publications/0d56a3a5/legal-analysis-of-the-governed-blockchain> accessed 8 July 2021

OpenLaw, 'The LAO: A For-Profit, Limited Liability Autonomous Organization' (2019), <https://medium.com/openlawofficial/the-lao-a-for-profit-limited-liability-autonomous-organization-9eae89c9669c> accessed 8 July 2021

Perez D and Livshits B, 'Smart Contract Vulnerabilities: Does Anyone Care?' (2019) arXiv:1902.06710

Peterson P, 'Selective Disclosure and Shielded Viewing Keys' (2018), <https://electriccoin.co/blog/viewing-keys-selective-disclosure/> accessed 8 July 2021

Pinch T, 'Technology and institutions: living in a material world' (2008) 37 *Theory and Society* 461

Posner RA, 'The Right of Privacy' (1978) 12 *Georgia Law Review* 393

Rao PK, *The Economics of Transaction Costs: Theory, Methods and Applications* (Macmillan 2003)

Raskin M, 'The Law and Legality of Smart Contracts' (2017) 1 *Georgetown Law Technology Review* 305

Rius ADDM, 'Towards a Sustainable ICO Process: Community Guidelines on Regulation and Best Practices' (2016–2017) <http://alfonso.digitalpapers.uk/> accessed 8 July 2021

—— 'Split Contracts: Bridging Legal Prose and Smart Contract Code' (2017) <http://alfonso.digitalpapers.uk/> accessed 8 July 2021

—— 'Governance in the Age of Blockchain' (2018) <http://alfonso.digitalpapers.uk/> accessed 8 July 2021

—— 'Foundations of Blockchain Technology' (2019) <http://alfonso.digitalpapers.uk/> accessed 8 July 2021

—— and Gashier E, 'On-Chain Options for Digital Assets' (Crypto Valley Conference on Blockchain Technology, 25 June 2019)

—— and Kulasinghe A, 'Responses to Public Consultations on Blockchain and Smart Contracts' (2019-2021) <http://alfonso.digitalpapers.uk/> accessed 8 July 2021

Russell S and Norvig P, *Artificial Intelligence: A Modern Approach* (3rd edn, Pearson 2016)

Shavell S, 'Why Breach of Contract May Not Be Immoral Given The Incompleteness of Contracts' (2009) 107 *Michigan Law Review* 1569

Stigler G, 'The Economics of Information' (1961) 69 *Journal of Political Economy* 213

Scholz L, 'Algorithmic Contracts' (2017) 20 *Stanford Technology Law Review* 101

Sklaroff JM, 'Smart Contracts and the Cost of Inflexibility' (2017) 166 *University of Pennsylvania Law Review* 263

Srivatsan B, 'De-Anonymizing the Bitcoin Blockchain' (2016) <https://bharathsrivatsan.com/files/bitcoin.pdf> accessed 8 July 2021

Stark J, 'Making Sense of Blockchain Smart Contracts' (CoinDesk, 4 June 2016) <https://www.coindesk.com/making-sense-smart-contracts> accessed 8 July 2021

—— 'Making sense of cryptoeconomics' (CoinDesk, 19 August 2017) <https://www.coindesk.com/making-sense-cryptoeconomics> accessed 8 July 2021

Surden H, 'Computable Contracts' (2014) 46 *UC Davis Law Review* 629

—— 'Machine Learning and Law' (2014) 89 *Washington Law Review* 87

Szabo N, 'Smart Contracts' (1994) <https://www.fon.hum.uva.nl/rob/Courses/InformationInSpeech/CDROM/Literature/LOTwinterschool2006/szabo.best.vwh.net/smart.contracts.html> accessed 8 July 2021

—— 'Smart Contracts: Building Blocks for Digital Markets' (1997) <https://www.fon.hum.uva.nl/rob/Courses/InformationInSpeech/CDROM/Literature/LOTwinterschool2006/szabo.best.vwh.net/smart_contracts_2.html> accessed 8 July 2021

—— 'Formalizing and Securing Relationships on Public Networks' (1997) 2 First Monday

—— 'Micropayments and Mental Transaction Costs' (1999) Workshop Paper, 2nd Berlin Internet Economics Workshop

—— 'A Formal Language for Analysing Contracts' (2002), <https://www.fon.hum.uva.nl/rob/Courses/InformationInSpeech/CDROM/Literature/LOTwinterschool2006/szabo.best.vwh.net/contractlanguage.html> accessed 8 July 2021

—— 'Wet code and dry' (2011) <https://unenumerated.blogspot.com/2006/11/wet-code-and-dry.html> accessed 8 July 2021

—— 'Small-game fallacies' (2015) <https://unenumerated.blogspot.com/2015/05/small-game-fallacies.html>

—— 'Money, Blockchains and Social Scalability' (2017), <https://unenumerated.blogspot.com/2017/02/money-blockchains-and-social-scalability.html> accessed 8 July 2021

—— 'Winning Strategies For Smart Contracts' (2017) A Blockchain Research Institute Big Idea Whitepaper

Tai ETT, 'Formalizing contract law for smart contracts' (2017) Tilburg Private Law Working Paper Series No. 6/2017

Taleb N, *Skin in the Game: Hidden Asymmetries in Daily Life* (Random House 2018)

The Economist, 'The great chain of being sure about things' (31 October 2015)

Tinn K, "Smart' Contracts and External Financing' (Western Finance Association meeting, 2018)

UKJT, 'Legal statement on cryptoassets and smart contracts' (2020)

Vatiero M, 'Smart contracts and transaction costs' (2018) Discussion Paper, University of Pisa, Dipartimento di Economia e Management, 2018/23

Vos G, 'End-to-End Smart Legal Contracts: Moving from Aspiration to Reality' (2019)

Walch A, 'Blockchain's Treacherous Vocabulary: One more Challenge for Regulators' (2017) 21 *Journal of Internet Law* 9

—— 'In Code(rs) We Trust: Software Developers as Fiduciaries in Public Blockchains' in Hacker P and others (eds), *Regulating Blockchain: Techno-Social and Legal Challenges* (OUP 2019)

Werbach K, and Cornell N, 'Contracts Ex Machina' (2019) 67 *Duke Law Journal* 313–82

Williamson OE, *The Economic Institutions of Capitalism* (Free Press 1985)

Williamson OE 'Opportunism and its Critics' (1993) 14 *Managerial and Decision Economics* 97

Williamson OE, 'The New Institutional Economics: Taking Stock, Looking Ahead' (2000) 38 *Journal of Economic Literature* 595

472 BIBLIOGRAPHY

Wood G, 'Ethereum: A Secure Decentralised Generalised Transaction Ledger' (2014) <https://ethereum.github.io/yellowpaper/paper.pdf> accessed 8 July 2021
World Bank, 'Smart Contract Technology and Financial Inclusion' (2019) Fintech Note No 6
Wright A, and de Filippi P, 'Decentralized Blockchain Technology and the Rise of Lex Cryptographia' (2015)
Z/Yen Group, 'A Wholesale Insurance Executive's Guide To Smart Contracts' (2017) <https://www.longfinance.net/publications/long-finance-reports/a-wholesale-insurance-executives-guide-to-smart-contracts/> accessed 8 July 2021

Chapter 7 (Blycha and Garside)

Allen JG, 'Wrapped and Stacked: "Smart Contracts" and the Interaction of Natural and Formal Language' (2018) 14(4) *European Review of Contract Law* 307
Bartoletti M and Pompianu L, 'An empirical analysis of smart contracts: platforms, applications, and design patterns' (18 March 2017) <https://arxiv.org/pdf/1703.06322.pdf>
Beale H (ed), *Chitty on Contracts* (29th edn, Sweet & Maxwell 2004) vol 1 & (32nd edn, Sweet & Maxwell 2017) vol 1
Carter JW, *Carter on Contract* (LexisNexis Butterworths Australia 2021)
Chamber of Digital Commerce, 'Smart Contracts: Is the Law Ready?' (September 2018) <https://digitalchamber.org/smart-contracts-whitepaper/>
Clack CD, 'Smart Contract Templates: legal semantics and code validation' (2018) 2(4) *Journal of Digital Banking* 338
Clack CD and others, 'Smart Contract Templates: Foundations, Design Landscape and Research Directions' (2016) <https://arxiv.org/pdf/1608.00771.pdf>
Garside A and others, 'Digital Infrastructure Integrity Protocol for Smart and Legal Contracts DIIP 2021' <https://papers.ssrn.com/sol3/papers.cfm?abstract_id=3814811> accessed 28 May 2021
Grigg I, 'The Richardian Contract' (2004) <https://iang.org/papers/ricardian_contract.html>
Hajkowicz S and Dawson D, 'Digital Megatrends: A perspective on the coming decade of digital disruption' (CSIRO Data61, Brisbane 2018) <https://data61.csiro.au/en/Our-Research/Our-Work/Future-Cities/Planning-sustainable-infrastructure/Digital-Megatrends-2019>
ISDA and King & Wood Mallesons, 'Smart Derivatives Contracts – From Concept to Construction (2018)' <https://www.isda.org/a/cHvEE/Smart-Derivatives-Contracts-From-Concept-to-Construction-Oct-2018.pdf>
ISDA and Linklaters, 'Smart Contracts and Distributed Ledger – A Legal Perspective' (2017) <https://www.isda.org/a/6EKDE/smart-contracts-and-distributed-ledger-a-legal-perspective.pdf>
Levy KEC, 'Book-Smart, Not Street-Smart: Blockchain-Based Smart Contracts and The Social Workings of Law' (2017) 3 *Engaging Science, Technology, and Society* 1 <https://doi.org/10.17351/ests2017.107>
Lipshaw JM, 'The Persistence of 'Dumb' Contracts' (2019) 2(1) *Stanford Journal of Blockchain Law & Policy* 45 <https://stanfordjblp.pubpub.org/pub/persistence-dumb-contracts>
McKinsey Global Institute, 'A Future That Works: Automation, Employment, and Productivity' (January 2017) <https://www.mckinsey.com/~/media/mckinsey/featured%20insights/Digital%20Disruption/Harnessing%20automation%20for%20a%20future%20that%20works/MGI-A-future-that-works-Executivesummary.ashx>

Molina-Jimenez C and others, 'Implementation of Smart Contracts Using Hybrid Architectures with On- and Off-blockchain Components' (31 July 2018) <https://arxiv.org/pdf/1808.00093.pdf>

Patterson D, 'The Philosophical Origins of Modern Contract Doctrine: An Open Letter to Professor James Gordley' (1991) 1432 *Wisconsin Law Review*

Raskin M, 'The Law and Legality of Smart Contracts' (2016) 1 *Georgetown Law Technology Review* 304 <https://papers.ssrn.com/abstract_id=2959166> accessed 27 May 2021

Robinson S, *Drafting: Its application to conveyancing and commercial documents* (1st edn, Butterworths Sydney 1973)

Szabo N, 'Smart Contracts: Building Blocks for Digital Markets' (1996) <http://www.fon.hum.uva.nl/rob/Courses/InformationInSpeech/CDROM/Literature/LOTwinterschool2006/szabo.best.vwh.net/smart_contracts_2.html>

Vos G, 'End- to- End Smart Legal Contracts: Moving from Aspiration to Reality' (2019–2020) 26(1) *Journal of Law Information & Science* EAP 4

Wilkinson S & Giuffre J, 'Six Levels of Contract Automation: The Evolution to Smart Legal Contracts—Further Analysis' (2021) <https://papers.ssrn.com/abstract_id=3815445>

Zhang GQ, *Elastic Language: How and Why We Stretch Our Words* (Cambridge University Press 2015)

Chapter 8 (Wilkinson and Giuffre)

Allen JG, 'Wrapped and Stacked: "Smart Contracts" and the Interaction of Natural and Formal Language' (2018) 14 *European Review of Contract Law* 331

Blycha N and Garside A, 'Smart Legal Contracts: A Model for the Integration of Machine Capabilities Into Contracts' (2020) <https://papers.ssrn.com/sol3/papers.cfm?abstract_id=3743932>

Buterin V, 'Ethereum White Paper', <https://blockchainlab.com/pdf/Ethereum_white_paper-a_next_generation_smart_contract_and_decentralized_application_platform-vitalik-buterin.pdf> accessed 12 March 2021

Cyber Infrastructure and Security, 'Understand Digital Signatures' (24 August 2020) <https://us-cert.cisa.gov/ncas/tips/ST04-018>

Garside A and others, 'Digital Infrastructure Integrity Protocol For Smart Legal Contracts DIIP 2021' (30 March 2021) <https://privpapers.ssrn.com/sol3/papers.cfm?abstract_id=3814811>

International Organisation for Standardization, *Blockchain and distributed ledger technologies—Overview of and interactions between smart contracts in blockchain and distributed ledger technology systems, Technical Report, ISO/TR23455:2019* (2019)

ISDA and Linklaters, 'Whitepaper: Smart Contracts and Distributed Ledger – A Legal Perspective' (August 2017) <www.isda.org/a/6EKDE/smart-contracts-and-distributed-ledger-a-legal-perspective.pdf>

Observatory of Public Sector Innovation, 'Rules as Code (RaC)' <https://oecd-opsi.org/projects/rulesascode/> accessed 12 March 2021

Rosic A, 'Smart Contracts: The Blockchain Technology That Will Replace Lawyers' (25 November 2020) <https://blockgeeks.com/guides/smart-contracts/>

Ryan P, 'Proposed new Taxonomy for Autonomous Smart Contracts' (12 August 2018) <www.linkedin.com/pulse/proposed-new-taxonomy-autonomous-smart-contracts-dr-philippa-ryan> accessed 19 December 2020

SAE International, 'SAE International Releases Updated Visual Chart for Its 'Levels of Driving Automation' Standard for Self-Driving Vehicles' (11 December 2018) <https://www.sae.org/news/press-room/2018/12/sae-international-releases-updated-visual-chart-for-its-%E2%80%9Clevels-of-driving-automation%E2%80%9D-standard-for-self-driving-vehicles> accessed 10 December 2020

—— 'Taxonomy and Definitions for Terms Related to Driving Automation Systems for On-Road Motor Vehicles J3016_201806' <www.sae.org/standards/content/j3016_201806/> accessed 10 December 2020

Szabo N, 'Smart Contracts: Building Blocks for Digital Markets' (1996) <http://www.fon.hum.uva.nl/rob/Courses/InformationInSpeech/CDROM/Literature/LOTwinterschool2006/szabo.best.vwh.net/smart_contracts_2.html> accessed 12 March 2021

The Law Commission, 'Smart contracts' <www.lawcom.gov.uk/project/smart-contracts/> accessed 19 December 2020

Tyurin A and others, 'Overview of the Languages for Safe Smart Contract Programming' (2019) <https://www.researchgate.net/publication/335689429_Overview_of_the_Languages_for_Safe_Smart_Contract_Programming>

UK Jurisdictional Taskforce, *Legal Statement on Crypto Assets and Smart Contracts* (The Law Tech Delivery Panel, November 2019)

Vos G, 'End- to- End Smart Legal Contracts: Moving from Aspiration to Reality' (2019) 26 *Journal of Law Information & Science* 1

Wilkinson S, 'Six Levels of Contract Automation: Evolution to Digitalised Smart (and Legal) Contracts' (December 14, 2020) <https://ssrn.com/abstract=3748266> or <http://dx.doi.org/10.2139/ssrn.3748266>

Chapter 9 (Tjong Tjin Tai)

Allen, JG, 'Wrapped and Stacked: "Smart Contracts" and the Interaction of Natural and Formal Language' (2018) 14 *ERCL* 307

Bhandari Neupane J, 'Characterization of Leptazolines A–D, Polar Oxazolines from the Cyanobacterium Leptolyngbya sp., Reveals a Glitch with the 'Willoughby–Hoye' Scripts for Calculating NMR Chemical Shifts' (2019) 21 *Organic Letters* 8449

Cannarsa M, 'Contract Interpretation' in DiMatteo LA, Cannarsa M, and Poncibò C (eds), *The Cambridge Handbook of Smart Contracts, Blockchain Technology and Digital Platforms* (Cambridge University Press 2019)

Casey AJ, Niblett A, 'Self- Driving Contracts' (2017) 43 *Journal of Corporation Law* 1

De Caria R, 'The Legal Meaning of Smart Contracts' (2018) 26 *ERPL* 731

De Caria R, 'Definitions of Smart Contracts: Between Law and Code' in DiMatteo LA, Cannarsa M, and Poncibò C (eds), *The Cambridge Handbook of Smart Contracts, Blockchain Technology and Digital Platforms* (Cambridge University Press 2019)

De Filippi P and Wright A, *Blockchain and the Law* (Harvard University Press 2018)

DiMatteo LA, Cannarsa M, and Poncibò C (eds), *The Cambridge Handbook of Smart Contracts, Blockchain Technology and Digital Platforms* (Cambridge University Press 2019)

Durovic M, and Janssen A, 'Formation of Smart Contracts under Contract Law', in DiMatteo LA, Cannarsa M, and Poncibò C (eds), *The Cambridge Handbook of Smart Contracts, Blockchain Technology and Digital Platforms* (Cambridge University Press 2019)

Giancaspro M, 'Is a "smart contract" really a smart idea? Insights from a legal perspective' (2017) 33 *Computer Law & Security Review* 825

Howarth D, *Law as Engineering* (Elgar 2013)

Jennejohn M, 'The Architecture of Contract Innovation' (2018) 59 *Boston College Law Review* 71

Levy KEC, 'Book-Smart, Not Street-Smart: Blockchain-Based Smart Contracts and The Social Workings of Law' (2017) 3 *Engaging Science, Technology, and Society* 1

Mik E, 'Smart Contracts: Terminology, Technical Limitations and Real World Complexity' (2017) 9 *Journal of Law, Innovation and Technology* 269

Mitchell C, *Contract Law and Contract Practice* (Hart 2013)

Morgan J, *Contract Law Minimalism* (Cambridge University Press 2013)

O'Shields R, 'Smart Contracts: Legal Agreements for the Blockchain' (2017) 21 *North Carolina Banking Institute* 177

Perugini ML and Dal Checco P, 'Smart Contracts: A Preliminary Evaluation' (2015) <ssrn.com/abstract=2729548> accessed 9 July 2021

Paech P, 'The Governance of Blockchain Financial Networks' (2017) 80 *Modern Law Review* 1072

Peyton Jones S, Eber JM, and Seward J, 'Composing Contracts: An Adventure in Financial Engineering', in: *ACM SIGPLAN International Conference on Functional Programming* (ICFP) 2000 (New York: ACM 2000)

Raskin MI, 'The Law and Legality of Smart Contracts' (2017) 1 *Georgetown Technology Review* 305

Reyes CI, 'Conceptualizing Cryptolaw' (2017) 96 *Nebraska Law Review* 384

Santos FJA, Baldus C, and Dedek H (eds), *Vertragstypen in Europa* (Sellier 2011)

Savelyev A, 'Contract Law 2.0: 'Smart' Contracts As the Beginning of the End of Classic Contract Law' (2016) <ssrn.com/abstract=2885241> accessed 9 July 2021

Sklaroff JM, 'Smart Contracts and the Cost of Inflexibility' (2017) 166 *University of Pennsylvania Law Review* 263

Surden H, 'Computable Contracts' (2012) 46 *UC Davis Law Review* 629

Szabo N, 'Formalizing and Securing Relationships on Public Networks' (First Monday, 1997) <firstmonday.org/ojs/index.php/fm/article/view/548/469/> accessed 9 July 2021

—— 'The Idea of Smart Contracts' <szabo.best.vwh.net/smart_contracts_idea.html> accessed 9 July 2021

Tjong Tjin Tai TFE, 'Formalizing contract law for smart contracts' (ICAIL 2017) https://ssrn.com/abstract=3038800 accessed 9 July 2021

—— 'Challenges of Smart Contracts: Implementing Excuses', in DiMatteo LA, Cannarsa M, and Poncibò C (eds), *The Cambridge Handbook of Smart Contracts, Blockchain Technology and Digital Platforms* (Cambridge University Press 2019)

—— 'Force Majeure and Excuses in Smart Contracts' (2018) 26 *European Review of Private Law* 787

Werbach K, and Cornell N, 'Contracts Ex Machina' (2017) 67 *Duke Law Journal* 313

Chapter 10 (Xu)

Al-Tawil T, 'English Contract Law and the Efficient Breach Theory' (2015) 22 *Maastricht Journal of European and Comparative Law* 396

—— 'The Efficient Breach Theory—The Moral Objection' (2011) 20 *Griffith Law Review* 449

Arrunada B, 'Blockchain's Struggle to Deliver Impersonal Exchange' (2018) 19 *The Minnesota Journal of Law, Science & Technology* 55

—— and Garicano L, 'Blockchain: The Birth of Decentralized Governance' (10 April 2018). *Pompeu Fabra University, Economics and Business Working Paper Series*, 1608 <https://ssrn.com/abstract=3160070> accessed 14 February 2019

Atzori M, 'Blockchain Technology and Decentralized Governance: Is the State Still Necessary' (1 December 2015) <http://ssrn.com/abstract=2731132> accessed 16 June 2019

Biais and others, 'The Blockchain Folk Theorem' (2019) 32 *The Review of Financial Studies* 1662 <https://doi.org/10.1093/rfs/hhy095> accessed 14 February 2019

Bigoni and others, 'Unbundling Efficient Breach: An Experiment' (2017) 14 *Journal of Empirical Legal Studies* 527

Buterin V, 'Ethereum: Platform Review—Opportunities and Challenges for Private and Consortium Blockchains' (2016) <http://www.smallake.kr/wp-content/uploads/2016/06/314477721-Ethereum-Platform-Review-Opportunities-and-Challenges-for-Private-and-Consortium-Blockchains.pdf> accessed 23 January 2019

—— 'A Next-Generation Smart Contract and Decentralized Application Platform' <https://github.com/ethereum/wiki/wiki/White-Paper> accessed 23 January 2019

Butler M and Garnett R, 'Teaching the Coase Theorem: Are We Getting It Right' (2003) 31 *Atlantic Economic Journal* 133

Casey A and Niblett A, 'Self-Driving Contracts' (2017) 43 *Journal of Corporation Law* 100.

Catalini C and Gans J, 'Some Simple Economics of the Blockchain' (2018) NBER Working Paper Series <http://www.nber.org/papers/w22952>

Coase R, 'The Problem of Social Coast' (2013) 56 *The Journal of Law & Economics* 837

Cutts T, 'Degenerate Contracts and Liberal Code' <https://www.academia.edu/38351785/Degenerate_Contracts_and_Liberal_Code> accessed 23 March 2019

De Filippi P and Loveluck B, 'The Invisible Politics of Bitcoin: Governance Crisis of a Decentralised Infrastructure' (2016) 5 *Internet Policy Review* <https://ssrn.com/abstract=2852691> accessed 24 January 2019

Dolan J, 'Tethering the Fraud Inquiry in Letter of Credit Law' (2006) 21 *Banking & Finance Law Review* 479

Eenmaa-Dimitrieva and Schmidt-Kessen, 'Creating markets in no-trust environments: The law and economics of smart contracts' (2018) 35 *Computer Law & Security Review: The International Journal of Technology Law and Practice* <https://doi.org/10.1016/j.clsr.2018.09.003> accessed 24 January 2019

Eicher F, '*Pacta Sunt Servanda*: Contrasting Disgorgement Damages with Efficient Breaches under Article 74 CISG' (2018) 3 *LSE Law Review* 29

Fries C and Kohl-Landgraf P, 'Smart Derivative Contracts (Detaching Transactions from Counterparty Credit Risk: Specification, Parametrisation, Valuation)' (15 April 2018) <https://ssrn.com/abstract=3163074> accessed 14 February 2019

Giancaspro M, 'Is a "Smart Contract" Really a Smart Idea? Insights From a Legal Perspective' (2017) 33 *Computer Law & Security Review* 825

Goldenfein J and Leiter A, 'Legal Engineering on the Blockchain: "Smart Contracts" as Legal Conduct' (2018) 29 *Law Critique* 141

Goode R, 'Abstract Payment Undertakings' in Cane P and Stapleton J (eds), *Essays for Patrick Atiyah* (Oxford University Press 1991)

Governatori and others, 'On Legal Contracts, Imperative and Declarative Smart Contracts, and Blockchain Systems' (2018) 26 *Artificial Intelligence Law* 377

Green S, 'Smart Contracts, Interpretation and Rectification' [2018] *Lloyd's Maritime and Commercial Law Quarterly* 234

Hart O, 'Incomplete Contracts and Control' (2017) 107 *American Economic Review* 1731

Horowitz D, *Letters of Credit and Demand Guarantees, Defences to Payment* (Oxford University Press 2010)

ISDA, 'ISDA Legal Guidelines for Smart Derivatives Contracts: Introduction' (January 2019) <https://www.isda.org/2019/01/30/legal-guidelines-for-smart-derivatives-contracts-introduction/> accessed on 7 February 2019

Kiviat T, 'Beyond Bitcoin: Issues In Regulating Blockchain Transactions' (2015) 65 *Duke Law Journal* 570

Klein B, 'Why Hold-ups Occur: The Self-Enforcing Range of Contractual Relationships' (1996) 34 *Economic Inquiry* 444

Levy K, 'Book-Smart, Not Street-Smart: Blockchain-Based Smart Contracts and the Social Workings of Law' (2013) 3 *Engaging Science, Technology and Society* 1

Lewin-sohn-Zamir D, Schwartz A, and Schweizer U, 'The Questionable Efficiency of the Efficient-Breach Doctrine' (2012) 168(1) *Journal of Institutional Theoretical Economics* 5

Loeb T, 'Judicial Application of the Efficient Breach Theory—A Critical Examination' (2017) 30 *Georgetown Journal of Legal Ethics* 893

Macneil I, 'Contracts: Adjustment of Long-Term Economic Relations under Classical, Neoclassical, and Relational Contract Law' (1978) 72 *Northwestern University Law Review* 854

McCloskey D, 'The So-Called Coase Theorem' (1998) 24(3) *Eastern Economic Journal* 367

Malek and others, *Jack: documentary credits: the law and practice of documentary credits including standby credits and demand guarantees* (4th edn, Haywards Heath 2009)

McNeel G, 'Pay Now, Argue Later' [1999] *Lloyd's Maritime and Commercial Law Quarterly* 5

Mik E, 'Smart contracts: terminology, technical limitations and real world complexity' (2017) 9(2) *Law, Innovation and Technology* 269, DOI: 10.1080/17579961.2017.1378468

Möslein F, 'Legal Boundaries of Blockchain Technologies: Smart Contracts as Self-Help?' (2018). A De Franceschi and others (eds), *Digital Revolution—New challenges for Law*, 2019 Forthcoming. Available at SSRN: https://ssrn.com/abstract=3267852 (accessed on 30 January 2019)

Satoshi N, 'Bitcoin: A Peer-to-Peer Electronic Cash System' (2008). Available at https://bitcoinsv.io/bitcoin (accessed on 24 January 2019)

Olivier G and Jacard B, 'Smart Contracts and the Role of Law' (2017) *Jusletter* IT 23

Ortolani P, 'Self-Enforcing Online Dispute Resolution: Lessons from Bitcoin' (2016) 36(3) *Oxford Journal of Legal Studies* 595

Paech P, 'Securities, Intermediation and the Blockchain: An Inevitable Choice Between Liquidity and Legal Certainty?' (2016) 21 *Uniform Law Review* 612

Paech P, 'The Governance of Blockchain Financial Networks' (2017) 80(6) *Modern Law Review*, 1073; LSE Legal Studies Working Paper No. 16/2017. Available at SSRN: https://ssrn.com/abstract=2875487 (accessed on 7 December 2018)

Peters G and Panayi E, 'Understanding Modern Banking Ledgers Through Blockchain Technologies: Future of Transaction Processing and Smart Contracts on the Internet of Money' (18 November 2015). Available at SSRN: https://ssrn.com/abstract=2692487 (accessed on 24 January 2019)

Posner R, *Economic Analysis of Law* (7th edn, Wolters Kluwer for Aspen Publishers 2007)

Raskin M, 'The Law And Legality Of Smart Contracts' (2017) 1(2) *Georgetown Law Technology Review* 306

Rozario A and Vasarhelyi M, 'Auditing With Smart Contracts' (2018) 18 *The International Journal of Digital Accounting Research* 1

Savelyev A, 'Contract Law 2.0: «Smart» Contracts As the Beginning of the End of Classic Contract Law' (December 14, 2016). *Higher School of Economics Research Paper No. WP BRP 71/LAW/2016*. <https://ssrn.com/abstract=2885241> accessed on 7 February 2019

Surden H, 'Computable Contracts' (2012) 46 *University of California, Davis Law Review* 629

Stefan T and Schwartz E, 'Smart Oracles: A Simple, Powerful Approach to Smart Contracts'. <https://github.com/codius/codius-wiki/wiki/White-Paper> accessed on 7 February 2019

Szabo N, 'Formalizing and Securing Relationships on Public Networks' (1997). <https://nakamotoinstitute.org/formalizing-securing-relationships/> accessed on 24 January 2019

Tirole J, 'Incomplete Contracts Where Do We Stand?' (1999) 67(4) *Econometrica* 741

Vatiero M, 'Smart Contracts and Transaction Costs' (25 September 2018). <https://ssrn.com/abstract=3259958> accessed 30 January 2019

Wall E and Malm G, 'Using Blockchain Technology and Smart Contracts to Create a Distributed Securities Depository'. <https://lup.lub.lu.se/student-papers/search/publication/8885750> accessed 24 January 2019

Werbach K and Cornell N, 'Contracts Ex Machina' (2017) 67 *Duke Law Journal* 313

Werbach K, 'Trust, But Verify: Why The Blockchain Needs The Law' (2018) 33 *Berkeley Technology Law Journal* 489

Wright A and de Filippi P, 'Decentralized Blockchain Technology and the Rise of Lex Cryptographia' (10 March 2015). <https://ssrn.com/abstract=2580664> accessed 24 January 2019

Chapter 11 (Herian)

Aldiss B, *Supertoys Last all Summer Long: And Other Stories of Future Time* (Orbit 2001)

Alexandre A, 'Decentralized Aragon Court Now Onboards Jurors to Settle Real Cases' (Coin Telegraph, 8 Jan 2020) <https://cointelegraph.com/news/decentralized-aragon-court-now-onboards-jurors-to-settle-real-cases> accessed 29 September 2021

Allen JG, 'Wrapped and Stacked: "Smart Contracts" and the Interaction of Natural and Formal Language' (2018) 14 *European Review of Contract Law* 307

Atiyah PS, *The Rise and Fall of Freedom of Contract* (Oxford University Press 1985)

Beale HG (ed), *Chitty on Contracts* (33rd edn, Sweet & Maxwell 2018)

—— Bishop WD and Furmston MP, *Contract Cases and Materials* (5th edn, Oxford University Press 2008)

Birks P, *Unjust Enrichment* (2nd edn, Oxford University Press 2005)

Böhme H, *Fetishism and Culture: A Different Theory of Modernity* (Galt A tr, De Gruyter 2014)

Buterin V, 'Persistent Scripts' (Twitter, 13 October 2018) <https://twitter.com/vitalikbuterin/status/1051160932699770882> accessed 29 September 2021

—— 'Panel 1: Law 2.0 Understanding Smart Contracts' (Chamber of Digital Commerce, YouTube, 9 July 2021) <https://www.youtube.com/watch?time_continue=463&v=ZuHZOryZ_f0> accessed 9 July 2021

Consensys, 'General Philosophy' (GitHub) <https://consensys.github.io/smart-contract-best-practices/general_philosophy/> accessed 29 September 2021

Dameron M, 'Beigepaper: An Ethereum Technical Specification' (GitHub, 16 August 2019) <https://github.com/chronaeon/beigepaper/blob/master/beigepaper.pdf> accessed 29 September 2021

Dikusar A, 'Smart Contracts: Industry Examples and Use Cases for Business' (XB Software, 17 October 2017) <https://xbsoftware.com/blog/smart-contracts-use-cases/> accessed 9 July 2021

Eisenberg MA, 'The Limits of Cognition and the Limits of Contract' (1995) 47 Stanford Law Review 214

Eno B and Varoufakis Y, 'Brian Eno meets Yanis Varoufakis: "Economists are more showbiz than pop stars now"' (The Guardian, 28 November 2015) <https://www.theguardian.com/lifeandstyle/2015/nov/28/conversation-brian-eno-yanis-varoufakis-interview> accessed 29 September 2021

Furmston M (ed), *The Law of Contract* (6th edn, LexisNexis 2017)

Granieri M, 'Technological Contracts' in Monateri PG (ed), *Comparative Contract Law* (Edward Elgar Publishing 2017)

Hart O, 'Incomplete Contracts and Control' (Nobel Prize Lecture, 8 December 2016) <https://www.nobelprize.org/uploads/2018/06/hart-lecture.pdf> accessed 29 September 2021

Herian R, *Regulating Blockchain: Critical Perspectives in Law and Technology* (Routledge 2018)

—— 'Smart contracts: a remedial analysis' (2021) 30 *Information & Communications Technology Law* 17

Hildebrandt M, 'Data-Driven Prediction of Judgment. Law's New Mode of Existence?' (OUP Collected Courses Volume EUI Summer-school, 2019) <https://papers.ssrn.com/sol3/papers.cfm?abstract_id=3548504> accessed 29 September 2021

Hillman RA and Rachlinski JJ, 'Standard-Form Contracting in the Electronic Age' (2002) 77 *New York University Law Review* 495

Hsiao JI, 'Smart Contract on the Blockchain-Paradigm Shift for Contract Law' (2017) 14 *US-China Law Review* 685

Khatwani S, 'These are the 5 Best Use Cases of Ethereum Smart Contracts' (Coin Sutra, 22 May 2018) <https://coinsutra.com/ethereum-smart-contract-usecases/> accessed 9 July 2021

Marino B and Juels A, *Setting Standards for Altering and Undoing Smart Contracts* (2016) <https://www.arijuels.com/wp-content/uploads/2016/06/Setting-Standards-for-Altering-and-Undoing-Smart-Contracts.docx> accessed 29 September 2021

McKinney SA, Landy R, and Wilka R, 'Smart Contracts, Blockchain, and the Next Frontier of Transactional Law' (2018) 13 *Washington Journal of Law, Technology & Arts* 313.

Mudge N, 'ERC1538: Transparent Contract Standard #1538' (GitHub, 30 October 2018) <https://github.com/ethereum/EIPs/issues/1538> accessed 9 July 2021

Narayanan A and others, *Bitcoin and Cryptocurrency Technologies* (Pre-Print 2016)

Sanitt A and Grigg I, 'Legal analysis of the governed blockchain' (Norton Rose Fulbright, Briefing, June 2018) <https://www.nortonrosefulbright.com/en/knowledge/publications/0d56a3a5/legal-analysis-of-the-governed-blockchain> accessed 9 July 2021

Schwartz A and Scott RE, 'Contract Theory and the Limits of Contract Law' (2003) John M Olin Center for Studies in Law, Economics, and Public Policy Working Papers Paper 275 <https://digitalcommons.law.yale.edu/lepp_papers/275/> accessed 28 March 2019

Sklaroff JM, 'Smart Contracts and the Cost of Inflexibility' (2017) 166 *University of Pennsylvania Law Review* 263

Radin MJ, *Boilerplate: The Fine Print, Vanishing Rights, and the Rule of Law* (Princeton University Press 2014)

Raskin M, 'The Law and Legality of Smart Contracts' (2017) 1 *Georgetown Law Technology Review* 305

Ream J, Chu Y, and Schatsky D, 'Upgrading blockchains: Smart contract use cases in industry' (Deloitte Insights, 8 June 2016) <https://www2.deloitte.com/insights/us/en/focus/signals-for-strategists/using-blockchain-for-smart-contracts.html> accessed 9 July 2021

Scott RE and Triantis GG, 'Anticipating Litigation in Contract Design' (2006) 115 *Yale Law Journal* 814

Slock.it, 'Decentralized Autonomous Organization (DAO) Framework' (GitHub, 3 July 2018) <https://github.com/slockit/DAO> accessed 9 July 2021

Szabo N, 'Formalizing and securing Relationships on Public Networks' (First Monday, 1997) <https://firstmonday.org/ojs/index.php/fm/article/view/548/469> accessed 20 September 2021

UK Jurisdiction Taskforce, 'Legal Statement on Cryptoassets & Smart Contracts' (Tech Nation, November 2019) <https://technation.io/lawtech-uk-resources/#cryptoassets> accessed 29 September 2021

Werbach K and Cornell N, 'Contracts Ex Machina' (2017) 67 *Duke Law Journal* 313

Wood G, '*Ethereum: A Secure Decentralised Generalised Transaction Ledger Byzantium Version 69351d5 - 2018-12-10* (2018)' (GitHub 2018) <https://ethereum.github.io/yellowpaper/paper.pdf> accessed 9 July 2021

World Economic Forum, 'Decentralized Finance (DeFi) Policy-Maker Toolkit, White Paper' (8 June 2021) <https://www.weforum.org/whitepapers/decentralized-finance-defi-policy-maker-toolkit> accessed 29 September 2021

Worthington S, *Equity* (2nd edn, Oxford University Press 2006)

Yurick S, *Metatron* (Semiotext(e) 1985)

Chapter 12 (Clack)

JR Abrial, SA Schuman, and B Meyer, 'A Specification Language', in AM Macnaghten and RM McKeag (eds), *On the Construction of Programs* (Cambridge University Press 1980)

Accord Project, 'Open Source Software Tools for Smart Legal Contracts' <https://accordproject.org> accessed 8 October 2021

Aeternity Sophia Language, 'Introduction' <https://aeternity-sophia.readthedocs.io/en/latest/contracts/> accessed 24 June 2021

Agarwal S and others, 'Computable Contracts' <http://compk.stanford.edu> accessed 24 June 2021

Al Khalil F and others, *A solution for the problems of translation and transparency in smart contracts* (Government Risk and Compliance Technology Centre 2017) <http://web.archive.org/web/20180701083330/http://www.grctc.com/wp-content/uploads/2017/06/GRCTC-Smart-Contracts-White-Paper-2017.pdf > accessed 24 June 2021

Allen JG, 'Wrapped and stacked: "Smart Contracts" and the Interaction of Natural and Formal Language' (2018) 14(4) *European Review of Contract Law* 307–43

Andersen J and others, 'Compositional specification of commercial contracts' (2006) 8(6) *International Journal on Software Tools for Technology Transfer* 485

Angelov K, Camilleri JJ, and Schneider G, 'A framework for conflict analysis of normative texts written in controlled natural language' (2013) 82(5–7) *The Journal of Logic and Algebraic Programming* 216

Arnold RT, van Deursen A, and Res M, 'An Algebraic Specification of a Language for Describing Financial Products' in *ICSE-17 Workshop on Formal Methods Application in Software Engineering* (IEEE Computer Society Press 1995)

Azzopardi S and others, 'Contract automata' (2016) 24 *Artif Intell Law* 203

Baier C and Katoen JP, *Principles of model checking* (MIT Press 2008)

Blawx, 'Blawx Alpha' <https://www.blawx.com>

Braine L and Clack C, 'Object-flow' in *1997 IEEE Symposium on Visual Languages (Cat No 97TB100180)* (IEEE 1997)

Braine L and others, 'Simulating an object-oriented financial system in a functional language' (1998) <https://arxiv.org/abs/2011.11593> accessed 24 June 2021

BSI Group, 'PAS 333:2020 PAS 333:2019, Smart Legal Contracts—Specification' (Web Archive 2020) <https://web.archive.org/web/20201230122114/https://standardsdevelopment.bsigroup.com/projects/2018-03267#/section> accessed 8 October 2021

Buterin V, 'A Next Generation Smart Contract & Decentralized Application Platform' (2013) *Ethereum Foundation Whitepaper* <https://cryptorating.eu/whitepapers/Ethereum/Ethereum_white_paper.pdf> accessed 24 June 2021

Camilleri JJ, Paganelli G, and Schneider G, 'A CNL for contract-oriented diagrams' in *International Workshop on Controlled Natural Language* (Springer 2014)

Chappell D, *Understanding JCT Standard Building Contracts* (8th edn, JCT 2007)

Clack CD, Bakshi VA, and Braine L, 'Smart Contract Templates: Foundations, Design Landscape and Research Directions' (2016) *arXiv preprint* <https://arxiv.org/abs/1608.00771v2> accessed 24th June 2021

Clack CD, Bakshi VA, and Braine L, 'Smart Contract Templates: Essential Requirements and Design Options' (2016) *arXiv preprint* <https://arxiv.org/abs/1612.04496> accessed 24 June 2021

Clack CD, 'Smart Contract Templates: legal semantics and code validation' (2018) 2(4) *Journal of Digital Banking* 338

Clack CD and Vanca G, 'Temporal Aspects of Smart Contracts for Financial Derivatives' (2018) 11247 *Lecture Notes in Computer Science, Springer* 339

Clack CD and McGonagle C, 'Smart Derivatives Contracts: the ISDA Master Agreement and the Automation of Payments and Deliveries' (2019) *arXiv preprint* <https://arxiv.org/abs/1904.01461> accessed 24 June 2021

Clack CD, Myers C, and Poon E, *Programming with Miranda* (Prentice Hall 1995)

Cummins J and Clack C, 'Transforming Commercial Contracts through Computable Contracting' (2020) *arXiv preprint* <https://arxiv.org/abs/2003.10400> accessed 24 June 2021

Daml, 'daml' <https://daml.com/> accessed 24 June 2021

Deon Digital, 'The Deon Digital CSL Language Guide' <https://deondigital.com/docs/v0.38.0/> accessed 24 June 2021

—— 'Your first CSL contract' <https://docs.deondigital.com/v0.60.0/src/guidechapters/yourfirstcontract.html> accessed 25 June 2021

van Deursen A, 'Executable Language Definitions: Case Studies and Origin Tracking Techniques' Ph.D. thesis (University of Amsterdam 1994)

——van Deursen A, and Klint P, 'Little Languages: Little Maintenance?' (1998) 10(2) *Journal of Software Maintenance: Research and Practice* 75

Diaz G, Cambronero ME, Martínez E, and Schneider G, 'Specification and Verification of Normative Texts Using C-O Diagrams' (2013) 40(8) *IEEE Transactions on Software Engineering* 795

Diedrich H, *Lexon Bible: Hitchhiker's Guide to Digital Contracts* (Wildfire Publishing 2020)

Eyers J, 'Laws should be published in code, says CSIRO' *The Australian Financial Review* (17 January 2020)

Fitting M, *First-order logic and automated theorem proving* (Springer Science & Business Media 2012)

Flood MD and Goodenough OR, 'Contract as Automaton: The Computational Representation of Financial Agreements' (2015) *Office of Financial Research Working Paper*

Fraser N, 'Google Blockly-A Visual Programming Editor' (Google 2014) <https://developers.google.com/blockly> accessed 25 June 2021

Fuchs NE and others, 'Attempto Controlled English: A Knowledge Representation Language Readable by Humans and Machines' in *Reasoning web* (Springer 2005)

Goodenough O, 'Developing a Legal Specification Protocol: Technological considerations and Requirements' CodeX white paper (Stanford University 2019) <https://law.stanford.edu/wp-content/uploads/2019/03/LSPWhitePaperJan1119v021419.pdf> accessed 24 June 2021

Governatori G, 'Representing Business Contracts in RuleML' (2005) 14(2–3) *International Journal of Cooperative Information Systems* 181

Grice HP, 'Logic and Conversation' in *Speech acts* (Brill 1975)

Grigg I, 'Financial Cryptography in 7 Layers' in *International Conference on Financial Cryptography* (Springer 2000)

——'The Ricardian Contract' in *First IEEE International Workshop on Electronic Contracting* (IEEE 2004) 25, 31 < http://iang.org/papers/ricardian_contract.html> accessed 24 June 2021

—— 'The Sum of All Chains—Let's Converge!' <http://financialcryptography.com/mt/archives/001556.html> accessed 24 June 2021

Grosof BN and Poon TC, 'SweetDeal: Representing Agent Contracts with Exceptions using XML Rules, Ontologies, and Process Descriptions' in *Proceedings of the 12th International Conference on World Wide Web* (2003) 340

Gulliksson R and Camilleri JJ, 'A Domain-Specific Language for Normative Texts with Timing Constraints' in *23rd International Symposium on Temporal Representation and Reasoning (TIME)* (IEEE 2016) 60

Haapio H, Plewe D, and deRooy R, 'Next Generation Deal Design: Comics and Visual Platforms for Contracting' in *Networks: Proceedings of the 19th International Legal Informatics Symposium IRIS* (2016) 373

Harley B, *Are Smart Contracts Contracts?* (Clifford Chance 2017)

Hazard J and Haapio H, 'Wise Contracts: Smart Contracts that Work for People and Machines' in Schweighofer E and others (eds), *Trends and Communities of Legal Informatics. Proceedings of the 20th International Legal Informatics Symposium IRIS 2017* (Osterriechische Computer Gesellschaft 2017)

Henglein F and others, 'POETS: Process-Oriented Event-Driven Transaction Systems' (2009) 78(5) *Journal of Logic and Algebraic Programming* 381

Hirai Y, 'Defining the Ethereum Virtual Machine for Interactive Theorem Provers' in *International Conference on Financial Cryptography and Data Security* (Springer 2017)

Hoare CAR, 'Communicating Sequential Processes' (1978) 21(8) *Communications of the ACM* 666

Horn F and Trypuz R, 'What is FIBO' (2020) *EDM Council* <https://wiki.edmcouncil.org/> accessed 24 June 2021

Hvitved T, 'Contract Formalisation and Modular Implementation of Domain-Specific Languages' (2012) PhD thesis, Department of Computer Science, University of Copenhagen (DIKU)

Idelberger F, 'Merging Traditional Contracts (or Law) and (Smart) e-Contracts – A Novel Approach' in *The 1st Workshop on Models of Legal Reasoning* (2020) <https://lawgorithm.com.br/wp-content/uploads/2020/09/MLR2020-Florian-Idelberger.pdf > accessed 24 June 2021

ISDA, *User's Guide to the ISDA 2002 Master Agreement* (ISDA 2003)

King & Wood Mallesons, 'Smart derivatives contracts: From concept to construction' (2018) <https://www.isda.org/a/cHvEE/Smart-Derivatives-Contracts-From-Concept-to-Construction-Oct-2018.pdf> accessed 24 June 2021

—— and Linklaters, *Smart contracts and distributed ledger—a legal perspective* (ISDA 2017) <http://www.isda.org/a/6EKDE/smart-contractsanddistributed-ledger-a-legal-perspective.pdf> accessed 24 June 2021

Juro, 'All-in-One Contract Automation' <https://juro.com/> accessed 24 June 2021

Karadotchev V, 'First Steps towards Logical English' MSc dissertation (Imperial College London (2019)

Knuth DE, 'Literate Programming' (1984) 27(2) *The Computer Journal* 97

Kowalski RA, 'Logic for Knowledge Representation' in *International Conference on Foundations of Software Technology and Theoretical Computer Science* (Springer 1984)

—— 'Logical English' in *Logic and Practice of Programming (LPOP)* (2020) <http://www.doc.ic.ac.uk/~rak/papers/LPOP.pdf> accessed 24 June 2021

—— and Datoo A, 'Logical English meets Legal English for Swaps and Derivatives' (2020) <http://www.doc.ic.ac.uk/~rak/papers/Logical%20English%20meets%20Legal%20English.pdf> accessed 24 June 2021

—— Sadri F, and Calejo M, 'How to do it with LPS (Logic-Based Production System)' in RuleML+ RR (Supplement) International Joint Conference on Rules and Reasoning (2017) <http://ceur-ws.org/Vol-1875/paper16.pdf> accessed 24 June 2021

—— and others, 'Logical English as Executable Computer Language' <http://www.doc.ic.ac.uk/~rak/papers/Logical%20English.pdf> accessed 24 June 2021

Kuhn T, 'A Survey and Classification of Controlled Natural Languages' (2014) 40(1) *Computational Linguistics* 121–70

Lauritsen M and Steenhuis Q, 'Substantive Legal Software Quality: A Gathering Storm?' in *ICAIL'19 Proceedings of the Seventeenth International Conference on Artificial Intelligence and Law*, 52–62 (ACM 2019)

Lee RM, 'A Logic Model for Electronic Contracting' (1988) 4(1) *Decision support systems* 27

Magazzeni D, McBurney P, and Nash W, 'Validation and Verification of Smart Contracts: A Research Agenda' (2017) 50(9) *IEEE Computer Journal Special Issue on Blockchain Technology for Finance* 50

Martin K, 'Deconstructing Contracts: Contract Analytics and Contract Standards' in *Data-Driven Law* (Auerbach Publications 2018)

Martínez E and others, 'A Model for Visual Specification of e-Contracts' in *2010 IEEE International Conference on Services Computing* (IEEE 2010)

Mellish CS and Clocksin WF, *Programming in PROLOG* (Springer 1981)

Milner R, *A calculus of communicating systems* (Springer Verlag 1980)

Milosevic Z, 'A Formal Analysis of a Business Contract Language' (2006) 15(04) *International Journal of Cooperative Information Systems* 659

Molina-Jimenez C and others, 'Run-Time Monitoring and Enforcement of Electronic Contracts' (2004) 3(2) *Electronic Commerce Research and Applications* 108

Morris J, 'Rules as Code: How Technology May change the Language in which Legislation is Written, and What it Might Mean for Lawyers of Tomorrow' (2021) <https://s3.amazonaws.com/us.inevent.files.general/6773/68248/1ac865f1698619047027fd22eddbba6e057e990e.pdf> accessed 24 June 2021

Oasis, 'Legal XML' <http://www.legalxml.org> accessed 8 October 2021

OasisOpen, 'OASIS LegalRuleML TC' <https://www.oasis-open.org/committees/tc_home.php?wg_abbrev=legalruleml> accessed 8 October 2021

OpenLaw, 'Real World Contracts for Ethereum' <https://www.openlaw.io> accessed 8 October 2021

Pace GJ and Schneider G, 'Challenges in the Specification of Full Contracts' in *International Conference on Integrated Formal Methods* (Springer 2009)

Pace G, Prisacariu C, and Schneider G, 'Model Checking Contracts–A Case Study' in *International Symposium on Automated Technology for Verification and Analysis* (Springer 2007)

Peyton Jones S (ed), *Haskell 98 Language and Libraries: The Revised Report* (Cambridge University Press 2003)

Peyton Jones S, Eber JM, and Seward J, 'Composing Contracts: An Adventure in Financial Engineering (Functional Pearl)' (2000) 35(9) *ACM SIGPLAN Notices* 280

Prakken H and Sartor G, 'The Role of Logic in Computational Models of Legal Argument: A Critical Survey' in *Computational Logic: Logic Programming and Beyond* (Springer 2002)

Prisacariu C and Schneider G, 'A Formal Language for electronic contracts' in *International Conference on Formal Methods for Open Object-Based Distributed Systems* (Springer 2007)

Rescher N and Urquhart A, *Temporal Logic* (Springer-Verlag 1971)

R3, 'Barclay's Smart Contract Templates – Presented by Dr Lee Braine, Introduced by Brad Novak' <https://vimeo.com/168844103> accessed 24 June 2021

Scott D and Strachey C, 'Toward a Mathematical Semantics for Computer Languages', Technical Monograph PRG-6 (Oxford University Programming Research Group 1971)

Seijas PL and Thompson S, 'Marlowe: Financial Contracts on Blockchain' in *International Symposium on Leveraging Applications of Formal Methods* (Springer 2018)

Sergot MJ and others, 'The British Nationality Act as a logic program' (1986) 29(5) *Communications of the ACM* 370

Skotnica M and Pergl R, 'Das Contract-A Visual Domain Specific Language for Modeling Blockchain Smart Contracts' in *Enterprise Engineering Working Conference* (Springer 2019)

Smith HE, 'Modularity in Contracts: Boilerplate and Information Flow' (2006) 104 Michigan Law Review <https://repository.law.umich.edu/cgi/viewcontent.cgi?article=1538&context=mlr> accessed 24 June 2021

Smucclaw, 'The Future Home of the L4 DSL' <https://github.com/smucclaw/dsl> accessed 24 June 2021

Stark J, 'Making Sense of Blockchain Smart Contracts' (2016) Coindesk.com <http://www.coindesk.com/making-sense-smart-contracts/> accessed 24 June 2021

Surden H, 'Computable Contracts' (2012) 46 *UCDL Review* 629

Szabo N, 'Smart Contracts: Building Blocks for Digital Markets' (1996) 16 EXTROPY: The Journal of Transhumanist Thought 50, 64 <https://archive.org/details/extropy-16/page/50/mode/2up> accessed 24 June 2021

Thompson S, *Haskell: The Craft of Functional Programming* (Addison-Wesley 1999)

Turner DA, 'Functional Programs as Executable Specifications' (1984) 312(1522) *Philosophical Transactions of the Royal Society of London. Series A, Mathematical and Physical Sciences* 363

Turner D, 'An Overview of Miranda' (1986) 21(12) *ACM Sigplan Notices* 158

UK Jurisidiction Taskforce, *Legal statement on cryptoassets and smart contracts* (The LawTech Delivery Panel 2019) <https://technation.io/about-us/lawtech-panel>< https://bit.ly/3gTORja> accessed 24 June 2021

von Wright GH, 'Deontic logic' (1951) 60(237) Mind 1

von Wright GH, 'And Next' (1965) *Fasc. XVIII Acta Philosophica Fennica* 293

von Wright GH, 'An Essay in Deontic Logic and the General Theory of Action' (1968) *Fasc XXI Acta Philosophica Fennica*
von Wright GH, 'The Logic of Action: A Sketch' in Rescher N (ed), *The Logic of Decision and Action* (Univ. Pittsburgh Press 1967)
Warren DH, Pereira LM, and Pereira F, 'Prolog-The Language and Its Implementation Compared with Lisp' (1977) 12(8) *ACM SIGPLAN Notices* 109
Wikipedia, 'Solidity' <https://en.wikipedia.org/wiki/Solidity> accessed 8 October 2021
Wong M and others, 'Computational Contract Collaboration and Construction' in *Co-operation: Proceedings of the 18th International Legal Informatics Symposium IRIS* (2015) 505
Wyner A and others, 'On Controlled Natural Languages: Properties and Prospects' in *International Workshop on Controlled Natural Language* (Springer 2009) 281
W3C, 'XML' <https://www.w3.org/TR/REC-xml/> accessed 8 October 2021
Yang X and others, 'Finding and Understanding Bugs in C Compilers' in *Proceedings of the 32nd ACM SIGPLAN Conference on Programming Language Design and Implementation* (ACM 2011) 283

Chapter 13 (Ma)

Accord Project, 'Ergo overview' <https://docs.accordproject.org/docs/logic-ergo.html> accessed 1 February 2020
—— 'Key Concepts' <https://docs.accordproject.org/docs/accordproject-concepts.html> accessed 1 October 2020
Allen LE, 'Symbolic Logic: A Razor-Edged Tool for Drafting and Interpreting Legal Documents' (1957) 66 *Yale Law Journal* 833
Austin JL, *How to Do Things with Words* (2nd edn, Harvard University Press 1975)
Baggio G, *Meaning in the Brain* (MIT Press 2018)
Blawx, 'Facts, Rules and Queries' <https://www.blawx.com/2019/09/facts-rules-and-queries/#page-content> accessed February 2020
—— 'Example: Using Blawx for Rules as Code' <https://www.blawx.com/2020/01/example-using-blawx-for-rules-as-code/#page-content> accessed 13 July 2021
Boole G, *The Laws of Thought* (1854)
Brill E and Mooney RJ, 'Empirical Natural Language Processing' (1997) 18 *AI Magazine* 4
Casey AJ and Niblett A, 'Self-Driving Contracts' (2017) 43 *Journal of Corporation Law* 101
Chomsky N, 'Remarks on Nominalization' in Jacobs RA and Rosenbaum PS (eds), *Readings in English Transformational Grammar* (Ginn and Company 1970)
—— *Cartesian Linguistics: A Chapter in the History of Rational Thought* (3rd edn, Cambridge University Press 2009)
Chou EY, Halevy N, and Murnighan JK, 'The Relational Costs of Complete Contracts' (2011) IACM 24th Annual Conference Paper <https://papers.ssrn.com/sol3/papers.cfm?abstract_id=1872569> accessed 30 September 2021
Derrida J, *Limited Inc.* (Northwestern University Press 1988)
Devlin K, *Goodbye Descartes: The End of Logic and The Search for a New Cosmology of the Mind* (John Wiley & Sons 1997)
Diedrich H, *Lexon: Digital Contracts* (Wildfire Publishing 2020)
Eigen ZJ, 'Empirical Studies of Contract' (2012) Northwestern University school of Law Faculty Working Paper 204 <https://scholarlycommons.law.northwestern.edu/cgi/viewcontent.cgi?article=1203&context=facultyworkingpapers> accessed 12 July 2021

Foucault M, *The Order of Things: An Archaeology of the Human Sciences* (Tavistock Publications 1970)

Frumer Y, 'Translating Worlds, Building Worlds: Meteorology in Japanese, Dutch, and Chinese' (2018) 109 *Isis* 326

Genie AI, 'Super Drafter' <https://genieai.co/home> accessed February 2020.

Hart HLA, *The Concept of Law* (Oxford University Press 1961)

Harvard Law School, 'Computer Programming for Lawyers' <https://hls.harvard.edu/academics/curriculum/catalog/default.aspx?o=75487> accessed February 2020

Hildebrandt M, 'Law as Computation in the Era of Artificial Legal Intelligence. Speaking Law to the Power of Statistics' (2017) *Draft for Special Issue of the University of Toronto Law Journal* <https://papers.ssrn.com/sol3/papers.cfm?abstract_id=2983045> accessed 29 September 2021

—— *Law for Computer Scientists and Other Folk* (Oxford University Press 2020)

Hofstadter D, *Gödel, Escher, Bach* (Twentieth-anniversary edn, Basic Books 1999)

—— 'The Shallowness of Google Translate' *The Atlantic* (30 January 2018), <https://www.theatlantic.com/technology/archive/2018/01/the-shallowness-of-google-translate/551570/> accessed 29 September 2021

Holmes OW, 'The Path of Law' (1897) 10 *Harvard Law Review* 457

Jasanoff S, *Can Science Make Sense of Life?* (Polity 2019)

Jeffrey M, 'What Would an Integrated Development Environment for Law look like?' (1.1 MIT Computational Law Report, 2020), <https://law.mit.edu/pub/whatwouldanintegrateddevelopmentenvironmentforlawlooklike> accessed 29 September 2021

Kantor I, 'Code Structure' (JavaScript Tutorial) <https://javascript.info/> accessed 1 April 2020

Kennedy D, 'A Semiotics of Legal Argument' (1994) 3 *Collected Courses of the Academy of European Law* 317

—— *Legal Reasoning: Collected Essays* (Davies Group Publishers 2008)

Kira, 'How Professional services Firms are using Kira' <https://kirasystems.com/forms/whitepapers/professional-services-use-cases/> accessed 29 September 2021

Lessig L, *Code 2.0* (2nd edn, Basic Books 2006)

Mabey R and Kovalevich P, 'Machine-readable contracts: a new paradigm for legal documentation' (Juro) <https://info.juro.com/machine-learning> accessed 1 February 2020

Markou C and Deakin S, 'Ex Machina Lex: The Limits of Legal Computability' (2019) Working Paper, <https://ssrn.com/abstract=3407856>

OpenLaw, 'Markup Language' (OpenLaw Docs) <https://docs.openlaw.io/markup-language/#variables> accessed 1 April 2020

Pasquale F, 'A Rule of Persons, Not Machines: The Limits of Legal Automation' (2019) 87 *George Washington Law Review* 2

Posner RA, 'The Law and Economics of Contract Interpretation' (2005) 83 *Texas Law Review* 1581

Postema GJ, 'Implicit Law' (1994) 13 *Law and Philosophy* 361

Rich B, 'How AI is Changing Contracts' (Harvard Business Review, 12 February 2018) <https://hbr.org/2018/02/how-ai-is-changing-contracts> accessed 29 September 2021

Richards NM and Smart WD, 'How should the law think about robots?' in Calo R and others (eds), *Robot Law* (Edward Elgar 2016)

Samuel G, 'Is Legal Reasoning like Medical Reasoning?' (2015) 35 *Legal Studies* 323

Smith HE, 'Modularity in Contracts: Boilerplate and Information Flow' (2006) 10 *Michigan Law Review* 1175

Surden H, 'Computable Contracts' (2012) 46 *UC Davis Law Review* 629
Wittgenstein L, *Philosophical Investigations* (2nd edn, Macmillan 1958)
World Justice Project, *World Justice Project Rule of Law Index* (2019)

Chapter 14 (Fina and Ng)

Adams K and Scherr R, 'Top Ten Tips in Drafting and Negotiating an International Contract', Thomson Reuters (online) <https://legal.thomsonreuters.com/en/insights/articles/top-10-tips-in-drafting-and-negotiating-international-contracts>
Adams KA, A Manual of Style for Contract Drafting (4th edn, American Bar Association, 2020)
Alibaba Cloud, *25 Things You Should Know About Developers in China* (Web Page) <https://www.alibabacloud.com/blog/25-things-you-should-know-about-developers-in-china_415712>
Bucerius Law School, *The Future of Law and Legal Services* (Web Page) <https://www.law-school.de/international/education/bucerius-summer-programs/legal-technology-and-operations>
Chen R, 'The 10 most popular programming languages, according to the Microsoft-owned GitHub', *Business Insider* (online at 6 November 2019) <https://www.businessinsider.de/international/most-popular-programming-languages-github-2019-11/?r=US&IR=T>
Ciobanu A and Dinu L, 'On the Romance Languages Mutual Intelligibility' (online) <http://citeseerx.ist.psu.edu/viewdoc/download?doi=10.1.1.675.6045&rep=rep1&type=pdf>
Dannen C, *Introducing Ethereum and Solidity: Foundations of Cryptocurrency and Blockchain Programming for Beginners* (Springer 2017)
Ethereum, *Developer Resources* (Web Page) <https://ethereum.org/developers/>
European Parliament, *Fact Sheets on the European Union* (Web Page) <http://www.europarl.europa.eu/factsheets/en/sheet/142/language-policy>
European Union, *The EU Motto* (Web Page) <https://europa.eu/european-union/about-eu/symbols/motto_en>
Finley K, 'A $50 Million Hack Just Showed That the DAO Was All Too Human', *Wired* (online at 18 June 2016) <https://www.wired.com/2016/06/50-million-hack-just-showed-dao-human/>
Harrisson KD, *When Languages Die* (Oxford University Press 2008) 11
Hornberger NH, 'Language Shift and Language Revitalization' in *The Oxford Handbook of Applied Linguistics* (2nd edn, Oxford University Press, 2010)
Hotdocs, <https://www.hotdocs.com/>
Istrup, P, 'Smart Contracts as Contracts' (Conference Presentation, 1st ICT 2020, 21 January 2020)
Kankaanranta A and Lu W, 'The Evolution of English as the Business Lingua Franca: Signs of Convergence in Chinese and Finnish Professional Communication' (2013) 27(3) *Journal of Business and Technical Communication* 288
Lampič J, 'Ricardian Contracts: A Smarter Way to do Smart Contracts?', *Schönherr* (online in 2019) <https://www.schoenherr.eu/publications/publication-detail/ricardian-contracts-a-smarter-way-to-do-smart-contracts/>
LegalSifter (Web Page) <https://www.legalsifter.com/>
Luminance, *Advisory* (Web Page) <https://www.luminance.com/advisory.html>
Luminance, *Market-leading AI platform, Luminance, used in 80 languages across the globe* (Web Page) <https://www.luminance.com/news/press/20191126_marketleading_ai.html>
Model Law on Electronic Commerce 1996 (United Nations Commission on International Trade Law)

Model Law on Electronic Transferable Records 2017 (United Nations Commission on International Trade Law)

Muzzy E, 'Measuring Blockchain Decentralization', *ConsenSys* (online) <https://consensys.net/research/measuring-blockchain-decentralization/>

Nickerson C, 'English as a Lingua Franca in International Business Contexts' (2005) 24(4) *English for Specific Purposes* 367

Ng I, 'The Art of Contract Drafting in the Age of Artificial Intelligence: A Comparative Study Based on US, UK and Austrian Law' (2017) 26 *TTLF Working Papers*

Ng I, 'UNCITRAL E-Commerce Law 2.0: Blockchain and Smart Contracts', *LawTech.Asia* (online at 22 April 2018) <https://lawtech.asia/author/ireneng/>

Ng I and Lampič J, 'UNCITRAL Model Law on Electronic Transferable Records, Contract Automation and Metadata' (Conference Presentation, 1st ICT 2020, 21 January 2020)

Ristikivi M, 'Latin: The Common Legal Language of Europe?' (2005) 10 *Juridica International* 199

Rozovics M, 'Drafting Multiple-Language Contracts', *American Bar Association* (online at 3 April 2019) <https://www.americanbar.org/groups/gpsolo/publications/gp_solo/2011/april_may/drafting_multiple-languagecontractswhenyouonlyspeakenglish/>

Sahota N, 'Will A.I. Put Lawyers Out of Business?', *Forbes* (online at 9 February 2019) <https://www.forbes.com/sites/cognitiveworld/2019/02/09/will-a-i-put-lawyers-out-of-business/>

Solidity (Web Page) <https://solidity.readthedocs.io/en/v0.6.2/>

Stanford Law School, *Law and Computing Science (Web Page)* <https://law.stanford.edu/education/degrees/joint-degrees-within-stanford-university/law-and-computer-science/>

Szabo N, 'Formalizing and Securing Relationships on Public Networks' (online in 1997) <https://nakamotoinstitute.org/formalizing-securing-relationships/#building-blocks-of-smart-contract-protocols>

Torbert P, 'Globalizing Legal Drafting: What the Chinese Can Teach Us About Ejusdem Generis and All That' (2007) 11 *Scribes Journal of Legal Writing* 41

Thomson Reuters, *Contract management solutions* (Web Page) <https://legalsolutions.thomsonreuters.co.uk/en/explore/document-management/contract-drafting-automation-management.html>

Try APL (Web Page) <https://tryapl.org/>

w3schools.com, *JavaScript if/else Statement* (Web Page) <https://www.w3schools.com/jsrcf/jsref_if.asp>

W3Cschool, 易语言教程 (Web Page) <https://www.w3cschool.cn/eyuyantutorials/>

UN Library, *What are the official languages of the United Nations?* (Web Page) <http://ask.un.org/faq/14463>

United Nations Commission on International Trade Law, *UNCITRAL Model Law ON Electronic Commerce (1996) with additional article 5 bis as adopted in 1998* (Web Page) <https://uncitral.un.org/en/texts/ecommerce/modellaw/electronic_commerce>

Chapter 15 (Koepsell)

Allen JG, 'Wrapped and Stacked: "Smart Contracts" and the Interaction of Natural and Formal Language' (2018) 14(4) *European Review of Contract Law* 307–43

Cong LW and He Z, 'Blockchain Disruption and Smart Contracts' (2019) 32(5) *The Review of Financial Studies* 1754–97

Ferraris M, 'Documentality, or Europe' (2009) 92(2) *The Monist* 286–314

Ferraris M, 'Perspectives of Documentality' (2012) 2 *Phenomenology and Mind* 34–40

Ferraris M, *Documentality: Why it is Necessary to Leave Traces* (Fordham University Press 2012)

Hamilton M, 'Blockchain Distributed Ledger Technology: An Introduction and Focus on Smart Contracts' (2020) 31(2) *Journal of Corporate Accounting & Finance* 7–12

Koepsell D and Smith B. 'Beyond Paper' (2014) 97(2) *The Monist* 222–35

Smith B, 'How to Do Things with Documents' (2012) *Rivista di estetica* 50, 179–98

Smith B, 'Searle and de Soto: The New Ontology of the Social World' from Barry Smith, David Mark, and Isaac Ehrlich (eds), *The Mystery of Capital and the Construction of Social Reality* (Open Court 2008) 35–51

Szabo N, 'Formalizing and Securing Relationships on Public Networks' *First monday* (1997)

Wang Q and others, 'Non-Fungible Token (NFT): Overview, Evaluation, Opportunities and Challenges' *arXiv preprint arXiv:2105.07447* (2021)

Zheng Z and others, 'An Overview on Smart Contracts: Challenges, Advances and Platforms' (2020) *Future Generation Computer Systems* 105, 475–91

Chapter 16 (Farrell, Glass, and Wells)

Allen JG, 'Wrapped and Stacked: "Smart Contracts" and the Interaction of Natural and Formal Languages' (2018) 14 *European Review of Contract Law* 4

Clack C, 'Smart Contract Templates: Legal semantics and code validation' (2018) 2 *Journal of Digital Banking* 4

Data61, 'Risks and Opportunities for Systems Using Blockchain and Smart Contracts' (White Paper, Data61, May 2017) <https://data61.csiro.au/~/media/052789573E9342068C5735BF604E7824.ashx>

De Filippi P and McMullen G, 'Governance of Blockchain Systems: Governance of and by Distributed Infrastructure' (White Paper, Coalition of Automated Legal Applications, June 2018) <https://coala.global/wp-content/uploads/2019/02/BRI-COALA-Governance-of-Blockchains.pdf>

Farrell, S, 'Blockchain Standards in International Banking: Understanding Standards Deviation' (2019) 7(3) *Journal of ICT Standardization* <https://www.riverpublishers.com/journal_read_html_article.php?j=JICTS/7/3/2>

—— and others, 'How to use humans to make "smart contracts" truly smart' (*King & Wood Mallesons*, 7 July 2016) <https://www.kwm.com/en/au/knowledge/insights/smart-contracts-open-source-model-dna-digital-analogue-human-20160630>

—— and others, 'Lost and found in smart contract translation—considerations in transition to automation in legal architecture' (2018) 33 *Journal of International Banking Law and Regulation* 1

—— and Warren, C, 'Smart Contracts: From concept to construction' (*King & Wood Mallesons*, 4 October 2018) <https://www.kwm.com/en/au/knowledge/insights/smart-derivatives-contracts-from-concept-to-construction-20181004>

International Organization for Standardization, 'Standards by ISO/TC 307: Blockchain and distributed ledger technologies' (*ISO*) <https://www.iso.org/committee/6266604/x/catalogue/p/0/u/1/w/0/d/0>

International Swaps and Derivatives Association, 'ISDA Papers on DLT and Smart Contracts' (*International Swaps and Derivatives Association*, 16 October 2019) <https://www.isda.org/2019/10/16/isda-smart-contracts/>

—— and others, 'Private International Law Aspects of Smart Derivatives Contracts Utilizing Distributed Ledger Technology' (Report, International Swaps and Derivatives Association, 13 January 2020) 20 <https://www.isda.org/a/4RJTE/Private-International-Law-Aspects-of-Smart-Derivatives-Contracts-Utilizing-DLT.pdf>

—— and King & Wood Mallesons, 'Smart Legal Contracts: From Concept to Construction' (White Paper, ISDA, October 2018) <https://www.isda.org/a/cHvEE/Smart-Derivatives-Contracts-From-Concept-to-Construction-Oct-2018.pdf>

—— and Linklaters, 'Whitepaper: Smart Contracts and Distributed Ledger—A Legal Perspective' (White Paper, ISDA, August 2017) <https://www.isda.org/a/6EKDE/smart-contracts-and-distributed-ledger-a-legal-perspective.pdf>

Jentzsch, C, 'Decentralized Autonomous Organization to Automate Governance' (White Paper, Slock.IT, 2016) 1 <https://web.archive.org/web/2019*/https://download.slock.it/public/DAO/WhitePaper.pdf>

King & Wood Mallesons, 'Project-DnA' (*Github,* 4 August 2016) <https://github.com/KingandWoodMallesonsAU/Project-DnA>

Reserve Bank of Australia, 'ISO 20022 Migration for the Australian Payments System – Conclusions Paper' (Conclusions Paper, Reserve Bank of Australia, February 2020) <https://www.rba.gov.au/publications/consultations/202002-iso-20022-migration-for-the-australian-payments-system/pdf/iso-20022-migration-for-the-australian-payments-system-conclusions-paper.pdf>

Chapter 17 (Butler and Maslin)

ABA Standing Committee on the Delivery of Legal Services, 'Results of the Legal Incubator Lawyers' Survey' (American Bar Association 2021)

Accord Project <https://www.accordproject.org/> accessed 8 May 2021

Accord Project's Cicero <https://accordproject.org/projects/cicero/> accessed 12 May 2021

Alarie B, Niblett A, and Yoon AH, 'How Artificial Intelligence Will Affect the Practice of Law' (2018) 68(1) *University of Toronto Law Journal* 106

Allen JG, 'Wrapped and Stacked: "Smart Contracts" and the Interaction of Natural and Formal Language' (2018) 14(4) *European Review of Contract Law* 307

Appenate <https://www.appenate.com/white-label//> accessed 12 May 2021

Bennett J and others, *Current State of Automated Legal Advice Tools* (Discussion Paper 1, Networked Society Institute, April 2018)

Brandt R, 'Birth of a Salesman, Behind the rise of Jeff Bezos and Amazon' *The Wall Street Journal* (New York, 15 October 2011) <https://www.wsj.com/articles/SB10001424052970203914304576627102996831 20> accessed 15 May 2021

Chin E, 'Three Strategies for Law Firms as NewLaw Reaches a Tipping Point' (2016) *Australasian Law Management Journal* 1 <http://www.lmhub.com.au/wp-content/uploads/2016/06/ALMJ-June2016-EricChin-PDF.pdf> accessed 12 May 2021

Cohen M, 'The Legal Industry is Starting to Collaborate—Why Now and Why It Matters' *Forbes* (New York, 22 July 2019) <https://www.forbes.com/sites/markcohen1/2019/07/22/the-legal-industry-is-starting-to-collaborate-why-now-and-why-it-matters/#378589ea343d> accessed 19 May 2021

Cohen M, 'What's A Lawyer Worth?' *Forbes* (New York, 4 December 2017) <https://www.forbes.com/sites/markcohen1/2017/12/04/whats-a-lawyer-worth/#7c28665377c4> accessed 7 May 2021

BIBLIOGRAPHY 491

Cohen S and Hochberg Y, 'Accelerating Startups: The Seed Accelerator Phenomenon' (March 2014) <http://seedrankings.com/pdf/seed-accelerator-phenomenon.pdf> accessed 9 May 2021

Constine J, '$75M Legal Startup Atrium Shuts Down, Lays Off 100' *TechCrunch* (Online, 4 March 2020) <https://techcrunch.com/2020/03/03/atrium-shuts-down/> accessed 9 May 2021

Constine J, 'Atrium Raises $65M from a16z to Replace Lawyers with Machine Learning' *TechCrunch* (Online, 11 September 2018) <https://techcrunch.com/2018/09/10/atrium-legal/> accessed 9 May 2021

Coumarelos C and others, *Legal Australia-Wide Survey: Legal Need in Australia* (Law and Justice Foundation of New South Wales 2012)

de Rond M, 'Why Less Is More in Teams' *Harvard Business Review* (Boston, 6 August 2012 <https://hbr.org/2012/08/why-less-is-more-in-teams> accessed 15 May 2021

Department of Industry, Science, Energy and Resources, 'National Blockchain Roadmap' (Australian Government 2020) <https://www.industry.gov.au/data-and-publications/national-blockchain-roadmap> accessed 11 May 2021

European Commission, 'ICT and Standardisation' <https://ec.europa.eu/digital-single-market/en/policies/ict-and-standardisation> accessed 11 May 2021

Gainor D, 'Why A White Label Solution Is Easier Than Building Your Own' *Forbes* (New York, 3 June 2014) <https://www.forbes.com/sites/theyec/2014/06/03/why-a-white-label-solution-is-easier-than-building-your-own/#77353700dd9e> accessed 13 May 2021

github Accord Project <https://github.com/accordproject> accessed 12 May 2021

Hagan M, 'A Human-Centered Design Approach to Access to Justice: Generating New Prototypes and Hypotheses for Intervention to Make Courts User-Friendly' (2018) 6(2) *Indiana Journal of Law and Social Equality* 199 <https://www.repository.law.indiana.edu/ijlse/vol6/iss2/2/> accessed 8 May 2021

HSBC UK, 'Annual law firm strategy and investment survey' (2020) <https://www.briefing.co.uk/wp-content/uploads/2020/10/Briefing2020-HSBC-Survey-Digital-1.pdf> accessed 7 May 2021

HSBC UK, 'Peer group analysis: Financing investments in legal tech' (2017) <https://www.business.hsbc.uk/corporate/-/media/library/business-uk/pdfs/financing-investments-in-legal-tech.pdf> accessed 4 May 2021

HSBC UK, 'Peer group analysis: Investment trends in legal technology' (2018) <https://www.business.hsbc.uk/corporate/-/media/library/business-uk/pdfs/financing-investments-in-legal-tech-2018.pdf> accessed 5 May 2021

Integra Ledger <https://integraledger.com/> accessed 8 May 2021

International Organization for Standardization, 'Benefits of Standards' <https://www.iso.org/benefits-of-standards.html> accessed 11 May 2021

International Organization for Standardization, 'Stages and Resources for Standards Development' <https://www.iso.org/stages-and-resources-for-standards-development.html> accessed 11 May 2021

ISO/TC 307 Blockchain and distributed ledger technologies, 'ISO/AWI TS 23259 Blockchain and distributed ledger technologies — Legally binding smart contracts' (International Organization for Standardization 2019) <https://www.iso.org/standard/75095.html?browse=tc> accessed 7 May 2021

ISO/TC 307 Blockchain and distributed ledger technologies, 'Overview of and interactions between smart contracts in blockchain and distributed ledger technology systems' (International Organization for Standardization 2019) <https://www.iso.org/standard/75624.html?browse=tc> accessed 7 May 2021

Maurya A, 'Love The Problem, Not Your Solution' *Medium* (Online, 12 August 2016) <https://blog.leanstack.com/love-the-problem-not-your-solution-65cfbfb1916b> accessed 8 May 2021

McMillan M and others, 'Smart(er) Contracts in 2020' (*McCullough Robertson*, 7 August 2020) <https://www.mccullough.com.au/2020/08/07/smarter-contracts-in-2020/> accessed 10 May 2021

Mordor Intelligence, 'Legal Services Market—Growth, Trends and Forecast (2020–2025)' (2019)

Mordor Intelligence, 'Legal Services Market—Growth, Trends, COVID-19 Impact, and Forecasts (2021–2026)' (2020)

Naden C, 'Blockchain technology set to grow further with International Standards in pipeline' (*ISO News*, 24 May 2017) <https://www.iso.org/news/Ref2188.htm> accessed 6 May 2021

Pawczuk L, Wiedmann P, and Simpson L, 'So, You've Decided to Join a Blockchain Consortium: Defining the Benefits of "Coopetition"' (*Deloitte*, 2019) <https://www2.deloitte.com/content/dam/Deloitte/us/Documents/technology/us-cons-blockchain-consortium.pdf> accessed 4 May 2021

Pawaczuk L, Massey R, and Holdowsky J, 'Deloitte's 2019 Global Blockchain Survey' (*Deloitte Insights*, 6 May 2019) <https://www2.deloitte.com/content/dam/Deloitte/se/Documents/risk/DI_2019-global-blockchain-survey.pdf> accessed 4 May 2021

Reynen Court, <https://reynencourt.com/> accessed 8 May 2021

Rogers J, Jones-Fenleigh H, and Sanitt A, 'Arbitrating Smart Contract Disputes' (*Norton Rose Fulbright*, October 2017) <https://www.nortonrosefulbright.com/en-au/knowledge/publications/ea958758/arbitrating-smart-contract-disputes> accessed 11 May 2021

Ryan P, 'Smart Contract Relations in e-Commerce: Legal Implications of Exchanges Conducted on the Blockchain' (2017) 7(10) *Technology Innovation Management Review* 10

Simms A and Nichols T, 'Social Loafing: A Review of the Literature' (2014) 15(1) *Journal of Management Policy and Practice* 58

Standards Australia, 'Roadmap for Blockchain Standards' (Report, March 2017) <https://www.standards.org.au/getmedia/ad5d74db-8da9-4685-b171-90142ee0a2e1/Roadmap_for_Blockchain_Standards_report.pdf.aspx> accessed 4 May 2021

Thomson Reuters, '2019 Australia: State of the Legal Market' (Report, 2019) <https://insight.thomsonreuters.com.au/legal/resources/resource/2019-australia-state-of-the-legal-market-report> accessed 10 May 2021

Thomson Reuters, '2020 Australia: State of the Legal Market' (Report, 2020) <https://legalprof.thomsonreuters.com/LEI_2020_State_of_Legal_Market_LP_010620> accessed 10 May 2021

Vos Sir G, 'End-to-End Smart Legal Contracts: Moving from Aspiration to Reality' (2019-2020) 26(1) *Journal of Law, Information and Science* 1

Yafimava D, 'What are Consortium Blockchains, and What Purpose do They Serve?' (*Blockchain Insights*, 15 January 2019) <https://openledger.info/insights/consortium-blockchains/> accessed 7 May 2021

Chapter 18 (Golding and Giancasparo)

Bacina M, 'When Two Worlds Collide: Smart Contracts and the Australian Legal System' (2018) 21 *Journal of Internet Law* 15

Borgogno O, 'Smart Contracts as the (New) Power of the Powerless' (2019) 6 *European Review of Private Law* 885

de Caria R, 'The Legal Meaning of Smart Contracts' (2019) 6 *European Review of Private Law* 731

Carter J, *Contract Law in Australia* (6th edn, LexisNexis Butterworths 2013)

Chapman A, Howe J and Ainsworth J, 'Organisational Policies and Australian Employment Law: A Preliminary Study of Interaction' (2015) University of Melbourne Centre for Employment and Labour Relations Law Working Paper No 53 <https://law.unimelb.edu.au/__data/assets/pdf_file/0003/1649019/Working-Paper-No-53.pdf> accessed 30 September 2021

Chilaeva M and Dutton P, 'Smart Contracts: Can They Be Aligned with Traditional Principles or are Bespoke Norms Necessary?' (2018) 8 *Journal of International Banking & Financial Law* 479

Deakin S and Morris G, *Labour Law* (6th edn, Hart Publishing 2012)

Dickens L, 'Exploring the Atypical: Zero Hours Contracts' (1997) 26 *Industrial Law Journal* 262

DiMatteo L and Poncibo C, 'Quandary of Smart Contracts and Remedies: The Role of Contract Law and Self-Help Remedies' (2019) 6 *European Review of Private Law* 805

Drescher D, *Blockchain Basics: A Non-Technical Introduction in 25 Steps* (Apress 2017)

Dutz M, Almeida R, and Packard T, *The Jobs of Tomorrow: Technology, Productivity, and Prosperity in Latin America and the Carribean* (World Bank Publications 2018)

Finck M, 'Smart Contracts as a Form of Solely Automated Processing under the GDPR' (2019) 9 *International Data Privacy Law* 78

Freedland M and Kountouris N, *The Legal Construction of Personal Work Relations* (Oxford University Press 2011)

Frey CB, *The Technology Trap: Capital, Labor, and Power in the Age of Automation* (Princeton University Press 2019)

Giancaspro M, 'Do Workplace Policies Form Part of Employment Contracts? A Working Guide and Advice for Employers' (2016) 44 *ABLR* 106

—— 'Is a Smart Contract Really a Smart Idea? Insights from a Legal Perspective' (2017) 33 *Computer Law & Security Review* 825

Golding G, 'The Origins of Terms Implied by Law into English and Australian Employment Contracts' (2020) 20 *Oxford University Commonwealth Law Journal* 163

Governatori G and others, 'On Legal Contracts, Imperative and Declarative Smart Contracts, and Blockchain Systems' (2018) 26 *Artificial Intelligence and Law* 377

Kemp R, 'Mobile Payments: Current and Emerging Regulatory and Contracting Issues' (2013) 29 *Computer Law & Security Review* 175

Krishna Balan R and Ramasubbu N, 'The Digital Wallet: Opportunities and Prototypes' (2009) 42(4) *IEEE Computer* 100

Marthews A and Tucker C, 'Blockchain and Identity Persistence' in Brummer C (ed), *Cryptoassets: Legal, Regulatory, and Monetary Perspectives* (Oxford University Press 2019)

McCarry G, 'The Employee's Duty to Obey Unreasonable Orders' (1984) 58 *Australian Law Journal* 327

McKinney S, Landy R, and Wilka R, 'Smart Contracts, Blockchain, and the Next Frontier of Transactional Law' (2018) 13 *Washington Journal of Law, Technology & Arts* 313

Mik E, 'Smart Contracts: Terminology, Technical Limitations and Real-World Complexity' (2017) 9 *Law, Innovation and Technology* 269

—— 'The Legal Problems Surrounding Blockchains' (2018) *SAL Practitioner* 13

Milnes M, 'Blockchain: Issues in Australian Competition and Consumer Law' (2018) 26 *Australian Journal of Competition and Consumer Law* 265
NewsBTC, 'Smart Contracts May Help Corporations Pay Their Employees' (Spnsored Post, 17 September 2018) <https://www.newsbtc.com/sponsored/smart-contracts-may-help-corporations-pay-their-employees/> accessed 12 May 2021
Organisation for Economic Co-operation and Development, *OECD Digital Economy Outlook 2017* (OECD Publishing 2017)
Owens R, Riley J, and Murray J, *The Law of Work* (2nd edn, Oxford University Press 2011)
Prassl J, *The Concept of the Employer* (Oxford University Press 2015)
—— *Humans as a Service: The Promise and Perils of Work in the Gig Economy* (Oxford University Press 2018)
Pratap M, 'Everything You Need to Know About Smart Contracts: A Beginner's Guide' (Hackernoon, 27 August 2018) <https://hackernoon.com/everything-you-need-to-know-about-smart-contracts-a-beginners-guide-c13cc138378a> accessed 12 May 2021
Raskin M, 'The Law and Legality of Smart Contracts' (2017) 1 *Georgetown Law Technology Review* 305
Rohr J, 'Smart Contracts and Traditional Contract Law, or: The Law of the Vending Machine' (2019) 67 *Cleveland State Law Review* 71
Ryan P, 'Smart Contract Relations in e-Commerce: Legal Implications of Exchanges Conducted on the Blockchain' (2017) 7 *Technology Innovation Management Review* 14
Stewart A and others, *Creighton and Stewart's Labour Law* (6th edn, Federation Press 2016)
Tai ETT, 'Force Majeure and Excuses in Smart Contracts' (2019) 6 *European Review of Private Law* 787
Werbach K and Cornell N, 'Contracts Ex Machina' (2017) 67 *Duke Law Journal* 313
Wiles J, '5 Ways Blockchain Will Affect HR' (Gartner, 27 August 2019) <https://www.gartner.com/smarterwithgartner/5-ways-blockchain-will-affect-hr/> accessed 12 May 2021

Chapter 19 (Gleeson)

Allen JG and Lastra RM, 'Border Problems: Mapping the Third Border' (2020) 83 *Modern Law Review* 505
Beale HG (ed), *Chitty on Contracts* (33rd edn, Sweet & Maxwell 2018)
Cartwright J, *Misrepresentation, Mistake and Non-Disclosure* (5th edn, Sweet & Maxwell 2019)
Fleckner A, 'Regulating Trading Practices', in Moloney N, Ferran E, and Payne J (eds), *The Oxford Handbook of Financial Regulation* (Oxford University Press 2015)
Kötz H, *European Contract Law* (Mertens G and Weir T trs, Oxford University Press 2017)
International Organization of Securities Commissions, 'Policies on Error Trades' (Final Report, October 2005) <https://www.iosco.org/library/pubdocs/pdf/IOSCOPD208.pdf> accessed 30 September 2021
Low K, 'Unilateral Mistake at Common Law and in Equity' [2005] *Lloyd's Maritime and Commercial Law Quarterly* 423
—— and Mik E 'Unpicking a Fin(e)tech Mess: Can old doctrines cope in the 21st Century?' (Oxford Business Law Blog, 8 November 2019), <https://www.law.ox.ac.uk/business-law-blog/blog/2019/11/unpicking-finetech-mess-can-old-doctrines-cope-21st-century> accessed 6 July 2021
McGhee J (ed), *Snell's Equity* (32nd edn, Sweet & Maxwell 2010)
Midwinter SB, 'The Great Peace and Precedent' (2003) 119 *Law Quarterly Review* 180

NasdaqTrader, 'Obvious Error Transactions Policy' <https://www.nasdaqtrader.com/Micro.aspx?id=ObviousErrorPolicy> accessed 6 July 2021

Scholz L, 'Algorithmic Contracts' (2017) 20 *Stanford Technology Law Review* 128

Yeo N and Farmer J, 'Mapping the Landscape: Cryptocurrency disputes under English law (pat 2)' (2019) 5 *Butterworths Journal of International Banking and Finance Law* 290

Yeo TM, 'Great Peace: A Distant Disturbance' (2004) 121 *Law Quarterly Review* 393

Chapter 20 (Morgan, Livingston, and Moir)

Allen D, Lane A, and Poblet M, 'The Governance of Blockchain Dispute Resolution' (2019) 25 *Harvard Negotiation Law Review* 75

Allen J, 'Wrapped and Stacked: "Smart Contracts" and the Interaction of Natural and Formal Language' (2018) 14 *ERCL* 307

Anderson M and Perrin A, 'Tech Adoption Climbs Among Older Adults' (Pew Research Center, 17 May 2017) <https://www.pewresearch.org/internet/2017/05/17/tech-adoption-climbs-among-older-adults/> accessed 7 June 2021

Barendrecht M and others, 'ODR and the Courts: The Promise of 100% Access to Justice?' (2016) IV *HIIL* 43

Chamber of Commerce (ICC) Commission on Arbitration and ADR Task Force, 'Information Technology in International Arbitration' (International Chamber of Commerce, 2017), 10 <https://iccwbo.org/content/uploads/sites/3/2017/03/icc-information-technology-in-international-arbitration-icc-arbitration-adr-commission.pdf> accessed 8 June 2021

Carneiro D and others, 'Online Dispute Resolution: An Artificial Intelligence Perspective' (2014) 41 *AIR* 211

Clark E, Cho G, and Hoyle A, 'Online Dispute Resolution: Present Realities, Pressing Problems and Future Prospects' (2003) 17 *IRLCT* 21

Condlin R, 'Online Dispute Resolution: Stinky, Repugnant, or Drab' (2017) 18 *CJCR* 717

Dhakappa B, 'Sagewise—Adding Dispute Resolution To Smart Contracts' (TechWeek, 9 September 2018) <https://techweek.com/sagewise-blockchain-los-angeles/> accessed 1 June 2021

Dickinson A, 'Cryptocurrencies and the Conflict of Laws' in Fox D and Green S (eds), *Cryptocurrencies in Public and Private Law* (Oxford University Press 2019)

Ebner N and Zeleznikow J, 'Fairness, Trust and Security in Online Dispute Resolution' [2015] *Hamline Uni Sch Law JPLP* 36

Ebner N and Zeleznikow J, 'No Sheriff in Town: Governance for Online Dispute Resolution' (2016) 32 *Negotiation Journal* 297

Farned DB, 'A New Automated Class of Online Dispute Resolution: Changing the Meaning of Computer-Mediated Communication' (2011) 2 *Faulkner Law Review* 335

Galloway P, 'Is Construction Arbitration ready for Online Dispute Resolution?' (2013) 30 *ICLR* 215

Hamann K and Smith R, 'Facial Recognition Technology: Where Will It Take Us?' (The American Bar Association, 2019) <https://www.americanbar.org/groups/criminal_justice/publications/criminal-justice-magazine/2019/spring/facial-recognition-technology/> accessed 3 June 2021

Hebert Smith Freehills, 'Update [8]: "Necessity is the Mother of Invention": Covid-19 Dramatically Accelerates Digitalisation of Arbitration Processes' (Herbert Smith Freehills, 10 July 2020) <https://hsfnotes.com/arbitration/2020/07/10/update-8-necess

ity-is-the-mother-of-invention-covid-19-dramatically-accelerates-digitalisation-of-arbi tration-processes/> accessed 25 May 2021

HM Courts & Tribunals Service, 'COVID-19: Overview of HMCTS response' (HM Courts & Tribunals Service, July 2020) < https://assets.publishing.service.gov.uk/government/uploads/system/uploads/attachment_data/file/896779/HMCTS368_recovery_-_COVID-19-_Overview_of_HMCTS_response_A4L_v3.pdf> accessed 26 May 2021

HM Courts & Tribunals Service, 'Guidance: HMCTS services: Video Hearings service' (HM Courts & Tribunals Service, 14 May 2021) < https://www.gov.uk/guidance/hmcts-servi ces-video-hearings-service> accessed 1 June 2021

HM Courts & Tribunals Service, 'New video tech to increase remote hearings in civil and family courts' (HM Courts & Tribunals Service, 1 July 2020)<https://www.gov.uk/gov ernment/news/new-video-tech-to-increase-remote-hearings-in-civil-and-family-cou rts> accessed 27 May 2021

Hong Y, 'Data Localisation: Deconstructing Myths and Suggesting a Workable Model for the Future: The Cases Of China and The EU' (2019) 5 BPH 17

Hynes J, '"Hello Dungavel!": Observations on the Use of Video Link Technology in Immigration Bail Hearings' (UK Administrative Justice Institute, 6 May 2019) <https:// ukaji.org/2019/05/06/hello-dungavel-observations-on-the-use-of-video-link-technol ogy-in-immigration-bail-hearings/> accessed 6 June 2021

JAMS, Rules Governing Disputes arising out of Smart Contracts (JAMS) <https://www.jams adr.com/rules-smart-contracts> accessed 14 September 2021

Jur, 'Whitepaper' (Jur, July 2019) <https://jur.io/wp-content/uploads/2019/05/jur-whitepa per-v.2.0.2.pdf> accessed 2 June 2021

JUSTICE, Delivering Justice in an Age of Austerity (JUSTICE 2015) < https://justice.org.uk/justice-age-austerity-2/> accessed 15 September 2021

Kandaswamy R and Furlonger D, 'Blockchain-Based Transformation: A Gartner Trend Insights Report' (Gartner, 27 March 2018) <https://www.gartner.com/en/doc/3869696-blockchain-based-transformation-a-gartner-trend-insight-report> accessed 1 June 2021

Katsh E and Rabinovich-Einy O, 'Blockchain and the Inevitability of Disputes: The Role for Online Dispute Resolution' (2019) *JDR* 47

Kaufmann-Kohler G, 'Online Dispute Resolution and its Significance for International Commercial Arbitration, Global Reflections On International Commerce And Dispute Resolution' (ICC Publishing 2005)

Kleros, 'One Pager' (Kleros 2018) <https://kleros.io/onepager_en.pdf> accessed 4 June 2021

Lessig L, 'Code Is Law, On Liberty in Cyberspace' (Harvard Magazine 2000) <http://harv ardmagazine.com/2000/01/code-is-law-html> accessed 25 May 2021

McKinsey Global Institute, 'Twenty-Five Years of Digitization: Ten Insights into How to Play It Right' (McKinsey 2019) <https://www.mckinsey.com/business-functions/mckin sey-digital/our-insights/twenty-five-years-of-digitization-ten-insights-into-how-to-play-it-right> accessed 24 May 2021

Mik E, 'Smart Contracts: A Requiem' [2019] *JCL* 36

Morgan C and Reed R, 'Dispute Resolution in the Era of Big Data and AI' (Herbert Smith Freehills, 18 September 2019) <https://www.herbertsmithfreehills.com/latest-thinking/dispute-resolution-in-the-era-of-big-data-and-ai> accessed 26 May 2021

Online Dispute Resolution Advisory Group, 'Online Dispute Resolution for Low Value Civil Claims: Report by the UK Civil Justice Council' (Civil Justice Council, February 2015), 26–27 <https://www.judiciary.uk/wp-content/uploads/2015/02/Online-Dispute-Res olution-Final-Web-Version1.pdf> accessed 22 May 2021

Pertoldi A and McIntosh M, 'Enforcement of judgments between the UK and the EU post-Brexit: where are we now?' (Thomson Reuters, 20 Jan 2020)<http://disputeresolutionblog.practicallaw.com/enforcement-of-judgments-between-the-uk-and-the-eu-post-brexit-where-are-we-now/> accessed 19 May 2021

ProPublica, 'Machine Bias: There's software used across the country to predict future criminals. And it's biased against blacks' (ProPublica, 23 May 2016) <https://www.propublica.org/article/machine-bias-risk-assessments-in-criminal-sentencing> accessed 8 June 2021

Schmitz A and Rule C, 'Online Dispute Resolution for Smart Contracts' [2019] *JDR* 103

Schmitz A, 'Measuring "Access to Justice" in the Rush to Digitize' (2020) 88 *Fordham Law Review* 2381

Schultz T, 'Does Online Dispute Resolution Need Governmental Intervention? The Case for Architectures of Control and Trust' (2004) 6 *NC JOLT* 71

Shieber J, 'Sagewise Pitches a Service to Verify Claims and Arbitrate Disputes over Blockchain Transactions' (Tech Crunch, 3 August 2018) <https://techcrunch.com/2018/08/03/sagewise-pitches-a-service-to-verify-claims-and-arbitrate-disputes-over-blockchain-transactions/> accessed 5 June 2021

<https://thesolicitorsgroup.co.uk/news/2020/racial-bias-in-immigration-algorithms> accessed 9 June 2021

Susskind R, *Online Courts and the Future of Justice* (OUP 2019)

Teitz L, 'Providing Legal Services for the Middle Class in Cyberspace: The Promise and Challenge of On-Line Dispute Resolution' (2001) 70 *Fordham Law Review* 985

The Solicitors Group, 'Racial bias in immigration algorithms: The Law Society described the decision announced by the Home Office as timely and has warned of the risk of discrimination' (The Solicitors Group, 10 August 2020)

Thomson Reuters, The Impact of ODR Technology on Dispute Resolution in the UK (Thomson Reuters 2016)

UKJT, 'The Digital Dispute Resolution Rules' (UKJT 2019) <https://35z8e83m1ih83drye28o09d1-wpengine.netdna-ssl.com/wp-content/uploads/2021/04/Lawtech_DDRR_Final.pdf> accessed 14 September 2021

Vos G, 'End-to-End Smart Legal Contracts: Moving from Aspiration to Reality' (2019–2020) 26 *JLIS*

Wahab A, Katsh E, and Rainey D, 'Online Dispute Resolution: Theory and Practice: A Treatise on Technology and Dispute Resolution' [2011] *EIP* 21

Zeleznikow J, 'Can Artificial Intelligence And Online Dispute Resolution Enhance Efficiency And Effectiveness In Courts' (2017) 8 *IJCA* 30

Index

Figures and boxes are indicated by *f* and *b* following the page number

Accord Project 2
accountability
  DAOs
    natural language governance documents, use of 365
    questions of responsibility, complex nature of 363–5
    traditional mechanisms to allocate accountability, use of 364, 365
  definition of 362
  smart contract legal architecture *see under* design of smart contract
agency costs 125–6
agentivity 12n, 12, 24
AI *see* artificial intelligence (AI)
air gaps 366–7
algorithms 74, 75–6, 310
algorithmic contracts 75, 115
  meaning 112–13
  self-performing algorithmic contracts as smart contracts 71
  unenforceability, arguments for 407
anonymity 3
  dispute resolution, optional anonymity in 85
  DLT, and 425, 437, 451
  enforcement, and 209
  smart contracts, and 44, 209, 387
  see also pseudonymity
applications of smart contracts *see* use cases for smart contracts
arbitration *see under* dispute resolution
artificial intelligence (AI) 81, 136, 247, 305, 307, 311
  AI-powered contract drafting 312, 340, 351
  algorithms, and 74, 429, 448
  chatbots 332
  contractual triggers fulfilled, determining 177
  dispute resolution, and 429, 448
    AI predicting outcomes of disputes 442
    AI tools used as first, non-binding step in 448
  efficiency of contractual due diligence, improving 185
  legal technology developments, and 351–2

AI dependent on data training sets 351
  embedding of metadata 351–2
  robotics, and 143
  'Turing test' for emergence of 337
  visa applications, use in 446–7
automated mistake *see* legal consequences of automated mistake
automation 1, 184–6
  contract automation *see* contract automation
autonomous performance 225–45
  comparative analysis of smart contracts and documentary credit 233–44
    closed system 235
    efficient breach 235–6–8
    internalized medium of exchange 233–5
    securing sufficient funds to enable contractual performance 243–4
  concept of autonomous performance 226
  documentary credit as analogue autonomous performance 226, 230–2
    core functionalities of documentary credit 231–2
    see also documentary credit
  invalid and illegal contracts 241–3
  lack of adaptability 238–41
  three core functionalities 227–9
    autonomous contractual performance as case for smart contracts 227–8
    closed system, mechanism operating as 226, 229
    internalized medium of exchange 226, 228–9
    legal concerns about autonomous nature of smart contracts 228
    securing funds to guarantee contractual performance 226, 229
autonomous vehicles 191–2

Bitcoin 7, 31, 31n, 114, 327, 330
  Bitcoin unit, nature of 103–4
  mode of operation 103, 114
Blawx 256, 297, 315, 319–21, 324–5
blockchain 8, 9, 10–11, 12, 30–1, 71, 105, 330–1
  blockchain-based functional alternatives to legal processes 82–4

blockchain (*cont.*)
  blockchain-based 'smart contracts' 1, 2, 3, 5, 80, 208–11, 385, 423–4
    decentralized nature of blockchain, consequences of 209–10
    increasing popularity of 341–2
    cryptocurrencies *see* Bitcoin; Ethereum
    nature/types of 327–8, 330
    social reality, and *see* documentality
boilerplate contracts 311–12, 254–5
  smart boilerplate examples *see under* smart legal contracts (SLC) model
  see also smart contract 'drafting'
Boolean logic/algebra 187, 311
business efficacy 73, 111

canonical form problem 289
certainty
  certainty of dispute resolution, importance of 101
  commercial certainty 416–19
  contract law 73, 101
  cryptoassets, legal uncertainty around 55, 57, 59
  smart contracts 249, 357–8
    need for legal certainty 73, 101, 357–8
chatbots 332–3
Chinese Room Argument 307–8, 337
code 5, 29, 118, 132–5, 155, 171, 215–16, 240
  agreed mechanisms for correcting code 156–7
  American Standard Code for Information Interchange (ASCII) 310–11
  choice of clauses to encode 175–6, 187
  coding limitations 447–8
  DAOs, and 133
  formal integration of code into contract 156, 187
  impact of specificity and inflexibility of 161–2
  indicative use cases 135*f*
  language, and *see under* languages for smart and computable contracts
  legal categorization of coded provisions 163–5
  legal enforceability 136
  meaning of smart contract code 118, 273
  natural language, smart contract code and 137–8, 278, 280, 282
  programming languages
    Blawx 319–21
    Ergo 316–18
    Lexon 318–19
  pseudo-code 221, 221*f*
  reasons to incorporate code 165–6
  rigidity of code, consequences of 155–6
  split contracts 118–19, 134
  translation, and 309

verification and validation 271–2, 283, 285–90, 299, 302
commercial certainty *see under* certainty
computable contracts 3, 5, 206, 312
  languages for
    controlled natural language 298–303
    domain specific programming languages 295–8
    drafting style in CSL and Marlowe 298*f*
    drafting style in Lexon 301*f*
    drafting style in logical English 300*f*
    markup languages and templates 293–5
  smart contracts as 'computable contracts' 208
'computational contracts' 5, 21
contract automation 12, 25
  analogy between automation of contracts and autonomous vehicles 191–203
  conceptual levels of contract automation 193–4
  features of different levels of contract automation 195–201
  features of digital execution mechanism or digital platform 202–3
  when a contract becomes a smart legal contract 201–2
  automation and digital transformation 184–6
  fusion of contractual terms with code 24, 25
  intention, and 75–6
  see also smart legal contracts, evolution of
contract stacks 1–2, 10, 11, 12–14, 25, 56, 188, 211, 272
  interaction between 'encoded' and 'conventional' components 3, 12–14, 25
    legal prose and machine-readable code in single instrument 148–9
    smart legal contracts, and 148–9
  'wrapped' or 'stacked' smart contracts 42–3
contracts/contract law 8, 9–10, 12, 73, 256
  certainty 73, 101
  consumer and commercial contracts 255–6
  conventional ('paper') contracts 42, 145, 211*f*
  definition of 'contract' 108, 255
  digital evolution of contracts *see* contract automation
  enforceability 73–4, 111, 150, 222
    conditions to be legally binding 109–10
    flexibility inherent in contractual form 260–1, 262
  formation 150, 185*f*, 406–9
  forms of legal contracts 112–13
  freedom of contract 10, 72–3
  functioning of contracts in society 211, 262–3
  future contract law, issues raised by smart contracts for 45–52

logical operators in contract drafting 45–6
semantic richness, intentional loss of 48–9
semantic richness, unintentional loss of 47–8
textualism and contextualism 49–51
translation of formal language into natural language 46–7
good faith and fair dealing 49
human conduct, and 259, 262
illegality, jurisdiction, and procedure 10, 43–5
implied terms 111, 112
interpretation 51, 214
role of interpretation 213–14, 215, 216
language *see under* language/natural language
jurisdiction 10, 43–5
oral contracts 37–9, 42, 112
party autonomy 72–3
remedies *see* remedies
smart contracts, English law and *see* smart contracts and English law/contract law
smart legal contracts *see* smart legal contracts
speech act(s) creating the contract 37–40
documents recording speech acts 39–40
written contracts 39–40
natural language, in 111–12
contractware
definition 28, 29
digital contractware 28–30
digitalization of payment and of goods themselves 29–30
evolution of 27–8
performance ensured by making breach impossible or expensive 27–8
COVID-19 370, 435
crypto-anarchy 138–40
agents, use of 138–9
cost of privacy 139–40
Decentralised Finance ('DeFi') movement 139
reputation systems, use of 139–40
risk of opportunistic behaviour 138–9
cryptoassets 8, 57, 60, 61, 66, 83
Bitcoin *see* Bitcoin
Ethereum *see* Ethereum
Legal Statement see Legal Statement on Cryptoassets and Smart Contracts
legal uncertainty around 55, 57, 59
property under English law, as 59–62, 63, 64, 111
cryptocurrencies 24, 27, 32, 55
Bitcoin *see* Bitcoin
Ethereum *see* Ethereum
cybersecurity
cybersecurity risk 134, 432
smart legal contracts, and 153–4, 172
cyberspace 85–7

Decentralised Autonomous Organisations ('DAOs') 248, 331, 337
accountability 363–5
nature of 133, 363–4
The DAO incident 50–1, 67, 116, 208
Decentralised Finance ('DeFi') movement 82, 139
design of smart contracts 3, 262
accountability 362–5
air gaps 365–7
certainty 357–8
design trade-offs 132–40
natural language and code, no overlap between 135–7
natural language and code, partial or complete overlap between 137–8
price of crypto-anarchy 138–40
erasure or capability to overwrite, need to accommodate 260
flexibility 256, 358–61, 263
interoperability 355–6
safety/safeguards 365–7
smart contract legal architecture 353–68
accountability 362–5
certainty 357–8
flexibility 358–62
interoperability 355–6
safety 365–7
standard form contracts/boilerplate 254–5, 258
see also smart legal contracts (SLC) model
developers, lawyers and *see* interdisciplinary collaboration
digital contractware *see under* contractware
digital economy 177–9
dispute resolution 79–87, 420–53
AI, and 429, 442, 448
alternative dispute resolution 67
arbitration 16, 80, 82, 85, 101, 251, 423, 426–7, 436, 438–45
arbitration systems 136, 429
background Online Dispute Resolution ('ODR')
consensual methods of resolving disputes 421, 422–3
distributed ledger technology 423–4
smart contracts' versus 'SLCs' and party intentions 424–8
blockchain-based dispute resolution systems 82–4
appeals 83, 83n
challenge for conventional law 81–2
certainty of dispute resolution, importance of 101
challenges to overcome 445–51

dispute resolution (*cont.*)
  coding limitations 447–8
  compatibility issues 448–9
  culture and people 445–7
  enforcement 450–1
  code-based dispute resolution alternatives integrated in legal system 87
  courts 67, 129
  DLT as an additional catalyst for ODR 435–51
    challenges to overcome 445–51
    defining concept of decentralized justice 436
    examples of DLT-based ODR offerings 441–5
    procedure for resolving SLC disputes 437–9
    substantive questions for smart contract and SLC dispute resolution 439–41
  drivers and obstacles to online dispute resolution 428–35
    AI, and 429
    automated platforms 429–30
    COVID-19 435
    electronic communications 428–9
    increased accessibility and fairness 433–4
    increased efficiency, accountability, and reduced costs 431–3
    key drivers for moving dispute resolution online 430–5
    scalability 434
  efficient breach, and 237–8
  examples of DLT-based ODR offerings 441–5
    categories of ODR procedures 441–2
    digitizing and automating recognized processes 442–3
    hybrid solution 444–5
    re-designing dispute resolution within a distributed network 443
  expedited dispute resolution process entrenched in code itself 68, 80
  halting smart contract's automatic performance 67
  in-built dispute resolution system 66–8, 80
  multidisciplinary collaboration as way forward 451–2
  need for dispute resolution 67
  recent developments in England and Wales 84–5
  UKJT *Digital Dispute Resolution Rules* 67n, 84–5, 87, 426–7
distributed ledger technology (DLT) 1, 3, 4, 5, 8, 11–12, 30–3, 115
  blockchain *see* blockchain
  cryptocurrencies *see* cryptocurrencies
  meaning 423–4

documentality
  social objects and documents 328–37
    blockchains and specific dependence 330–1
    computability and documentality 331–2
    documentality as prescriptive requirements 334–5
    inscriptions that (re)write themselves 332–3
    inspectability and endurance 333–4
    issues of intentionality and Chinese rooms 337
    role of records in making the social world 329–30
    smart legal contracts 335–6
  social reality
    documentality describing 328
    meaning of 328–9
  theory of documentality 328
documentary credit 230–2
  comparative analysis of smart contracts and documentary credit 233–44
    closed system 235
    efficient breach 235–8
    internalized medium of exchange 233–5
    securing sufficient funds to enable contractual performance 243–4
  core functionalities of documentary credit 231–2
  differences between documentary credit and smart contracts 232
  nature of 226, 230, 237
drafting contracts *see* boilerplate contracts; design of smart contracts; languages for smart and computable contracts; mathematization of legal writing; smart contract 'drafting'; smart legal contracts (SLC) model

efficient breach 235–8
  dispute resolution, application of 237–8
  efficient breach relying on specific performance order 236–7
  kill switch, triggering 237
  nature of efficient breach theory 235, 236
  smart contracts making economically efficient breaches impossible 235–6
employment and smart contracts 383–96
  background to smart contracts in employment 385–8
  advantages for employers 387–8
  advantages of smart contracts 386–7
  inability of smart contracts to accommodate change 391–2
  functional vulnerabilities 393–4
  Inevitability of structural change 394–5
  inflexibility 392–3

unsuitability of smart contracts for
        employment 388–95
    inability to accommodate change 391–2
    inability to account for managerial
        prerogative 388–9
    inability to allow for employer's exercise of
        discretions 389–90
    inability to performance manage, discipline,
        and dismiss for misconduct 391
enforceability of smart contracts 73–7
    blockchain based smart contracts 208–10
    consideration and exchange problem 76
    intention and automation 74, 75–6
    smart legal contracts need to provide for legal
        enforceability 79–80
    vitiating factors and smart contracts 76–7
enforcement costs 127–32
    benefits of smart legal contracts 131
    legal institutions to enforce
        commitment 129–30
    opportunism 112, 128
        mitigation in smart contracts 131, 229
    reputation systems, use of 128–9
    risk of default 127–8
    smart contracts avoiding enforcement costs
        and injustices 130–2
EOS 136–7
equity
    equitable doctrines, smart contracts and 52
    equitable relief—Lord Mance's
        remedy 414–16
    equity or restitution, importance of 257–8
    remedy for mistake, as 409–11, 414–16
    uncertainties as to remedies at law and in
        equity 249
Ergo 294, 315, 316–18, 321, 322–3
escape hatches 134
Ethereum 7–8, 31, 31n, 81, 83
    persistent scripts 114
    smart contracts 8, 103, 114, 248, 269, 342,
    Solidity 23, 29, 36, 47, 133, 134, 301, 342, 343,
        345, 346, 352

fair dealing 49, 265
FinTech Delivery Panel 62
flexibility
    contractual form, flexibility inherent
        in 260–1, 262
    lack of adaptability/flexibility in smart
        contracts 238–41, 256
    smart contract legal architecture *see under*
        design of smart contracts

good faith 49, 265

hacking 330
    smart legal contracts, and 153–4, 156
    vulnerability of smart contracts 217
homogenization of language *see under* smart
    contract 'drafting'
hybrid contracts 113, 132

interdisciplinary collaboration 369–82
    emerging taxonomy of interdisciplinary
        collaboration 371–4
    developers and lawyers, divide between 371
    global consortia models 372–3
    strategic partnerships 373–4
    lawyers, standards, and emerging
        technologies 379–81
    new standards framework for 'legally
        binding smart contracts' 380–1
    relative benefits of different ways of
        working 374–8
    benefits of collaboration for smart legal
        contracts 376–8
    going it alone 375–6
    smart legal contracts as development
        domain 378
International Organization for Standardization
    108, 186
Internet of Things (IoT) devices 160, 178, 200, 352
    meaning of 355n
interoperability *see under* design of smart
    contracts
interpretation
    courts' interpretation of contracts 130, 213
    interpretation of smart contracts 350–2
    language/natural language 51
    'formal' versus 'contextual' interpretation of
        contractual language 49–50
    smart contracts *see under* smart contracts
invalid and illegal contracts 241–3
    allocation of risk of contractual
        invalidity 241–2
    permissionless and permissioned
        networks 241
    transactions void/unenforceable for reasons of
        public policy 242–3
isomorphism problem 289

Java 95, 98, 106, 342, 346
Javascript 29, 301, 313, 343f, 346, 348

kill switches 237, 366

language/natural language 1, 29, 51
    agreed, constrained syntax, need for 45–6
    barrier to entry, language as 346–7

language/natural language (cont.)
  code avoiding the semantic ambiguity of
    natural language 132–3
  contracts in natural/human language 144,
    151–2, 153, 154
  interpretation 49–50, 51
  language homogenization *see under* smart
    contract 'drafting'
  legal writing *see* mathematization of legal
    writing
  natural language 273–4
    allowing contracts to be intentionally and
      unintentionally incomplete 322
    controlled natural language 279, 298–303
    natural and formal languages 36–7
    'natural' or 'ordinary' meaning of
      contractual language 45, 50
    translation of formal language into natural
      language, need for 46–7
  natural language and code
    no overlap between 135–7
    partial or complete overlap between 137–8
  natural language documents as authoritative
    record 111–12, 134
  natural language governance documents, use
    of 365
  Natural Language Processing (NLP) 311
  semantic richness, loss of
    intentional loss of 48–9, 149
    unintentional loss of 47–8, 149
  smart contracts *see* languages for smart and
    computable contracts
  smart legal contracts *see* languages for smart
    and computable contracts
  textualism and contextualism 49–51, 149
languages for smart and computable
  contracts 11–14, 269–304
  computable contracts 292–303
    controlled natural language 298–303
    domain specific programming
      languages 295–8
    drafting style in CSL and Marlowe 298*f*
    drafting style in Lexon 301*f*
    drafting style in logical English 300*f*
    markup languages and templates 293–5
  contract to code 279–80
  language homogenization *see under* smart
    contract 'drafting'
  language stack 271–8
    executable language and human-readable
      code 272–3
    natural language 273–4
    programming language 275–6
    runtime systems, virtual machines,
      interpreters, and byte code 277–8
  specification language 274–5
  verification and validation of code 271–2
  legal language, smart contracts and 263–4
  natural and formal expression 278–82
    contract to code, from 279–80
    internal or external model 280–1
    practical aspects of validating changes in
      code or agreement 281–2
  programming languages examples *see* Blawx; Ergo;
    Java; Javascript; Lexon; Python; Solidity
  semantics 283–91
    ante hoc and post hoc analysis 284–5
    consequences for validation 285–6
    different perspectives 284–5
    semantics and validation 286–7
    semantics of the agreement 287–90
    semantics of the code 290–1
    separability, isomorphism, and canonical
      form 289–90
  unavoidability of translation 212–13, 220
  validation
    creation and validation of smart contract
      code 285–6
    formal methods of 286–7
    semantics, and 286–7
    valid by design 287
  see also language/natural language, smart
    contract 'drafting'
Law Commission 14, 65
LawtechUK Panel 2, 62, 426
lawyers 4, 8
  agency costs 125–6
  AI software in dispute resolution, using 312,
    351, 447
  coders and lawyers 15, 283, 294, 359, 371
    divide between coders and lawyers 57–8
  computer scientists, and 45–7, 49, 283
  cryptoassets, approach to 59
  contract drafting 19, 156, 297, 303–4, 342
    impact of smart contracts on legal
      professions 350
    language, and 24, 26, 340–2
    programming language or a DSL,
      using 287, 298
    smaller number of native speakers creating
      greater monopoly 341
  developers, working with 369–82
    developers and lawyers, divide between 371
    emerging taxonomy of interdisciplinary
      collaboration 371–4
    global consortia models 372–3
    lawyers, standards, and emerging
      technologies 379–81
    strategic partnerships 373–4

interpretation, and 10, 130, 212, 264, 351
language as a barrier to entry 346
online dispute resolution 422, 429, 431, 433, 447
remedies, and 26, 60, 223
Ricardian contract, and 88–106
relative benefits of different ways of working 374–8
benefits of collaboration for smart legal contracts 376–8
going it alone 375–6
smart legal contracts as development domain 378
smart/smart legal contracts 23–4, 56, 84, 145, 150, 156, 183, 188, 204, 270, 297
new standards framework for 'legally binding smart contracts' 380–1
standards and emerging technologies, and 379–81
new standards framework for 'legally binding smart contracts' 380–1
systems enabling lawyers to work productively from home after COVID-19 370
legal consequences of automated mistake 397–419
commercial certainty 416–19
duty of common law to preserve contracts 416
error trades 416–18
price formation process in trading markets 416
integrating cyber-contracts with the law of mistake 412–16
constructive or deemed knowledge as a solution 413—14
equitable relief—Lord Mance's remedy 414–16
law of mistake 403–12
cyber-contract formation 406–9
equity as a remedy for mistake in English law 409–11
mistake and equity in Singapore law 411–12
Quoine Pte Ltd v B2C2 Ltd 398–403
decision 400–3
facts 398–400
Legal Statement on Cryptoassets and Smart Contracts 2, 4, 5, 14, 62–3, 84, 107, 266
conditions for agreement to be legally binding 109–110
embodying 'legal contract' and automated mechanism of performance 12
English law accommodating smart contracts through principles of contract law 14
smart contracts 9, 118, 138

legal systems/institutions and law
adjudicating disputes 67, 129
digital transformation of law 3, 185
enforcement 129, 130, 140
interpretation of contracts by courts 130, 213, 350-2
litigation as costly and time-consuming 129–30
see also dispute resolution and smart contracts; rule of law
legal writing, mathematization of *see* mathematization of legal writing
Lexon 301, 304, 315, 318–19, 323–4
example drafting style in Lexon 301*f*
extract of contract drafted in Lexon 318*f*
libraries 218–19
Linux Foundation 2
mathematization of legal writing 305–26
code, observations and implications 322–5
Blawx 324–5
Ergo 322–3
Lexon 323–4
code, study of 315–21
Blawx 319–21
Ergo 316–18
Lexon 318–19
logical ancestors and the formalistic return 310–14
early signs 310–11
logical roots of drafting 314
market uptake 312
modern variations 311–14
new environments 312
primer on translation 307–9
context 308–9
semantics 307–8
see also smart contract 'drafting'

measurement costs 123–4
mistake
automated mistake *see* legal consequences of automated mistake
doctrine of 76–7, 403–9
equitable relief—Lord Mance's remedy 414–16
equity as remedy for 409–11
monitoring and verification costs 126–7
moral hazard 125, 126, 247

nature of smart legal contracts *see* concept/nature of smart legal contracts
natural language *see* language/natural language
Natural Language Processing (NLP) 311
negotiation costs 124

non-operational terms
  common non-operational terms best expressed in natural language 187
  standards of behaviour 135–6

'off-chain' 9, 14
  judgments or awards 'off-chain' 426
  'off-chain' assets 61, 133
off-ramps 366, 367
'on-chain' 14, 83
  decisions
    enforcement of 'on-chain' determination 445
    'on-chain' implementation of decisions 426–7
    'on-chain' process enforced within DLT system 423
  dispute resolution, and 85, 426, 439
online dispute resolution *see* dispute resolution
opportunism
  counterparty opportunism 112, 128
  mitigation in smart contracts 131, 229
  lexical opportunism 155–6
oracles 217–18, 253, 385, 394
  'oracle problem' 253, 262, 267

persistent scripts 8, 11, 114
privacy 140, 172, 202, 378
  cost of privacy 109, 139–40
  monetary privacy 89
  ODR platforms, and 449
  PGP (Pretty Good Privacy) tool 94–5
  privacy breaches 179
  socially undesirable behaviour, and 140
property law, English *see under* smart contracts and English law/contract law
pseudo-code 221, 221f
pseudonymity 3, 82, 140
  DLT networks, default configuration for participants in 138
  miners 387
  permanent pseudonymity, relaxing requirement for 140
  transaction costs, and 109, 120, 126
  user pseudonymity
    exploitation of deliberate vulnerabilities in code 126
    obfuscating socially undesirable activities 120, 140
  see also anonymity
Python 29, 218, 315, 342, 343, 346

record-keeping *see* documentality
remedies 58, 60, 249, 251, 255, 257–62
  adaptability of 258
  contract law remedies and risk-allocation 260–2

damages and compensation 257, 261
dispute resolution *see* dispute resolution
equity 261
  equitable relief—Lord Mance's remedy 414–16
  equity or restitution, importance of 257–8
  remedy for mistake, as 409–11
injunctions 261
rectification 111, 261
rescission 260, 261
restitution 257–8, 261
smart contracts
  ability of smart contracts to be self-enforcing 257
  legal weaknesses in smart contract design, remedies and 259–60
  remedies giving legitimacy to smart contracting as legal process 251
  smart contract ideals and contingent reality 258–9
specific performance 261
tokenization *see* tokenization
unjust enrichment 61, 257, 261
utility or welfare maximization, and 255
vital role in contract law 255, 258
reputation
  counterparty risk, and 139–40
  implicit contracts, and 110n
  reputation capital 128–9, 255
  reputation signals 125, 125n, 128
  reputation systems 128, 139–40
  reputational consequences 232
    hearings in open court 430
    parties' wish to main excellent reputation 255
    purchasing decisions based on business's reputation 267
Ricardian Contract 88–106
  developments in design 102
  future research, points for 105–6
  nature of 11, 119
  natural language and smart contract code 138
  origins 89–93
    deep dive into bonds 91–2
    research choice of bonds 90–1
  random experiences 100–2
  smart contracts 102–5, 119
    Bitcoin unit 103–4
    sum of all chains 104–5
  split contracts, and 119
  war of the wordsmiths 93–100
    Bow-Tie model of Ricardian Contract 100f
    form of the contract 99–100
    identifier 98, 99
    mark-up 96–7

INDEX 507

Ricardian 'stablecoin' dollar contract showing tag-value pairs 97*f*
signed digital, readable document 94–6
simplification as principle 93–4
Zooko's Triangle 99*f*
rule of law 68, 84
enforcement, and 130, 131

safety/safeguards *see under* design of smart contracts
search costs 122
semantics
languages for smart and computable contracts 283–91
ante hoc and post hoc analysis 284–5
consequences for validation 285–6
different perspectives 284–5
semantics and validation 286–7
semantics of the agreement 287–90
semantics of the code 290–1
separability, isomorphism, and canonical form 289–90
semantic richness
intentional loss of 48–9
semantic richness, unintentional loss of 47–8
translation, and 307–8
separability problem 289
smart contract code *see* code
smart contract 'drafting' 339–52
AI-powered contract drafting 312, 340, 351
impacts of language homogenization by smart contracts 347–52
embedding of metadata 351–2
interpretation of smart contracts by courts 350–2
legal profession and industry, impact on 350
loss of linguistic diversity 347–8
notarized (smart) contracts 348–50
language, contract drafting, and lawyers 340–2
language homogenization 344–7
language as a barrier to entry 346–7
programming standardization 345–6
smart contracts and language homogenization 340, 342–4
impacts of language homogenization by smart contracts 347–52
smart contracts as impetus to standardize language in contract drafting 342
standardization of programming language 343–4
see also languages for smart and computable contracts; mathematization of legal writing

smart contracts
advantages 10, 131, 221, 386
automation of contractual performance 12, 127
transactions visible to all miners within blockchain 386–7
agentive function 12, 24
algorithmic contracts *see* algorithmic contracts
automation of contract performance *see* automation
autonomous performance *see* autonomous performance
blockchain-based *see under* blockchain
business efficacy, promotion of 73
characteristics of 206–11
blockchain-based smart contracts 208–11
smart contracts as 'computable contracts' 208
vending machines as implied semi-smart contracts 207
choice of platform 173–4
code *see* code
contract taxonomy 109–19
legal contracts, conditions for 109–10
ontological clarification 111–12
use of 'contract' in economics 110
criticisms of 145
economically efficient breaches, impossibility of 235–6
increasing capital cost of transactions 244
inefficient outcomes 236, 238–9
internalized medium of exchange imposing inherent limitations 233–4
lack of adaptability/flexibility 238–41, 256
lack of contingent intelligence 253
open-textured terms incompatible with autonomous performance 234–5
removing parties' ability to adapt to external changes 238
smart contracts used to execute invalid and illegal contracts 241–3
'unstoppable' nature of closed systems 235
definitions of smart contract 4, 26–33, 71–3, 120, 206–11, 216*f*
agreement whose performance is automated, as 70, 108
automatable and enforceable agreement, as 27
automated transaction comprised of code, script or programming language that executes the terms of an agreement 253
broad definition 71–2, 80
computer code which on specified condition runs automatically to pre-specified functions 144

508 INDEX

smart contracts (*cont.*)
  computer program that directly controls some digital asset, as 248
  computerized transaction protocol that executes terms of a contract, as 71, 113
  contract stored as electronic record verified by the use of blockchain, as 248
  contracts expressed in executable code, as 33
  enforceable legal agreements expressed in computer code, as 54, 248
  event-driven program on a distributed ledger that can take custody over and instruct transfer of assets 254
  instruments of promise and agreement, as 248
  narrow definition of smart contracts 70
  no consensus on 23–4, 109
  legal agreement in human-intelligible and machine-readable language, as 25, 32–3, 55, 71–2, 188
  programming conventions, as 248
  programs executed on blockchain to perform contractual obligations 207
  recording of legal agreement written in a formal, machine-readable language whose text incorporates an algorithm automating some or all performance of the agreement 27
  set of promises, specified in digital form, as 54
  software code that embodies a contract, as 33
  design of *see* design of smart contracts
  design trade-offs *see under* design of smart contracts
  DLT, and 55, 115
  documentality *see* documentality
  drafting *see* smart contract 'drafting'
  economic case for smart contracts 236
  efficiency 256–7
    ability of smart contracts to be self-enforcing 257
    electronic contracts surpassing human cognitive capacity 256–7
    smart contracts too simple compared to demands of contract law 257
  employment, and *see* employment and smart contracts
  enforceability *see* enforceability of smart contracts
  English law, and *see* smart contracts and English law/contract law
  evolution of term 'smart contracts' 113–15
  extensions to smart contracts 217–19
    libraries 218–19
    oracles 217–18
  fetishization of smart contracts 249, 249n, 252, 268
  homogenization of language *see under* smart contract 'drafting'
  inherent traits and misconceptions 115–17
    autonomous/decentralized/trustless 116–17
    immutable/tamper-proof/tamper-resistant 116
    self-executing/self-enforcing 117
  interpretation 11–14
    courts' interpretation of smart contracts 350–1
    evolving canon of interpretation 51
    logical operators in contract drafting 45–6
    role of interpretation 211–17
    semantic richness, intentional loss of 48–9
    semantic richness, unintentional loss of 47–8
    smart boilerplate/examples 168–71, 167*b*
    textualism and contextualism 49–51
    translation of formal language into natural language 46–7
  invalid and illegal contracts 241–3
  language *see* languages for smart and computable contracts
  legal architecture *see* design of smart contracts
  legal certainty 249
  limitations 217
  making smart contracts a reality 70–8
    enforceability *see* enforceability of smart contracts
    policy considerations driving smart contracts 72–3
  mistake *see* legal consequences of automated mistake
  nature of smart contracts 7–8, 10, 11, 25, 26–33, 217
    concept of legal contract not incorporated in 145
    contractware *see* contractware
    efficiency as key definitional marker 256
    ideological commitment to non-contestability 44–5
    immutability 67, 71, 263, 392–3
    pre-packaged automated trading programme, as 398
    self-executing 44, 81, 385
    'strong' and 'weak' smart contracts 44
    text-based instrument, as 10–11
    unique features of 362, 385

whether really a 'contract' *see under* smart contracts and English law/contract law
party autonomy 72–3
present position 56–8
remedies *see* remedies
smart legal contracts, and 370, 424–8
static and dynamic market individualism, smart contracts amplifying 256
statutory regulation *see* statutory regulation of smart contracts
Szaboian smart contract *see* Szaboian smart contract
techno-legal supertoys, smart contracts as *see* techno-legal supertoys
transaction costs *see* transaction costs
types of 118–19
    legally binding and not legally binding 118
    Ricardian contracts 119
    smart legal contracts and smart contract code 118
    split contracts 118–19
use cases for 3–4
smart contracts and English law/contract law 9, 44, 58, 266
accommodating smart contracts through contract law principles 14, 26, 58, 78
certainty, need for 73, 101
consideration and exchange 77
conventional contract law, smart contracts and 43–52
    illegality, jurisdiction, and procedure 43–5
    towards smart(er) contract law 44–52
current developments in English Law 62–4
design of smart contracts 65–6
see also design of smart contracts
dispute resolution *see* dispute resolution
enforceability of smart contracts *see* enforceability of smart contracts
equity *see* equity
errors 76–7, 258
    flawed contracts, reasons for 256–7
execution, smart contracts as *see* smart contracts as execution instead of expression
in-built dispute resolution system for smart contracts 66–8
interpretation *see under* smart contracts
interrelationship between cognition and contract 256–7
mistake, doctrine of 76–7, 403–9
    automated mistake *see* legal consequences of automated mistake
    equitable relief—Lord Mance's remedy 414–16

equity as remedy for 409–11
no barrier to a single instrument 25, 80–1
property in English law
    cryptoassets as property 59–62, 63
    personal property, definition of 61
    real and personal property and choses in action 61
    statutory definition of property 60–1
removal of fundamental legal impediment to smart contract use 64–5
rights and remedies 58, 60
see also remedies
risk-allocation 260–2
rule of law *see* rule of law
smart contracts too simple compared to demands of contract law 257
vitiating factors and smart contracts 76–7
whether a smart contract capable of giving rise to binding legal obligations 63–4
whether a smart contract is really a 'contract' 25, 33–43
    natural and formal languages 36–7
    smart contracts as 'legal contracts' 40–1
    speech act(s) creating the contract 37–40
    'wrapped' or 'stacked' smart contracts 42–3
smart contracts as execution instead of expression 205–24
definition and principal characteristics of smart contracts 206–11
    blockchain-based smart contracts 208–11
    smart contracts as 'computable contracts' 208
    vending machines as implied semi-smart contracts 207
extensions to smart contracts 217–19
    libraries 218–19
    oracles 217–18
implementing contract law in smart contracts 219–23
    complexity of implementing contractual doctrines 22–2
    doctrines outside execution chain 220
    lack of ex post protection 222–3
    role of interpretation, smart contracts and 211–17
    role of interpretation 213–17
    unavoidability of translation 212–13, 220
smart legal contracts
active function components 153–4
allocation of liability 157
autonomous performance *see* autonomous performance
blockchain-based 'smart contracts' 1, 2, 3, 5
concept/nature of 3, 186–7, 425

smart legal contracts (*cont.*)
  key components of 146–55, 188–90
  machine-readable and digital 5, 151
  subset of smart contract code, as 118
  when a contract constitutes a smart legal contract 201–2
contract stacks, smart legal contracts as *see* contract stacks
code *see* code
customizable 149
cybersecurity
  data management architecture 172
  need for 153–4
data management architecture 172
data ownership and IP rights 154
definitions of 147, 186, 188, 370
design *see* design of smart contracts
dispute resolution *see* dispute resolution
documentality *see* documentality
drafting protections/secure digital hosting, need for 150
end-to-end smart legal contracts 54–69
  current development sin English law 62–4
  current position 56–8
  design of smart legal contracts 65–6
  legal impediments, removal of 64–5
  property law *see under* smart contracts and English law/contract law
  nature of 143–4
evolution of *see* smart legal contracts, evolution of
flow-through effects of related contracts and networks 154
hacking, risks from 153–4
interdisciplinary collaboration, and *see* interdisciplinary collaboration
methodologies of legal and digital domains, supporting both 145
language *see* languages for smart and computable contracts
language 11–14
  choice of primacy between smart and natural language terms 158–60
  code components' relationship with natural language 156
  formal integration of code into contract 156
  pairing natural language terms with coded expression of obligation 157, 189–90
  primacy of natural language with code creating efficiencies in execution 155
  natural language and algorithmic instructions 151–2
  see also languages for smart and computable contracts
law, and 3
  legal instruments to manage data reliance, smart legal contracts as 178–9
  legal status of automated contract performance 176–7
  legal uncertainty around smart legal contracts 59
  legal void of digital economy 177–9
  legally binding agreement, smart legal contract as 149–50, 187
mistake *see* legal consequences of automated mistake
model *see* SLC model for integration of machine capabilities into contracts 142–81
Paired Method 149, 157, 189–90, 191
platforms
  choice of platform 173–4
  features of digital execution mechanism or digital platform 202–3
reasons to adopt smart legal contracts 188
remedies *see* remedies
social reality, and 335–6
see also documentality
smart contracts, and 370, 424–8
transaction costs *see under* smart contracts
Unified Method 149, 190
variation 150, 171–2
  variation outside parties' intention 153–4
see also smart contracts
smart legal contracts, evolution of 182–204
  analogy between automation of contracts and autonomous vehicles 191–203
  conceptual levels of contract automation 193–4
  features of different levels of contract automation 195–201
  features of digital execution mechanism or digital platform 202–3
  when a contract constitutes a smart legal contract 201–2
automation and digital transformation 184–6
  digital technologies across contract lifecycle 184–6
  digital transformation of law 184
  simple contract life cycle 185*f*
drafting *see* smart contract 'drafting'
features of different levels of contract automation 195–201
  Level 0 (paper contract) 195–6
  Level 1 (digitally accessible) 196–7
  Level 2 (meaning can be processed) 197–8
  Level 3 (specialized digital platform) 198–9
  Level 4 (automated performance) 199–200
  Level 5 (fully autonomous) 200–1

INDEX   511

smart legal contracts 186–91
  necessary components of 188–90
  Unified Method vs Paired Method 190–1
smart legal contracts (SLC) model 142–81
  active function 153–4
    cybersecurity, need for 153–4
    data ownership and IP rights 154
    flow-through effects of related contracts and networks 154
    'live' machine-based performance of terms 153
    meaning 153
    reliance on contract itself to perform recorded rights and obligations 154
  clause classification 175–6, 187
    future auto-coding of natural language provisions 175–6
    human oversight, role of 176
    parties' agreed/preferred level of generality vs precision of terms 175
  conjoined method 157–65
    ability to arbitrate impact of specificity and inflexibility of code 161–2
    application of conjoined method 160
    choice of primacy between smart and natural language terms 158–60
    definition of conjoined term 158
    legal categorization of coded provisions 163–5
    outcome-based drafting for conjoined terms 162–3
    reasons supporting use of 160–1
    structure and operation of a conjoined term in an SLC 159f
  summary of conjoined method 165
  drafting principles 155–7
    agreed mechanisms for correcting code 156–7
    allocation of liability for damage 157
    broad governance, meaning of 156
    code components' relationship with natural language 156
    formal integration of code into contract 156
    pairing natural language terms with coded expression of obligation 157, 189–90
    primacy of natural language with code creating efficiencies in execution 155
    rigidity of code, consequences of 155–6
    specific governance, meaning of 156
  foundational components 146–55
    active components 147, 148, 148f
    active function 153–4
    containing natural language and algorithmic instructions 151–2
    direct impact of chosen digital operating environment on contractual terms 154–5
    legally binding agreement 149–50
    machine-readable and digital 151
    model's relation to other smart contract models 148–9
    rule-making components 147–8, 148f
    summary of key interconnected components 147
  legal status of automated contract performance 176–7
  legal void of digital economy 177–9
    SLCs as legal instruments to manage data reliance 178–9
  smart boilerplate/examples 165–74
    choice of platform 173–4
    data management architecture 172
    definitions 167–8, 167b
    interpretation 168–71, 167b
    lifecycle of SLC Performance 174f
    malfunctioning code and data source provisions 171
    recitals 166–7
    reasons to incorporate code 165–6
    variations and unintended variations 171–2
  smart legal contract concept 146
  Unified Method and Paired Method 149, 157, 189–90, 190–1
social reality see under documentality
Solidity 29, 36, 47, 133, 134, 301, 342, 343, 345, 346, 352
split contracts 118–19, 134
  American Information Exchange (AMIX) as early example of 118–19
  nature of 118
  Ricardian contracts, and 119
statutory regulation of smart contracts
  enforceability, clarifying 78
  need for a legislative framework 78
  simple legislative reform required 58, 79
stored procedures 8.269
Szaboian smart contract 5–8, 11
  automating and guaranteeing performance 6
  basic concept of 6–7
  definition and meaning 71, 113–14
  economic incentives circumventing conventional legal processes 6
  properly determined contract, as 6–7
  structure informed by cost of breach 6
  vending machine example 7, 114

techno-legal supertoys 246–68
  categories of smart contracts
    smart contracts as instruments of promise and agreement 248–9

techno-legal supertoys (cont.)
  smart contracts as programming
    conventions 248
  electronic agreements promoting false sense of
    'legal' certainty 249
  fetishization of contractual perfectibility and
    totality 249
  remedies 251, 255, 257–62
    contract law remedies and
      risk-allocation 260–2
    equity or restitution, importance of 257–8
    expectation damages 257
    legal weaknesses in smart contract design,
      and 259–60
    rescission 260, 261
    smart contract ideals and contingent
      reality 258–9
    unjust enrichment 257, 261
  smart contracts and good faith 265
  smart contracts and legal language 263–4
  smart contracts as techno-legal
    supertoys 251–2
  smart, but not intelligent, contracts 252–7
    duality of smart contracts as 'tools' and
      'instruments' 253
    emerging definitions of 'smart
      contracts' 253–6
    lack of contingent intelligence leading to
      reliance on 'data feeds' or 'oracles' 253
    lack of facility to adjust program to deal
      with contingencies 252–3
    rhetoric of efficiency 256–7
  smart contracts privileging performance and
    notions of perfectibility 251
textualism and contextualism 49–51, 149
The DAO incident see under Decentralised
  Autonomous Organisations ('DAOs')
tokenization 133–4, 261–2, 444
transaction costs
  smart contracts entailing lower transaction
    costs 386
  technology leading to reduction in 254
  transaction costs approach to contract
    law 119–32
    agency costs 125–6
    enforcement costs see enforcement costs
    measurement costs 123–4
    monitoring and verification costs 126–7
    moral hazard 125, 126
    negotiation costs 124
    overview of transaction costs 121f
    pseudonymity 109, 120, 126
    search costs 122
transactional scripts 8, 9

translation see under language
Turing
  'Turing-complete' blockchains 328, 331
  'Turing-complete' smart contracts 81–2, 331
  'Turing complete' virtual machine 31n
  Turing machine 311
  Turing test for AI 337

UK Jurisdiction Taskforce (UKJT) 2, 62–3, 84, 426
  Digital Dispute Resolution Rules see under
    dispute resolution and smart contracts
  Legal Statement see Legal Statement on
    Cryptoassets and Smart Contracts

vending machines 10
  contract stacks 10
  implied semi-smart contracts, as 207
  'industrial-age smart contract' as 24
  modern vending machines governed by rules
    written in formal language 29
  responding to actions by agents with
    predetermined conditional output 28
  smart contracts as continuation of vending
    machine model 208
  Szaboian smart contract 7, 114
validation 283, 285–90, 299, 303
  community validation 330
  computable contracts 292–3, 302
  creation and validation of smart contract
    code 285–6
  difficulties of 272
  DSML assisting 275
  exhaustive validation 286
  formal methods of 286–7
  internal or external models, and 280
  language stack, and 271–2, 278
  practical aspects of validating changes in code
    or agreement 281–2
    attaching source code as appendix to
      contract 281
    distributing the source code throughout
      contract 281–2
    expressing contract entirely in source
      code 282
    keeping contract and source code
      separate 281
  reducing burden of 291
  semantics, and 280, 285–7
    application of formal methods 286–7
    consequences for validation 285
    exhaustive validation 286
    making smart contracts valid by design 287
  verification, and 272
verification 7, 386

DLT removing need for verification of
    evidence 432
  formal methods of 286-7
  identity, of 385
  legal effect of smart contracts, of 358
  processes and procedures of verification
    defined by traditional contract law 266
  smart contract code verification likely to be
    insufficient 283
  validation, and 272
verification costs 126-7

'Wrapped and Stacked' (Allen) 23-53
  contract stacks *see* contract stacks
  issues raised by smart contracts for future
    contract law 45-52
    equitable doctrines, smart contracts and 52
    evolving canon of interpretation 51
    keeping contracts based in relationships
      between (human) agents 49
    logical operators in contract drafting 45-6
    semantic richness, intentional loss of 48-9
    semantic richness, unintentional loss
      of 47-8
  textualism and contextualism 49-51
  translation of formal language into natural
    language 46-7
  nature of a 'smart contract' 26-33
    digital contractware 28-30
    distributed ledger technology 30-2
    evolution of 'contractware' 27-8
    working definition of 'smart
      contract' 32-3
  smart contracts and conventional contract
    law 43-52
    illegality, jurisdiction, and procedure 43-5
    towards smart(er) contract law 44-52
  whether a smart contract is really a
    'contract' 33-43
    natural and formal languages 36-7
    smart contracts as 'legal contracts' 40-1
    speech act(s) creating the contract 37-40
    'wrapped' or 'stacked' smart contracts 42-3

zero
  atomic unit of finance, as 89
  zero coupon bonds 89-90, 91
  zero-hours contracts 388